SUBSCRIPTS

C: Call option or consol

F: Risk-free bond

g: Growth rate in industrial production

H: Highest possible value for ending stock price

i: ith possible state of nature

J: Jth stock

L: Lowest possible value for ending stock price

M: Market portfolio or proxy for market portfolio

P: Any portfolio of two or more securities

S: Stock

t: Time or term

Z: Minimum variance, zero beta portfolio

MODERN INVESTMENT THEORY

SECOND EDITION

ROBERT A. HAUGEN

Professor of Finance
University of California at Irvine

 PRENTICE HALL, Englewood Cliffs, New Jersey 07632

This book is dedicated
to Marilyn and Richard.

CONTENTS IN BRIEF

v

PART FOUR
INTEREST RATES AND BOND MANAGEMENT

PART FIVE
THE PRICING OF COMPLEX SECURITIES

PART SIX
ISSUES IN INVESTMENT MANAGEMENT

CONTENTS

3 SOME STATISTICAL CONCEPTS 42

PART TWO
PORTFOLIO MANAGEMENT

4 COMBINING INDIVIDUAL STOCKS INTO PORTFOLIOS 70

5 FINDING THE EFFICIENT SET 97

6 INDEX MODELS *152*

PART THREE

RISK, EXPECTED RETURN, AND PERFORMANCE MEASUREMENT

7 THE CAPITAL ASSET PRICING MODEL *197*

PART FOUR
INTEREST RATES AND BOND MANAGEMENT

PART FIVE

THE PRICING OF COMPLEX SECURITIES

16 AMERICAN OPTION PRICING *464*

17 ADDITIONAL ISSUES IN OPTION PRICING *479*

18 FINANCIAL FORWARD AND FUTURES CONTRACTS *509*

PART SIX
ISSUES IN INVESTMENT MANAGEMENT

19 THE EFFECT OF TAXES ON INVESTMENT STRATEGY AND SECURITIES PRICES *540*

20 STOCK VALUATION *561*

21 ISSUES IN ESTIMATING FUTURE EARNINGS AND DIVIDENDS *580*

22 MARKET EFFICIENCY: THE CONCEPT *600*

23 MARKET EFFICIENCY: THE EVIDENCE *620*

APPENDIX 8: ADDITIONAL PROPERTIES OF THE MINIMUM VARIANCE SET *672*

GLOSSARY *681*

INDEX *689*

PREFACE

This book is intended for the introductory graduate or intermediate undergraduate course in investment management. It requires a minimal level of training in mathematics and statistics. A knowledge of basic calculus is useful but not required, since it is used only in the appendices to the main discussions in the chapters. All the statistical concepts required for an understanding of the text are provided in a review of Chapter 3.

The book differentiates itself in the following respects. First, the coverage of portfolio theory is complete and detailed, covering three chapters including a unique graphical explanation of the Markowitz procedure. The material on portfolio selection is backed up by computer problems and powerful and easy-to-use portfolio analysis modules within the software that accompanies this book. The extensive coverage given to index models reflects the growing use of these models in the industry and, at the same time, paves the way for an easy grasp of the assumptions underlying the arbitrage pricing theory.

Second, extensive coverage is given to the issues related to capital asset pricing. The capital asset pricing model is covered in great detail. Emphasis is given to discriminating between the properties of the model that derive from economics and the properties that derive from definitional identities. The coverage of the arbitrage pricing theory is both complete and up to date. The issues involved in testing both CAPM and APT are also explored in detail. Emphasis is given to inherent problems associated with both the CAPM and the APT. It is my feeling that we no longer need to convince students that a study of modern finance will increase their human capital. Most of the theories and models in this book are widely employed in the real world. Rather than trying to convince them of their merits, they should thoroughly understand their weaknesses as well as their strengths, so they will know which models to lean on in making their investment decisions and how hard.

Third, the book presents four chapters on interest rates and bond management. It is no secret that in recent years interest rates have become increasingly volatile.

This has increased both the complexity and excitement of bond portfolio management. Two full chapters are devoted to the economic forces which push both the general level and term structure of interest rates around. Then two more chapters are devoted to aggressive and defensive bond portfolio management. In the first of these chapters the students learn how to integrate bonds into the Markowitz approach. In the second chapter they will learn how to immunize their portfolio against the threat of changing interest rates. There is great interest in immunization among pension funds and other financial institutions. A knowledge of interest immunization is now an essential weapon in the modern portfolio manager's arsenal.

Finally, as befitting the increasing popularity of these contracts, the coverage of options and forward and futures contracts is very extensive. Three full chapters are devoted to option pricing. In the first chapter, devoted to the pricing of European options, the students are taken through simplified valuation frameworks. They learn the behavioral characteristics of option prices, the concept of pricing an option to provide those who hedge with the risk-free rate of return, and finally the framework of the Black-Scholes option pricing model. In the second chapter, devoted to American options, they learn why American options may be exercised early and how the value of American puts and calls may exceed the values of their European counterparts. The third options chapter addresses sources of bias in option pricing and option strategies including portfolio insurance. In the greatly simplified chapter on forward and futures contracts, emphasis is given to the *pricing* and use of these contracts in hedging.

In addition to these distinctions in coverage, the book presents many *mini case studies* which show students how the techniques explored in the book are actually used in the real world. The individuals and firms discussed in these case studies are real. In addition to motivating the student to learn the material, they are likely to provoke in-class discussion of the material.

Completion of a book of this size is a considerable task involving the participation of many people. I would like to thank my secretary, Robin Smith, for a truly terrific job of assembling, organizing, and editing the book. Thanks also to Tiffany Haugen, Brian Archibald, Jim Berens and Bill Lepley for participation in writing the instructors manual and the end-of-chapter questions and problems. A word of thanks to the many reviewers of this book: Simon M. Wheatley, University of Washington; John S. Howe, University of Kansas; William P. Dukes, Texas Technical University; Donald H. Wort, California State University at Hayward, Amir Banea, University of Wisconsin; George A. Racette, University of Oregon, and Norman P. Obst, Michigan State University. I also greatly appreciate the work David Tan did in redesigning and reprogramming much of the software and thanks to Eli Talmor and Amir Barnea for beta-testing the software for three quarters at UCLA and Wisconsin. Finally, a special thanks goes to all the professionals who participated in the *Out on the Street* segments of the book. These people devoted their time freely to the project, and their stories should be a source of inspiration to the students who will follow in their footsteps.

WELCOME TO INVEST SOFTWARE

Background Reading

Modules 1 and 2: *Modern Investment Theory,* Chapters 5 and 6.
Module 3: *Modern Investment Theory,* Chapters 15 and 16.
Module 4: *Modern Investment Theory,* Chapter 20.
Module 5: *Modern Investment Theory,* Chapters 12 and 14.

Modern Investment Theory 2/e is accompanied by extremely powerful, efficient, and easy to use, software designed to run on most I.B.M. compatible machines. This software is not only an invaluable learning tool, but, as you will see, it can be used after graduation for professional security and portfolio analysis.

The four principle areas covered in the software are:

I. Portfolio Analysis
II. Fixed Income Analysis
III. Options Analysis
IV. Dividend Discount Stock Valuation

The ***Portfolio Analysis*** modules compute mean-variance efficient sets employing both the Markowitz and the single-index approaches. Both approaches accommodate restrictions on short selling. The user can (a) input estimates of expected returns, standard deviations, correlations, betas, residual standard deviations, etc., (b) input security returns and have these estimates calculated, or (c) draw from a data base, included in the software, covering individual securities, indices, and mutual funds. Inputs are made into a convenient spread-sheet format. Files can be saved, printed, and they can be exported or imported to and from Lotus 123. Modifications to the inputs are very easily made, so the student can assess the sensitivity of their results to changes in assumptions. When in the single-index mode, actual as well as estimated values for portfolio standard deviation are provided to enable the student to assess the accuracy of the single-index model's assumption of residual orthogonality. The user can also easily graph the efficient sets and the relative positions of the individual securities.

The *Fixed Income Analysis* module provides plots of the term structure in terms of both internal and geometric mean yields to maturity as well as forecasts and graphs of forward interest rates. These forecasts accommodate user assumptions regarding liquidity premiums. The programs also can be used to calculate the internal yields and durations of bond portfolios in the manner discussed in the text. Thus, students can use the programs to construct immunized bond portfolios.

The *Options Analysis* module is especially powerful. Both American and European put and call option pricing models are provided. Implicit volatility calculations can be made via the Black-Scholes model (a European model) or the binomial model (an American model). Since the American and European values are shown side by side, the student can clearly see the value of the right to early exercise for call options on stocks that pay dividends and on put options. Once again inputs are made via a spread-sheet format, and the sensitivity of the outputs to changes in assumptions or option characteristics is easily assessed. A position analysis program is also provided to enable the uses to establish complex positions and assess the sensitivity of the value of these positions to changes in the value of the underlying stock and the passage of time. Students can use the implicit volatility and valuation programs to identify over- and under-valued options, and then use the position analysis program to put together a delta neutral position. The position can then be tracked to assess its profitability.

The *Dividend Discount Stock Valuation* module provides one, two, or three stage dividend discount valuation. The module has the attractive feature of being able to compute any missing input when the others are provided. Thus, it can compute expected return, for example, if market price and the required elements of the dividend growth profile are provided.

To start the *INVEST* program, simply boot up and enter ''INVEST''.

To Begin Program

Insert DOS 3.2 or a later version into Drive A.
Turn the computer on.
At "A>" replace DOS disk with the INVEST disk and type "INVEST".
Press "RETURN".

Hard Disk Setup

INVEST may be installed on a hard disk by copying the following files into the desired subdirectory.

INVEST.EXE
INV1.EXE
INV2.EXE
INV3.EXE
INV4.EXE
INV5.EXE
BRUN40.EXE
COLORS.DAT (optional—if this is left out a new one will be created)

Printing Graphs from INVEST 1 & 2

The graphs of the bullet may be printed from within the program. To do this you must be using graphics settings 2 or 3 (CGA graphics). *Before* starting INVEST load the DOS program GRAPHICS into memory by typing "GRAPHICS" with DOS disk in the default drive. Then start INVEST in the normal way. When you have calculated the efficient portfolios, Press F3 to graph the bullet press "SHIFT" "PRTSC". The graph should print. Refer to your DOS manual for greater detail and information on compatibility with various printers.

Importing a Returns File into LOTUS 123 from INVEST 1&2

Assuming you are in Module 1 of INVEST and you are at the screen which shows the list of returns data;

1. To save this data, press "F4".
2. You will be prompted for a filename. Enter a name (e.g. "TEST.PRN") A path may also be specified if you wish to save the file on a different drive or subdirectory (e.g. "B:\FILES\TEST.PRN").
3. Press "RETURN" and the file will be saved.

Exit INVEST.

Start LOTUS 123

1. Position the cursor at the top left hand corner of the spreadsheet.
2. Press "\" then select "FILE", "IMPORT", "NUMBERS".
3. You will then be prompted for the name of the file to be imported. Enter the full filename (and path if necessary) (e.g. "TEST.RTN" or "B:\FILES\TEST.RTN").
4. Press "RETURN". The file will be imported into the spreadsheet.

With this method the name of each security will be lost but the order and format of the returns is left intact. If you wish, you can manually reenter the names in the top line of the spreadsheet.

Experienced 123 users can import the file together with the names using the commands "FILES", "IMPORT", "TEXT" and then using the "DATA", "PARSE" command to split the entries into individual columns.

Format of Data for Loading into INVEST 1&2

Once the data has been imported into LOTUS 123, it may be manipulated in any way and then exported again provided the following rules are observed:

- The top row always contains the names of the securities. It may be left blank if you wish.
  IMPORTANT: SECURITY NAMES MUST BE ONE WORD. Any two-word names must be connected by a non-blank space character e.g. "ACME INC" must be entered as "ACME_INC". This is because the program interprets a space as the end of one name and the start of the next.
- All the securities must have exactly the same number of observations.
- There are at least two securities and not more than twenty-eight.
- There are at least two return observations for each security and not more than sixty.
- Each column of returns must have one or more spaces between them.

EXPORTING a returns file from LOTUS 123 to INVEST 1

Make sure that the format of the spreadsheet to be exported conforms to the requirements outlined earlier.

Assuming you are in LOTUS 123 and (for example) you have just imported a file, added another column of securities, and are ready to export it again.

1. Press "\" then select "PRINT", "FILE".
2. You will be prompted for a print filename. Enter the name (and path if required) (e.g. "TESTOUT.PRN" or "b:\FILES\TESTOUT.PRN").
3. Press "RETURN".
4. Select "RANGE" and then highlight the entire area to be exported.
5. Select "OPTIONS", "MARGINS", "LEFT", "0".
6. Select "MARGINS", "RIGHT", "240".
7. Select "OTHER", "UNFORMATTED".
8. Select "QUIT" to return to previous menu level, then select "GO". The file will be exported in a format that can be read by INVEST 1&2.

EXIT LOTUS 123.

START INVEST 1.

1. To import returns select option 2 from the INVEST 1&2 menus.
2. When prompted for the number of securities and observations, you can enter any legal number. The program will automatically reset these values when the file is loaded.
3. Press "F3" and enter the filename (and path if necessary). e.g. "TESTOUT.PRN" (or "b:\FILES\TESTOUT.PRN").
4. The program will load the file.

Note: If there are any problems in loading, it is most likely due to errors in the format, hidden characters, etc. When exporting from Lotus, make sure that it is printed as an UNFORMATTED file.

C H A P T E R

1

INTRODUCTION TO MODERN INVESTMENT THEORY

This is a book about the theory of investment management. Among other things, the theory provides the tools to enable you to manage investment risk, detect mispriced securities, minimize taxes, and measure the performance of investment managers.

Perhaps in no other area of business education have theories and techniques that have been developed in economics departments and business schools had such a profound effect on professional behavior and practice in the real world. Modern investment theory is widely employed throughout the investment community by investment and portfolio analysts who are becoming increasingly sophisticated. Admittedly, many of the models and techniques are complex and difficult to master, but they are effective. They can help you capture extra returns. They can be used to create new products and land new accounts. A deep understanding of them can mean the difference between success and failure in your investment career.

In part, an understanding of investment theory will help you learn how to accomplish goals in portfolio management. You will learn how to set up a hedged position using options or futures contracts. You will learn how to guarantee that pensioners will be assured of getting all their promised retirement benefits. You will also learn how to squeeze the most return out of a portfolio given the level of risk or how to make the returns on one portfolio mimic the returns on another.

In addition, as you master the theory, you will gain a deeper understanding of the way securities are priced by the market. You will understand the forces that push interest rates up and down and why short-term rates may be above or below the level of long-term rates. You will understand how to measure the risk of an investment and the influence this risk has on security prices. You will see how options behave in relation to the stocks they are written on and gain some insight into the elements behind a futures price. The more knowledge you have about the nature of securities pricing, the easier it will be for you to detect deviations from this pricing structure and thereby capture superior returns on your investments.

THE DEVELOPMENT OF MODERN INVESTMENT THEORY

The beginnings of modern portfolio theory date back to 1952 when Harry Markowitz (1952) published a paper entitled "Portfolio Selection." In it, he showed how to create a frontier of investment portfolios, such that each of them had the greatest possible expected rate of return, given their level of risk. The technique was, computationally, very complex, especially given the technology of the time. A student of Markowitz named William Sharpe (1963) developed a simplified version of the technique which is now referred to as the **single-index model.** The simplified version made portfolio theory practical, even when managing large numbers of securities. In the 1970s, after techniques for estimating the required inputs to the model were perfected, packaged, and marketed as computer software, modern portfolio theory took off in terms of practical application in the real world. Now the single-index model is widely employed to allocate investments in the portfolio between individual common stocks, while the original, more general model of Markowitz is widely used to allocate investments between types of securities, such as bonds, stock, venture capital, and real estate.

Prior to the dissemination of portfolio theory into the real world, three individuals simultaneously and independently asked themselves the following question: "Suppose everyone managed their investments using portfolio theory and invested in the portfolios on the frontier. How would this impact on the pricing of securities?" In answering this question, Sharpe (1964), Lintner (1965), and Mossin (1966) developed what became know as the **capital asset pricing model.** This model reigned as the premier model in the field of finance for nearly 15 years. In addition to finding its way into the elementary textbooks in finance, it became widely used in the real world to measure portfolio performance, value securities, make capital budgeting decisions, and even regulate public utilities. In 1976, however, the model was called into question by Richard Roll (1977, 1978), who argued that the model should be discarded because it was impossible empirically to verify its single economic prediction. This controversial issue is still the subject of heated debate today. At the same time, an alternative to the capital asset pricing model was being developed by Steve Ross (1976). This model was called the **arbitrage pricing theory.** This theory argued that expected return must be related to risk in such a way that no single investor could create unlimited wealth through arbitrage. The theory was less demanding in terms of its assumptions, and both Roll and Ross (1984) argue that it's testable, at least in principle. At this point, although it is being called into question, the capital asset pricing model is still widely used in the real world. The arbitrage pricing theory, however, seems to be gaining momentum.

The question of how to price option contracts to buy and sell securities long puzzled researchers in finance until a paper by Fisher Black and Myron Scholes was published in 1973. They argued that you can create a riskless hedged position with an option by taking a position in both the option and the stock it is written on. It will cost you money to set up the hedge, but since it is riskless, the option must be priced relative to the stock so that you get the riskless rate of return on your hedged investment. They developed a model which would price the option so as to produce this result. The Black-Scholes model has since become extremely popular in the investment community. Options have literally exploded in terms of variety and volume of trading. Option traders are extremely sophisticated. The Black-Scholes model remains the most widely used, but since 1973 many alternative models have been developed. Some of these more sophisticated approaches to valuing options are beginning to affect the behavior of traders and options prices on the floors of the options exchanges.

Even as researchers were attempting to determine the nature of the pricing structure in the securities markets, the issue of how efficient the market was in pricing to its structure was called into question. In 1965, the Ph.D. dissertation of Eugene Fama was published in the *Journal of Business*. In it, he persuasively made a startling argument. There are literally thousands of intelligent, well-informed professional investors actively searching for mispriced securities. Since, upon finding them, these professionals trade and thereby affect prices, it's likely that security prices, at any given time, reflect the collective wisdom of those who invest in them. If information rapidly and efficiently becomes impounded into the prices of securities, then it becomes impossible to "beat" the market through any form of security analysis. This controversial issue became known as the efficient market controversy, and it still remains to be settled to this day. The debate spawned an extremely large number of empirical studies directed at determining the quantity and quality of information reflected in security prices. Initially, the weight of the evidence clearly favored the view that the market was highly efficient. The results of these studies had their effect in the real world. Mutual funds were established which made no attempt to beat the market. Their philosophy was that this was a waste of time and money, and they would only attempt to match the market's performance. Gradually, however, as better data became available and statistical techniques were refined, some holes were punched through the efficient market hypothesis. At this point, the prevailing view is that while the market appears to be clearly more efficient than was thought prior to the publication of Fama's dissertation, security prices reflect less than the complete set of information available to the diligent investor.

OUT ON THE STREET

TERMINAL INVESTING

The bright glow of the computer terminal seemed to turn everything it touched in the dimly lit office a pale green, including the face and hands of Terry Lange-tieg.

It was 8:00 P.M., and Terry was finding it difficult to think. He had arrived at his Salomon Brothers office at 8:00 A.M. that morning. Twelve-hour days were new to him, after spending the last decade as a finance professor at the University of Southern California. They were new, but they weren't uncommon in the three years he had been working for the firm.

Terry was only one of several academics in finance who had recently made the switch from the classroom to the real world of investment analysis. New faces seemed to be popping up all over, and these weren't the traditional pinstriped M.B.A. investment types you'd normally expect to see. These people had Ph.D. degrees, and not just in finance or economics either. Increasingly, you'd see new colleagues with terminal degrees in mathematics, statistics, and even physics. The feeling was that these people would pick up the finance they'd need to know on the job during their first few years with the firm. The important thing was they had the advanced quantitative skills to contribute to the highly sophisticated investment analysis Salomon Brothers was using to create new financial products and new securities and to detect and take advantage of arbitrage opportunities.

The computer age in investments was definitely here. Terry normally spends half his working day before a computer terminal. The models and valuation techniques, which were developed by professors like Terry over the last 20 years, are about to be applied by the practitioners in a big way. Students desiring to enter the world of investment analysis would be advised to prepare by expanding their programming abilities in the various computer languages.

Terry himself has been spending the past four months applying modern investment theory in building bond portfolios that track and beat, in the sense of earning 50 or more annual basis points, the Broad Investment Grade Bond Index recently developed by Salomon Brothers. The main index is divided into three subindices, one consisting of treasury and government agency securities, a second consisting of corporate bonds rated BBB or better and having total market values of $25 million or more, and a third consisting of generic mortgage-backed securities, like Ginnie Mae passthroughs. Surprisingly, the size of the market for mortgage-backed securities now rivals the market for tradable corporate bonds. The broad index consists of $2 trillion worth of securities.

Terry tries to *track* movements in the index by using a measure of the average maturity of the payments associated with a bond issue called "duration" (which we will learn more about in Chapter 14). Roughly speaking, he tries to build bond portfolios that have the same duration as the duration of the index.

One way he tries to *beat* the return produced by the index is by analyzing spreads between the yields on individual bonds and the yields on nearly identical treasury issues that have comparable durations.

During the course of the past four months, Terry has developed a feel for the efficiency of the bond market. He sees a bond market consisting of thousands of traders who expect instant access to information and analysis of any security in any tradable market. They are hooked into sophisticated systems that compute yields based on a multiplicity of reinvestment assumptions and then compute duration-based yield spreads matched to the treasury yield curve. Some systems, based on a forecast of interest rates over some time horizon, determine the impact of the forecasted change in rates on the outlook for the bonds being called by the issuing firms at their call prices. This analysis is used to develop a rate of return profile for any menu of bonds over the time horizon. Some, more sophisticated programs, use Monte Carlo techniques to simulate the effects of different interest rate patterns on bond returns to develop probability distributions for returns on the bonds over the horizon period.

Terry has come to believe, given the number of analysts employing sophisticated technology, the market has achieved a tremendous degree of efficiency. Yes, opportunities for arbitrage do exist, but they certainly don't last long. Terry doubts very much the viability of the so-called market segmentation theory of the term structure (which we will learn about in Chapter 12). There is very little scientific evidence supporting the theory, and he sees many, many traders arbitraging across the entire term structure. Although there is clientele for bonds of specific maturity ranges, even banks are somewhat heterogeneous in terms of their desired maturities.

Which bonds, long or short, are viewed as being riskier? In Terry's view, it's long bonds for sure. Yes, some institutions have long-term liabilities, but the performance of most money managers is still evaluated on an annual basis, and given this, they will be concerned with their returns during the course of a year. Long-term bonds contribute the most to the variability of these returns.

It's possible, however, the new bond indices may change this perception. The broad index has a duration of approximately five years. To the extent performance is measured in terms of the deviation of a manager's return from the return on the index, bonds with average maturities of greater or less than five years, may be viewed as comparatively risky.

The day is finally done! As Terry makes his way to the elevator, he notices many lights still on in other offices. It's 11:00 P.M. No question about it, this is definitely not the university.

WHY SHOULD YOU LEARN MODERN INVESTMENT THEORY?

Rapid advances in computer technology have revolutionized professional investment management. Managers can sit at terminals and access detailed data relating to myriad companies in all sectors of the market. This has had two important implications.

First, information is channeled more rapidly from its source to the analysts and traders who process and act on it. The probable effect of this is to reduce the lag between the incidence of an event and its effect on security prices. In discussions with professional traders, you come away with the distinct impression that the efficiency of the markets in processing information has increased significantly in the last few years. This seems especially true in the option markets.

Second, the explosive growth in computers and computer software has made possible the everyday use of extremely sophisticated financial models. Hundreds of services have appeared specializing in the writing of software based on stock, bond, or option valuation models, routines which optimize portfolio composition, and sophisticated statistical procedures to obtain estimates of the required inputs for techniques such as the single-index model.

The computer age has had a dramatic impact on both the speed and sophistication of investment management, and there is no reason to think the process won't continue to move in this direction.

There are plenty of people out there who are more than willing to take your job, your money, or both, if you choose to make them available to them. To survive in tomorrow's market, you have to be both alert and sophisticated in your techniques of analysis. If you don't believe a deep understanding of modern investment theory is important to your survival, read a copy of the last chartered financial analysts examination or talk to a floor trader on the Chicago Board Options Exchange.

As you learn the theory, it's important to concentrate on the weaknesses and the biases in the models. Although they are widely used, these models are by no means perfect. If you understand their strengths and weaknesses, you will know when and how hard to lean on them. You will be in the best position to critique the presentations made by the representatives of the financial software companies. You will be in a position to lead your firm in new directions. You may even want to start your own investment management firm.

The techniques of modern investment theory will enable you to do some things which may surprise you but which many investors out there may find to be very attractive. Here are some examples:

1. You will learn how to obtain a forecast of the market's estimate of future interest rates from the current structure of security prices.
2. You will learn how to get the market's estimate of the future variability of a stock price from the price of an option written on the stock.
3. The return on a common stock is a composite of dividend income and price appreciation. You will learn how to separate a stock into two securities, one paying only dividends and the other only capital gains. You can market the securities to two clients who, for tax or other reasons, want one and not the other.

4. You will learn how to provide clients with the following service. For a fee they can invest their money in a portfolio which almost matches the performance of their existing portfolio without your service. I say almost matches because their new portfolio increases in value with their old portfolio. On the other hand, if the old portfolio goes down in value, the value of the client's new portfolio will remain constant. Aside from payment of the fee, the clients face the attractive prospect of the possibility of dramatic gains but no losses. This is called portfolio insurance, and it is only one of many things that can be done with futures contracts written on stock and bond market indices. This product has run into some recent problems, but billions of dollars in assets are still insured in this way.

Products like these aren't hard to create. You can create them and others like them by applying the techniques of modern investment theory and your own imagination.

Throughout this book you will find stories about individuals like Peter Thayer, Larry Davanzo, Tom Dumphy, Elaine Garzarell, and Joe Gorman, who are trading the markets and marketing products like these. The people are real, and their stories are true. Investment management is an exciting industry populated by intelligent, dynamic, determined individuals. You can become one of them. You can make money, *if* you are well informed.

REFERENCES

BLACK, F., and SCHOLES, M., "The Pricing of Options and Corporate Liabilities," *Journal of Political Economy* (May–June 1973).

FAMA, E. F., "The Behavior of Stock Prices," *Journal of Business* (January 1965).

FAMA, E. F., "Efficient Capital Markets: A Review of Theory and Empirical Work," *Journal of Business* (May 1970).

LINTNER, J., "The Valuation of Risk Assets and the Selection of Risky Investments in Stock Portfolios and Capital Budgets," *Review of Economics and Statistics* (February 1965).

MARKOWITZ, H. M., *"Portfolio Selection," Journal of Finance* (December 1952).

MOSSIN, J., "Equilibrium in a Capital Market," *Econometrica* (October 1966).

ROLL, R., "A Critique of the Asset Pricing Theory's Tests. Part I: On the Past and Potential Testability of the Theory," *Journal of Financial Economics* (March 1977).

ROLL, R., "Ambiguity When Performance Is Measured by the Security Market Line," *Journal of Finance* (September 1978).

ROLL, R., and ROSS, S., "A Critical Reexamination of the Empirical Evidence on the Arbitrage Pricing Theory: A Reply," *Journal of Finance* (June 1984).

ROSS, S. A., "The Arbitrage Theory of Capital Asset Pricing," *Journal of Economic Theory* (December 1976).

SHARPE, W. F., "A Simplified Model of Portfolio Analysis," *Management Science* (January 1963).

SHARPE, W. F., "Capital Asset Prices: A Theory of Market Equilibrium Under Conditions of Risk," *Journal of Finance* (September 1964).

C H A P T E R

2

SECURITIES AND MARKETS

This chapter provides the institutional background for the rest of the book. The nature of the various securities that are traded in the capital markets and the structure, procedures, and rules of the markets themselves will be discussed.

The ultimate objective is to learn how to construct an optimal portfolio of investments. To do this, you will have to be aware of the various investment alternatives available and be able to make estimates of the returns you expect to get from the individual securities in the portfolio as well as their risk. Since each security is a claim on the wealth of a firm or government, in making these estimates, you will need to understand the contractual provisions of the claims. In executing your decision to invest in various securities, you will also need to know where they are traded and the procedures through which the trades can be consummated.

Fixed income securities, like bonds, have a defined, limited, dollar claim. The dollar receipts from these investments will never exceed the promised claim, although they can fall short of the promise in the case of default. *Variable income securities,* like common stock, have a residual claim to the earnings of a company. These claimants are entitled to whatever is left after all the other security holders have exercised their claims to the firm's earnings. While the stockholder's claim to the earnings is residual, it is also unlimited in amount. If the firm proves to be a huge success, the stockholders may reap huge gains, while the bondholders receive only their fixed claim. On the other hand, if the firm doesn't do too well, the stockholders are first to feel the pinch, in the form of their income (lowered dividends) and their wealth (lowered market price).

Primary securities are issued by governments or firms. They obligate the firm to the payment of some part of its income. *Secondary securities* are issued by individual traders rather than firms. An example of a secondary security is an option contract, giving its holder the right to buy or sell a primary security at a certain price. For every trader buying a secondary security as an asset, there is another trader selling the security as a liability. If we were to add up all the positive and negative positions in these securities, we would find their total value sums to zero. On the other hand, if we were to add up the total value of all the primary securities, we would find their total value sums to the total value of the assets of all the firms and governments issuing them.

Securities are issued by *governments* and *private firms.* Governments issue securities to finance deficits in their budgets when revenues fall short of expenditures. Government securities are almost invariably bond issues of various types. These bonds are issued by governments at all levels; federal, state, and municipality. Because it can print money, the securities of the federal government are not subject to default. The securities of the state and municipal governments, however, are only as sound as the abilities of these governments to raise revenue through taxation and other means. Private firms issue a wide variety of different types of securities from bonds to common stock. The quality of these issues is based on the quality of the earning power of the firms issuing them.

Government Bonds

Securities issued by the *federal* government include U.S. savings bonds, U.S. Treasury bills, U.S. Treasury notes, U.S. Treasury bonds, and bonds issued by the various agencies of the U.S. government.

U.S. savings bonds are usually sold to individual investors. They can be redeemed at any time at specified amounts which gradually increase from the original purchase price to the maximum redemption value at their maturity. Series EE bonds pay no periodic, cash interest payments to their investors. Your interest received is based on the difference between the original purchase price and the value of the

9

bond when redeemed. The redemption values are usually structured to provide an incentive to hold the bond until maturity. Series HH bonds pay interest semiannually and mature in 10 years with the payment of principal.

Treasury bills have very short maturities, with the maximum being 1 year. These securities can be redeemed only at maturity. Unlike savings bonds, there is a very active market for these issues, and they can be easily sold at prices that reflect prevailing interest rates prior to maturity. You buy a treasury bill at a discount from its promised payment at maturity. Your interest on the investment is represented by the difference between the promised payment and your purchase price.

The annual rates of return produced by treasury bills in the years 1926 through 1987 are presented in Figure 2.1(a). The frequency distribution for these returns is presented in Figure 2.1(b). Notice treasury bill returns have been fairly stable over the years but also quite modest. These returns tend to go up and down with the expected rate of inflation. Thus, treasury bills are considered by some to be the best hedge against inflation currently available in the U.S. security markets.

Treasury notes have maturities of up to 7 years. They are issued in denominations of $1000 or more. Unlike treasury bills, notes pay cash interest payments on a semiannual basis. As with all U.S. government securities, aside from savings bonds, these securities are traded in an active market, so your investment in them can be easily liquidated at any time. As with any bond, when you buy a treasury note, you must pay the seller of the bond not only the prevailing market price but also any interest that has accrued. For example, suppose you are buying a treasury note that has a semiannual interest payment of $100. It has been exactly 60 days since the last interest payment, and it will be 120 days until the next payment. The seller has accrued interest on the bond of $33.33 = (60/180) × $100. You must

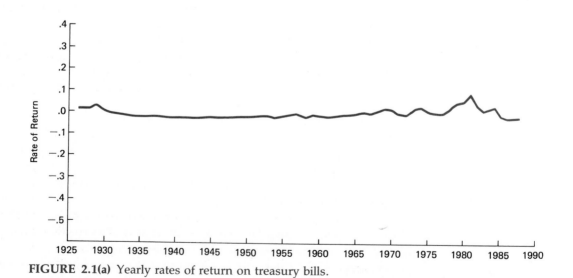

FIGURE 2.1(a) Yearly rates of return on treasury bills.

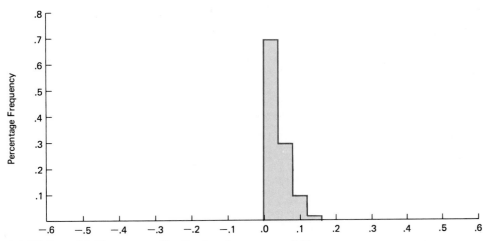

FIGURE 2.1(b) Frequency distribution for treasury bill returns.

pay the seller the accrued interest, in addition to the market price, when you buy the bond.

There is no maximum maturity for a ***treasury bond.*** These securities are identical to treasury notes in form, with two possible distinguishing features. These bonds are sometimes issued with call provisions attached. The call provision gives the government the option to retire the issue at a stated call price prior to maturity. The call option doesn't become active until a stated date, perhaps 5 years prior to actual maturity. Certain designated treasury bonds can be used to pay federal estate taxes, dollar for dollar, on the basis of their *principal* values. These bonds were originally issued when interest rates were much lower than they are today. Because of their very small interest payments, the bonds sell at prices discounted below their principal values, making them advantageous for purposes of paying the inheritance tax. Unless you are planning to use them for this purpose, however, these bonds are unattractive as investments because their yields are usually well below those of conventional treasury bonds.

Annual rates of return to a portfolio of long-term U.S. Treasury bonds and their frequency distribution are presented in Figures 2.2(a) and (b). Note, these returns are considerably more variable than are the treasury bill returns. These returns reflect both annual interest payments and capital gains or losses. In the years where the total return is negative, the capital loss has been large enough to more than offset the annual interest payment. The capital losses are the result of increases in the rate of interest, which drives down the market value of these bonds. Interest rates go up in times of high inflation; thus, these bonds produce their lowest returns when the inflation rate is unexpectedly high. Therefore, treasury bonds should be considered a poor inflation hedge.

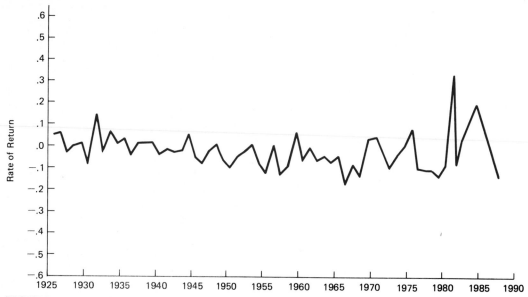

FIGURE 2.2(a) Yearly rates of return on long-term treasury bonds.

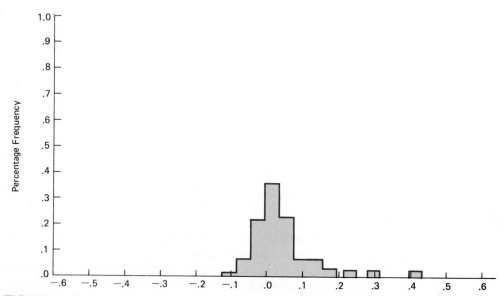

FIGURE 2.2(b) Frequency distribution for treasury bond returns.

The various agencies of the federal government also issue bonds which, with exceptions (such as Federal Home Loan Bank Consolidated Obligations), are backed with the full faith and credit of the U.S. government. Among others, these agencies include the Federal Housing Administration, the Federal Land Banks, and the Government National Mortgage Association. Although these bonds are backed by the U.S. government, they usually sell at slightly higher interest rates than the direct obligations of the government, such as treasury bills. Most of the bonds issued by these agencies are conventional in form. However, some, such as those issued by the Government National Mortgage Association, are participation certificates. These particular securities are called Ginnie Mae passthroughs. A group of residential mortgages is pooled, and certificates are issued. The payments on certificates are based on the payments associated with the individual mortgages. Default on the payments of the passthroughs themselves is no problem because the payments are guaranteed by the association and backed by the federal government. The holder of the passthroughs receives a monthly annuity until maturity.

State and municipal governments also issue debt to finance their expenditures. *General obligation bonds* are backed by the full faith and credit of the issuing government or agency. The interest and principal payments for these bonds may be paid from any source of revenue of the particular government. The interest and principal payments on *revenue bonds,* on the other hand, may be paid only from the revenues associated with a particular project, such as a toll bridge. If the project fails to produce sufficient revenue to make the scheduled payments, the bondholders have no access to the other sources of revenue of the issuing government or agency. When seeking to finance short-term expenditures, governments may frequently issue *tax-anticipation notes* which are secured by taxes already due but not yet paid.

Some quotations for tax-exempt bond issues of local governments and agencies are given in Figure 2.3. The column labeled ''Coupon'' lists the annual interest payment as a percentage of the face or principal payment. The next column, ''Mat,'' lists the year in which the bond matures. The ''Bid'' and ''Asked'' columns list the price dealers are willing to buy and sell the individual bonds for. This price is expressed as a percentage of face or principal value. The last column, ''Chg,'' lists the change in price of the bond from the preceding day.

Corporate Fixed Income Securities

The debt issued by business firms comes in a wide variety of forms. *Mortgage bonds* are backed by the pledge of specific property as security. Should the firm be unable to fulfill its pledge to make the scheduled payments on the bond, the bondholders are entitled to sell the property and retain the proceeds. Typically, however, the property pledged is illiquid, and the real protection behind the bonds is the earning power of the assets and not their liquidating value.

On the other hand, *equipment trust certificates* are usually backed by a particular piece of equipment, such as a railroad car, which is both readily transported and readily marketable. In some cases, title to the equipment resides with the creditors

Tax-Exempt Bonds

Thursday, May 1, 1986

Here are current prices of several active tax-exempt revenue bonds issued by toll roads and other public authorities.

Agency	Coupon	Mat	Bid	Asked	Chg.
Alabama G.O.	8⅜s	'01	107	110	....
Bat Park City Auth NY	6⅜s	'14	84	89	− ½
Chelan Cnty PU Dist	5s	'13	83½	85½	....
Clark Cnty Arpt Rev	10½s	'07	111	114	....
Columbia St Pwr Exch	3⅞s	'03	93	95	....
Dela River Port Auth	6½s	'11	93½	96½	....
Douglas Cnty PU Dist	4s	'18	61½	64½	+ ½
Ga Mun El Auth Pwr Rev	8s	'15	97	100	....
Intermountain Pwr	7½s	'18	93	97	....
Intermountain Pwr	10½s	'18	123	127	....
Intermountain Pwr	14s	'21	136	141	....
Jacksonville Elec Rev	9¼s	'13	107	111	....
Loop	6½s	'08	76	79	....
MAC	7½s	'92	100½	104½	....
MAC	7½s	'95	102	106	....
MAC	8s	'86	99	103	....
MAC	8s	'91	100	104	....
MAC	9.7s	'08	111½	115½	....
MAC	9¾s	'92	102	106	....
MAC	10¼s	'93	107	111	....
Mass Port Auth Rev	6s	'11	88	92	....
Massachusetts G.O.	6½s	'00	97	100	....
Mass Wholesale	6⅜s	'15	73	76	....
Mass Wholesale	13⅜s	'17	121	124	....
Metro Transit Auth	9¼s	'15	106	125	....
Michigan Public Pwr	10⅝s	'18	120	125	....
Nebraska Pub Pwr Dist	7.1s	'17	91	95	....
NJ Turnpike Auth	4¾s	'06	80	83	....
NJ Turnpike Auth	5.7s	'13	85½	88½	....
NJ Turnpike Auth	6s	'14	90	93	....
NY Mtge Agency Rev	9½s	'13	102	107	....
NY State Pwr Escr	5½s	'10	83	88	− ½
NY State Pwr	6⅝s	'10	90	95	− ½
NY State Pwr Escr	9½s	'01	109	114	− ½
NY State Pwr	9⅞s	'20	109	114	− ½
NY State Thruway Rev	3.1s	'94	82	85	....
NY State Urban Dev Corp	6s	'13	77½	82½	....
NY State Urban Dev Corp	7s	'14	88½	93½	....
NC East Mun Pwr Agcy	11¼s	'18	122	126	....
Okla Tpke Auth Rev	4.7s	'06	80	82	....
Port of NY & NJ	4¾s	'03	75	80	− ½
Port of NY & NJ	6s	'06	86	90	− ½
Port of NY & NJ	7s	'11	97	102	− ½
Port of NY-Delta	10½s	'08	114	119	....
Salt River-Arizona	9¼s	'20	103	108	....
SC Pub Svc Auth	10¼s	'20	115	118	....
Texas Munic Pwr Agcy	9½s	'12	107	111	....
Valdez (Exxon)	5½s	'07	79½	82½	....
Valdez (Sohio)	6s	'07	80	83	....
Wshngtn PPSS #4-5	f6s	'15	9	12	....
Wshngtn PPSS #4-5	f7¾s	'18	9½	12½	....
Wshngtn PPSS #4-5	f9⅞s	'12	10	13	....
Wshngtn PPSS #4-5	f12½s	'10	11	13½	....
Wshngtn PPSS #2	6s	'12	69	72	....
Wshngtn PPSS #1	7¾s	'17	85	87	....
Wshngtn PPSS #2	9¼s	'11	99	103	....
Wshngtn PPSS #3	13⅞s	'18	121	124	....
Wshngtn PPSS #2	14¾s	'12	127	130	....
Wshngtn PPSS #1	15s	'17	136	140	....

Trades flat without payment of current interest.

FIGURE 2.3 Quotations for tax-exempt bonds.

SOURCE: *The Wall Street Journal,* May 2, 1986, p. 36. Reprinted by permission of *The Wall Street Journal,* © Dow Jones & Company, Inc., 1986. All rights reserved.

through a trustee. The corporation receives title to the equipment only when all the scheduled payments are made.

Debenture bonds are unsecured by real property. Their claim is fixed but based only on the firm's ability to generate cash flow. Given the illiquid status of the security backing most mortgage bonds, however, the unsecured status of debenture bonds should not be a source of concern. One meaningful difference between the two types of issues occurs in technical default, where the firm is profitable but has insufficient cash to make the scheduled payments on its debt issues. In this case, the claim of the mortgage bondholder takes priority over the government's claim to the corporate income tax. The government's claim, on the other hand, takes priority over the claim of the debenture bondholder.

The interest payments on *income bonds* need only be paid if the income of the firm is sufficient to make payment. Failure to pay, when earnings are insufficient, doesn't result in bankruptcy. Failure to pay principal at maturity, however, does result in bankruptcy, irrespective of the level of the firm's income.

Convertible bonds give their holders the option of exchanging their bonds for the common stock of the firm. The ratio of the number of shares of stock you may acquire for each bond surrendered is called the conversion ratio. The bonds may be convertible as of a certain future date, and there is frequently a provision for the conversion ratio to fall as the bonds approach maturity.

When corporate bonds are issued, they are backed by an *indenture* in which the firm promises to the bond *trustee* that it will comply with certain provisions. Among these are the payment of scheduled interest and principal. There may also be restrictions on the amounts of dividends that can be paid to stockholders. There may be restrictions on the use of the proceeds of the bond issue, guarantees on the acquisition of insurance, and restrictions on investments by the firm in the capital market.

The vast majority of corporate bonds are *callable*. As with treasury bonds, this gives the issuing firm the option to retire the bonds at a stated call price. The call option usually becomes operative after a stated period of call protection, which is usually either 5 or 10 years after original issuance. The call price usually begins at a value close to the sum of the principal plus one annual interest payment, and it steadily declines to the value of the principal at maturity.

Corporate bonds may also contain *sinking fund provisions*. The sinking fund provision requires the firm to retire a stated fraction of the issue each year. In complying with this provision, the firm can usually exercise one of three options. It can (1) retire the bonds at a stated sinking fund call price. If this action is taken, the bonds retired will be determined by lottery. It can also (2) purchase the required quantity of the bonds in the open market. Many sinking funds give the firm a third option of (3) acquiring bonds of other firms of similar quality in the market. The third option is designed to prevent financial institutions from buying large blocks of the bonds in an effort to force the firm to exercise option 1, when it would be more advantageous for them to exercise option 2. This strategy is called "cornering the sinking fund," and it enables the financial institution to sell the bonds to the firm for considerably more than they are worth, based on prevailing interest rates.

Commercial paper is a short-term promissory note issued by a corporation. The maximum maturity of commercial paper is 270 days, and is issued in denominations of $100,000 or more. The quality of commercial paper can be variable and depends on the quality of the issuing firms and their access to other forms of credit. Commercial paper can be placed through the market or through dealers. In the case of dealer placed paper, the dealer sets the rate and stands behind the payments.

Corporate bonds are rated as to quality by two major rating agencies, Standard & Poor's Corporation and Moody's. The ratings are based on an analysis of the

TABLE 2.1 Moody's Rating System

Aaa Bonds which are rated Aaa are judged to be of the best quality. They carry the smallest degree of investment risk and are generally referred to as "gilt edge." Interest payments are protected by a large or by an exceptionally stable margin, and principal is secure. While the various protective elements are likely to change, such changes as can be visualized are most unlikely to impair the fundamentally strong position of such issues.

Aa Bonds which are rated Aa are judged to be of high quality by all standards. Together with the Aaa group they comprise what are generally known as high-grade bonds. They are rated lower than the best bonds because margins of protection may not be as large as in Aaa securities or fluctuation of protective elements may be of greater amplitude or there may be other elements present which make the long-term risks appear somewhat larger than in Aaa securities.

A Bonds which are rated A possess many favorable investment attributes and are to be considered as upper-medium-grade obligations. Factors giving security to principal and interest are considered adequate, but elements may be present which suggest a susceptibility to impairment sometime in the future.

Baa Bonds which are rated Baa are considered as medium-grade obligations; that is, they are neither highly protected nor poorly secured. Interest payments and principal security appear adequate for the present, but certain protective elements may be lacking or may be characteristically unreliable over any great length of time. Such bonds lack outstanding investment characteristics and in fact have speculative characteristics as well.

Ba Bonds which are rated Ba are judged to have speculative elements; their future cannot be considered as well assured. Often the protection of interest and principal payments may be very moderate and thereby not well safeguarded during both good and bad times over the future. Uncertainty of position characterizes bonds in this class.

B Bonds which are rated B generally lack characteristics of the desirable investment. Assurance of interest and principal payments or of maintenance of other terms of the contract over any long period of time may be small.

Caa Bonds which are rated Caa are of poor standing. Such issues may be in default or there may be present elements of danger with respect to principal or interest.

Ca Bonds which are rated Ca represent obligations which are speculative in a high degree. Such issues are often in default or have other marked shortcomings.

C Bonds which are rated C are the lowest-rated class of bonds, and issues so rated can be regarded as having extremely poor prospects of ever attaining any real investment standing.

SOURCE: *Moody's Bond Record,* July 1984, p. 1.

TABLE 2.2 Standard & Poor's Rating System

AAA Debt rated AAA has the highest rating assigned by Standard & Poor's. Capacity to pay interest and repay principal is extremely strong.

AA Debt rated AA has a very strong capacity to pay interest and repay principal and differs from the higher-rated issues only in small degree.

A Debt rated A has a strong capacity to pay interest and repay principal, although it is somewhat more susceptible to the adverse effects of changes in circumstances and economic conditions than debt in higher-rated categories.

BBB Debt rated BBB is regarded as having an adequate capacity to pay interest and repay principal. Whereas it normally exhibits adequate protection parameters, adverse economic conditions or changing circumstances are more likely to lead to a weakened capacity to pay interest and repay principal for debt in this category than in higher-rated categories.

BB, B, CCC, CC Debt rated BB, B, CCC, and CC is regarded, on balance, as predominantly speculative with respect to capacity to pay interest and repay principal in accordance with the terms of the obligation. BB indicates the lowest degree of speculation and CC the highest degree of speculation. While such debt will likely have some quality and protective characteristics these are outweighed by large uncertainties or major risk exposures to adverse conditions.

C The rating C is reserved for income bonds on which no interest is being paid.

D Debt rated D is in default, and payment of interest and/or repayment of principal is in arrears.

SOURCE: Standard & Poor's *Corporation Bond Guide,* August 1984, p. 9.

firm's financial statements and other factors such as the nature of its industry and its position in the industry. Of major concern is the extent to which the firm can be expected to weather economic adversity, such as a major recession. A listing of the ratings by each agency is provided in Tables 2.1 and 2.2.

Figure 2.4 is a partial listing of quotations for corporate bonds. The first column identifies the issuer of the bonds, the annual interest payment as a percentage of face or principal, and the year of maturity. The second column, "Cur Yld," lists the bond's current yield or the ratio of the annual interest payment to the current market value of the bond. The next three columns list the highest traded price, the lowest traded price, and the closing price for the day. The final column lists the change in the closing price from the previous day.

Annual rates of return and the frequency distribution of returns to a portfolio of long-term corporate bonds are given in Figures 2.5(a) and 2.5(b). These returns are affected, for the most part, by fluctuations in prevailing interest rates, although changes in the anticipated probabilities for default also play a role.

Corporate Stock

Preferred stock is a hybrid of sorts between a fixed and a variable income security. Its claim isn't really fixed and definite in the sense it can force the firm into bankruptcy if it isn't paid in full. On the other hand, its claim *is* limited in size to a

CORPORATION BONDS
Volume, $39,120,000

Bonds	Cur Yld	Vol	High	Low	Close	Net Chg.
AMR 10¼06	10.4	2	99	99	99	...
Advst 9s08	cv	225	115	113	114¾	− 1¼
AetnLf 8⅛07	8.6	10	95	95	95	+ 1¾
AlaP 9s2000	9.3	7	97¾	96⅞	96⅞	+ ½
AlaP 7¾s02	8.9	20	87¼	87⅛	87⅛	...
AlaP 8⅞s03	9.3	20	95¾	95¾	95¾	+ ⅜
AlaP 10⅞05	10.6	4	103	103	103	...
AlaP 10½05	10.2	9	103⅜	103⅜	103⅜	+ ½
AlaP 8¾07	9.3	17	94⅜	94⅛	94⅜	+ 1⅜
AlaP 9¼07	9.3	12	99	99	99	+ ⅛
AlaP 9½08	9.5	40	99¾	97⅛	99¾	+ 1⅛
AlaP 9⅝08	9.7	11	98¾	98¾	98¾	− ¼
AlaP 12⅝10	11.6	6	109¼	109¼	109¼	− ¼
AlaP 15¼10	13.6	96	112¼	112¼	112¼	...
AlaP 18¼89	16.9	42	108	107½	108	+ 1
AlskA 9s03	cv	10	114	114	114	− 3
AlskH 16¼99	14.4	13	113	113	113	...
AlskH 17¾91	14.8	13	119¾	119¾	119¾	− 1¼
AlskH 18⅜01	16.4	190	115	110⅜	111⅞	− 3⅛
AlskH 15¼92	14.5	28	105	105	105	...
AlskH 12⅞93	12.3	10	105	105	105	+ 1
Alco 8½10	cv	10	113	113	113	− 1½
AllgWt 4s98	6.8	3	59⅛	59⅛	59⅛	+ ⅝
Allgl 10.4s02	12.5	27	83⅞	83¼	83¼	− ⅝
Allgl 9s89	9.8	4	91⅜	91⅜	91⅜	+ ⅞
AlldC 6.6s93	7.3	1	90¼	90¼	90¼	...
AlldC 7⅞96	8.2	25	96½	96½	96½	− 1½
AlldC zr87	...	30	90⅞	90⅞	90⅞	...
AlldC zr92	...	16	58⅝	58⅜	58⅜	− ⅝
AlldC zr96	...	40	43½	43	43	− 1⅜
AlldC zr98	...	3	33½	33½	33½	+ ⅛
AlldC zr2000	...	45	27¾	27⅜	27¾	+ ⅛
AlldC d6s88	6.3	5	94⅞	94¾	94⅞	+ ⅛
AlldC d6s90	6.5	8	92½	92½	92½	+ 1¾
AlldC zr91	...	50	64	64	64	− 1
AlldC zr95	...	50	44⅛	44⅛	44⅛	+ ⅛
AlldC zr05	...	5	17¾	17¾	17¾	+ ¼
AlldC zr09	...	65	13	13	13	+ ⅛
AlsCha 16s91	14.3	27	111½	111½	111½	...
Alcoa 7.45s96	8.2	1	91⅜	91⅜	91⅜	− ⅛
AMAX 8½96	10.3	20	82⅝	82⅝	82⅝	...
AMAX 14¼90	13.3	60	107⅝	107⅜	107⅜	− ¼
AMAX 14½94	13.2	46	110⅛	110	110	− ⅝
AAirl 4¼92	5.6	4	76⅛	76	76	+ ¾
ABrnd 4⅝90	5.2	1	88⅛	88⅛	88⅛	+ ⅛
ABrnd 5⅞92	6.6	2	89⅜	89⅜	89⅜	+ ⅜
ACan 6s97	7.6	6	79⅛	79	79	− ½
ACan 11⅜10	10.5	4	108	108	108	+ 1
ACan 13¼93	12.0	25	110½	110½	110½	+ ½
ACeM 6¾91	cv	10	67½	67½	67½	− 2⅞
AExC 14¾92	12.4	17	119	119	119	...
AmGn 11s07	cv	3	210	210	210	+ 1
AHoist 5½93	cv	38	73	73	73	...
AmMed 9½01	cv	170	106	105	105	− 1
AmMed 8¼08	cv	37	96¾	96½	96¾	...
AmMot 6s88	cv	4	89½	89¼	89½	+ ⅛

FIGURE 2.4 Quotations for corporate bonds.

SOURCE: *The Wall Street Journal,* May 2, 1986, p. 38. Reprinted by permission of *The Wall Street Journal,* Dow Jones & Company, Inc., 1986. All rights reserved.

specified amount. In general, the only leverage a preferred stockholder has over the firm is that no dividends can be paid on the common stock until the specified dividends have been paid on the preferred stock. Preferred stocks are usually perpetual securities having no maturity date, although there are exceptions to this general rule. Preferred stocks are commonly callable, however.

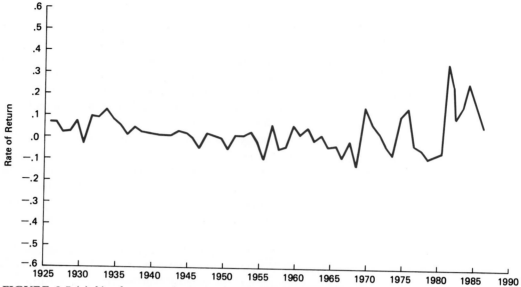

FIGURE 2.5.(a) Yearly rates of return on corporate bonds.

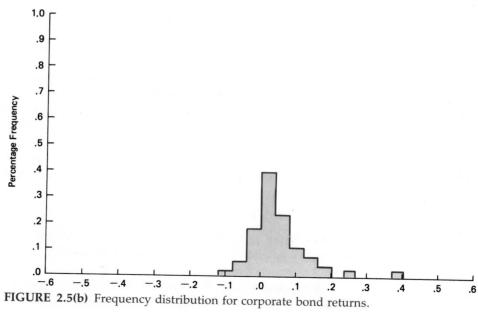

FIGURE 2.5(b) Frequency distribution for corporate bond returns.

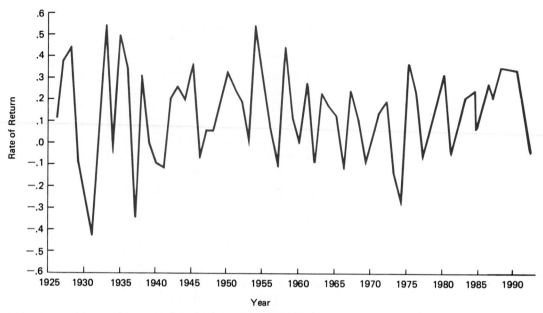

FIGURE 2.7(a) Yearly rates of return on common stocks.

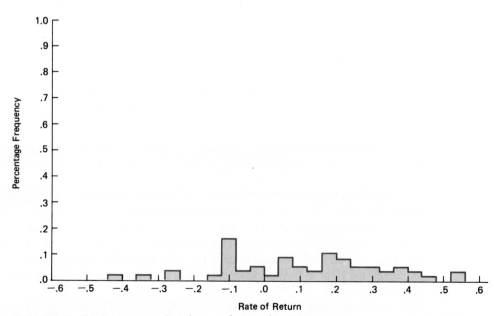

FIGURE 2.7(b) Frequency distribution for stock returns.

Library of Congress Cataloging-in-Publication Data

Haugen, Robert A.
  Modern investment theory / Robert A. Haugen. — 2nd ed.
    p.   cm.
  ISBN 0-13-594797-9
  1. Investment analysis.   2. Portfolio management.   I. Title.
  HG4529.H38   1989
  332.6—dc20   89-22849
                                                           CIP

Editorial/production supervision: Carolyn Kart
Interior design: Judith A. Matz - Coniglio
Cover design: Judith A. Matz - Coniglio
Manufacturing buyer: Ed O'Dougherty and Mary Ann Gloriande

© 1990, 1886 by PRENTICE-HALL, INC.
A Division of Simon & Schuster
Englewood Cliffs, N.J. 07632

Printed in the United States of America

10 9 8 7 6 5 4 3 2 1

0-13-594797-9

Prentice-Hall International (UK) Limited, *London*
Prentice-Hall of Australia Pty. Limited, *Sydney*
Prentice-Hall Canada Inc., *Toronto*
Prentice-Hall Hispanoamericana, S.A., *Mexico*
Prentice-Hall of India Private Limited, *New Delhi*
Prentice-Hall of Japan, Inc., *Tokyo*
Simon & Schuster Asia Pte. Ltd., *Singapore*
Editora Prentice-Hall do Brasil, Ltda., *Rio de Janeiro*
Prentice-Hall, Inc., *Englewood Cliffs, New Jersey*

CHICAGO BOARD

Option & NY Close	Strike Price	Calls—Last			Puts—Last		
		May	Jun	Jul	May	Jun	Jul
Amrtch	115	r	r	r	5/8	r	r
118 7/8	120	1	r	3 5/8	r	r	r
Atl R	45	s	s	7 1/2	s	s	r
52 7/8	50	r	3 1/2	4	1/4	15/16	1 1/16
52 7/8	55	5/16	7/8	1 5/8	r	3 1/2	4 1/4
52 7/8	60	r	r	3/8	r	r	r
BankAm	12 1/2	r	s	5	r	s	1/16
17 1/4	15	r	r	2 3/4	1/16	3/16	3/8
17 1/4	17 1/2	7/16	1	1 3/8	11/16	1	1 3/8
17 1/4	20	1/8	7/16	3/4	2 5/8	r	3
BellAtl	60	r	r	4 3/4	1/4	r	r
63 7/8	62 1/2	r	s	3	r	s	r
63 7/8	65	3/8	r	2 1/4	r	r	r
63 7/8	70	1/16	r	3/4	r	r	r
Citicp	50	s	s	9 3/4	s	s	3/8
59 1/8	55	r	r	5 7/8	r	1 1/8	1 1/4
59 1/8	60	1	2 1/2	3	1 15/16	2 5/8	3
59 1/8	65	1/4	11/16	1 1/8	5 7/8	6 5/8	r
Cullin	12 1/2	1 1/2	r	r	r	r	9/16
13 5/8	15	1/4	3/4	1	r	r	2
13 5/8	17 1/2	r	1/4	3/8	r	r	r
Delta	40	r	r	r	r	1/8	7/16
47	45	2 3/8	3 3/8	4	3/8	1 1/4	1 1/2
47	50	3/8	1	1 1/2	r	3 3/4	r
EKodak	50	s	s	8 1/2	s	s	3/4
57	55	2 7/8	3 3/4	4 5/8	5/8	1 5/8	2
57	60	9/16	1 1/2	2 1/2	3 3/8	4 1/2	4 7/8
57	65	1/8	11/16	1 1/8	r	r	8 3/8
Exxon	50	6 5/8	s	6 1/2	r	s	1/4
56 5/8	55	1 1/2	2 1/8	2 7/8	9/16	1 1/4	1 1/2
56 5/8	60	1/8	1/2	13/16	r	r	4 7/8
FedExp	45	s	s	r	s	s	1/16
62 3/4	55	7 1/8	s	r	1/8	s	1
62 3/4	60	3 1/4	4 5/8	6 1/8	5/8	1 3/4	2 1/4
62 3/4	65	11/16	2 1/2	3	3	4 1/2	5 1/8
62 3/4	70	1/8	3/4	1 1/2	r	r	r
62 3/4	75	s	s	11/16	s	s	r
Grumm	25	r	3 1/2	r	r	r	7/8
27 3/4	30	1/4	5/8	7/8	r	r	r
27 3/4	35	s	s	1/4	s	s	r
Halbtn	20	r	r	2 1/2	3/8	5/8	3/4
22	25	1/16	3/16	3/8	r	r	3 1/2
22	22 1/2	r	1	1 3/4	1 1/8	r	1 1/2
22	30	s	s	1/16	s	s	r
Homstk	20	r	2 1/2	2 1/2	3/8	3/4	1 3/16
21 5/8	22 1/2	3/8	3/4	13/16	1 3/8	1 3/4	2 1/8
21 5/8	25	1/16	3/16	1/2	r	r	4
21 5/8	30	r	s	1/8	r	s	8 3/8
I B M	130	s	s	r	s	s	3/16
156 3/4	135	s	s	23	s	s	3/8
156 3/4	140	16 3/4	s	18 3/4	1/16	s	5/8
156 3/4	145	11 7/8	12 1/4	14 1/2	1/8	7/8	1 1/2
156 3/4	150	7 3/8	9 1/4	11	11/16	2	3
156 3/4	155	3 3/8	6 1/4	7 7/8	2 1/8	4	5
156 3/4	160	1 5/16	3 7/8	5 1/2	5 1/8	6 1/2	7 1/2
156 3/4	165	3/8	2 3/16	3 5/8	r	9 5/8	10 1/2
In Pap	55	2 3/4	3 3/4	4	1	r	1 3/4
57	60	5/8	1 11/16	2 3/8	r	r	4 3/4
57	65	1/16	r	7/8	r	r	r
57	70	s	s	5/8	s	s	r

FIGURE 2.8 Quotations for put and call options.

SOURCE: *The Wall Street Journal,* May 2, 1986, p. 42. Reprinted by permission of *The Wall Street Journal,* © Dow Jones & Company, Inc., 1986. All rights reserved.

written on, as well as current market price for the stock. The second column lists the exercise or strike price for the option. Then the closing market prices for three different call options, all with the given exercise price but expiring in the months of May, June, and July, are given. The symbol ''r'' indicates that the option was not traded on the previous day. The symbol ''s'' indicates that no option exists for this stock at that expiration date and strike price. Closing market prices for put options are provided in the final three columns.

A *warrant,* on the other hand, is a primary security. It is issued by a firm, and it is a claim on the assets of the firm. A warrant, is in all other respects, identical to a call option, although warrants usually have longer lives than call options. A warrant gives its holder the right to purchase shares of stock in the firm at a particular price before a particular date. If the warrant is exercised, the firm must issue new shares of common stock to the holder of the warrant. Thus, the effect of exercise is to dilute the per share value of the stock.

Warrants are often given to executives as part of their compensation. They are also frequently attached to other securities, such as bonds, when originally issued to make the issue more attractive to investors.

Forward and Futures Contracts

Forward and *futures contracts* obligate you to buy or sell a particular commodity at a particular price on a particular day. These are to be distinguished from options in that they don't give you the *right* to buy or sell; they *obligate* you to buy or sell.

Because of this, forward contracts can do something none of the other contracts discussed earlier can do. Their values can become negative! If you have obligated yourself to buy a commodity at a price of $100 and the commodity is currently selling at a price of $70, the value of your forward contract to buy is negative. You would actually pay someone to take it off your hands. If you buy a forward or futures contract, you have obligated yourself to buy the commodity at the stated price. On the other hand, if you sell such a contract, you have obligated yourself to sell the commodity at the stated price.

When originated, the contracted price you must later buy or sell for is set such that the buyer and seller will exchange the contract with no associated cash payment. That is, the forward or futures price is set to make the current market value of the contract equal to zero. The market value of a *forward* contract is allowed to subsequently become positive or negative as the commodity price goes up or down. In the case of a *futures* contract, however, one aspect of the contract is changed each day to keep the market value of the contract at zero. The aspect of the contract that is revised is the futures price, in a process called *marking to market.*

The process of marking to market is an important feature which differentiates a futures from a forward contract. To see how it works, consider the following example.

Suppose you buy a futures contract on June 1 to buy wheat in September at $10 a bushel. On June 2 other futures contracts are being negotiated at $11 a bushel. The terms of your contract would now be revised to $11, and you would have the difference of $1 added to your account. If instead, the negotiated price went down to $9, you would have to make up the difference by adding $1 to your account. This process continues on a daily basis.

Futures contracts are written on commodities such as gold, silver, and agricultural products as well as on various financial contracts such as treasury bills, treasury bonds, Ginnie Mae passthroughs, and even stock market indices. In fact, the market for financial futures is currently exploding in terms of types of contracts traded, volume of trading, and investor interest.

The Shares of Investment Companies and Mutual Funds

The investments already described are individual securities. You would normally not invest in these one at a time. Rather, you would combine many of them into a well-diversified portfolio to reduce the risk of your overall investment. It may be possible, however, that you don't have the funds to spread over many individual investments or the time to manage such a portfolio. If this is the case, you may want to consider investing in a closed-end investment company or a mutual fund. Both these institutions manage a diversified portfolio for you. When you invest with these institutions you, in effect, buy into a piece of the portfolio. The difference between them is in the way this is accomplished.

A *closed-end investment company* makes an initial sale of shares to investors much in the way any corporation does when it commences operations or finances a new investment project. The investment company takes the proceeds of the sale of shares and invests it in a diversified portfolio of securities. To buy into the portfolio, you must buy shares of the portfolio from individual investors who already own them. These shares are traded in the financial markets. To buy them, you must pay the same types of brokerage commissions you would pay to buy stock. Closed-end investment companies are conceptually identical to nonfinancial corporations, except that they make financial investments, while nonfinancial corporations make real, economic investments in things such as plant and equipment.

Closed-end investment companies have an interest feature which, at times, can make them attractive investments. From time to time, these companies publish the total market value of the securities in their portfolios. If you compare these total market values with the total market value of the shares in the closed-end investment company, you will often find big differences. More often than not, the market value of the shares in the investment company is less than the market value of the securities in the company's portfolio. In fact, at times, the market value of the shares can be as little as 60 percent of the market value of the securities. This means, if you invest in the investment company, you acquire the securities at bargain prices. Thompson (1978) has shown the shares of these deeply discounted investment companies which produce abnormally large rates of return to their investors *after* the discounts have been established. It seems to be an investment opportunity worth watching.

There are many more *mutual funds* than there are closed-end investment companies. You buy shares in the mutual fund directly from the fund itself. The price you pay for each share is equal to the total market value of the securities in the fund divided by the number of shares currently outstanding. As a consequence, there are no opportunities for ''bargains'' in mutual fund shares. Some mutual funds charge a sales fee, or a ''load,'' to buy into the fund. For many other funds, there is no such fee. All mutual funds, however, charge a management fee to cover the expenses incurred by the fund for analysis and administration. Management fees can range from 2 percent of the total market value of the portfolio per year to as little as $\frac{1}{2}$ percent.

There are many types of mutual funds with different investment objectives. Money market funds invest in short-term, high-quality, fixed income securities. The market value of these funds is quite stable, but their yields fluctuate on a daily basis. There are also mutual funds that invest in long-term U.S. government bonds, corporate bonds, municipal bonds, bonds and stock, and common stock of different types.

As an investor in a mutual fund, you can typically arrange to write checks on your account with the fund. Many mutual funds manage several different types of

	NAV	Offer NAV Price Chg.
AARP Invest Program:		
Cap Grw	22.34	N.L.− .06
Gen Bnd	16.05	N.L.− .02
Ginnie M	16.11	N.L. ...
Gro Inc	21.39	N.L.− .13
TxFr Bd	16.21	N.L.− .02
TxF Shrt	15.51	N.L.+ .01
ABT Midwest Funds:	.....	
Emrg Gr	9.38	10.25− .04
Growth I	13.48	14.73− .03
Int Govt	10.73	10.74− .01
LG Govt	10.79	11.24− .02
Sec Inc	10.98	12.00− .05
Util Inc	14.36	15.69+ .04
Acorn Fnd	41.01	N.L.− .04
Adtek Fd	12.02	N.L.− .05
Advest Advantage:	....	
Govt	10.08	N.L.− .02
Growth	10.55	N.L.− .03
Income	10.32	N.L.+ .02
Specl	10.33	N.L.− .02
Afuture Fd	14.98	N.L.− .04
AIM Funds:		
Conv Yld	12.90	13.80− .05
Grnway	10.48	11.21− .05
HiYld Sc	10.08	10.78+ .01
Summit	7.08	(z) − .03
Alliance Capital:		
Alli Gov	9.33	9.87− .04
Alli HiY	10.58	11.20− .02
Alli Intl	21.77	23.79− .46
Alli Mtge	9.78	10.35 ...
Alli Tech	23.88	26.10− .18
Chem Fd	9.15	10.00− .05
Survevr	16.75	18.31− .06

FIGURE 2.9 Quotations for mutual funds.

SOURCE: *The Wall Street Journal,* May 2, 1986, p. 40. Reprinted by permission of *The Wall Street Journal,* © Dow Jones & Company, Inc., 1986. All rights reserved.

portfolios. If you wish to transfer some or all of your funds from the money market portfolio to the long-term U.S. government bond portfolio, or any of the other portfolios run by the fund, you can arrange to do this simply by making a telephone call to the fund.

Mutual funds provide a very convenient way to manage your money. If you are a small investor, they provide an economical way to diversify your portfolio broadly. To the extent the fund's investment decisions are made by skillful analysts who can spot undervalued securities, they may also be able to provide additional, abnormal returns for you. This latter point is the subject of much controversy, and we will talk about this more in Chapter 23.

A partial listing of some quotations for mutual funds is provided in Figure 2.9. At the top of each list the organization is identified in boldface type. The individual types of funds sponsored by the organization are provided below. For example, the AARP Invest Program has a capital growth stock fund, a general bond fund, a fund that invests in Ginnie Mae passthroughs, a growth-income fund that invests in bonds as well as stocks, a state and municipal bond fund, and a fund that invests in short-term tax-exempt securities. The column labeled ''NAV'' (net asset value) lists the total market value of the securities owned by the fund divided by the number of outstanding shares in the fund. The offer price includes this net asset value plus the maximum charge required to buy the fund, if any is so assessed on the investor.

THE FINANCIAL MARKETS

The Difference Between Primary and Secondary Markets

When securities are initially offered to the public, they are said to be sold in the **primary market**. In the primary market, the proceeds of sale are used by the seller, perhaps a corporation, to make investments in real capital goods or for other purposes allowed under its corporate charter.

Investment banking firms are important institutions in the primary market. They stand between the corporation and its potential security holders and provide the corporation with a number of important services in marketing its securities. They have a knowledge of the current state of the market, and they provide the firm with information about how much money can be currently raised and what types of securities would be most effective in raising it. They prepare a prospectus, which is a brochure disclosing information relevant to the valuation of the securities by potential investors. They may also organize a group of individual investment bankers to work together on the actual distribution, or sale of the securities and the collection of the proceeds. If after the initial offering some securities remain unsold, the investment bankers are allowed to maintain order in the market for the securities for up to 10 days after the initial offering.

Investment bankers may be compensated in two ways. In a fixed price offering, they promise the firm a fixed amount of proceeds from the sale, and they take title to the issue and receive the difference between this fixed amount and what they actually are able to raise. Alternatively, in a best efforts agreement the bankers do not take title and promise only to give the best possible effort in marketing the securities for a fixed fee.

Securities are frequently *privately placed* in the primary market. If the investment bankers contact a minimum number of potential buyers for the offering, many of the costly disclosure requirements of the Securities and Exchange Commission, such as the prospectus, are waived. Also, the issue can frequently be better tailored to meet the needs of the issuing firm and the investors who make the final purchase. Private placements are usually made to financial institutions, and in the vast majority of cases, they involve bond issues.

Financial institutions, such as commercial banks and savings and loans, also participate in the primary market when they make loans to business firms and even to individuals for purposes of home construction. These institutions stand as an intermediary between individual savers and the borrowers of the funds. The intermediaries act as agencies who collect information (which might not otherwise be publicly disclosed) from borrowers, analyze information (using techniques and skills which might not be available to the general public), and repackage investments (such as loans and mortgages) into forms (checking and savings deposits) which are more attractive to individual investors.

After securities are initially offered in the primary market, they are then traded from investor to investor in the *secondary market.* The role of the secondary market is to provide investors with liquidity for their investments, enabling them to move quickly, and without substantial loss in market value, from security to cash and from one security to another. In buying or selling in the secondary market, you will either trade in an organized exchange or in the over-the-counter market. Organized exchanges are centralized auction-type markets, while the over-the-counter market is an intricate network of security dealers that take positions in various securities and buy and sell from their own portfolios.

The Organized Exchanges for Common Stock and Bonds

There are several organized stock exchanges in the United States and Canada. By far, the largest is the New York Stock Exchange, in which the shares of approximately 1600 companies are traded. The second largest stock exchange is the American Stock Exchange (AMEX). The other exchanges are much smaller and are called regional exchanges.

Most of the exchanges deal in a variety of security types in addition to common stock. You can buy or sell corporate bonds on the NYSE as well as warrants. In addition to these, you can trade in options on the AMEX and on some of the regional exchanges, such as the Pacific Coast Stock Exchange.

Suppose you want to buy 100 shares of International Business Machines stock. You would first call a brokerage house in your town. This will probably be a branch of a large firm such as the Milwaukee Company. If you don't have an account there, they will ask you to open one. You will fill out a form disclosing information about your personal income and finances. You will deal with a broker who will probably be your connection with the market for some time to come. The broker will provide you with information about the company you are interested in, about general economic trends, and about other investments of interest. The brokerage house may also have attractive investment packages such as tax shelters of various forms and will also provide you with information about these.

It is important for you to understand that brokers are, for the most part, salespeople. They are a very heterogeneous group in terms of their training in finance and investments. If you are going to rely on a broker for investment advice, as opposed to a mere link between you and the market, it's important for you to determine the broker's formal training and experience before you act on his or her recommendations.

From the brokerage house, your order will be called to the floor of the exchange to a person called a *floor broker.* These individuals actually buy and sell securities on the floor of the exchange. The floor broker will buy your 100 shares of IBM from a person called a *specialist.* The specialist keeps an inventory in one or more stocks and buys and sells out of that inventory. The specialists publicize prices at which they are willing to buy a stock (bid prices) and prices at which they are willing to sell (asked prices). These prices are based on the orders to buy and sell the stock *at specific prices* other traders have made before you or the price the specialists are ready to buy or sell the stock for from their own accounts. In any case, the specialist must trade on the basis of the price which is more advantageous to you.

After seeing the bid and asked prices, the floor broker will call out a price he or she is willing to pay for the stock. The stock may be bought from the specialist, or for that matter, anyone else on the floor of the exchange who is willing to sell the stock at that price. If the trade is consummated, you get the shares for that price.

To execute the trade for you, you will be charged a commission by the brokerage house. The commission will be anywhere from 1 percent to 10 percent of the total market value of the transaction, depending on the price per share and the number of shares you buy. In general, the smaller the transaction, the larger the commission. If you buy or sell in less than a round lot (100 shares), you will be charged an additional fee. If you want to minimize your commissions, you may want to deal with a *discount broker* as opposed to a *full-service broker.* Full-service brokers provide you with investment advice and with investment packages such as tax shelters, and they are willing to hold your securities for you in safe keeping until you are ready to trade again. Discount brokers provide none of these services. They just execute your trade, but they do it at a lower price.

You can make your trade by employing any one of a number of different orders. If you use a *market order,* the broker will buy or sell the number of securities directed at the best available price. If you use a *limit order,* the trade will be executed only at a price at least as advantageous as a stated price. If the trade can't be completed at that price, it is delayed until it is possible to execute it under those conditions. A *stop loss order,* on the other hand, is an order to sell a stock you already own as soon as its price falls to a specified level. Orders can also be differentiated on the basis of allowable time for completion. An order is *good until canceled* if it remains in effect indefinitely. A *day order* must be executed by the end of the day, or it is cancelled. A *fill or kill* order must be executed immediately or cancelled.

OUT ON THE STREET

GETTING STARTED

Lightning in a snowstorm. Tom Dumphy knew what that meant from past experience. At least 6 inches of snow would fall tonight. The first real snow of the winter. Just in time, this being the beginning of the holiday season.

Tom stared out his window, which was really part of the outer wall of the glass-enclosed First Wisconsin Bank Building in Madison, Wisconsin. Directly across the street was the State Capitol Building, an almost exact replica of the Capitol building in Washington, D.C. Floodlights illuminated the building from four sides. It was eerie. The floodlights, the lightning, the snow created a scene that Tom would remember for some time to come.

From the outside, the light in Tom's room was a single beacon on the western wall of the building. It was 6 P.M., and nearly everyone had already left for home. Tom was about to leave as well.

For Tom life was good. He lived comfortably, felt secure, fulfilled. Over the years as a broker for the Milwaukee Company, he had built up a solid clientele.

But it hadn't always been this way.

He started in the business in January 1973, after graduating with a bachelor's degree in finance from the state university. After 4 or 5 months of training and correspondence courses and passing two exams, Tom received his license and officially entered the business. Many people have the conception that stockbrokers become rich overnight. Not true. Tom found himself at ground zero. While he was guaranteed a salary for his first year, after that he was going to be strictly on his own, receiving 40 percent of all the commissions he could generate. Here at ground zero he had *no* customers, and he needed a "system" to generate some.

There are many different "systems." You can cold-call people on the telephone. You can walk the streets and introduce yourself to likely prospects. You can use mass mailings or even seminars. As one of Tom's colleagues is fond of saying, "The name of this game is exposure. Expose yourself any way you can, short of indecent."

Tom's system was to go through the city directory looking for the names of the executives of the major corporations. Even before he got his license, he compiled an extensive list of names and addresses. Then he would send out 10 to 15 pieces of mail a day, containing some research information and a letter introducing himself and saying he'd be calling in the future. The future was the next day.

Landing clients wasn't easy. Tom remembers contacting one person eight

Organized Exchanges for Options

Options are traded on four organized exchanges in the United States: the Chicago Board Options Exchange, the American Stock Exchange, the Philadelphia Stock Exchange, and the Pacific Coast Stock Exchange.

times. Each time the prospective client showed interest, but Tom would never get an order. Finally, Tom convinced him to invest in Westinghouse Electric stock and he became Tom's first customer. The next week, Westinghouse announced some really bad news and the price of the stock fell by half. After picking his heart up from the floor, Tom bit the bullet, picked up the phone, and explained the situation to the client. The client was impressed with his sincerity, realized the situation couldn't be anticipated in advance, and stayed on until this very day. Honesty is very important in this business; if something is going wrong, don't try to hide it. Tell them!

In January 1973 the Dow hit 1050. It wouldn't see that level again for many years. These were rough times in the business. Of the eight young brokers Tom started with, all now have left the business. Tom stuck it out, and he's glad he did.

The best thing about being a broker is that you are your own person. You have the freedom of basically running your own business. You can work when you want and as hard as you want. Some brokers who stay in the business make as little as $30,000. But others make 10 times that much, even in a relatively small community like Madison. In larger cities the big producers make $600,000, with a few exceptions in the $1 million to $2 million range.

The worst thing is the uncertainty of the market and the stress that comes with it. No matter how hard you try to do a good job, no matter how sound your advice is, the market may always turn on you. You must then watch your clients lose money and know it's beyond your control. It affects your personal relationship with them. You lose sleep. It's difficult to shake that feeling.

Tom has long passed the initial building stage of his career, but the building never really stops. He now builds on referrals and looks toward bigger accounts like pension and profit-sharing plans. You never really do stop cold calling, however. In fact, he spent the entire morning introducing himself to people who hopefully had some holiday spirit.

Now it's time for Tom to have some holiday spirit.

He rises from his desk and hits the light switch.

The western glass wall of the building is now a solid mirror, reflecting the spectacle of the lights, the lightning, and the snow falling on the capitol.

As you recall, an option is a contract to buy or sell a stock at a stated exercise price. Normally, when you acquire an option to buy something such as a house, you are dealing with a particular individual. If you decide to exercise your option, you will buy the house from that particular individual. When you buy or sell options through an organized options exchange, however, an *exchange clearing house* stands between you and the other party to the contract. If you decide to exercise the option you have acquired, the clearing house will randomly match you up with some-one who sold the option you want to exercise.

This process of matching requires the options be standardized with respect to their characteristics. For any given stock, the options outstanding on the stock will have a few specific exercise prices, usually differentiated by $10 amounts, and a few specific expiration dates, usually approximately three months apart, with the maxi-mum being nine months off.

The clearing house guarantees to the buyer of an option that the terms of the contract will be honored if it is exercised. The clearing house backs the contract with its own financial resources. It also requires the sellers of the option to escrow the proceeds of sale and to put up an additional amount of money as a margin to guar-antee they will be able to honor the contracts if they are exercised.

Organized Exchanges for Futures Contracts

Among the organized exchanges that trade in futures contracts are the Chicago Mer-cantile Exchange, the Chicago Board of Trade, and the New York Futures Exchange.

As with the options exchanges, a clearing house stands between the buyers and sellers of futures contracts. Because of the presence of the clearing corporation, buy-ers of the contracts need not be concerned about the creditworthiness of sellers, and vice versa. However, since buyers and sellers once again are randomly matched, the terms of the contract must be standardized—this time with respect to expiration date, since the exercise price is the same for all futures contracts after marking to market.

Membership in the exchange itself can be divided between *commission brokers* who execute trades for customers, and *locals,* who trade for their own accounts.

Locals are typically classified on the basis of their trading horizon. Those with the shortest trading horizons are called *scalpers.* These individuals operate on the basis of a heavy volume of trading and try to take advantage of the smallest trade-to-trade fluctuations in the price of the commodity. *Day traders* look to wider price swings that occur during the course of a day, but they rarely carry a position over-night. A *position trader* holds a position over the course of days or even weeks. They are concerned with extended price movements which result from fundamental changes in supply and demand relationships for the commodity. A *spreader,* on the other hand, watches the shifting relationships between prices for different delivery dates for the same commodity. When these relationships move away from their typ-ical patterns, these traders will move in and sell the high market and buy the low market.

Futures contracts are seldom actually executed. Normally buyers and sellers liquidate their positions through the clearing corporation before the expiration date. If you are a buyer and choose to take delivery on the contract, you must notify the clearing corporation two business days before the first day allowed for making deliv-ery. Sellers of the contract must also notify the clearing house if they intend to deliver. The clearing house then matches buyers and sellers and notifies both parties of their identities. The sellers then acquire the commodity for delivery and make delivery, and title passes from seller to buyer.

The sellers actually have a limited choice of commodities or financial securities they can deliver. Thus, if you are going to deliver a treasury bond futures contract, you don't have to deliver a particular bond. Rather, you have a choice of delivering any treasury bond that has 15 or more years to maturity or earliest call date. If a *particular* bond were called for, the seller might find that the market for the bond was difficult to purchase when needed. To avoid this risk, the seller of a financial futures contract is usually given a limited choice of deliverable bonds.

The Over-the-Counter Market

Securities which aren't traded on organized exchanges are traded in the **over-the-counter market.** This market consists of a network of thousands of dealers in particular securities. Each dealer maintains inventories of one or more securities and has a bid price for which he or she is willing to buy the stock to add to inventory and an asked price for which he or she is willing to sell the stock from inventory. There are two levels of prices: wholesale and retail. Retail prices are offered to individual investors who are usually executing orders through brokers. Wholesale prices are offered to other dealers who wish to make changes in their inventory positions.

The terms of trade are communicated throughout the market system through the National Association of Security Dealers Automated Quotations System. This allows all brokers in the network to know the terms being offered by all dealers in a given stock at any given point in time. Actual trades are subject to negotiation between brokers and dealers, but the system does report completed transactions.

Computerized Trading Techniques

You may have already heard the terms "program trading," "index arbitrage," and "portfolio insurance" in the media over the past few years. These **computerized trading techniques** have been the subject of a great deal of controversy and discussion, especially since the stock market "crash" of October 1987.

Many people use the three computerized trading terms interchangeably. Actually, however, they represent three distinctly different techniques, each with its own desired objectives.

Program trading isn't really an investment strategy. Rather, it is a *trading technique* for buying or selling long lists of stocks simultaneously. Program trading evolved to meet the needs of large-scale traders like pension funds. Program trades are usually executed via computers. When a pension fund trades a "portfolio" of stocks simultaneously, the particular specialists on the exchange floor or the dealers in the over-the-counter market begin receiving the orders simultaneously. The portfolio is traded much more quickly than with a more conventional sequence of separate trades. Program trading is usually employed by managers who are attempting to replicate the performance of a particular stock index—like the Dow Jones Industrial Average—with their portfolios. These managers have to make periodic adjustments in their portfolios to ensure they behave as much like the target index as possible. Program trading is also used to transfer money from one type of market to another.

OUT ON THE STREET

IN THE EYE OF A HURRICANE

The Dow is down 200 points. 200 points!

Unbelievable! Charles Downing was off the map and into a place he had never been. Friday had been bad enough. The Dow had dropped more than 100 points, registering its largest one-day dollar decline in history. Now here we are at 10:30 A.M. on Monday, October 19, and the Dow had already doubled its performance for Friday.

Charles is a New York broker, trading for institutional accounts. Having sailed successfully through the whirlwind markets of the 1980s, he was used to contending with storms.

But this is his first time inside a hurricane.

"Charles, we've got a program trade on line 3."

Charles picked up his phone to get the details. The clients wanted to sell a $40 million portfolio of common stock. The portfolio consists of approximately 50 individual stocks, all of which the client wants to be sold at market.

Normally, this was a routine trade on the Super Dot system. Super Dot is the New York Stock Exchange's computerized trading system. The Dot is designed to break the portfolio into its component parts and route each issue directly to the post of the specialist dealing in the stock on the floor of the exchange. The trade is handled by machines rather than by brokers, which means it can go through in rapid fashion. An entire portfolio of stock can be sold or assembled in a matter of minutes.

That's precisely what this particular client has in mind, but today there is a slight problem.

Super Dot has derailed. The system is overwhelmed and experiencing hard disk failure. From time to time it would come back to life, but its order execution is unreliable to say the least. That means it's time to go back to doing things by hand.

The alternative to Super Dot is to route trades to one of his firm's floor booths. The trades sent to each booth are arranged in logical order and then printed for physical hand routing. Logical order means that the stack of trading tickets are sequenced so the broker can make an orderly trip through the trading room. Charles' firm's main booth would handle the major portion of this trade, but some portions would be handled by other booths in other trading rooms.

For all intents and purposes this was program trading only in concept. Charles would be dealing with people and not computers. And so far today he hadn't heard much from the people he'd have to be dealing with. The people on the floor weren't talking; they were too busy trading.

As he began to execute the trade, Charles felt as though he were in a void. He found it was a real struggle to get reports back from the floor. Did the trade go through or not? The routine of trading is normally characterized by care and caution. Execute with the greatest possible accuracy and at the best possible price, given the constraints imposed on the trade by the client.

Today was anything but routine.

What was the status of *these* orders? The people on the floor were too busy trying to execute the next order to report on the status of the last. In some cases hours passed before Charles could pin down exactly what had happened to a given sell order.

Trades on the NYSE were bad enough today, but the over-the-counter market was even worse. The OTC market was very manual, even under normal circumstances. You had to watch things very carefully to make sure details were punched in accurately. Amid the chaos of October 19, it was becoming very difficult to discern whether he had failed to enter an order or whether it was really out there somewhere temporarily lost in the storm. The danger, of course, was in issuing two orders to sell the same stock *twice!*

Reports on the execution of the "program trade" began to come in. Many of the trades went through with little or no problem, executed at perhaps an eighth under the previous trade. However, at the client's request, the orders were to be executed at market. This meant that the brokers would continue to attempt to fill the order until the block was sold, even if they had to sell at successively lower bids.

This is fine if there is an active market on both sides of the trade, but what if the market's buy side suddenly and mysteriously disappears?

"Charles, take a look at this fill on Lone Star!"

The report that came back on Lone Star Industries was difficult to believe. At the inception of the trade, Lone Star was selling at $25 per share. This was a stock that normally trades 100,000 shares a day. Charles was trying to sell only 10,000 shares, but there was little or no one on the buy side for Lone Star. The block was executed piece by piece at successively lower and lower bid prices. The final piece went through at $18 per share.

Liquidity on the New York Stock Exchange was beginning to evaporate.

Charles eventually successfully executed his program trade on overall terms that proved to be acceptable to the client. However, it took him most of the day to do a trade that would have normally flashed by in a matter of minutes.

If liquidity was evaporating on Monday, it had all but disappeared on Tuesday when many of the listed stocks didn't open until late in the afternoon. Not that investors had lost interest in them. The specialists serving the stocks had suffered such catastrophic losses in the value of their positions on Monday that they were afraid to open amid continued chaos on Tuesday.

On Tuesday, October 20, the New York Stock Exchange *unofficially* closed.

For example, if a particular manager decides the performance of the stock market is going to be unfavorable in the coming year, he or she may sell large pieces of the stock portfolio and use the proceeds simultaneously to buy the individual issues that will comprise his or her new bond portfolio.

Unlike program trading, **index arbitrage** is a *trading strategy* whereby trades are made to take advantage of discrepancies between the prices of stock indices like the Standard & Poor's 500 and futures contracts written on them. For example, suppose the value for a particular stock index is $45. (This is called the cash price.) On the other hand, the futures price written in a contract to "buy" or "sell" the index is $44. Based on what they know about the normal relationship between the cash price and the futures price, the traders of a particular firm believe the futures contracts should have a price of $43. At $44 they believe the futures contracts are selling "dear"—the futures price is higher than it should be, and in their view, it is likely to fall. Given their beliefs, they may wish to engage in index arbitrage. In doing so, they will sell futures contracts and simultaneously buy a stock portfolio which replicates the behavior of the index. To buy the stock portfolio, they may employ program trading, because this is the easiest means of accomplishing what they want. But this is the only connection between the two trading techniques. Given that the index arbitragers have simultaneously bought "the index" and sold futures contracts on the index, they are hedged against movements in the value of the index. If the index goes up in value, they will make money on their cash investment in the replicating index portfolio, and they will lose approximately the same amount of money on their short positions in the futures contracts. If the value of the index goes down instead, the opposite will happen—they will win on the futures contracts they sold (money will be added to their accounts in marking to market), but they will lose a nearly identical amount on their cash positions in the replicating index portfolio. You might ask, "How are they going to make money on this strategy?" They expect to make money by a widening of the gap between the cash price and the futures price. Going in, the gap was only $1. Based on their research or experience, they believed the normal value for the gap to be $2. If the gap widens as expected, the index arbitragers should make a net profit on their futures positions, irrespective of what happens to the value of the index itself.

Portfolio insurance is another *investment strategy*. In this strategy, an attempt is made to reduce the downside risk associated with holding a portfolio—usually a stock portfolio. If you are employing portfolio insurance, and the value of your stock portfolio begins to fall, you begin selling stock from the portfolio (ideally, you should sell some of each of the stocks in the portfolio proportionately, to keep the character of the portfolio constant) and moving the money into what is referred to as the safe asset, usually treasury bills. With each successive decline in the value of the stock portfolio, more money is shifted from stocks to treasury bills. Finally, if the stock portfolio falls far enough, the investor's entire position is in treasury bills. The value of the treasury bill position at that time is called the "floor" for the insurance strategy. Obviously, further declines in the stock portfolio have no further impact on the insured investors, because their positions are completely in bills. Should the stock portfolio begin to increase in value, portions of the bill portfolio are liquidated and moved back into stocks. As the stock portfolio continues to rise, increasing amounts of money are shifted from bills to stocks, until at some point the insured investors are completely invested in stock. Should the situation again reverse, the insured investors are gradually moved back into bills. In this way, portfolio insurance offers investors the upside potential of stock portfolio investments with a degree of downside protection against disastrous declines in the value of their portfolios. In order to economize on transactions costs, in shifting from stock to bills and back again, the mechanics of portfolio insurance are usually carried out with futures contracts. That is, rather than selling off actual cash positions in stock investments, the insured investors take increasingly heavy short positions in stock index futures contracts. In this way they increasingly hedge themselves against further reductions in the value of their stock portfolios which are associated with general stock market declines.

Some people believe the severity of the stock market crash of October 1987 was related to the extensive use of these trading strategies at the time. Taking them one at a time, it seems unlikely program trading, which merely facilitates the simultaneous trading of portfolios of stocks, would act to promote or exacerbate a downward movement in the stock market. Index arbitrage merely acts to keep cash prices and futures prices in line with one another. It's also unlikely this trading technique promoted the downward spiral in stock prices witnessed on October 19. Portfolio insurance strategies, on the other hand, could have conceivably contributed to the decline. Going into the month of October 1987, as much as $60 billion in assets were covered by some form of portfolio insurance. As the stock market declined on October 19, many of these insured investors were told to sell stock and move to the safety of treasury bills. Many investors obeyed the orders given to them by their insurance programs. Many did not however, especially those implementing insurance strategies through the futures markets. This is because on the morning of October 19, futures prices were selling at very deep discounts relative to cash prices. Some defenders of portfolio insurance point to the limited amount of futures contracts executed by portfolio insurers on October 19 as evidence supporting the limited effect insurance had in helping the market decline. However, many investors executed their insurance strategies by selling stock on the stock exchanges. For example, according to *The Wall Street Journal*,[1] as much as 7 percent of the total trading volume on the New York Stock Exchange on October 19 was accounted for by the pension plan of General Motors. According to the *Wall Street Journal* the plan sold off more than $1.2 billion in stock in 13 waves of selling of nearly $100 million each. One can't be sure this massive exodus from the stock market was related to portfolio insurance, but the General Motors' plan had in fact an insurance program in place at the time through Wells Fargo Investment Advisors, which the *Journal* states sold 1.3 billion in stock on October 19, most of which was for a single client.

---

[1]*The Wall Street Journal*, January 15, 1988.

SUMMARY

In this chapter, we have attempted to provide some institutional background on financial securities and their markets. Securities can be divided into fixed income, stock, options, and forward and futures contracts. Fixed income securities, or bonds, are issued by the federal government, state and municipal governments, and corporations. The two major types of stock are preferred and common, with preferred offering a prior but limited claim and the common taking whatever remains after all other security holders have taken their rightful share.

Options are contracts to buy or sell a particular commodity on or before a particular date. A put option gives you the right to sell, and a call option gives you the right to buy. Neither has to be exercised. You do so only if it's in your interest. Otherwise the contract may be discarded.

Forward and futures contracts obligate you to buy or sell a commodity at a specified price on a particular date. The buyer of the contract is obligated to buy, and the seller is obligated to sell the commodity. The main difference between forward and futures contracts is in the way your account is handled. The futures price is changed each day to the value being used for contemporary contracts. To compensate for the change in the terms of the contract, your account is credited or debited in a process called marking to market.

Investment companies and mutual funds invest in diversified portfolios of securities. You can buy shares in either type of fund and thereby obtain diversification with a small amount of capital. In the case of a closed-end investment company, you would buy shares from another investor who holds them. In the case of a mutual fund, you buy shares from the fund itself.

Securities are traded in the primary and secondary markets. When originally issued to finance capital investment, securities are marketed through investment banking firms in the primary market. The primary market therefore connects the users of capital with the suppliers or savers. Securities are traded from one investor to another in secondary market. The secondary market serves as a source of liquidity for securities that already exist.

The secondary market consists of organized exchanges and the over-the-counter market. The organized exchanges are centralized auction markets, while the over-the-counter market consists of a nationwide network of dealers who make markets by taking positions in individual securities.

QUESTION SET 1

1. Why is the return associated with common stock referred to as a *residual claim?* Contrast this kind of claim with a *fixed claim.*
2. How do investors in a U.S. Treasury bill receive their returns?
3. Why are U.S. government securities viewed differently from state and local government securities in terms of default risk?

4. Why might the general obligation bonds of a state yield a return different from revenue bonds issued by the same state?

5. Explain the meaning of a call provision on a bond.

6. What is the priority of claims on the corporation's earnings held by (a) common stockholders, (b) bondholders, and (c) preferred stockholders?

7. Contrast an option with a forward or futures contract. Could either or both of these contracts have *negative* value to you?

8. What is the basic difference between a forward contract and a futures contract?

9. What is a mutual fund? Why might a person buy shares in a mutual fund rather than buy shares of individual corporations?

10. Define the following:
    Limit order
    Stop loss order
    Day order

11. What apparatus exists to facilitate purchases and sales of futures contracts?

12. What is a *private placement?* What are the potential advantages of this for the firm issuing securities?

QUESTION SET 2

1. What is the difference between a fixed income security and a variable income security, and which would get preference upon the liquidation of a company?

2. If a company has some extra cash that is lying idle, and wants liquidity and safety in a government investment, what type of investment is likely to be chosen?

3. What types of backing are given by firms for their debt instruments?

4. A certain executive made so much money per year that the extra $100,000 income offered to him in his latest position would mostly go to taxes. The executive asked for warrants as part of his compensation. What did he get and how might this affect his tax situation?

5. What are the main differences between options and warrant contracts and forward and futures contracts?

6. As an investor, you looked at the published list of securities held by an investment company and noted that the price of the stock was less than the market value of the securities held. You immediately decided to purchase shares of the company. What type of investment company was it?

7. As the same investor, you put in a limit order to purchase the above company at $12.00 per share at 12:00 P.M. on June 15. At 3:00 P.M. the stock was selling for 11¾. Was your order executed?

8. The frost that was predicted to hit the Florida orange crop missed its mark, and the weather outlook is good for the rest of the season. Suppose you are a position trader on the CBOE. What are you likely to do upon hearing this news?

9. Explain briefly what is meant by program trading, index arbitrage, and portfolio insurance.

10. Explain the effect program trading had on the stock market crash of October 1987.

ANSWERS TO QUESTION SET 2

1. A fixed income security represents the *debt* of a company; a variable income security is a share in the *equity* of a company. A fixed income security will provide its holder with a specific dollar amount of interest, whereas a variable income security will provide its holder with a dividend, which is discretionary on the company's part. A fixed income security has priority in the event that a company goes bankrupt.

2. The most liquid government investment that a company can invest in are treasury bills, since there is a very active market for these issues and they can be easily sold at prevailing interest rates prior to maturity.

3. The types of backing given for corporate debt are real estate (mortgage bonds), property (equipment trust certificates), and debentures (backed by cash flows).

4. You would get stock options, or generally the ability to purchase the company's stock at specific price by or before a specific date. Thus, if the stock were selling for $50.00 a share, and your option price was $40.00 a share, you can make $10.00 per share profit if you sell the stock when you exercise the option. If you hold the stock for the required length of time, you can turn your earnings into a long-term capital gain, which is often taxed at a reduced rate from ordinary income (although such earnings are currently taxed at the same rate).

5. Options and warrants contracts give the holder the *right* (but not the obligation) to buy or sell a security at a specific price by a specific date. They are written on stocks, treasury bonds, stock indices, and futures contracts. Forward and futures contracts *obligate* the holder to buy or sell a particular *commodity* at a specific price on a particular date. Hence, the value of a forward or futures contract can take on a *negative* value.

6. This is an example of a closed-end investment company, which is identical to a nonfinancial corporation except for the fact that they make financial investments.

7. Your order would be executed. In a limit order, a trade is executed at a price at least as advantageous as the stated price. Since the stock is selling at $11.75, this is cheaper than the $12.00 you were willing to pay for it.

8. A position trader deals in futures (commodities) contracts and holds a position over the course of days or weeks. Upon hearing optimistic predictions for the orange juice, you would probably sell contracts for orange futures, anticipating that the price of the contracts would fall in the coming weeks, and you could purchase them back at a lower price. This assumes that the weather forecast is not already reflected in the futures price.

9. Program trading is a technique for buying or selling whole lists of stocks simultaneously. Index arbitrage is a technique designed to take advantage of discrepancies between stock indices and futures contracts written on them. Portfolio insurance is a strategy designed to reduce the downside risk of a portfolio by moving into a safe asset when the value of the portfolio begins to fall.

10. Program trading is merely a technique which facilitates the trading of portfolios of stocks. Thus, it was likely not a cause in the crash. However, it may have increased the magnitude of the crash because it allows a greater volume of trading to occur in a given time period.

REFERENCES

AMLING, F., *Investments: An Introduction to Analysis and Management.* Englewood Cliffs, N.J.: Prentice Hall, 1984.

CAMPBELL, T. S., *Financial Institutions, Markets, and Economic Activity.* New York: McGraw-Hill, 1982.

POLAKOFF, M. E., and DURKIN, T. A., *Financial Institutions and Markets.* Boston: Houghton Mifflin, 1981.

STEVENSON, R. A., and JENNINGS, E. H., *Fundamentals of Investments.* St. Paul, Minn.: West, 1984.

THOMPSON, R., ''The Information Content of Discount and Premiums on Closed-End Investment Fund Shares,'' *Journal of Financial Economics* (September 1978).

3

SOME STATISTICAL CONCEPTS

In studying portfolio theory we're going to be interested in what happens when you combine individual securities into a portfolio. The risk of a portfolio is usually measured in terms of the variability in its returns. As a consequence, one of the major questions we will be asking is: "What happens to the variability in the returns to our portfolio as we add one or more stocks to the bundle?" The purpose of this chapter is to introduce you to the basic statistical concepts required to answer this question.

THE SIMPLE OR MARGINAL PROBABILITY DISTRIBUTION

Suppose we are looking across some period of time in the future, say, over the next month, and we are contemplating the potential for getting various rates of return on our investment. We might ask, for example, "What is the probability of getting a rate of return in the next month that is less than zero?" If we explore questions like this thoroughly, we might be able to envision what is called a *simple probability distribution* for the investment. The simple probability distribution shows the probabilities of getting various rates of return over the course of some period of time, in this case a month.

The distribution might look like the one in Figure 3.1. On the horizontal axis of this figure, we are plotting the rates of return that might develop on the investment, which we will presume is a common stock. The symbol r_i relates to the ith possible rate of return a stock may produce in the course of the month.

The rate of return is the percentage increase in your wealth associated with holding the stock for the period. Your dollar return is equal to cash dividends received during the period plus the change in the value of the stock in the period. Your percentage rate of return is equal to the dollar return divided by the market value of the stock at the beginning of the period.

$$r = \frac{\text{Dividends} + \text{change in market value}}{\text{Beginning market value}}$$

On the vertical axis of Figure 3.1 we're measuring the probability h_i of getting any given ith rate of return. The graph is drawn as if the returns were continuous along

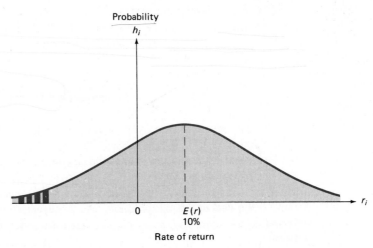

FIGURE 3.1 Marginal probability distribution for rates of return.

the horizontal axis. Actually, assume there is a series of discrete possible rates of return, each associated with one of the vertical bars drawn on the left side of the graph. The length of the bar represents the probability of getting the particular rate of return represented below the bar. If you summed the probabilities represented by all the bars, the sum would equal 1.00, or 100 percent, because the returns plotted on the horizontal axis constitute everything that can happen to the stock in the next month.

The Population Expected Value and Variance

Now consider two computations you can make to describe what a distribution like this looks like. Suppose we are interested in telling someone where the returns (weighted by probabilities) were centrally located along the horizontal axis. The parameter describing the central location is the expected value, or in this case the *expected rate of return*. As its name would imply, the expected rate of return tells what we expect to get from the stock as a rate of return in the course of the next month. The formula for the expected rate of return is

$$E(r) = \sum_{i=1}^{n} h_i r_i$$

To compute the expected rate of return, you go from the lowest possible return to the highest. You take the lowest possible return and multiply it by the probability of its occurrence in the next month. Then you go to the next lowest and again multiply that return by its probability. You sweep the distribution in this fashion from the left to the right, and then you add up all the products. The sum is the expected rate of return. For the particular stock in Figure 3.1 the expected rate of return is 10 percent.

A second parameter that describes the nature of the probability distribution is the *variance*. The variance tells us about the potential for deviation of the return from its expected value. How much dispersion is there about the expectation? The formula for the variance is

$$\sigma^2(r) = \sum_{i=1}^{n} h_i [r_i - E(r)]^2$$

To compute the variance, you again sweep the distribution from the left to the right. You first take the difference between the lowest rate of return and the expected rate of return. Then square the deviation, and multiply the squared deviation by the probability of appearance of the lowest possible rate of return. You then go to the next lowest and do the same thing. Again, sweep the distribution from left to right. Then add up all the products to get the variance of the return. The bigger the variance, the more the propensity for rates of return to deviate from their expected value.

The Sample Mean and Variance

Suppose, however, you can't see the actual probability distributions that are supposedly producing the returns. Is there any way to infer what the underlying distributions look like if you can't actually see them? This is an important question because when we're dealing with stocks in the real world we can't see the underlying probability distributions. We cannot see the probabilities as they exist in the example depicted in Figure 3.1. Consequently, you usually have to estimate those values by sampling. You must compute sample estimates of the expected return and the variance of the return, and these estimates are used as inputs when you employ the techniques of portfolio management. In taking your sample estimate, you assume the underlying probability distribution for the returns is constant. If you're dealing with a probability distribution for monthly rates of return, you assume the distribution doesn't change as time goes by. You then observe the rates of return that are supposedly drawn from this distribution month after month.

In Figure 3.2, we have plotted a time series of such returns for a stock. Rates of return are plotted vertically, and time is plotted horizontally for 6 months. To illustrate the diagram, note the stock produces a positive return equal to 6 percent in period 1. Given the returns produced in the 6 months, you can get an estimate of the expected value of the underlying distribution by taking the sample mean of the returns:

$$\bar{r} = \frac{\sum\limits_{t=1}^{N} r_t}{N}$$

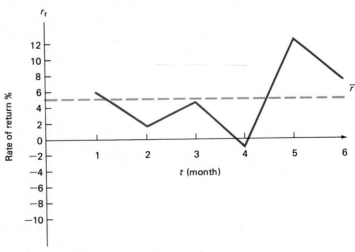

FIGURE 3.2 Time series of rates of return.

Here N is the number of months over which you take the sample. In this example N is equal to 6, and the sample mean is computed as the average of 6 percent, 2 percent, 4 percent, -1 percent, 12 percent, and 7 percent for a value of 5 percent. Note that the actual expected rate of return from the stock is in fact 10 percent. The difference between this value and our estimate is due to what is called sample error. The sample mean gives an unbiased estimate of the expected value, but obviously it's not perfectly accurate. We would expect accuracy to increase, however, as the size of the sample becomes larger (as we increase N). Thus, if you observe the stock for a longer period of time, you may get a better estimate of $E(r)$. Keep in mind, however, you have made the assumption that the underlying probability distribution does not change its shape as time goes by. This assumption becomes more and more unrealistic the longer the period over which you take the sample. In general, the sample estimate should be taken for as long a period for which you are confident there has not been a significant change in the shape of the underlying distribution.

The same is true with the variance. You can't see the actual distribution, so you can't compute what the actual variance is. You must once again resort to a sampling procedure. The sample variance is computed using the following formula:

$$\sigma_r^2 = \frac{\sum_{t=1}^{N} (r_t - \bar{r})^2}{N - 1}$$

You again observe the stock's returns over a number of periods. In each period you subtract, from the return produced, the sample mean rate of return. You square the differences and sum them up. Then you divide the sum by $N - 1$. You divide by $N - 1$ because you're using an *estimate* in the computation of the variance. The estimate is the sample mean. Dividing by $N - 1$ gives you an unbiased estimate for the variance when you are dealing with a relatively small sample. In the case of our example, the computation would be as follows:

$$(.06 - .05)^2 = .0001$$
$$(.02 - .05)^2 = .0009$$
$$(.04 - .05)^2 = .0001$$
$$(-.01 - .05)^2 = .0036$$
$$(.12 - .05)^2 = .0049$$
$$(.07 - .05)^2 = \underline{.0004}$$
$$\text{Total} = .0100$$

$$\frac{.0100}{6 - 1} = .0020 = \sigma_r^2$$

THE JOINT PROBABILITY DISTRIBUTION

The expected rate of return and the variance provide us with information about the nature of the probability distribution associated with a single stock or for a portfolio of stocks. However, these numbers tell us nothing about the way the returns on securities *interrelate*. Suppose in some given month one stock produces a rate of return above its expected value. If we know in advance this is going to happen, what does it do to our expectation for the rate of return produced on some other stock? When one stock produces a rate of return above its expected value, do other stocks have a propensity to do so as well? A statistic which provides us with some information about this question is the covariance between two stocks.

The Sample Covariance

To illustrate the concept of ***covariance,*** suppose we have two stocks called A and B. In a period of 5 months the stocks produce the following rates of return:

		Month				
	1	2	3	4	5	Mean
Stock A	.04	− .02	.08	− .04	.04	.02
Stock B	.02	.03	.06	− .04	.08	.03

The five pairs of monthly returns are plotted against one another in Figure 3.3. The mean rates of return on the two stocks are plotted where the broken horizontal and vertical lines intersect the two axes.

Let's assume we can't see the underlying probability distributions for the returns on these two stocks, so we must estimate the covariance from the sample of five monthly returns. In this case we compute the sample covariance using the following formula:

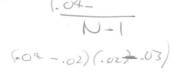

$$\text{Cov } r_A, r_B = \frac{\sum_{t=1}^{N} [(r_{A,t} - \bar{r}_A)(r_{B,t} - \bar{r}_B)]}{N - 1} \tag{3.1}$$

To compute the covariance, go to the first pair of monthly returns marked 1 in the graph. In this month stock A is producing 4 percent, while stock B is producing 2 percent. We first compute the deviation these returns represent from the mean returns of each stock. Note that stock A is 2 percent above its mean, while stock B is 1 percent below its mean of 3 percent. After expressing the two deviations as decimals, we multiply them to get a product of − .0002. We now do the same for each of the other four return pairs and sum them up as follows:

$$(.04 - .02)(.02 - .03) = -.0002$$
$$(-.02 - .02)(.03 - .03) = .0000$$
$$(.08 - .02)(.06 - .03) = .0018$$
$$(-.04 - .02)(-.04 - .03) = .0042$$
$$(.04 - .02)(.08 - .03) = \underline{\quad.0010\quad}$$
$$\text{Total} = .0068$$

We then divide this total by the number of observations, less one, to obtain the covariance:

$$\frac{.0068}{5 - 1} = .0017$$

As a number, the covariance doesn't tell you much about the relationship between the returns on the two stocks. In this case, since it is a positive number, it tells you that when one stock produces a return above its mean return, the other tends to do so as well. Figure 3.3 can be divided into four quadrants on the basis of the mean returns on the two stocks. The quadrants are labeled I, II, III, and IV. In quadrant I, both stocks are above their mean returns. In III they are both below. In II, stock A is below, and B is above. Finally, in IV, B is below, and A is above. Note that in I and III the deviations from the mean for both stocks are of the same sign. In I, the

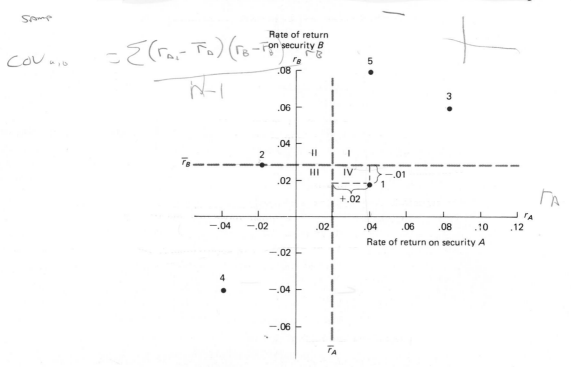

FIGURE 3.3 Relationship between the returns on two stocks over time.

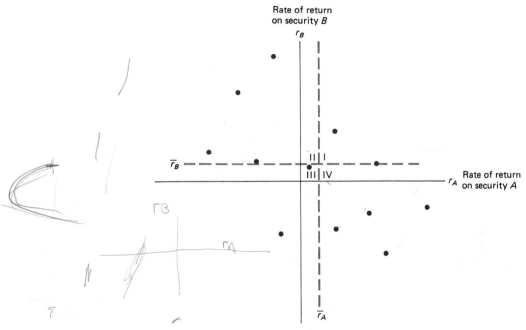

FIGURE 3.4 The case of negative covariance.

deviations are both positive, and in III they are both negative. In these two quadrants, when we take the products of the deviations, we get positive numbers. Contrast this with the other quadrants, II and IV, where the deviations are of opposite sign, and we get negative products.

If the majority of the observations are in quadrants I and III, as they are in this case, the sum of the products will tend to be positive, as will the covariance. Again, a positive covariance tells you that when one stock is above its mean, the other tends to be also.

To further illustrate the concept of covariance, consider Figures 3.4 and 3.5. The covariance between the stocks of Figure 3.4 is negative. In this case the observations of quadrants II and IV dominate those of I and III. When one stock is above its mean, the other tends to be below and vice versa. On the other hand, the covariance between the stocks of Figure 3.5 is approximately zero. The observations are scattered pretty uniformly throughout the four quadrants, and the negative products pretty much offset the positive products in the sum. Thus, the products of the deviations sum to approximately zero.

The Population Covariance

Equation (3.1) tells you how to compute an *estimate* of the true covariance from a sample of paired returns. Suppose, however, you somehow knew the actual probabilities of getting various pairs of returns on the two stocks at the same time. That

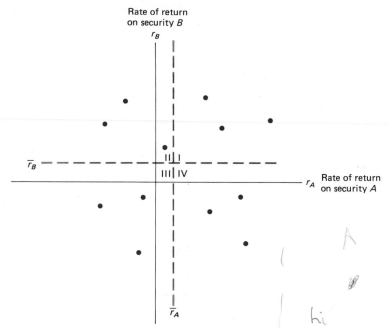

FIGURE 3.5 The case of zero covariance.

is, suppose you knew that, in the next month, the probability of getting a −4 percent return on stock A and a −3 percent return on stock B was 6 percent. The probabilities of getting various pairs of returns on two investments at the same time are represented in the *joint probability distribution*. The joint distribution is drawn in three dimensions, where paired returns are plotted on the base of the diagram and probabilities are plotted vertically. The joint distribution for stocks A and B is depicted in Figures 3.6 and 3.7. Figure 3.6 shows the probability associated with only one of the many possible pairs of returns, $r_A = 8\%$ and $r_B = 6\%$. The probability of these two returns coming up in the same month is shown to be 6 percent. The probability is given by the length of the vertical bar at the point on the base representing the pair of returns. There are, of course, many other possible pairs of returns. Each pair has an associated probability. Figure 3.7 shows the complete joint distribution where all possible pairs of returns are represented. Since all possible events for the two stocks are represented, the sum of the probabilities for all of the bars is equal to 1.00 or 100 percent.

If you can see the actual probability distribution, as we can in Figure 3.7, rather than take a sample estimate, you can compute the true or population covariance of the underlying joint distribution. The formula for the population covariance is given as follows:

$$\text{Cov}(r_A, r_B) = \sum_{i=1}^{m} h_i[r_{A,i} - E(r_A)][r_{B,i} - E(r_B)]$$

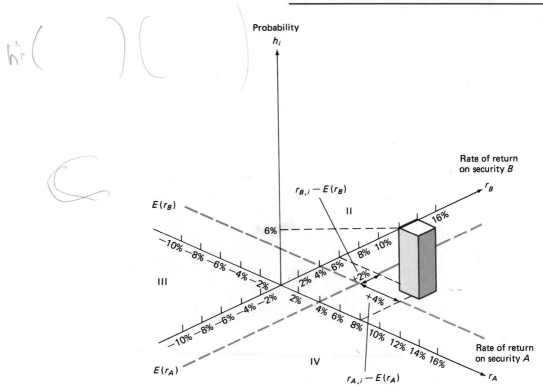

FIGURE 3.6 One of the probability bars in the joint distribution.

To illustrate the computation, consider the single pair of returns depicted in Figure 3.6. The broken lines drawn on the base of the figure represent the expected rates of return for the two stocks, just as the broken lines of Figure 3.3 represent the sample mean returns. It is evident that, given the pair of returns represented, both stocks have simultaneously produced rates of return above their expected values. Since both stocks have an expected value of 4 percent, the deviation from the expected value for stock *A* is 4 percent, and for *B* it is 2 percent. To compute the population covariance, you multiply the two deviations. You then multiply the product by the probability of getting this particular pair of returns at the same time, 6 percent.

$$(.04)(.02)(.06) = .000048$$

Next, perform this same operation for each of the possible pairs of return represented in Figure 3.7. Then sum up all the products, and you have the population covariance.

Once again, if the probabilities are such that pairs of returns are more likely in quadrants I and III than they are in II and IV, the population covariance is likely to be a positive number.

The covariance number is an important one for us to know, because it's a critical input in determining the variance of a portfolio of stocks. As a number on its

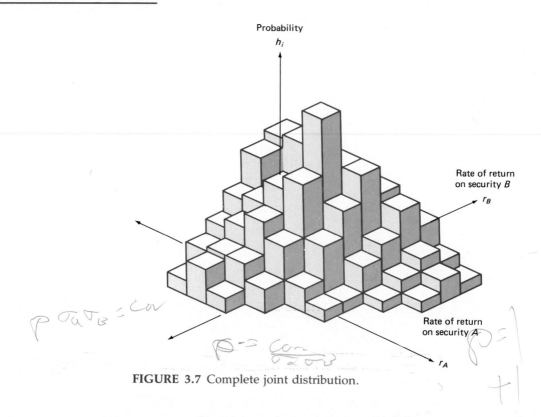

FIGURE 3.7 Complete joint distribution.

own, however, it doesn't describe very fully the nature of the joint distribution or the relationship which exists between the two investments. We can, however, standardize the covariance and obtain a better descriptor called the correlation coefficient.

The Correlation Coefficient

The covariance number is unbounded. Theoretically, its range extends all the way from minus to plus infinity. We can bound it, however, by dividing it by the product of the standard deviations for the two investments:

$$\rho_{A,B} = \frac{\text{Cov}(r_A, r_B)}{\sigma(r_A)\sigma(r_B)} \tag{3.2}$$

The resulting number is called the ***correlation coefficient,*** and it falls within the range -1 to $+1$. Figures 3.8 through 3.12 represent samples of paired returns taken from stocks. The correlation coefficients for the stocks of Figure 3.8 and 3.9 are both equal to $+1$. In both cases, you can pass a straight line through every observation in the figure. This is the unique characteristic of perfect positive ($+1$) or perfect negative (-1) correlation. If the slope of the line passing through all the observations is positive, we have perfect positive correlation; if it's negative, we have perfect

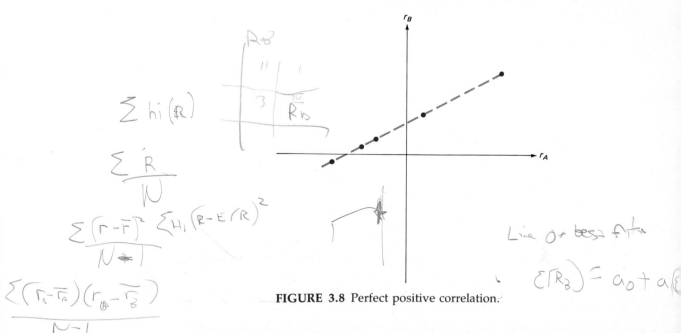

FIGURE 3.8 Perfect positive correlation.

negative correlation. Other than that, the magnitude of the slope is immaterial. Thus, Figures 3.8 and 3.9 both represent cases of perfect positive correlation, but Figure 3.10 represents perfect negative correlation.

If you can't pass a straight line through all the observations, the correlation is imperfect, falling somewhere in between -1 and $+1$. You can still pass a line

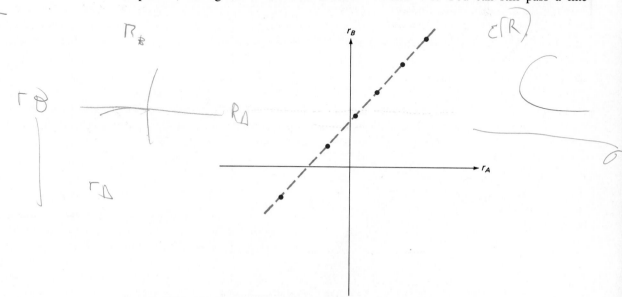

FIGURE 3.9 Perfect positive correlation.

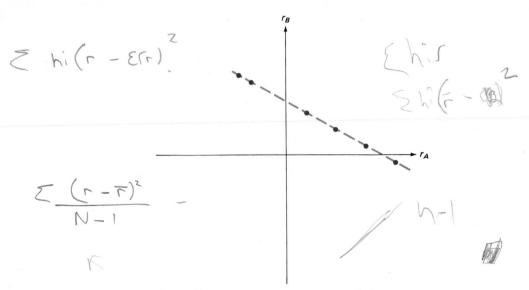

$\sum hi(r - \mathcal{E}(r))^2$

$\sum \frac{(r - \bar{r})^2}{N-1}$ —

FIGURE 3.10 Perfect negative correlation.

through the scatter of observations which is called the *line of best fit*. This line minimizes the sum of the squared vertical distances from each individual observation to the line. The distance labeled ϵ in Figure 3.11 is one of these vertical distances, and the line drawn through the scatter is the line of best fit. If this line has a positive

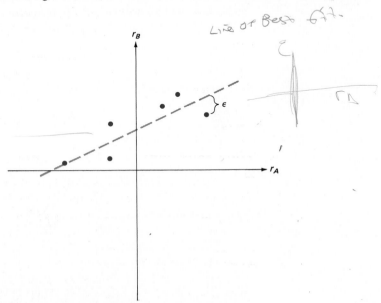

FIGURE 3.11 Imperfect positive correlation.

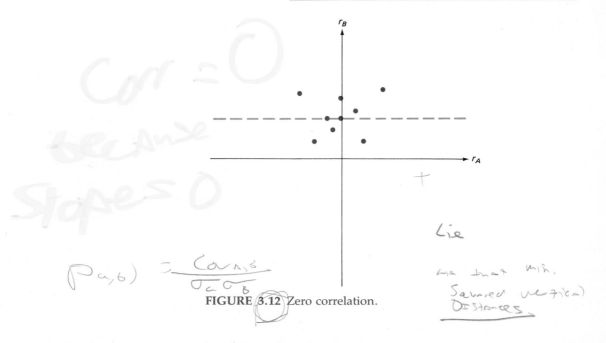

FIGURE 3.12 Zero correlation.

slope, with the individual observations scattered about it, the correlation coefficient between the two stocks falls between 0 and +1. In the case of Figure 3.11, the correlation coefficient is approximately .90. The correlation coefficient approaches 1 as the fit about the line becomes tighter and tighter. If the line of best fit has a slope of zero, the correlation coefficient is also equal to zero. This is the case of Figure 3.12.

Before moving on, we should note that, given the definition for the correlation coefficient provided in Equation (3.2), we can write the covariance as the product of the correlation coefficient and the standard deviations of the two stocks:

$$\text{Cov}(r_A, r_B) = \rho_{A,B}\sigma(r_A)\sigma(r_B)$$

The Coefficient of Determination

If we square the correlation coefficient, we obtain a number called the ***coefficient of determination.*** This number tells us the fraction of the variability in the returns on the one investment that can be associated with variability in the returns on the other. For example, since the correlation coefficient for Figure 3.11 is +.90, we can say that approximately 81 percent of the variability in the returns on stock A can be associated with, or explained by, the returns on stock B. Note that the coefficient of determination for the cases represented by Figures 3.8 through 3.10 is 100 percent. Thus, if we knew what the return on one of the stocks was going to be in the next month, we could predict exactly the return on the other stock.

THE RELATIONSHIP BETWEEN A STOCK AND THE MARKET PORTFOLIO

Up to this point we have been talking about the relationship between the returns on two stocks. Now we're going to consider some statistics that describe the relationship between the returns on a stock and what we shall call the **market portfolio.** The market portfolio contains every single risky asset in the international economic system, and it contains each asset in proportion to the total market value of that asset relative to the total value of all other assets. This kind of portfolio is commonly called a value weighted portfolio. In this portfolio, General Motors will be a much bigger fraction of the total than a smaller company such as American Motors. Suppose you want to construct your own index of the market portfolio. You can do it in the following way. You buy some arbitrary percentage, perhaps .01 percent of the total market value of every single risky asset in existence. While you own the same fraction of the total value of each company, your dollar holdings of General Motors are much larger than your dollar holdings of American Motors, because GM is a much larger company. Moreover, the proportion of money you have invested in GM is larger than the proportion you invested in AMC. You can think of the market portfolio as the ultimate market index.

Consider now the relationship that exists between a stock and the market portfolio. We'll designate the rates of return on stock J as r_J and the rates of return to the market portfolio as r_M. Suppose you observe the returns to stock J and to the market portfolio over 5 months and you see this:

	Month				
	1	2	3	4	5
Stock J	2%	3%	6%	−4%	8%
Market portfolio	4%	−2%	8%	−4%	4%

For convenience, these are the same pairs of returns we looked at earlier for stocks A and B.

The Characteristic Line

The pairs of returns are plotted in Figure 3.13. The broken line passing through the observations is the line of best fit as defined earlier. This line helps describe the relationship between the stock and the market portfolio or the *market*. When you relate an individual stock to the market in this way, the line of best fit is also referred to as the stock's **characteristic line.** The characteristic line shows the return you expect the stock to produce, given that a particular rate of return appears for the market. For example, we see in Figure 3.13, if the market produces a 2 percent rate of return, we expect stock J to produce a 3 percent rate of return, given the position of its characteristic line.

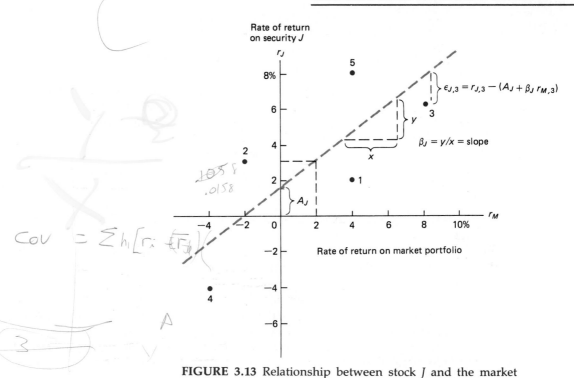

FIGURE 3.13 Relationship between stock *J* and the market portfolio.

The Beta Factor

Since the characteristic line is a straight line, it can be fully described by its *slope* and the point where it passes through the vertical axis, its *intercept. The slope of the characteristic line is commonly referred to as the stock's **beta factor** or* $\boldsymbol{\beta}$. We shall refer to the intercept by the symbol *A*.

The beta factor and the intercept can be computed directly using the following formulas:

$$\hat{\beta}_J = \frac{\text{Cov}\, r_J,\, r_M}{\sigma^2_{r_M}}$$

$$\hat{A}_J = \bar{r}_J - \hat{\beta}_J \bar{r}_M$$

In the case of our example using stock *J*, the sample variance of the five rates of return to the market portfolio is computed as

$$\sigma^2 r_M = \sum_{t=1}^{N} \frac{(r_{M,t} - \bar{r}_M)^2}{N - 1}$$

$$(.04 - .02)^2 = .0004$$
$$(-.02 - .02)^2 = .0016$$
$$(.08 - .02)^2 = .0036$$
$$(-.04 - .02)^2 = .0036$$
$$(.04 - .02)^2 = \underline{.0004}$$

$$\text{Total} = .0096$$

$$\frac{.0096}{5 - 1} = .0024 = \sigma^2_{r_M}$$

Thus, the beta factor and intercept can be computed as

$$\hat{\beta}_J = \frac{.0017}{.0024} = .708$$

$$\hat{A}_J = .0300 - .708(.0200) = .0158$$

The beta factor of the stock is an indicator of the degree to which the stock responds to changes in the return produced by the market. For stock J the beta factor is .708. This would indicate that if we knew the return for the market was going to be higher by 1 percent next month, we would increase our expectation for stock J's return by .708 percent.

The intercept serves only as a convenient reference point to fix the position of the line. It should be interpreted only as our expected rate of return to the stock should the market happen to produce a zero rate of return in any given month.

The characteristic line we draw, based on the computed slope and intercept, is identical to the line of best fit that minimizes the sum of the squared vertical distances from the line for each of the five pairs of returns.

Residual Variance

Another dimension of the relationship between the stock and the market is the propensity of the stock to produce returns which deviate from the characteristic line. The statistic describing this propensity is called the ***residual variance***. While the stock's variance describes the stock's propensity to produce returns which deviate from its expected value, the residual variance describes the stock's propensity to produce returns which deviate from its characteristic line.

Residual variance is the variance in the stock's **residuals** or **shock terms**. A residual, or shock term, is the vertical distance between the pair of returns and the characteristic line. To compute a *residual,* you use the following formula:

$$\epsilon_{J,t} = r_{J,t} - (\hat{A}_J + \hat{\beta}_J r_{M,t})$$

The first term on the right-hand side of the formula is the return actually produced by the stock in the given month. The second term, in parentheses, represents our expectation for the stock's return, given its characteristic line and the market's return.

To illustrate, consider the third month in our example. In this month the stock produces a 6 percent rate of return, while the market produces a return of 8 percent. Based on the stock's characteristic line, the residual is computed as

$$\epsilon_{J,3} = .06 - [.0158 + .708(.08)]$$

$$\epsilon_{J,3} = .06 - .0724 = -.0124$$

In this month, the stock is producing a return less than we would normally expect, given the performance of the market in the month. Perhaps some negative information about the company behind the stock has been released during the month, and it has had a depressing effect on the stock price. Given a market return of 8 percent and the stock's characteristic line, we would expect the stock to produce a return of 7.24 percent. Instead the return is only 6 percent. The difference of -1.24 percent is the residual for the third month. The residuals for the other months are computed in the same way:

Month	Residual	
1	$.02 - [.0158 + .708(.04)]$	$= -.0241$
2	$.03 - [.0158 + .708(-.02)]$	$= .0284$
3	$.06 - [.0158 + .708(.08)]$	$= -.0124$
4	$-.04 - [.0158 + .708(-.04)]$	$= -.0275$
5	$.08 - [.0158 + .708(.04)]$	$= .0359$

Just as the stock's variance is computed by squaring the deviations from the expected value, the residual variance is computed by squaring the residuals or the deviations from the stock's characteristic line:

$$\sigma^2_{\epsilon_J} = \frac{\sum_{t=1}^{N} \epsilon^2_{J,t}}{N - 2}$$

We divide the sum of the squared residuals by $N - 2$ instead of $N - 1$ because we are employing two estimates instead of one in making the computation. When we compute the sample variance, we employ an estimate of the expected value, the sample mean. Here we employ estimates of both the intercept and the slope of the characteristic line in order to compute the residuals.

In our example, the residual variance is computed as follows:

Month	Squared Residual
1	$(-.0241)^2 = .00058$
2	$(.0284)^2 = .00081$
3	$(-.0124)^2 = .00015$
4	$(-.0275)^2 = .00076$
5	$(.0359)^2 = .00129$
	Total $= .00359$

$$\frac{.00359}{5 - 2} = .0012 = \sigma^2_{\epsilon_J}$$

In Figures 3.14 and 3.15 we are plotting the relationship between two stocks, American Telephone & Telegraph and United Airlines, and a proxy for the market portfolio. The proxy is a value weighted portfolio of 500 stocks called the Standard & Poor's 500 Stock Index. Each observation plotted represents the pair of returns for each stock and the 500 for a particular month. You can think of these returns as being generated by an underlying joint probability distribution for each respective stock. In those areas of the graph where you have a greater concentration of pairs of returns, you have higher probabilities of occurrence for the pairs in the underlying probability distribution. The broken lines going through both figures are the lines of best fit or the characteristic lines for the two stocks. These lines are drawn based on sample estimates of the covariances, market (500) variances, and mean returns for the two stocks and the 500. Note that AT&T has a beta factor of about .5 and an intercept of approximately zero. The intercept for United Airlines is also approxi-

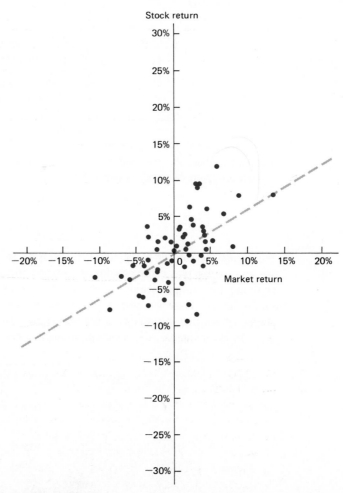

FIGURE 3.14 Estimate of the characteristic line for AT&T.

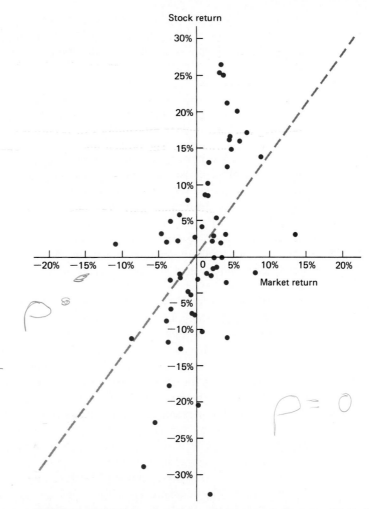

FIGURE 3.15 Estimate of the characteristic line for United Airlines.

mately zero, but its beta factor is much larger at 1.5. In fact, the great majority of stocks have betas between these two rather extreme values.

If you recall the discussion on the correlation coefficient, you may note that as the residual variance of a stock approaches zero, the correlation coefficient approaches either $+1$ or -1, depending on whether the characteristic line has a positive or negative slope. It is also true for large samples that if the correlation coefficient is zero, the stock's residual variance is approximately equal to its variance, because with zero correlation or covariance, the stock's beta factor is equal to zero as well. Referring back to the formula for the intercept, we see that with a zero beta, the characteristic line intercepts the vertical axis at the stock's sample mean rate of return. The characteristic line is perfectly horizontal at this level. The vertical deviations from the characteristic line are equal to deviations from the mean. The total of the squared deviations from the mean is equal to the total of the squared residuals. The only difference between variance and residual variance in this case is that for variance you divide the total by $N - 1$ and for residual variance you divide by $N - 2$.

SUMMARY

At this point we have reviewed all the statistical concepts you need to know for an understanding of the material in the remainder of the text. To summarize, you need to be familiar with the properties of a simple probability distribution and a joint probability distribution. The three statistics that we use to describe the simple probability distribution are the expected value, the variance, and the standard deviation. If you can observe the distribution and its associated probabilities, then you can compute the population values for these statistics. If you can't see the probability distribution, then you must infer its shape by taking sample estimates of these statistics.

The joint probability distribution depicts the relationship between two stocks or between a single stock and the market portfolio. Three of the statistics that describe the properties of the joint distribution are the covariance, the coefficient of correlation, and the coefficient of determination. The covariance is unbounded and provides us with information only about the direction of the relationship. The correlation coefficient can be thought of as a standardized covariance. It ranges between $+1$ and -1. If we square the correlation coefficient, we get the coefficient of determination, which tells us the percentage of the variability in the returns on one investment that can be explained by variability in the returns on another investment. With perfect correlation ($+1$ or -1), all the variability in one investment can be associated with variability in the returns on the other.

The relationship between a stock and the market portfolio is, in part, described by the stock's characteristic line. The slope of the characteristic line is called the stock's beta factor. It tells us the extent to which a stock's return will change if the market's return changes. A stock's residual variance gives us an indication of the propensity of a stock's returns to deviate from its characteristic line. Stocks, which are perfectly correlated with the market, have residual variances equal to zero.

As you shall see, we will be using all these statistical concepts in the next seven chapters on portfolio theory and capital asset pricing.

QUESTION SET 1

1. It is equally probable that stock A will have a $+10$ percent or -10 percent rate of return. The only other possibility is that it will return 0 percent. The probability of 0 percent is twice that for a return of 10 percent. What is the expected return and standard deviation of return for stock A?

2. Consider stock B, which has three possible returns $+50$ percent, 0 percent, and -50

percent. The three possible returns are equally probable. What is the expected return and standard deviation of return for stock *B?*

Refer to the following information on joint stock returns for stocks *A, B,* and *C* for Questions 3 through 6:

Probability	A	B	C
.25	.10	.15	− .05
.25	− .05	0	.10
.25	.20	.25	− .15
.25	0	.05	.05

3. Compute the expected returns to each stock.
4. Compute the standard deviation of returns for each stock.
5. Compute the covariances between returns on each pair of stocks.
6. If the return on stock *A* turns out to be greater than expected, would you expect the return on stock *C* to be greater or less than expected?

Refer to the following observations for stock *Y* and the market portfolio (*M*) for Questions 7 through 14:

Time Period	Observed Returns	
	Y	M
1	.10	.02
2	.14	− .02
3	.12	.08
4	.08	.17

7. Compute the sample mean returns for *Y* and *M*.
8. Compute the sample standard deviations for *Y* and *M*.
9. Compute the sample covariance between returns for *Y* and *M*.
10. Compute the sample beta factor of stock *Y*.
11. What is the equation for stock *Y*'s characteristic line?
12. Compute the sample correlation coefficient between the returns of *Y* and *M*.
13. Compute the sample coefficient of determination associated with stock *Y*'s characteristic line. What does this statistic tell us?
14. Compute the sample residual variance associated with stock *Y*'s characteristic line.
15. Explain what the residual variance associated with a stock's characteristic line is supposed to tell you.

QUESTION SET 2

1. What two sources of income go into determining the rate of return on a security?
2. Through what means do we estimate the parameters of a probability distribution, and what are the limitations on these estimates?

3. What does a probability distribution describe, and what is the difference between a simple probability distribution and a joint probability distribution?

4. What does covariance measure, and if two securities are said to have negative covariance, what does it mean?

5. What does the coefficient of determination measure? If the correlation coefficient for two stocks is .50, what is the coefficient of determination?

6. Describe the beta factor. What would probably have a greater beta, an airline stock or a utility stock, and do the characteristic lines of such stocks tend toward the horizontal or vertical axis?

ANSWERS TO QUESTION SET 2

1. The dividends and the change in market value are divided by the initial market value to determine a security's rate of return.

2. The parameters of a population are estimated through statistics on a sample. The limitations on these measures are the validity of the sample drawn and the time frame in which the sample is studied. If a population parameter is estimated from a poorly drawn sample, or the time frame studied is either too short or too long, incorrect assumptions about the population may be drawn.

3. A probability distribution describes the probability of obtaining various rates of return from a security over a given period of time. A simple probability distribution describes a single security, a joint probability distribution describes the probability of getting various pairs of returns on two securities at the same time.

4. Covariance measures the degree to which two variables move together. If two securities have a negative covariance, this means that a high rate of return on one will tend to be associated with a low rate of return on the other, and vice versa.

5. The coefficient of determination tells us the fraction of variability in one investment that can be associated with variability in returns on another. If the correlation coefficient for two stocks was .50, then the coefficient of determination would be .25, which indicates that 25 percent of the variability in one stock can be associated with the variability in returns on the other stock.

6. The beta factor is a measure of the association between a security's expected rate of return and the return on the market portfolio, and is represented by the slope of the characteristic line. The airline stock would probably have the greater beta factor, and its characteristic line would tend toward the vertical axis; the utility toward the horizontal axis.

PROBLEM SET

1. As an investor, you purchased a stock for $60 a share at the beginning of the year and sold it at the end of the year for $72. At the end of the year you received dividends totaling $4 per share. What was your dollar return and the percentage rate of return on your investment?

The following table is for Problems 2 through 4:

h_i Probability	Rates of Return on Stocks		
	1	2	3
.20	.24	.16	.02
.25	.18	.12	.07
.30	.10	.08	.10
.15	−.01	.04	.13
.10	−.12	.02	.21

$\cdot E(R)$ $E(R)$

2. Compute the expected rate of return for each of the three stocks.
3. Compute the variance and standard deviation for the three stocks.
4. Compute the population covariance and the correlation coefficient between stocks 1 and 2 and between stocks 1 and 3.

The accompanying table lists the annual rates of return on General Motors stock and the S&P 500 Index (a proxy for the market portfolio). Refer to it to answer Problems 5 through 9.

$.031$

	Annual Rates of Return	
Year	General Motors	S&P 500
1976	.474	.238
1977	−.114	−.072
1978	−.054	.065
1979	.023	.184
1980	−.044	.324
1981	−.099	−.049

$-.042$ $.175$

5. Calculate the sample mean returns for General Motors and the S&P 500 Index.
6. Calculate the sample covariance between returns for General Motors and the S&P 500 Index.
7. Compute the sample beta factor for General Motors.
8. Plot a graph showing the annual rates of return on General Motors against the annual returns of the S&P 500 Index. Draw in the characteristic line.
9. Compute the sample residual variance.

ANSWERS TO PROBLEM SET

1. The dollar return is the sum of the dividends received plus the gain in the market value of the stock:

$$\$4 + (\$72 - \$60) = \$16$$

The percentage rate of return is the dollar return per share of the stock dividend by the market value of the stock at the beginning of the period.

$$\frac{\$16}{\$60} = .2667 = 26.7\%$$

2. The equation for the expected rate of return is

$$E(r) = \sum_{i=1}^{n} h_i r_i$$

The expected return for stock 1 is computed as follows:

$$
\begin{aligned}
.20(.24) &= & .0480 \\
.25(.18) &= & .0450 \\
.30(.10) &= & .0300 \\
.15(-.01) &= & -.0015 \\
.10(-.12) &= & \underline{-.0120} \\
\text{Total} &= & .1095 \text{ or } 10.95\%
\end{aligned}
$$

The expected rates of return are 9.40 percent for stock 2 and 9.20 percent for stock 3.

3. The variance of the return is calculated using the following equation:

$$\sigma^2(r) = \sum_{i=1}^{n} h_i[r_i - E(r)]^2$$

The variance of stock 1 is

$$
\begin{aligned}
.20(.24 - .1095)^2 &= .0034 \\
.25(.18 - .1095)^2 &= .0012 \\
.30(.10 - .1095)^2 &= .0000 \\
.15(-.01 - .1095)^2 &= .0021 \\
.10(-.12 - .1095)^2 &= \underline{.0053} \\
\text{Total} &= .0120
\end{aligned}
$$

The variances of return are .0021 for stock 2 and .0027 for stock 3.
The standard deviation is simply the square root of the variance:

$$
\begin{aligned}
\text{Stock 1:} \quad \sigma &= .1095 \\
\text{Stock 2:} \quad \sigma &= .0458 \\
\text{Stock 3:} \quad \sigma &= .0520
\end{aligned}
$$

4. Covariance describes the relationship between two variables. The magnitude of the covariance measures the strength of the common movement. Using the equation in the text, we can compute the population covariance as follows:

$$
\begin{aligned}
.20(.24 - .1095)(.16 - .0940) &= .0017 \\
.25(.18 - .1095)(.12 - .0940) &= .0005
\end{aligned}
$$

$$.30(.10 - .1095)(.08 - .0940) = .0000$$

$$.15(-.01 - .1095)(.04 - .0940) = .0010$$

$$.10(-.12 - .1095)(.02 - .0940) = \underline{.0017}$$

$$\text{Total} = .0049$$

$$\text{Cov}(r_1, r_2) = .0049$$

The covariance for stocks 1 and 3 is $-.0054$.

The correlation coefficient is obtained by dividing the covariance by the product of the standard deviations of the two stocks.

$$\rho_{1,2} = \frac{\text{Cov}(r_1, r_2)}{\sigma(r_1)\sigma(r_2)} = \frac{.0049}{(.1095)(.0458)} = .9970$$

$$\rho_{1,3} = \frac{\text{Cov}(r_1, r_3)}{\sigma(r_1)\sigma(r_3)} = \frac{-.0054}{(.1095)(.0520)} = -.9484$$

5. The equation for the sample mean is

$$\bar{r} = \frac{\sum\limits_{t=1}^{N} r_t}{N}$$

Using this equation, the sample mean return for General Motors is

$$\frac{(.474) + (-.114) + (-.054) + (.023) + (-.044) + (-.099)}{6}$$

$$= .031 \text{ or } 3.1\%$$

The sample mean return for the S&P 500 is .115.

6. The equation for the sample covariance is

$$\text{Cov}_{A,B} = \frac{\sum\limits_{t=1}^{N} (r_{A,t} - r_A)(r_{B,t} - r_B)}{N - 1}$$

The value of the numerator is calculated as follows:

$$(.474 - .031)(.238 - .115) = \quad .0545$$

$$(-.114 - .031)(-.072 - .115) = \quad .0271$$

$$(-.054 - .031)(.065 - .115) = \quad .0043$$

$$(.023 - .031)(.184 - .115) = -.0006$$

$$(-.044 - .031)(.324 - .115) = -.0157$$

$$(-.099 - .031)(-.049 - .115) = \quad \underline{.0213}$$

$$\text{Total} = .0909$$

Next, divide the total by the number of observations, less one, to get the covariance:

$$\frac{.0909}{6 - 1} = .0182$$

7. The formula for the sample beta is

$$\beta_{GM} = \frac{\text{Cov}_{GM,M}}{\sigma^2_{r_M}}$$

First, compute the sample variance of the S&P 500:

$$(.238 - .115)^2 = .0151$$
$$(-.072 - .115)^2 = .0350$$
$$(.065 - .115)^2 = .0025$$
$$(.184 - .115)^2 = .0048$$
$$(.324 - .115)^2 = .0437$$
$$(-.049 - .115)^2 = \underline{.0269}$$

$$\text{Total} = .128$$

$$\frac{.128}{6 - 1} = .0256$$

From Problem 6 we know $\text{Cov}_{GM,M} = .0182$. Therefore,

$$\beta_{GM} = \frac{\text{Cov}_{GM,M}}{\sigma^2_{r_M}} = \frac{.0182}{.0256} = .7109$$

8.

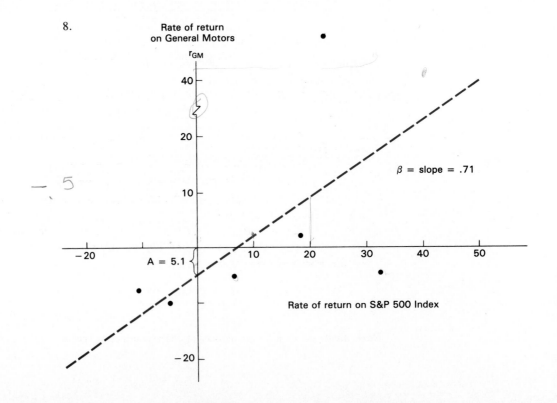

Rate of return
on General Motors

r_{GM}

β = slope = .71

A = 5.1

Rate of return on S&P 500 Index

9. From Problem 7 we know $\beta_{GM} = .7109$. We can calculate A_{GM} using the formula

$$A_{GM} = \bar{r}_{GM} - \beta_{GM}\bar{r}_M$$

$$= .0310 - (.7109)(.1150) = -.0508$$

We are now able to calculate the annual residuals by applying the equation:

$$\epsilon_t = r_{GM,t} - (A + \beta_{GM}r_{M,t})$$

$Y = -.0508 + .7109 X^{.10}$

Year	Residual
1976	$.474 - [-.0508 + .7109(\ .238)] = \ \ .3556$
1977	$-.114 - [-.0508 + .7109(-.072)] = -.0120$
1978	$-.054 - [-.0508 + .7109(\ .065)] = -.0494$
1979	$.023 - [-.0508 + .7109(\ .184)] = -.0570$
1980	$-.044 - [-.0508 + .7109(\ .324)] = -.2235$
1981	$-.099 - [-.0508 + .7109(-.049)] = -.0134$

Year	Squared Residual
1976	$(\ \ .3556)^2 = .1265$
1977	$(-.0120)^2 = .0001$
1978	$(-.0494)^2 = .0024$
1979	$(-.0570)^2 = .0032$
1980	$(-.2235)^2 = .0500$
1981	$(-.0134)^2 = \underline{.0002}$
	Total $= .1824$
	$\dfrac{.1824}{6-2} = .0456$

REFERENCES

DANIEL, W. E., and TERRELL, J. C., *Business Statistics: Concepts and Methodology,* 2nd ed. Boston: Houghton Mifflin, 1979.

HUNSBERGEER, D. V., CROFT, D. J., and BILLINGSLEY, P., *Statistical Inferrence for Management and Economics,* 2nd ed. Boston: Allyn & Bacon, 1980.

LEVY, H., and BEN-HORIM, M., *Statistics: Decisions and Applications in Business and Economics.* New York: Random House, 1984.

MANSFIELD, E., *Statistics for Business and Economics.* New York: W. W. Norton, 1983.

WONNACOTT, T. H., and WONNACOTT, R. J., *Introductory Statistics for Business and Economics.* New York: John Wiley, 1984.

4

COMBINING INDIVIDUAL SECURITIES INTO PORTFOLIOS

Suppose we have two individual securities with underlying probability distributions like those of Figures 4.1 and 4.2. We're going to construct a portfolio by investing some of our money in one security and the rest in the other. The question we're going to ask in this chapter is: "What will the probability distribution of returns to the portfolio in Figure 4.3 look like?" Actually, we are going to restrict the question to just two properties of the distribution, the expected rate of return and the variance or standard deviation. If you are willing to accept standard deviation as a reasonable measure of the risk of a portfolio, we're going to find out how to predict the risk and expected rate of return of a *portfolio* based on the characteristics of the securities we put into it.

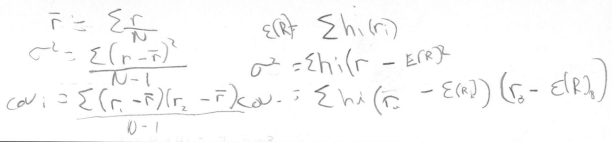

$$\bar{r} = \frac{\sum r}{N}$$

$$\sigma^2 = \frac{\sum (r - \bar{r})^2}{N-1}$$

$$cov_i = \frac{\sum (r_1 - \bar{r})(r_2 - \bar{r})}{N-1}$$

$$E(R) \quad \sum h_i(r_i)$$

$$\sigma^2 = \sum h_i (r - E(R))^2$$

$$cov. = \sum h_i (r_A - E(R_A))(r_B - E(R_B))$$

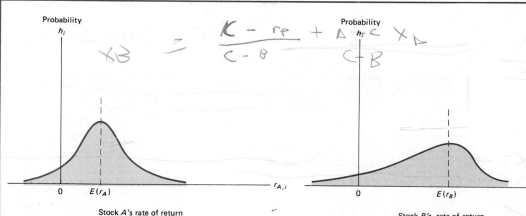

$$X_B = \frac{K - r_P}{C - B} + A \frac{h_T C}{C - B} X_A$$

FIGURE 4.1 Probability distribution for stock A.

Stock A's rate of return

FIGURE 4.2 Probability distribution for security B.

Stock B's rate of return

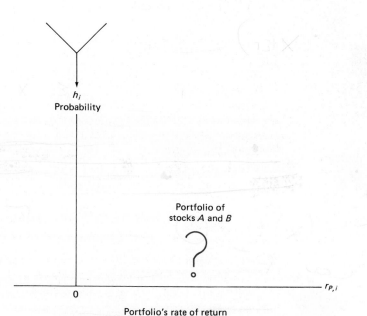

h_i
Probability

Portfolio of stocks A and B

?

Portfolio's rate of return

FIGURE 4.3 Probability distribution for a portfolio of A and B.

THE RISK AND EXPECTED RETURN OF A PORTFOLIO

The Portfolio's Rate of Return

Let's start with something basic. Suppose we consider a single period of time; let's again say a month. If the individual securities in the portfolio produce various rates of return, what will be the return to the portfolio as a whole? Let's consider a portfolio of two securities and first consider the *dollar* return to the portfolio. We'll assume we have $1000 to invest, and we put $400 of it in security A and $600 in security B. In the next month, A produces a rate of return of 10 percent (a dollar return of $40), and B produces a rate of return of 6 percent ($36). What is the *dollar* rate of return to the portfolio? The dollar return to the portfolio is obviously the sum of the dollar returns to the two securities:

$$\$76 = (\$400 \times .10) + (\$600 \times .06)$$

$$\$76 = \quad \$40 \quad + \quad \$36$$

The percentage *rate* of return to the portfolio is given by the dollar return divided by the amount we have invested, which in this case is $1000. Dividing both sides of the above equation for $1000, we get

$$7.6\% = \frac{\$76}{\$1000} = \left(\frac{\$400}{\$1000} \times .10\right) + \left(\frac{\$600}{\$1000} \times .06\right)$$

$$r_P = \quad x_A \times r_A \quad + \quad x_B \times r_B$$

The term x is the fraction of money you are investing in each security. Thus, the rate of return to our portfolio, in any given period of time, is a weighted average of the rates of return that are being produced by the securities in the portfolio, where we are weighting by the fraction of our own money that we are investing in each security. These fractions are also called *portfolio weights*. When summed, they add up to 100 percent, and they are computed as

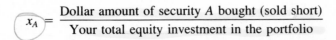

$$x_A = \frac{\text{Dollar amount of security } A \text{ bought (sold short)}}{\text{Your total equity investment in the portfolio}}$$

A portfolio weight can be either positive or negative. A positive weight means you are buying the security; we also refer to this as taking a *long* position in the security. The opposite of taking a long position is taking a short position or *selling short*. In this case, the portfolio weight is negative because the numerator is negative.

Selling a security short isn't quite the same as selling some security that you happen to own. For example, when you sell stock short, you borrow *shares* of stock from someone (usually through your broker). You're obligated to return to this person, after a certain period of time, the same number of shares you borrowed. Suppose, for example, you borrow 100 shares of Blue Steel stock from me. Then you turn around and sell it for $10 per share, collecting $1000. After a period of time the stock falls $5 per share. You then go back into the market and buy the 100 shares back for a total of $500. You then return the 100 shares that you borrowed from me, and the short sale is completed. You have made a profit on this short sale, the difference between the $1000 you got for the borrowed stock when you sold it and the $500 it took to buy the stock back later in the market. However, if the stock paid any dividends between the time you sold it and the time you bought it back, you would have to pay cash, in the amount of these dividends, to me, the person from whom you borrowed the stock.

You might ask, "What are you allowed to do with the $1000 proceeds between the time you short sell and the time you buy the stock back?" If you or I were to sell short, we would have to set the proceeds aside, and, in addition, we would have to set aside some of our own money (perhaps 30 percent, or $300, in this case) as a margin on the transaction. Large financial institutions, however don't suffer from the same limitations on the use of the proceeds of short sales. Since financial institutions are the principal users of the techniques of portfolio management, we will assume that when you sell short, you are free to use the proceeds to invest in other securities and that no margin account is required on the transaction.

Suppose you have $1000 of your own money and you sell short $600 of stock B and use this money in addition to your own money to buy $1600 of stock A. What are your portfolio weights? You're buying $1600 of stock A, which is 160 percent of your $1000 equity investment. Thus, x_A is 1.6. At the same time you're *selling* $600 of stock B, which is -60 percent of your equity investment. The sign is negative because you're doing the opposite of buying the stock—you're selling it. Note that the two portfolio weights still add up to 100 percent.

Now suppose that in the period of time you're holding this position, stock A produces a 20 percent rate of return and stock B produces a 10 percent rate of return. What's your rate of return on the "portfolio" of the two stocks?

$$r_P = (x_A \cdot r_A) + (x_B \cdot r_A)$$
$$.26 = (1.6 \times .20) + (-.6 \times .10)$$

To verify this, consider that we've got a profit on our long position of $320 (.20 × $1600). We've also got a $60 loss on the short sale, since we sold stock B for $600 and repurchased it for $660 (a 10 percent increase). Our net profit, therefore, is $260. Since we initially invested $1000 of our own money, this represents a 26 percent rate of return on our investment.

To summarize, we can say that in any given period of time, the rate of return on our portfolio is a weighted average of the rates of return on the stocks in the portfolio. In taking the average, the weights are given by the fraction of our own money that we are investing in each stock. If we are buying the stock in question, the weight assigned to the stock is positive; if we are short-selling the stock, the weight is negative. In any case, the sum of the weights is 100 percent.

The Portfolio's Expected Rate of Return

In Appendix 1 at the end of this chapter, we show that the expected rate of return to a portfolio is a simple weighted average of the expected rates of return to the securities that are included in the portfolio. The weights are again equal to the fractions of our own money that we are investing in each security. If there are M securities in the portfolio,

$$E(r_P) = \sum_{J=1}^{M} x_J E(r_J)$$

Thus, if security A has a 20 percent expected return and B has a 10 percent expected return and we allocate half our money to each security, the expected return to the portfolio is 15 percent:

$$.15 = (.5 \times .2) + (.5 \times .1)$$

On the other hand, suppose we have $1000 of our own money, we sell short $1000 of security B, and use the proceeds, in addition to our own money, to invest $2000 in security A. The expected rate of return to our portfolio is now 30 percent:

$$.30 = (2.0 \times .2) + (-1.0 \times .1)$$

Note that if we don't sell short, the expected portfolio return is always somewhere in between the two securities, depending on how much of the two securities we buy. However, if we sell one of the two securities short, our expected return is unlimited on the upside or the downside. We can make the expected return to the portfolio as big as we want it simply by selling short huge amounts of the security with the lower expected rate of return. However, you should also understand that as we increase our expected return, we also usually increase the risk of the portfolio. This brings us to the next section.

The Portfolio's Variance

To compute the variance of a portfolio of securities, you need to have the covariance matrix for the securities you are putting in the portfolio. The covariance matrix gives you the covariances between each of the securities in the portfolio. For example, the covariance matrix among three stocks A, B, and C is as follows:

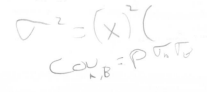

Stock	A	B	C
A	$\mathrm{Cov}(r_A, r_A)$	$\mathrm{Cov}(r_B, r_A)$	$\mathrm{Cov}(r_C, r_A)$
B	$\mathrm{Cov}(r_A, r_B)$	$\mathrm{Cov}(r_B, r_B)$	$\mathrm{Cov}(r_C, r_B)$
C	$\mathrm{Cov}(r_A, r_C)$	$\mathrm{Cov}(r_B, r_C)$	$\mathrm{Cov}(r_C, r_C)$

Each element of the matrix tells you the covariance between the returns to the stock(s) given at the top of the column(s) and the returns to the stock given at the left of the row(s). To illustrate, as we go down the diagonal of the matrix from the extreme north-west corner to the extreme southeast corner, we are looking at the covariance between each stock and itself. This may seem strange at first, but if you consider the formula for covariance, you will realize that the covariance between a stock and itself is simply its own variance:

$$Cov(r_A, r_A) = \sum_{i=1}^{m} h_i[r_{A,i} - E(r_A)][r_{A,i} - E(r_A)] = \sum_{i=1}^{m} h_i[r_{A,i} - E(r_A)]^2 = \sigma^2(r_A)$$

Thus, all the numbers going down the diagonal of the matrix represent the variances for the individual stocks.

It is also true that for each number above the diagonal there is a corresponding and equal number below the diagonal. This is true because

$$Cov(r_A, r_B) = \sum_{i=1}^{m} h_i[r_{A,i} - E(r_A)][r_{B,i} - E(r_B)]$$

$$= \sum_{i=1}^{m} h_i[r_{B,i} - E(r_B)][r_{A,i} - E(r_A)] = Cov(r_B, r_A)$$

To determine what the variance of a portfolio is going to be, we need to know the portfolio weights for each stock, and we need to have estimates (perhaps sample estimates) for the numbers in the covariance matrix. We then set up the matrix in the following way:

	Stock	x_A A	x_B B	x_C C
x_A	A	$\sigma^2(r_A)$	$Cov(r_B, r_A)$	$Cov(r_C, r_A)$
x_B	B	$Cov(r_A, r_B)$	$\sigma^2(r_B)$	$Cov(r_C, r_B)$
x_C	C	$Cov(r_A, r_C)$	$Cov(r_B, r_C)$	$\sigma^2(r_C)$

Computing the variance is now a comparatively simple operation. You simply take each of the covariances in the matrix and multiply it by the portfolio weight at the top of the column and then again by the portfolio weight at the left side of the row. For example, in the case of $Cov(r_A, r_B)$ you would compute the following product:

$$Cov(r_A, r_B) \cdot x_A \cdot x_B$$

When you have obtained such a product for each element of the matrix, you add up all the products, and the resulting sum is the variance of the portfolio.

By recognizing that each of the elements above the diagonal is paired with an identical element below the diagonal, the formula for the variance of a three-stock portfolio is given as follows:

$$\sigma^2(r_P) = x_A^2 \sigma^2(r_A) + x_B^2 \sigma^2(r_B) + x_C^2 \sigma^2(r_C) + 2x_Ax_B Cov(r_A, r_B)$$
$$+ 2x_Ax_C Cov(r_A, r_C) + 2x_Bx_C Cov(r_B, r_C)$$

The number of elements in the sum is equal to the square of the number of stocks in the portfolio. With three stocks there are 9 elements, with four stocks there are 16

OUT ON THE STREET

ESTIMATING RISK AND RETURN

"Would you like something to drink, Mr. Davanzo?"

"No thanks, but I would like a copy of *Business Week* or *Forbes,* if you have one, please."

Larry Davanzo settles back into the relatively comfortable first-class seat of the DC-10. He is flying from Chicago to Los Angeles after stops in Washington, D.C., and New York. Larry is the director of consulting to public and private pension plans at Wilshire Associates, Inc., a consulting firm specializing in the application of modern portfolio techniques.

This has been a successful trip. This time it has pretty much been a case of helping clients allocate their assets among basic investment types. Each pension client has an associated stream of projected benefit liabilities. Larry shows the client the impact that different asset mixes will have on asset values, benefits, and future required contributions by the plan sponsor, usually a corporation, and in some cases a state or municipality.

Using Wilshire's computer programs, Larry can specify any arbitrary mix of portfolio investments, estimates of risk and expected rates of return for each mix are then produced for the client, given certain minimum and maximum amounts of investments in different types of assets.

The programs can consider up to 20 basic asset categories. These include stocks, bonds, real estate, venture capital, options, international stocks and bonds, or any other quantifiable asset category. In making the asset allocation decision, the objective is not to determine the specific stock investments but rather to determine how much money to invest in one asset category as opposed to another.

To run the programs, Larry must come up with estimates of the expected rate of return on each asset category, the standard deviation of returns to each category, and the correlation coefficient between the categories.

The estimates of expected return are made in consultation with each client separately. Larry tries to get a feel for the individual client's expectation for the

elements, and so on. Obviously, to compute the standard deviation of the portfolio, you need only take the square root of the preceding equation.

COMBINATION LINES

A ***combination line*** is drawn on a graph where you are plotting $E(r)$ against $\sigma(r)$. Each point on the line shows you the expected rate of return and standard deviation of a portfolio of two stocks with given portfolio weights. Each point on the line represents a different set of portfolio weights in the two stocks. Thus, the combination line tells us how the expected return and risk of a two-stock portfolio changes

rate of inflation over the client's horizon period. On this particular trip, expectations ranged from 4 percent to as high as 7 percent for the next three to five years. Then, using Wilshire's data base, an estimate is made of the real, inflation-adjusted, expected rate of return in each asset category. These estimates are based, to a considerable extent, on the historical record. For example, over the last 61 years or so, the real rate of return to stock investments has been 6.8 percent. However, in the last decade, this has increased to about 9 percent. Thus, Wilshire may project about 5 percent to 6 percent, depending on the economic outlook. Based on current interest rates, fixed income securities have a real rate of interest of nearly 5 percent, but to obtain a forecast consistent with its stock forecast, Wilshire will project this to fall to three percent over the next three years or so. In any case, all these projections are developed jointly with the client.

The projections for standard deviation are also based, to a great extent, on historical returns. For example, over the last 61 years the standard deviation of rates of return to long-term bonds has been 5 percent to 6 percent. However in the last 10 years it has been 10 percent to 12 percent. Wilshire assumes a continued higher level of risk in the fixed income markets and usually forecasts in the neighborhood of 10 percent to 12 percent.

Turning to correlation coefficients, the long-term correlation coefficient between stocks and bonds has been 20 percent, but in the last 10 years it has been up to 30 percent. In each case, Wilshire looks at the history and then imposes some kind of subjective correction where they think the past doesn't adequately reflect the best estimate of prospects for the future. Investment categories such as venture capital present special problems, because there are no decent data on the past rates of return to these types of investments. The correlation with stocks is probably positive. They feel it is more positive for more aggressive stock portfolios because these are usually invested in smaller stocks, which themselves resemble venture operations.

as we change the weights in the two stocks. The combination line is really a plot of the equations for $E(r_P)$ and $\sigma(r_P)$ for a two-stock portfolio.

By recognizing that in a portfolio of two stocks $x_B = (1 - x_A)$, the equations for expected return and standard deviation are given by

$$E(r_P) = x_A E(r_A) + (1 - x_A)E(r_B)$$

and

$$\sigma(r_P) = [x_A^2 \sigma^2(r_A) + (1 - x_A)^2 \sigma^2(r_B) + 2x_A(1 - x_A)\text{Cov}(r_A, r_B)]^{1/2}$$

As shown in Chapter 3,

$$\text{Cov}(r_A, r_B) = \rho_{A,B}\,\sigma(r_A)\sigma(r_B)$$

Therefore, we can rewrite the equation for the standard deviation as

$$\sigma(r_P) = [x_A^2\, \sigma^2(r_A) + (1 - x_A)^2\, \sigma^2(r_B) + 2x_A(1 - x_A)\rho_{A,B}\, \sigma(r_A)\, \sigma(r_B)]^{1/2} \quad (4.1)$$

To illustrate the concept of a combination line, suppose we have two stocks with the following characteristics:

	Stock A	Stock B
$E(r)$	.10	.04
$\sigma(r)$	.05	.10

To construct a combination line for the two stocks, we need to make an assumption about the degree to which they are correlated. Let's assume the correlation coefficient between the two stocks is zero. Filling in the preceding numbers for the corresponding values in our equations for expected return and standard deviation gives

$$E(r_P) = x_A \times .10 + (1 - x_A) \times .04$$

$$\sigma(r_P) = [x_A^2 \times .05^2 + (1 - x_A)^2 \times .10^2]^{1/2}$$

Note that the covariance term has disappeared from the formula for standard deviation because the correlation is presumed to be zero.

Assume that you have $1000 to invest, you short-sell $500 of stock B and you use the proceeds in addition to your equity to invest $1500 in stock A. Your portfolio weight in A is, thus, 1.5. Substituting this value into the formulas, we get the following values for the expected rate of return and standard deviation:

$$E(r_P) = 1.50 \times .10 - .5 \times .04 = .13$$

$$\sigma(r_P) = [1.50^2 \times .05^2 + (-.50)^2 \times .10^2]^{1/2} = .09$$

By making the same computations for other values for x_A, we obtain the following schedule:

x_A	$E(r_P)$	$\sigma(r_P)$
1.50	.130	.090
.75	.085	.045
.50	.070	.056
.25	.055	.076
$-.50$	.010	.152

The points in the preceding schedule are plotted in Figure 4.4. If still more such points were plotted for different values for x_A, they would trace out the bullet-shaped curve drawn in the diagram. This curve is called the *combination line* for the two stocks. It shows what happens to the risk and expected return to a portfolio of two stocks as the portfolio weights are shifted from one value to another. The two stocks

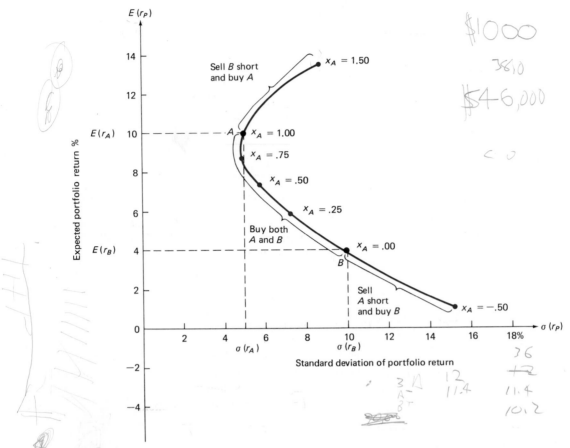

FIGURE 4.4 Combination line between stocks A and B for the case of zero correlation.

are positioned at points A and B. At these points, x_A is equal to 1.00 and .00, respectively. For points along the curve to the northeast of point A, we are short-selling stock B and investing in stock A. For points on the curve between points A and B, we are taking positive positions in both stocks. For points to the southeast of B, we are short-selling stock A and investing in stock B. While these points represent unattractive portfolios, in the sense that risk is high and expected return is low, nevertheless they are available, given the assumed position of the two stocks. You also should understand that the curve extends out indefinitely toward the northeast and toward the southeast. The more of stock B we short-sell, the farther we move on the curve to the northeast, and the more of stock A we short-sell, the farther we move to the southeast.

To see what is happening as we move along the combination line, consider Figure 4.5. In this figure probability distributions are shown for three portfolios along the combination line, portfolios C, D, and E. Note that as you move from C to D to

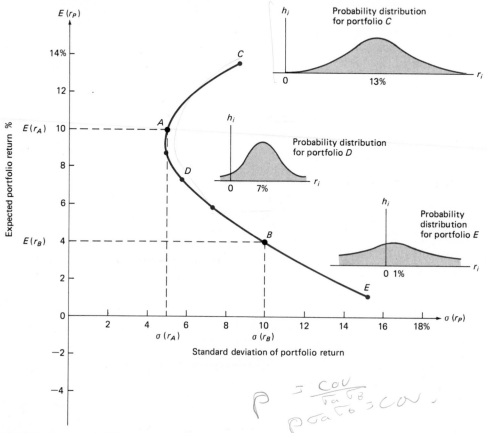

FIGURE 4.5 Probability distributions corresponding to positions on the combination line.

E, the expected rate of return becomes smaller and smaller. The standard deviation of the distribution grows smaller as you move from portfolio C to D, but then it increases in magnitude as you go from portfolio D to E.

The Cases of Perfect Positive and Negative Correlation

The combination line of Figure 4.4 is drawn for an assumed 0 value, for the correlation coefficient between the two stocks. If we assume a different value for the correlation coefficient, the schedule of $\sigma(r_P)$ values would change, and we would obtain a different combination line. In fact, there is a family of combination lines, one line for each assumed value for the correlation coefficient.

Suppose, for example, we assume the two stocks are perfectly positively correlated. The assumed relationship between the two stocks is depicted in Figure 4.6. If the stocks are perfectly positively correlated, pairs of returns produced by the

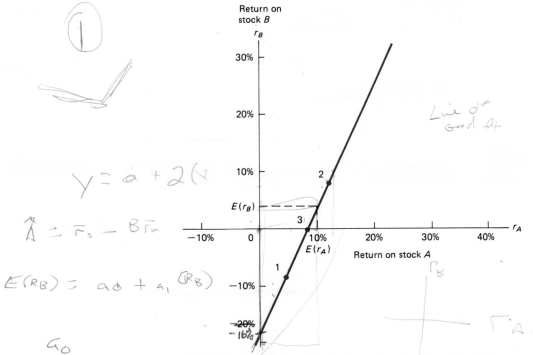

FIGURE 4.6 Relationship between stocks A and B with perfect positive correlation.

stocks must all fall on a straight line with a positive slope, as they do with the points labeled 1, 2, and 3. If we are dealing with a case of perfect correlation, the slope of the line must reflect the relative standard deviations for the two stocks. In our example, stock B has twice the standard deviation of stock A. A line with a slope equal to 2.00 is consistent with these relative standard deviations. In this case, a change in the return on stock A is always accompanied by a change in the return on stock B that is twice as great. The line must intercept the vertical axis at a value that is consistent with the relative expected rates of return on the two stocks. Denoting the slope of the line as a_1 and its intercept as a_0, the relationship between the expected returns is given by

$$E(r_B) = a_0 + a_1 E(r_A)$$

Since a_1 is equal to 2.00 in this case and since the expected returns to A and B are 10 percent and 4 percent, respectively, we have

$$.04 = a_0 + 2.00 \times .10$$

or

$$a_0 = -.16$$

$\sigma = x\sigma + x\sigma$

Now consider the equation for the standard deviation of a two-stock portfolio as given by Equation (4.1). When the correlation coefficient is assumed to be 1.00, the terms in parentheses become a perfect square in the sense that $[x_A\sigma(r_A) + (1 - x_A)\sigma(r_B)]$ multiplied by itself produces the expression in brackets. Thus, for the case of perfect positive correlation, we can say the standard deviation of a portfolio is a simple weighted average of the standard deviations of the stocks we are putting in the portfolio:

$2.0(.08) - 11$

$$\sigma(r_P) = x_A \, \sigma(r_A) + (1 - x_A) \, \sigma(r_B)$$

Technically speaking, since the standard deviation is always a positive number (it's the square root of the variance), the portfolio's standard deviation is equal to the absolute value of the right-hand side of the equation.

Given the preceding expression, we can again develop a schedule of values for $E(r_P)$ and $\sigma(r_P)$, given different values for x_A:

$3.00(.10)$ $-2(.04)$

$.3 - .08$

$.22$

x_A	$E(r_P)$	$\sigma(r_P)$
3.00	.220	.0500
2.00	.160	.0000
1.50	.130	.0250
.75	.085	.0625
.50	.070	.0750
.25	.055	.0875
-.50	.010	.1250

$x\sigma_A$

These points are plotted on the black combination line of Figure 4.7. Note that you can achieve a riskless portfolio by selling B short in an amount equal to 100 percent of your equity investment and using the proceeds to add to your equity investment in A. To see this, consider the three pairs of returns labeled 1, 2, and 3 in Figure 4.6. Assume these pairs are observed in three successive months:

$E(R) = 2 x\sigma$

	Month		
	1	2	3
Return to stock A	.04	.12	.08
Return to stock B	-.08	.08	.00

Now consider the corresponding returns to a portfolio with weights that are adjusted to $x_A = 2.00$ and $x_B = -1.00$ at the beginning of each month:

$$r_{P,t} = x_A \cdot r_{A,t} + X_B \cdot r_{B,t}$$

$$.16 = 2.00 \times .04 + (-1.00) \times (-.08)$$

$$.16 = 2.00 \times .12 + (-1.00) \times .08$$

$$.16 = 2.00 \times .08 + (-1.00) \times .00$$

 Michael P. Kelle

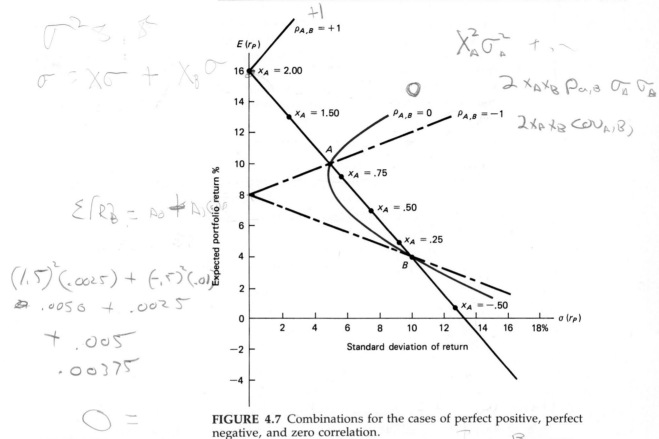

FIGURE 4.7 Combinations for the cases of perfect positive, perfect negative, and zero correlation.

The portfolio's return is perfectly stable at 16 percent. This is true no matter what pairs of returns we take from the line of Figure 4.6. With these weights we have created a portfolio that produces a constant rate of return period after period. We can always do this by selling one of the two stocks short to some degree, provided the stock's standard deviations are not equal and the stocks are perfectly positively correlated.

Now suppose, instead, the two stocks are perfectly *negatively* correlated. In this case all pairs of returns must come from a straight line which has a negative slope. Again, the slope of the line must be equal to −2.00 because stock *B* has twice the standard deviation of stock *A*. The intercept of the line again must be consistent with the expected returns on the stocks. Thus,

$$.04 = a_0 - 2.00 \times .10$$

and

$$a_0 = .24$$

The relationship between stocks A and B of perfect negative correlation is drawn in Figure 4.8.

Consider again Equation (4.1) for the standard deviation of a two-stock portfolio. If we assume a value of -1.00 for the correlation coefficient, the terms in brackets again become a perfect square in the sense that the term $[x_A\sigma(r_A) - (1 - x_A)\sigma(r_B)]$, when multiplied by itself, produces the bracketed expression. Thus, in this case, the formula for the standard deviation of a two-stock portfolio reduces to

$$\sigma(r_P) = x_A\ \sigma(r_A) - (1 - x_A)\ \sigma(r_B)$$

This expression is almost the same as the expression for the case of perfect positive correlation, except that a negative sign now separates the two terms on the right-hand side. The standard deviation is again equal to the absolute value of the right-hand side of the expression.

We can again derive a schedule, graphed as the broken line in Figure 4.7, showing $E(r_P)$ and $\sigma(r_P)$ values corresponding to various values for x_A:

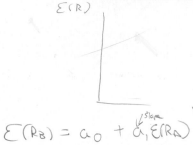

x_A	$E(r_P)$	$\sigma(r_P)$
3.000	.220	.3500
2.000	.160	.2000
1.500	.130	.1250
.667	.080	.0000
.250	.055	.0875
$-.500$	.010	.1750

With perfect negative correlation, we can create a riskless portfolio by taking positive positions in both stocks. Whenever the return on stock B increases, the return on stock A decreases, so if we invest positive amounts in both stocks, variability in their returns will tend to cancel. Note, however, that when the return on A changes by a given amount, the return on B changes by twice the amount. Consequently, to make the cancelling complete, we must invest twice as much in A as we do in B. This is the case when the portfolio weights are $x_A = .667$ and $x_B = .333$.

To see this, consider the three pairs of returns plotted in Figure 4.8. Again, assume they are realized in three successive months:

	Month		
	1	2	3
Return on stock A	.04	.12	.08
Return on stock B	.16	.00	.08

If, at the beginning of each month, we adjust to portfolio weights equal to $x_A = .667$ and $x_B = .333$, the portfolio will produce an 8 percent return in each of the three periods:

$$r_{P,t} = x_A \cdot r_{A,t} + x_B \cdot r_{B,t}$$
$$.08 = .667 \times .04 + .333 \times .16$$
$$.08 = .667 \times .12 + .333 \times .00$$
$$.08 = .667 \times .08 + .333 \times .08$$

No matter which pair of returns are drawn from the line of Figure 4.8, with these weights the portfolio will always produce an 8 percent rate of return.

Contrast the risk associated with short selling under conditions of perfect positive and negative correlation. If we are short in either stock, the risk of our portfolio is higher if the correlation is negative. Remember, if you are short, it is better for the return to be low than high. With perfect negative correlation, when the return on one stock is high relative to its mean, the return on the other stock is invariably low relative to its mean. If you are short in the high stock and long in the low, you're suffering in both parts of your portfolio. On the other hand, if you're long in the high and short in the low, you're prospering in both parts. It's a feast or famine situation! It's also highly risky.

We have the opposite situation with perfect positive correlation. Here, when the return on one stock is high, the other will be also. You will prosper from your long position but suffer from your short. Moreover, when the returns on both stocks are low, you will suffer from your long but prosper from your short. The returns

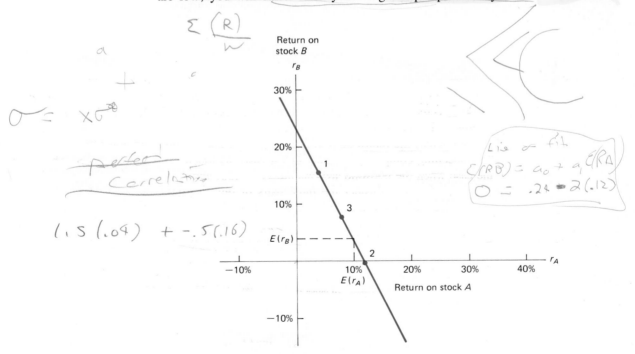

FIGURE 4.8 Relationship between stocks A and B with perfect negative correlation.

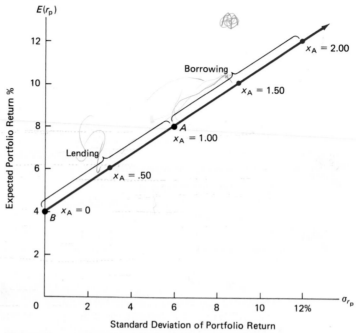

FIGURE 4.9 Effect of borrowing and lending on risk and expected return.

from your long and short positions will cancel, and the return to your overall position will be stabilized.

Borrowing and Lending at a Risk-Free Rate

Consider Figure 4.9. Two investments are plotted. A risky stock is plotted at point A, with an expected return of 8 percent and a standard deviation of 6 percent, and a risk-free bond is plotted at point B. Assume that the return on the bond is guaranteed by the government, so the probability of getting a 4 percent rate of return on the bond is 100 percent. The standard deviation of the returns on the bond is, therefore, equal to 0 percent.

Now consider again Equation (4.1) for the standard deviation of a portfolio of two stocks. If we set $\sigma(r_B) = 0$, the second and third terms in brackets drop out, leaving

$$\sigma(r_P) = [x_A^2 \, \sigma^2(r_A)]^{1/2}$$

This reduces to

$$\sigma(r_P) = x_A \, \sigma(r_A)$$

Given the preceding expression, we can again produce a schedule showing the risk and expected return to our portfolio, given various values for x_A:

x_A	$E(r_P)$	$\sigma(r_P)$
.00	.040	.000
.50	.060	.030
1.00	.080	.060
1.50	.100	.090
2.00	.120	.120

These points are plotted in Figure 4.9 on the combination line between the two investments. When one of the two investments is risk-free, as it is here, the combination line is always a straight line. Correlation is obviously meaningless when one of the investments has no variability in its return.

If you take a position between points *A* and *B*, you are investing positive amounts in both the stock and the risk-free bond. In this case, you are said to be *lending* to the person from whom you bought the bond. When you take positions on the combination line to the northeast of point *A*, you are said to be *borrowing*, because you are selling the bond to raise money to add to your investment in stock *A*. The more you borrow, the farther out on the combination line you go, increasing your risk as well as your expected rate of return.

Remember that if a risk-free borrowing and lending opportunity exists, such as the one in Figure 4.9, you can attain any position on a straight line extending out from the risk-free rate through any investment opportunity which exists in $E(r)$, $\sigma(r)$ space.

SUMMARY

In this chapter, we examined how individual securities combine into a portfolio. We concentrated on determining the expected rate of return and variance (or standard deviation) of a portfolio based on the characteristics of the stocks we put into the portfolio.

The expected portfolio return is simply a weighted average of the expected rates of return of the stocks in it. The weights are the fractions of our own investment we commit to each security in our portfolio. If you buy (go long) a security, the weight for the security is positive; if you sell the security short, the weight is negative.

The portfolio variance is determined on the basis of a covariance matrix for the individual stocks in the portfolio. For each covariance element in the matrix, we multiply the covariance by the two portfolio weights for the associated stocks. Then we sum up all the products to obtain the variance of the portfolio.

A combination line shows you what happens to the expected return and standard deviation of a two-security portfolio as we change the portfolio weights in the two securities. Combination lines are linear for the cases of perfect positive or perfect negative correlation between the returns on the two securities. For correlation coefficients between these limits, combination lines are curved. When one of the two investments is risk-free, the combination line is a straight line extending out from the risk-free rate and passing through the position of the other risky investment.

To this point we have only learned how to determine the positions of portfolio opportunities available to us, given a selection of stock investments. We haven't learned how to determine the *best* opportunities. That is left to the next chapter.

APPENDIX 1

FORMULAS FOR THE EXPECTED RATE OF RETURN AND VARIANCE OF A PORTFOLIO

Expected Rate of Return to a Portfolio

We know that the rate of return to a portfolio in any ith state of nature is given by

$$r_{P,i} = x_A r_{A,i} + x_B r_{B,i} \tag{1.A.1}$$

The statistical definition for the expected rate of return to a portfolio is given by

$$E(r_P) = \sum_{i=1}^{n} h_i r_{P,i} \tag{1.A.2}$$

Substituting Equation (A.1) into (A.2), we obtain

$$E(r_P) = \sum_{i=1}^{n} h_i(x_A r_{A,i} + x_B r_{B,i}) \tag{1.A.3}$$

Since the sum of X plus Y is equal to the sum of X plus the sum of Y, we can bring the summation sign into the parentheses and factor x out of the sums $\sum_{i=1}^{n} x_A h_i r_{A,i}$ and $\sum_{i=1}^{n} x_B h_i r_{B,i}$:

$$E(r_P) = x_A \sum_{i=1}^{n} h_i r_{A,i} + x_B \sum_{i=1}^{n} h_i r_{B,i}$$

Recognizing the formulas for expected rates of return on stocks A and B, we obtain

$$E(r_P) = x_A E(r_A) + x_B E(r_B)$$

Generalizing to a portfolio of M stocks, we obtain

$$E(r_P) = \sum_{J=1}^{M} x_J E(r_J)$$

Variance of Return to a Portfolio

The statistical definition of portfolio variance is given by

$$\sigma^2(r_P) = \sum_{i=1}^{n} h_i[r_{P,i} - E(r_P)]^2$$

Substituting Equations (1.A.1) and (1.A.4) into (1.A.5), we obtain

$$\sigma^2(r_P) = \sum_{i=1}^{n} h_i\{(x_A r_{A,i} + x_B r_{B,i}) - [x_A E(r_A) + x_B E(r_B)]\}^2$$

Bringing together terms involving the individual stocks and factoring out the portfolio weights, we obtain

$$\sigma^2(r_P) = \sum_{i=1}^{n} h_i\{x_A\underline{[r_{A,i} - E(r_A)]} + x_B\underline{[r_{B,i} - E(r_B)]}\}^2$$

The squared term tells us to multiply the two underscored terms in brackets. Doing so, we obtain two squared terms and two cross-product terms:

$$\sigma^2(r_P) = x_A^2 \sum_{i=1}^{n} h_i[r_{A,i} - E(r_A)]^2 + x_B^2 \sum_{i=1}^{n} h_i[r_{B,i} - E(r_B)]^2$$

$$+ 2x_A x_B \sum_{i=1}^{n} h_i[r_{A,i} - E(r_A)][r_{B,i} - E(r_B)]$$

The first two terms are the variances of stocks A and B. The second two are the covariances between the two stocks. Thus,

$$\sigma^2(r_P) = x_A^2\,\sigma^2(r_A) + x_B^2\,\sigma^2(r_B) + 2x_A x_B\,\text{Cov}(r_A, r_B)$$

QUESTION SET 1

1. Explain the concept of short selling.
2. Suppose you purchase $1000 of stock A, purchase $500 of stock B, and borrow $500. If these transactions constitute your entire portfolio, what are the portfolio weights for each component of the portfolio?
3. Compute the variance and expected return of the portfolio in Question 2, given the following additional information:

	A	B
Variance	.25	.49
E(r)	.10	.16

The correlation of A with B is .7. Borrowing takes place at a risk-free interest rate of .05.

4. Write out the formula that would be required to compute the variance on a five-stock portfolio.

Assume the following information for Questions 5 through 7:

Stock	$E(r)$	Std Dev.	Correlation Coefficients
1	.05	.20	1 with 2 = −.2
2	.10	.10	1 with 3 = .3
3	.20	.15	1 with 4 = .5
4	.15	.30	2 with 3 = .2
			2 with 4 = −.5
			3 with 4 = 0

A portfolio is formed as follows: Sell short $2000 of stock 1 and buy $3000 of stock 2, $2000 of stock 3, and $3000 of stock 4. The cash provided by the owner of the portfolio is $2000, and any additional funds required to finance the portfolio are borrowed at a risk-free interest rate of 5 percent. There are no restrictions on the use of short sale proceeds.

5. Compute the portfolio weights for each component of the portfolio.
6. Compute the expected return of the portfolio.
7. Compute the standard deviation of the portfolio.
8. Consider two securities, A and B, which have the following characteristics:

	A	B
$E(r)$	.12	.06
Std dev.	.12	.06

Correlation coefficient of A with $B = -1.0$. Compute the expected returns and standard deviations of each of the following portfolios of A and B. Also plot securities and the portfolios of A and B on a graph with expected return and standard deviation on the axes.

Portfolio 1: $x_A = 2, x_B = -1$
Portfolio 2: $x_A = .5, x_B = .5$
Portfolio 3: $x_A = \frac{1}{3}, x_B = \frac{2}{3}$
Portfolio 4: $x_A = -.5, x_B = 1.5$

9. Consider two stocks with the following characteristics:

	Stock X	Stock Y
Expected return	.10	.14
Standard deviation	.25	.30

Suppose you build a portfolio with equal dollar amounts in the two stocks. Compute the expected return and variance of the portfolio under each of the following assumptions about the correlation between returns on X and Y:

Correlation = 1
Correlation = 0
Correlation = −1

10. Assume that two stocks have a correlation coefficient of -1.0.
    a. What would be the lowest possible standard deviation that could be achieved by constructing a portfolio of these two stocks?
    b. Use your answer to part (a) and Equation (4.1) to derive an expression for the lowest standard deviation portfolio weights for the stocks. (The weights for the stocks will be a function of the standard deviations of the two stocks.)
11. Two stocks, L and M, are perfectly negatively correlated. L's standard deviation is .6 and M's standard deviation is .8. Find the portfolio of L and M that will result in the lowest possible standard deviation.
12. What does a combination line for two stocks tell you?
13. Suppose you construct a combination line for two assets, with one of the assets having a zero standard deviation. What is a feature of this particular combination line which is not true for any arbitrary combination line?
14. If two stocks were perfectly positively correlated, would it be possible to construct a portfolio of the two stocks with zero standard deviation? Explain.

QUESTION SET 2

1. Define a portfolio weight.
2. How can short selling increase a portfolio's expected return?
3. If there is a positive covariance between stocks A and B, and stock A produces a return above its expected rate of return, what does that do to your expectations for stock B?
4. What does a combination line show?
5. Every time a certain airline stock sees a 1 percent jump in rate of return, a certain food company sees a .5 percent increase. What does this tell you about the correlation between the stocks? What do you expect the combination line to look like?
6. Given that you can invest in only two securities, describe how to put together a portfolio of a risk-free and a risky security.

ANSWERS TO QUESTION SET 2

1. A portfolio weight is the fraction of your total equity investment in a particular security.
2. Short selling increases portfolio expected return if the proceeds from a short sale are invested in an investment with a higher expected rate of return than the stock that was sold short.
3. You would expect stock B to also produce a return above its expected rate of return, although not necessarily in the same degree as stock A.
4. A combination line shows the relationship between the expected return and the standard deviation for a portfolio of two assets. It indicates, for differing portfolio weights for each of the two assets, how the expected rate of return and standard deviation change.
5. The stocks are perfectly positively correlated. The combination line is a straight line.
6. You invest in one security which may be a government-backed bond with a guaranteed rate of return. The other investment is made in a risky security. If you invest positive amounts

in both securities, you are said to be lending; if you invest more than 100 percent of your equity in the risky security, you are said to be borrowing. The more you borrow from the risk-free rate security, the greater the variability associated with the return to your equity investment.

PROBLEM SET

1. You have $10,000 invested, 30 percent of which is invested in Company X, which has an expected rate of return of 15 percent, and 70 percent of which is invested in Company Y, with an expected return of 9 percent.
   a. What is the dollar return to your portfolio?
   b. What is the expected percentage rate of return?

2. Suppose you invest in four stocks equally. Company A has an expected return of 20 percent, Company B has an expected return of 10 percent, Company C has an expected return of 12 percent, and Company D has an expected return of 9 percent. You have a total of $40,000 invested. What is the expected rate of return on your portfolio?

3. As an investor, you saw an opportunity to invest in a new stock with excellent growth potential. Wanting to invest more than you had, which was only $1000, you sold another stock short with an expected rate of return of 5 percent. The total amount you sold short was $4000, and your total amount invested in the growth stock, which had an expected rate of return of 24 percent, was thus $5000. Assuming no margin requirements, what is your expected rate of return on this portfolio?

4. Assume the investor in Problem 2 wants to determine how risky his portfolio is and wants you to compute the portfolio variance. If the respected correlations and variances of the stocks are as follows, what is the variance of the portfolio? Remember that $\text{Cov}(r_A, r_B) = \rho_{A,B}\, \sigma(r_A)\sigma(r_B)$.

Correlations:		A	B	C	D
	B	.50			
	C	.60	.30		
	D	− .30	− .20	− .10	
Variances:		.04	.16	.02	.10
		.2	.4	.1414	.316

5. Draw a combination line for a portfolio of two stocks which have the following characteristics, assuming no correlation between the two:

Stock	A	B
E(r)	.12	.02
σ(r)	.08	.10

6. In Problem 5, suppose you have $10,000 to invest and would like to sell $5,000 in stock B short to invest in A. Calculate the expected rate of return and standard deviation.

$\dfrac{15}{10}$ $\dfrac{-5}{10}$

ANSWERS TO PROBLEM SET

1. a. The dollar rate of return is the percentage of the portfolio invested in a stock multiplied by its expected rate of return. Thus, of the $10,000 invested
   Company X—30 percent of total with 15 percent rate of return:

$$.30 \times \$10,000 \times .15 = \$450$$

   Company Y—70 percent with a 9 percent rate of return:

$$.70 \times \$10,000 \times .09 = \$630$$

   The total dollar return is $450 + $630 = $1080.

   b. The expected percentage rate of return is the dollar return divided by the amount invested:

$$r = \frac{\text{Dollar return}}{\text{Total amount invested}}$$

$$r = \frac{\$1080}{\$10,000} = 10.8\%$$

2. The expected rate of return is the weighted average of the expected rates in the portfolio:

$$E(r_P) = \sum_{J=1}^{M} x_J E(r_J)$$

   The portfolio weights are first determined by the formula

$$x_A = \frac{\text{Dollar amount of } A \text{ bought}}{\text{Total equity investment}}$$

   Since you have invested equally in four stocks and your total investment is $40,000, the portfolio weights are equal ($x_A = x_B = x_C = x_D$) and are determined:

$$x_A = \frac{\$10,000}{\$40,000} = .25$$

   Plugging in the expected returns on the individual stocks and the expected rate of return on the portfolio is

$$r_P = (x_A \times r_A) \quad + (x_B \times r_B) \quad + (x_C \times r_C) \quad + (x_D \times r_D)$$

$$= (.25 \times .20) + (.25 \times .10) + (.25 \times .12) + (.25 \times .09)$$

$$= .1275 = 12.75\%$$

3. Computing the portfolio weights for each stock with the formula

$$x_A = \frac{\text{Dollar amount in } A \text{ bought (sold short)}}{\text{Total equity investment}}$$

   we find

$$x_A = \frac{-4000}{1000} = -4.0$$

$$x_B = \frac{5000}{1000} = 5.0$$

$$r_P = (x_A \times r_A) \qquad + (x_B \times r_B)$$

$$= (-4.0 \times .05) + (5.0 \times .24)$$

$$= 1.0 = 100\%$$

You can thus expect to double your money in one year if you have guessed correctly in choosing to invest in the growth stock.

4. To compute the variance, you need to make a covariance matrix. Using the square roots of the variances and the correlations given, the covariances are calculated:

$$\text{Cov}(r_J, r_K) = \qquad \rho_{J,K} \times \sigma(r_J) \times \sigma(r_K)$$

$$\text{Cov}(r_A, r_B) = \qquad .500 \times .200 \times .400 = \qquad .040$$

$$\text{Cov}(r_A, r_C) = \qquad .600 \times .200 \times .141 = \qquad .017$$

$$\text{Cov}(r_A, r_D) = -.300 \times .200 \times .316 = -.019$$

$$\text{Cov}(r_B, r_C) = \qquad .300 \times .400 \times .141 = \qquad .017$$

$$\text{Cov}(r_B, r_D) = -.200 \times .400 \times .316 = -.025$$

$$\text{Cov}(r_C, r_D) = -.100 \times .141 \times .316 = -.004$$

Plugging in the given variances and the portfolio weights, the covariance matrix is as follows:

	Stock	.25 A	.25 B	.25 C	.25 D
.25	A	.04	.040	.017	−.019
.25	B	.040	.16	.017	−.025
.25	C	.017	.017	.02	−.004
.25	D	−.019	−.025	−.004	.10

Multiplying each covariance by the weight at the top of the column and at the left of the row and summing, we get

$$.25 \times .25 \times \qquad .04 = \qquad .0025$$

$$.25 \times .25 \times \qquad .040 = \qquad .0025$$

$$.25 \times .25 \times \qquad .017 = \qquad .0011$$

$$.25 \times .25 \times -.019 = -.0012$$

$$.25 \times .25 \times \qquad .040 = \qquad .0025$$

$$.25 \times .25 \times \qquad .160 = \qquad .0100$$

$$.25 \times .25 \times \quad .017 = \quad .0011$$
$$.25 \times .25 \times -.025 = -.0016$$
$$.25 \times .25 \times \quad .017 = \quad .0011$$
$$.25 \times .25 \times \quad .017 = \quad .0011$$
$$.25 \times .25 \times \quad .020 = \quad .0013$$
$$.25 \times .25 \times -.004 = -.0003$$
$$.25 \times .25 \times -.019 = -.0012$$
$$.25 \times .25 \times -.025 = -.0016$$
$$.25 \times .25 \times -.004 = -.0003$$
$$.25 \times .25 \times \quad .100 = \quad \underline{.0063}$$

Total portfolio variance =   .0233

After computing the variance for a four-stock portfolio, aren't you glad there are computers for most other portfolios?

5. Assuming no correlation between the stocks, we use the following equations:

$$E(r_P) = x_A E(r_A) + (1 - x_A)E(r_B)$$
$$\sigma(r_P) = [x_A^2 \sigma^2(r_A) + (1 - x_A)^2 \sigma^2(r_B)]^{1/2}$$

Using the given characteristics:

Stock	A	B
$E(r)$	.12	.02
$\sigma(r)$	.08	.10

$$E(r) = x_A \times .12 + (1 - x_A) \times .02$$
$$\sigma(r_P) = [x_A^2 \times .08^2 + (1 - x_A)^2 \times .1^2]^{1/2}$$

For a series of values for A, we can make a schedule:

x_A	$E(r_P)$	$\sigma(r_P)$
1.5	.170	.130
1.0	.120	.080
.75	.095	.065
.50	.070	.064
.00	.020	.100
−.50	−.030	.155

The graph of the combination line looks as in the following figure:

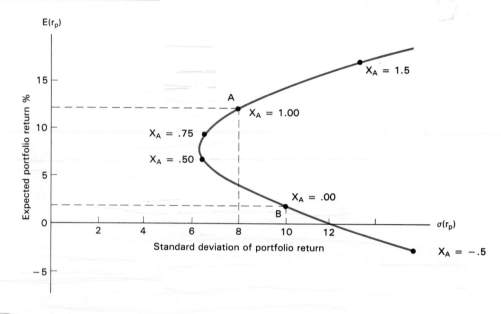

6. Expected return: $E(r_P) = x_A E(r_A) + x_B E(r_B)$

$$\frac{15,000}{10,000} .12 - \frac{5,000}{10,000} .02 =$$

$$.18 \quad - \quad .01 \quad = .17$$

Standard deviation: $(x_A^2 \sigma^2(r_A) \quad + \quad x_B^2 \sigma^2(r_B))^{1/2} \quad = \sigma(r_P)$

$$[(1.5)^2 \times (.08)^2 + (-.5)^2 \times (.10)^2]^{1/2} = .130$$

REFERENCES

BREALEY, R. A., and HODGES, S. D., "Playing with Portfolios," *Financial Analysts Journal* (March 1974).

CLARKSON, G. P., *Portfolio Selection: A Simulation of Trust Investment.* Englewood Cliffs, N.J.: Prentice Hall, 1962.

HESTER, D. D., and TOBIN, J., *Risk Aversion and Portfolio Choice.* New York: John Wiley, 1967.

LEVY, H., "Does Diversification Always Pay?" *TIMS Studies in Management Science* (1979).

RENSHAW, E. F., "Portfolio Balance Models in Perspective: Some Generalizations that Can Be Derived from the Two-Asset Case," *Journal of Financial and Quantitative Analysis* (June 1967).

SHARPE, W. F., "Portfolio Analysis," *Journal of Financial and Quantitative Analysis* (June 1967).

WAGNER, W., and LAU, S., "The Effect of Diversification on Risk," *Financial Analysts Journal* (November–December 1971).

C H A P T E R

5

FINDING THE EFFICIENT SET

In the previous chapter we learned how individual securities combined to form portfolios. We were seeking the answer to the question, "If we combine a group of securities together to form a portfolio, what will the portfolio look like in terms of its risk and expected return?" In this chapter we will direct our attention to answering the following question: "Given an available group of securities, how do we determine the *best* way to combine the securities into portfolios?" In answering this question, we will be seeking those portfolios that are expected to produce the maximum amount of return given the level of risk exposure.

The Minimum Variance and Efficient Sets

The points plotted in Figure 5.1 denote the positions of individual stock investments. To illustrate, the stock denoted by point *A* has an expected rate of return of 10 percent and a standard deviation of 15 percent. These individual stocks can be combined into portfolios. For example, we can invest in stocks *A* and *B* and attain positions anywhere along the broken combination line. As you might imagine, by taking positive positions in some of the stocks and short positions in others, we can form a wide variety of portfolios that would be positioned at various points on the graph.

All of these attainable portfolio positions represent the set of investment opportunities available to us. We would, of course, prefer some of these positions to others. Given the level of risk, or standard deviation, we prefer positions with higher expected rates of return; given the level of expected return, we prefer positions of lower risk. In any case, given the characteristics of the available population of stocks, the investment opportunity set has a perimeter that is represented by the bullet-shaped curve. From now on, we're going to refer to this *perimeter* as the ***minimum variance set.***

Each point on the minimum variance set represents a portfolio, with portfolio weights allocated to each of the stocks in the population. Each of the portfolios in

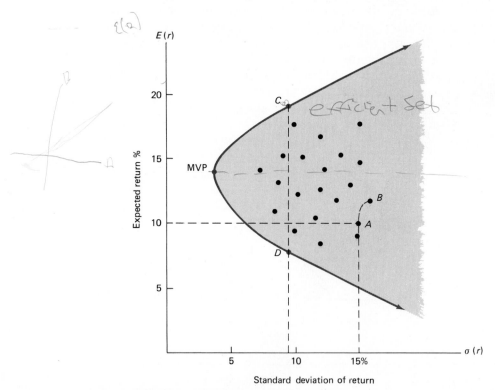

FIGURE 5.1 Minimum variance set.

the minimum variance set meets the following criterion: *Given a particular level of expected rate of return, the portfolio on the minimum variance set has the lowest standard deviation (or variance) achievable with the available population of stocks.* As befitting its shape, from time to time we shall refer to the minimum variance set as the *bullet*. We will refer to the bullet as the minimum variance set irrespective of whether standard deviation or variance is being measured along the horizontal axis. Since the portfolios that minimize *variance* given expected return are identical to the portfolios which minimize *standard deviation,* the terms *minimum variance set* and *minimum standard deviation set* can be used interchangeably.

The minimum variance set can be divided into two halves, a top and a bottom. The halves are separated at the point *MVP*. This point represents the single portfolio with the lowest possible level of standard deviation, the **global minimum variance portfolio.** The most desirable portfolios for us to hold are those in the top half of the bullet. The most undesirable are those in the bottom half.

The top half of the bullet is called the **efficient set.** All the portfolios in the efficient set meet the following criterion: *Given a particular level of standard deviation, the portfolios in the efficient set have the highest attainable expected rate of return.* Thus, while portfolios C and D both meet the criterion for the minimum variance set (lowest standard deviation, given expected return), only C meets the criterion for the efficient set (highest expected return, given standard deviation). Portfolio D actually has the lowest expected return, given its standard deviation level.

FINDING THE EFFICIENT SET WITH SHORT SELLING

In practice, you will find the minimum variance and efficient sets using a computer. To illustrate the process employed by your software, we shall consider an example where we build portfolios from three available stocks: *A,* Acme Steel; *B,* Brown Drug; and *C,* Consolidated Electric. The three stocks have the following expected rates of return:

$$\text{Acme Steel: } E(r_A) \qquad = 5\%$$

$$\text{Brown Drug: } E(r_B) \qquad = 10\%$$

$$\text{Consolidated Electric: } E(r_C) = 15\%$$

The covariance matrix for the stocks is given by

	A	B	C
A	.25	.15	.17
B	.15	.21	.09
C	.17	.09	.28

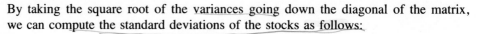

By taking the square root of the variances going down the diagonal of the matrix, we can compute the standard deviations of the stocks as follows:

$$\text{Acme Steel: } \sigma(r_A) = .50$$

$$\text{Brown Drug: } \sigma(r_B) = .46$$

$$\text{Consolidated Electric: } \sigma(r_C) = .53$$

The expected returns and standard deviations of the three stocks are plotted in Figure 5.2. The minimum variance set of portfolios of the three stocks is plotted as the solid curve. We shall now examine the procedure a computer might follow in finding the portfolios in the minimum variance set.

In Figure 5.3 we are plotting the portfolio weights in Acme Steel and Brown Drug. The portfolio weight in Consolidated Electric is not represented on the diagram, but it is implied by the values for x_A and x_B. For example, if we are at point U, the portfolio weight in Brown is equal to .30, and the portfolio weight in Acme is given by .00. Since there are only three stocks, the portfolio weight in Consolidated is always equal to $1 - x_A - x_B$ and is therefore .70. Each point in Figure 5.3 represents a portfolio with particular weights allocated to each of the three stocks.

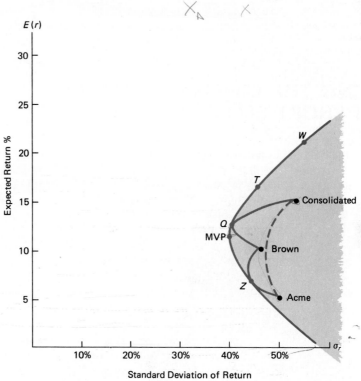

FIGURE 5.2 Minimum variance set for Consolidated, Brown, and Acme.

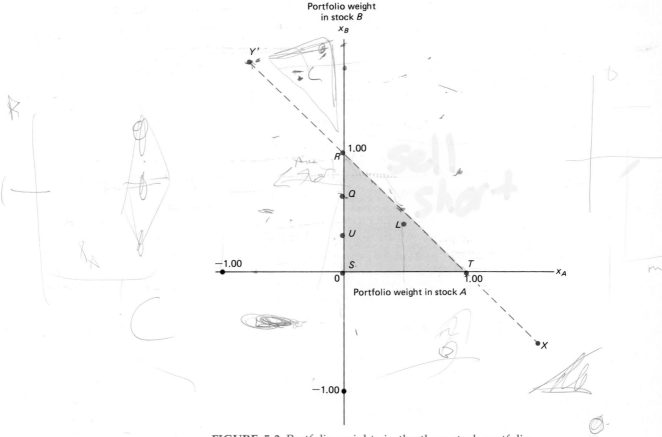

FIGURE 5.3 Portfolio weights in the three-stock portfolio.

Now consider the triangle drawn in Figure 5.3. The points of the triangle are given by R, S, and T. All positions inside the triangle represent portfolios where we have invested positive amounts of money in each of the three stocks. To illustrate, consider the point labeled L. This point represents a portfolio where we are investing 50 percent of our money in Acme, 45 percent of our money in Brown, and the remaining 5 percent of our money in Consolidated. For portfolios on the perimeter of the triangle, we are investing a combined total of 100 percent of our money in two of the stocks, and we aren't taking any position at all in the third. At point Q on perimeter RS, we're investing 60 percent in Brown, 40 percent in Consolidated, and nothing in Acme. On perimeter RT we are taking no position in Consolidated.

If we are outside the triangle, at any point to the northeast of the line labeled $Y'X$, we are selling Consolidated short. If we are positioned to the west of the figure's vertical axis, we are selling Acme short, and if we are anywhere to the south of the horizontal axis, we are selling Brown short. At point Y', we are selling Acme short and adding the proceeds to our equity to invest in Brown.

The Iso-expected Return Lines

Suppose we wish to find a set of portfolios all of which have the same expected rate of return. The weights for these portfolios are given by one of the *iso-expected return lines*.[1] There is a family of such lines, each representing a given expected rate of portfolio return. The lines are drawn in $x_A x_B$ space, and any of them can be expressed by the following relationship with intercept a_0 and slope a_1:

$$x_B = a_0 + a_1 \cdot x_A$$

Given a value for x_A, we solve the preceding equation for a value for x_B (and an implied value for x_C) which will produce a portfolio with the desired expected rate of return. The values for a_0 and a_1 are determined by the relative expected rates of return on the three stocks. To compute a_0 and a_1, we start with the formula for the expected return on a three-stock portfolio:

$$E(r_P) = x_A E(r_A) + x_B E(r_B) + (1 - x_A - x_B)E(r_C)$$

Multiplying through by $E(r_C)$ and solving for x_B as a function of x_A, we get

$$x_B = \underbrace{\frac{E(r_C) - E(r_P)}{E(r_C) - E(r_B)}}_{a_0} + \underbrace{\left(\frac{E(r_A) - E(r_C)}{E(r_C) - E(r_B)}\right)}_{a_1} x_A$$

In the case of the three stocks of our example, the slope is computed as

$$a_1 = \frac{.05 - .15}{.15 - .10} = -2.00$$

The intercept is computed as

$$a_0 = \frac{.15 - E(r_P)}{.15 - .10}$$

Thus, the value for the intercept depends on the desired expected rate of return on the portfolio. Let's assume we want to find the set of portfolio weights that will give us an expected rate of return of 10 percent. In this case the value for a_0 is given by 1.00:

$$a_0 = \frac{.15 - .10}{.15 - .10} = 1.00$$

The formula for the 10 percent iso-expected return line is thus

$$x_B = 1.00 - 2.00 x_A$$

---

[1]The process of finding the minimum variance set described in this chapter was originally developed by Harry Markowitz (1952).

Suppose we invest 50 percent of our money in Acme. According to the preceding formula, we must invest 0 percent of our money in Brown and the remaining 50 percent in Consolidated to construct a portfolio with an expected return of 10 percent:

$$E(r_P) = x_A E(r_A) \quad + x_B E(r_B) \quad + (1 - x_A - x_B) E(r_C)$$

$$.10 = .50 \times .05 + .00 \times .10 + .50 \times .15$$

These, of course, are not the only weights which will produce a 10 percent expected rate of return. For example, the combination $x_A = 1.00$, $x_B = -1.00$, and $x_C = 1.00$ will also do the job. Think of all the combinations of weights in the three stocks that represent portfolios with 10 percent expected rates of return. These are plotted as the iso-expected return line labeled 10 percent in Figure 5.4.

If we want to see the combinations of weights which are consistent with a different value for the portfolio expected return, we must look to a different iso-

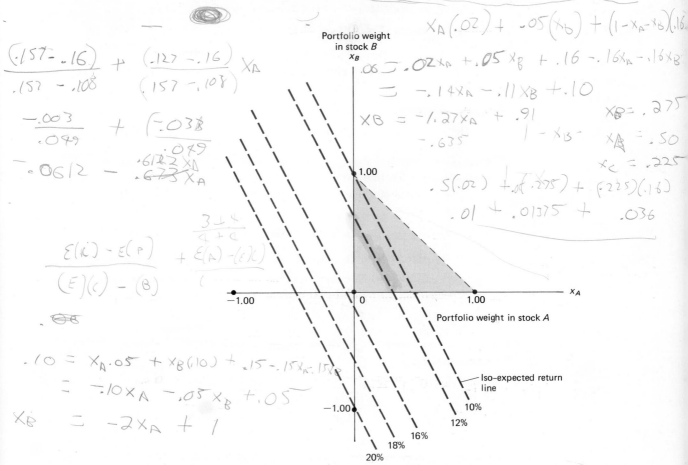

FIGURE 5.4 Iso-expected return lines.

expected return line. For example, all of the combinations of weights represented by the line labeled 12 percent are those which provide a 12 percent expected return on the portfolio.

In the case of this example, as we move to the northeast, we move to iso-expected return lines with lower and lower expected rates of return. The iso-expected return lines also have a negative slope. In general, however, the slope and relative position of the iso-expected return lines are dependent on the relative expected returns of the three stocks considered. To see this, suppose we switched the expected returns on Acme and Consolidated. In this case, while the lines would still have a negative slope, we now move to iso-expected return lines with higher and higher expected returns as we move in a northeasterly direction.

The Isovariance Ellipses

Now, suppose we want to find a set of portfolios all of which have the same *variance* of return. The portfolio weights for members of this set are given by one of the *isovariance ellipses*. As with the iso-expected return lines, there is a family of these ellipses, each representing a different level of portfolio variance.

To find the isovariance ellipse representing a given level of portfolio variance, we begin with the equation of the variance for a three-stock portfolio:

$$\sigma^2(r_P) = x_A^2\, \sigma^2(r_A) + x_B^2\, \sigma^2(r_B) + (1 - x_A - x_B)^2\, \sigma^2(r_C) + 2x_Ax_B\, \text{Cov}(r_A, r_B)$$

$$+ 2x_A(1 - x_A - x_B)\, \text{Cov}(r_A, r_C) + 2x_B(1 - x_A - x_B)\, \text{Cov}(r_B, r_C)$$

Suppose we want to find the ellipse of portfolio weights consistent with a 30 percent portfolio variance. To find two points on the ellipse, select an arbitrary value for x_A (say, .00) and substitute this and the values for the variances and covariances into the variance formula:

$$.30 = .00^2 \times .25 + x_B^2 \times .21 + (1 - .00 - x_B)^2 \times .28 + 2 \times .00 \times x_B \times .15$$

$$+ 2 \times .00 \times (1 - .00 - x_B) \times .17 + 2 \times x_B \times (1 - .00 - x_B).09$$

or, after simplifying,

$$.03 = .28 - .38x_B + .31x_B^2$$

The equation now has only one unknown value, that being x_B. This is a quadratic equation, so two values for x_B will make the right-hand side equal to the left-hand side. The two values are

$$x_B = 1.28$$

and

$$x_B = -.05$$

Two portfolios that both have a 30 percent variance are thus

$$x_A = .00, \qquad x_B = 1.28, \qquad \text{and} \qquad x_C = -.28$$

and

$$x_A = .00, \qquad x_B = -.05, \qquad \text{and} \qquad x_C = 1.05$$

These portfolios are plotted in Figure 5.5 at the points labeled W and X. These are two of the many portfolios on the 30 percent isovariance ellipse. To find two more, we merely select another arbitrary value for x_A, say, 1.00. We substitute this new value for x_A in the portfolio variance equation and solve once again for two values for x_B.

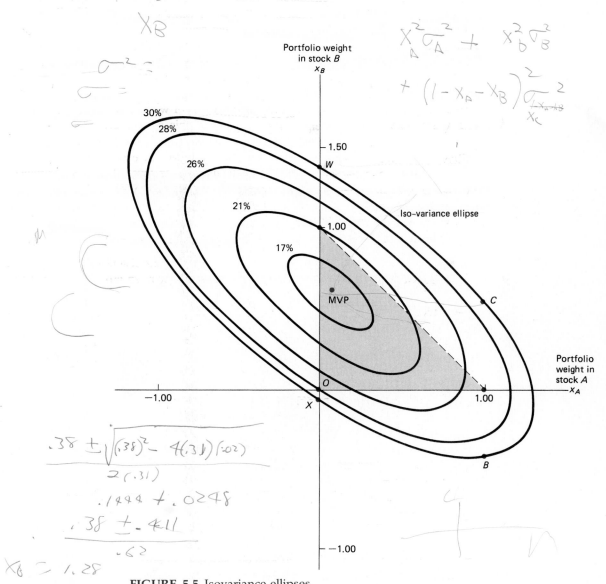

FIGURE 5.5 Isovariance ellipses.

These solutions are plotted at the points labeled C and B in Figure 5.5. By repeating the process, we can produce as many points in the ellipse as desired. Suppose we find there are no solutions for x_B, given the arbitrarily chosen value for x_A. This means that, given the characteristics for the stocks, it is impossible to construct a portfolio with a variance as low as 30 percent with x_A equal to the chosen value. The chosen value for x_A, therefore, must be outside the horizontal range of the ellipse.

To produce another ellipse consistent with a different value for $\sigma^2(r_P)$, simply select another desired value, substitute it in the portfolio variance equation, and go through the same process just described. If a portfolio variance level of less than 30 percent is selected, the new ellipse will be found inside the 30 percent ellipse. Note that the ellipse for the 28 percent variance is inside the ellipse for the 30 percent variance. As smaller values for the portfolio variance are selected, the ellipses become smaller and smaller in size, converging on the point labeled MVP. This point represents the lowest possible portfolio variance level achievable, given the covariance matrix for the three stocks. If we were to attempt to construct an ellipse for a still lower portfolio variance, we would find no solutions, no matter what values for x_A were arbitrarily chosen.

Note that the ellipses are all concentric about the point MVP. Aside from this, in a way, the ellipses are similar to lines denoting points of equal altitude on a topographic map. Such a map is drawn in Figure 5.6. By studying the map, we can determine that the body of water is positioned at the top of a hill, at an altitude of approximately 500 feet above sea level. In Figure 5.5 the isovariance ellipses repre-

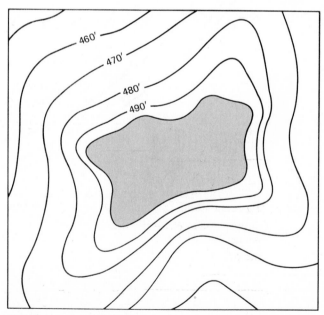

FIGURE 5.6 Topographic map.

sent points of constant variance, instead of altitude, with the *MVP* point positioned at the bottom of a valley rather than at the top of a hill.

The Critical Line

The iso-expected return lines are superimposed on the isovariance ellipses in Figure 5.7.

The ***critical line*** is drawn as line *NY* in Figure 5.7. It shows the portfolio weights for the portfolios in the minimum variance set. The critical line can be found by tracing out the points of tangency between the iso-expected return lines and the isovariance ellipses. We can say that finding the minimum variance set is tantamount to finding the location of the critical line.

To find the minimum variance set with a computer, you might provide the computer with the following set of instructions:

1. Find the portfolio weights which minimize portfolio variance, subject to the constraint that the expected rate of return on the portfolio is equal to some predetermined level.
2. For any given portfolio constructed, the sum of the portfolio weights for all stocks in the portfolio must be equal to 1.
3. The portfolio weight assigned to any one stock may take any value from plus to minus infinity. (This allows the computer to sell short in unlimited amounts.)
4. The expected rate of return to a portfolio is given by

$$E(r_P) = x_A E(r_A) + x_B E(r_B) + (1 - x_A - x_B)E(r_C)$$

5. The variance of return to the portfolio is given by

$$\sigma^2(r_P) = x_A^2\,\sigma^2(r_A) + x_B^2\,\sigma^2(r_B) + (1 - x_A - x_B)^2\,\sigma^2(r_C) + 2x_A x_B\,\text{Cov}(r_A,\,r_B)$$
$$+ 2x_A(1 - x_A - x_B)\,\text{Cov}(r_A,\,r_C) + 2x_B(1 - x_A - x_B)\,\text{Cov}(r_B,\,r_C)$$

6. You provide the computer with estimates of the expected rates of return on the three stocks as well as estimates of the numbers in the covariance matrix.

You now provide the computer with some target expected rate of return. The computer's task is to minimize the variance of the portfolio subject to having an expected rate of return on the portfolio equal to the target. Assume the first target expected rate of return is equal to 20 percent. The computer "knows" the portfolio weights which provide the solution to the problem lie somewhere on the 20 percent iso-expected return line. The process of finding the solution begins at a position on the line corresponding to some arbitrary value for x_A. Let's assume this value for x_A is equal to .00, so we begin at the position labeled D on the 20 percent line in Figure 5.7.

The point D represents three portfolio weights for the three stocks. The computer substitutes these weights, along with the given variances and covariances from the covariance matrix, into the formula you have provided for portfolio variance. The portfolio variance consistent with the weights of point D is computed. The computer

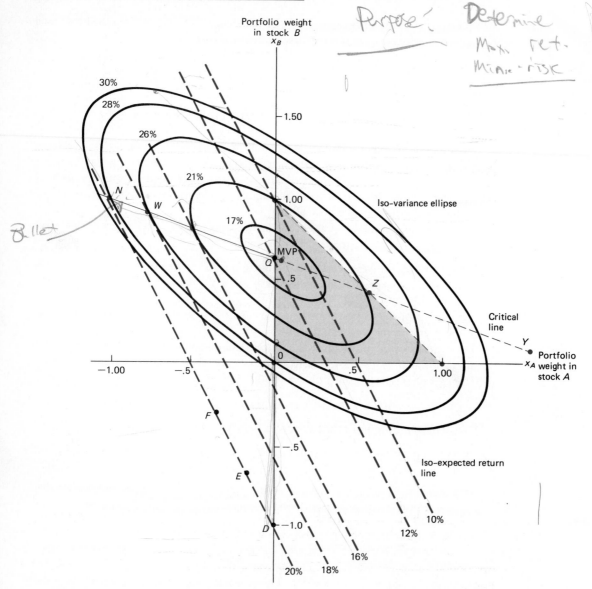

FIGURE 5.7 Portfolio weights in the minimum variance set.

now moves by some predetermined distance toward either the southeast or the north-west along the 20 percent iso-expected return line. Suppose it moves to the southeast and recomputes the portfolio variance for the new point. If you move to the southeast along the 20 percent iso-expected return line, you move out of the "valley" toward higher variance positions. Thus, the variance consistent with the portfolio weights of the new point will be greater than that of point *D*. The computer now knows it has moved in the wrong direction along the line. It retraces its steps and moves to a point toward the northwest of *D*, say, to point *E*. It again computes the variance and finds that it's lower than the variance of point *D*. It now "knows" it's moving in the right direction, so it takes another jump to point *F*. The computed variance is again smaller because we are continuing to move deeper into the valley.

The computer continues to move to the northwest until it takes a jump past point *N*. Beyond *N* the computed variance will begin to increase, because we have gone beyond the iso-expected return line's deepest penetration into the valley. The sizes of the jumps are now reduced, and the computer now reverses direction toward the southeast. The process is repeated until the computer gradually iterates to point *N*. This point represents the lowest variance position on the iso-expected return line, a portfolio variance of 28 percent. Point *N* is also the point where the 28 percent isovariance ellipse is tangent to the 20 percent iso-expected return line.

We have found one of the portfolios in the minimum variance set. Reading from the graph, we find that the portfolio weights for the portfolio that minimizes variance, given a 20 percent expected rate of return, are approximately

$$x_A = -1.00$$
$$x_B = 1.00$$
$$x_C = 1.00$$

This portfolio has a 28 percent variance and a 53 percent standard deviation. The portfolio is plotted in the $E(r_P)$, $\sigma(r_P)$ mapping of Figure 5.2 at point *N*.

To find another point on the minimum variance set, we select another target expected rate of return, perhaps 18 percent. The 18 percent iso-expected return line again can be found in Figure 5.7. In the same fashion described, the computer iterates to point *W*, the line's deepest penetration into the "valley." This is the point of tangency between the line and the 26 percent isovariance ellipse. Since a 26 percent variance is consistent with a 51 percent standard deviation, this minimum variance portfolio is plotted at point *W* in Figure 5.2.

This process is repeated to find as many points as desired on the minimum variance set. In actual practice, extremely efficient computer algorithms are employed so computers can find the solutions quickly and accurately. However, the description furnished here should give you a rough idea of what is being accomplished.

As said before, the line passing through the portfolio weights in the minimum variance set is called the critical line. In Figure 5.7, as we move from point *W* to point *Q*, we move along the minimum variance set of Figure 5.2 from corresponding points *W* to Q.

Note, at point *Q* we are on the western border of the triangle of Figure 5.7. Therefore, we are taking no position at all in Acme, and we are investing *positive* amounts of money in both Brown and Consolidated. This means portfolio *Q* must be on the combination line between Brown and Consolidated, somewhere between the

OUT ON THE STREET

ALLOCATING ASSETS

Jeff Diermeier, a managing director at First Chicago Investment Advisors, walks into the office of his boss, Gary Brinson. Gary is president of First Chicago Investment Advisors, a wholly owned subsidiary of the First Chicago Corporation. First Chicago is at the forefront of the application of sophisticated techniques of modern portfolio analysis to investment management.

First Chicago's reputation in this area is due, in large part, to the leadership of Gary Brinson. It was Gary who initially steered First Chicago away from the traditional techniques of security analysis toward the more quantitative approach that now guides most of the firm's investment decisions.

Jeff begins his discussion of the results of his latest computer run. The output indicates recommended positions invested in various types of investments. Given various risk levels, the computer has calculated overall portfolio weights in each type of asset. The weights are determined on the basis of the efficient set, found through the Markowitz portfolio technique. The computer is constrained to avoid short selling, and, in some cases, it is constrained to limit the total amount of the investment in any one type of investment.

Nine classes of investments are used in the analysis:

1. The common stocks of large companies.
2. The common stocks of small companies.
3. Venture capital investments.
4. Foreign common stocks.
5. Domestic fixed income securities. These include corporate bonds, government and agency securities, and mortgages.
6. Eurodollar investments. These are international bonds denominated in dollars but issued by or in non-U.S. provinces.

positions of the two stocks. In Figure 5.2 we see portfolio Q lies at the point of tangency between the minimum variance set and the combination line between Brown and Consolidated.

For all the portfolios between N and Q, we are short-selling Acme and investing positive amounts of money in Brown and Consolidated. As we move past point Q into the triangle, we begin taking positive positions in all three of the stocks. When we reach the point MVP, we have reached the lowest point in the "valley," the global minimum variance portfolio. This portfolio is also labeled MVP in Figure 5.2. As we move beyond MVP on the critical line, we move to the inferior positions on the bottom half of the minimum variance set.

At point Z in Figure 5.7, the critical line passes through the northeastern edge of the triangle. At this point we are taking no position at all in Consolidated, and we are investing positive amounts of money in Acme and Brown. Thus, portfolio Z must

7. Nondollar bond investments. These are bonds, for example, issued by a German manufacturer, denominated in a nondollar currency such as Swiss franks. This classification would also include straight foreign bonds.
8. Real estate investments.
9. Money market investments.

Jeff and his staff estimate the expected rates of return on each class of investments on the basis of historical rates of return, current yields to maturity, estimates of the normal return relationships across markets, and forecasts of general economic conditions currently being made by the firm.

The covariance matrix is estimated on the basis of sample estimates taken from historical returns associated with portfolios of securities in each investment class. Some of the classes, such as venture capital, are problematic in this respect. In the case of venture capital, Jeff uses estimates of ventures capital funds and partnerships returns that his firm has accumulated.

The expected returns and covariances are supposedly representative of the reward and risk associated with each general investment classification. At this point in time, interest rates are expected to remain in a narrow range around current levels. The estimates of the expected rates of return on domestic bonds and common stocks are fairly normal. Due to other factors, the computer's recommended portfolio weights in real estate, and foreign securities are lower than usual. The weights help him to determine the general structure of the portfolios managed by the firm at each level of desired risk. After the general asset allocation decisions have been made, the analysis becomes more micro in nature, as individual investments within each classification are selected.

be positioned in Figure 5.2 at point Z where the combination line between Acme and Brown is tangent to the minimum variance set.

Note that the critical line doesn't pass through the southern edge of the triangle, so the combination line between Acme and Consolidated isn't tangent to the minimum variance set.

As we move past point Z on the critical line, we begin selling Consolidated short and investing positive amounts in Acme and Brown. Eventually, where the critical line passes through the horizontal axis, we begin to sell both Consolidated and Brown short and use the proceeds to invest in Acme.

It is important to recognize that the critical line represents all the portfolios in the minimum variance set. The portfolios we are interested in as investors are those in the efficient set. In Figure 5.7 the part of the critical line representing portfolios in the efficient set is represented by the solid portion of the line.

FINDING THE MINIMUM VARIANCE WITHOUT SHORT SELLING

Some financial institutions do not sell short as a matter of policy. Consequently, it may be of interest to discuss how the minimum variance set is determined when you are constrained not to sell short.

If you can't sell any stock short, the portfolio weight for each stock must be no less than 0 and no greater than 1. This means you are constrained to stay on, or within, the boundaries of the triangle of Figure 5.3. Consequently, those positions on the minimum variance set, which correspond to points on the critical line which are outside of the triangle (such as point N in Figure 5.7), are no longer available to you.

However, since the critical line passes through the triangle, some of the portfolios which were available before will still be available, even though you can no longer sell short. These will be the portfolios for which you were investing either positive amounts in each stock or positive amounts in two of the stocks with no position at all in the third.

The triangle of Figure 5.3 is reproduced in Figure 5.8. Let's start with portfolio

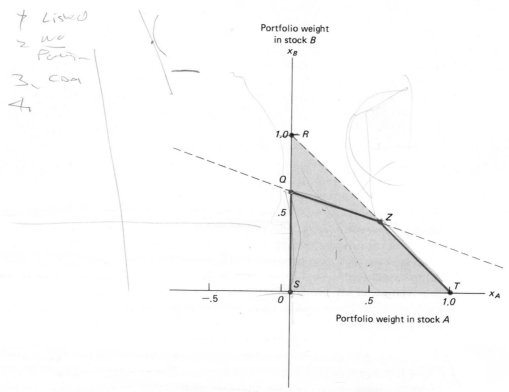

FIGURE 5.8 Critical line with no short selling.

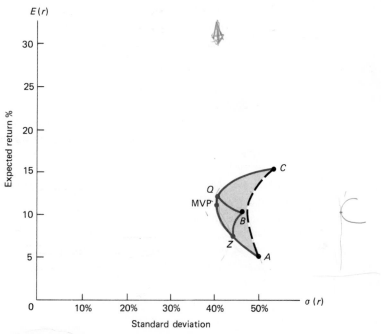

FIGURE 5.9 Minimum variance set with no short selling.

Z on the northeastern edge of the triangle. This portfolio is positioned at point Z in Figure 5.9 on the bottom half of the bullet. As we move from point Z to point Q on the critical line of Figure 5.8, we move from point Z to point Q in the minimum variance set of Figure 5.9. This section of the minimum variance set is identical to the case where short selling is allowed. Once we get to point Q, however, we can't continue toward the northwest on the critical line. Consider your options at this point. You can either (1) move up the western edge to point R, (2) move down the western edge to point S, or (3) move back inside the triangle somewhere.

Let's first consider option (1), moving up the western edge. As you move up the western edge, you are taking positive positions in Brown and Consolidated and no position at all in Acme. As you move closer to point R, your portfolio weight in Brown becomes larger and larger, finally reaching 1.00 when you reach point R. In Figure 5.9 you have been moving on the combination line between Brown and Consolidated from point Q to the position of Brown's stock at point B. The portfolios on this segment of the combination line aren't minimum variance portfolios. The portfolios between Q and Z have lower variances for the same expected return, and they are available, even though you can't sell short.

Now let's consider option 3, moving back inside the triangle. We already know, given any portfolio inside the triangle, other portfolios positioned on the same iso-expected return line but closer to the critical line have lower variance, given their expected return. Therefore, any portfolio inside the triangle, that is off the critical line, can't be minimum variance.

This leaves us with option 2, moving down the western edge toward point *S*. If we take this option, we are again taking positive positions only in Brown and Consolidated, but now we are moving up the combination line between the two stocks in Figure 5.9 toward the position of Consolidated at point *C*. Given our constraint not to sell short, these portfolios represent the lowest variance positions we can attain, given the expected returns, and they are part of the constrained minimum variance set. Given that we can't sell short, we can't move beyond point *C*, so the minimum variance set runs from point *C*, through point *Q*, to at least point *Z*. To see where it goes from *Z*, let's take a closer look at the portfolio position represented by that point.

At point *Z* we are investing positive amounts in Acme and Brown and nothing at all in Consolidated. Point *Z*, therefore, lies on the combination line between Acme and Brown as drawn in Figure 5.9. If we move up the northeastern edge of the triangle toward point *R*, we move along the combination line toward the position of Brown's stock at point *B*. These aren't minimum variance portfolios because some of the portfolios on the bullet between *Q* and *Z* have lower variance and the same expected return. However, if we move down the northwestern edge instead, toward

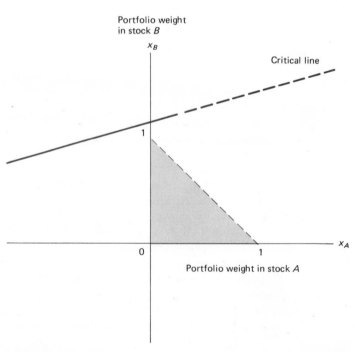

FIGURE 5.10 Case where critical line doesn't pass through triangle.

point *T,* we move along the combination line of Figure 5.9 from *Z* to the position of Acme's stock at *A.* These are minimum variance portfolios, given our no-short-selling constraint.

Thus, the minimum variance set begins at point *C* and runs through points *Q* and *Z,* finally ending at point *A.* Note the minimum variance set for the case of no short-selling falls inside of the bullet drawn on the basis of unrestricted short selling. This is true because the unconstrained minimum variance set took full advantage of all possible strategies in terms of the weights allocated to the three stocks. When you rule out most of these strategies by disallowing short sales, you rule out many opportunities to further reduce variance, given the level of expected return, or to increase expected return, given the level of variance.

In the case of this example, the minimum variance set without short selling partially coincides with the minimum variance set where short selling is allowed. This is true because in this case the critical line goes through the triangle. If the critical line doesn't pass through the triangle, as is the case in Figure 5.10, the minimum variance set without short selling will fall inside the unconstrained minimum variance set as in Figure 5.11.

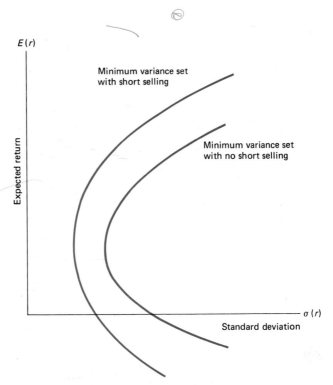

FIGURE 5.11 Corresponding minimum variance sets.

TWO IMPORTANT PROPERTIES OF THE MINIMUM VARIANCE SET

Property I If we combine two or more portfolios on the minimum variance set, we get another portfolio on the minimum variance set.

This important property follows directly from the fact that the critical line is a straight line. Recall the critical line traces out the points of highest expected return on the iso–standard deviation ellipses. The critical line is linear because the iso–standard deviation ellipses are all symmetric about a common point (the minimum variance portfolio). As a result, when we trace out the points of highest expected return, we trace out a straight line.

To illustrate property I, consider portfolios 1 and 3 in Figure 5.12, where the portfolio weights for Acme and Brown are plotted on the horizontal and vertical axes, respectively. Suppose we combine these two portfolios by investing $1000 in each. The portfolio weights for the two portfolios are given by

	x_A	x_B	x_C
Portfolio 1	−1.50	1.20	1.30
Portfolio 3	.00	.70	.30

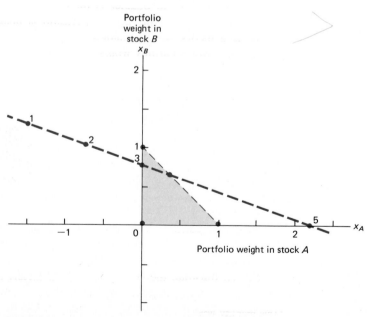

FIGURE 5.12 Portfolio weights in Acme and Brown.

Given a $1000 investment in each portfolio, these portfolio weights are consistent with the following dollar commitments:

	Acme	Brown	Consolidated
Portfolio 1	− $1500	$1200	$1300
Portfolio 3	$0	$700	$300
Combined portfolio 2	− $1500	$1900	$1600

Because we are investing a total of $2000 in the combined portfolio, the dollar positions in the three stocks are consistent with the following portfolio weights for the three stocks:

	A	B	C
Portfolio 2	− .75	.95	.80

If we plot the combined portfolio in Figure 5.12, it plots at point 2. Note this point is on the critical line, so the combined portfolio is also a member of the minimum variance set. This same thing will happen no matter which, or how many, of the minimum variance portfolios are combined. We can, in fact, sell short some of the portfolios and use the proceeds to invest in others. As long as all the portfolios are in the minimum variance set, the combined portfolio will also be on the bullet.

As we will see in Chapter 7, the central prediction of the capital asset pricing model (CAPM) is that the market portfolio is positioned on the efficient set. The CAPM is a theory which assumes everyone can short sell without restriction and predicts the way securities would be priced if everyone used portfolio theory and invested in efficient portfolios. Keep in mind that the market portfolio is a combination of all the portfolios of every investor in the economy. Given property I, we know that if each investor holds an efficient portfolio, the combination of all of them will be efficient as well. In this sense, property I drives the central prediction of the CAPM.

Property II Given a population of securities, there will be a simple linear relationship between the beta factors of different securities and their expected (or average) returns if and only if the betas are computed using a minimum variance market index portfolio.[2]

The **beta factor** of a security describes the response of the security's returns to changes in the rates of return to the market portfolio, which is a portfolio composed of all risky (e.g., having positive standard deviations) investments in the economic system. To illustrate the concept of a beta factor, suppose we expect the return to

---

[2]This property was originally discovered by Sharpe (1964). Its implications were not fully appreciated, however, until the publication of an important paper by Roll (1977).

the market portfolio to be 6 percent greater next month than it was last month. If this causes us to revise upward our expectation for the rate of return on an individual stock by 12 percent, we can say the stock has a beta factor of 2.00. If, instead, our expectation for the stock increased by only 3 percent, the stock would have a beta of only .50.

Property II states that if we estimate betas by using a minimum variance portfolio as a proxy for the market portfolio, the relationship between our estimated betas for individual stocks and their average rates of return will be exactly linear. To see this, suppose we sample the returns to Acme, Brown, and Consolidated over a six-year period and find that the stocks produce the following rates of return:

Year	Acme	Brown	Consolidated
1	36%	35%	53%
2	−11	−8	−37
3	−18	−20	69
4	70	28	50
5	25	76	16
6	−72	−51	−61
Mean	5	10	15
Standard deviation	49.6	45.3	53.0

The sample covariance matrix for the three stocks for the six-year period can be computed from these returns as

Stock	Acme	Brown	Consolidated
Acme	.246	.179	.178
Brown	.179	.205	.112
Consolidated	.178	.112	.281

Based on these numbers we can now compute the minimum variance set. The minimum variance set and the positions of the three stocks are plotted on the left-hand side of Figure 5.13.

Now suppose we want to compute beta factors, with reference to some index portfolio, for the three stocks. Assume we select, as such an index portfolio, one of the portfolios in the minimum variance set, say, portfolio M in Figure 5.13.

Portfolio M is represented by a set of portfolio weights, one weight for each of the three stocks:

Portfolio Weights in Portfolio M	
Acme	−1.000
Brown	1.139
Consolidated	.861

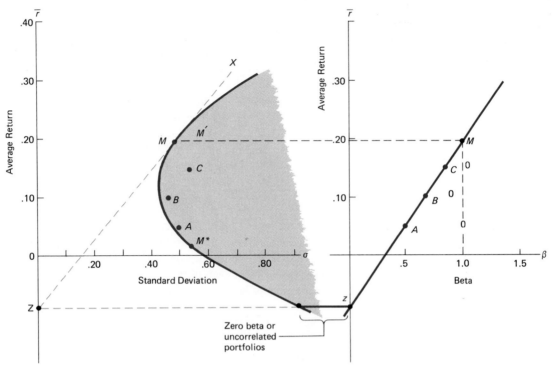

FIGURE 5.13 The positioning of stocks in average return—beta space.

Because we have six yearly returns for each of the three stocks, we can compute the corresponding six yearly returns to portfolio M. For each year we multiply the return to each stock by its portfolio weight and sum up the products. For example, the portfolio's return in the first year can be computed as

$$49.5\% = -1.00 \times 36\% + 1.139 \times 35\% + .861 \times 53\%$$

In this way the six portfolio returns can be computed as

Year	Return to Portfolio M
1	49.5%
2	−29.9
3	54.6
4	4.9
5	75.3
6	−38.6
Mean	19.3
Standard deviation	47.3

Now we can compute the beta factor for each stock by relating the individual stock's returns to portfolio M's returns, as we do for Acme, Brown, and Consolidated in Figures 5.14a, b, and c. The broken line in each figure is our estimate of the characteristic line for the stock. The slope of these lines is our estimate of the beta factor (computed as the ratio of each stock's sample covariance with portfolio M to portfolio M's sample variance). The betas are given by

	Beta Factor
Acme	.493
Brown	.670
Consolidated	.848

At this point we plot the betas against the average rates of return for each stock. Given the position of the three stocks and portfolio M, as drawn in the left side of Figure 5.13, the plot *must* look like the right side of Figure 5.13. Note we can draw a straight line through the positions of each of the three stocks on the right side. This will always be the case, no matter how many stocks we are dealing with, as long as the market index we select is in the minimum variance set for the stocks considered. In fact, we don't even have to go through the trouble of computing the betas for each of the stocks and then plotting them to find the line. The position of the line on a graph relating average or expected return to beta can be found directly.

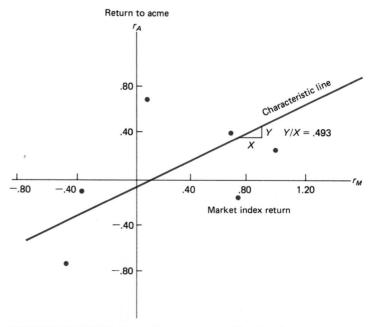

FIGURE 5.14(a) Estimated characteristic line for Acme.

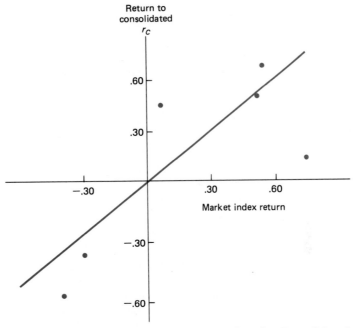

FIGURE 5.14(b) Estimated characteristic line for Consolidated.

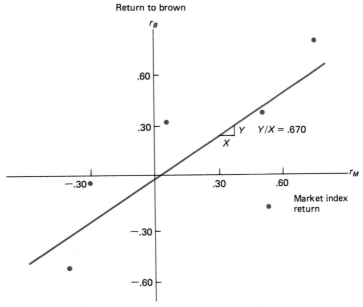

FIGURE 5.14(c) Estimated characteristic line for Brown.

To find the line relating average return to beta, first draw a line tangent to the bullet at the position of the index portfolio you have selected. The broken line ZX in Figure 5.12 is such a line. Now consider point Z, where the line of tangency intersects the vertical axis. Plot this same level of average return on the vertical axis of the right-hand graph of Figure 5.13 at z. Now plot the index portfolio on the right-hand side. To do this, think of a plot like those in Figures 5.14a through 5.14c for the market index itself.

Because, in this case, we are plotting the same returns on both the horizontal and vertical axes, all points will fall on a 45-degree line extending from the origin of the graph. The slope of this line, of course, would be equal to 1. The index portfolio, therefore, has a beta equal to 1 and is plotted at point M in the right side of Figure 5.13.

The relationship between beta and average return for all securities can now be found by drawing a straight line through points Z and M. *Every* security in the population considered will be positioned on this line. The position of each security on the line (and, therefore, the beta factor for each stock) is determined completely by the average return for the security in the time period observed.

Note all securities with an average return equal to Z will have a beta equal to 0. Given that beta is equal to security covariance with the index portfolio divided by the index portfolio's variance, we know all securities positioned on the solid segment of the horizontal line passing through the bullet are completely uncorrelated with the index portfolio. One of these portfolios has the lowest variance and is therefore positioned on the bullet. We shall refer to this portfolio as the *minimum variance, zero beta portfolio*.

You should be able to see that if the index portfolio is positioned on the bullet above the minimum variance portfolio, the line on the right side of Figure 5.13 will be positively sloped. If it is positioned below the minimum variance portfolio, the line will be negatively sloped. With a market index like M, Consolidated has the largest beta because it has the largest average return. On the other hand, if we selected an index portfolio like M*, Acme would have the largest beta, because it has the smallest average return.

The relationship of property II stems from the fact that the combination lines between each of the individual securities and the index portfolio must be tangent to the bullet at the position of the index portfolio, as in Figure 5.15(a). If the combination lines didn't reflect *off* the bullet at this point but rather went *through* it, the bullet couldn't be efficient or minimum variance, as we have defined it.

In Figure 5.15(b) we are dealing with an index portfolio that is *inefficient*. Now the combination lines for the various stocks can move through the position of the portfolio at various angles relative to one another. It is no longer true that, for changes in the weight assigned to each individual stock, the average return and variance of the portfolio change in the same proportion.

If the index portfolio is minimum variance, however, the combination line for all the securities must have the same slope at the position of the index portfolio on the bullet. This means, if we slightly change the portfolio weight assigned to *any* security, the standard deviation and average return of the index portfolio will change

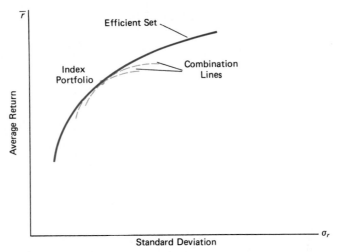

FIGURE 5.15(a) Combination lines for efficient index portfolio.

in the same proportions relative to one another for each and every security. Suppose, for example, we slightly change the weight in the index portfolio assigned to Acme, and we find the change in the average return to the index portfolio is twice as great as the change in its standard deviation. We will find this is also the case when we change the weights assigned to Brown and Consolidated.

Consider, first, what determines the extent to which the portfolio's expected return changes as we change the portfolio weight. The magnitude of the change

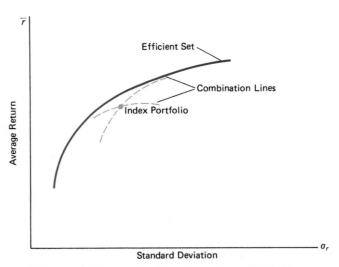

FIGURE 5.15(b) Combination lines for inefficient index portfolio.

increases with the differene between the expected return to the stock and the index. At the extreme, where they have the same expected return, there would be no change as we change the weight.

Now consider the effect of a change in the weight assignment on the index portfolio's *standard deviation*. In this case the larger the covariance between the stock and the index portfolio, the larger will be the impact of a change in weight assignment on the portfolio's standard deviation. Because beta is computed as the ratio of this covariance to the variance of the market index, we can also say the effect on the portfolio's standard deviation is directly related to beta.

Thus, as we change the portfolio weight, the impact on portfolio expected return depends on the expected return to the stock (relative to the index, which is a constant across all the stocks). The impact on portfolio standard deviation increases with the beta of the stock. If the index is minimum variance, the change in expected return is in the same proportion to the change in standard deviation as we make slight changes in the portfolio weights assigned to each and every stock in the population. This can be true only if security betas are linearly related to security expected rates of return. This relationship exists under property II.

A proof of property II is given in Appendix 4 following this chapter. Additional properties of the minimum variance set are given in Appendix 8 following Chapter 23.

Property II is extremely important and will be referred to many times throughout this book. To appreciate the importance of this property, consider the fact that, armed with properties I and II, we can get a sneak preview of the essential characteristics of the capital asset pricing model, which is more completely discussed in Chapter 7.

The capital asset pricing model describes the way expected returns on different securities will relate to their risks if everyone in the economy used portfolio theory, as we have described it, to determine his or her investment positions. In such an event, we all would take positions scattered along the efficient set. If I am more aggressive than you, my position would be higher on the bullet than yours, but we would both be positioned somewhere on the bullet. The market portfolio is a portfolio containing all the capital investments in the economic system. It is, therefore, the aggregate of everyone's portfolio. On the basis of property I, we know that combinations of efficient portfolios are also efficient. This means, when we aggregate the efficient portfolios of all investors to obtain the market portfolio, it too will be efficient. The market portfolio will be sitting on the skin of the bullet.

In the capital asset pricing model, beta is taken to be the appropriate measure of risk of an individual security or investment. Betas are obtained by relating individual security returns to the returns of the market portfolio. We know, on the basis of property II, because the market portfolio is efficient, there will be a simple linear relationship between the beta of any security and its expected rate of return. In the context of the CAPM, this relationship is referred to as the security market line. Thus, if index portfolio M on the left-hand side of Figure 5.13 is the market portfolio, we have the CAPM, and the solid line on the right-hand side is the security market line.

SUMMARY

Given a plot of portfolio investment opportunities in expected return–standard deviation space, the bullet-shaped minimum variance set represents those portfolios which have the lowest possible variance, given a particular level of expected return. The portfolio in the minimum variance set with the lowest variance, or standard deviation, is called the minimum variance portfolio. All portfolios in the minimum variance set that have expected returns equal to or greater than the minimum variance portfolio are in the efficient set. Portfolios in the efficient set have the highest possible expected return, given their level of standard deviation.

The critical line provides the portfolio weights for the portfolios in the minimum variance set. This line traces out the points of tangency between the iso-expected return lines and the isovariance ellipses. An iso-expected return line shows the combinations of portfolio weights, all of which provide for a particular portfolio expected rate of return. An isovariance ellipse shows the combinations of portfolio weights, all of which provide for a particular portfolio variance. The slope and relative positions of the iso-expected return lines depend on the relative expected returns of the stocks considered. The shapes of the iso-variance ellipses depend on the covariances between the stocks considered.

In the next chapter we will examine some of the properties of the minimum variance set.

APPENDIX 2

A THREE-DIMENSIONAL APPROACH TO FINDING THE EFFICIENT SET

The Expected Return Plane

The expected rate of return to a portfolio is a simple weighted average of the expected rates of return to the securities we are putting in the portfolio. Thus, securities combine in a linear fashion in terms of their expected rates of return.

Consider Figure A.2.1. This is a two-dimensional diagram. Now think of adding a third dimension that comes directly out from the page. We will plot expected portfolio return on this dimension. We now have three axes. On the floor or base of the diagram (which is actually Figure A.2.1) we have our two horizontal axes, which show the portfolio weights in Acme and Brown. On the vertical axis we are plotting the expected portfolio return, which corresponds to each combination of portfolio weights plotted on the base.

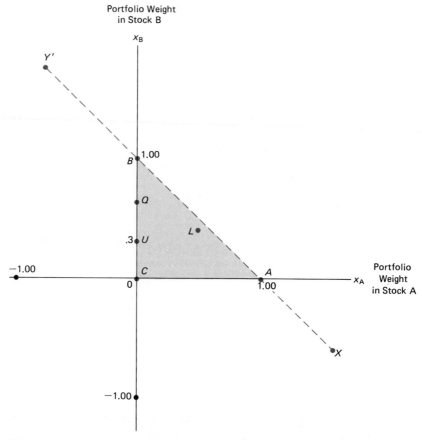

FIGURE A.2.1 Portfolio weights in the three-stock portfolio.

This three-dimensional diagram is depicted in Figure A.2.2. The plane depicted in the diagram is situated directly above the triangle covering positive positions in the three stocks. It is a flat surface sloping down toward you. The plane shows you the expected return to portfolios of Acme, Brown, and Consolidated, which are plotted on the base of the diagram.

Let's first consider the three points of the triangular plane. Consider point A on the base of the diagram. At A, you are investing all of your money in Acme and nothing in the other two stocks. Because you have formed a portfolio that is actually Acme and nothing else, it will have an expected return that is equal to 5 percent, the expected return for Acme. To find the expected portfolio return corresponding to point A, move directly up from the base at point A. You will hit the plane at a 5 percent rate of return relative to the vertical axis. Similarly, at point C, where you are investing everything in consolidated, moving directly up from the base you hit the plane at a 15 percent expected return, the expected

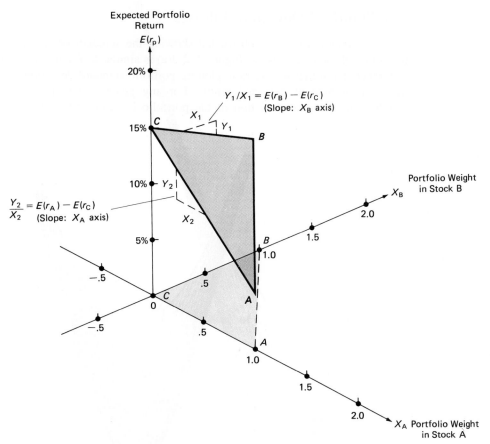

FIGURE A.2.2 The expected return plane.

return to Consolidated. Moving up from *B*, where you are investing everything in Brown, you hit the plane at Brown's 10 percent expected return. Moving up from a point inside the triangle, where you are combining an investment in all three of the stocks, you find the portfolio's expected rate of return is a linear combination of the expected returns to the three stocks. Remember, the expected return to a portfolio is a simple weighted average of the expected returns to the stocks in the portfolio.

You should be able to see that the plane is sloping down toward you only because Acme has the lowest expected rate of return. If Acme's expected return were, instead, the highest, the plane would then be sloping in an upward direction.

The plane actually extends indefinitely north, south, east, and west. For convenience, however, we have drawn only that segment positioned directly over the triangle, representing positive positions in each of the stocks.

number in the covariance matrix and multiplying it by the portfolio weights for the two stocks associated with the covariance, (2) adding up the products, and (3) taking the square root of the sum. This is not, as in the case of the expected portfolio return, a simple linear process. Therefore, it shouldn't surprise us that the surface depicting the standard deviation of the portfolios represented on the base isn't flat either.

If portfolio standard deviation is repeatedly calculated for the various combinations of portfolio weights on the base of the diagram, a plot of the resulting portfolio standard deviations would produce the three-dimensional surface of Figure A.2.3(a). This surface looks like a net holding a watermelon. The net has a somewhat elliptical shape.

If you pick a point on the base of the diagram representing a particular set of portfolio weights for the three stocks, the distance you would have to move directly upward to hit the three-dimensional net would correspond to the standard deviation of a portfolio with the selected weights.

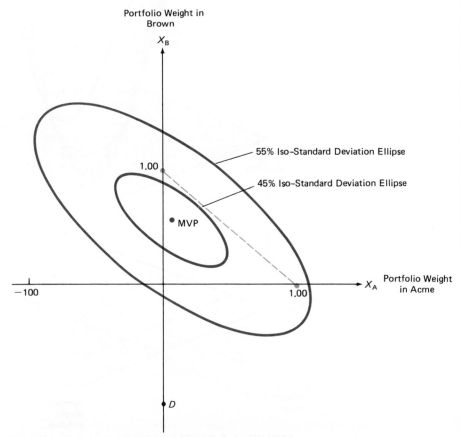

FIGURE A.2.4 Two iso–standard deviation ellipses.

In Figure A.2.3(b) we have sliced the net with a horizontal plane at a particular level of portfolio standard deviation (55 percent). The points of intersection between the net and the horizontal plane trace out as a portion of an ellipse. When the ellipse is superimposed on the base of the diagram, as in Figure A.2.3(b), it indicates those combinations of portfolio weights, all of which represent portfolios with 55 percent standard deviations. This ellipse is called an *iso–standard deviation ellipse*. If we sliced the net of Figure A.2.3(b) with another horizontal plane at a different level of portfolio standard deviation, we would get another iso–standard deviation ellipse representing a different portfolio standard deviation.

Two members of the family of iso–standard deviation ellipses for Acme, Brown, and Consolidated are drawn in Figure A.2.4. The ellipses are centered about point *MVP*. The larger ellipse represents a larger portfolio standard deviation. Point *MVP* represents the one set of portfolio weights that produces the smallest possible portfolio standard deviation or variance. We have called this portfolio the *global minimum variance portfolio*. It is positioned at the lowest point of the net of Figure A.2.3(a) at point *MVP*. Drop a marble into the net, and it will settle at a position directly over *MVP*.

THE CRITICAL LINE

Now consider Figure A.2.5. In this figure we are again plotting expected portfolio return on the vertical axis, as in Figure A.2.2. In this figure, the iso–standard deviation ellipses of Figure A.2.4 have been superimposed on the expected return plane of Figure A.2.2. For reasons that will become obvious, the plane has now been drawn to extend farther out toward the northwest.

Our objective is to find the portfolio with the highest expected return, given the level of standard deviation. Suppose we want the standard deviation of our portfolio to be 45 percent. Given this constraint, we want the expected return on the portfolio to be as high as possible. If we want a 45 percent portfolio standard deviation, we must position ourselves somewhere on the 45 percent iso–standard deviation ellipse. Given the location of the ellipse on the plane, we reach the highest possible point on the plane at point *T*. This is the portfolio with the highest possible expected return, given a 45 percent standard deviation. To construct this portfolio we must short sell Acme and invest the proceeds in Brown and Consolidated. We know this is the case because point *T* is positioned over a point on the base of the diagram that represents a negative weight in Acme and a weight between 0.00 and 1.00 in Brown. The remaining portfolio position consists of a positive investment in Consolidated.

Because this portfolio provides the highest possible expected return, given a 45 percent standard deviation, it can be found on the efficient set of Figure A.2.6 at point *T*. If we want a portfolio with a larger standard deviation, say, 55 percent, we move to the 55 percent ellipse. Moving along the ellipse, we reach the highest point on the plane at point *W*. We are now selling additional amounts of

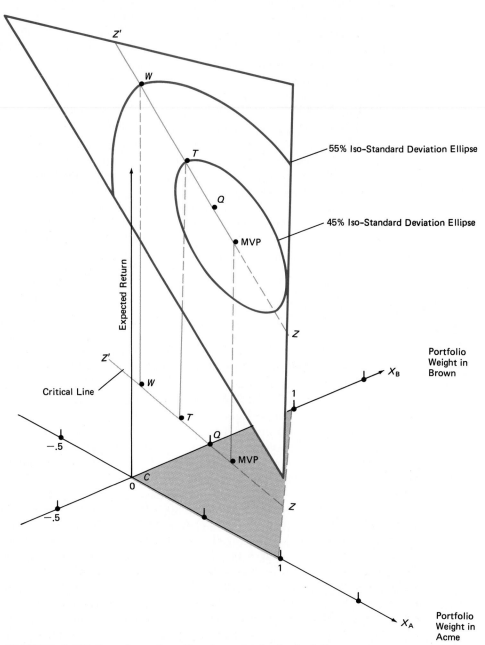

FIGURE A.2.5 Superimposing the iso–standard deviation ellipses on the expected return plane.

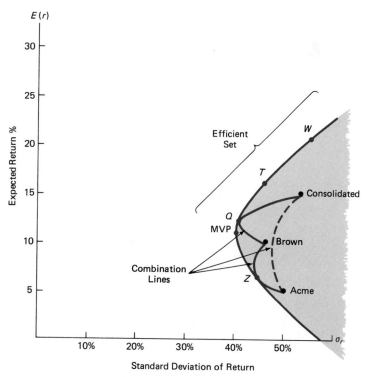

FIGURE A.2.6 The minimum variance set for Consolidated, Brown, and Acme.

Acme short, using the proceeds to increase our long position in both Brown and Consolidated. This portfolio can be found on the efficient set of Figure A.2.6 at point W.

Because the expected return plane is flat, and the iso–standard deviation ellipses are concentric about point MVP, we can pass a straight line through the points on each ellipse representing the highest possible expected return. This is line $Z'Z$ in Figure A.2.5. This line, called the *critical line,* is superimposed on the base of the diagram and then plotted in two dimensions in Figure A.2.7. The portfolios in the efficient set (highest expected return, given standard deviation) are represented by the solid portion of the critical line. The broken portion of the line represents the remaining portfolios in the minimum variance set. These portfolios have the lowest possible expected return, given their standard deviation. Remember that each point in Figure A.2.7 represents the portfolio weights for a given portfolio. The points on the critical line represent the portfolio weights for all the portfolios in the minimum variance set.

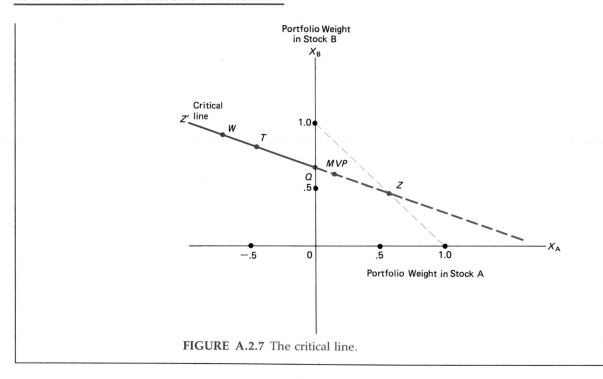

FIGURE A.2.7 The critical line.

APPENDIX 3

USING LAGRANGIAN MULTIPLIERS TO FIND THE MINIMUM VARIANCE SET

In Appendix 2, a graphic model of the procedure used to find the minimum variance set was presented. This model has considerable intuitive content but lacks mathematical precision. In this appendix we present a numerical procedure for finding the minimum variance set for a three-stock portfolio. Once understood, the extension of this model to portfolios containing more than three stocks should be fairly straightforward.

Finding the minimum variance portfolio for a given level of expected rate of return is a constrained optimization problem. In the case of a three-stock portfolio, our objective is to minimize the portfolio variance.

$$\text{Minimize } \sigma^2(r_p) = x_A^2\, \sigma^2(r_A) + x_B^2\, \sigma^2(r_B) + x_C^2\, \sigma^2(r_C)$$

$$+ 2x_Ax_B\, \text{Cov}(r_A,\, r_B) + 2x_Ax_C\, \text{Cov}(r_A,\, r_C)$$

$$+ 2x_Bx_C\, \text{Cov}(r_B,\, r_C)$$

subject to a target expected return $E(r^*_p)$

$$E(r^*_p) = \sum_{J=1}^{3} x_J E(r_J)$$

so that the sum of the portfolio weights must be 1.00:

$$1.00 = \sum_{J=1}^{3} x_J$$

The first of these three equations is called the **objective function** and the last two equations the **constraints**.

To begin to solve the problem we rewrite the objective function in Lagrangian form:

Minimize $\sigma^2(r_p) = x_A^2\sigma^2(r_A) + x_B^2\sigma^2(r_B) + (1 - x_A - x_B)^2\sigma^2(r_C)$

$$+ 2x_Ax_B \,\mathrm{Cov}(r_A, r_B) + 2x_A(1 - x_A - x_B) \,\mathrm{Cov}(r_A, r_C)$$

$$+ 2x_B(1 - x_A - x_B) \,\mathrm{Cov}(r_B, r_C)$$

$$+ b[E(r_p) - x_AE(r_A) - x_BE(r_B) - (1 - x_A - x_B)E(r_C)]$$

where

$$x_C = 1 - x_A - x_B$$

$$b = \text{the Lagrangian multiplier}$$

If we set the the target expected return $E(r^*_p) = .15$ and substitute in the values for the variances, covariances, and expected returns given earlier, we have

minimize $\sigma^2(r_p) = .25x_A^2 + .21x_B^2 + .28(1 - x_A - x_B)^2$

$$+ .30x_Ax_B + .34x_A(1 - x_A - x_B)$$

$$+ .18x_B(1 - x_A - x_B)$$

$$+ b[.10 - .05x_A - .10x_B - .15(1 - x_A - x_B)]$$

Simplifying,

$$\sigma^2(r_p) = .19x_A^2 + .31x_B^2 - .22x_A - .38x_B + .34x_Ax_B$$

$$+ .28 + b(-.05 + .10x_A + .05x_B)$$

Next, take the partial derivatives, set them equal to zero, and solve simultaneously:

$$.38x_A + .34x_B + .10b - .22 = 0$$

$$.34x_A + .62x_B + .05b - .38 = 0$$

$$.10x_A + .05x_B \qquad - .05 = 0$$

We get

$$x_A = .24$$

$$x_B = .52$$

$$x_C = .24$$

$$b = -.48$$

If we plug the portfolio weights into the original objective function, we find

$$\sigma^2(r_p) = .1668$$

Technically, the Lagrangian multiplier, b, indicates the incremental change in the value of the objective function solution due to an infinitesimally small change in the constraint (in this instance, the target expected return). Because the objective function is nonlinear, its slope changes continuously and so should b.

APPENDIX 4

PROOF OF PROPERTY II

Given a population of stocks, the cross-sectional relationship between the beta factors of the stocks and their expected returns will be perfectly linear and deterministic as long as the betas are computed with reference to any portfolio in the minimum variance set for the population of stocks.

The minimum variance set of Figure A.4.1 is drawn on the basis of the assumption that short selling is allowed. We have selected an arbitrary portfolio in the minimum variance set, at point M. We have also selected an arbitrary stock J from the many in the population. Since M is on the minimum variance set and since short selling is allowed, the combination line between M and J must be tangent to the bullet at point M. The portfolio weight of stock J in portfolio M can be either positive or negative. In any case, for purposes of this proof, we are going to be interested in portfolios where we combine stock J with portfolio M in various proportions. However, the position of J in M is already nonzero. Because we want to distinguish portfolio M from stock J, we're going to redefine the portfolio weight of J in a portfolio allocated between portfolio M and stock J. We're going to define the weight to be the fraction of our money committed to J beyond what is already committed to J in portfolio M. In this sense, when we are at point M on the combination line, $x_J = .00$. When we are at a point such as M', the portfolio weight is negative. For points on the line between M and J, the portfolio weight is positive.

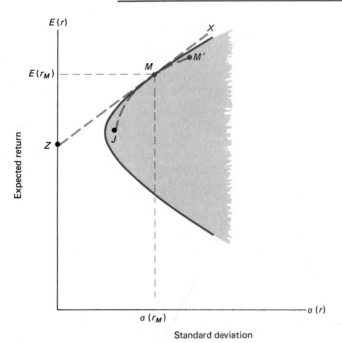

FIGURE A.4.1 Combination line between stock J
and portfolio M.

Given this definition of the portfolio weight, the expected rate of return to a
portfolio in which we combine M and J is given by

$$E(r_P) = x_J E(r_J) + (1 - x_J)E(r_M)$$

and the standard deviation of the portfolio is given by

$$\sigma(r_P) = [x_J^2 \, \sigma^2(r_J) + (1 - x_J)^2\sigma^2(r_M) + 2 \, \text{Cov}(r_J, r_M)x_J(1 - x_J)]^{\frac{1}{2}}$$

Note that $(1 - x_J)^2 = 1 + x_J^2 - 2x_J$, so that

$$\sigma(r_P) = [x_J^2 \, \sigma^2(r_J) + \sigma^2(r_M) + x_J^2\sigma^2(r_M) - 2x_J\sigma^2(r_M)$$

$$+ 2 \, \text{Cov}(r_J, r_M)x_J - 2 \, \text{Cov}(r_J, r_M)x_J^2]^{\frac{1}{2}}$$

We know that the combination line between J and M' is tangent to the bullet at
point M, because if it weren't tangent, it would penetrate the bullet, and this
would be a violation of the definition of the bullet. The slope of the bullet at M
is given by the slope of line ZM. Thus, the combination line JM' and line ZM
have equal slopes at M. We will use the equality between the slopes to prove
property II.

Our first step will be to get an expression for the slope of the combination
line JM' at point M. We will then equate this expression to the slope of ZM. As

you move along the combination line, both $\sigma(r_P)$ and $E(r_P)$ are changing in response to changes in x_J. Thus, we first derive expressions for the response of standard deviation and expected return to changes in the portfolio weight.

First, we take the derivative of $\sigma(r_P)$ with respect to x_J. The derivative of the nth power of a function is equal to the product of n, the $n - 1$ power of the function [in this case the function is $\sigma^2(r_P)$], and the derivative of the function. Thus, the derivative is the product of three terms. The first term is n:

$$n = \tfrac{1}{2}$$

The second term is the $n - 1$ power of the function.

$$[\sigma^2(r_P)]^{-1/2} = \frac{1}{\sigma(r_P)}$$

The third term is the derivative of the function $(\sigma^2(r_P)$:

$$\frac{\partial \sigma^2(r_P)}{\partial x_J} = 2x_J\sigma^2(r_J) + 2x_J\sigma^2(r_M) - 2\sigma^2(r_M) + 2\,\mathrm{Cov}(r_J, r_M) - 4\,\mathrm{Cov}(r_J, r_M)x_J$$

We are interested in the derivative at point M in Figure 4.A.1. At that point $\sigma^2(r_P) = \sigma^2(r_M)$ and $x_J = .00$, so the derivative of the function reduces to

$$\frac{\partial \sigma^2(r_P)}{\partial x_J} = -2\sigma^2(r_M) + 2\,\mathrm{Cov}(r_J, r_M)$$

Thus, the product of the three terms is given by

$$\frac{\partial \sigma(r_P)}{\partial x_J} = \frac{1}{2}\frac{1}{\sigma(r_P)}\,[-2\sigma^2(r_M) + 2\,\mathrm{Cov}(r_J, r_M)]$$

which reduces to

$$\frac{\partial \sigma(r_p)}{\partial x_J} = \frac{-1}{\sigma(r_M)}\,[\sigma^2(r_M) - \mathrm{Cov}(r_J, r_M)]$$

Now we know that $\beta_J = \mathrm{Cov}(r_J, r_M)/\sigma^2(r_M)$, so it follows that $\mathrm{Cov}(r_J, r_M) = \beta_J\sigma^2(r_M)$. Substituting this value for the covariance in the derivative and canceling, we get

$$\frac{\partial \sigma(r_P)}{\partial x_J} = -[\sigma(r_M) - \sigma(r_M)\beta_J]$$

Now we're going to take the derivative of the *expected value* of the portfolio with respect to x_J. By multiplying through by $E(r_M)$, we can write the expected return to the portfolio as

$$E(r_P) = x_J E(r_J) + E(r_M) - x_J E(r_M)$$

Thus,

$$\frac{\partial E(r_P)}{\partial x_J} = E(r_J) - E(r_M) = -[E(r_M) - E(r_J)]$$

To find the change in portfolio expected return accompanying a change in portfolio risk along the combination line at point M, we take the derivative of $E(r_P)$ with respect to $\sigma(r_P)$ using the chain rule:

$$\frac{\partial E(r_P)}{\partial \sigma(r_P)} = \frac{\partial E(r_P)/\partial x_J}{\partial \sigma(r_P)/\partial x_J} = \frac{E(r_M) - E(r_J)}{\sigma(r_M) - \sigma(r_M)\beta_J}$$

Referring back to Figure A.4.1, we draw line ZM tangent to the minimum variance set at point M. The slope of this line is given by

$$\frac{E(r_M) - Z}{\sigma(r_M)}$$

Remember that at the point of tangency the slope of ZM is equal to the derivative of $E(r_P)$ with respect to $\sigma(r_P)$. Thus,

$$\frac{\partial E(r_P)}{\partial \sigma(r_P)} = \frac{E(r_M) - E(r_J)}{\sigma(r_M) - \beta_J\sigma(r_M)} = \frac{E(r_M) - Z}{\sigma(r_M)}$$

or by transposing,

$$\frac{\sigma(r_M) - \beta_J\sigma(r_M)}{\sigma(r_M)} = \frac{E(r_M) - E(r_J)}{E(r_M) - Z}$$

Factoring $\sigma(r_M)$ from the left-hand side of the equation, canceling, and multiplying both sides by $E(r_M) - Z$, we get

$$[E(r_M) - Z](1 - \beta_J) = E(r_M) - E(r_J)$$

Solving for $E(r_J)$, we have property II:

$$E(r_J) = Z + [E(r_M) - Z]\beta_J$$

Thus, given that we are using as a market index a portfolio in the minimum variance set, the beta factor for any stock in the population from which we constructed the minimum variance set is deterministically related to its expected return in a linear fashion. In fact, by solving for β_J, we see that the beta of any stock can be computed as

$$\beta_J = \frac{E(r_J) - Z}{E(r_M) - Z}$$

QUESTION SET 1

1. What criterion must a portfolio meet to be in the minimum variance set? *Given Rez Low σ*
2. Contrast the minimum variance set with the efficient set. *Given σ highest Ret*
3. Referring to Figure 5.7,
   a. What part of the figure corresponds to portfolios having negative weight for stock C? *hope Rtzl*
   b. What are the portfolio weights corresponding to point D?

A = 0
B = -1
C = 2

c. Could a portfolio variance of 30 percent be achieved if short selling were not permitted?

4. Suppose the expected returns on three stocks are as follows:

	X	Y	Z
E(r)	.07	.11	.16

a. Find the equation of the iso-expected return line which corresponds to a portfolio expected return of .15 for these three stocks. (The line is to be expressed in terms of the weights on X and Y.)

b. If the weight on stock Y were restricted to be zero, what weights for stocks X and Z would result in a portfolio expected return of .15?

5. What criterion must a portfolio meet to be located on the critical line?

6. Refer to Figure 5.7. What would the critical line for stocks A, B, and C look like if you were restricted from selling A and B short but were permitted to sell C short?

7. Refer to Figure 5.7 and the data that were the basis for that figure.

a. Find the portfolios that have variance of 26 percent and that have zero weight for stock A.

b. Which, if any, of the portfolios you find in part a would constitute possible investments if short selling were not allowed?

8. Referring to Figure 5.7 and the relevant data for that figure, write out the equation that corresponds to the *particular* isovariance ellipse associated with a variance of 21 percent.

9. Referring to Figure 5.9, why does the minimum variance set "stop" at points A and C?

10. Which points on the minimum variance set depicted in Figure 5.9 correspond to portfolios in which all three of the stocks are used? Also, which points on the critical line depicted in Figure 5.8 correspond to these same portfolios?

11. Consider the following statement: "The geometry of the critical line is such that points on the line are always points of tangency between iso-expected return lines and isovariance ellipses." Is this statement true or false? Explain.

12. For an arbitrary set of stocks, suppose someone had constructed two minimum variance sets—one with short selling permitted and one with short selling not permitted. Even without knowing the details of the stocks' characteristics, what general statement could you make about the difference between the two minimum variance sets?

13. In finding the portfolios that make up the minimum variance set, what is the general approach that you need to employ?

QUESTION SET 2

1. What can be said of a portfolio in the minimum variance set?

2. What criterion defines the global minimum variance portfolio?

3. How does the efficient set differ from the minimum variance set? If you could not obtain a portfolio on the efficient set, would you prefer a portfolio of the same expected standard deviation on the remaining minimum variance set or inside the bullet?

4. What is an iso-expected return line? An isovariance ellipse?

5. Define the critical line. How is it found?

6. Intuitively, why should it be true that, when short selling is allowed, most securities will have either a positive or a negative weight?

7. How can we separate the decision of how much variance to assume from what stocks to purchase?

8. Given that a riskless asset is available, you are given instructions by your client to get the highest rate of return with the minimum variance available. What point on the graph do you choose?

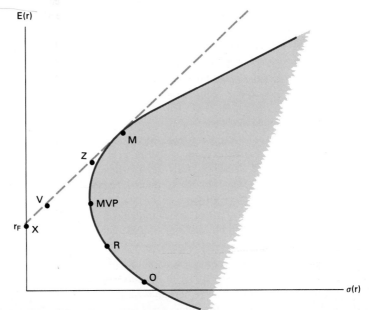

9. a. Given the graphs below, what points are necessary to draw the line showing the risk-reward trade-off for the individual stocks A, B, and C?

   b. What can we say about the relationships between the betas of stocks A, B, and C?

   c. What does the beta of C tell us about stock C? Is C more likely to be a utility or an emerging technology company?

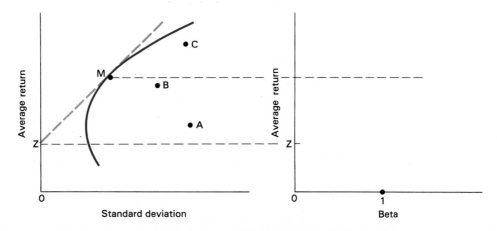

10. Why, intuitively, would most of the stocks in a portfolio on the minimum variance set with no short selling allowed have zero portfolio weights?

ANSWERS TO QUESTION SET 2

1. A portfolio in the minimum variance set has the least possible variance for a given level of expected return.

2. The global minimum variance portfolio has the least possible variance given the universe of securities available.

3. The efficient set includes only those portfolios on the top half of the "bullet," having the highest possible expected return given a level of portfolio variance. Given that you cannot have a portfolio on the efficient set, you would prefer a portfolio inside the bullet rather than on the lower half of the minimum variance set, since these represent the least desirable portfolios.

4. An iso-expected return line shows the set of portfolios all of which have the same expected rate of return. Different lines, showing different expected rates of return, are parallel to each other. An isovariance ellipse shows the set of portfolios all of which have the same variance of return. These ellipses are concentric around the global minimum variance portfolio.

5. The critical line shows the portfolio weights for portfolios in the minimum variance set. It is found by tracing out the points of tangency between the iso-expected return lines and the isovariance ellipses.

6. Given a definite expected rate of return with a definite variance, most securities will fall into the categories of desirable investments or undesirable investments. The undesirable investments are sold short to place more funds in the desirable investments.

7. Given a population of risky assets and a riskless asset which we can either buy or sell, there exists a unique portfolio on the minimum variance set that is the one best portfolio of risky assets for the investor to hold. We can separate out the variance factor by taking a position in a risk-free asset. The more risk averse we are, the more of our portfolio we invest in the risk-free asset. All investors, however, if they hold any risky assets, still would prefer to invest a proportion of their assets in the unique portfolio on the minimum variance set.

8. You would choose point x, or the point where you get the highest rate of return for the lowest variance, in this case, *no* variance. This is a point on the new minimum variance set, which has been created by the addition of the possibility of investing in a riskless asset.

9. a. M and Z are necessary to tell us about the linear relationship of betas in the portfolio. M is the index portfolio, and a tangent to it intersects the vertical axis at point Z.
   b. The relationship between the betas is perfectly linear and deterministic.
   c. C is a stock with a higher beta, or risk factor. It is more likely to be an emerging technology company (i.e., a growth company) than it is to be a utility company (probably a stable stock with small, but certain, growth and dividends).

10. Unlike the case with short selling allowed, the portfolios with no short selling allowed do not allow the advantage of selling the less desirable securities to invest in the more desirable ones.

PROBLEM SET

1. The Figure below depicts in X_A, X_B space the possible portfolio weights in a three-stock portfolio. Indicate the areas of positive, negative, and zero portfolio weights for each of the three securities.

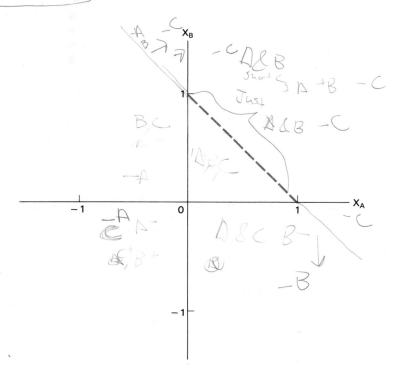

2. The following Figure shows the critical line for portfolio containing stocks A, B, and C when there are no restrictions on short selling.
   What would the critical line look like in each of the following cases:
   a. No short selling allowed.
   b. Short selling not allowed in stock A.
   c. Short selling not allowed in stock A and C.
   d. Short selling not allowed in stocks B and C.

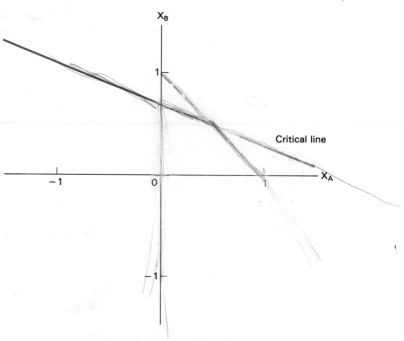

3. Utilizing the accompanying diagram, what portfolios, by letter, would you choose under the following constraints from your customer:

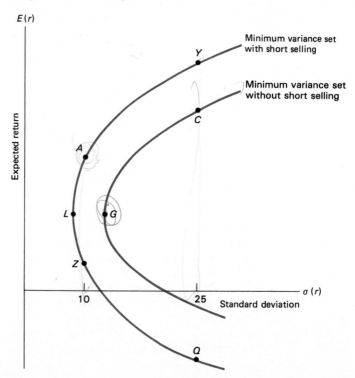

a. You are allowed to short sell stocks, but you can't have a standard deviation of more than 10.
b. Your client wants the highest expected return, with a variance of no more than 25.
c. Your client does not allow short selling, and simply wants the best expected return along with the lowest variance.

4. Suppose that we have two portfolios known to be on the minimum variance set for a population of three stocks, A, B, and C. There are no restrictions on short sales. The weights for each of the two portfolios are as follows:

	X_A	X_B	X_C
Portfolio 1	.24	.52	.24
Portfolio 2	−.36	.72	.64

a. What would the stock weights be for portfolio constructed by investing $2000 in portfolio 1 and $1000 in portfolio 2?
b. Plot portfolios 1 and 2 and the combined portfolio in X_A, X_B space. Is the combined portfolio on the critical line?
c. Suppose you invest $1500 of the $3000 in stock A. How will you allocate the remaining $1500 between stocks A and B to ensure that your portfolio is on the minimum variance set?

Refer to the accompanying diagrams for Problems 5 and 6. The bullet represents the minimum variance set for a population of stocks. A line drawn tangent to the bullet at M intersects the mean return axis at .06.

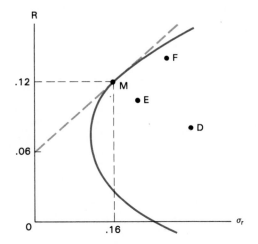
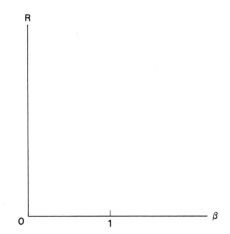

5. Assuming that short selling is allowed and that all betas of stocks and portfolios are computed with reference to M, draw the implied relationship between beta values and mean returns.

6. Suppose the mean returns for stocks D, E, and F are .08, .10, and .14, respectively. What would be the implied betas for these three stocks?

ANSWERS TO PROBLEM SET

1.

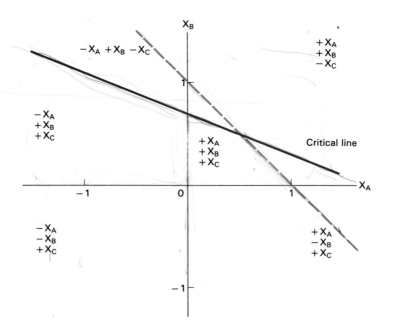

2.

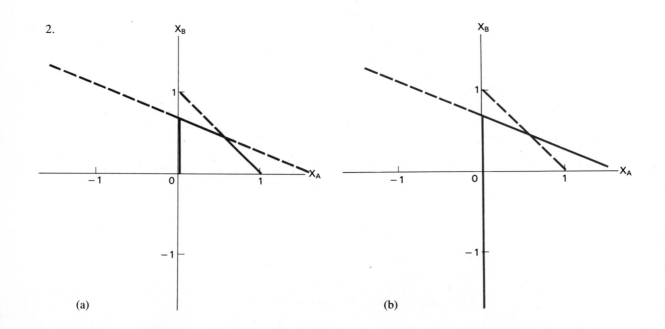

(a)   (b)

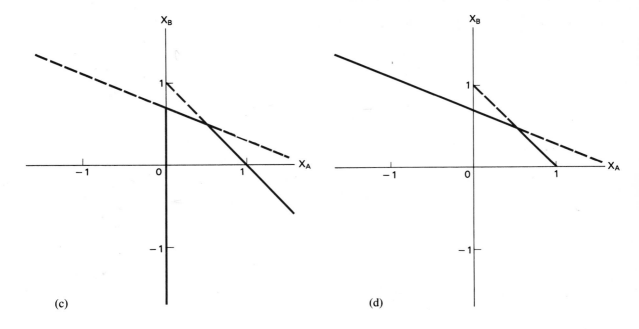

(c)

(d)

3. a. Point Z represents the optimal portfolio in which you could invest given the constraint of a standard deviation of no more than 10.

b. To get the highest rate of return with a standard deviation allowed of 25, you would pick point Y, which represents the portfolio on the minimum variance set that is also a part of the efficient set.

c. In this case, the no short-selling constraint does not allow you to be on the minimum variance set, and you would choose point G on the inside curve, which represents the smallest variance given the short selling constraint.

4. a. Given a $2000 investment in portfolio 1 and a $1000 investment in portfolio 2, the dollars commited to each stock would be

	A	B	C	Total
Portfolio 1	$480	$1040	$ 480	$2000
Portfolio 2	− 360	720	640	1000
Combined portfolio	$120	$1760	$1120	$3000

Since we are investing a total of $3000 in the combined portfolio, the dollar positions in the three stocks are consistent with the following portfolio weights.

	X_A	X_B	X_C
Combined portfolio	.04	.59	.37

b.

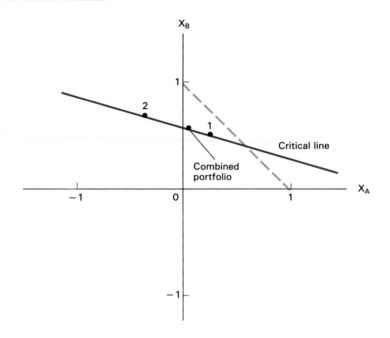

The combined portfolio is on the critical line.

c. Recall from Chapter 5 that if a portfolio is on the minimum variance set, it is also, by definintion, on the critical line. In (b) we plotted the critical line for our population of stocks in x_A, x_B space. The equation for the critical line takes the following form:

$$x_B = a + bx_A$$

Substituting in the values for x_A and x_B from portfolios 1 and 2, we get

$$.52 = a + .24b$$
$$.72 = a + -.36b$$

We can solve these equations simultaneouly to obtain the slope and the intercept of the critical line

$$x_B = .6 - \tfrac{1}{3} x_A$$

Using this equation, we can find x_B for any given value x_A if we invest half our funds in stock A ($x_A = .5$), then

$$x_B = .6 - \tfrac{1}{3}(.5) = .43$$

Since $x_A + x_B + x_C = 1$, we know $x_C = 1 - x_A - x_B$. Substituting in our values for x_A and x_B, we find

$$x_C = 1 - .5 - .43 = .07$$

The minimum variance portfolio is

$$x_A = .50$$

$$x_B = .43$$

$$x_C = .07$$

5.

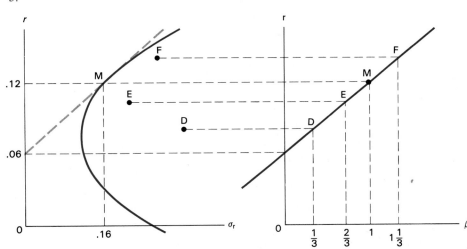

6. From property II we know that the relationship between beta factors of the stocks and their mean returns will be linear since the betas were computed with reference to an index portfolio on the minimum variance set. The equation for a straight line can in β, $\bar{r}$ space can be written

$$\bar{r}_J = .06 + (.12 - .06)\beta_J$$

Solving for β_J

$$\beta_J = \frac{(\bar{r}_J - .06)}{(.12 - .06)} = \frac{\bar{r}_J - .06}{.06}$$

By substituting in the mean returns of the three stocks for $\bar{r}_J$, we can find their implied betas

$$\beta = \frac{.08 - .06}{.06} = .333$$

$$\beta_E = \frac{.10 - .06}{.06} = .666$$

$$\beta_F = \frac{.14 - .06}{.06} = 1.333$$

COMPUTER PROBLEM SET

1. You received $10,000 from a rich uncle and have decided to invest the money in the stock market. Your broker recommends you buy stock in three companies: A, B, and C. He tells you that at current market prices the stocks have an expected annual return of 20.4 percent, 24.5 percent, and 19.7 percent, respectively. Based on the stock's annual rates of return over the past 10 years, you construct the following covariance matrix:

	A	B	C
A	.0301	.0160	.0112
B	.0160	.0139	.0101
C	.0112	.0101	.0171

   a. Using the data in the matrix, find the standard deviation and calculate the correlation coefficient for each pair of stocks. (The formula is given in Chapter 3.)
   b. Using the Markowitz mean-variance program in the computer software package for this text, generate a series of 20 or more efficient portfolios. Plot the portfolios in mean–standard deviation space.
   c. Plot the portfolios generated by the computer program in $x_A - x_B$ space. Draw in the critical line and locate the minimum variance portfolio.
   d. If you were to draw the minimum variance set without short selling in mean–standard deviation space, would it coincide anywhere with the minimum variance set where short selling is allowed?

2. Just as you are about to decide how to allocate your uncle's money among the three stocks, you broker telephones. His firm's research department has just upgraded its estimate of the expected return on stock A to 30.0 percent from 20.4 percent. How will this new piece of information affect your investment decision? Plot the new efficient set for the three stock portfolio and interpret the results.

3. In the years 1981–1984 the NYSE, the AMEX, and the OTC markets produced the following rates of return for investors:

	1981	1982	1983	1984
NYSE	−4.22	20.72	23.00	6.88
OTC	−6.10	4.93	28.27	−5.45
AMEX	−0.01	21.87	22.17	−9.31

   From the Markowtiz mean-variance model, input the returns for the three indices for the years 1981–1984. Print the charts showing (a) the annual rates of return and (b) the estimated rate of return and standard deviation. After viewing the first 10 portfolios that are generated, select an expected return of 13.515% and print the first new portfolios generated.

   a. For portfolios 1 and 5 of the second set of portfolios generated, calculate two market indices with the weights (investment proportions) given in the table multiplied by the annual rates of return for each of the stocks in each year from the table you printed earlier. (Make sure to convert the percentages to decimals in the annual rates of return before multiplying.) Carry your calculations to 6 decimal places.

b. With your market index for the *MVP* (minimum variance portfolio), run the single-index program, which will compute betas for you. Choose format 2. Input the indices you calculated and the annual rates of return. If you have done your calculations correctly, the betas should all be one.

c. Return to the single-index model program with your second market index, again choosing format 2. Input your indices and annual rates of return. Print the estimated model parameters and note the betas.

d. Make two graphs, side by side. On the left-hand graph, plot the portfolios calculated and printed out in expected return, standard deviation space from the Markowitz model. This will display the minimum variance set (bullet) for these three securities. To the right of that graph, on the second graph, plot the relationship between expected return and beta. Your graphs should prove property II.

REFERENCES

BAWA, V. S., ELTON, E. J., and GRUBER, M. J., "Simple Rules for Optimal Portfolio Selection in a Stable Paretian Market," *Journal of Finance* (September 1979).

COHEN, K. J., and ELTON, E. J., "Inter-Temporal Portfolio Analysis Based on Simulation of Joint Returns," *Management Science* (September 1967).

ELTON, E. J., and GRUBER, M. J., "Simple Criteria for Optimal Portfolio Selection," *Journal of Finance* (December 1976).

ELTON, E. J., and GRUBER, M. J., "Simple Criteria for Optimal Portfolio Selection: Tracing Out the Efficient Frontier," *Journal of Finance* (March 1978).

HOGAN, W., and WARREN, J. M., "Computation of the Efficient Boundary in the E-S Portfolio Selection Model," *Journal of Financial and Quantitative Analysis* (September 1972).

MAO, J. C. T., "Essentials of Portfolio Diversification Strategy," *Journal of Finance* (December 1970).

MARKOWITZ, H. M., "Portfolio Selection," *Journal of Finance* (December 1952).

PORTER, R. B., and BEY, R., "An Evaluation of the Empirical Significance of Optimal Seeking Algorithms in Portfolio Selction," *Journal of Finance* (December 1974).

ROLL, R., "A Critique of the Asset Pricing Theory's Tests: Part I: On the Past and Potential Testability of the Theory," *Journal of Financial Economics* (March 1977).

SHARPE, W. F., "Capital Asset Prices: A Theory of Market Equilibrium Under Conditions of Risk," *Journal of Finance* (September 1964).

6

INDEX MODELS

The technique we have been using to construct the efficient set is called the **Markowitz model,** named after the individual who introduced it in 1952. Markowitz showed how to squeeze the maximum amount of expected return from our portfolio, given our level of risk exposure.

Remember that the Markowitz model uses a matrix of covariances to compute the variance of a portfolio of securities. Each element of the matrix represents the covariance between the rates of return for two of the securities. To compute the variance of a portfolio of the securities, you multiply the covariance number by the fraction of the money you are investing in each of the two securities. You obtain a similar product for each element in the matrix and add them up to obtain the variance of the portfolio.

This procedure is perfectly accurate, given the accuracy of the covariance estimates. Suppose, for example, the covariance numbers are sample estimates taken from the returns on the stocks over the last 12 months. This being the case, the portfolio variance we get is the actual variance of the portfolio for the 12 months of the preceding year. While it may not be an accurate prediction of what the variance is going to be in the coming year—depending on the stability of the covariance numbers over time—it is a perfectly accurate estimate of the variance in the year in which the sample estimates of the covariance are taken.

However, there is a problem in computing portfolio variance in this way. The problem becomes apparent when the number of securities in the population becomes large. When this happens, the number of elements in the covariance matrix becomes extremely large. Suppose, for example, we tried to determine the efficient set for the approximately 1600 stocks on the New York Stock Exchange. The matrix would be 1600 by 1600, and it would contain more than 2.5 million covariance numbers. Granted, for each covariance on one side of the diagonal, there is a matching number on the other side of the diagonal, but we still would have to estimate nearly 1.3 million variances and covariances.

Even if we went to the trouble of making that many estimates, our problems are just beginning. Think of the process a computer goes through in finding the efficient set. Every time it needs to compute the variance of a portfolio, it must add more than 2.5 million products. Even when we use the fastest computers and the most efficient computer programs, until recently the problem exceeded the practical capacity of nearly all machines.

The problem with the Markowitz model is that it is complex.[1] It employs an equation for portfolio variance which is perfectly accurate, but also *intractable* when we are dealing with a large number of securities. What we need is an alternate formula for portfolio variance that is capable of dealing with large populations of stocks. We get such a capability with index models.

THE SINGLE-INDEX MODEL

Although the single-index model gives a simple formula for portfolio variance, it also makes an assumption about the process generating security returns. The accuracy of the single-index model's formula for portfolio variance is as good as the accuracy of its assumption.

The Assumption of the Single-Index Model

Essentially, the single-index model assumes security returns are correlated for only one reason. Each security is assumed to respond, in some cases more and in other cases less, to the pull of a single index which is usually taken to be the market portfolio. As the market portfolio makes a significant movement upward, nearly all stocks go up with it. Some stocks rise in price more than others, but as we observe the movement of stock prices over time, it is assumed that variability in the market portfolio accounts for all of the co-movement we see among the stocks. This is, in

[1]Actually, this may not be the only problem with the Markowitz model. If there are no constraints on portfolio weights, to invert the covariance matrix needed to calculate portfolio variance, the number of observations in the time series of sample rates of return must be greater than the number of securities represented in the matrix. This can present data problems when the number of securities being considered is very large.

fact, the assumption of the single-index model: The model assumes all the numbers in the covariance matrix can be accounted for by the fact that all the stocks are responding to the pull of this single, common force.

To state the assumption of the single-index model more precisely, consider Figure 6.1, where we have related the returns on an arbitrarily selected stock to the returns on the market portfolio. The broken line running through the scatter is the line of best fit (minimizing the sum of the squared vertical deviations of each observation from the line), or an estimate of the stock's characteristic line. The intercept of the characteristic line is given by A, and the slope by the beta factor, β. As defined in Chapter 3, the vertical deviations from the characteristic line are called residuals or shock terms, ϵ.

The rate of return for the stock in any one month can be written as

$$r_t = A + \beta r_{M,t} + \epsilon_t$$

where r_t is the rate of return to a security or portfolio and $r_{M,t}$ is the rate of return to the market portfolio.

The single-index model assumes that two types of events produce the period-to-period variability in a stock's rate of return. We refer to the first type of event as a *macro event*. Examples might include an unexpected change in the rate of inflation, a change in the Federal Reserve discount rate, or a change in the prime rate of

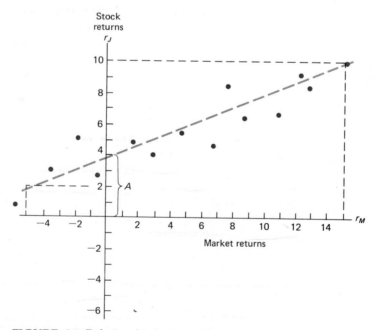

FIGURE 6.1 Relationship between the returns on an individual investment and the returns on the market portfolio.

interest. In any case, macro events are broad or sweeping in their impact. They affect nearly all firms to one degree or another, and they may have an effect on the general level of stock prices. They produce a change in the rate of return to the market portfolio, and through the pull of the market, they induce changes in the rates of return on individual securities. Thus, in Figure 6.1, if the return to the market portfolio in a given period were equal to −5 percent, we would expect the return to the stock to be 2 percent. If the market's return were 15 percent instead, we would expect the stock's return to be 10 percent. The difference in the stock's expected return can be attributed to the difference in the pull of the market from one period to the other.

The second type of event which produces variability in a security's return in the single-index model is micro in nature. *Micro events* have an impact on individual firms but no generalized impact on other firms. Examples include the discovery of a new product or the sudden obsolescence of an old one. They might also include a local labor strike, a fire, or the resignation or death of a key person in the firm. These events affect the individual firm alone. They are assumed to have no effect on other firms, and they have no impact on the value of the market portfolio or its rate of return. Micro events do affect the rate of return on the individual security affected, however. They cause the stock to produce a rate of return which might be higher or lower than normal, given the rate of return produced by the market portfolio in the period. Micro events, therefore, are presumed to cause the appearance of the residuals or deviations from the characteristic line.

Other types of events have been assumed away by the model. One might be referred to as an *industry event,* an event which has a generalized impact on many of the firms in a given industry, but is not broad or important enough to have a significant impact on the general economy or the value of the market portfolio. Events of this nature also may, conceivably, cause the appearance of a residual, but the single-index model assumes residuals are always caused by micro events.

The foregoing scenario is consistent with the assumption that the residuals or shock terms for different companies are uncorrelated with one another, as is depicted in Figure 6.2. The residuals will be uncorrelated if they are caused by micro events that have impact on the individual firm alone but not on other firms.

As noted, the single-index model assumes all the numbers in the covariance matrix for the returns on securities can be accounted for by the fact that each of the stocks responds, to its own degree, to the pull of a single common factor, the market. In fact, given the assumption of the single-index model, we can write the covariance between any two securities, J and K, as

$$\text{Cov}(r_J, r_K) = \beta_J \beta_K \, \sigma^2(r_M)$$

The right-hand side of this equation is the product of three terms. The third, which is the variance of the rate of return to the market, specifies the magnitude of the market's movement or the strength of its pull; the first two, which are the beta factors for the two securities, specify the extent to which each of the two securities responds to the pull.

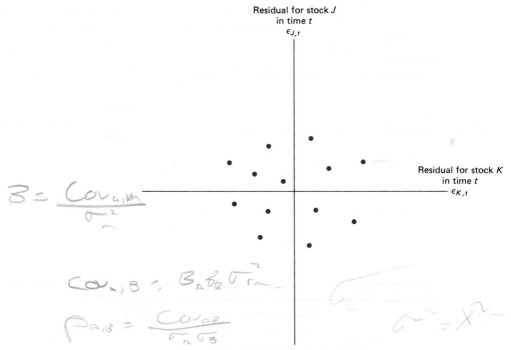

FIGURE 6.2 Relationship between residuals on stocks *J* and *K*.

The Single-Index Model's Simplified Formula for Portfolio Variance

Based on the foregoing assumptions and conditions, we can derive an alternative formula for the variance of a portfolio which is much less demanding in terms of estimation and computation time. We begin by noting that, after passing a line of best fit through points representing pairs of returns between security or portfolio returns and market returns, as in Figure 6.1, we can always split the variance of the return on a security or portfolio into two parts:

$$\sigma^2(r) = \beta^2 \sigma^2(r_M) + \sigma^2(\epsilon) \tag{6.1}$$

Total variance = Systematic risk + Residual variance

The first term on the right-hand side of Equation (6.1) is called the systematic risk of the investment. Under the assumptions of the single-index model, it accounts for that part of the security's variance which cannot be diversified away. This part of the variance is contributed to the variance of a well-diversified portfolio of many different stocks. The second term is called residual variance or unsystematic risk. It represents the part of a security's total variance that disappears as we diversify. It is mainly because of residual variance that the variance of a portfolio is less than the weighted average of the variances of the securities in the portfolio.

We can see from the equation that variability in return is accounted for by two things. The systematic risk accounts for the part of the total variability that is due to market movement pulling the security *along* its characteristic line. Note, systematic risk itself is the product of two terms. The first term involves the security's beta, which tells us the extent to which the security responds to the up and down pull of the market. The second term is the market's variance, which tells us the extent to which the market is pulling up and down. The second part of a security's variance is the residual variance. This accounts for the part of the variability which is due to deviations *from* the characteristic line. Thus, when we think of the total variability in a security's returns under the single-index model, part of it is due to movement by the security along its characteristic line and part of it is due to deviations from the characteristic line.

Equation (6.1) holds for an individual security and for a portfolio as well. Rewriting the equation for the case of a portfolio, we get

$$\sigma^2(r_P) = \beta_P^2 \, \sigma^2(r_M) + \sigma^2(\epsilon_p) \tag{6.2}$$

At this point, we need equations for the beta factor and residual variance of a portfolio as functions of the characteristics of the securities we put in the portfolio. Once we have these equations, we can substitute them for portfolio beta and residual variance and obtain a more simple, alternative expression for portfolio variance to use in finding the minimum variance set.

The beta factor for a portfolio of M securities is a simple weighted average of betas of the stocks in the portfolio, where the weights are the relative amounts invested in each security.

$$\beta_P = \sum_{J=1}^{M} x_J \beta_J$$

Portfolio beta = Weighted average of security betas

Thus, if we have two stocks, one with a beta of 1.00 and the other with a beta of 0.00, and we invest 75 percent of our money in the stock with the larger beta and 25 percent in the other stock, the portfolio would have a beta of .75.

Now consider the formula for the residual variance of a portfolio. To determine what the residual variance is, we can, if we wish, use the same procedure we used to determine the variance of the portfolio's returns (as opposed to its residuals) in the Markowitz model. That is, we could employ the covariance matrix for the residuals on the various stocks. For the case of a three-security portfolio, the matrix would look like this:

	Security	x_A A	x_B B	x_C C
x_A	A	$\sigma^2(\epsilon_A)$	$\text{Cov}(\epsilon_B, \epsilon_A)$	$\text{Cov}(\epsilon_C, \epsilon_A)$
x_B	B	$\text{Cov}(\epsilon_A, \epsilon_B)$	$\sigma^2(\epsilon_B)$	$\text{Cov}(\epsilon_C, \epsilon_B)$
x_C	C	$\text{Cov}(\epsilon_A, \epsilon_C)$	$\text{Cov}(\epsilon_B, \epsilon_C)$	$\sigma^2(\epsilon_C)$

You might object at this point and say, "Wait a minute! I thought the whole idea of the single-index model was to get away from this matrix. Why are we bringing it back in to compute residual variance?" This is where the *assumption* of the single-index model comes into play. The covariance between the residuals on any two securities is assumed to be equal to zero. Given this assumption, all the covariances in the matrix that are *off* the diagonal are equal to zero. This means, to compute the residual variance of a portfolio, we need only go down the diagonal of the matrix, taking each security's residual variance and multiplying it by the portfolio weight at the top of the column and again by the portfolio weight at the left-hand side of the row. Because both these two weights are equal to the portfolio weight for the security itself, we have the following relationship:

$$\sigma^2(\epsilon_J) = \sum_{J=1}^{M} x_J^2 \, \sigma^2(\epsilon_J)$$

(6.3)

Portfolio residual $=$ "Weighted average" of security residual
variance $\quad$ variances where portfolio weights are squared

Thus, the residual variance of a portfolio is also a weighted average (or sorts) of the residual variances of the securities in the portfolio. However, this time, in taking the average, we square the portfolio weights.

Given the assumption of uncorrelated residuals among securities, the residual-variance of a portfolio begins to disappear as the number of securities in the portfolio is increased. Consider the residual variance formula, and suppose we have a large number of securities, each with a residual variance equal to 10 percent. If we invest half our money equally in two of the securities, the residual variance of the two-security portfolio is 5 percent according to the foregoing formula.

$$\sigma^2(\epsilon_P) = (.50^2 \times .10) + (.50^2 \times .10) = .05$$

In the same sense, if we invest a third of our money in each of three of the securities, the residual variance of the portfolio would be 3.33 percent and so on, as shown by the solid curve in Figure 6.3.

As we diversify, the residual variance of the equally weighted portfolio approaches, but never quite reaches, zero. This is because the residuals in the portfolio are presumed to be uncorrelated, and the good things happening to some of the securities are being offset by the bad things happening to others. Some are above their characteristic lines, but others are below; the residual of the portfolio, being the average of the residuals of the individual securities, is always quite small if the number of securities is large. In fact, when we are dealing with a portfolio that is weighted *equally* among the various securities, the residual variance of the portfolio is equal to the average residual variance of the stocks, divided by the number of securities in the portfolio. Of course, as the residual variance of the portfolio gets smaller and smaller, the correlation of the portfolio's returns with the market gets larger and larger, as shown in Figure 6.4.

These relationships depend crucially on our assumption that the residuals for different securities are uncorrelated. Suppose this is an invalid assumption. Suppose that industry-type events frequently occur, and the covariance between the residuals

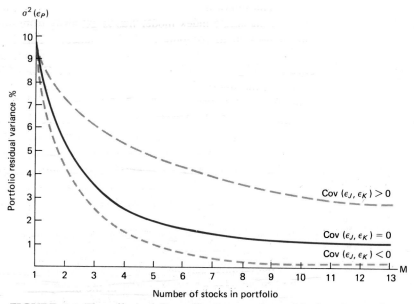

FIGURE 6.3 The effect of diversification on the residual variance of a portfolio.

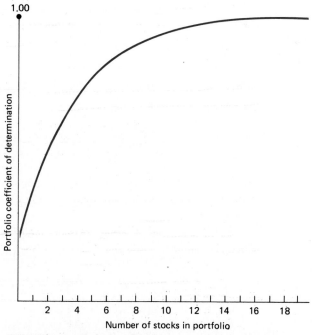

FIGURE 6.4 Relationship between the coefficient of determination and the number of stocks in the portfolio in the single-index model.

for different securities is typically *positive* and not zero. In this case, the off-diagonal elements of the matrix for residual covariances will be predominantly positive numbers. If we follow the single-index model formula for portfolio residual variance and simply go down the diagonal of the matrix, we will underestimate the true residual variance of the portfolio. The actual residual variance will be larger than the single-index model tells us it is, based on its assumption, because it is ignoring the positive elements in the sum that are off the diagonal. The relationship between the true residual variance and the number of securities in the portfolio may really look like the upper broken line of Figure 6.3.

Suppose, on the other hand, the covariances between the residuals for the securities in the population are typically *negative*. This might be the case for two stocks issued by companies that are competitors. In this case, any event that has a positive impact on one of the companies is negative for the other. If the numbers off the diagonal in the covariance matrix for the residuals are predominantly negative, the single-index model gives an overestimate of the true residual variance of the portfolio. The actual residual variance, obtained by summing the products obtained for each element in the matrix, would be smaller than the sum obtained by simply going down the diagonal. The actual relationship between residual variance and the number of securities in the portfolio might then look like the lower broken line of Figure 6.3.

To summarize, the beta factor of a portfolio is equal to a weighted average of the betas of the securities in the portfolio, where the weights are equal to the fractions of the money we invest in each security. The residual variance under the single-index model is assumed to be given by a similar weighted average, but this time, in taking the average, we square the portfolio weights.

We know that in the context of the single-index model we can split the variance of any investment, including a portfolio, into two components, systematic risk and residual variance, as in Equation (6.2). Substituting the expressions we have derived for the portfolio's beta and residual variance, we obtain the single-index model's simplified formula for portfolio variance:

$$\sigma^2(r_P) = \left(\sum_{J=1}^{M} x_J \beta_J \right)^2 \sigma^2(r_M) + \sum_{J=1}^{M} x_J^2 \sigma^2(\epsilon_J)$$

$$\begin{array}{ccccc} \text{Total portfolio} & = & \text{Portfolio systematic} & + & \text{Portfolio residual} \\ \text{variance} & & \text{risk} & & \text{variance} \end{array}$$

Contrast this expression with the procedure for computing portfolio variance under the Markowitz model. For 1600 stocks, we need approximately 1.3 million variance and covariance estimates under Markowitz. Under the single-index model, we need only 1600 estimates of beta for each stock, 1600 estimates of residual variance, and one estimate for the variance of the market portfolio. In addition, the computation time required to compute the variance is dramatically reduced.

However, the reduction in the complexity of the model comes at a price. As we said before, the variance number obtained from the Markowitz formula is perfectly accurate, given the accuracy of the covariance estimates. The model makes no assumptions regarding the process generating security returns. The single-index model, on the other hand, assumes the residuals, or deviations from the characteristic line are uncorrelated across different companies. The variance number obtained from the single-index model, therefore, is only an approximation of the true variance. Even if the estimates of beta and residual variance that we feed into the model are perfectly accurate, the estimate of portfolio variance we obtain from the model is only as accurate as our assumption regarding the residuals.

- It is obvious that the assumption isn't strictly accurate. After all, suppose something good happens to General Motors. This has an immediate impact not only on General Motors itself, but also on the company's suppliers and competitors. Many companies would be affected simultaneously, some positively and others negatively. The residuals that appear for these firms would not be independent, but rather would be generated by a common event. We know, therefore, the residuals are correlated to some degree. We hope, however, that the degree of correlation is small enough that the inaccuracy of the single-index model's portfolio variance equation doesn't transcend its relative efficiency.

An Example in Which the Single-Index Model Works

Consider two hypothetical stocks, Blue Steel and Black Rubber companies. In Table 6.1 are the rates of return for these companies, for the market portfolio, and for an equally weighted portfolio of the two stocks for five periods of time. The two-stock portfolio is assumed to be rebalanced to equal weights at the beginning of each period. Given this, the return for the portfolio is a simple average of the returns to the stocks in each period.

The returns for each stock and for the portfolio are plotted against the returns for the market in Figures 6.5, 6.6, and 6.7. Note that the beta factor for Blue Steel is equal to 1.00, the beta for Black Rubber is equal to .50, and the beta for the portfolio is the average of the two, or .75. The intercept of the portfolio (15 percent) is also the weighted average of the intercepts on Blue Steel (10 percent) and Black Rubber (20 percent).

Recall that the general statistical procedure for computing residual variance is first to compute the differences between the actual rates of return to the investment and the rates of return you expect the investment to produce, given its characteristic

TABLE 6.1 Rates of Return to the Market, Two Stocks, and a Portfolio

Period	Market Portfolio r_M	Blue Steel r_S	Black Rubber r_R	Two-Stock Portfolio r_P
1	30%	30%	55%	42.5%
2	40	60	40	50
3	20	50	30	40
4	35	45	27.5	36.25
5	25	15	22.5	18.75

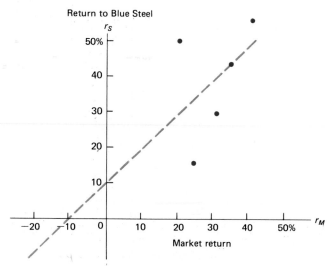

FIGURE 6.5 Blue Steel.

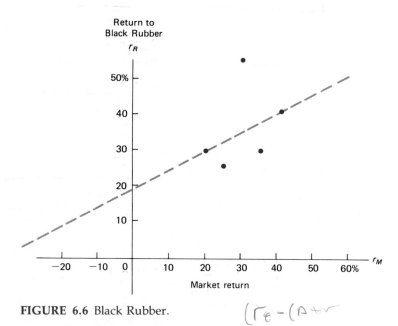

FIGURE 6.6 Black Rubber.

line and the market return for the period. The difference for any one period would be equal to

$$r_t - (A + \beta r_{M,t})$$

The differences for each period are then squared and the squared differences summed. The sum is divided by the number of periods observed, less 2. Therefore,

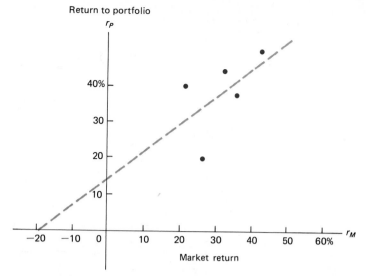

Return to portfolio

FIGURE 6.7 Two-stock portfolio.

the residual variance of Blue Steel can be computed as

$$
\begin{array}{c}
[.30 - (.10 + 1.00 \times .30)]^2 \\
+ [.60 - (.10 + 1.00 \times .40)]^2 \\
+ [.50 - (.10 + 1.00 \times .20)]^2 \\
+ [.45 - (.10 + 1.00 \times .35)]^2 \\
+ [.15 - (.10 + 1.00 \times .25)]^2 \\
\hline
.1000
\end{array}
$$

$$.1000/(5 - 2) = .0333$$

and the residual variance for Black Rubber as

$$
\begin{array}{c}
[.55 \quad - (.20 + 0.50 \times .30)]^2 \\
+ [.40 \quad - (.20 + 0.50 \times .40)]^2 \\
+ [.30 \quad - (.20 + 0.50 \times .20)]^2 \\
+ [.275 - (.20 + 0.50 \times .35)]^2 \\
+ [.225 - (.20 + 0.50 \times .25)]^2 \\
\hline
.0600
\end{array}
$$

$$.0600/(5 - 2) = .0200$$

The residual variances for the portfolio are given by

$$
\begin{array}{c}
[.425 \quad - (.15 + 0.75 \times .30)]^2 \\
+ [.500 \quad - (.15 + 0.75 \times .40)]^2 \\
+ [.400 \quad - (.15 + 0.75 \times .20)]^2 \\
+ [.3625 - (.15 + 0.75 \times .35)]^2 \\
+ [.1875 - (.15 + 0.75 \times .25)]^2 \\
\hline
.0399
\end{array}
$$

$$.0399/(5 - 2) = .0133$$

163

The portfolio's residual variance conforms to the value predicted by the single-index model, a weighted average of the residual variances of each stock, where we square the portfolio weights.

$$.0133 = (.50)^2 \times .0333 + (.50)^2 \times .0200$$

This is true because the example was constructed so the correlation coefficient between the residuals was equal to zero.

An Example of a Potential Problem with the Single-Index Model

To illustrate the potential problem with the single-index model, consider the following example. Suppose we have two stocks, Unitech (U) and Birite (B). The stocks have the following characteristics:

	Beta	Residual Variance
Unitech	0.50	.0732
Birite	1.50	.0548
Market index variance	.0600	

Given this information, the variance of the two stocks can be written as the sum of their respective systematic risks and residual variances:

$$\sigma^2(r_J) = \beta_J^2\, \sigma^2(r_M) + \sigma^2(\epsilon_J)$$

$$\text{Unitech } .0882 = .50^2 \times .060 + .0732$$

$$\text{Birite } .1898 = 1.50^2 \times .060 + .0548$$

The covariance matrix for the *rates of return* to the two stocks is assumed to be given by

Stocks	Unitech	Birite
Unitech	.0882	.0594
Birite	.0594	.1898

Under the assumption of the single-index model, the covariance between the *returns* on the two stocks is equal to the product of their betas and the variance of the market index.

$$\text{Cov}(r_U, r_B) = \beta_U \times \beta_B \times \sigma^2(r_M)$$

$$.0450 = 0.50 \times 1.50 \times .060$$

The actual covariance between the rates of return is greater than this number, which means the residuals for the two stocks are positively correlated. The covariance matrix for the *residuals* is in fact assumed to be given by

Stocks	Unitech	Birite
Unitech	.0732	.0144
Birite	.0144	.0548

Now suppose we form an equally weighted portfolio of the two stocks. The beta factor of the portfolio is given by

$$\beta_P = x_U \times \beta_U + x_B \times \beta_B$$

$$1.00 = .50 \times .50 + .50 \times 1.50$$

Under the assumption of the single-index model, the residual variance can be *estimated* by going down the diagonal of the covariance matrix for the residuals.

$$\sigma^2(\epsilon_P) = x_U^2 \times \sigma^2(\epsilon_U) + x_B^2 \times \sigma^2(\epsilon_B)$$

$$.032 = .25 \times .0732 + .25 \times .0548$$

To compute the *true* residual variance of the portfolio, we would have to add to this number the two products from the two off-diagonal elements of the covariance matrix for the residuals.

$$\sigma^2(\epsilon_P) = .032 + 2 \times .50 \times .50 \times .0144 = .0392$$

Under the assumption of the single-index model, we would estimate the variance of the equally weighted portfolio as

$$\sigma^2(r_P) = \beta_P^2 \times \sigma^2(r_M) + \sigma^2(\epsilon_P)$$

$$.092 = 1.00 \times .060 + .032$$

This is really an underestimate of the true portfolio variance. To find the true variance, we use the Markowitz technique, multiplying each element in the covariance matrix of returns by the portfolio weights for the two stocks.

$$
\begin{array}{r}
.50 \times .50 \times .0882 \\
+ .50 \times .50 \times .0594 \\
+ .50 \times .50 \times .0594 \\
+ .50 \times .50 \times .1898 \\
\hline
.0992
\end{array}
$$

The difference between the actual portfolio variance and our estimate using the single-index model (SIM) is equal to our underestimate of the residual variance.

$$\text{Markowitz variance} - \text{SIM variance}$$
$$.0992 - .0992 \qquad\qquad = .0072$$

$$\text{Actual residual variance} - \text{SIM residual variance}$$
$$.0392 - .032 \qquad\qquad = .0072$$

In actual practice, portfolio managers employ the single-index model in determining which individual securities to buy and how much to invest in them. They tend to use the more general Markowitz model for the problem of asset allocation—that is, allocating investments in the portfolio to various classes of assets, such as bonds, stocks, real estate, venture capital, and the like. Usually for this problem up to 10 classes of assets are considered, so the covariance matrix is of manageable size. Once the Markowitz model dictates a percentage allocation of the portfolio to stocks, then the managers must deal with a stock population much larger in terms of the number of members. At this point, the single-index model is used to optimize the stock portfolio.

This approach can be criticized, however. In estimating the covariance matrix for the various classes of assets, samples of rates of return on various indices, such as Standard & Poor's 500, are employed. These indices are not themselves optimal portfolios. Thus, the final ending portfolio resulting from the two-stage application of the Markowitz and single-index models is inferior to what would have been obtained under a general application of the Markowitz model.

What is the Correlation Between the Residuals of Different Companies?

Firms are interconnected through either customer/supplier or competitive relationships. This being the case, it cannot be strictly true that the unique events affecting one firm have absolutely no effect on any others. The interesting question is whether we can account for a sufficient fraction of the covariances between the returns with the single market index, so as to make the single-index model's formula for portfolio variance a useful approximation.

Fisher Black, Michael Jensen, and Myron Scholes (BJS) conducted an empirical investigation (1972) of the properties of stock returns that sheds some light on the question of residual correlation. BJS began their study by computing beta factors, using monthly rates of return, for every stock on the New York Stock Exchange (NYSE) from 1926 through 1930. They then ranked all the stocks by their betas and separated the stocks into 10 groups or portfolios. Each portfolio was equally weighted between each of the stocks. Portfolio 1 contained the 10 percent of the stocks with the highest beta factors. Portfolio 2 contained all the stocks ranked in the second decile. Finally, portfolio 10 contained the 10 percent of the stocks with the lowest beta factors.

They then recorded the rates of return on each of the portfolios in each of the next 12 months of 1931. At the end of the year they recomputed the beta factors for each of the stocks, reranked on the basis of beta, and reformed the 10 portfolios, getting 12 more rates of return for 1932. They continued this process through 1965, obtaining a series of monthly returns on each of the portfolios from 1931 through 1965. From these monthly returns, they then computed the beta factor for each of the portfolios by relating its returns to their market index, an equally weighted portfolio of all stocks on the NYSE.

In the process of computing the beta for each portfolio, BJS also computed the coefficient of determination for each portfolio, or the percentage of the variability in each portfolio's return that could be accounted for by variability in the return to the market. The relationship between the beta factors for the ten portfolios and their coefficients of determination are plotted in Figure 6.8.

The number of stocks in each portfolio changed as time went by and the number of stocks listed on the NYSE increased. At any given point in time, each portfolio contained a number of stocks equal to somewhat less than 10 percent of the total number of stocks on the exchange. (The number is somewhat less because in order to qualify for entry into a portfolio, a stock had to be listed on the exchange during the preceding five years to obtain an estimate of its beta.) Thus, the number of stocks in each portfolio is quite large. In fact, it is large enough so that if the assumption of the single-index model were strictly accurate, the residual variance of each portfolio would be close to zero. We see from Figure 6.8, however, a substantial amount of residual variance remains for many of the portfolios. We know this is true because if the residual variance were approximately equal to 0, the coefficient of determination would be approximately equal to 1. That is, virtually all of the variability in the portfolio's return could be accounted for by variability in the market's return.

The residual variance for all the portfolios is larger than we would expect, given the formula for residual variance under the single-index model. Considering our discussion of Figure 6.3, it must be the case that the covariances between the residuals for stocks are predominantly positive numbers. If the numbers off the diagonal in the covariance matrix are generally positive, you get a larger total by summing all the products associated with each element of the matrix than by summing the products associated with only those elements going down the diagonal. The equation for residual variance under the single-index model tells us to sum only those products going down the diagonal. To obtain the *actual* residual variance, we sum all the products, *including* those off the diagonal. Thus, if the off-diagonal covari-

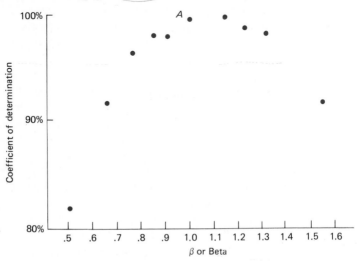

FIGURE 6.8 Coefficients of determination for well-diversified portfolios with different beta factors.

ances are positive, the actual portfolio residual variance is greater than that estimated by the single-index model.

Note from Figure 6.8 the problem of correlated residuals is more severe for portfolios of very low and very high degrees of beta risk. This result is confirmed in a number of other unrelated studies conducted by other researchers. This finding is probably due, in part, to the fact that the portfolios at the extremes of risk are concentrated heavily in companies from the same industry. The low-beta portfolios are probably heavily invested in the utility industry, and the high-beta portfolios are probably heavily invested in industries like the airline industry. The returns to the stocks within each of these industries are probably responsive to common factors distinctive from the market factor.[2]

MULTI-INDEX MODELS

The Assumption of Multi-Index Models

In the single-index model, we attribute the covariances between the returns on stocks to a single factor, usually market index. In a multi-index model, we attribute the covariances to two or more factors, usually including the market. Suppose, for example, we assume stocks tend to move up and down together because they are simultaneously responding to two factors, movement in the rate of return to the market portfolio and movement in the economywide growth rate in industrial production. The rate of return to any stock J in any period t is given by

$$r_{J,t} = A_J + \beta_{M,J}\, r_{M,t} + \beta_{g,J} g_t + \epsilon_{J,t} \tag{6.4}$$

where $\beta_{M,J}$ is the stock's market beta. It measures the response of the stock to changes in the market portfolio's rate of return. The term g_t is the unexpected growth rate in industrial production in any given period, and $\beta_{g,J}$ measures the stock's response to unexpected changes in the growth rate in industrial production. We say *unexpected* changes because the price of the stock is likely to be affected only by changes in industrial production not already anticipated by investors and discounted into the price of the stock. Just as in the context of the single-index model the beta factor is estimated by relating the returns of the stock to the returns to the market index over a number of previous periods, so in a multi-index model the betas can be estimated by relating the stock's returns to both the market's returns and to the unexpected growth rate in industrial production. One way of obtaining numbers for the latter series is to take the difference between the actual growth rate in industrial production and the average growth rate which was forecasted by some group of professional economists.

In the context of a single-index model, we slide a line of best fit through the data (stock returns versus market returns). Similarly, in the context of a double-index model, like the foregoing one, we slide a plane of best fit through the data (stock

[2]The presence of an industry factor in stock returns was first investigated by B. F. King in 1966.

returns versus market returns and unexpected changes in industrial production). If the plane is drawn to minimize the sum of the squared deviations from it, the residuals, or vertical deviations from the plane, will be uncorrelated with both the market returns and industrial production.

The Equation for Portfolio Variance Under the Multi-Index Model

If we assume, in addition, the rate of return to the market and the unexpected growth rate in industrial production are also uncorrelated with each other, we can write the variance of a portfolio of M stocks as

$$\sigma^2(r_P) = \beta_{M,P}^2 \sigma^2(r_M) + \beta_{g,P}^2 \sigma^2(g) + \sigma^2(\epsilon_P) \quad (6.5)$$

$$\underset{\text{variance}}{\text{Total}} = \underset{\text{(market)}}{\text{Systematic risk}} + \underset{\text{(industrial production)}}{\text{Systematic risk}} + \underset{\text{variance}}{\text{Residual}}$$

The market beta for the portfolio is again a weighted average of the market betas of the stocks in the portfolio. This is also true of the portfolio's beta with respect to unexpected changes in industrial production.

If we now assume the residuals on any two stocks are also uncorrelated with each other, as with the single-index model, we can write the residual variance of a portfolio as

$$\sigma^2(\epsilon_P) = \sum_{J=1}^{M} x_J^2 \sigma^2(\epsilon_J)$$

The final equation for residual variance is based on the presumption that we have now fully considered all the factors that account for the interrelationships among the returns on stocks. This being the case, the residuals for different companies will now be uncorrelated. If we should find, to our dismay, that the covariances between the residuals are still significantly different from zero, we haven't taken into account all the relevant factors. We need to move to a tri-index model or beyond. The search for such factors is now a matter of intense interest among researchers in finance. The best evidence to date seems to indicate the covariances among stock returns can be explained by at least as many as four or five factors.

Estimating Portfolio Variance Using a Multi-Index Model: An Example

Recall our earlier discussion of Unitech (U) and Birite (B) corporations. In the example, we estimated the variance of an equally weighted portfolio of the two stocks using the single-index model. The single-index model underestimated the actual variance of the portfolio because the residuals for the two stocks were positively correlated. A single index was apparently inadequate in terms of explaining the covariance between these two stocks. The actual covariance between the two stocks was .0594, greater than the covariance predicted by the single-index model.

$$Cov(r_U, r_B) > \beta_U \times \beta_B \times \sigma^2 r_M$$

$$.0594 > .50 \times 1.50 \times .06$$

Suppose the covariance between the residuals is caused by the presence of a second index, say, unanticipated changes in the rate of inflation. The betas for the two stocks with respect to the market and inflation and the true residual variances are assumed to be given by

	Market Beta	Inflation Beta	Residual Variance
Unitech	.50	1.20	.030
Birite	1.50	.40	.050

The variance of the market index remains at 6 percent. The variance of the index of unanticipated inflation is assumed to be 3 percent.

The variance of each stock can be expressed as

Systematic risk

Total variance = (market) + (inflation) + residual variance

$$\sigma^2(r) = \beta_M^2 \sigma^2(r_M) + \beta_i^2 \sigma^2(i) + \sigma^2(\epsilon)$$

Unitech: $.0882 = .25 \times .06 + 1.44 \times .03 + .03$

Birite: $.1898 = 2.25 \times .06 + .16 \times .03 + .05$

Suppose we again form an equally weighted portfolio of these two stocks. The portfolio's betas with respect to the two indices is given by

Market beta: $1.00 = .50 \times .50 + .50 \times 1.50$

Inflation beta: $.80 = .50 \times 1.20 + .50 \times .40$

Given the assumption that the residuals are now truly uncorrelated, the residual variance of the portfolio can be computed as the weighted average of the true residual variances of the two stocks, where we square the portfolio weights.

Portfolio residual variance $= .50^2 \times .03 + .50^2 \times .05 = .02$

The total variance of the portfolio is estimated as the sum of the two systematic risk terms and the residual variance.

Systematic risk

Total variance = (market) + (inflation) + residual variance

$$\sigma^2(r) = \beta_M^2 \sigma^2(r_M) + \beta_i^2 \sigma^2(i) + \sigma^2(\epsilon)$$

$$.0992 = 1.00^2 \times .06 + .80^2 \times .03 + .02$$

If you recall, this is the answer we got when we computed the variance using the Markowitz technique. We get the correct answer this time, because the example has been constructed assuming a double-index framework.

USING INDEX MODELS TO TRACK A TARGET

We have already seen how index models can be used as an alternative to the Markowitz model to find portfolios that closely approximate the risk-return characteristics of the portfolios in the Markowitz efficient set. Another popular use of index models is to build portfolios which can track a target.

By "tracking a target," we mean the rates of return on the portfolio are (1) highly correlated with the percentage changes in the value of the target and (2) the returns on the portfolio change in the desired proportion with respect to percentage changes in the value of the target.

To illustrate, suppose the target was the S&P 500 Composite Stock Index, and you wanted the changes in the returns to your portfolio to equal the changes in the returns to the S&P 500. If this is the case, then the tracking relationship of Figure 6.9 would be undesirable (not enough correlation) as would the relationship of Figure 6.10 (wrong slope). The relationship you want would be Figure 6.11 (high correlation and correct slope).

To use an index model to track a target, you're going to need the right kind of indices. If you restrict yourself to a *single* index, it should probably be the target itself. If the target is the S&P 500, the index should be the returns to the S&P 500. You would then compute betas and residual variances based on this index for a large group of stocks, and then find the portfolio that minimized residual variance, subject to the constraint that the beta on the portfolio was equal to 1.00.

Of course, to compute the *estimate* of the residual variance of your index portfolio, you would use Equation (6.3). As you know, this equation assumed individual stock residuals are uncorrelated, and they may not be. To allow for this, you may wish to move to a multi-index model by adding another index. Let's assume you pick inflation as the second index. You will first have to recompute your estimates of betas and residual variance by running a regression with one dependent variable (individual stock return) and two independent variables (S&P 500 return and per-

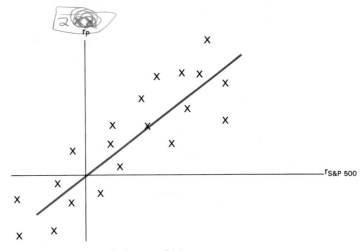

FIGURE 6.9 Too little correlation.

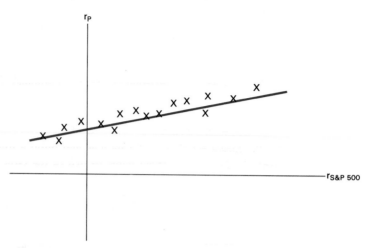

FIGURE 6.10 Not enough slope.

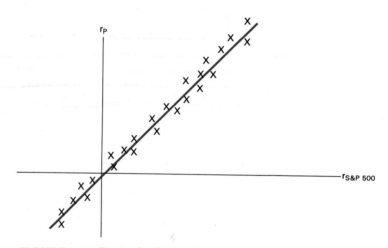

FIGURE 6.11 Desired relationship.

centage changes in the consumer price index). Now you have estimates of the S&P beta, inflation beta, and residual variance for each of the stocks that are candidates for inclusion into the portfolio. The desired portfolio will be the one which minimizes residual variance subject to the constraint that the portfolio's S&P 500 beta is equal to 1.00 and the inflation beta is equal to 0.00. If you can get residual variance small enough, the returns on this portfolio will be predominantly affected by changes in the returns to the S&P 500. Because its inflation beta is 0.00, it will be unaffected by inflation, and if its residual variance is very small, it will also be affected little by the idiosyncratic events happening to the individual stocks inside the portfolio. Should you feel the need for additional factors to reduce correlation further between the residuals of the individual stock candidates, you may include them. This means you must estimate an additional set of betas, and find the portfolio which minimizes residual variance subject to the constraint that the target index beta is equal to 1.00, and all other index betas are equal to 0.00.

Now suppose your target is the rate of inflation rather than the S&P 500. This merely means your instructions to the computer will change. You now minimize residual variance subject to the constraint that the betas of all indices are equal to zero, except the inflation index, which should be equal to 1.00.

Alternatively, if your target is not one of indices, you can estimate the betas for the target relative to the indices and build a minimum residual variance tracking portfolio that has identical betas to that of the target.

Using A Full Covariance Approach[3] to Track a Target

You should be aware of the fact that the full covariance matrix for returns can also be used to track a target. One way to do this is to merely subtract from the returns of each of the population of stocks the percentage changes in the value of the target. You then compute the matrix of covariances between these *differences* over all the stocks in the available population. Then, given the matrix of covariances between the differences of the returns to the stocks and the returns to the target, the computer finds the global minimum variance portfolio as in Figure 6.12. If you're lucky enough to find a global minimum variance portfolio with a zero variance, you have found a portfolio with one of the two relationships represented in Figures 6.13(a) and (b). The returns to portfolio A are always identical to the percentage changes in the

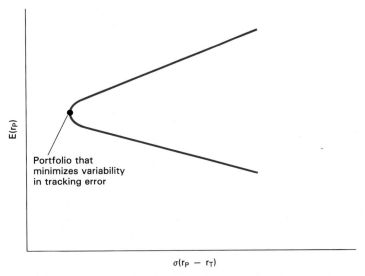

FIGURE 6.12 Using the full covariance approach to track a target.

[3]Patent applied for in the U.S. Patent Office

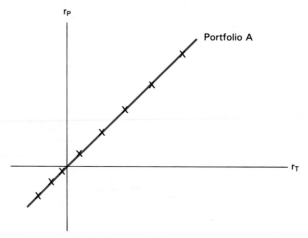

FIGURE 6.13(a) Zero tracking error.

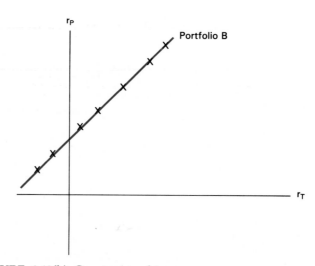

FIGURE 6.13(b) Constant tracking error.

index, while the difference between the returns to portfolio B and the percentage changes in the value of the index is always a constant.

The full covariance procedure will again give you a more accurate answer to the question, "Which portfolio has the lowest degree of tracking error relative to the target?" This is because it makes no assumptions regarding the nature of the covariances between the returns on the stocks and the returns and the index. On the other hand, you are once again faced with a potential tractability problem. As the number of stocks considered grows very large, you are faced with more difficult computing problems.

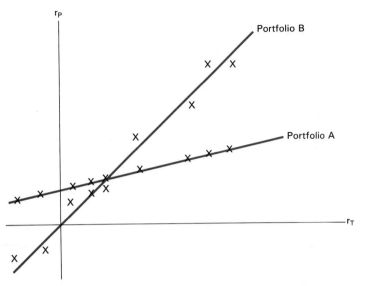

FIGURE 6.14 Correlation versus tracking error volatility.

Using A Full Covariance Approach to Find the Portfolio Most Highly *Correlated* with the Index[4]

Rather than attempting to minimize variability in tracking error (the *variability* in the differences between the returns on your portfolio and the returns on the index), you may want to maximize correlation.

Maximizing correlation is not the same as minimizing variability in tracking error. To see this, consider the two portfolios in Figure 6.14. Portfolio *A* has perfect correlation with the index, but a relatively high variability of tracking error. Note that the differences between the returns to this portfolio and the returns to the index can be quite variable over time. On the other hand, portfolio *B* has a lower degree of correlation, but also a lower degree of tracking error.

The formula for the correlation coefficient between the portfolio and the target is

$$\rho_{P,T} = \frac{\text{Cov}(r_P, r_T)}{\sigma(r_P)\ \sigma(r_T)}$$

Note the correlation coefficient is the ratio of the covariance and the product of the standard deviations. Now consider Figure 6.15. This figure plots the covariance vertically and the product of the standard deviations horizontally. Point *P* in this figure is a portfolio. Its correlation with the index may be expressed as the slope of a line drawn from the origin of the graph to the position of the portfolio. This slope is equal to the ratio of the horizontal distance marked *A*, divided into the vertical distance marked *B*, and, as explained, this ratio is equal to the correlation coefficient.

[4]Patent applied for in the U.S. Patent Office

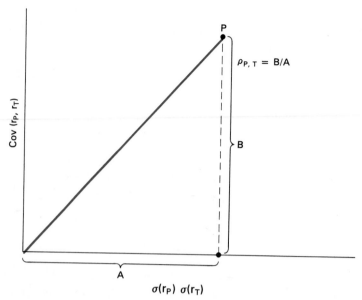

FIGURE 6.15 Find the correlation of P.

The standard deviation of the target is a constant over all the different portfolios we might build. Therefore, to move to the left on this graph we must reduce the standard deviation of the returns to the portfolio itself. In fact, given a value for the covariance with the target, we can find the one portfolio that has the lowest possible standard deviation. Since, as with expected return, the covariance between a portfolio and a target is a simple weighted average of the covariances of its stocks with the target, we can use exactly the same procedures here as we did in Chapter 5 to find the portfolio in the minimum variance set. This time we merely substitute covariance for expected return.

Thus, we find another bullet; this time drawn in terms of covariance, as in Figure 6.16. The maximum correlation portfolio will be the one with the greatest slope for a line drawn from the origin to the portfolio. In Figure 6.16, this will be portfolio P^*. To find the portfolio, pivot a line anchored at the origin down until it touches the "new bullet." The point of tangency is the maximum correlation portfolio.

This technique is useful when you are dealing with a prospective client whose objective is correlation as apposed to tracking error—as in "Find me the portfolio that has maximum correlation with changes in the consumer price index."

Using the Multi-Index Model to Optimize Portfolios

Whenever you employ a multi-index model to find the minimum variance set, you supply the computer with an equation for portfolio variance similar to the one given. You also supply the computer with estimates of each of the factor betas for each of the companies and with estimates of residual variance for each company. The com-

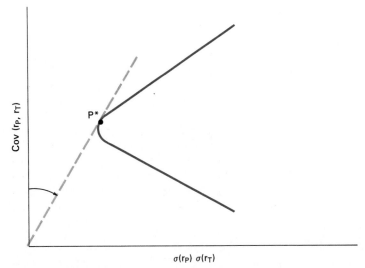

FIGURE 6.16 Finding maximum correlation portfolio.

puter then attempts to minimize portfolio variance, given a target expected rate of return.

Another use for a multi-index model is to construct optimal portfolios, given forecasts of the performance of your indices. For example, suppose among your indices you had factors like changes in the real price of oil, changes in the rate of growth in the money supply, or changes in the rate of inflation. Suppose, in addition, you feel that in the coming months the real (inflation-adjusted) price of oil will be down, but the rate of growth of the money supply will be up, as will be the rate of inflation. To take an optimal portfolio posture relative to this forecast, you will want to construct a portfolio of stocks with relatively small "oil betas" and relatively large "money and inflation betas." If your forecast for these variables materializes, the return on your portfolio should be substantial, especially if you have adequately diversified to minimize unexpected shocks coming from residual variance.

How to Use Index Models to Find Optimal Portfolios Conditional on an Economic Forecast

Index models can do at least one thing that the Markowitz model simply cannot do. They can enable you to find the optimal portfolio based on a client specified scenario for the future of the economy.

To use an index model in this way, you will first have to specify a set of economic indices. Candidates for this set might include the following:

1. The rate of inflation
2. The change in level of unemployment
3. The growth in industrial production
4. The change in the trade deficit

OUT ON THE STREET

SELLING FUNDAMENTAL BETAS

"Ms. Sawyer will see you now, Mr. Stevens."

Tom Stevens opened the door and walked into the impressively large office of June Sawyer, the newly appointed president of the trust division of one of the nation's largest banks. Behind June's desk was a spectacular view of the skyline of the city of Chicago. In fact, just two floors above them a low-level cloud was floating by.

"How do you do, Tom; I've been looking forward to your call. As you know, I've been president of this division for only three weeks. I want to make some changes, major changes. You see, I don't particularly like our image—it's too traditional, too antiquated. We're sitting right in the middle of banks like First Chicago, Harris Trust, and Northern Trust—some of the premier institutions in the use of modern quantitative techniques of investment analysis. In this group we stick out like a sore thumb. Most of our analysts haven't seen a beta since their fraternity days, which, in most cases, are a long time past. I want to change direction, and you may be the one to help me change. Now what can you do for me?"

Tom hadn't had an opening like this in years. "Well, as you know, I represent Wilshire Associates. Our firm has a broad array of services spanning both quantitative and computer-assisted more traditional tools of investment management like income and balance sheet analysis. Perhaps I should begin with my own area of specialization. One of the services we offer is a quantitative assessment of the risk of individual stocks and portfolios. We call this the fundamental beta."

"I know what a beta is, but what on earth is a fundamental beta?"

"It's an estimate of beta that's not only based on the stock's past relationship with the market but also on the characteristics of the company behind the stock. We look at 48 factors, such as variability in earnings per share, company size, and financial leverage, and relate these factors to company betas in the past to find the relationship between them. In the case of balance sheet and income statement items, we use up to five years of past ratios. In the case of market value items, we use up to 60 past monthly prices. After modeling the relationship, we estimate the company's current beta by plugging the company's 48 characteristics into the model."

"What advantage do fundamental betas have over straight historical beta estimates?"

5. The change in the federal budget deficit
6. The change in the level of interest rates
7. The change in the difference between long-term rates and short-term rates
8. The change in the value of the dollar

"They have greater predictability. Now they're far from being perfectly accurate, but they do a better job than the straight historical model alone."

"What do I do with them?"

"Well, when averaged to obtain the fundamental portfolio beta, they are becoming increasingly accepted as a measure helpful in describing the character of the portfolio. For example, a growth manager may wish to demonstrate to clients just how much orientation his or her portfolios have had toward growth. The fundamental beta of the portfolio may be useful in a comparison against the market or against other managers. In another situation, suppose you think you're approaching a major bull market, and you want to check the posture of your portfolio to see how responsive your investments will be to the general price level increase. The fundamental beta of your portfolio gives you useful information in this regard. By keying on a certain market index and moving toward a portfolio beta equal to 1.00, you can create a portfolio that will track the index. Overall, I think I can honestly say that fundamental beta has grown to become one of the *basic* parameters describing a portfolio's orientation. Today, it's regarded on a par with the price-earnings ratio and the dividend yield."

"What are the weaknesses of these fundamental betas?"

"Well, I think they're more useful in capturing the character of a portfolio as a whole than they are for individual companies. Just like any model, depending on how they are picked up by the model, a certain stock's characteristics can interact to create a beta estimate that's clearly out of line. Because of this, some people have been known to get frustrated when using beta to estimate things like discount rates that are to be applied to income streams. Currently, we are stressing its use in portfolios rather than individual stock application. To give you another example, we use fundamental betas in the assessment of the performance of portfolio managers."

"To your knowledge, does First Chicago employ fundamental betas in its quantitative investment analysis?"

"As a matter of fact, one of the key people in First Chicago's trust department is a friend of mine. They've not only employed fundamental betas for many years now but they've been highly successful with them."

As Tom watches the cloud move away toward the Sears Tower and the First National Bank of Chicago Plaza, he feels his confidence growing. His story is far from over, but Wilshire will have one more account by the end of the day.

Your next task will be to compute individual stock betas in relation to each of the economic indices. As we learned, the beta of a portfolio with respect to each of the indices is a simple weighted average of the betas of the stocks comprising the portfolio.

The expected return to any given portfolio can be written as

$$E(r_P) = \beta_{P,1}E(I_1) + \beta_{P,2}E(I_2) + \cdots + \beta_{P,N}E(I_N) \tag{6.6}$$

where $\beta_{P,1}$ is the portfolio's beta with respect to the first economic index and $E(I_1)$ is the expected change in the value for the index in the course of the next month.

The equation for the variance of any given portfolio would be similar to Equation (6.5), but with additional indices.

Armed with estimates of the betas and residual variances for individual stocks, you can now interview clients, trying to extract from them their feelings for the future values of the economic indices. "What do you expect to happen to the unemployment rate in the course of the next quarter?" Their responses will help you specify *expected values* for the various economic indices. These expected values can then be inserted into Equation (6.5) to find expected returns for various stock portfolios.

The values for the variances of your economic indices in Equation (6.6) can be obtained by sampling the past behavior of the indices themselves. These sample estimates can then be customized to the individual client by asking such questions as, "What's your feeling about the current environment regarding *uncertainty* about the rate of inflation? Do you think uncertainty has increased, decreased, or remained about the same?" Based on the client's answers to questions like these, you can modify your sample estimates accordingly.

Given the stock betas and residual variances, and the expected values and variances for each of the economic indices, you can now use the multi-index procedure to find the efficient set which is consistent with the client's outlook for the future. Given the client's economic forecast, these are the optimal portfolios for them to own.

ESTIMATING BETAS AND RESIDUAL VARIANCES FOR INDEX MODELS

In actual practice, many investors who use modern portfolio theory find that the single-index model is acceptable for their purposes. To operationalize the model, however, they need to have accurate estimates of the required inputs into the model.

Consider the time frame depicted in Figure 6.17. Assume we are at the end of year t. Our investment planning horizon is the month of January for year $t + 1$. We are attempting to find the minimum variance set for rates of return on stocks over this month. Because our time horizon is one month, we will want to sample using rates of return that are also measured over a single month. Keep in mind that we want to estimate the population values for the variances of the returns for different portfolios in the next month. We are using the single-index model, so we will need estimates of population values for betas and residual variances for the next month.

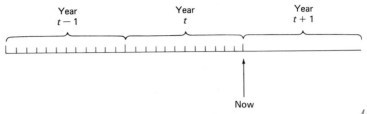

FIGURE 6.17 Time frame for estimating beta.

Sample Estimates for Population Values

The most straightforward approach to obtaining estimates of these inputs is to take sample estimates over some past period of time. The *Value Line Investment Survey* uses this approach in obtaining the beta estimates for the stocks it reviews in its weekly publication. *Value Line* uses weekly rates of return and estimates beta by relating each stock's returns to the New York Stock Exchange Index over the preceding five-year period, if that much data are available on the company. Thus, it computes a sample covariance and then divides this number by the sample covariance of returns to the New York Stock Exchange Index. To be technically correct, dividends in the rates of return should be included. However, because the preponderance of the variability in the series is due to the capital gain or loss component of the return, it really makes little difference to the estimate whether or not dividends are included.

Suppose we decide to sample the 12 returns for each stock in year t; we compute the sample covariance of the returns to each stock with our market index and divide this by the sample estimate of the variance of our market index to obtain our sample estimates of beta. Based on this straightforward approach, our estimation of the population value, β_{t+1}, is simply equal to the unadjusted sample estimate.

$$\beta_{t+1} = \hat{\beta}_t$$

Modified Sample Estimates

There may be a systematic relationship between the value for beta, as computed in a given period, and its value in the next. If this is true, you may want to take the relationship into account in your estimate of beta in the future period.[5] To do this, of course, you must first estimate the relationship between beta factors for stocks in successive periods of time. We can do this, in the context of the time frame of Figure 6.17, by taking sample estimates of the betas for our stocks in the 12 months of year $t - 1$ and relating them to the sample estimates in year t. The relationship might look like that of Figure 6.18.

Each observation point in the figure represents one of the stocks in the sample. For example, the stock at point A has a beta of .60 in period $t - 1$ and .90 in

[5]See Blume (1971) for an early example of estimating such a relationship.

OUT ON THE STREET

A "DEFENSIVE" STRATEGY

Michelle Clayman was talking on the phone to one of Salomon Brothers' many institutional clients. In her association with Salomon Brothers, Michelle was a vice president in the stock research department. She worked in an area called Strategy System, which was a quantitative research group consisting of five people.

Michelle's office was on the fortieth floor of a building located at the southernmost tip of Manhattan. The view from her office was spectacular, overlooking Governor's Island and the Statue of Liberty. Michelle spent much of her time talking to the many investors across the country who manage literally billions of dollars with the aid of quantitative models developed by the Strategy Systems group.

This morning she was discussing the "fundamental factor model" with a client on the West Coast. The model worked in the context of the multifactor process that generates returns in the multi-index model.

The model broke the systematic risk of a stock into components deriving from five basic factors. The five factors included unexpected changes in

1. The rate of growth in real gross national product.
2. The rate of inflation.
3. The real rate of interest.
4. The rate of change in real oil prices.
5. The rate of growth in real defense spending.

Salomon Brothers had an interesting and unique method of determining the responsiveness of stocks to these factors. Rather than estimate the factor betas through factor analysis or time series regression, they employed a type of sensitivity analysis. The sensitivity analysis was based on a sophisticated input-output model of the U.S. economy. Given inputs relating to housing starts or retail automobile sales, for example, the input-output model was capable of estimating intermediate demands for such products as plastics, glass, aluminum, and steel. In fact, given what is called a *base case forecast* for the general economy provided by Salomon Brothers' economists, the input-output model could provide disaggregated forecasts for different sectors of the economy over the next five years. Based on the model, estimates were obtained of the impact of various macroeconomic changes on accounting statements at the individual firm level.

The factor betas were estimated as the product of two elasticities. The first measured the expected change in the rate of growth in earnings per share accom-

period t. If, for every stock, the sample estimate of beta was the same in each period, then every observation would fall on the broken, 45-degree line. Because the observations are scattered, we know we obtain different sample estimates of beta as we go from one period to the next. To obtain an estimate of the relationship between

panying a given change in one of the factors. This elasticity was estimated through the input-output model by observing the estimated change in the earnings per share for a given firm accompanying a change in one of the factors. The second elasticity measured the expected change in the price accompanying a given change in the rate of growth in earnings per share. This second elasticity was estimated on the basis of the duration of the dividend stream for the stock. Duration will be discussed in more detail later in the book. You can think of it as a measure of the average period of time before the dividends in the stream are expected to be paid. Under certain assumptions, duration also serves as a measure of the expected response of the stock price to changes in either the rate at which dividends are capitalized to a present value or the rate at which they are expected to grow.

When the two elasticities (response of earnings growth to the factor and response of the stock price to the change in earnings growth) are multiplied together, the product can be taken as the factor beta, depicting the expected change in the stock price accompanying a change in the factor.

Salomon Brothers had back-tested the model and had found that in periods where there were large, unanticipated changes in the factors, relative rates of return on individual stocks could be successfully predicted on the basis of the estimated factor betas.

Salomon Brothers used the fundamental factor model for two types of applications. First, the model was useful for the managers of index funds. These managers tried to build a portfolio that mimics, as closely as possible, the performance of a stock index, such as the Standard & Poor's 500. In using the model, the first step was to estimate the factor betas for the component stocks in the 500 and then set up an indexed portfolio that had a factor beta structure that was as close as possible to that of the 500. In this way the indexed portfolio would mimic the responses of the 500 to changes in the factors that occurred over time.

Second, the model could be used to position clients to best take advantage of their forecasts for changes in the macroeconomic climate. Suppose, for example, a portfolio manager is predicting a sharp increase in gross national product. The model can isolate those stocks which can be expected to show the greatest price appreciation should the prediction regarding the growth in GNP materialize. At this moment, Michelle was using the model in this very way to advise her client on the strategy to take which was to provide optimal advantage of a forecast of a rapid increase in defense spending.

beta values in successive periods, we slide a line of best fit through the observations. Because the line can be described by its slope and its intercept, we have

$$\hat{\beta}_t = a_0 + a_1\hat{\beta}_{t-1}$$

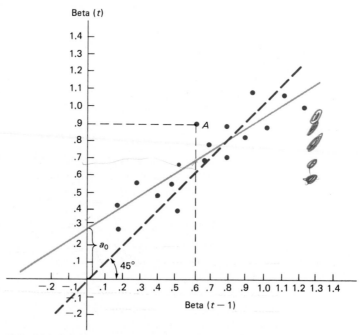

FIGURE 6.18 Relationship between betas for different stocks in successive periods.

If we assume the relationship between betas in successive periods remains constant over time, we can use the coefficients a_0 and a_1 to modify our sample estimate of beta in period t to obtain an estimate of its population value in period $t + 1$.

$$\beta_{t+1} = a_0 + a_1\hat{\beta}_t$$

For example, in Figure 6.18, $a_0 = .25$ and $a_1 = .75$; so if our sample estimate for the beta of a stock were 1.50 in period t, we would estimate its population value to be 1.38 for the next period.

$$1.38 = .25 + .75 \times 1.50$$

Employing Firm Characteristics to Estimate Population Values

In the two methods just described, we used only the past series of rates of return on the stock to estimate its beta. Presumably, however, the beta factor and residual variance of a stock are fundamentally determined by the characteristics of the company behind the stock. Given this, we should take these characteristics into consideration in estimating the population values. Before we can do this, however, we need to estimate the relationship between different company characteristics and the values for beta and residual variance.

To illustrate the procedure, suppose we feel the size of a company is an important determinant of the risk of the company. We want to include this consideration in estimating the beta factors for our stocks. To do this, we estimate the relationship between the size of each company at the end of period $t - 1$ and the sample estimate of beta in period t, much in the same way as we estimated the relationship between the betas in successive periods. We can, in fact, estimate the relationship for both variables (company size and beta in the previous period) at the same time. Rather than slide a line through a scatter of observations in two dimensions ($\hat{\beta}_t$ and $\hat{\beta}_{t-1}$) as we did before, we now slide a plane through a scatter of points in three dimensions ($\hat{\beta}_t$, $\hat{\beta}_{t-1}$, and SIZE). The equation for the plane is given by

$$\hat{\beta}_t = a_0 + a_1\hat{\beta}_{t-1} + a_2 \text{ SIZE}_{t-1}$$

As before, if we assume this relationship remains constant over time, we can estimate the population value for beta in the next period through the following equation:

$$\beta_{t+1} = a_0 + a_1\hat{\beta}_t + a_2 \text{ SIZE}_t$$

Size isn't, of course, the only company characteristic that may have an effect on stock risk. Stability of earnings, financial leverage, and the liquidity position of the company are only a few of the many variables we may wish to take into account in making our estimates. Thus, the size of the final equation may become very large. Commercial services are available that estimate beta factors for stocks in nearly this same way. These services employ a wide variety of firm characteristics in their beta estimates.

Although the equation is used to estimate the beta factor for a given stock, nearly identical procedures can be employed to estimate residual variances.[6]

SUMMARY

The Markowitz and index models are both used in constructing the minimum variance set. The difference between the two methods is the formulas used in each to determine the variance of a portfolio. The formula used by Markowitz is perfectly accurate; the formulas used by the index models are approximations that are as accurate as is their assumption that the residuals for different stocks are perfectly uncorrelated with each other.

The Markowitz model makes no assumptions regarding the source of the covariances between stocks in the covariance matrix. They could be due to any number or kind of interrelationships that exist between the stocks. The index models, however, assume that all the covariances can be accounted for by the relative responses of each stock to common forces, such as the movement in the market itself. If this is true, then the residuals, or deviations from the characteristic lines, will indeed be uncorrelated with each other.

In using the Markowitz model to find the efficient set, you provide the computer with estimates of the covariances among all of the stocks in the population from which you want to choose. If this population is large, you have an extremely large number of covariances to estimate, and a large amount of computation time is

---

[6]This procedure to estimate fundamental beta and residual variance estimates was originally developed by Barr Rosenberg (1974).

required to compute the variance of any given portfolio. This is the problem with the Markowitz model.

If you are trying to find the minimum variance set using the single-index model, you provide the computer with the model's alternative formula for portfolio variance. You also supply it with estimates of the beta factor for each stock, the residual variance for each stock, and the variance of the market portfolio. With a large population of stocks from which to choose, the number of required estimates has been greatly reduced, and the time required to compute the variance has been similarly reduced. It must be recognized, however, that the minimum variance set you obtain is not likely to be the *true* minimum variance set. Unless the residuals are truly uncorrelated, if you recomputed the variance of your portfolios using the *correct* formula as given by the Markowitz model, you would find that these portfolios lie inside the true bullet, as found with the Markowitz model.

Empirical evidence seems to indicate that the covariances between the residuals for different companies are predominantly positive. This means the residual variance of a portfolio is likely to be larger than one might predict it to be on the basis of the equation of the single-index model. This appears to be especially true for portfolios having unusually low or high beta factors.

If correlation between the residuals is a problem, you can attempt to overcome it by using multi-index models. The single-index model assumes the correlations between the rates of return on different stocks can all be accounted for by the fact that all stocks respond to some degree to variability in the returns to the single index. Multi-index models bring in additional factors to account for the correlations. The covariances that may exist between the residuals in the single-index model can presumably be accounted for by the presence of these other factors. Once these factors are accounted for, in the context of a multi-index model, the remaining residuals may be uncorrelated. In any case, the problem of residual correlation hasn't been sufficiently severe to prevent the use of the single-index model by practicing portfolio analysts.

In estimating the inputs for index models, you can simply use sample estimates, or you can employ more sophisticated procedures that take into account the relationship between beta and residual variance and the fundamental characteristics of the company behind the stock.

QUESTION SET 1

1. What assumption serves as the foundation of the single-index model?
2. Given the following information and the assumption of the single-index model, what is the covariance between stocks 1 and 2?

$$\beta_1 = .85$$

$$\beta_2 = 1.30$$

variance of the market index $= .09$

3. Assume the following:

	Residual Variance	
Stock X	.02	$\text{Cov}(\epsilon_X, \epsilon_Y) = .01$
Stock Y	.06	

   Also assume that a portfolio of X and Y is constructed, with a 2/3 weight for X and a 1/3 weight for Y.
   a. What is the residual variance of the portfolio if the single-index model is assumed?
   b. What is the residual variance of the portfolio without the single-index model assumption?

4. Suppose you had estimated the following relationship for firm J's return as a function of the return on a market index.

$$r_J = .03 + 1.3 \, r_M + \epsilon_J$$

   a. If the return on the market index should fall by two percentage points, what is the expected change in firm J's return?
   b. What is the name given to the graphic representation of the preceding equation?
   c. What might account for J's *actual* return being different from that expected on the basis of the first two terms of the equation?

Refer to the following data for Questions 5 through 8.

Security	Beta	Residual Variance	σ_r^2
A	.5	.04	.0625
B	1.5	.08	.2825

   Suppose an equally weighted portfolio of A and B is formed.
5. What is the beta coefficient for the portfolio?
6. Compute the residual variance of the portfolio assuming the single-index model.
7. Compute the variance of the portfolio assuming the single-index model.
8. Fill in the missing columns in the following table. Assume the variance of the market index (M) to be .0016.

Security i	Variance of i	Correlation of i with M	Beta	Systematic Risk	Unsystematic Risk
$i = 1$	.006	.9			
$i = 2$	.006	.3			
$i = 3$	.006	0			

9. What is the meaning of "unsystematic risk"?

Refer to the following data for Questions 10 through 15.

Correlation coefficient between stocks A and B = .50

Standard deviation of the market index (M) = .10

	Correlation of Stock with M	Standard Deviation
Stock A	0	.10
Stock B	.5	.20

10. What are the beta values for A and B?

11. What is the covariance between A and B, assuming the single-index model?

12. What is the true covariance between A and B?

13. Suppose a portfolio was constructed, with weights of .40 for A and .60 for B. What is the beta of this portfolio?

14. Compute the variance of the portfolio in Question 13, assuming the Markowitz model.

15. Compute the variance of the portfolio in Question 13, assuming the single-index model.

16. What is an index model (either a single index or multi-index) supposed to accomplish? What is the potential advantage of the multi-index approach, in comparison with the single-index model?

17. What kind of systematic relationship between market betas and residual variance of well-diversified portfolios was discovered in the work of Black, Jensen, and Scholes?

18. Suppose you employed a two-index model to estimate the following relationship for the percentage return on stock K

$$r_K = .5 + .8\, r_M + .2\, g + \epsilon_K$$

where r_M represents the percentage return on the market index and g represents the unexpected growth rate of industrial production.

a. If the market index's return is 5 percent and the unexpected growth of industrial production is 2 percent, what return would you expect for stock K?

b. What kind of *change* in stock K's return would you expect if there were to be no change in g and a two-percentage-point decrease in r_M?

19. Write the formula for the variance of a portfolio, assuming that a two-factor model has been used to explain returns and that the covariance between the factors is zero. Also, write the *general* expression for the portfolio's residual variance. If the two-factor model is really appropriate to account for the interrelationships among returns on individual stocks, what simplification occurs in the general expression for the portfolio's residual variance?

20. Compute the variance of stock X using the expression derived from the two-index model and the following information. The two factors consist of the return on a market index and an index of unexpected growth in industrial production.

Stock X's market beta = .75

Stock X's growth beta = .40

Growth index variance = .10

Market index variance = .08

Stock X's residual variance = .03

Refer to the following data for Questions 21 through 25. A two-factor model is being employed, one being a market index (M) and the other being an index of unexpected changes in the growth of industrial production (g).

	Market Beta	Growth Beta	Residual Variance
Stock 1	.6	.2	.05
Stock 2	.9	.1	.02

$$\text{Variance of the market index} = .12$$

$$\text{Variance of the growth index} = .10$$

$$\text{Covariance between residuals of stocks 1 and 2} = .02$$

$$\text{Covariance between } M \text{ and } g = 0$$

21. Compute the variance of stock 1.

22. Assume you had constructed an equally weighted portfolio of stocks 1 and 2. Compute the residual variance of this portfolio in two ways:
    a. Making the simplifying assumption of the two-index model about residual covariance.
    b. Without making the simplifying assumption about residual covariance.

23. Compute the market beta and the growth beta for an equally weighted portfolio of stocks 1 and 2.

24. For an equally weighted portfolio of stocks 1 and 2, compute the variance of the portfolio in two ways:
    a. Making the simplifying assumption of the two-index model about residual covariance.
    b. Without making the simplifying assumption about residual covariance.

25. Why would you want to compute portfolio variance by a single- or multi-index model rather than by the Markowitz model?

26. Discuss how we would arrive at an estimated beta value for a stock based on historical information. Further, try to speculate on potential difficulties in using historical information to estimate beta.

27. For a given stock, you have estimated the following time series relationship for market betas
$$\beta_t = .20 + .85\, \beta_{t-1}$$
where t indicates the year of interest.
    a. If you relied on this relationship for prediction purposes, and the beta in 1987 was 1.2, what would your predicted beta be for 1988?
    b. What are you implicitly assuming in using this relationship for predictive purposes?

28. Question 27 discussed a relationship between betas at different points in time. What other variables might be used in an attempt to predict future beta values for a stock?

QUESTION SET 2

1. How are the Markowitz and single-index models used in portfolio selection?

2. If you had a portfolio of 20 stocks from which to choose, which model should you employ in determining the relative weights of the stocks in the portfolio and why?

3. A new law in Brazil makes the construction and operation of steel factories a real bargain; however, the steel may only be used in the construction of South American automobiles, which rapidly become popular in the United States. If you were managing a portfolio which had three classes of securities—drugs, services, and machinery manufacturing—and used the single-index model, would you expect the systematic or unsystematic variance to be affected by this event?

4. Under the single-index model the relationship between returns to the market and returns to a security on a portfolio is expressed by the equation

$$r_i = A + \beta r_{M,i} + \epsilon_i$$

a. What is the name given this regression line?

b. Define each term in the equation.

c. What type of event is assumed to cause period-to-period movement along this line? What term in the equation accounts for this variability?

d. What type of event produces deviations from this line? Explain. What term in the equation accounts for this variability?

5. What is the single-index model's key assumption and what does it imply about the residual returns to securities in a portfolio?

6. Suppose you are managing a portfolio consisting entirely of aerospace stocks. Is the single-index model likely to accurately estimate the portfolio's residual variance? Explain.

7. If, in a portfolio of stocks, those of a given industry respond in a similar manner to an industrywide event, what is true of the SIM estimate of the portfolio's residual variance?

8. Suppose the stock of two highly competitive companies is held in a portfolio. Would the SIM over- or underestimate this portfolio's residual variance?

ANSWERS TO QUESTION SET 2

1. In general, the Markowitz model is used for asset allocation between the classes of securities and the single-index model for portfolio optimization within a class of securities (usually common stocks).

   First, the more general Markowitz model is used to choose classes of assets that will be included in the portfolio and determine the fraction each hold in the portfolio.

   Second the single-index model is used to select, within each class of assets, individual securities and determine the investment in each that will optimize the portfolio.

2. The Markowitz model, because the population is small enough and the assumptions of the single-index model do not need to be dealt with.

3. The systematic risk would be affected, since not only would the developments affect the automobile manufacturers, but also their suppliers of parts and the steel industry.

4. a. The regression line expressed by the equation

$$r_i = A + \beta r_{M,i} + \epsilon_i$$

   is called the *characteristic line*.

   b. r_i = rate of return to a security (or portfolio) in period i.

   A = point at which the characteristic line intercepts dependent (r_i) axis. This point represents the expected rate of return to the security (or portfolio) if the market rate of return in the period is zero.

β = beta is the slope of the characteristic line, measuring the extent that returns to a security (or portfolio) change in response to changes in rate of return to the market.

$r_{M,i}$ = rate of return to the market in period i.

ϵ_i = residual; the extent the actual return to the security (or portfolio) in period i differs from the expected rate of return.

c. *Macro events,* which affect the rate of return to the market, are assumed to be the cause of movement along the characteristic line. The term $\beta r_{M,i}$ accounts for this variation.

d. Vertical deviations from the characteristic line are caused by *micro events*. Company-specific factors which cause the rates of return of individual securities to differ from the expected rate of return during a given period, i. The term ϵ_i accounts for this residual variance.

5. The single-index model assumes that the returns to individual securities are correlated for one reason only: each security is assumed to respond, in varying degrees, to the pull of the market. In the model, the degree of response is expressed as the security's beta factor. The implication of this assumption is that the residual returns of individual securities are uncorrelated.

$$\text{Cov}(\epsilon_J, \epsilon_K) = 0$$

That is to say, the cause of the covariance among individual securities is due solely to the common influence of macro events in the economy. Residual returns are the result of firm-specific microevents.

6. Industry events, such as an industrywide rise in labor costs, could affect all the stocks in the portfolio but not have an appreciable effect on the market. Because of this, the covariance between the residuals of the stocks may be nonzero. The single-index model, however, ignores the covariance of residuals among individual stocks and consequently will misestimate both the residual variance and total variance of the portfolio.

7. When returns to two stocks of a given industry change in the same direction in response to an event that affects the entire industry but not the general economy, the covariance between the residuals of firms in the industry is likely to be nonzero.

Since the SIM ignores any covariance between the residuals for different stocks, it does not take this covariance into account, and consequently it overestimates the portfolio residual variance and total variance.

8. When two companies are highly competitive, what is gained by one is usually lost to the other. Thus the covariance between their returns is likely to be negative. The SIM ignores this negative covariance between stocks and thus overestimates the portfolio residual variance.

PROBLEM SET

1. Given the following information and the assumption of the single-index model, what is the beta factor of stock 1?

$$\beta_2 = 1.20$$

$$\sigma(r_M) = .3162$$

$$\text{Cov}(r_1, r_2) = .09$$

Refer to the following table for Problems 2 through 7.

Stocks	Portfolio Weight	Beta	Expected Return	$\sigma^2(r)$
A	.25	.50	.40	.07
B	.25	.50	.25	.05
C	.50	1.00	.21	.07

$$\sigma^2(r_M) = .06$$

2. Given the assumption of the single-index model, what is the residual variance of each of the above stocks?

3. What is the beta factor of the three-stock portfolio?

4. What is the variance of the portfolio?

5. What is the expected return on the portfolio?

6. Given the actual (Markowitz) covariance between the stocks' returns, what is the actual portfolio variance?

$$\text{Cov}(r_A, r_B) = .020$$

$$\text{Cov}(r_A, r_C) = .035$$

$$\text{Cov}(r_B, r_C) = .035$$

7. Why might the actual covariance differ from those found using the single-index model formula?

ANSWERS TO PROBLEM SET

1. Given the assumption of the single-index model, we can write the covariance between any two stocks as

$$\text{Cov}(r_1, r_2) = \beta_1 \beta_2 \sigma^2(r_M)$$

By rearranging the terms, we can solve for

$$\beta_1 = \frac{\text{Cov}(r_1, r_2)}{\beta_2 \sigma^2(r_M)}$$

$$= \frac{.09}{1.20(.3162)}$$

2. We know

$$\sigma^2(r) = \beta^2 \sigma^2(r_M) + \sigma^2(\epsilon)$$

or

$$\sigma^2(\epsilon) = \sigma^2(r) - \beta^2 \sigma^2(r_M)$$

Plugging in the known variables on the right-hand side of the equation, we find

$$\sigma^2(\epsilon_A) = \sigma^2(r_A) - \beta_A^2 \sigma^2(r_M) = .07 - (.50)^2(.06) = .055$$

$$\sigma^2(\epsilon_B) = \sigma^2(r_B) - \beta_B^2 \sigma^2(r_M) = .05 - (.50)^2(.06) = .035$$

$$\sigma^2(\epsilon_C) = \sigma^2(r_C) - \beta_C^2 \sigma^2(r_M) = .07 - (1.0)^2(.06) = .010$$

3. The beta factor for the portfolio is simply the weighted average beta of the three stocks. From the text we know

$$\beta_P = \sum_{J=1}^{M} x_J \beta_J$$

Therefore,

$$\beta_P = x_A \beta_A + x_B \beta_B + x_C \beta_C$$
$$= (.25)(.50) + (.25)(.50) + (.50)(1.00) = .75$$

4. The variance of the portfolio can be split into two components, systematic risk and residual variance.

$$\sigma^2(r_P) = \beta_P^2 \sigma^2(r_M) + \sigma^2(\epsilon_P)$$

From Problem 3, we know the beta of the stock portfolio is .75. Knowing this and the variance of the market, we can find the portfolio's systematic risk.

$$\text{Systematic risk} = \beta_P^2 \sigma^2(r_M) = (.75)^2(.06) = .0338$$

The portfolio residual variance under the single-index model is the weighted sum of the elements on the diagonal in the covariance matrix.

$$\text{Residual variance} = \sigma^2(\epsilon_P) = \sum_{J=1}^{M} x_J^2 \sigma^2(\epsilon_J)$$

Note that the weights used are the square of the portfolio weights.

Using the residual variances computed in Problem 2, we can find the residual variance of the three-stock portfolio:

$$\sigma^2(\epsilon_P) = x_A^2 \sigma^2(\epsilon_A) + x_B^2 \sigma^2(\epsilon_B) + x_C^2 \sigma^2(\epsilon_C)$$
$$= (.25)^2(.055) + (.25)^2(.035) + (.50)^2(.010)$$
$$= .0081$$

With this information, we can now find the variance of the portfolio.

$$\sigma^2(r_P) = \beta_P^2 \sigma^2(r_M) + \sigma^2(\epsilon_P) = .0338 + .0081 = .0419$$

5. The expected rate of return on the portfolio is a weighted average of the expected returns on each stock in the portfolio.

$$E(r_P) = x_A E(r_A) + x_B E(r_B) + x_C E(r_C)$$

$$= (.25)(.40) + (.25)(.25) + (.50)(.21)$$

$$= .2675 \text{ or } 26.75\%$$

6. The actual (Markowitz) portfolio variance includes the off-diagonal terms in the covariance matrix as well as the terms along the diagonal:

$$\sigma^2(r_P) = \sum_{J,K=1}^{M^2} x_J x_K \text{ Cov}(r_{J,K})$$

$$= x_A^2 \sigma^2(r_A) + x_B^2 \sigma^2(r_B) + x_C^2 \sigma^2(r_C)$$

$$+ 2x_A x_B \text{ Cov}(r_A, r_B) + 2x_A x_C \text{ Cov}(r_A, r_C)$$

$$+ 2x_B x_C \text{ Cov}(r_B, r_C)$$

$$= (.25)^2(.07) + (.25)^2(.05) + (.50)^2(.07)$$

$$+ 2(.25)(.25)(.020) + 2(.25)(.50)(.035) + 2(.25)(.50)(.035)$$

$$= .0450$$

7. The actual (Markowitz) portfolio variance can differ from the portfolio variance found using the single-index model if the single-index model does not account for all the covariance among the portfolio's stocks.

COMPUTER PROBLEM SET

1. The following table represents rates of return to four securities and an index of world wealth. Use the Markowitz program to construct the efficient set consisting of the four securities. Use the annual returns from 1974 to 1988 to estimate the model parameters. Print the table containing the estimated rate of return and standard deviation of the four securities as well as the tables for the 10 efficient portfolios. Draw a diagram of the efficient set in return/standard deviation space.

Annual Rates of Return (%)

Year	Index	1	2	3	4
1974	5.52	1.31	−18.14	−12.23	− 9.04
1975	14.62	15.81	17.86	37.19	27.33
1976	13.88	17.77	5.18	20.35	16.45
1977	2.10	−16.92	−30.09	−28.47	− 7.78
1978	2.31	−26.80	−37.61	−32.71	−23.34
1979	16.00	37.72	38.77	33.76	44.78
1980	10.01	26.26	28.25	29.20	− 7.56
1981	11.35	− 4.81	9.80	10.53	21.26
1982	15.95	7.39	16.95	15.81	25.51
1983	16.13	21.82	58.47	31.91	15.38
1984	20.94	32.70	30.61	37.38	14.53
1985	− 3.18	− 4.22	− 6.10	− 0.01	− 8.93
1986	11.96	20.72	4.93	21.87	5.74
1987	7.66	23.00	28.27	22.17	22.84
1988	5.17	6.88	− 5.45	− 9.31	1.67

2. Use the SIM program to construct the efficient set consisting of the same four securities as in Problem 1. Use the world market wealth portfolio as your index and the annual returns for the years 1970 to 1984 to estimate the model parameters. Print the table containing the annual returns to the index and four securities as well as tables containing the estimated model parameters and investment proportions of the 10 portfolios on the efficient set.

   Draw the SIM efficient set on the diagram you prepared for Problem 1 (plot the return against the true standard deviation). Compare the two curves and explain your findings.

3. Using the computer output from Problem 2, calculate the covariance between security 1 and the other three securities using the formula for covariance found in the Markowitz and SIM models.

4. Use the estimated model parameters in Problem 2 to calculate the single-index models assumed correlation coefficients for the four securities. Carry out your calculations to six decimal places. Load the Markowitz program into the computer and input the expected returns and the standard deviations of the four equities as well as the correlation coefficients you just estimated. Run the program and draw a graph of the efficient set and compare your results with the graph you prepared for Problem 2.

REFERENCES

BLACK, F., JENSEN, M. C., and SCHOLES, M. "The Capital Asset Pricing Model: Some Empirical Tests," in *Studies in Theory of Capital Markets,* ed. M. C. Jensen. New York: Praeger, 1972.

BLUME, M. E., "On the Assessment of Risk," *Journal of Finance* (March 1971).

BRENNER, M., and SMIDT, S., "Asset Characteristics and Systematic Risk," *Financial Management* (Winter 1978).

CHEN, S., "Beta Non-Stationarity, Portfolio Residual Risk and Diversification," *Journal of Financial and Quantitative Analysis* (March 1981).

COHEN, K., and POGUE, J., "An Empirical Evaluation of Alternative Portfolio Selection Models," *Journal of Business* (April 1967)

CORNELL, B., and DIETRICH, J. K., "Mean-Absolute-Deviation Versus Least-Squares Regression Estimation of Beta Coefficients," *Journal of Financial and Quantitative Analysis* (March 1978).

EUBANK, A. A., and ZUMWALT, J., "How to Determine the Stability of Beta Values," *Journal of Portfolio Management* (Winter 1979).

FAMA, E. F., "A Note on the Market Model and the Two Parameter Model," *Journal of Finance* (December 1973).

FRABOZZI, F. J., and FRANCIS, J. C., "Beta as a Random Coefficient," *Journal of Financial and Quantitative Analysis* (March 1978).

FRANKFURTER, G. M., "The Effect of 'Market Indices' on the Ex-Post Performance of the Sharpe Portfolio Selection Model," *Journal of Finance* (June 1976).

HILL, N. C., and STONE, B. K., "Accounting Betas, Systematic Operating Risk, and Financial Leverage: A Risk Composition Approach to the Determinants of Systematic Risk," *Journal of Financial and Quantitative Analysis* (September 1980).

KING, B. F., "Market and Industry Factors in Stock Price Behavior," *Journal of Business* (January 1966).

KLEMKOSKY, R. C., and MARTIN, J. D., "The Adjustment of Beta Forecasts," *Journal of Finance* (September 1975).

LINDAHL-STEVENS, M., "Some Popular Uses and Abuses of Beta," *Journal of Portfolio Management* (Winter 1978).

MCCLAY, M., "The Penalties of Incurring Unsystematic Risk," *Journal of Portfolio Management* (Spring 1978).

ROBICHEK, A. A., and COHN, R. A., "The Economic Determinants of Systematic Risk," *Journal of Finance* (May 1974).

ROENFELDT, R. L., GRIEPENTROF, G. L., and PFLAUM, C. C., "Further Evidence on the Stationarity of Beta Coefficients," *Journal of Financial and Quantitative Analysis* (March 1978).

ROSENBERG, B., "Extra-Market Components of Covariance Among Security Returns," *Journal of Financial and Quantitative Analysis* (March 1974).

ROSENBERG, B., and GUY, J., "Beta and Investment Fundamentals—II," *Financial Analysts Journal* (July–August 1976).

SCHOLES, M., and WILLIAMS, J., "Estimating Beta from Nonsynchronous Data," *Journal of Financial Economics* (December 1977).

SHARPE, W. F., "A Simplified Model of Portfolio Analysis," *Management Science* (January 1963).

THEOBALD, M., "Beta Stationarity and Estimation Period: Some Analytical Results," *Journal of Financial and Quantitative Analysis* (December 1981).

UMSTEAD, D. A., and BERGSTROM, G. L., "Dynamic Estimation of Portfolio Betas," *Journal of Financial and Quantitative Analysis* (September 1979).

WEINSTEIN, M., "The Systematic Risk of Corporate Bonds," *Journal of Financial and Quantitative Analysis* (September 1981).

C H A P T E R

7

THE CAPITAL ASSET PRICING MODEL

The previous three chapters were devoted to portfolio models or techniques with which you can find the portfolios in the efficient set. We shall now shift gears somewhat and talk about theories concerning the way assets are priced by the market. We are concerned now about the *structure* of asset prices. In particular we are asking about the pricing structure as it relates to risk. If two stocks differ with respect to their risk, how will they differ in terms of the price investors are willing to pay for them? How will they differ in terms of the rate of return investors expect to get from them?

In this chapter we will discuss the *capital asset pricing model.** This is a theory about the way assets are priced in relation to their risk. Essentially, the theory is based on the following premise: Suppose all investors employed Markowitz portfolio theory to find the portfolios in the efficient set, and then, based on their individual risk aversion, each of them invested in one of the portfolios in the efficient set. How then would we measure the relevant risk of an individual stock, and what then would be the relationship between risk and the returns investors expect and require from their investments?

*The capital asset pricing model was simultaneously and independently discovered by John Lintner (1965a), Jan Mossin (1966), and William Sharpe (1964).

THE ASSUMPTIONS OF THE CAPITAL ASSET PRICING MODEL

Assumption I: Investors Can Choose Between Portfolios on the Basis of Expected Return and Variance

In Figure 7.1 we have drawn the probability distributions for two portfolios. The distributions are obviously very different. Portfolio A has a higher expected value. It has a higher variance, and its distribution is skewed to the left instead of to the right. Assumption I states that if you had to choose between these two portfolios as an investment, the only things you would have to know about the portfolios are their expected returns and variances.

Investors *can* choose on the basis of expected return and variance if *either* of two conditions holds.[1]

The first condition is that the probability distributions for portfolio returns are all *normally distributed*. This means they all look something like the *bell-shaped* distribution of Figure 7.2. A **normal distribution** has only two relevant parameters, the expected value and the variance. If you tell me the expected value and the variance and that the distribution is normal, I know everything I need to know to accurately describe the distribution. A normal distribution is fully specified by its expected value and its variance. All normal distributions are identical in every respect other than their expected value and variance. They are all, for example, perfectly symmetric, having no skewedness in either direction. Thus, even if we had a preference for distributions that were skewed to the right, it would be immaterial, because none of the distributions would be skewed in either direction.

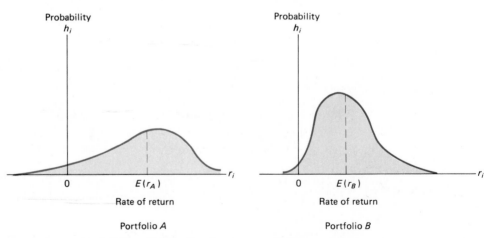

FIGURE 7.1 Probability distribution for two portfolios.

[1]This was first proven by Tobin (1958).

198

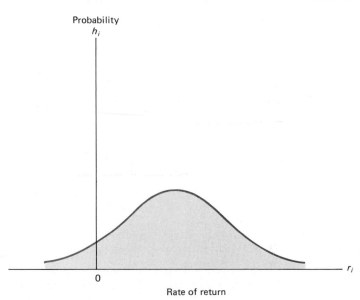

FIGURE 7.2 Normal probability distribution.

The assumption of normality isn't unreasonable in some cases. While the possible range for the return is truncated at the lower end (the lowest possible return is −100%, but there is no bound on the highest possible return), this is of no *practical* consequence if the time horizon is relatively short, say a month. Stocks rarely more than double in price or fall by more than 50% in such a short period of time. As a consequence, if you were to observe the monthly returns on a typical stock over a period of time where there was no change in the underlying variance of the series, the frequency distribution for the returns would not depart significantly from that of a normal distribution.[2]

For longer intervals, such as for yearly returns, the distribution of returns for individual stocks does tend to be skewed to the right. However, keep in mind the assumption relates to *portfolios* rather than individual stocks. Even if the distributions for individual stocks are not normal, when we combine many of these stocks into a well-diversified portfolio, we know, from the central limit theorem, that the distribution for the portfolio itself will be *approximately* normal.[3]

The second condition, which alllows you to choose between portfolios solely on the basis of expected return and variance, is that the relationship between your utility u and the value of your portfolio V is *quadratic* in form. If this is true, then

[2]See, for example, Hsu, Miller, and Wichern (1974). There is some evidence of the existence of skewedness however in the distribution of daily and weekly returns.

[3]This argument is weakened when one recognizes that the strong form of the central limit theorem requires that the objects being combined are uncorrelated. Security returns are, of course, correlated to some degree.

the utility associated with any ith value for your portfolio is given by the following equation:

$$u_i = a_0 + a_1 V_i + a_2 V_i^2 \tag{7.1}$$

In this equation, if the coefficient a_i were positive and a_2 were negative, the relationship between your utility and the value of your portfolio would look like the parabola of Figure 7.3. Utility increases as portfolio value increases, but it increases at a decreasing rate, finally reaching a maximum at V'.

In choosing between portfolios, you want to maximize your expected well-being or utility. The formula for expected utility is given by

$$E(u) = \sum_{i=1}^{n} h_i u_i \tag{7.2}$$

In the formula, h_i represents the probability of attaining the ith possible level of utility, which is associated with the ith possible portfolio value. Substituting Equation (7.1) into Equation (7.2), we get

$$E(u) = \sum_{i=1}^{n} h_i (a_0 + a_1 V_i + a_2 V_i^2)$$

By bringing the summation into the parentheses and factoring out constants from the sums, we get

$$E(u) = a_0 \sum_{i=1}^{n} h_i + a_1 \sum_{i=1}^{n} h_i V_i + a_2 \sum_{i=1}^{n} h_i V_i^2$$

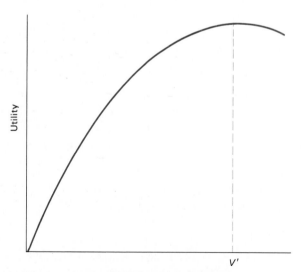

FIGURE 7.3 Quadratic utility function.

Recognizing the formulas for expected values and the fact that the probabilities sum to 1.00, we obtain

$$E(u) = a_0 + a_1 E(V) + a_2 E(V^2) \tag{7.3}$$

We shall now employ the following mathematical identity:

$$E(V^2) \equiv E(V)^2 + \sigma^2(V) \tag{7.4}$$

Substituting (7.4) into (7.3), we find that

$$E(u) = a_0 + a_1 E(V) + a_2 E(V)^2 + a_2 \sigma^2(V)$$

Thus, if you have a quadratic utility function, the utility you'd expect to get from investing in a portfolio is related only to the expected value and variance of the portfolio. Even if the probability distribution of ending portfolio values (and, therefore, of portfolio returns as well) is skewed left or right, it makes no difference to you. Given two portfolios with the same variance, you prefer the one with the higher expected rate of return. Since a_2 is assumed to be a negative number, given two portfolios with the same expected return, you prefer the one with the lower variance.

In fact, given that you have quadratic utility, we can plot points of indifference for you on an expected return, standard deviation graph similar to Figure 7.4. In the figure you are indifferent to portfolio A and portfolio B. While B has a higher level of standard deviation, it has just enough additional expected return to make you

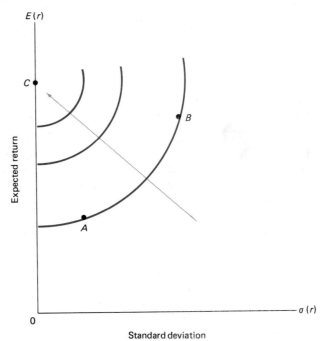

FIGURE 7.4 Indifference curves in $E(r)$, $\sigma(r)$ space.

indifferent between investing in it or portfolio *A*. In fact you would be indifferent toward investing in any portfolio that was positioned on the circle going through the two points. The circle is called an ***indifference curve***. Each indifference curve represents a given level of expected utility. As you move to the northwest on the graph, you are moving to more desirable positions. If your utility function is quadratic, your indifference curves will always be concentric circles surrounding a single point, C. The point denotes the rate of return required to bring the value of the portfolio to the position of maximum utility, as in V' in Figure 7.3.

Thus, we can justify making investment choices on the basis of expected return and variance if (1) we constrain the probability distributions for portfolio returns to be normal or (2) we constrain utility functions to be quadratic.

Actually the former constraint is preferable to the latter, because the quadratic utility function has some undesirable properties. In the first place, utility reaches a maximum at some wealth level and then actually declines. While it may be possible to be saturated with a single commodity such as bananas, you probably have never met anyone who was saturated with *money,* which can be turned into any number of different commodities. Second, with a quadratic utility function, as your wealth level increases, your propensity or willingness to take on risk decreases. You can see this by imagining that you are at wealth level V' in Figure 7.3. At this point your willingness to take on risk is zero, or your risk aversion is infinite. If you take on any gamble, you lose in terms of utility whether you win or lose the bet in terms of dollar return. Utility comes down whether wealth increases or decreases. This is contrary to what we observe in terms of human behavior. In general, rich people are more willing to take on risk than poor people. Consequently, it may be unrealistic to assume people have quadratic utility functions. If we're going to assume investment choices are made on the basis of expected return and variance, it's probably safer to base our assumption on normal probability distributions for portfolio returns.

Assumption II: All Investors Are in Agreement Regarding the Planning Horizon and the Distributions of Security Returns

We are going to assume all investors plan their investments over a single period of time that is the same for all. Furthermore, we all agree on the numbers required as inputs to our Markowitz portfolio models. We all agree on the expected rates of return for each stock. We all agree on the numbers in the covariance matrix for all the securities in the market. To some extent, this assumption is consistent with the assumption made below; information about securities flows freely throughout the capital market.

Assumption III: There Are No Frictions in the Capital Market

Frictions are defined as impediments to the free flow of capital and information throughout the market. Thus, we will assume that there are no transactions costs associated with buying or selling securities. We will also assume there are no taxes imposed on dividends, interest income, or capital gains. Moreover, we assume information flows freely to everyone in the marketplace, and there are no restrictions on short selling.

In general, these assumptions are made so that we can obtain a *definitive* picture of the relationship between *risk* and expected return in the market. We want to see the effect of risk on expected return. We don't want expected returns to be affected by the costs of transacting, and we don't want expected returns to be influenced by the degree to which the income from a security is exposed to taxes. Also, we don't want the picture to be clouded by market inefficiencies caused by impediments in the flow and processing of information. In the presence of these assumptions we will get a "clean" picture of the risk-return relationship.

Many of the assumptions of the capital asset pricing model are admittedly unrealistic. However, it should be stressed that the model can be derived without the need of making many of these assumptions. For example, the model has been derived in the presence of transactions costs, taxes, and differing beliefs regarding probability distributions.[4] In each case, the final form of the model is essentially similar to the form we obtain on the basis of the assumptions made here. We are making the assumptions, because the model is easier to derive on this basis.

THE CAPITAL ASSET PRICING MODEL WITH UNLIMITED BORROWING AND LENDING AT A RISK-FREE RATE

The Capital Market Line

We will derive the capital asset pricing model first by assuming that a risk-free bond exists. You can assume that it's a bond which matures at the end of the planning horizon and its payment is guaranteed by the government. Its rate of interest is equal to r_F. We will also assume all investors can buy or sell as much of the bond as they desire. If you sell the bond, you are free to use the proceeds to invest in other securities. This is consistent with our general assumption that investors are free to short-sell any security without restriction.

Consider first the portfolio opportunities available to investors. On the basis of assumption I, we can represent them in terms of their expected return and standard deviation. The points in Figure 7.5 represent individual securities. The solid curve represents the minimum variance set based on the population of securities. On the basis of assumption II, we know all investors see this same picture of portfolio opportunities. They all make their investment decisions based on the *same* minimum variance set.

If a risk-free asset didn't exist, investors would take positions at various points on the efficient set. The composition of each portfolio, held by each investor, would

---

[4]See Chen, Kim, and Kon (1975) for a derivation of the CAPM under transaction costs, Brennan (1973) for a derivation under personal income taxes, and Lintner (1970) for a derivation under heterogeneous expectations.

$$R = R_F + B_1(R_1 - E(RF)).$$

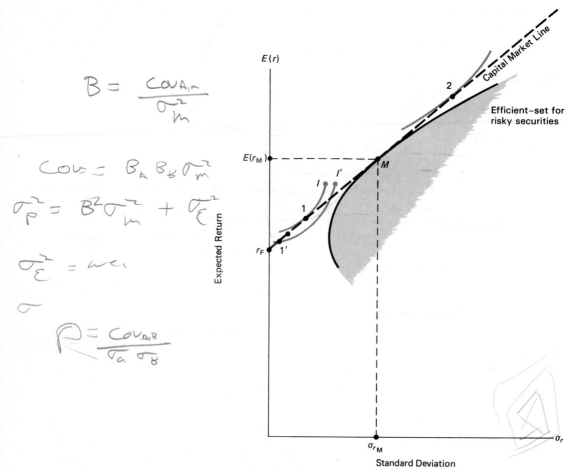

$$B = \frac{COV_{A,m}}{\sigma_m^2}$$

$$COV = B_A B_B \sigma_m^2$$

$$\sigma_P^2 = B^2 \sigma_m^2 + \sigma_E^2$$

$$\sigma_E^2 = wc_i$$

$$\sigma$$

$$P = \frac{COV_{A,B}}{\sigma_a \sigma_B}$$

FIGURE 7.5 Investor portfolio positions in the capital asset pricing model.

be different. If a risk-free bond exists, however, we know, on the basis of property AIII from Appendix 8, that it makes sense for everybody in the market to hold the same portfolio of risky assets. This portfolio is the one portfolio in the efficient set that has the highest value for the following ratio:

$$\frac{E(r_P) - r_F}{\sigma(r_P)}$$

In Figure 7.5, the portfolio with the highest value for this ratio is portfolio M. To find this portfolio, extend a straight line vertically from r_F and gradually tilt it to the right until it touches the bullet. The portfolio at the point where it touches the bullet is the best portfolio on the efficient set for everyone to hold regardless of their relative risk preferences. The efficient set now becomes the straight line extending from r_F through portfolio M. You can attain positions between r_F and M by investing some of your money in portfolio M and the rest of it in the risk-free bond. For these positions you are *buying* the risk-free bond. You can attain positions on the line beyond point M by selling the risk-free bond and using the proceeds of sale, in addition to your own funds, to buy portfolio M.

If you are highly risk averse, you will have indifference curves which look like I and I'. To maximize your utility, you want to attain a position on an indifference curve as far to the northwest as possible. You can do this if you take a position where the line between r_F and M is tangent to your indifference curve. This position is labeled point 1 on the graph. Notice that if you move away from point 1 in either direction along the line, you move to an indifference curve representing a lower amount of utility, such as with point $1'$.

If you have a lower degree of risk aversion, the point of tangency with the new linear efficient set may be one where you are selling the risk-free bond or *borrowing* to invest in portfolio M, as with point 2 in Figure 7.5.

In equilibrium, the prices for all assets must adjust so there is as much buying of the risk-free bond as there is selling. This means the risk-free rate and the shape of the bullet must adjust with respect to one another so the points of tangency between investors' indifference curves and the linear efficient set are distributed uniformly on both sides of point M. We know from property AI (Appendix 8) that when drawn in terms of standard deviation, the bullet is hyperbolic in shape, extending out to the northeast and southeast at equal angles relative to the horizontal. If investors in the market are, in general, highly risk averse, the angles will be large, as drawn in Figure 7.6. If investors are less risk averse on average, the angles will be smaller, as drawn in Figure 7.7. The greater the degree of risk aversion on the part of investors, the greater the differences between the expected rates of return on stocks of different risk in the market. In any case, prices will adjust until the market clears for all assets, including the risk-free asset.

In Figure 7.5, the straight line extending from r_F through portfolio M is called the ***capital market line***. All investors take portfolio positions on this line by borrowing or lending. However, regardless of our positions on the capital market line, all of us are investing in portfolio M. The ratio of the market value of stock X to stock Y in my portfolio is exactly the same as in yours. We are all holding the same portfolio of *risky* assets, portfolio M.

We know whenever we aggregate the portfolio holdings of everyone in the market, we get the market portfolio. Given this, since we are all holding the same portfolio of risky assets, the portfolio weights in this portfolio must be identical to those of the market portfolio. When you can buy or sell a risk-free asset, everyone in the market holds the same portfolio of risky assets, and that portfolio is the market portfolio.

Measuring the Risk of an Individual Asset

Since, as an investor, your ultimate concern is your final portfolio position, you will assess the risk of an individual security on the basis of its contribution to the variance of your portfolio. Since we are all holding the market portfolio, a security's risk can

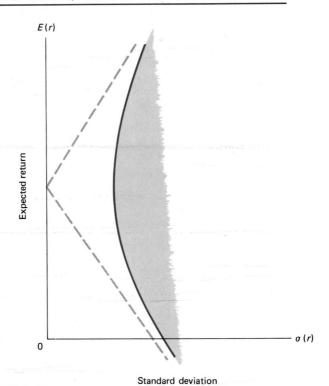

FIGURE 7.6 Minimum variance set with high risk aversion.

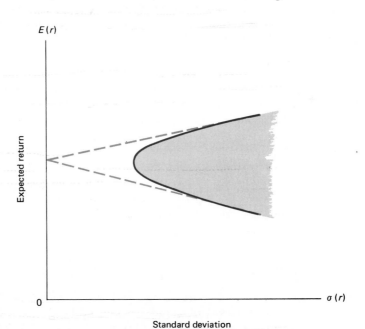

FIGURE 7.7 Minimum variance set with low risk aversion.

be measured on the basis of its contribution to the variance of the market. In Chapter 6 on index models, we showed, as a general case, that the beta of any portfolio with the market is a simple weighted average of the beta of the stocks in the portfolio with the market. This also holds for covariance.:

$$\text{Cov}(r_P, r_M) = \sum_{J=1}^{M} x_J \text{Cov}(r_J, r_M) \tag{7.5}$$

This equation holds for any market index, including your own portfolio P. Thus, we can write it as

$$\text{Cov}(r_P, r_P) = \sigma^2(r_P) = \sum_{J=1}^{M} x_J \text{Cov}(r_J, r_P) \tag{7.5a}$$

From Equation (7.5a) you can see that the contribution that a security J makes to your portfolio can be measured by the covariance of its returns with the returns on your portfolio. The variance, after all, is simply the weighted sum of these covariances. In this simple version of the CAPM, everyone is holding the same portfolio of risky securities, the market portfolio. Thus, we can replace P with M, obtaining

$$\text{Cov}(r_M, r_M) = \sigma^2(r_M) = \sum_{J=1}^{M} x_J \text{Cov}(r_J, r_M) \qquad \beta = \frac{}{\sigma^2} \tag{7.6}$$

This equation shows us that the contribution an individual stock makes to the variance of the market portfolio is measured by the covariance between the stock and the market. Since the beta factor of a stock is equal to this covariance divided by the market's variance, and since the market's variance is the same for all stocks, we can measure the risk of a stock by either its covariance with the market or by its beta. Since beta is more intuitively appealing, we shall use it as the measure of stock risk in the majority of cases.

     Thus, in the capital asset pricing model, the risk of an investor's portfolio is measured in terms of its variance and the risk of an individual stock in terms of its beta. Only a fraction of a stock's variance is of concern to a portfolio investor. If you will recall our discussion of the single-index model, the variance of any stock can be split into two parts, systematic risk $\beta_J^2 \sigma^2(r_M)$ and residual variance $\sigma^2(\epsilon_J)$. The part of the variance that concerns investors is systematic risk because only that part is contributed to the variance of the portfolio they all hold. Residual variance disappears under diversification. It is of no concern to investors, and under the capital asset pricing model it has no effect on the price of a stock or its expected rate of return.

The Relationship Between the Risk of an Asset and Its Expected Rate of Return

If beta is the appropriate measure of the risk of a stock, what is the relationship between beta and expected rate of return? Based on property II of the minimum variance set, discussed in Chapter 5, it is easy to answer this question. We know the market portfolio is positioned at point M in Figure 7.8 on the skin of the bullet. If the market portfolio is efficient, then a perfect linear relationship should exist between the beta factors for stocks and their expected rates of return. Given property II, the relationship can be found by drawing a line tangent to the bullet at M. The line of tangency is, in fact, the capital market line, and it intercepts the vertical axis at r_F. The line relating betas to expected rates of returns, therefore, will also intercept the vertical axis at r_F, as in Figure 7.9. Given that the market portfolio is on the efficient set, every security in the market must be positioned on this line.

The relationship of Figure 7.9 is called the ***security market line.*** The security market line is drawn in $E(r)$, β space, and it shows the relationship between a stock's risk and its expected rate of return.

While only the portfolios which are candidates for those to be held by investors are positioned on the capital market line [drawn in $E(r)$, $\sigma(r)$ space], all portfolios and individual securities are positioned on the security market line [drawn in $E(r)$, β space].

Since the security market line is linear, it can be expressed in terms of its intercept and its slope. The intercept of the line is, of course, the risk-free rate. The slope is the vertical distance required to return to the line, divided by the horizontal distance you have moved away from the line. In Figure 7.9, if we move horizontally from 0 to 1.00 in terms of beta, we must move vertically by a distance equal to $E(r_M) - r_F$ in order to return to the line. Thus, the slope is equal to $[E(r_M) - r_F]/1.00$, or $E(r_M) - r_F$. The equation for the security market line relating expected

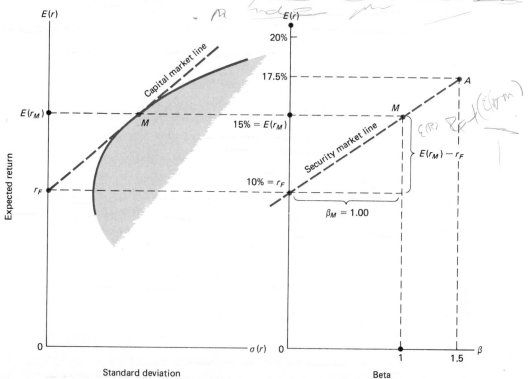

FIGURE 7.8 Capital market line.   FIGURE 7.9 Security market line.

return to beta, therefore, is given by

$$E(r_J) = r_F + [E(r_M) - r_F]\beta_J \tag{7.7}$$

The equation states that the expected rate of return on a stock is equal to the risk-free rate (compensating investors for delaying consumption over the planning horizon), plus a risk premium (compensating them for taking on the risk associated with the investment). The risk premium itself can be broken into two parts. The term in brackets, on the right-hand side of the equation, is the risk premium for the market portfolio. It can also be thought of as the risk premium for an average, or representative, security. To get the risk premium for security J, we multiply the risk premium for an average security by the other term, the risk measure for security J.

To see the logic of this, consider Equation (7.6). If we divide both sides of this equation by the variance of the market, we get

$$\frac{\sigma^2(r_M)}{\sigma^2(r_M)} = 1.00 = \sum_{J=1}^{M} x_J \frac{\text{Cov}(r_J, r_M)}{\sigma^2(r_M)} = \sum_{J=1}^{M} x_J\beta_J$$

Thus, the weighted average beta factor for all securities in the market is equal to 1. Given the equation for the security market line, if a security is of average risk, having a beta equal to 1, it will carry the average risk premium. If it is twice the average risk, it will carry twice the average risk premium.

In Figure 7.9, security A has a beta of 1.5. The risk-free rate is assumed to be 10 percent and the expected rate of return to the market portfolio is assumed to be 15 percent. Given this, the expected rate of return to security A is equal to

$$17.5\% = 10\% + (15\% - 10\%) \times 1.50$$

The Positioning of Characteristic Lines Under the Capital Asset Pricing Model

The relationship between expected return and beta as given by the security market line implies a particular alignment, relative to one another, of the characteristic lines of different stocks. Recall that the characteristic line describes the relationship between the returns on a stock and the returns on the market portfolio. The slope of the characteristic line is, of course, the beta factor. If we multiply each of the terms in brackets on the right-hand side of Equation (7.7) by β_J, collect terms involving r_F, and factor, we get

$$E(r_J) = r_F(1 - \beta_J) + \beta_J E(r_M)$$

This is the formula for the *expected* rate of return to the stock. The corresponding formula for the rate of return in any given period t is given by

$$r_{J,t} = \underbrace{r_F(1 - \beta_J)}_{A_J} + \beta_J r_{M,t} + \epsilon_{J,t}$$

This is the formula for the rate of return to the stock under the single-index model. Given that stocks are priced on the basis of the capital asset pricing model, the intercept term A_J for each stock will be given by $r_F(1 - \beta_J)$. It's important to keep

OUT ON THE STREET

HUNTING FOR BARGAINS

Jeff Diermier sits at his desk on the ninth floor of the First National Plaza in downtown Chicago. Jeff is a managing director at First Chicago Investment Advisors, which is a division of First National Bank of Chicago's holding company.

Jeff is carefully studying some computer output in which the market prices of various stocks are compared with estimates of their intrinsic values. Jeff is looking for "bargain" stocks with market prices considerably below the computer's estimate of intrinsic value.

The intrinsic value estimate is based on the discounted value of a stream of future dividends. Dividends are projected to grow at three distinct rates in three distinct future periods. The projected future dividends are then discounted to a present value, using a discount rate that reflects the risk of each individual stock.

First Chicago uses the capital asset pricing model to determine the proper discount rate for each stock.

To estimate the discount rate, Jeff uses the equation for the security market line. He employs the current yield to maturity on long-term government bonds as an estimate of the risk-free rate. The bank subscribes to a service that provides them with estimates of beta factors on a wide variety of different stocks. This service estimates betas on the basis of past-stock returns as well as a large number of other company characteristics such as earnings volatility and financial leverage, in the manner described in Chapter 6.

The remaining estimate required for the security market line equation is the expected rate of return to the common stock market portfolio. The estimate for the common stock market portfolio evolves from a more comprehensive index made up of several different types of investments. Included are common stocks, real estate, treasury bills and other government bonds, corporate bonds, and even venture capital. Their proxy is a value weighted portfolio of all these investments.

To estimate the expected rate of return on this portfolio, Jeff employs the following equation:

$$E(\hat{r}_M) = d + [E(g) - E(n)] + E(f)$$

in mind at this point, however, that while the preceding equation takes the form of the single-index model, the CAPM doesn't make the single-index model's assumption regarding the independence of the residuals (ϵ) across different companies. *These residuals could well be correlated in the CAPM*.

Suppose the risk-free rate is 10 percent, and stock A has a beta of 2.00. Its intercept will be equal to -10 percent, and its characteristic line will be positioned as in Figure 7.10. Stock B, with a beta of .50, will have an intercept of 5 percent, and stock C, with a beta of .00, will have an intercept of 10 percent. The characteristic lines of all the stocks intercept at a common point, with coordinates r_F, r_F. The fact that the characteristic lines intercept at a common point follows from the fact

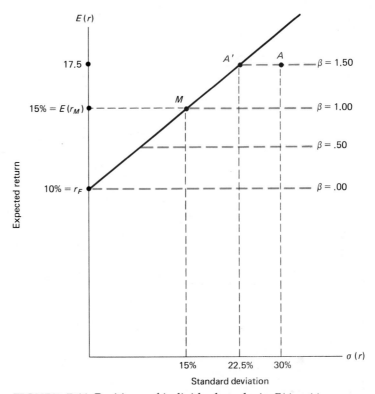

FIGURE 7.11 Positions of individual stocks in $E(r)$, $\sigma(r)$ space.

7.11 labeled $\beta = 1.50$ toward point A'. A stock positioned at point A' has a standard deviation of 22.5 percent and a variance of .0506. Given that it has a beta of 1.50, it must have a residual variance of 0:

$$.0506 = 1.50^2 \times .0225 + .00$$

Since its residual variance is 0, it must be perfectly correlated with the market portfolio. This, in fact, is the required condition for a security to be positioned on the capital market line. If a security has any residual variance at all, it must be positioned to the right of the capital market line. The more residual variance it has, the farther to the right is its position.

Thus, there is a series of horizontal isobeta lines, each representing a given level of beta. Any security, for example, with a beta of .50 must be positioned on the line labeled $\beta = .50$. The greater the level of residual variance for the security, the farther to the right on the line it is positioned.

We can also position securities in $E(r)$, $\sigma(r)$ space on the basis of their correlation coefficient with the market portfolio. We start with the equation for the security market line:

$$E(r_J) = r_F + [E(r_M) - r_F]\beta_J$$

We know that $\beta_J = \text{Cov}(r_J, r_M)/\sigma^2(r_M)$, so by substitution,

$$E(r_J) = r_F + \frac{E(r_M) - r_F}{\sigma^2(r_M)} \text{Cov}(r_J, r_M)$$

We also know that $\text{Cov}(r_J, r_M) = \rho_{J,M}\,\sigma(r_J)\,\sigma(r_M)$, so by substitution and cancellation,

$$E(r_J) = r_F + \left[\frac{E(r_M) - r_F}{\sigma(r_M)} \rho_{J,M} \right] \sigma(r_J)$$

This equation shows the relationship between expected return and standard deviation for stocks having identical values for their correlation coefficient. The relationship is linear with an intercept equal to r_F and a slope equal to the term in brackets.

To illustrate, consider Figure 7.12. Suppose, first, we were considering a group of stocks that were all perfectly correlated with the market portfolio. In this case, $\rho_{J,M} = 1.00$ and the term in brackets would be equal to the slope of the capital market line. The relationship between $E(r_J)$ and $\sigma(r_J)$ for these stocks would then be given by the capital market line.

Now suppose we are dealing with stocks all of which have a correlation with the market of .50. The slope of the relationship between $E(r_J)$ and $\sigma(r_J)$ for these stocks is half that of the capital market line. All stocks with a correlation coefficient equal to .50 are positioned somewhere on the line labeled $\rho = .50$. Their exact positions on the line are determined by their standard deviations.

Note that stocks which are negatively correlated with the market sell at expected rates of return that are below the risk-free rate. Their expected rates of return conceivably could even be negative. You might find it hard to believe anyone would be willing to invest in a security that had a negative expected rate of return. However, you might be surprised to know that you probably regularly invest in a security of sorts which has an expected rate of return as low as -50 percent! It's your automobile insurance. In some cases, for every dollar you pay the insurance company, you can *expect* to get back 50 cents in benefits. The remainder goes to pay company expenses and underwriting profits. Why do you engage in such a transaction? Because it reduces the risk of your overall portfolio of assets. The returns on your insurance policy are negatively correlated with the value of at least one of the other assets in your portfolio, your car.

As you drive down the road, your car is worth a lot, and your policy pays off nothing. Drive off the road and into a tree, and your car is now worth little, but your insurance policy pays off a lot.

Investors are willing to invest in stocks that are negatively correlated with other stocks at low expected returns for the same reason. Because they are negatively correlated, they reduce the overall risk level of their portfolios. This is the central message of the capital asset pricing model. In assessing risk, to price stocks, investors consider more than the expected return and variance of the individual stock itself. They also consider the *interrelationships* that exist between the returns on different stocks.

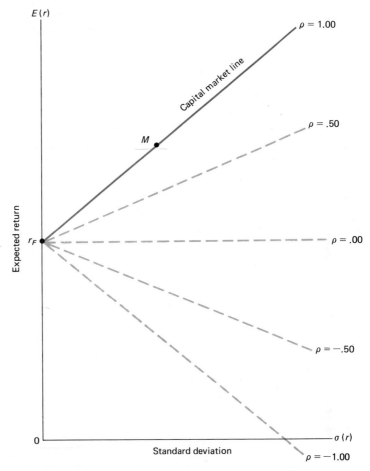

FIGURE 7.12 Positioning of stocks according to their correlation coefficients.

Market Pressure to Assume Equilibrium Prices

As we can see from the discussion above, each stock has a precise equilibrium position in $E(r)$, $\sigma(r)$ space. If a stock assumes its equilibrium position, there will be no buying or selling pressure in the market to force the price of the stock up or down. If, however, the stock is somehow incorrectly priced, in the sense that its expected return is too high or too low, given its covariance with the market portfolio, buying or selling pressure will immediately force the price back to its equilibrium level.

The relationship between the market price of a stock and its expected rate of return can be written as follows:

$$E(r) = \frac{E(\text{dividend} + \text{ending market price})}{\text{beginning market price}} - 1$$

In the capital asset pricing model, we take the numerator of the fraction on the right-hand side of the equation as given. We have a market expectation regarding the income (dividends and ending stock value) to be produced by the stock. The risk associated with the stock is also taken as given. Based on the expected income and the risk, the market sets a current price for the stock, and through the price it sets the expected rate of return. As the beginning market price goes up, the expected rate of return goes down.

Now consider the stock positioned at point C in Figure 7.13. Stock C is selling at a market price consistent with its equilibrium expected rate of return. Given its position, we know that its returns are negatively correlated with the market portfolio, because its expected return is below the risk-free rate. The combination line between

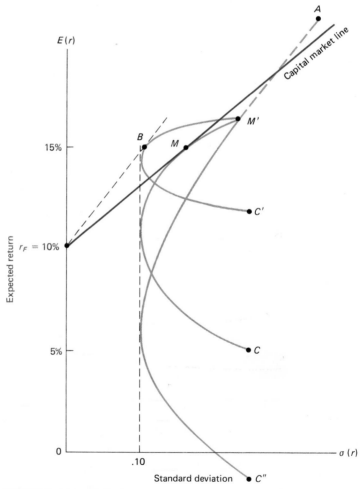

FIGURE 7.13 Market pressure to force a stock to its equilibrium price.

stock C and the market portfolio is given by the curve labeled CM'. The market portfolio is positioned at M. Stock C is, of course, in the market portfolio, so its combination line passes through point M and extends to point M'. At point M', the portfolio weight for stock C has been reduced to zero, so we can consider M' as the market portfolio with stock C completely removed.

Consider what happens to the portfolio weight for stock C as we move along the combination line from M' to C. At M', the portfolio weight in C is zero. At M, the portfolio weight is equal to the total market value of stock C divided by the grand total market value of all stocks. At point C the portfolio weight is equal to 1.00. Note that if the stock is selling at its equilibrium price, its combination line with the market portfolio will reflect *off* the capital market line. Given this, if you increase or decrease the portfolio weight to a level that is greater or less than the stock's fraction of the total market value of all stocks, you move inside the efficient set to an inferior position (such as M' or C). In this sense, it's in everyone's interest to hold the stock in proportion to its fraction of the total market.

Suppose something happens to move the stock from its equilibrium position. Assume initially the stock's expected dividend and expected market price are $5.00 and $100.00, respectively. The beginning market price is $100.00, and, consequently, the expected rate of return is 5 percent:

$$.05 = \frac{\$5.00 + \$100.00}{\$100.00} - 1$$

Now suppose an item of good news is received by the marketplace. The information does nothing to change the market's assessment of the *risk* characteristics of the stock, but it does change its assessment of the dividend and ending price. The new expected dividend is $7.00, and the new expected ending price is $105.00. If there is no change in the beginning price, the new expected rate of return is 12 percent:

$$.12 = \frac{\$7.00 + \$105.00}{\$100.00} - 1$$

At a market price of $100.00 the stock is now positioned at point C' in Figure 7.13. The combination line between stock C and the market portfolio is now given by curve $C'M'$. Since the good news did nothing to change the market's opinion regarding the stock's covariance, the lowest standard deviation achievable on the combination line is the same as it was before, 10 percent. The combination line looks different now because the stock's expected return has changed. It is now in everyone's interest to increase their investment in the stock, moving to point B on the new combination line, where they can achieve their preferred portfolio positions by borrowing or lending at the risk-free rate. The buying pressure on the stock will force its price up and its expected rate of return down, until it resumes its equilibrium position at point C. The market price at that point will be $106.67:

$$.05 = \frac{\$7.00 + \$105.00}{\$106.67} - 1$$

Now suppose that instead of receiving good news about the stock, the market receives bad news. Again the news doesn't change its opinion regarding risk, but it does change its opinion regarding expected income. The expected return falls to -2 percent:

$$-.02 = \frac{\$3.00 + \$95.00}{\$100.00} - 1$$

The stock moves to point C'' in Figure 7.13. Its combination line with the market portfolio is now given by curve $C''M'$. At the new expected return of -2 percent, we will not want to hold any of the stock. In fact, if we short sell the stock, we can move out on the broken portion of the combination line to hold a portfolio such as A. Then we can borrow or lend once again to our preferred risk position. Everyone in the market will attempt to do this, and in the process of attempting to sell the stock, they will lower its price to $93.33 and drive the stock back to its equilibrium position at C:

$$.05 = \frac{\$3.00 + \$95.00}{\$93.33} - 1$$

This same kind of market pressure holds each stock in its equilibrium position. Should anything disturb the stock from its position, opportunities will arise to earn superior returns by either buying more of the stock or selling it short. The buying or selling pressure immediately forces the stock back to its equilibrium price.

THE CAPITAL ASSET PRICING MODEL WITH NO RISK-FREE ASSET

It's important to realize that much of the structure of the capital asset pricing model derives from the properties of the minimum variance set. Remember these properties are merely mathematical identities, and they do not reflect or predict the behavior of portfolio investors. As a consequence, while, on the surface, the capital asset pricing model appears to be rich in economic content and predictive power, it really makes only one interesting economic prediction: *All* investors hold portfolios that are on the efficient set, and as a result the market portfolio is itself on the efficient set.

We can see this most easily in the context of a version of the model where we assume there is no risk-free bond available to buy or sell. We will assume all the other assumptions of the model are intact.

The minimum variance set available to all investors is depicted in the graph at the upper left of Figure 7.14. On the basis of the assumption that all investors choose between portfolios on the basis of expected return and variance or standard deviation, they all take positions on the efficient set above the minimum variance portfolio. Surprising as it may seem, we are now finished with the economic analysis of the model! Everything we say from here on follows on the basis of identity relationships.

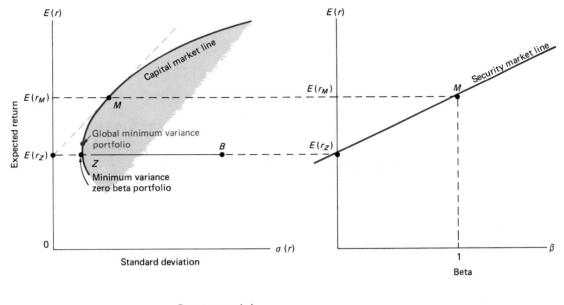

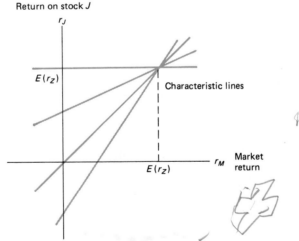

FIGURE 7.14 Capital asset pricing model with no risk-free rate.

From property I, we know the market portfolio is efficient because it is the aggregate of all portfolios, held by all investors, all of which are efficient. From property II we know that if the market portfolio is efficient, there will be a deterministic, linear relationship between the beta factors of individual stocks and their expected returns, as in the graph at the upper right of Figure 7.14. This relationship (the security market line) has a positive slope (the market portfolio is not only on the minimum variance set; it is efficient), and it intercepts the expected return axis at the point labeled $E(r_Z)$, which is expected return at which a line drawn tangent to the

bullet at M intersects the vertical axis. On the basis of property AVI (Appendix 8), we know that all the investments inside the bullet falling on the broken line ZB will be perfectly *uncorrelated* with the market portfolio. Of these, the portfolio having the lowest variance is portfolio Z. This portfolio is called the *minimum variance, zero beta portfolio*. Its beta is zero of course, because its correlation is zero. In this version of the model the security market line intersects the expected return axis at the expected return to the minimum variance, zero beta portfolio.

Given a linear relationship between expected return and beta, all the characteristic lines must intersect at a common point, as in the lower graph of Figure 7.14. In this version of the model, the common point has coordinates $E(r_Z), E(r_Z)$.

As you can see, the structure of the entire model automatically falls into place as soon as we specify that all investors are holding efficient portfolios. This is the real prediction *(and assumption!)* of the capital asset pricing model. Is this a reasonable assumption/prediction, and how hard does the model lean on it?

Intelligent investors may hold portfolios that are not efficient in expected return–standard deviation space. These investors may knowingly hold portfolios that are inside of, rather than on the skin of, the bullet. Their reasons for doing this might include the following:

1. They may not be able to sell any securities short in unlimited amounts, or they may not be able to invest the proceeds of their short sales without restriction. In this case they would be facing a bullet, constructed on the basis of some form of a short-selling constraint, that would be positioned inside the bullet of Figure 7.14. Even if they were to take efficient positions with respect to the constrained bullet, these positions would be inefficient with respect to the unconstrained bullet. Moreover, combinations of these positions would in turn be inefficient relative to the constrained bullet.

2. Security returns may not be normally distributed, and investors may have preferences with respect to the shape of the probability distributions for the returns on their portfolios that go beyond expected return and standard deviation. If they have a preference for portfolios with positive skewness, they may hold portfolios that are inefficient in expected return–standard deviation space, but efficient nonetheless in expected return–standard deviation–skewness space.

3. Investors may optimize their portfolios in terms of returns net of trading costs, including taxes. To the extent that these costs differ from investor to investor, each faces a different "net of cost" bullet, and efficient positions on these bullets may well imply inefficient positions with respect to the "gross of cost" bullet in Figure 7.14.

4. Investors may hold capital assets that are indivisible, such as their human capital (present value of their future earnings). These investors will want to build optimal portfolios around these indivisible assets. (For example, they may not want to invest very heavily in the company for which they work to avoid keeping all their eggs in one basket.) Viewed in terms of the discussion of Chapter 5, these investors are constrained to take specific positions in certain assets, and these positions are likely to be off the unconstrained critical line. Thus, although these investors may be expected to optimize as best they can given the constraint, their overall

portfolios, as well as their portfolios of divisible assets, will be off the unconstrained critical line as well.

Alternative versions of the CAPM have been derived to take account of these problems. It is easy to take account, for example, of the effect on the risk–expected return relationship of putting constraints on short selling. However, you should recognize that, when the constraints are considered, we are no longer dealing with a simple security market line (SML), as in Figure 7.14. Rather, we are facing a "security market cloud," where the positioning of securities in expected return–beta space is more complex.

It can be argued that using, as most do, a simple SML as a benchmark to assess the adequacy of expected return given the degree of exposure to risk, is a reasonably good approximation to the security market cloud that should actually be employed.

Those who believe this should recognize a fundamental difference between CAPM and other models in finance and economics. Later in this book we shall learn about models for the pricing of put and call options. These models are very popular, and they are powerful. They differ fundamentally from CAPM in that a few powerful floor traders with sufficient capital can push option prices to the values predicted by these models. Most of the models make no assumptions about human behavior other than to assume that, if free money exists, we will reach for it.

Other models in economics are similar in the sense that they appeal to the trading behavior of rational buyers and sellers at the margin, who ultimately set the relative prices predicted by the models.

With CAPM we seem to be dealing with something fundamentally different. To see this, return to the clean environment with no restrictions on short selling, no taxes or transactions costs, no indivisible assets, and normal distributions. Even in this clean environment, CAPM pricing cannot be enforced by a few powerful floor traders on the floor of the New York Stock Exchange. Nor can we appeal to the behavior of rational, marginal traders in each separate issue. They have no incentives whatsoever to set prices in accord with the predictions of the CAPM. The model predicts that the market portfolio is efficient. It will be if, and only if, we *all* hold efficient portfolios. *All of us*. If some take positions off the critical line, when we aggregate wealth, the market portfolio will be off the critical line as well. It will then be inefficient, and we will no longer have a security market line in expected return–beta space.

THE CAPITAL ASSET PRICING MODEL WHEN A RISK-FREE ASSET EXISTS BUT WE CAN'T SELL IT

In this form of the model,[5] we assume investors can short-sell risky assets but they can't sell the riskless bond. Presumably, the bond is issued by the government to finance deficit spending, and there are restrictions on investors, preventing them from

---

[5]The no borrowing form of the capital asset pricing model was independently derived by Black (1972) and Vasicek (1971).

selling it short (although they can sell everything else short in this model). They can, however, buy the bond if they want. This form of the model is of interest, because its prediction regarding the position of the security market line relative to the risk-free rate is supported by some of the traditional empirical studies discussed in Chapter 8.

   We begin with the minimum variance set of portfolios of risky securities as given by curve $ZP'M$ in the diagram in the upper left of Figure 7.15. The risk-free bond we can buy, but not sell, is positioned at r_F. Those investors with indifference curves like the one labeled I will find it in their interests to construct portfolios out of the risk-free bond and the risky security portfolio with the largest value for the

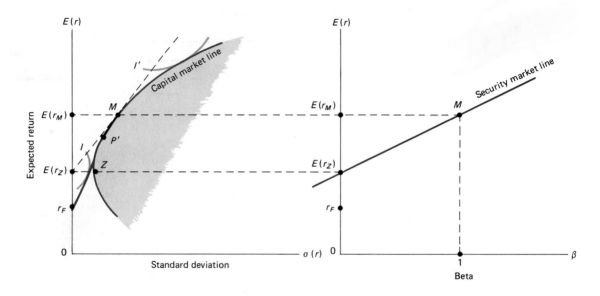

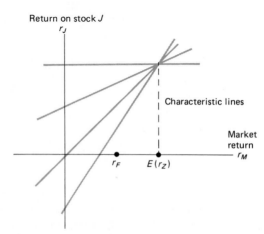

FIGURE 7.15 Capital asset pricing model with lending but no borrowing.

ratio $[E(r_P) - r_F]/\sigma(r_P)$. This portfolio is portfolio P' on the graph. These conservative investors will be investing some of their money in the risk-free bond and the remainder in portfolio P'.

In this context, the efficient set or capital market line begins at r_F, runs as a straight line to P', and then bends back along the bullet through point M.

Now consider the portfolios of *risky securities* that investors in this market will be holding. There will be many conservative investors holding portfolio P'. However, there will be many others, with indifference curves like that of I', who will be holding portfolios positioned on the bullet above P'. These portfolios consist of risky securities alone. Investors will be scattered all along the efficient side of the bullet from P' on up.

When we aggregate these portfolios to obtain the market portfolio, on the basis of property I, we will find that the market portfolio is efficient. Since investors are scattered from P' on up, the market portfolio will be positioned *above* P' on the bullet at point M. On the basis of property II, since the market portfolio is efficient, there will be a linear relationship between beta and expected return (depicted in the upper right of Figure 7.15) which has a positive slope and intercepts the expected return axis at $E(r_Z)$, the expected return on the minimum variance, zero beta portfolio. Note that $E(r_Z)$ lies above r_F because the market portfolio is positioned above portfolio P' on the bullet. In the diagram at the bottom of Figure 7.15 we see the characteristic lines going through a common point with coordinates $E(r_Z)$, $E(r_Z)$.

It appears from the security market line of Figure 7.15 that the zero beta portfolio at $E(r_Z)$ dominates (having higher expected return for the same risk) the risk-free bond at r_F. After all, they both have a zero beta, but the zero beta portfolio has a higher expected rate of return. It must be remembered, however, that while the zero beta portfolio has no systematic risk, it does have residual variance and a positive standard deviation. It is positioned on the minimum variance set of Figure 7.15 at point Z, and when viewed from this perspective, it does not dominate the risk-free bond.

SUMMARY

The portfolio models of previous chapters can be viewed as tools to find the efficient set in expected return, standard deviation space. The capital asset pricing model can be viewed as a theory of the way stocks would be priced if everyone in the market used these tools and took positions on the efficient set. In a world where short selling is permitted, when we aggregate everyone's efficient portfolio to obtain the market portfolio, we will find that the market portfolio, itself, is on the efficient set. This then automatically implies a linear, positively sloped relationship between expected stock return and beta.

Either of two conditions is sufficient to ensure that rational investors will take positions on an expected return–standard deviation efficient set. The first is that the probability distributions for portfolio returns are *normal*. In this case, the probability distributions are fully described by their expected returns and standard deviations.

The second is that the relationship between investor utility and portfolio wealth is *quadratic* in form. In this case, the only attributes of the probability distribution that the investor is concerned with are the expected return and the standard deviation. In any case, to operate in the domain of expected return and standard deviation, you must constrain *either* the shape of the probability distribution *or* the investor's preference function.

In the capital asset pricing model, the risk of a portfolio that is held by an investor is measured in terms of its standard deviation or variance. On the other hand, the risk of an individual security is measured in terms of the contribution that the security makes to the variances of the portfolios that investors hold. This contribution can be measured by the beta factor for the stock.

The capital market line is drawn in expected return, standard deviation space. When investors are permitted to borrow and lend at a risk-free rate, the capital market line is linear and positively sloped. The portfolios held by investors are positioned on this line. Unless a stock happens to be perfectly positively correlated with the market, it is positioned to the right of the capital market line. The greater a stock's residual variance, the farther to the right of the capital market line it is positioned.

The security market line is drawn in expected return–beta space. It is linear and positively sloped, irrespective of whether investors can borrow or lend at a risk-free rate. All individual securities and portfolios are positioned on the security market line.

The greater the degree of risk aversion of investors in the market, the greater are the slopes of both the capital market line and the security market line. At the extreme, if investors have zero risk aversion or are risk neutral, the slope of both lines will be zero, and all securities will sell at prices to produce the same expected rate of return.

QUESTION SET 1

1. What are the two alternative assumptions covered in the chapter that would allow us to claim that investment choices can be evaluated solely on the basis of expected return and variance?

2. In the context of the CAPM with unlimited borrowing and *lending* at the risk-free rate of interest, explain the meaning of the capital market line.

3. If the risk-free rate of interest is 6 percent and the return on the market portfolio is 10 percent, what is the equilibrium return on an asset having a beta of 1.4, according to the CAPM (with no constraints on riskless borrowing and lending)?
   Refer to the following information for Questions 4 through 7.

Stock i	Correlation Coefficient i with M	Standard Deviation of i
1	.3	.4
2	.8	.3

$$E(r_M) = .11$$
$$r_F = .06$$

Variance of market portfolio's return = .25.

4. Compute betas for
   a. Stock 1.
   b. Stock 2.
   c. A portfolio consisting of 60 percent invested in stock 1 and 40 percent invested in stock 2.

   According to the CAPM, how would you rank these securities according to risk?

5. Compute the equilibrium expected return according to the CAPM for
   a. Stock 1.
   b. Stock 2.
   c. The portfolio indicated in Question 4(c).

6. Sketch the security market line and indicate the positions of stock 1, stock 2, and the portfolio in Question 4(c).

7. Sketch the characteristic lines for stock 1, stock 2, and the portfolio in Problem 4(c).

   For questions 8 through 11 refer to the following diagram:

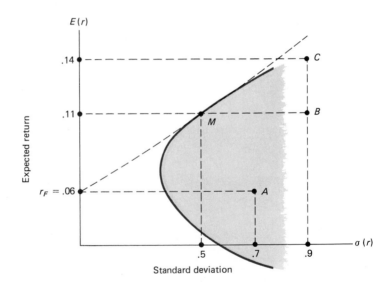

8. What are the beta values of stocks A, B, and C?

9. What are the residual variances of stocks A, B, and C?

10. Consider a portfolio consisting of 20 percent invested in A and 80 percent invested in C.
    a. What is the beta of this portfolio?
    b. According to the CAPM, what should the portfolio's equilibrium return be?

11. Evaluate the following Statement: "Stocks B and C should be viewed as equally risky, since they have the same standard deviation."

12. Suppose that the relevant equilibrium model is the CAPM with unlimited borrowing and lending at a riskless rate of interest. Suppose, further, that you discovered a security that was located *below* the security market line.

a. What would you conclude about the pricing of this particular security?

b. Describe any changes you would expect to occur in its price.

13. Suppose that the relevant equilibrium model is the CAPM with unlimited borrowing and lending at a riskless rate of interest. Complete the blanks in the following table:

Asset	Expected Return	Standard Deviation	Beta	Residual Variance
A	.08	.10	—	0
B	.12	—	2	.49
C	—	—	1	0
D	.05	—	0	.36

14. Assume the CAPM with *no* riskless asset.

a. Contrast the capital market line in this model with the capital market line when there *is* a riskless asset that can be bought or sold.

b. What is the interpretation of the market portfolio in this model?

15. Assume the CAPM with risk-free lending but no risk-free borrowing. Suppose the return on the market portfolio is 9 percent, and the return on a zero beta portfolio is 5 percent. You have combined two assets in a portfolio with equal weights. The expected returns on the two assets are 7 percent and 15 percent. What is the beta of this portfolio?

QUESTION SET 1

1. Suppose you feel equally at ease having a portfolio with a guaranteed rate of return of 5 percent or one with an expected return of 25 percent, as long as the standard deviation is 18 percent. Which portfolios would you pick on the accompanying graph? What is your set of equally desirable portfolios along CFA called?

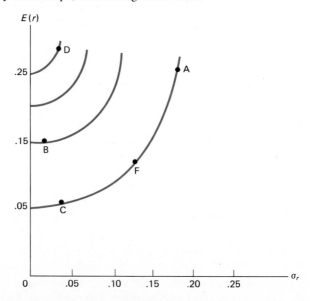

2. Under the CAPM, what is the efficient set called? If there is buying and selling of a risk-free asset, what happens to the efficient set?

3. If the market portfolio is efficient, what is the relationship between the beta factors for stocks and their expected rates of return?

4. Under the CAPM, at what common point do the characteristic lines of individual stocks intersect?

5. The stock A is positioned off the security market line on the accompanying graph. What does this tell us about the stock?

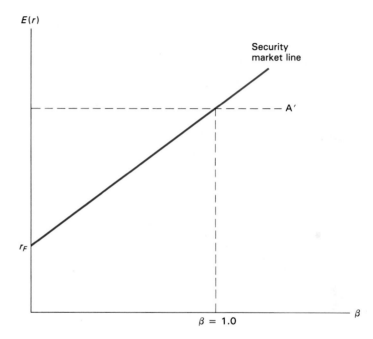

6. You choose to invest in the company which is going to turn garbage into vehicle fuel through decomposing gases. The worldwide outlook for natural gas and oil is good for the next 20 years, and the stock of the company is negatively correlated with the market portfolio. If the company has a correlation coefficient of -1.00, what does this mean? If the stock has an expected return of -10 percent why would you purchase it?

ANSWERS TO QUESTION SET 2

1. You could pick A, F, or C. All the portfolios you would pick are on your indifference curve.

2. The efficient set under the CAPM is called the capital market line. Under the conditions of buying and selling a riskless asset short, the capital market line becomes linear.

3. If the market portfolio is efficient, a perfect linear relationship exists between the beta factors for the stocks and their expected rates of return. The security market line describes this relationship.

4. The characteristic lines of the stocks intersect at a point whose coordinates are the risk-free rate (r_F, r_F).

5. Since A is off the security market line, we know that its beta was calculated with reference to an inefficient portfolio.

6. A correlation coefficient of -1.0 means that the stock is perfectly negatively correlated with the market portfolio; for example, if the market goes up 10 percentage points, the price of the company will go down a given multiple of 10 percentage points. You would invest in this stock to diversify your portfolio to reduce your overall portfolio risk. There is a slight chance that the predictions for the future in oil and natural gas could be totally off, at which point an alternative energy source might take off. If this were the case, your investment could really pay off.

PROBLEM SET

Refer to the following data for Problems 1 and 2.

Stock i	Correlation Coefficient i with M	Standard Deviation of i
A	.5	.25
B	.3	.30

$$E(r_M) = .12.$$

$$r_F = .05.$$

$$\sigma^2(r_M) = .01.$$

1. Compute betas for
   a. Stock A.
   b. Stock B.
   c. For an equally weighted portfolio of stocks A and B.

2. Compute the equilibrium expected return according to the CAPM for
   a. Stock A.
   b. Stock B.
   c. The portfolio indicated in Problem 1(c).

3. Suppose that the relevant equilibrium model is the CAPM with unlimited borrowing and lending at the riskless rate of interest. Complete the blanks in the following table.

Stock	Expected Return	Standard Deviation	Beta	Residual Variance
1	.15	—	2.00	.10
2	—	.25	0.75	.04
3	.09	—	0.50	.17

4. Assume the CAPM with risk-free lending but no risk-free borrowing. The return on the market portfolio is 10 percent and the return on the zero beta portfolio is 6 percent. The market's standard deviation is 30 percent. Complete the following table.

Stock	Expected Return	Standard Deviation	Beta	Residual Variance
x	.16	—	—	.0375
y	.08	—	—	.0775

5. Based on your answer to Problem 4 and Cov $(E_x, \epsilon_y) = 0$, what is the expected return, beta, and standard deviation of a portfolio with equal amounts in stocks x and y?

ANSWERS TO PROBLEM SET

1. Recall from Chapter 3 that

$$\text{Cov}(r_i, r_M) = \rho_{i,M} \, \sigma(r_i) \, \sigma(r_M)$$

and

$$\beta_i = \frac{\text{Cov}(r_i, r_M)}{\sigma^2(r_M)}$$

a. $\text{Cov}(r_A, r_M) = (.5)(.25)(.01)^{.5} = .0125$

$$\beta_A = \frac{.0125}{.0100} = 1.25$$

b. $\text{Cov}(r_B, r_M) = (.30)(.30)(.01)^{.5} = .009$

$$\beta_B = \frac{.009}{.010} = .90$$

c. $\beta_P = (.5)(1.25) + (.5)(.90) = 1.075$

2. The equation for the expected return can be written as

$$E(r_i) = r_F + [E(r_M) - r_F]\beta_i$$

or alternatively as

$$E(r_i) = r_F + \left[\frac{E(r_M) - r_F}{\sigma^2(r_M)} \rho_{i,M} \right] \sigma(r_i)$$

We will use the latter equation to find the equilibrium expected return, but both are perfectly satisfactory.

a. $E(r_i) = .05 + \left[\dfrac{(.12 - .05)}{(.01)^{.5}} (.5) \right] .25 = .1375$

b. $E(r_i) = .05 + \left[\dfrac{(.12 - .05)}{(.01)^{.5}} (.3) \right] .30 = .1130$

c. $E(r_P) = (.5)(.1375) + (.5)(.1130) = .1253$

3. Given our assumptions, we know that the relationship between the expected rate of return and beta is linear.

From the information we have for stocks 1 and 3, we know the risk premium accorded the market portfolio must be

$$[E(r_M) - r_F] = \frac{E(r_1) - E(r_2)}{\beta_1 - \beta_2} = \frac{.15 - .09}{2.0 - 0.5} = .04$$

Knowing this, we can use the information we have for stock 1 to find the risk-free rate

$$E(r_1) = r_F + [E(r_M) - r_F]\beta_1$$

$$r_F = E(r_1) - [E(r_M) - r_F]\beta_1$$

$$= .15 - (.04)(2.00)$$

$$= .07$$

We can now find the expected return for stock 2

$$E(r_2) = .07 + (.04)(.75) = .10$$

The information given for stock 2 allows us to estimate the variance of returns to the market.

$$\sigma^2(r_2) = \beta_2^2 \sigma^2(r_M) + \sigma^2(\epsilon_2)$$

$$\sigma^2(r_M) = \frac{\sigma^2(r_2) - \sigma^2(\epsilon_2)}{\beta_2^2} = \frac{(.25)^2 - (.04)}{(.75)^2} = .04$$

The standard deviations of stocks 1 and 3 can now be found:

$$\sigma^2(r_1) = (2.0)^2(.04) + .10 = .26$$

$$\sigma(r_1) = (.26)^{.5} = .5099$$

$$\sigma^2(r_3) = (.05)^2(.04) + .17 = .18$$

$$\sigma(r_3) = (.18)^{.5} = .4243$$

The completed table should look like this:

Stock	Expected Return	Standard Deviation	Beta	Residual Variance
1	.15	.51	2.00	.10
2	.10	.25	.75	.04
3	.09	.42	.50	.17

4. Given the assumptions of the CAPM, we know there is a linear relationship between the expected return to a security and beta.

Using the equation for the security market line where selling the risk-free asset is not allowed we can find the betas of the two securities.

$$E(r_i) = E(r_Z) + [E(r_M) - E(r_Z)]\beta_i$$

$$\beta_i = \frac{E(r_i) - E(r_Z)}{E(r_M) - E(r_Z)}$$

$$\beta_x = \frac{.16 - .06}{.10 - .06} = \frac{.10}{.04} = 2.5$$

$$\beta_y = \frac{.08 - .06}{.10 - .06} = \frac{.02}{.04} = 0.5$$

With the security betas, we can now solve for the standard deviations

$$\sigma^2(r_x) = (2.5)^2(.30)^2 + .0375 = .60 \qquad \sigma(r_x) = .7746$$

$$\sigma^2(r_y) = (.5)^2(.30)^2 + .0775 = .10 \qquad \sigma(r_y) = .3162$$

5. $E(r_p) = .5(.16) + .5(.08) = .12$

$\beta_p = .5(2.5) + .5(.5) = 1.5$

$\sigma^2(r_p) = (1.5)^2(.30)^2 + (.5)^2(.0375) + (.5)^2(.0775) = .2313$

$\sigma(r_p) = (.2313)^5 = .4809$

REFERENCES

BLACK, F., "Capital Market Equilibrium with Restricted Borrowing," *Journal of Business* (July 1972).

BRENNAN, M. J., "Capital Market Equilibrium with Divergent Borrowing and Lending Rates," *Journal of Financial and Quantitative Analysis* (December 1971).

BRENNAN, M. J., "Taxes, Market Valuation and Corporate Finance Policy," *National Tax Journal* (December 1973).

CHEN, A. H., KIM, E. H., and KON, S. J., "Cash Demand, Liquidation Costs and Capital Market Equilibrium Under Uncertainty," *Journal of Financial Economics* (September 1975).

CONSTANTINIDES, G. M., "Intertemporal Asset Pricing with Heterogeneous Consumers and Without Demand Aggregation," *Journal of Business* (April 1982).

FAMA, E. F., "Risk, Return and Equilibrium: Some Clarifying Comments," *Journal of Finance* (March 1968).

FRIEND, I., and WESTERFIELD, R., "Co-Skewedness and Capital Asset Pricing," *Journal of Finance* (September 1980).

HAGGERMAN, R. L., and KIM, E. H., "Capital Asset Pricing with Price Level Changes," *Journal of Financial and Quantitative Analysis* (September 1960).

HARRINGTON, D., "Trends in Capital Asset Pricing Model Use," *Public Utilities* (August 1981).

HECKERMAN, D. G., "Portfolio Selection and the Structure of Capital Asset Prices When the Prices of Consumption Goods May Change," *Journal of Finance* (March 1972).

HOGAN, W. W., and WARREN, J. M., "Toward the Development of an Equilibrium Capital-Market Model Based on Semi-Variance," *Journal of Financial and Quantitative Analysis* (January 1974).

HSU, D., MILLER, R., and WICHERN, D., "On the Stable Paretian Character of Stock Market Prices," *Journal of the American Statistical Association* (March 1974).

JARROW, R., "Heterogeneous Expectations, Restrictions on Short Sales, and Equilibrium Asset Prices," *Journal of Finance* (December 1980).

JENSEN, M. C., *Studies in the Theory of Capital Markets*. New York: Praeger, 1972.

JENSEN, M. C., "Capital Markets: Theory and Evidence," *Bell Journal of Economics and Management Science* (Autumn 1972).

KRAUS, A., and LITZENBERGER, R. H., "Market Equilibrium in a Multiperiod State Preference Model with Logarithmic Utility," *Journal of Finance* (December 1975).

KRAUS, A., and LITZENBERGER, R. H., "Skewness Preference and the Valuation of Risk Assets," *Journal of Finance* (September 1976).

LEE, C. F., "Investment Horizon and the Functional Form of the Capital Asset Pricing Model," *Review of Economics and Statistics* (August 1976).

LEROY, S. F., "Expectations Models of Asset Prices: A Survey of Theory," *Journal of Finance* (March 1982).

LINTNER, J., "The Valuation of Risk Assets and the Selection of Risky Investments in Stock Portfolios and Capital Budgets," *Review of Economics and Statistics* (February 1965).(a)

LINTNER, J., "Security Prices, Risk, and Maximal Gains from Diversification," *The Journal of Finance* (December 1965).(b)

LINTNER, J., "The Aggregation of Investors' Diverse Judgments and Preferences in Purely Competitive Security Markets," *Journal of Financial and Quantitative Analysis* (December 1970).

MOSSIN, J., "Equilibrium in a Capital Market," *Econometrica* (October 1966).

SHARPE, W. F., "Capital Asset Prices: A Theory of Market Equilibrium," *Journal of Finance* (September 1964).

TOBIN, J., "Liquidity Preference as Behavior Towards Risk," *Review of Economic Studies* (February 1958).

TREYNOR, J. L., "Toward a Theory of Market Value of Risky Assets," unpublished manuscript, 1961.

VASICEK, O., "Capital Asset Pricing Model with No Riskless Borrowing," unpublished manuscript, Wells Fargo Bank, March 1971.

WESTON, J. F., "Investment Decisions Using the Capital Asset Pricing Model," *Financial Management* (Spring 1973).

WILLIAMS, J. T., "Capital Asset Prices with Heterogeneous Beliefs," *Journal of Financial Economics* (November 1977).

8

EMPIRICAL TESTS OF THE CAPITAL ASSET PRICING MODEL

The capital asset pricing model (CAPM) predicts all investors hold portfolios which are efficient in expected return, standard deviation space. As a consequence, the market portfolio is predicted to be efficient as well. To test the CAPM, we must test the prediction that the market portfolio is positioned on the efficient set.

Keep in mind that the CAPM is specified in terms of investor expectations. That is, the market portfolio is predicted to be efficient over some holding period into the *future*. Obviously, in conducting a test, we can't read the minds of investors to see if the portfolios they are holding are efficient from their points of view. Instead, we assume the probability distributions for the returns on stocks do not change their shapes over time. If this is true, the expected values, variances, and covariances can be estimated through the sampling of past returns. We then can construct a sample estimate of the efficient set as well as a sample estimate of the position of the market portfolio relative to it.

We must recognize that our sample estimates are subject to sampling error. Expectations for the future are never fully realized, because unforeseen events do happen. As a consequence, even if the market portfolio is *expected* to be efficient at the beginning of each period of time, it is not likely to *turn out* to be efficient over a sequence of past periods. After all, some stocks may unexpectedly triple in price, while others may become nearly valueless. In computing the efficient set based on these past returns, the computer will be short-selling the negative return stocks and taking positive positions in the stocks with large positive returns. The market portfolio will be dominated by such portfolios on the basis of *historical* returns, even though it was efficient on the basis of *expected future* returns.

Consequently, in testing the theory, we must determine whether the observed deviation of the market portfolio's position from the efficient set is due to something other than chance. If the degree of inefficiency is so great that it is highly unlikely to have been caused by unexpected events, then we can say that the market portfolio was *expected* to be *inefficient*. On the basis of this finding, we would reject the capital asset pricing model as a valid theory.

We should note that in taking our sample estimates, we must choose a time interval over which we measure returns. The time interval we choose should correspond to the length of investors' horizons. If the horizons are 1 month long, we should sample using monthly rates of return. This is important, because portfolios (such as the market portfolio) that are expected to be efficient over the next month are not likely to be expected to be efficient over the next year as well. In taking sample estimates we must assume the horizon of all investors is of a particular length and that it begins and ends at the same calendar times. If we guess incorrectly, even if the CAPM holds over the right interval, the market portfolio will not be expected to be efficient over any of *our* intervals.

TRADITIONAL TESTS OF THE CAPITAL ASSET PRICING MODEL

Rather than test the single prediction of the CAPM directly, initial testing of the model centered on the properties of the security market line which follow, given the efficiency of the market portfolio. We know from property II, Chapter 5, that if the market portfolio is efficient, then there will be a linear, positive relationship between the beta of any security and its expected rate of return. This relationship is called the security market line.

In testing theory, the initial tests used a two-pass regression technique. The betas of securities or portfolios were estimated in the first pass. The first pass was a time series regression, where security or portfolio returns were related to the returns to a market index. The line of best fit passing through the observations taken from each period serves as an estimate of the security's characteristic line, and the slope of the characteristic line is the estimate of the security's beta. The second pass regression is cross-sectional in nature. Each observation here was an individual security or portfolio. In the second pass beta is related to average return. The line of best fit through the observations in this pass is an estimate of the security market line. The researchers then try to determine whether the properties of this estimate are in accord with the CAPM predictions.

The Test of Black, Jensen, and Scholes (1972)

Black, Jensen, and Scholes (BJS) do not directly test the prediction that the market portfolio is on the efficient set. They concentrate, instead, on the security market line. We know that if the market portfolio is efficient, it follows automatically that a linear, positively sloped relationship should exist between betas and expected rates of return. If investors can borrow and lend at a risk-free rate, it also follows that a zero beta stock or portfolio should be expected to produce a return equal to the risk-free rate. The empirical test of BJS is designed to test these properties of the security market line.

BJS restrict their initial sample to all stocks traded on the New York Stock Exchange (NYSE) during the period 1926 through 1965. They start their study with the subperiod 1926 through 1930. They compute betas for all stocks that were on the exchange throughout this period, using as a market index, an equally weighted portfolio of all stocks on the NYSE. They then rank the stocks on the basis of beta and form 10 portfolios. The 10 percent of the stocks with the highest betas go into portfolio 1 and so on, through portfolio 10.

They now compute the rates of return to each of the portfolios in each of the 12 months of 1931. At the end of this year, they again compute the betas for every stock on the exchange in the period 1927 through 1931, and they reform the 10 portfolios. They repeat this process in each of the years 1931 through 1965, obtaining a series of monthly rates of return for each of the 10 portfolios. They now attempt to estimate the expected rates of return and beta factors for each of the portfolios by taking sample estimates from the rates of return.

The sample estimate of the expected value is, of course, the arithmetic mean rate of return. This is the unbiased estimator of the expected rate of return at the beginning of each of the individual months. They estimate the beta of each portfolio by relating the portfolio returns to their market index. While they take sample estimates over various subintervals in the period, we will concentrate on their sample estimates for the overall period 1931 through 1965.

The relationship they find between beta and average rate of return is depicted in Figure 8.1. The fit is remarkably good for a cross-sectional relationship. The graphing can be interpreted as an estimate of the security market line for the overall period. Recall that if investors can borrow and lend at a risk-free rate, the security market line is given by

$$E(r_J) = r_F + [E(r_M) - r_F]\beta_J$$

where $E(r_J)$ is the expected return to stock J, r_F is the risk-free rate, $E(r_M)$ is the expected rate of return to the market portfolio, and β_J is the beta factor of stock J.

On the other hand, if investors can't borrow at a risk-free rate, it is given by

$$E(r_J) = E(r_Z) + [E(r_M) - E(r_Z)]\beta_J$$

where $E(r_Z)$ is the expected rate of return on the minimum variance, zero beta portfolio.

Recall also that r_F (the rate of return on a risk-free bond) is expected to be less than $E(r_Z)$.

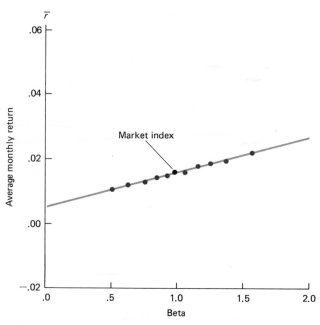

FIGURE 8.1 Estimate of the security market line.

SOURCE: F. Black, M. C. Jensen, and M. Scholes, ''The Capital Asset Pricing Model: Some Empirical Tests,'' *Studies in Theory of Capital Markets* (New York: Praeger, 1972).

The slope of the security market line is equal to the expected risk premium on the market portfolio. The slope of the BJS estimated security market line is .01081, reflecting a market risk premium of 1.081 percent per month or 12.972 percent per year.

The intercept is supposed to be equal to the rate of return on a risk-free bond or the expected rate of return on a zero beta portfolio. The intercept of the estimated security market line is .00519, reflecting a rate of return of .519 percent per month or 6.225 percent per year. This number is significantly greater than the average interest rate on riskless bonds during the overall period. BJS conclude that their results are consistent with the form of the CAPM which allows for riskless lending but precludes riskless borrowing.

Overall, their result *appears* to offer strong support for the CAPM. There is little or no evidence of nonlinearity in their estimated security market line; the slope is highly significant and positive. Moreover, nearly 100 percent of the cross-sectional differences in the average returns on the portfolios can be explained by differences in beta factors. On the surface, at least, there appears to be little room for other risk variables to explain differences in expected rates of return. Recall that in the CAPM, beta should be the *only* determinant of differences in expected rates of return.

The Fama-MacBeth Study (1974)

Fama and MacBeth (FM) also direct their attention to the properties of the security market line. Their study, however, differs fundamentally from that of BJS in that they attempt to predict the *future* rates of return to portfolios on the basis of risk variables estimated in *previous* periods.

Their data base is the same as that of BJS. They also use the same index of the market portfolio, an equally weighted portfolio of all stocks on the NYSE. They begin by computing the beta factor for every stock that was listed on the NYSE in the period 1926 through 1929. They then rank the stocks by beta and form 20 portfolios in the manner of BJS. Then they estimate the beta of each of the portfolios by relating their monthly returns to their market index in the period 1930 through 1934. At the end of 1934 they have an estimate of the beta factor for each of the portfolios, and they use these betas to *predict* the portfolio returns in the subsequent months of the period 1935 through 1938. For *each* of the months, they relate the monthly returns on the portfolios to the betas to obtain monthly estimates of the security market line. Thus, for the month of January 1935 (J35), they might see the relationship of Figure 8.2. Each observation in the figure is one of the 20 portfolios. The equation for portfolio return based on the security market line passing through the observations is given by

$$r_{P,J35} = a_0 + a_1 \hat{\beta}_P + \epsilon_{P,J35} \tag{8.1}$$

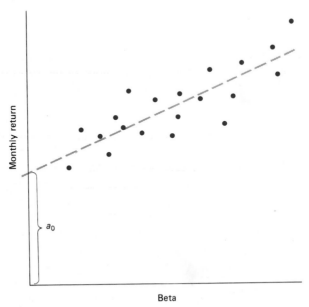

FIGURE 8.2 Relationship between beta and return for a given month in the Fama-MacBeth study.

In this equation, the term on the left-hand side represents the rate of return on portfolio P in January, 1935. The term $\hat{\beta}_P$ is the estimate of the beta factor for the portfolio, as estimated in the period 1930 through 1934, and $\epsilon_{P,J35}$ is an error term associated with each portfolio during the month.

To determine whether the security market line exhibits any evidence of nonlinearity, FM now add on an additional term to the relationship, the square of the beta factor. The relationship is now three-dimensional with the returns to the portfolios on one axis and with beta and beta squared on the other two. The equation for portfolio return based on the plane of best fit passing through the 20 observations is given by

$$r_{P,J35} = a_0 + a_1\hat{\beta}_P + a_2\hat{\beta}_P^2 + \epsilon_{P,J35} \tag{8.2}$$

The CAPM would predict that FM will find that the coefficient a_2 is not significantly different from zero and that the percentage of the differences in portfolio returns explained by the relationship doesn't improve significantly when we add the beta squared term to the relationship.

The CAPM also predicts that beta or systematic risk is the only determinant of expected security returns. Residual variance is supposedly unimportant in determining the price and expected rate of return of a stock because portfolio investors can diversify it away. FM test this prediction of the capital asset pricing model by including a residual variance term in the relationship. The 20 portfolios are equally weighted and include a large number of stocks, so the residual variance for each *portfolio* should be relatively small. However, to determine whether the residual variance of a stock affects its price and, therefore, its parent portfolio's expected rate of return, FM include in the relationship the average residual variance of the stocks they put in each portfolio. The variable is computed as follows,

$$RV_P = \frac{\sum_{J=1}^{M} \sigma^2(\epsilon_J)}{M}$$

where M is the number of stocks in the portfolio and $\sigma^2(\epsilon_J)$ is the residual variance for stock J.

With three variables explaining differences in the month's return for the 20 portfolios, the relationship looks like this:

$$r_{P,J35} = a_0 + a_1\hat{\beta}_P + a_2\hat{\beta}_P^2 + a_3 RV_P + \epsilon_{P,J35} \tag{8.3}$$

Remember that Equations (8.1)–(8.3) are estimated by sliding lines, planes, and so on, of best fit through 20 observations, each observation being 1 of the 20 portfolios. FM estimate the three equations for each of the 48 months of the period 1935 through 1938.

At the end of this period, they calculate fresh estimates of the beta coefficients for the portfolios by repeating the entire process. That is, they estimate stock betas in the period 1930 through 1933. They then form portfolios and estimate portfolio betas in the period 1934 through 1938. And then they estimate Equations (8.1)–(8.3) in the months of the period 1939 through 1942.

The process of estimating stock betas, reforming portfolios, and then estimating monthly security market lines is repeated a total of nine times, to obtain a total of 390 sets of estimates of the coefficients a_0 through a_3 for each of the months between January 1935 and June 1968. FM then compute the mean value for each of the coefficients and attempt to determine whether the means are significantly different from zero.

The capital asset pricing model makes the following predictions regarding the coefficients:

1. Depending on the form of the model, the intercept, or a_0, should be equal to or greater than the risk-free rate in the bond market.
2. The average slope of the security market line, or a_1, should be positive.
3. The security market line should be linear, so the mean value for the coefficient a_2 should not be significantly different from zero.
4. Residual variance should not affect the equilibrium value or expected rate of return of a stock, so the mean value for the coefficient a_3 should not be significantly different from zero.

The central results of the FM test are displayed as follows. The mean values for the coefficients are provided. The symbol * indicates that we can say with greater than 90 percent confidence that the mean value is really different from zero.

$$r_{P,t} = \underset{.0061^*}{a_0} + \underset{.0085^*}{a_1\hat{\beta}_P} + \epsilon_{P,t}$$

$$r_{P,t} = \underset{.0049^*}{a_0} + \underset{.0105^*}{a_1\hat{\beta}_P} + \underset{-.0008}{a_2\hat{\beta}_P^2} + \epsilon_{P,t}$$

$$r_{P,t} = \underset{.0020}{a_0} + \underset{.0114^*}{a_1\hat{\beta}_P} + \underset{-.0026}{a_1\hat{\beta}_P^2} + \underset{.0516}{a_3RV_P} + \epsilon_{P,t}$$

The results are consistent with the predictions of the theory. It appears we can predict that portfolios with greater than average beta factors will tend to produce greater than average rates of return in subsequent periods. There is little or no evidence of non-linearity in the relationship between beta and return. Moreover, we can't predict future return on the basis of the residual variance of the stocks in the portfolio. Given the CAPM, we don't expect residual variance to affect stock prices or expected rates of return, and, based on these results, there's no apparent propensity for stocks with greater than average residual variances to produce greater than average rates of return on future periods.

Like Black, Jensen, and Scholes, FM do find that the mean value for the coefficient a_0 is significantly greater than the mean value for the risk-free rate of interest during the period. This finding is again consistent with the form of the CAPM where lending at the risk-free rate is permitted but borrowing is precluded.

It's important to distinguish between the methodology of BJS and FM. In the case of BJS, the betas and average rates of return are computed in the same periods of time. In the case of FM, betas and returns are computed in different periods. The betas as estimated in one period are used to predict the rates of return in a later period.

The results of both of these tests appear to be very comforting. In fact, the CAPM gained much support among academics as well as professionals after the publication of these results. However, the honeymoon was short-lived.

As we shall see in the next section, these results are not really as supportive of the model as they appear to be on the surface.

ROLL'S CRITIQUE OF TESTS OF THE CAPITAL ASSET PRICING MODEL

In 1976 Richard Roll wrote an extensive working paper in which he criticized (1) empirical testing of the capital asset pricing model, (2) the use of beta as a risk measure, and (3) measures of portfolio performance employing the security market line as a benchmark. The three parts of the paper were later published separately. We will discuss part (1) here. Parts (2) and (3) are essentially the same argument and will be discussed in Chapter 10 on portfolio performance measurement.

Roll's critique of tests of the CAPM can be divided into two parts. First, he claims that the results of tests like those of BJS and FM are *tautological*. By this he means that it is not improbable that we would obtain results like these no matter how stocks were priced in relation to risk in the real world. If this is true, we have learned little or nothing about the structure of stock prices from these tests, and the capital asset pricing model has never really *been* tested.

Second, he claims that since the only real prediction of the CAPM is that the market portfolio is efficient, *this* is the prediction that should be tested. However, the market portfolio contains every asset in the international economic system. It is simply impossible to determine if such a portfolio is efficient in expected return, standard deviation space. If this is true, it follows that the capital asset pricing model can never *be* tested.

Previous Tests as Tautologies

Suppose we have a hat and many small pieces of paper. On each piece we write a number which represents a rate of return over a period of time, let's say a month. We put all the pieces into the hat and mix them up. Now pull 12 pieces of paper from the hat. The number on each piece will represent the rate of return on a stock in each of 12 months. Call this first stock 1, and put the pieces of paper back into the hat. Now do the same thing for another stock called 2, and repeat the process through stock 100. You now have 100 series of monthly returns, one for each stock. The series might look like that in Table 8.1. Since we have pulled only 12 returns from the hat for each "security," the sample mean returns for the individual securities will differ, even though their expected rates of return are all the same.

The mean monthly return represents the rate of return to our market index, an equally weighted portfolio of the 100 stocks. This index is constructed in the same way as the index used by BJS and FM.

TABLE 8.1   An Example Pulled from a Hat

Stock	Month					Stock Beta	Average Return
	1	2	3	...	12		
1	12%	5%	20%		−14%	1.30	7%
2	8	16	2		3	.70	2
.	.	.	.		.	.	.
.	.	.	.		.	.	.
.	.	.	.		.	.	.
100	20	1	7		10	1.05	10
Mean monthly return:	8	3	7		, 4		

Now we will compute beta factors for each of the 100 stocks. We relate the returns of each stock to the 12 returns of our market index. The line of best fit passing through the relationship is our estimate of the stock's characteristic line, and the slope of the line is our estimate of the stock's beta. We will find the average beta for all of the stocks is exactly equal to 1.00 and the betas for the individual stocks are scattered above and below 1, just as in the real world. They might look like the beta factors listed in Table 8.1. The average returns to the right of the beta factors are obtained by simply totaling the monthly returns on each stock and dividing by 12.

At this point we form 10 portfolios in the manner of BJS. We rank the stocks by beta and put the 10 percent of the stocks with the highest betas into the first portfolio, and so on. As with BJS, the portfolios are equally weighted, so the return on each portfolio, in each month, is the average of the returns on its 10 stocks. We also compute the beta for each portfolio by relating its returns to the returns of our market index. The schedule of betas and average rates of return to the portfolio might look like Table 8.2.

Suppose we now test the capital asset pricing model by examining the properties of the security market line. We estimate the security market line by relating beta to average return, first across the 100 individual stocks and then across the 10 portfolios.

The nature of our results depends on the position of our market index relative to the minimum variance set for our sample of stocks. Even though our stocks

TABLE 8.2   Betas and Average Returns to the 10 Portfolios

Portfolio	Beta	Average Return
A	1.30	12%
B	1.25	10
.	.	.
.	.	.
.	.	.
J	.40	3

were pulled from a hat, they still have an associated minimum variance set. Based on the numbers in Table 8.1, we can compute a covariance matrix for the 100-stock population. Given the covariance matrix and the average returns for the stocks, we can construct the minimum variance set. It might look like the one depicted in Figure 8.3.

Suppose our market index portfolio happens to be one of the portfolios in the minimum variance set, positioned at point M in Figure 8.3. It is extremely unlikely this would happen exactly, but suppose that it did. This being the case, we know, on the basis of property II (Chapter 5), that a perfect relationship will exist between beta factors and average returns for both individual stocks and for portfolios. Given our market index is positioned at M, the relationship will look like that of Figure 8.4. Each point in Figure 8.4 represents the position of a stock or portfolio. Note that the security market line intercepts the vertical axis at $\bar{r}_Z$, which is the average rate of return of portfolio Z, positioned on the minimum variance set of Figure 8.3. We will find (on the basis of property AII in Appendix 8) that this portfolio is perfectly uncorrelated with our market index, and we will call this portfolio the minimum variance, zero beta portfolio.

Note that we will think our results are consistent with the form of the CAPM where borrowing at the risk-free rate is disallowed, because $\bar{r}_Z$ happens to be greater than r_F. If our market index happened to be positioned at P' instead, we would have accepted the CAPM in its most basic form.

The results of our test are consistent with the CAPM even though the returns

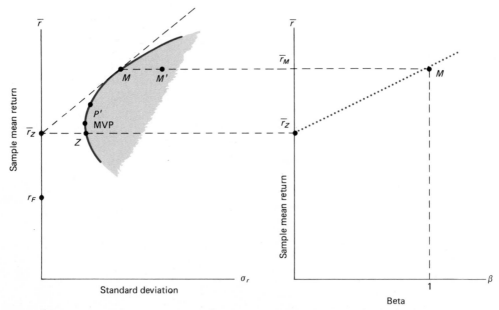

FIGURE 8.3 Minimum variance set for stocks drawn, from the hat.

FIGURE 8.4 Security market line corresponding to market index M.

were pulled from a hat! *This* is the problem. The results of tests such as these can well be consistent with the CAPM no matter what the actual pricing structure looks like in the market!

At this point you might object and say, "But you have assumed the market index is on the efficient set, and this is extremely unlikely." True enough, but if we look at our *portfolios,* we will obtain results which are likely to be consistent with CAPM as long as our market index has an average return greater than the average return to the global minimum variance portfolio, positioned at *MVP* in Figure 8.3.

Suppose, for example, our market index is positioned at point *M'* in Figure 8.3. Since the index is inside the bullet, we know the relationship between beta and average return for the individual stocks will look something like the scatter of Figure 8.5. Each point in the scatter represents 1 of the 100 stocks in our example. The broken line running through the scatter is the line of best fit.

BJS and FM did not look at individual stocks; they looked at portfolios. The Xs in Figure 8.5 represent the 10 stocks with the highest betas, all of which we put into portfolio A. Note that some of the stocks are above the line of best fit and some are below. This, of course, will tend to be true, given the properties of a line of best fit. Since the return on the portfolio is the average of the returns on the component stocks, the portfolio itself will be positioned very close to the line of best fit in Figure 8.6. This also will be true of the other portfolios such as *B, C,* and so on. Thus, even though the market index is well inside the bullet, the relationship between *port-*

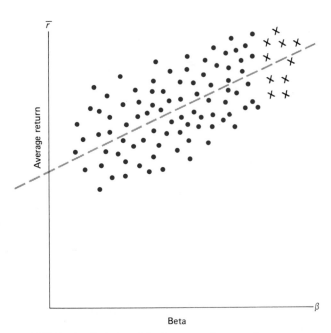

FIGURE 8.5 Relationship between beta and average return for stocks drawn from the hat.

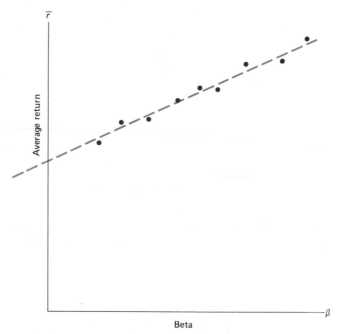

FIGURE 8.6 Relationship between beta and average return for portfolios drawn from the hat.

folio beta and average rate of return may well be _approximately_ consistent with the prediction of the capital asset pricing model.

What will be the propensity of these portfolios to line up in a straight line? Property AV of Appendix 8 provides some insight into this question. This property says that even if the portfolio used as a proxy for the market is inefficient, the relationship between the expected returns and betas of _minimum variance_ portfolios will be deterministic and linear. The portfolios studied by Black, Jensen, and Scholes were big, equally weighted, highly diversified portfolios. If these portfolios were positioned close to the bullet, they would tend to line up as a straight line irrespective of the efficiency of the true, value weighted market portfolio.

There is at least one condition under which equally weighted portfolios of large numbers of stocks are always nearly efficient, relative to a bullet constructed from the stocks, even when a _value_ weighted portfolio of the same stocks is not. This is the condition of the single-index model. In the context of this model the residual variance of equally weighted portfolios of hundreds of stocks will be infinitesimal, and these portfolios will have a propensity to take positions close to the bullet. The same is true of an equally weighted market proxy. It will tend to be close to the bullet even when its value weighted counterpart is not.

Just as the preceding test conducted failed to indicate that the returns on the stocks were pulled from a hat, the tests conducted on real data tell us little about the properties of the pricing structure in the stock market. While they indicate that the market indices employed were likely positioned above the global minimum variance portfolio, in terms of expected return, they tell us little about the relative efficiency of the index. In fact, it's doubtful if we are really interested in the efficiency of the index employed by BJS and FM in any case. To test the CAPM, we need to test the efficiency of the value weighted market portfolio. BJS and FM were employing an equally weighted portfolio of all stocks on a single exchange, the NYSE.

The problem here is that BJS and FM didn't directly test the CAPM's single prediction: The market portfolio is on the efficient set. Instead, they examined the properties of a security market line constructed on the basis of an equally weighted proxy for the market. Now it is true that if the market portfolio is efficient, the relationship between beta and expected return will be perfectly linear and positively sloped. Unfortunately, however, the reverse isn't also true. As we can clearly see from the foregoing example, if we find that the relationship between *portfolio* beta and average return is (nearly) perfectly linear, this does not imply that the market portfolio, or even the market proxy, is efficient.

Can the Capital Asset Pricing Model Ever Be Tested?

Roll's second point is that the CAPM is, in principle, an untestable theory. To see this, suppose that you recognize the problem with the earlier tests of the model and you seek instead to determine directly whether your market index is efficient. Assume that you restrict yourself to the NYSE. You construct a value weighted portfolio of all the stocks on the exchange. You compute its average return and its standard deviation over some past period of time and then position the index relative to the minimum variance set. Since there are well over 1000 stocks on the exchange, to compute the minimum variance set, you are going to be dealing with a huge covariance matrix. However, assume that you spend the computer time required to find the set. Your next job is to determine whether the degree of inefficiency exhibited by your index is statistically significant.

Assume that your index plots inside the bullet, as in Figure 8.7. Given the risk of your index, if it were efficient, its average return would be $\bar{r}_{M'}$; instead it is $\bar{r}_M$. What is the probability that the difference is due to chance? Suppose you run a statistical test and conclude that the probability is remote. You come to me and say, "I can reject the CAPM on the basis of this test." My response would be, "No you can't, because you haven't tested the prediction of the CAPM." You see, the CAPM predicts that the *market portfolio* is efficient. It doesn't predict that the NYSE index will be efficient relative to the minimum variance set based on NYSE stocks alone.

Suppose you have a population of assets and the market portfolio for these assets is efficient in terms of the minimum variance set for the *population*. If you now take a subset of these assets, it is highly unlikely that a value-weighted portfolio of the subset is going to be efficient in terms of the minimum variance set for the *subset of the population*. Thus, even if the true market portfolio is efficient, it's highly unlikely the NYSE index is going to be efficient relative to a minimum variance set based on NYSE stocks. Thus, you can't reject the CAPM on the basis of your finding.

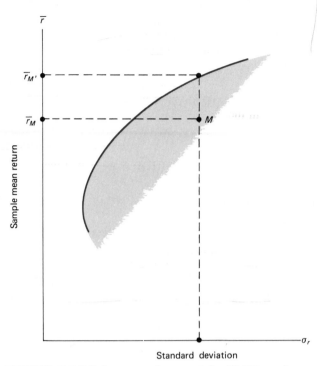

FIGURE 8.7 Minimum variance set for NYSE stocks.

To reject the CAPM, you've got to reject the efficiency of the true market portfolio. This is going to be extremely difficult, if not impossible. You will have to expand your study to include stocks on all other exchanges as well as in the over-the-counter markets. You will also have to include bonds, preferred stocks, and other types of securities. Many bonds are held privately by firms and are, consequently, never traded. You won't be able to observe the returns for these securities. You also won't be able to observe the returns on many other assets you will have to include, such as farms and proprietorships. Remember also that portfolio investors can diversify internationally, so you must include in your market portfolio all the capital assets of every country in the world. You indeed face an impossible task!

There are two important points to remember here. First, there is no reason to believe a market portfolio containing even a large fraction of the total assets in the economic system is going to be efficient based on the minimum variance set for the fraction even if the CAPM is the true underlying model. Second, given available information, we can observe the returns on only a tiny fraction of the total number of capital assets in existence. Shanken (1984) has argued that it's not the *fraction* of the total market value of all assets that's included in the proxy for the market that's important. Rather it's the *correlation* between the proxy returns and the market portfolio returns that counts. The fraction may be small, but the correlation could conceivably still be high. He also shows that the assets which are uncorrelated with the securities used in the empirical test of the CAPM need not be included in the proxy for the market portfolio. These are valid points, and they temper the critique of the model to some degree. However, it should be pointed out that we will never be able to observe the returns to the true market portfolio. Consequently, we shall never know the degree to which any proxy is correlated with those returns. Morever, we shall never know to what extent assets, which are correlated with securities included in the test, are present in the market portfolio but not included in the proxy.

Based on these arguments, many in the profession have concluded that no one has ever come close to constructing a valid test of the capital asset pricing model and that no one ever will. They feel that the CAPM is simply not a testable theory!

THE OTHER SIDE OF THE ISSUE

Roll's critique goes directly to the heart of financial theory. His points are obviously controversial, and they have been the subject of a great deal of debate in the profession in the years since his original paper was released. In the sections that follow, we discuss a few of the counterpoints which have been offered in support of the capital asset pricing model.

Tautologies Can't Predict the Future

Roll argues that the results of previous tests of the CAPM are tautological because, given the procedure used to form portfolios in the tests, you are likely to see a linear relationship between average return and beta irrespective of the relative efficiency of your market index or the nature of the actual pricing structure that exists.

Some have argued that while this may be true of the methodology employed by Black, Jensen, and Scholes, it is not true of the methodology employed by Fama and MacBeth.[1] If you recall, the essential difference between the two studies is that BJS related average returns to betas measured in the same period of time, while FM predicted *future* returns on the basis of betas measured over a *past* period. While a tautological relationship (property II, Chapter 5) exists between average return and beta measured in the same period, no such relationship exists when the two variables are measured over successive or different periods. Fama and MacBeth *predicted* next month's return on the basis of the past beta factors of their portfolios. Some have argued their success can't be attributed to the tautological relationship, because tautologies are merely definitional and, as such, have no predictive power.

You can see the point clearly if you recall our example with the hat. When average returns and betas were measured over the same 12-month period, if an *efficient* market index is employed, it is automatically true that the greater the beta of a portfolio, the greater will be its average rate of return. Suppose, however, we run the experiment in a slightly different way. This time we will compute the beta factors

---

[1]This point was suggested to me by Robert Litzenberger.

on the basis of the returns in the initial 12-month period, and then we will pull one additional return from the hat for each of the 10 portfolios. Since the returns are pulled at random, we should obviously expect to see no relationship between the beta of the portfolio and the next return pulled from the hat for the portfolio. There is no tautological relationship between the previous beta and the *next* return.

Note that FM did something very similar to this. They measured the betas for their portfolios using monthly returns over a 5-year period. They then used these betas to predict the returns on the portfolios in the individual months of the next few years. They find that you can expect to get a higher return in the future on portfolios of stocks that have had greater than average betas in the past. On the surface, at least, this relationship doesn't seem to be a mere product of property II.

But property II, in fact, may be working its way in through the back door.[2] To see this, suppose that all investors were risk neutral but that securities still had differential expected rates of return. One *possible* source of the differentials in the expected returns might be taxes. In the presence of taxes on investment income, securities with greater degrees of tax exposure might sell at greater pretax expected rates of return so as to produce competitive returns on an after-tax basis. Suppose dividends are taxed at a greater rate than capital gains. If this is true, stocks which pay out a greater percentage of their earnings as dividends expose their investors to a greater tax burden than stocks with lower payouts and greater rates of market price appreciation. Under these assumptions, if we fix the supply of dividends distributed in the market, we would expect that stocks with higher dividend payouts should have greater expected rates of return. We have no risk premiums, but we do have *tax-induced* differentials in expected rates of return.

Now suppose we compute betas for portfolios of stocks over some given period of time. We would expect that the portfolios more heavily invested in high-dividend-paying stocks should produce the greatest average rates of return. Based on the tautological relationship of property II these portfolios should also have the largest beta factors. Beta, in this case, is serving as sort of a proxy for the average rate of return.

What would we expect to happen if we relate the portfolio betas to returns produced in subsequent periods? Based on the tax factor, we would predict that the portfolios containing stocks with the highest dividend payouts will produce the greatest rates of return in the future. Since these portfolios also have the largest betas in the past, we should expect to see a relationship between past beta and future return that stems from the identity relationship of property II.

We are able to predict future return on the basis of past beta, not because of the presence of the CAPM (investors are, in fact, assumed to be risk neutral) but rather because the beta of the past period is serving as a proxy for average return in the past period. If we related average return in the past to future return, we would probably find an even stronger relationship, because, unless our market index was on the minimum variance set, beta will serve as an *imperfect* proxy for average return in the past period.

In the same sense, while FM find a significant relationship between past beta

[2]I became aware of this possibility in a discussion with Richard Green.

and future return, the relationship may be based on the identity relationship between beta and average return in the past period. They may find they can predict future returns with greater accuracy simply on the basis of past average returns.

Can You Reject the CAPM If You Find No Efficient Portfolios with Positive Portfolio Weights?

It may be argued that Roll is stretching the argument when he says that we must be able to observe the true market portfolio to test the CAPM. Since, in equilibrium, all assets in a given class (such as all stocks on the NYSE) must be held, it would seem the CAPM could be rejected by rejecting the existence of any portfolio with all positive portfolio weights that could be expected to be efficient.

The problem with this argument is that the relevant efficient set is the one based on the totality of all capital assets in the economic system. If we find no positively weighted portfolios in this set, then we can indeed reject the CAPM. However, this is the set we know is impossible to construct! The CAPM doesn't predict that the efficient set based on NYSE stocks alone should have any portfolios with all positive portfolio weights. Instead, it predicts the efficient set based on the entire population of assets should have portfolios with all positive portfolio weights. One of these portfolios is, of course, the market portfolio.

In a recent paper, Tiemann (1988) has made some progress in this regard. He shows, *if we assume that stocks are priced exactly according to the arbitrage pricing theory* discussed in the next chapter, rejection of the hypothesis that there are no all-positive weighted portfolios on an efficient set for a subset of assets implies rejection for the global efficient set as well. We must assume in addition, however, the subset is representative of the global set in terms of its covariances. However, again, since the global set is unobservable, we will never know how much confidence to place in this assumption.[3]

Testing a Contained CAPM

It can be argued that we can *contain* the theory to apply to a segment of the market. For example, I could hypothesize that the NYSE is a self-contained or segmented market with a pricing structure characterized by the capital asset pricing model. Since I can observe the market portfolio of New York Stock Exchange stocks, I now have a theory I can test.

The problem with this argument is that we can reject the contained theory out of hand. Suppose only a few investors looked outside the NYSE to form efficient portfolios based on a wider population of assets. For these investors, their NYSE stock portfolios are unlikely to be efficient relative to the efficient set based on NYSE

---

[3]The exact assumption is that the covariance between the value-weighted portfolio of missing assets and the individual assets in the subset can be replicated by a positively weighted portfolio of the assets in the subset. Keep in mind that a major component of the missing assets, human capital is usually not represented at all in the subset.

stocks alone. We know the market portfolio sums the portfolio holdings of all investors. (In this case the NYSE market portfolio sums the portfolio holdings of NYSE stocks of all investors.) If the portfolios of NYSE stocks were all efficient, the market portfolio would be efficient as well. However, since at least some investors hold inefficient portfolios of NYSE stocks alone, we know in advance that the NYSE market portfolio will be inefficient relative to the NYSE efficient set.

Sensitivity Analysis to Alternative Market Indices

Stambough (1982) has conducted a sensitivity analysis to determine whether changing the nature of the market proxy has a significant impact on the results of tests of the CAPM. He expands the types of investments included in his proxy from stocks on the NYSE to corporate and government bonds to real estate to durable consumer goods such as house furnishings and automobiles. His results indicate that the nature of your conclusions aren't materially affected as you expand the composition of your proxy for the market portfolio.

These results at first appear to be comforting until you realize that even in the broadest indices examined, many, many investments were not included at the domestic level, including human capital. More importantly, the market portfolio is internationally diversified, and the total invested capital of the United States is only a small fraction of invested capital worldwide. Moreover, many of these investments can be expected to exhibit a low degree of correlation with returns on investments in the United States. Stambough's results tell us only that when we move from using a market proxy which represents a very small fraction of the market portfolio to a proxy that represents only a larger but still very small fraction, empirical results don't tend to change much. Beginning from a mile away, it appears our results don't change when we move a foot closer to our destination.

MORE RECENT TESTS OF THE CAPM

More recent tests of the CAPM have addressed its central prediction: "The market portfolio is on the global mean-variance efficient set." In particular, Shanken (1987) provides a clever approach to a potential empirical test of the model.

Suppose you have a proxy for the market portfolio and a population of securities from which the proxy portfolio is constructed. Assume also that the subpopulation is only a small fraction of the global population of all capital investments in the international economy and the efficient set based on this subpopulation is likely to be well inside the global efficient set based on the global population based on all capital investments, as we have drawn in Figure 8.8. In the figure, point M represents the proxy for the market portfolio, and point M^* denotes the position of the true global market portfolio. As you can see, neither M nor M^* is efficient relative to its respective efficient sets. As we discussed, in the presence of unexpected developments during the period in which M is observed, this must always be the case. The issue at hand is whether M^* was *expected* to be inefficient relative to the *global* efficient set.

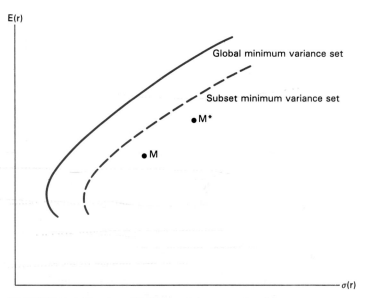

FIGURE 8.8 Testing CAPM based on a prior for $\rho_{P,M}$.

Now neither M^* nor the global efficient set can be observed, but you *can* observe M and the efficient set for the subpopulation. You can also determine whether M was *expected* to be inefficient relative to the subpopulation efficient set.

As Shanken points out, you can also do something else. Given a prior opinion regarding the correlation between the returns to M and M^*, *and the assumption that expected returns are linearly related to covariance with M^**, you can determine whether M^* was expected to be inefficient relative to the subpopulation efficient set. Because it comes from a subpopulation, the subpopulation efficient set *must* lie within the global efficient set. Therefore, if M^* was expected to be inefficient with respect to the subpopulation efficient set, it must also have been expected to be inefficient with respect to the global efficient set. It seems possible to reject CAPM, given the assumed relationship for expected returns and a prior for the correlation coefficient between M and M^*. Shanken goes on to demonstrate that CAPM can be rejected with 95 percent confidence, if you are willing to accept the prior that the correlation coefficient between the proxy used by Fama and MacBeth and by Black, Jensen, and Scholes is greater than approximately .8.

This is an interesting idea, but it still leaves us with a serious problem. Since a great fraction of the market portfolio is nonmarketable and therefore unobservable in its return, how are we to know whether .8 is a reasonable prior opinion about the correlation coefficient? Given that the market portfolio includes human capital and other very important and completely unobservable components, it is easy to make a case for the notion that the correlation of observable proxies and the true market portfolio may be very low. Given that it is, is a non-rejectable prior an improvement over a non-rejectable theory?

SUMMARY

The single, independent prediction of the capital asset pricing model is that the market portfolio is positioned on the efficient set. Several other conditions follow automatically, given this prediction, including a linear, positively sloped relationship between beta and expected rates of return. Unfortunately, this relationship between beta and expected return is a necessary but not a sufficient condition for the efficiency of the market portfolio. Given the methodology employed in early tests of the CAPM to construct portfolios, we would expect to see the CAPM's beta-return relationship irrespective of the relative efficiency of the market portfolio. These early tests of the model, therefore, tell us little about the structure of stock prices, other than the fact that the average return to their market proxies was probably greater than the average return to the minimum variance portfolio during the periods studied.

To test the CAPM, you must directly test whether the market portfolio is on the efficient set. The most recent tests of the CAPM are directed at answering this question. It must be said, however, that these tests are not likely to provide convincing empirical support for the model. The inherent problem with the CAPM is that the market portfolio contains every single capital asset in the economic system. There is no possible way to determine whether such a portfolio is efficient relative to the minimum variance set for the entire capital asset population. The observable market portfolio is only a tiny fraction of the true market portfolio. Moreover, even if the true market portfolio *is* efficient with respect to the total population, there is no reason to believe a submarket portfolio is going to be efficient with respect to a subpopulation of assets, even though the subpopulation is a very large fraction of the total. Because of this, we shall never be able to empirically test the single economic prediction of the capital asset pricing model.

CAPM follows logically from its assumptions, and it comes to a conclusion that is intuitively appealing. It makes sense that investors will price securities according to the contribution each makes to the risk of their overall portfolios. Thirty years ago we believed the risk of an individual security could be measured on the basis of the properties of its simple or marginal probability distribution, without regard to its relationships with other securities. The insight provided by the CAPM was a *major* step forward in our understanding of the way securities are priced in the market place.

It is also true that the CAPM is an *accepted* model in the securities industry. It is used by firms to make capital budgeting and other decisions. It is used by some regulatory authorities to regulate utility rates. It is used by rating agencies to measure the performance of investment managers. It would not be so widely used if it were not regarded as an extremely useful benchmark. It is, therefore, extremely important for you to understand the model in terms of both its strengths and weaknesses.

Work on deriving alternatives to the CAPM is underway. The arbitrage pricing theory is an alternative that captures the appealing intuition of the CAPM while purporting, at least by some, to be testable at the empirical level. We will examine this model in the next chapter.

QUESTION SET 1

1. Black, Jensen, and Scholes interpreted their estimated security market line as giving support for the CAPM with riskless lending but no riskless borrowing. In what way would their results have had to be different in order for them to find support for the basic CAPM (allowing unlimited borrowing and lending at a riskless rate)?

2. In what ways did the experimental design of the Fama-MacBeth study differ from that of Black, Jensen, and Scholes?

3. Fama-MacBeth tried to test whether residual variances of the stocks in a portfolio affect the portfolio's expected rate of return. Why does the CAPM lead you to believe that residual variance of a stock is not related to its expected return?

4. In the Fama-MacBeth study, what is the purpose of including a β^2 as an independent variable in some of their regressions? From the results reported in the text on the estimated coefficient of β^2, what can be concluded?

5. What is the central prediction of the CAPM? Based on the central prediction, what ought to be the nature of the security market line?

6. What is a potential difficulty in using *portfolio* data to test for the goodness of fit of the return-beta relationship?

7. Suppose you have data for all New York and American Stock Exchange issues. You construct the minimum variance set for the stocks. You also construct a value weighted index of all these stocks and find that your index is on the efficient part of the minimum variance set. Can you conclude that the CAPM is a valid theory? Explain.

8. Why would Richard Roll (and others) argue that tests of the CAPM like those of Black, Jensen, and Scholes are tautological?

9. With respect to the Fama-MacBeth approach,
   a. Why might someone argue that this set of tests is *not* subject to the criticism that the results may occur tautologically?
   b. How would you respond to the argument in part a to argue that the Fama-MacBeth approach *is* subject to the tautology criticism?

10. a. What does it mean to say that the "market portfolio is efficient?"
   b. What approach have studies such as Fama-MacBeth and Black, Jensen, and Scholes taken to testing whether the market portfolio is efficient?

11. The CAPM conclusions are couched in terms of *expectations* of the future. How can we then proceed to test the theory with historical data?

QUESTION SET 2

1. In the computer program for the Markowitz model, you can use as an index the New York Stock Exchange. Why might this not be a good index to use in determining whether the CAPM was valid?

2. You are an expert testifying at a hearing to support the utility's request for a rate increase. The opposition states that the utility is not earning enough on its investments and points to a high beta on the utility's portfolio, utilizing the CAPM. How do you respond?

3. The CAPM asserts that the total market portfolio is positioned on the efficient set, and

hence each and every portfolio held by investors must also be on the efficient set. You decide to study the portfolios of retired persons living in apartment buildings. Intuitively, what factors pertaining to these investors would make you question the basis of the CAPM?

4. What if BJS and FM had studied individual stocks to test the CAPM instead of portfolios? How might their results have been different?

5. Suppose BJS had restricted their study to portfolios traded on the NYSE from 1929 to 1933 and, instead of getting an upward-sloping security market line, produced a downward-sloping one. What implications would this have had on the CAPM?

6. FM utilized prior betas on portfolios to predict the returns on the portfolios in future months, and found that you can expect a higher return on such portfolios in the future. Even if investors were risk neutral, why might there still be differential rates of return on portfolios of stock which would be predictable using beta in the absence of the CAPM model?

ANSWERS TO QUESTION SET 2

1. The CAPM assumes the *total* market portfolio, including *all* assets, is mean-variance efficient. As such, it must include such things as all capital assets for every country, which the New York Stock Exchange doesn't include, and additional assets which are never traded, such as human capital.

2. You point out that the beta of a stock is related to the index portfolio against which it is measured. Since there is no one index portfolio of all assets in the economic system through which to test the CAPM, an index portfolio must be chosen. You can choose an alternative portfolio as an index, and just as legitimately assert that the beta of the utility's portfolio is too low!

3. The two types of market assets likely to be *not* included in the portfolios of retired persons living in apartment houses are human capital (the present value of future earnings) and real estate holdings. Hence, if these investors hold portfolios which are inefficient for a subset of securities in expected return–standard deviation space, they must also be inefficient relative to the global bullet. Therefore, you can reject CAPM on the basis of this finding.

4. Since portfolios studied by BJS and FM were the average of returns on the component stocks, the portfolios themselves were positioned very close to a line of best fit, or the security market line. Hence the portfolio beta and average rate of return could be approximately consistent with the prediction of the CAPM. However, the deviations from the security market line when studying separate stocks probably would not reflect this "averaging" factor (or the tendency to make things equalize in the long run), and thus not support the prediction of the CAPM.

5. The CAPM's predictions may be validated only when the market index has an average return that is greater than the average return to the global minimum variance portfolio. When the stock market crashed in 1929, market average returns were probably less than the average returns to the *MVP*. This would result in a downward-sloping security market line.

6. A possible source of differentials in expected returns might be differential tax treatment. If taxes discriminate between investment opportunities, then investors would require the same after-tax rate on an investment, even in a risk-neutral state. In this case, beta would be serving as a proxy for average return in the past, and we could predict the same result as the CAPM without its assumptions.

REFERENCES

BLACK, F., JENSEN, M. C., and SCHOLES, M., "The Capital Asset Pricing Model: Some Empirical Tests," in Ed. Jensen, M. C. *Studies in Theory of Capital Markets.* New York: Praeger, 1972.

CHENG, P. L., and GRAUER, R. R., "An Alternative Test of the Capital Asset Pricing Model," *American Economic Review* (September 1980).

FAMA, E. F., and MACBETH, J., "Tests of Multiperiod Two Parameter Model," *Journal of Political Economy* (May 1974).

FOSTER, J., "Asset Pricing Models: Further Tests," *Journal of Financial and Quantitative Analysis* (March 1978).

FRIEND, I., WESTERFIELD, R., and GRANITO, M., "New Evidence on the Capital Asset Pricing Model," *Journal of Finance* (June 1978).

GRAUER, R. R., "Generalized Two Parameter Asset Pricing Models: Some Empirical Evidence," *Journal of Financial Economics* (March 1978).

JAHANKHANI, A., "E-V and E-S Capital Asset Pricing Models: Some Empirical Tests," *Journal of Financial and Quantitative Analysis* (September 1976).

JENSEN, M., "Risk, The Pricing of Capital Assets, and the Evaluation of Investment Portfolios," *Journal of Business* (April 1969).

LEVY, H., "The Capital Asset Pricing Model: Theory and Empiricism," *The Economic Journal* (March 1983).

MULLINS, D. W., "Does the Capital Asset Pricing Model Work?," *Harvard Business Review* (January–February 1982).

REINGANUM, M. R., "A New Empirical Perspective on the Capital Asset Pricing Model," *Journal of Financial and Quantitative Analysis* (November 1981).

ROLL, R., "A Critique of the Asset Pricing Theory's Tests: Part I: On the Past and Potential Testability of the Theory," *Journal of Financial Economics* (March 1977).

ROLL, R., "Ambiguity When Performance is Measured by the Security Market Line," *Journal of Finance* (September 1978).

ROSS, S. A., "The Capital Asset Pricing Model (CAPM), Short Sale Restrictions and Related Issues," *Journal of Finance* (March 1977).

ROSS, S. A., "The Current Status of the Capital Asset Pricing Model (CAPM)," *The Journal of Finance* (June 1978).

SHANKEN, J., "On the Exclusion of Assets from Tests of the Mean Variance Efficiency of the Market Portfolio: An Extension," Working Paper, Graduate School of Business Administration, University of California, Berkeley, 1984.

SHANKEN, J., "Multivariate Proxies and Asset Pricing Relations," *Journal of Financial Economics,* Vol. 18 (1987).

STAMBOUGH, R., "On the Exclusion of Assets from Tests of the Two-Parameter Model," *Journal of Financial Economics* (November 1982).

TIEMANN, J., "Exact Arbitrage Pricing and the Minimum-Variance Frontier," *Journal of Finance* (June 1988).

9

THE ARBITRAGE PRICING THEORY

In the previous chapter we found there is a fundamental problem associated with the capital asset pricing model—it may not be possible to support or contradict the model with empirical evidence. This problem has stimulated interest in an alternative model of asset pricing called the (APT), which was first introduced by Ross (1976).

Proponents of the APT argue that it has two major advantages over the CAPM. First, it makes assumptions regarding investors' preferences toward risk and return that some would argue are less restrictive. If you recall, one of the assumptions of the CAPM was that investors could choose between alternative portfolio investments solely on the basis of expected return and standard deviation. The APT requires that bounds be placed on investors' utility functions, but the bounds are less restrictive. Second, the proponents of the APT argue that the model can be refuted or verified empirically. As we shall see, this point of view has been the subject of much dispute, but to many the testability of the APT is an open question.

DERIVING THE ARBITRAGE PRICING THEORY

The fundamental assumption of the APT is that security returns are generated by a process identical to the single- or multi-index models discussed in Chapter 6. We assume that the covariances that exist between security returns can be attributed to the fact that the securities respond, to one degree or another, to the pull of one or more factors. We don't specify exactly what these factors are, but we do assume that the relationship between the security returns and the factors is linear, as in the case of a multi-index model. Thus, the rate of return to stock J in any given period t is assumed to be given by

$$r_{J,t} = A_J + \beta_{1,J} I_{1,t} + \beta_{2,J} I_{2,t} + \cdots + \beta_{n,J} I_{n,t} + \varepsilon_{J,t} \qquad (9.1)$$

In this equation, I represents the value of any one of the indices, or factors, which affects the rate of return to the stock. The number of indices is assumed to be equal to n. Actually the number of indices is unimportant to the *theory* (except we need to assume there are many more securities than there are indices), although it may be important to empirical implementation of the theory. The intercept term A_J should be interpreted as it was before. It is the expected rate of return on the stock, conditioned on the fact that all of the indices take on a zero value (have no impact on the stock) during the period. The individual betas can be positive or negative from factor to factor and from stock to stock.

Since it is assumed that all of the covariances between the rates of return to the securities are attributable to the effect of the factors, the residual term $\varepsilon_{J,t}$ will be uncorrelated between companies. Given this, the residual variance for any portfolio of individual securities is given by the familiar expression

$$\sigma^2(\varepsilon_P) = \sum_{J=1}^{M} x_J^2 \, \sigma^2(\varepsilon_J) \qquad (9.2)$$

Moreover, the variance of portfolio *return* is given by the formula for portfolio variance under the multi-index model[1]:

$$\sigma^2(r_P) = \beta_{1,P}^2 \, \sigma^2(I_1) + \beta_{2,P}^2 \, \sigma^2(I_2) + \cdots + \beta_{n,P}^2 \, \sigma^2(I_n) + \sigma^2(\varepsilon_P) \qquad (9.3)$$

And, as with the multi-index model, the portfolio's beta with respect to any one of the factors is a simple weighted average of the betas of the securities in the portfolio:

$$\beta_{1,P} = \sum_{J=1}^{M} x_J \beta_{1,J}$$

[1]Actually, this equation assumes that the covariance between the factors is equal to zero. This is not a necessary assumption for the APT. Even with nonzero covariances between the factors, while the following equation will have some additional terms relating to factor covariances, these terms will all drop out for zero beta portfolios, leaving the variance of the portfolios equal to the residual variance.

The APT with an Infinite Number of Securities

Given that we have imposed the preceding constraints on the process generating security returns, we need only assume there is an infinite number of securities and there are no restrictions on short selling to derive the approximate relationship between expected return and risk under the APT.

To derive the APT risk-return relationship, suppose a single factor can explain all the covariances that exist between stocks. What will the relationship between the expected rate of return to stocks and their responsiveness β_1 to the factor look like?

Suppose it looks like the nonlinear relationship of Figure 9.1. It can be shown that such a nonlinear relationship is infeasible, given the assumptions we've made thus far. If the relationship looked like that of Figure 9.1, any of us could make unlimited sums of money with no required investment and no assumed risk.

There are an infinite number of securities scattered along the curved line of Figure 9.1. Six of these securities are labeled at points A, B, C, D, E, and F. Since both beta and expected portfolio return are simple weighted averages of the betas and expected rates of return of the securities we put in the portfolio, combination lines can be drawn as straight lines passing through the points on the graph. Thus, the combination line for stocks C and E is given by the line passing through points $E(r_{Z'})$, C, and E. Positions between C and E are taken by investing positive amounts of money in both stocks. Positions between $E(r_{Z'})$ and C are taken by selling stock E short and using the proceeds to invest in stock C.

Note that by selling stock E short and investing in C, we can construct a port-

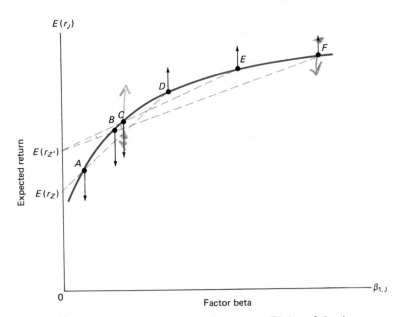

FIGURE 9.1 Infeasible relationship between $E(r_J)$ and $\beta_{1,J}$ in a one-factor model.

folio positioned on the graph at point $E(r_{Z'})$. The beta of this portfolio is equal to zero. We have assumed the position at $E(r_{Z'})$ by using two stocks, C and E, but we could have also assumed it by using four, shorting stocks E and F and using the proceeds to invest in stocks C and B. In fact, we can assume a position at $E(r_{Z'})$ by using as many pairs of stocks as we want. Since there is an infinite number of securities scattered along the line, we can use an infinite number of pairs to assume the position. If we do, the portfolio will have a zero variance. This is true because its beta is zero by construction, and its residual variance is zero on the basis of Equation (9.2). Since M is equal to infinity, the individual portfolio weights are so small that when we square them, in taking the weighted average, the residual variance sums to approximately zero:

$$\sigma^2(\varepsilon_P) = \sum_{J=1}^{\infty} x_J^2 \, \sigma^2(\varepsilon_J) \approx 0$$

The portfolio has no systematic risk and almost no residual variance, but it has an expected (riskless) rate of return equal to $E(r_{Z'})$.

Note that we can construct another portfolio positioned at $E(r_Z)$ by selling stock D short and investing in stock A. Again, by employing an infinite number of pairs of stocks, we can construct a portfolio positioned at $E(r_Z)$ with virtually no systematic risk or residual variance.

We have now constructed two zero-variance, or riskless, portfolios with two different expected rates of return. A position in *either* portfolio requires a positive capital commitment, but we can take a position in *both* portfolios with no capital commitment at all. We can do this by selling a given amount of the portfolio positioned at $E(r_Z)$ short and using the proceeds (with no equity investment of our own) to invest in the portfolio positioned at $E(r_{Z'})$.

Assume that $E(r_Z) = 10\%$ and $E(r_{Z'}) = 14\%$ and we sell short \$1 million of the 10 percent portfolio and use the proceeds to invest in the 14 percent portfolio. The certain loss in the short sale of the 10 percent portfolio is

$$10\% \times (-\$1,000,000) = -\$100,000$$

while the certain gain on the investment in the 14 percent portfolio is

$$14\% \times \quad \$1,000,000 \quad = \$140,000$$

The difference of \$40,000 is a pure and riskless profit, which is available to us all. Assuming there are no restrictions on short sales, we can all become as rich as we please!

Needless to say, we'll all be trying to take advantage of this opportunity, selling short stocks such as D, E, and F while buying stocks such as A, B, and C. In our attempts to make money, we will drive down the prices of stocks such as D, E, and F and drive up their expected rates of return. In the same sense, our buying activity will drive up the prices of stocks such as A, B, and C and drive down their expected rates of return in the direction indicated by the arrows on the graph.

The effect of all this will be to "unbend" the line until the general relationship between expected return and factor risk becomes approximately linear, as in

Figure 9.2. Given *this* relationship, any riskless portfolio we construct with any of the stocks will always have the same expected return, $E(r_Z)$. Pure, riskless arbitrage opportunities are unavailable when the general relationship between expected return and factor risk is linear, as it is in Figure 9.2.

Thus, in a single-factor APT, the relationship between factor risk and expected rates of return is given by

$$E(r_J) \approx E(r_Z) + \lambda_1\beta_{1,J}$$

The expression is written as an approximation because, while the general relationship between factor risk and expected return will be linear, there may still be individual deviations from the relationship so long as there isn't a sufficient number of them to open up riskless arbitrage opportunities.

In the preceding approximation, λ_1 is the slope of the relationship between factor risk and expected return. The magnitude of the slope depends on how risk averse investors are and how important they regard the factor as a source of stock co-variability. Some factors may not be priced, and in this case the slope will be zero. From time to time we will refer to the slope of the relationship between the factor risk and the expected rate of return as the factor price.

Now let's add a second factor to the model. We are now assuming that the covariances that exist between the returns on securities are attributable to the fact that the returns respond to two factors. Again, what will be the feasible relationship between factor risk and expected rates of return?

Suppose the relationship is given by the curved, three-dimensional surface in Figure 9.3. Again, we assume that an infinite number of securities are distributed over the surface. In the diagram, expected return increases with the degree of re-

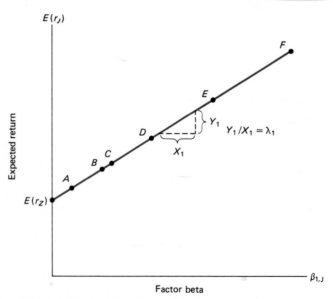

FIGURE 9.2 A feasible relationship between $E(r_j)$ and $\beta_{1,J}$.

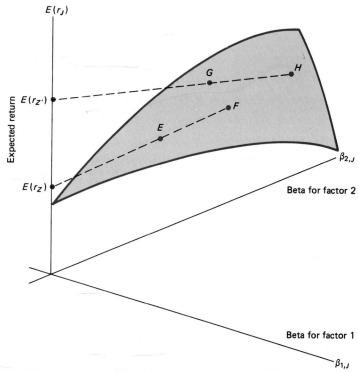

FIGURE 9.3 Infeasible relationship between $E(r_j)$ and $\beta_{1,J}$ and $\beta_{2,J}$ in a two-factor model.

sponsiveness of a security's return to each of the two factors. However, expected return increases at a decreasing rate. Given this nonlinear relationship between factor risk and expected return, we can again create riskless arbitrage opportunities which promise unlimited wealth.

By selling short securities such as H and using the proceeds to invest in securities such as G, we can create a zero beta position for *both* factors with an expected return equal to $E(r_{Z'})$. By doing this with an infinite number of pairs of securities, we can drive the variance of our zero beta portfolio to zero. At the same time, by short-selling securities such as F and investing in securities such as E, we can construct a zero beta, zero variance portfolio with an expected return equal to $E(r_Z)$. We then short-sell the portfolio with the lower expected return and use the proceeds to invest in the higher-return portfolio. Our arbitrage profit is equal to the difference in expected return multiplied by the dollar amount we sold short. Since it is assumed we can short-sell in unlimited amounts, we can create unlimited amounts of wealth for ourselves in this manner.

In the process of short-selling securities such as F and H and buying securities such as E and G, investors will affect prices and expected rates of return and begin to unbend the surface, making it into a linear plane like that of Figure 9.4. Given a linear relationship between expected return and the factor risks, no arbitrage op-

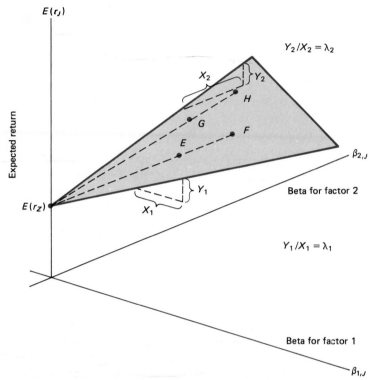

FIGURE 9.4 Feasible relationship between expected return and factor risk in a two-factor model.

portunities are available. All zero beta portfolios have the same expected rate of return, $E(r_Z)$.

The equation for the risk–expected return relationship is now given by the approximation for the plane:

$$E(r_J) \approx E(r_Z) + \lambda_1 \beta_{1,J} + \lambda_2 \beta_{2,J} \tag{9.4}$$

In the approximation the coefficients λ_1 and λ_2 represent the factor prices. In Figure 9.4 they are given by

$$\lambda_1 = \frac{Y_1}{X_1}$$

$$\lambda_2 = \frac{Y_2}{X_2}$$

In the diagram, the coefficients are both positive, but they need not be. In a multifactor model, many of the coefficients can be negative as well as positive.

As we move beyond two factors, we move to multidimensional hyperplanes, which are impossible to visualize. Nevertheless, it is still the case that, unless the relationship between factor risks and expected returns is approximately linear, unlimited arbitrage opportunities may become available. This is the central message of the APT. If security returns are generated by a process equivalent to that of a linear multifactor model with n priced factors, the relationship between expected return and factor risk must be approximately linear.

$$E(r_J) \approx E(r_Z) + \sum_{I=1}^{n} \lambda_I \beta_{I,J}$$

In the context of the APT, it must be impossible to construct two different portfolios, both having zero variance, with two different expected rates of return. This will be the case if the relationship between the factor betas and the expected rates of return is linear. It will not be the case if the relationship is generally nonlinear, *as in the examples cited*. As we have stressed, the absence of arbitrage opportunities doesn't ensure *exact* linear pricing, however. For example, we may have a few securities positioned above and below the plane of Figure 9.4. Because their number is fewer than is required to drive the residual variance of the arbitrage portfolio to zero, we no longer have a riskless arbitrage opportunity and no required market pressure forcing their expected returns to conform to the APT equation. While the linear relationship prices most assets with negligible error, it can be highly inaccurate in pricing some of them. It has been shown by Connor (1983) and others, however, that we *can* get more exact APT pricing if we (1) put bounds on investors' utility functions, (2) assume that everyone makes investment and consumption decisions that maximize their utility, and (3) assume that the market clears in the sense that there is no excess supply or demand for securities. In the context of these restrictions, however, we have a model that is more in the spirit of an equilibrium model, like the CAPM, than it is in the spirit of an arbitrage model, like the Black-Scholes option pricing model discussed later in the book.

The APT with a Finite Number of Securities

If we don't have an unlimited number of securities to work with, we can't reduce the residual variance of our zero beta arbitrage portfolios to zero in *any* case. If the number of securities is very large, we can reduce residual variance to a very small number, but we still must bear some risk in capturing our arbitrage profit.

Under these conditions, Dybvig (1983) and Grinblatt and Titman (1983) have shown that relationships of the form of Equation (9.4) understate the actual expected rate of return. Although they quantify the understatement for the general case, in the special case of normal distributions for security returns the understatement for security J is equal to

$$R \cdot x_J \cdot \sigma^2(\varepsilon_J) \tag{9.5}$$

In this expression, x_J is the portfolio weight of security J in the market portfolio, $\sigma^2(\varepsilon_J)$ is the residual variance of security J, and R is a measure of investor risk aversion. The term R is measured in terms of the relationship between investor utility and investor wealth. It is equal to the negative of per capita wealth multiplied by the ratio of the second derivative of the utility function to the first derivative.

To get a feel for R, consider the case of a quadratic utility function. Assume the function takes the following form:

$$U_i = .50V_i - .000001V_i^2$$

In the equation U_i is the utility associated with the level of portfolio wealth V_i in the ith possible state of nature. This utility function is plotted in Figure 9.5. As you can see, the coefficient in front of the term, V_i^2, is actually quite significant in its effect in absolute terms, implying satiation with wealth at a wealth level of $250,000.00. The first derivative of the utility function is given by

$$.50 - 2 \times .000001V_i$$

and the second derivative is given by

$$-2 \times .000001 = -.000002$$

Assuming a per capita wealth level of $50,000.00, R is given by

$$R = -\$50,000.00 \times \frac{-.000002}{.50 - 2 \times .000001 \times \$50,000.00} = .25$$

Assuming that the security is that of a very large company, representing .01 percent of the market portfolio and that the residual variance of the security is as large as .50, the APT equation will understate the true expected return by only .00125 percent.

Intuitively, the expression for the understatement can be explained as follows. The deviation from the linear APT relationship is caused by the presence of unavoid-

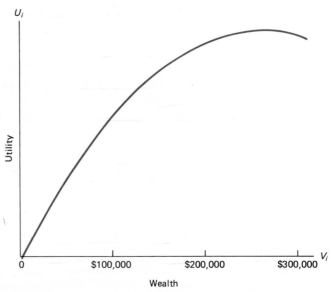

FIGURE 9.5 Utility function: $U_i = .5V_i - .000001\, V_i^2$.

able residual variance in the arbitrage portfolios. This residual variance will be greater when the residual variance of the security (the third term in the product) is greater and when the portfolio weight assigned to the security (second term) is greater. If investors were risk neutral, they wouldn't care about unavoidable residual variance, and it wouldn't affect expected returns. The greater their risk aversion (first term), the greater the impact of unavoidable residual variance on expected return.

Thus, the APT also works as an approximation if the number of securities is less than infinite. For the model to work, we need some weak restrictions on investor preferences and the distribution of security returns. These restrictions serve to prevent Expression (9.5) from blowing up. If we assume that investors have concave utility functions, we contain the first term in the product. We know that security returns are truncated from below at -100 percent. If we assume they are truncated from above at some point, we contain the third term in the product (the residual variance must then be finite). These restrictions seem less severe than those we must impose on preferences or probability distributions to derive the capital asset pricing model.

EMPIRICAL TESTS OF THE APT

Initial Empirical Tests

The initial empirical test of the APT was conducted by Roll and Ross (RR) (1980). Their methodology is, in a sense, similar to that used by Black, Jensen, and Scholes in testing the CAPM, since they first estimate the factor betas for securities, and then they estimate the cross-sectional relationship between security betas and average rates of return.

RR estimate the factor betas using a statistical technique called factor analysis. The input to factor analysis is the covariance matrix between the returns to the securities in the sample. The factor analysis determines the factor betas which best explain the covariances existing between the securities in the sample. Each index can be thought of as consisting of the systematic portions of the returns to a differently weighted portfolio of the securities in the sample.[2] The analysis determines a set of index portfolios and index betas such that the covariances between the residual returns are as small as possible. The program continues to add additional index portfolios until the probability that the next portfolio explains a significant fraction of the covariances between stocks goes below some predetermined level.

In a multifactor model, the covariance between the rates of return on any two stocks is assumed to be given by

$$\text{Cov}(r_J, r_K) = \beta_{1,J}\beta_{1,K}\,\sigma^2(I_1) + \beta_{2,J}\beta_{2,K}\,\sigma^2(I_2) + \cdots + \beta_{n,J}\beta_{n,K}\,\sigma^2(I_n)$$

Factor analysis makes the working assumption that the individual factor variances are equal to 1.00, and then it finds the set of factor betas for each stock which will make

---

[2] The indices can actually be considered as portfolios of the securities in the sample, where the residuals on each security have been subtracted from the returns.

the covariance matrix, as given by the preceding equation, correspond as closely as possible to the sample covariance matrix, as computed directly from the returns.

After obtaining estimates of the factor betas, the next step is to estimate the value of the factor price λ associated with each factor. This is done by cross sectionally relating the factor betas to average returns, using a procedure similar to that employed by Black, Jensen, and Scholes in the previous chapter.

Because of its complexity, factor analysis can only be employed on a relatively small number of stocks at a time. RR applied the analysis to 42 groups of 30 stocks in the period July 1962 through December 1972. They found that four or possibly five different factors have significant explanatory power. Moreover, they found that the residual variance of securities is unrelated to average returns.

The APT would predict that the estimates of the intercept term $E(r_Z)$ and the values for the λs should be the same for each sample tested. In a later study, Brown and Weinstein (1983) test this prediction and find ambiguous results. At this point, it is safe to say empirical testing of the APT is at an early stage of development, and there is no conclusive evidence either supporting or contradicting the model.

Is the APT Testable in Principle?

Several authors have raised the issue of the testability of the APT. One problem is the necessity of conducting the factor analysis on relatively small samples of firms. In dividing up the overall sample, factors which explain covariances between securities in different groups may be ignored. Dhrymes, Friend, and Gultekin (DFG) (1984) find, that as the number of securities included in the factor analysis increases from 15 to 60, the number of significant factors increases from 3 to 7. As Roll and Ross (1984) point out, however, there are many reasons why we should expect this to happen. In any group of, say, 30 stocks there may be only one cosmetics company. You would not likely find a "cosmetics factor" until you expanded your sample to include additional cosmetics companies. They argue that this does not necessarily mean that conducting the tests on small samples is inappropriate, because unless the factors are pervasive, they can be diversified away, and they will not be priced. As such they are not of interest in testing the theory.

DFG also find that your conclusion as to whether the intercept term is the same or different across different samples depends on the way you group the stocks. In a later paper Dhrymes, Friend, Gultekin, and Gultekin (1984) find that the number of *priced* factors you find is also dependent on the number of observations in your time series and that the number of *priced* factors increases with the number of securities factor analyzed. Overall, these initial empirical results indicate that the APT may be difficult to test if we employ factor analysis to conduct the test.

In a more recent paper, Grinblatt and Titman (1987) have shown that there is a crucial difference between the CAPM and the APT in terms of inherent testability. As we know, the CAPM predicts that the market portfolio is on the efficient set based on the global population of all assets. The problem with CAPM is that it is completely silent with respect to the efficiency of market proxies based on subpopulations of securities. It does not predict that the NYSE index (which is value weighted) should be efficient relative to the efficient set based on all NYSE stocks. In fact, it would be *remarkable* if this were true even if CAPM was the valid model.

APT, on the other hand, makes definite predictions about efficiency for sub-populations. Suppose, for example, we are dealing with a factor structure with n different factors, and suppose further we employ factor analysis on a subpopulation of investments to determine the identity of n portfolios each of which serves as a proxy for one of the n factors. Grinblatt and Titman show that these n portfolios can be expected to be on the efficient set for the subpopulation, if and only if the APT holds. Thus, APT is inherently more testable than CAPM because it does not rely on the observation of a particular portfolio (the market portfolio) which is inherently unobservable.

As an alternative to using factor analysis to test the APT, you can hypothesize that a given set of *specified* factors explains the covariance matrix between securities. If you take this approach, you can use large samples to estimate the factor betas and the factor prices (the λs). Chen, Roll, and Ross (1983) have employed this procedure and have determined a large fraction of the covariances that exist between securities can be explained on the basis of unanticipated changes in four specified factors[3]:

1. The difference between the yield on a long-term and a short-term treasury bond
2. The rate of inflation
3. The difference between the yields on BB-rated corporate bonds and treasury bonds
4. The growth rate in industrial production

One problem with this approach to testing the APT is that the theory, itself, is completely silent with respect to the identity of the factors in the factor structure that are priced. Consequently, even if you have found four factors that explain all the covariances between returns for stocks in some subpopulation, and you have rejected APT because of different risk-free rates and factor prices in still further subgroupings of the stocks, I can raise fundamental objections to your test. Perhaps your subpopulation isn't large enough. If you include more factors, you may find that these four factors no longer fully explain the covariance matrix. Moreover, it is the missing factors that account for the inconsistencies between the subgroups. (They may be more important to some groups than to others.) In addition, even if I am willing to buy the argument that there *are* only four factors that are priced, how do you know you have identified the right ones? Errors in factor identification may have also led to the inconsistencies.

Shanken (1982) has raised another serious issue relating to the testability of the APT. He argues that the shares of stock traded in the market place are actually portfolios of the individual units of production in the economy. These portfolios were created through merger and by the adoption of multiple capital budgeting projects by individual firms. Consequently, given a factor structure that relates to the returns on

---

[3]It should be noted that once you take the approach of preselecting the factors, on the basis of a theoretical model or framework, the APT becomes indistinguishable from the multiperiod CAPM first derived by Merton (1973).

the individual units of production, we may not be able to recognize it on the basis of the portfolios (the stocks traded in the marketplace).

It's easy to construct an example to show that this problem could lead to a false rejection of the APT. Suppose now we have a two-factor structure with two different factor prices. We test the theory by doing a factor analysis with two separate samples. In the first sample the firms have combined in such a way that their betas, with respect to the first factor, are zero. The firms in the second sample have combined to make their second factor betas equal to zero. In running a factor analysis in each sample, you will conclude that there is only one factor. Moreover, when you relate factor betas to average returns you will conclude that the pricing of the factor is different, as between the two samples. You will incorrectly reject the APT, because you unknowingly are observing two different factors at work in each of the two samples.

THE CONSISTENCY OF THE APT AND THE CAPM

The capital asset pricing model and the arbitrage pricing theory are not mutually exclusive. Suppose, for example, we can fully explain the covariance matrix on the basis of two stock portfolios which serve as indices or factors. When aggregated, the portfolio weights for individual securities in the two portfolios sum to the weights for individual securities in the market portfolio. We will call these portfolios 1 and 2.

Assume the expected return to any security is given by the following equation:

$$E(r_J) = E(r_Z) + \lambda_1 \beta_{1,J} + \lambda_2 \beta_{2,J} \tag{9.6}$$

Under the CAPM, λ_1 and λ_2 will take on particular values. They are

$$\lambda_1 = x_1[E(r_M) - E(r_Z)] \tag{9.7}$$

and

$$\lambda_2 = x_2[E(r_M) - E(r_Z)] \tag{9.8}$$

where x_1 and x_2 are the weights for portfolios 1 and 2 in the market portfolio.

Now, just as it is true that

$$\text{Cov}(r_P, r_M) = \sum_{J=1}^{m} x_J \, \text{Cov}(r_J, r_M)$$

and

$$\beta_P = \sum_{J=1}^{M} x_J \beta_J$$

so is it true that

$$\text{Cov}(r_M, r_J) = \sum_{P=1}^{M} x_P \, \text{Cov}(r_P, r_J)$$

and

$$\beta_{M,J} = \sum_{P=1}^{M} x_P \beta_{P,J} \tag{9.9}$$

where x_P is the weight for portfolio P in the market portfolio. Substituting Equations (9.7) and (9.8) into (9.6), multiplying through by the portfolio weights, recognizing the relationship of Equation (9.9), and simplifying, we get the equation for the security market line in the CAPM:

$$E(r_J) = E(r_Z) + [E(r_M) - E(r_Z)]\beta_{M,J} \tag{9.10}$$

This should come as no surprise, since we didn't assume security returns were generated by a single-index model to derive the CAPM. In the CAPM the covariance matrix between security returns can be accounted for by multiple factors. There also can be a linear relationship between expected returns and the betas with reference to these factors. However, the factor prices, or λs, must be such that a linear relationship still exists between the betas with reference to the market portfolio and expected rates of return.

Thus, in a test of the APT, a result which indicates the presence of multiple factors which influence expected rates of return should not be taken as a rejection of the CAPM. You would have to show that the factor prices are inconsistent with Equation (9.10). However, to show that, you must be able to observe the market portfolio. We are back to the problem of Chapter 8. It is impossible to support or reject the capital asset pricing model empirically.

While the two theories are completely consistent with one another, it is not the case that the CAPM can be considered as a special case of the APT. The CAPM assumes nothing about the structure of security returns other than possibly that they are normally distributed. Normal distributions, however, do not necessarily imply the linear factor structure that is required for the APT.

SUMMARY

The capital asset pricing model is intuitively pleasing, but it can be argued that it isn't testable. The arbitrage pricing theory has been suggested as a testable alternative. It captures some of the intuition of the CAPM (that only nondiversifiable risk affects expected security returns), but, while testing it may be an extremely hazardous business at best, the question of its testability, at least in principle, is still an open question.

The APT assumes that security returns are produced by a process identical to a linear single- or multi-index model. In the presence of such a return-generating process, the relationship between expected return and factor risk(s) must be approximately linear. If we put restrictions on investor utility, we can improve the approximation. If we limit the number of assets in the economy, the APT still works as an approximation, provided we bound investor risk aversion and if we place some limit on the highest possible return on a security. The approximation works with an error term that grows smaller as the relative size of the asset in the economy grows smaller.

Many of the APT models (Connor, Dybvig, and Grinblatt and Titman) assume that the residuals are either approximately or exactly uncorrelated with the return to the market portfolio. As pointed out by Shanken, if you consider a test of the APT to be tantamount to a test of this *assumption,* then you are back in the same empirical bind as with the CAPM. Since the return to the market portfolio is forever unobservable, we shall never know how reasonable is the assumption.

Others would argue that models should not be judged on the basis of the accuracy of their assumptions, but rather on the basis of their predictive power. The CAPM makes a single prediction, the efficiency of the market portfolio, which has been argued to be untestable.

Thus far, empirical tests of the APT have produced inconclusive results. It appears that an extensive number of factors may account for the covariances that exist between securities. There is some evidence that these factors affect the prices that investors are willing to pay for securities. In some studies pricing seems to be consistent across different samples. In others it is not. The empirical results also appear to be highly dependent on the methodology employed in the tests.

In one important respect both models exhibit a similar vulnerability. In the case of both models, we are looking for a benchmark for purposes of comparing the expost performance of portfolio managers and the exante returns on real and financial investments. In the case of the CAPM, we can never determine the extent to which deviations from the security market line benchmark are due to something real or are due to the obvious inadequacies in our proxies for the market portfolio. In the case of the APT, since the theory gives us no direction as to the choice of factors, we can't determine whether deviations from an APT benchmark are due to something real or are merely due to inadequacies in our choice of factors.

QUESTION SET 1

1. Suppose that three factors were sufficient to describe stock returns adequately. A large portfolio (with n stocks) has been formed. You have already computed the factor betas for each of the component stocks in the portfolio.
   a. How would you use this information to compute the factor betas for the *portfolio?*
   b. How would you represent the portfolio variance (using the factor betas for the portfolio) assuming that (i) the residual variance of the portfolio has been "diversified" to zero and (ii) the covariance between any pair of factors is zero?
2. What do we mean by a *riskless arbitrage opportunity?*
3. Suppose asset returns were described by the relationship in the accompanying graph (from a one-factor model).
   a. Why would such a relationship open up the possibility of riskless arbitrage?
   b. What qualifications to part a are required?

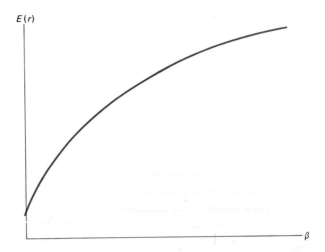

4. Assume a two-factor APT model is appropriate and there are an infinite number of assets in the economy. The cross-sectional relationship between expected return and factor betas indicates the price of factor 1 is .15 and the price of factor 2 is $-.2$. You have estimated factor betas for stocks X and Y as follows:

	β_1	β_2
Stock X	1.4	.4
Stock Y	.9	.2

Also, the expected return on an asset having zero betas (with respect to both factors) is .05. According to the APT, what are the approximate equilibrium returns on each of the two stocks?

5. You have concluded that a two-factor APT model is appropriate, and the cross-sectional relationship between return and each factor is as indicated in the accompanying graphs. What should the equilibrium return be on an asset having $\beta_1 = .75$ and $\beta_2 = .5$?

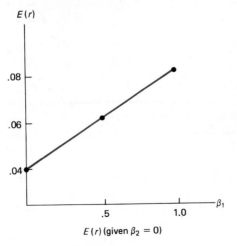

$E(r)$ (given $\beta_2 = 0$)

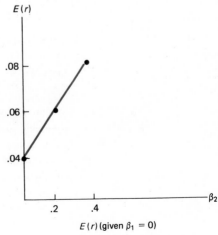

$E(r)$ (given $\beta_1 = 0$)

6. If the number of assets in the economy is less than infinite, what is the implication for the use of an APT expected return relationship?

7. Suppose investors' utility functions were linear, as in the accompanying diagram.
   a. What can you say about R, the measure of relative risk aversion?
   b. What would the implications be for the APT approximation for the expected return relationship?

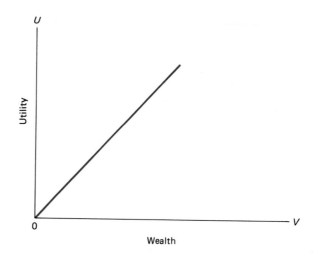

8. Assume a three-factor APT model is appropriate and that there are an infinite number of assets. The expected return on a portfolio with zero beta values is 5 percent. You are interested in an equally weighted portfolio of two stocks, A and B. The factor prices are indicated in the accompanying table, along with the factor betas for A and B. Compute the approximate expected return of the portfolio.

Factor i	β_{iA}	β_{iB}	Factor Prices
1	.3	.5	.07
2	.2	.6	.09
3	1.0	.7	.02

9. What was the finding of Dhrymes, Friend, and Gultekin concerning the number of factors that were significant in explaining returns?

10. The APT expected return relationship looks much like the security market line which was derived in the capital asset pricing model. How would one discriminate between the APT and the CAPM?

11. With regard to the number of different factors that are priced,
   a. What do the *theoretical* results in the APT say about the number of factors?
   b. What did the empirical evidence of Roll and Ross indicate about the number of factors?

12. Suppose that two factors have been deemed appropriate to "explain" returns on stocks and the covariance between the factors is zero. You have the information below on two stocks, X and Y, and the two factors, 1 and 2. What is the variance of a portfolio consisting of $1000 invested in X and $2000 invested in Y?

	Beta (Factor 1)	Beta (Factor 2)	Residual Variance
Stock X	1.1	.5	.02
Stock Y	.2	.8	.05

Variance of factor 1 = .15.

Variance of factor 2 = .10.

13. Assume a one-factor APT model having the expected return-beta relationship graphed below.
    a. Find a portfolio of A and C that would result in a beta of zero. What is the expected return on this portfolio?
    b. Find a portfolio of B and C that would result in a beta of zero. What is the expected return on this portfolio?
    c. What action would be suggested by your answers to parts a and b?

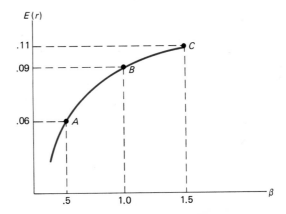

QUESTION SET 2

1. What is the basic assumption behind the APT?
2. Why is it necessary that the relationship between the expected return on a stock and its beta be linear under the model?
3. a. Why does the APT's estimate of expected return to a portfolio sometimes underestimate the return? Dybvig and Grinblatt and Titman show that the understatement for the actual

expected rate of return to an APT portfolio in the case of normal distributions for security returns for any security J is given by the equation

$$R \cdot x_J \cdot \sigma^2(\varepsilon_J)$$

b. Explain each of the terms in the equation.

c. What is the relationship between investor's risk aversion and the effect on the residual variance under this equation?

4. You are a mathematical whiz and factor analyze 10 stocks over the previous 10-year period, finding five factors which explain the covariance between them. Feeling confident, you look for five factors to explain the covariance between 25 different stocks. Are five factors likely to be sufficient?

5. In recent years there has been a growth in the number of specialized mutual funds, such as energy funds, small company funds, and so on. How might the APT be useful to you in predicting the performance of these funds?

6. The APT asserts that the relationship between the security returns and the factors is linear. If it were not, explain how you could obtain a risk-free return, utilizing the function given below, assuming you can sell short without restriction and there are no transactions costs.

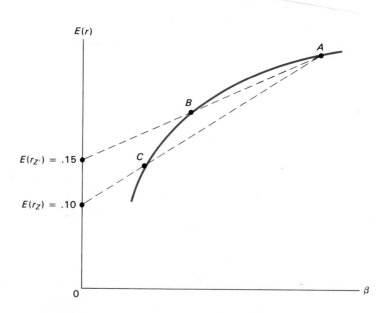

7. You determine that there are two factors under the APT which affect the portfolios you have constructed for your limited clientele, who invest only in energy stocks: the rate of inflation and the growth rate of all energy stocks in relation to the growth rate of all oil and gas stocks. You determine the market price of the factors to be .07 and .05, respectively, with zero covariance between the two factors, and the zero beta portfolio's expected

rate of return is 10 percent. The beta for your energy portfolio is 2.5 with respect to both factors. Calculate the expected rate of return for your portfolio.

8. How is the APT model consistent with the CAPM model?

ANSWERS TO QUESTION SET 2

1. The APT assumes that security returns are generated by a process similar to the single- or multi-index model, that is, that covariances between security returns can be attributed to the response of the securities to one or more factors.

2. Without a linear relationship, unlimited opportunities would exist for arbitrage since you could create risk-free portfolios with different expected rates of return.

3. a. The APT's estimate of expected returns to a portfolio sometimes underestimates the return to the portfolio because we cannot reduce the residual variance of the portfolio to zero with a limited number of securities.

   b. Dybvig and Grinblatt and Titman's equation quantifies this understatement for a normalized distribution of security returns. In this equation,

   $$R = \text{the measure of risk aversion, derived from the relationship between investor utility and investor wealth}$$

   $$x_J = \text{the portfolio weight of security } J \text{ in the market portfolio}$$

   $$\sigma^2(\varepsilon_J) = \text{the residual variance of security } J$$

   c. If the risk aversion is great, the greater the impact will be of unavoidable residual variance on expected return.

4. Probably not. Dhrymes, Friend, and Gultekin found that, as the number of securities in a factor analysis increased from 15 to 60, the number of significant factors increased from 3 to 7. If the number of factors you have found in your limited analysis is insufficient to explain the covariance matrix between the stocks, then your original sample may have failed to capture the effects of other factors.

5. Since you are limiting your analysis to a specified group of stocks, there probably are fewer factors affecting them than a general portfolio of equities would have. In line with the "Out-on-the-Street" vignette on page 178 of Chapter 6, you may find some fundamental factors affecting your stocks in a given portfolio. If a rise or fall in a given factor can be shown to affect your portfolio, you can predict changes in the value of the fund as soon as you have a forecast in a factor change.

6. You would construct a portfolio at $E(r_z')$ by selling short many stocks like A and investing in many stocks like B. This portfolio will have a zero beta. You then construct a second portfolio by selling short stocks like A and investing in many other stocks like C. This will give you a portfolio at $E(r_z)$. Now you can sell the *entire* second portfolio short, investing in $E(r_z')$. For example, by selling short $100,000 at 10 percent, we lose $10,000 in income but gain $100,000 at 15 percent or $15,000 in income, for a net riskless profit of $5,000.

7. The expected rate of return is given by

$$E(r_P) \approx E(r_2) + \lambda_1 \beta_{1,P} + \lambda_2 \beta_{2,P}$$

$$= .10 + 2.5(.07) + 2.5(.05)$$

$$= .40$$

8. If the covariance matrix of the CAPM can be explained by factors as under the APT, then the two models are consistent. For the APT to be inconsistent with the CAPM, factor prices would have to be shown to be inconsistent with the equation

$$E(r_J) = E(r_Z) + [E(r_M) - E(r_Z)] \beta_{M,J}$$

where

$E(r_Z) =$ the expected rate of return to the minimum variance zero beta portfolio

$E(r_M) =$ expected rate of return to the market portfolio

$\beta_{M,J} =$ beta factor with respect to returns on the market portfolio

REFERENCES

BROWN, S. J., and WEINSTEIN, M. I., ''A New Approach to Testing Asset Pricing Models: The Bilinear Paradigm,'' *Journal of Finance* (June 1983).

BROWN, STEPHEN J. and WARNER, J., ''Measuring Security Price Performance,'' *Journal of Financial Economics* (September 1980).

CHAMBERLAIN, G., ''Funds Factors and Diversification in Arbitrage Pricing Models,'' *Econometrica*, Vol. 51 (1983), pp. 1305–1323.

CHAMBERLAIN, G., and ROTHSCHILD, M., ''Arbitrage, Factor Structure, and Mean-Variance Analysis on Large Asset Markets,'' *Econometrica*, Vol. 51 (1983), pp. 1281–1304.

CHEN, N. F., ''Some Empirical Tests of the Theory of Arbitrage Pricing,'' *Journal of Finance* (December 1983).

CHEN, N. F., ROLL, R., and ROSS, S., ''Economic Forces and the Stock Market,'' unpublished manuscript, Yale University, New Haven, Conn., 1983.

CHO, D. C., ELTON, E. J., and GRUBER, M. J., ''On the Robustness of the Roll and Ross APT Methodology,'' *Journal of Financial and Quantitative Analysis* (March 1984).

CONNOR, G., ''A Factor Pricing Theory for Capital Assets,'' working paper, Northwestern University, Evanston, Ill., 1983.

CONNOR, G., and KORAJCZYK, R., ''Risk and Return in an Equilibrium APT: Theory and Tests,'' working paper, Northwestern University, Evanston, Ill., 1986.

DHRYMES, P., FRIEND, I., and GULTEKIN, N., ''A Critical Reexamination of the Empirical Evidence on the Arbitrage Pricing Theory,'' *Journal of Finance* (June 1984).

DHRYMES, P., FRIEND, I., GULTEKIN, N., and GULTEKIN, M., ''New Tests of the APT and Their Implications,'' working paper, Wharton School of Finance, Philadelphia, July 1984.

DYBVIG, P. H., "An Explicit Bound on Individual Assets Deviations from APT Pricing in a Finite Economy," *Journal of Financial Economics* (December 1983).

DYBVIG, P., and ROSS, S. 1985. "Approximate Factor Structures: Interpretations and Implications for Empirical Tests," *Journal of Finance,* Vol. 40 (1985), pp. 1367–1373.

GRINBLATT, M., and TITMAN, S., "Factor Pricing in a Finite Economy," *Journal of Financial Economics* (December 1983).

GRINBLATT, M., and TITMAN, S., "The Relation Between Mean-Variance Efficiency and Arbitrage Pricing," *Journal of Business* (January 1987).

INGERSALL, J., "Some Results in the Theory of Arbitrage Pricing," working paper, University of Chicago, 1982.

JOBSON, J. D., "A Multivariate Linear Regression Test for the Arbitrage Pricing Theory," *Journal of Finance* (September 1982).

KRYZANOWSKI, L., and CHAU, T., "General Factor Models and the Structure of Security Returns," *Journal of Financial and Quantitative Analysis* (March 1983).

MERTON, R. C., "An Intertemporal Capital Asset Pricing Model," *Econometrica* (September 1973).

MORRISON, D. F., *Multivariate Statistical Methods*. New York: McGraw-Hill, 1976.

REINGANUM, M. R., "The Arbitrage Pricing Theory: Some Empirical Results," *Journal of Finance* (May 1981).

ROLL, R., and ROSS, S. A., "An Empirical Investigation of the Arbitrage Pricing Theory," *Journal of Finance* (December 1980).

ROLL, R., and ROSS, S., "A Critical Reexamination of the Empirical Evidence on the Arbitrage Pricing Theory: A Reply," *Journal of Finance* (June 1984).

ROSS, S. A., "The Arbitrage Theory of Capital Asset Pricing," *Journal of Economic Theory* (December 1976).

ROSS, S. A., "Return, Risk, and Arbitrage," in *Risk and Return in Finance,* eds., I. Friend and J. L. Bicksler. Cambridge, Mass.: Ballinger, 1977.

SHENKEN, J. "The Arbitrage Pricing Theory: Is It Testable," *Journal of Finance,* (December 1982).

10

MEASURING PORTFOLIO PERFORMANCE

In this chapter we will learn how to measure the performance of a portfolio manager. Presumably, skillful managers have access to information about investments that is unavailable to the public at large. They derive their information by either probing sources of private information or processing publicly available information, using their own proprietary techniques of analysis. In any case, they know more than the average investor, and on the basis of their knowledge, they can discriminate between profitable and unprofitable investments.

We expect skillful managers to produce relatively high rates of return for their portfolios, but how do we discriminate between a manager that is truly skillful and one that has been merely lucky? How do we discriminate between skillful managers and ones that produce high returns because they merely capture the expected risk premiums in the equilibrium returns on their high-risk investments?

The performance measures discussed in this chapter will help us discriminate among those who have skill, those who are lucky, and those who earn higher returns merely because they take risks. The performance measures are widely used in the security markets. Billions of dollars are actually shifted from investment firm to investment firm because some get higher marks on the basis of these measures than do others. Someday you may win or lose accounts on the basis of *your* marks. You may even be promoted or demoted because of them.

Thus, it's imperative for you to understand how the performance measures work, the nature of their assumptions, and their relative strengths and weaknesses.

MEASURING THE RATE OF RETURN
TO A PORTFOLIO

We have typically measured the rate of return to a portfolio as the sum of cash received (dividend or interest income) during the period and the change in the portfolio's market value (capital gain or loss) divided by the market value of the portfolio at the beginning of the period. This method of calculating the return works well for "static" portfolios that have no cash flows coming in from or going out to their investors.

However, managed portfolios typically receive additional amounts to be invested in the course of the period (a month or perhaps a quarter) over which return is to be measured, and their investors may also withdraw funds from the portfolio. If a portfolio begins the quarter with $1 million invested, and an additional $1 million is added at the end of the first month, and then $1.5 million is withdrawn at the end of the second month, how is the return to be calculated for the quarter?

One of two methods are typically employed. The first is called a *time-weighted rate of return*. With this method, the portfolio is treated as though it were a mutual fund. Mutual funds have deposits and withdrawals nearly every day, but their returns are computed on the basis of cash distributions to and the change in market value of a single share in the fund. The number of shares outstanding changes with deposits and withdrawals each day, but the time-weighted return is computed by dividing the beginning value of a share into the cash distributions to, and change in value of a share during the course of the period. Thus, to compute the time-weighted rate of return, you divide the portfolio into "shares" or "units" and compute the return to a single share in the portfolio across the period, in much the same way you would compute the return to a mutual fund.

The second method is called the *value-weighted rate of return*. While the time-weighted method ignored interim deposits and withdrawals to and from the portfolio, the value-weighted method takes them into account. If W_T is a withdrawal made at time T, and D_t is a deposit made at time t, and if it is assumed that cash dividends and interest payments to the portfolio are received at the end of the period, the annualized, value-weighted rate of return is found by solving for r in the following equation:

$$\text{Beginning portfolio value} = \sum_{t=1}^{n} \frac{D_t}{(1 + r)^t} + \sum_{t=1}^{m} \frac{W_T}{(1 + r)^t}$$
$$+ \frac{\text{Total ending value of portfolio}}{(1 + r)^t}$$

where n is the number of deposits made during the period, m is the number of withdrawals, and t is the length of time in years, or fractions thereof, to deposit, withdrawal, or end of the period. The value-weighted rate of return can also be referred to as the internal rate of return, and it will be discussed in more detail in Chapter 12.

THE NEED FOR RISK-ADJUSTED PERFORMANCE MEASURES

Why can't we measure performance on the basis of the rate of return produced by the portfolio? Perhaps you've seen rankings of mutual funds in some of the financial magazines. The rankings are usually based on the rates of return produced by the funds in the preceding year. Sometimes the funds are ranked on the basis of their average rate of return over several preceding years.

You have to be very careful in interpreting rankings based purely on rate of return or even average rate of return. The funds may be ranked by their rate of return, but it's highly unlikely that these rankings even roughly correspond to rankings based on the skill level of the portfolio managers. In fact, the position of a portfolio in a ranking based on rate of return is more likely to depend on (1) the target risk level of the portfolio and (2) the performance of the market than it does on (3) the skill level of the portfolio manager.

To see this, consider the two mutual funds of Table 10.1. In each of the 10 years, the two funds are ranked by their rate of return. Note how the rankings flip-flop from year to year. Surely the relative skill of the funds' management isn't changing in such a volatile way. The real reason behind the instability in the rankings is the fact that the beta factors for the two funds are very different, and the performance of the market is changing dramatically from year to year.

The two funds probably have different beta factors, causing them to respond in different degrees to changes in the return to the market portfolio. If one has a higher than average beta and the other a lower than average beta, their characteristic lines may plot as in Figure 10.1.

Assume, for simplicity, that investors are risk neutral, and the two characteristic lines intersect at a point on the graph that is positioned directly over the expected return to the market. This being the case, both mutual funds will have the same *expected* rate of return $E(r_P)$. While their *expected* returns are the same, their *realized* returns will nearly always be different. In a bear market (when the market produces a rate of return that is less than expected, such as r'_M), the fund with the lower beta will produce the greater rate of return and will rank first. In a bull market (when the market's return is greater than expected, such as r^*_M), the higher beta fund will rank on top. The relative returns, and the rankings based on them, are highly dependent on market performance and relative beta. In fact, they are so dependent on these factors, they are nearly useless for judging the relative skill of the managers.

TABLE 10.1 Rankings of Two Mutual Funds Based on Rate of Return in Each Year

	Year														
	1988	1987	1986	1985	1984	1983	1982	1981	1980	1979	1978	1977	1976	1975	1974
Nicholas Fund	2	1	1	1	2	2	1	1	2	2	1	1	2	1	2
Omega Fund	1	2	2	2	1	1	2	2	1	1	2	2	1	2	1

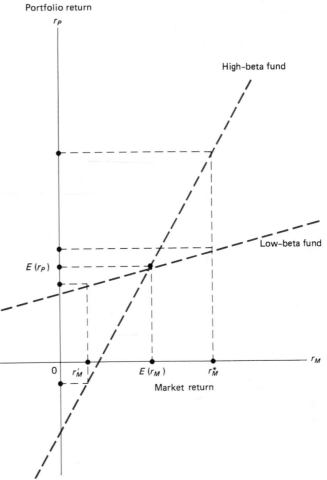

FIGURE 10.1 Characteristic lines of a high- and low-beta fund.

We need a measure of performance that is insensitive to relative risk and the strength of the market. Such a measure will adjust the portfolio's return by the amount that is attributable to the relative risk of the portfolio, given the strength of the market in the period that performance is evaluated. A *risk-adjusted measure of performance* should be insensitive to the risk of a portfolio. That is, in using such a measure, there should be no propensity for portfolios with unusually high or low levels of risk to earn unusually high or low marks, irrespective of the performance of the market.

In constructing a risk-adjusted performance measure, you have to make assumptions about the nature of risk and the relationship between return and risk. You have to assume that stocks are priced according to a given pricing model. We have discussed two such models, the CAPM and the APT.

RISK-ADJUSTED PERFORMANCE MEASURES BASED ON THE CAPITAL ASSET PRICING MODEL

Let's assume that, for the set of information relevant to the valuation of any given stock, we can divide the information into two parts: (1) public information, which is freely available to everyone, and (2) private information, which is available only to select individuals, possibly at some cost.

Also assume that stock prices reflect only publicly available information and that the pricing structure is that of the standard CAPM where borrowing and lending at a risk-free rate are both permitted. This implies that if we were to estimate expected returns, variances, and covariances based on a thorough analysis of publicly available information alone, we would see the market portfolio positioned on the capital market line (CML), as it is in Figure 10.2, and every stock and portfolio would be positioned on the security market line (SML), as in Figure 10.3.

Now consider two professionally managed portfolios, Alpha Fund and Omega Fund. The managers of Alpha Fund have acquired private information relating to a *single* company. The information is favorable in the sense that the expected rate of return to the stock is higher than you would think based on public information alone.

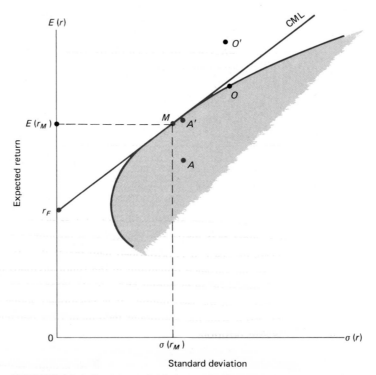

FIGURE 10.2 Position of Alpha and Omega relative to capital market line.

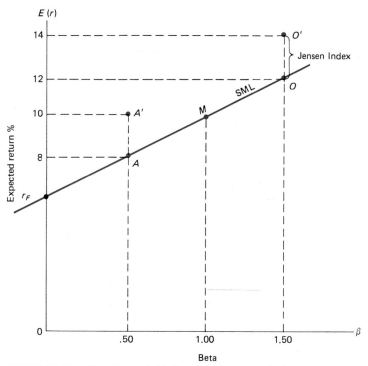

FIGURE 10.3 Position of Alpha and Omega relative to security market line.

The managers of Alpha Fund know the stock's expected rate of return is 10 percent, and analysis based on publicly available information alone would lead you to conclude that the expected return was only 8 percent. The private information is assumed to have no bearing on your assessment of the risk of the stock. The stock's beta factor is .50, and its residual variance is .075 percent.

The managers of Alpha Fund have invested 100 percent of the money in their portfolio in this single stock. If you were to plot the portfolio's position, based on public information alone, it would plot at the points labeled A in Figures 10.2 and 10.3. Note that while the portfolio is positioned on the security market line (as is everything else), it is positioned well inside the efficient set due to the large amount of residual variance remaining in the (undiversified) portfolio.

Based on *both* public and private information, Alpha Fund plots at the points labeled A' in the two figures. It is positioned above the security market line. However, even with the additional increment of 2 percent in its expected rate of return, it is still positioned *inside* the efficient set.

The managers of Omega Fund are either more skillful or better endowed, in the sense that they have been able to acquire private information on many more companies. It is assumed, in this case also, the private information affects only estimates of expected return and not estimates of risk. In any case, the managers of

Omega Fund have put together a well-diversified portfolio, taking appropriate positions in the various stocks. As it turns out, the expected rate of return on the portfolio, based on private as well as public information, is 14 percent. However, as naive investors possessing public information alone, if you or I were to estimate the portfolio's expected return, we would think it was only 12 percent. Omega's beta is 1.50, and we will assume, because it is broadly diversified, its residual variance has been driven to a negligible level. Omega is positioned in Figures 10.2 and 10.3 at the points labeled O and O', based on public information alone and both public and private information, respectively.

Note that Omega is not only positioned above the security market line but, because it has only a minimal level of residual variance, the 2 percent increment in expected return is sufficient to lift it to a position outside the efficient set. Remember that only those with private information see it at this position. Omega doesn't look very special to those of us who only have public information to make our estimates.

We are looking for a yardstick by which we can rank the funds on the basis of the skill of their managers. We know the managers of Omega are more skillful than the managers of Alpha. We hope our yardstick will tell us this.

Three risk-adjusted performance measures have been introduced and are in widespread use. All three are based on the capital asset pricing model. The measures are named after those who introduced them. They are the Jensen Index, the Treynor Index, and the Sharpe Index.

The Jensen Index

The Jensen Index (1969) uses the security market line as a benchmark. The index is actually the difference between the expected rate of return on the portfolio and what its expected return would be if the portfolio were positioned on the security market line. The equation for the Jensen Index is as follows:

$$J_P = E(r_P) - \{r_F + [E(r_M) - r_F]\beta_P\}$$

If we were to analyze the ability of the managers based on both public and private information, we would conclude that both Alpha and Omega are managed by individuals with equal skill levels, since they both have Jensen indices of 2 percent:

$$.02 = .10 - [.06 + (.10 - .06) \times .50]$$

$$.02 = .14 - [.06 + (.10 - .06) \times 1.50]$$

In Figure 10.2, the Jensen Index is given by the vertical distance of each fund from the security market line. If the fund has a positive Jensen Index, it is positioned above the security market line, and it is considered to have good performance. A negative Jensen Index indicates bad performance and a position below the security market line.

In actual practice, of course, we wouldn't know the expected returns or betas for the funds. We would, therefore, have to compute sample estimates by observing the rates of return produced by the portfolios over a successive number of periods. Since 10 percent and 14 percent are the "true" expected returns on Alpha and Omega, based on the market values of their stocks and the full set of available information relating to their future returns, the sample estimates should serve as unbiased estimates of these true expected returns.

Based on the sample estimates, the formula for the Jensen Index is given by

$$\hat{J}_P = \bar{r}_P - [\bar{r}_F + (\bar{r}_M - \bar{r}_F)\hat{\beta}_P]$$

In the formula, $\bar{r}_M$ is the average rate of return to a portfolio we have selected to serve as a proxy for the market portfolio, $\hat{\beta}_P$ is our estimate of the beta for the fund based on the proxy, and $\bar{r}_F$ is the average periodic return on risk-free bonds in the period we do the sampling. So if we are looking at monthly rates of return, we will use the average of the 30-day treasury bill rates at the beginning of each month of the period.

The simple rate of return is defective as a performance index because rankings based on this measure depend more on the risk of the fund and the performance of the market than they do on the skill of the fund's managers. In theory at least, rankings based on the Jensen Index should be insensitive to fund risk and market performance. Suppose we have a bull market, where realized returns are unexpectedly high. In this case we would expect that high-beta funds should have much greater rates of return than low-beta funds. After all, beta measures the responsiveness of a fund to the pull of the market, and in a bull market the market is pulling hard. However, while the rate of return to a high-beta stock should be larger than that of low-beta stocks, there's no reason to expect the same to be true of *excess returns*.

In Figure 10.4 we have drawn a sample estimate for the security market line

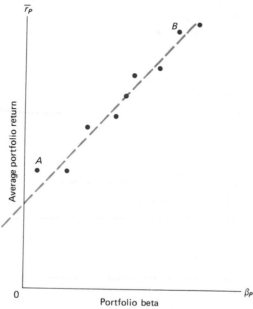

FIGURE 10.4 Estimated SML (bull market).

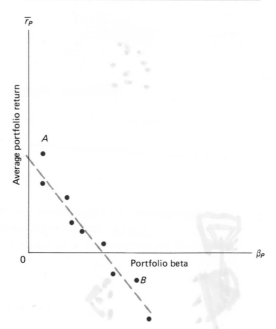

FIGURE 10.5 Estimated SML (bear market).

for a bull market period. The return to the market index is very high, so the slope of the security market line is very large. However, while the rate of return to low-beta fund *A* is lower than its high-beta counterpart *B*, the Jensen Index for *A* is actually greater than that of *B*. The ranking of the two funds remains the same as we go to the bear market condition of Figure 10.5. Here the return to the market index is low, the market is pulling down, and the slope of the *estimated* security market line is negative, but fund *A* still has the larger Jensen Index. In theory, the magnitude of the Jensen Index should be insensitive to either the risk of the fund or the performance of the market.

However, while the Jensen Index is insensitive to risk and market performance, even if our sample estimates are perfectly accurate, if we are asking the question, ''Which fund has the more skillful managers?'' the Jensen Index gives us the wrong answer. It tells us the managers of Alpha and Omega are equally skillful. They are not.

We can think of a portfolio manager's performance in terms of depth and breadth. The depth relates to the magnitude of the excess return captured by the manager. Breadth relates to the number of different securities for which a manager can capture excess returns. The Jensen Index is sensitive only to depth and not breadth. The managers of Alpha have less breadth than those of Omega, but they get the same marks under Jensen because they have the same depth.[1]

---

[1]The Jensen Index can be used to detect breadth of performance if you are willing to go to the trouble of computing the index separately for each of the fund's individual investments. Then you can note the number and proportion of the investments that have significantly positive indices.

However, if you are asking a different question, "Which fund is the best investment?" it may be desirable to ignore breadth and look only at depth because your investment in the fund is only one of many potential investments you might make. Given that you, yourself, are diversifying, you might well be most attracted to the funds with the greatest depth, irrespective of their breadth. But if you are ranking managers on the basis of their ability, you will want to consider both breadth and depth in assessing their skills.

The Treynor Index

The Treynor Index (1965) is also insensitive to the breadth dimension of performance, but it has an advantage over the Jensen Index. Alpha and Omega are plotted relative to the security market line in Figure 10.6. While both funds have the same excess rate of return (2 percent), Alpha has a greater rate of return per unit of risk exposure. Given that we can borrow at the risk-free rate r_F, we can lever a position in Alpha Fund by selling the risk-free bond and using the funds to invest in Alpha to attain a position at point A^*. While this position has the same beta as Omega Fund, it has a higher expected rate of return. We can therefore dominate Omega

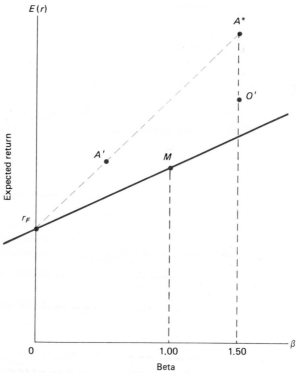

FIGURE 10.6 Levering Alpha to dominate Omega.

Fund (at least in β space) by levering our position in Alpha Fund. In this sense, Alpha is a more desirable portfolio investment.

The Treynor Index takes the opportunity to lever into account in its performance rankings. The Treynor Index is, in fact, the risk premium earned per unit of risk taken. Risk is measured in terms of the beta factor of the portfolio. The formula for the Treynor Index for portfolio P is given by

$$T_P = \frac{E(r_P) - r_F}{\beta_P}$$

Once again, since we can't see the actual distributions of returns, we have to take sample estimates after observing portfolio returns over a successive number of periods. The sample estimate of the Treynor Index is given by

$$\hat{T}_P = \frac{\bar{r}_P - \bar{r}_F}{\hat{\beta}_P}$$

On a graph like Figure 10.6, the Treynor Index is equal to the slope of a straight line connecting the position of the fund with the risk-free rate. Obviously, while both Alpha and Omega have the same Jensen Index, Alpha Fund has the greater Treynor Index. Alpha can be viewed as providing a superior position for portfolio investors because of their opportunity to lever the position by borrowing at the risk-free rate.

Note, however, that we are again getting the wrong answer to the question as to which group of managers has the greater ability. Treynor gives us the wrong answer because it too measures risk in terms of the beta factor. The beta factor of a portfolio is a simple weighted average of the securities in the portfolio. There is no propensity for beta to grow smaller as the number of securities in the portfolio increases. So there is no propensity for the Treynor Index to grow larger as we increase the number of securities in the portfolio, given a fixed value for the excess rate of return. The Treynor Index, therefore, is also insensitive to the breadth dimension of portfolio performance.

To obtain a risk-adjusted measure that is sensitive to breadth, we need to employ a risk measure that is sensitive to breadth. This brings us to the Sharpe Index.

The Sharpe Index

The Sharpe Index (1966) uses the capital market line as a benchmark. The index is computed by dividing the risk premium for the portfolio by its standard deviation. It measures the risk premium earned per unit of risk exposure. The formula for the Sharpe Index is given by

$$S_P = \frac{E(r_P) - r_F}{\sigma(r_P)}$$

and the sample estimate of the Sharpe Index by

$$\hat{S}_P = \frac{\bar{r}_P - \bar{r}_F}{\sigma_{r_P}}$$

Consider Alpha and Omega positioned relative to the capital market line of Figure 10.7. The Sharpe Index is equal to the slope of a straight line connecting the position of the fund with the risk-free rate. To determine the quality of performance, you compare the Sharpe Index for the manager's portfolio with the Sharpe Index for the market. A higher Sharpe Index would indicate that the manager has outperformed the market, while a lower Sharpe Index would indicate underperformance.

Note that any portfolio that is positioned on the capital market line has a Sharpe Index equal to that of the market and, therefore, is characterized by neutral performance. This makes sense under the CAPM, because on the basis of public information alone, any investor can construct a portfolio that is positioned on the capital market line.

Omega Fund ranks higher than Alpha under the Sharpe Index, so we get the correct answer to our question regarding relative management skills. On the other hand, it would be a mistake to conclude that because Alpha has a Sharpe Index less than that of the market, the managers of this fund have no skill or are, in fact, even doing something systematically wrong. The managers of Alpha do have some (limited) skill. The Sharpe Index is sensitive to both breadth and depth. In this case, its sensitivity to Alpha's lack of breadth is overcoming its sensitivity to Alpha's (limited) ability to capture excess return.

We can see the Sharpe Index's sensitivity to breadth by asking what would

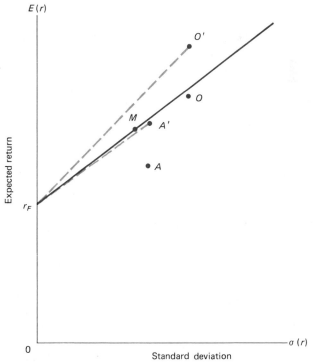

FIGURE 10.7 Performance of Alpha and Omega according to Sharpe Index.

happen to Alpha's index if the managers acquired private information for many more stocks. Suppose each additional stock has a 2 percent excess return and a beta identical to the one they already hold in their portfolio. In this case, the expected rate of return to the portfolio would remain at 10 percent, but the portfolio's standard deviation would become smaller because the residual variance of the portfolio becomes smaller with diversification. The portfolio's position moves to the west on the graph, and the Sharpe Index increases.

PITFALLS IN MEASURING PERFORMANCE WITH THE JENSEN, TREYNOR, AND SHARPE INDICES

Misspecifying the Market Pricing Structure

The three risk-adjusted performance measures are based on the standard form of the CAPM. When you use the measures, you must assume securities are priced in accord with *this* model. If your assumption is wrong, rankings based on the measures are likely to be biased.

Suppose, for example, securities are actually priced in accord with the form of the CAPM where investors can lend but cannot borrow at the risk-free rate. Under this form of the model, the security market line is drawn as in Figure 10.8. Note the

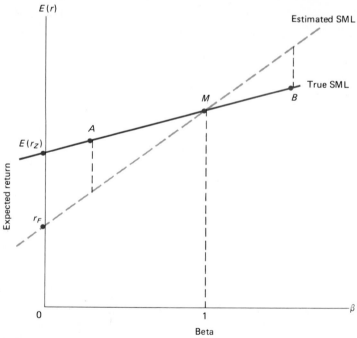

FIGURE 10.8 Bias in the Jensen Index due to misspecification of pricing structure.

line intercepts the vertical axis above the risk-free rate at $E(r_Z)$. If we use the standard form of the Jensen Index, we will measure performance on the basis of deviations from a ''security market line,'' which we will *assume* runs along the *broken* line between the risk-free rate and the position of the market portfolio. A fund such as *A* will have a positive Jensen Index even though it is positioned directly on the true security market line. The managers of the fund have no skill. They receive good marks under the Jensen Index merely because they are low risk. In the same sense, a high-risk fund such as *B* receives low marks merely because it is high risk. Under these conditions *neither* the Jensen nor the Treynor Index is truly *risk adjusted*.

This problem can be corrected if we use, as a benchmark, a security market line anchored at the expected rate of return to the zero beta portfolio rather than at the risk-free rate. The problem is that we have to estimate the expected return to the zero beta portfolio. One method commonly employed is to follow an approach similar to that of the Black, Jensen, and Scholes (1972) study. For the period over which you are measuring performance, construct several nonmanaged portfolios with widely divergent beta factors. Next, relate beta to average portfolio return by sliding a line of best fit through the scatter of portfolio positions in average return, beta space, as in Figure 10.9. The vertical intercept of the line of best fit serves as your estimate of the average return to the zero beta portfolio. In fact, in the case of the Jensen Index, the line of best fit can actually serve as your benchmark from which to measure performance.

The Sharpe Index can also give biased measures of performance if we misspe-

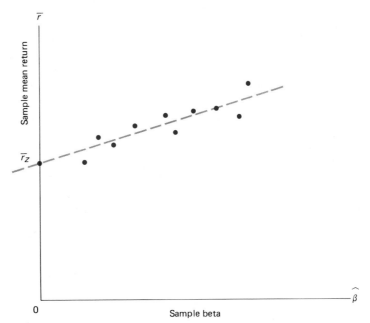

FIGURE 10.9 Estimating the average return to the zero beta portfolio.

OUT ON THE STREET

ASSIGNING A GRADE

Peter Dietz sits at his desk in Tacoma, Washington, trying to make a unified picture out of the mass of data before him. Peter is senior vice president and director of Research and Development at the Frank Russell Company. Among other things, the Frank Russell Company evaluates the performance of the managers of some 40 pension funds throughout the United States. Included in its accounts are the pension funds of American Telephone & Telegraph and General Motors Corporation. Their bigger accounts typically average approximately $2.5 billion in assets.

Peter has a Ph.D. from Columbia University and was a professor at Northwestern University and the University of Oregon before joining Frank Russell. He has written several articles on portfolio evaluation in journals such as the *Journal of Finance*, the *Journal of Portfolio Management*, and the *Financial Analysts Journal*. Now he puts into practice what he previously wrote about and taught.

This morning he is preparing an assessment of a management team for one of the firm's clients. The Frank Russell Company segregates common stock portfolio managers into five basic styles:

1. Aggressive growth managers would hold at least 70 percent of their invested assets in companies with less than $1 billion in total market value and portfolio betas greater than 1.20.
2. Quality growth managers hold relatively low-payout, larger, technology-oriented stocks with betas ranging from 1.05 to 1.2.
3. Broadly diversified managers participate in all sectors of the market and have betas ranging from .95 to 1.05.
4. A rotating manager shifts from one style to another depending on his or her assessment of economic conditions. Their portfolios display high turnover, and their beta factors tend to be unstable.
5. A defensive yield manager invests in stocks in stable industries with high payouts and lesser growth. Their portfolio betas are typically .95 or less.

Peter has classified this morning's management team as mostly quality growth.

Ranked with all other managers on the basis of the Jensen or Treynor indices, the team falls in the lowest quartile. To compute the indices, Peter uses the treasury bill rate for the period of assessment as the risk-free rate. Beta is measured on the basis of a sampling of historical returns going back various periods into the past. Various indices are also employed for the market, including the Standard & Poor's Composite Index of 500 Stocks, the New York Stock Exchange Index, and the Wilshire 5000 Index. Peter is well aware of Roll's contention that performance rankings can be influenced by the analyst's choice of a market index. In fact he is planning to participate in a major seminar to discuss potential problems associated with a methodology developed to get around the

"Roll problem." The methodology was developed by a firm called Barra Associates. They attempt to define the natural habitat of a portfolio manager, and from this they construct a normal "market" portfolio to serve as a benchmark for the manager. For example, if a manager normally chooses investments from a population of 300 quality growth stocks, the manager's performance will be judged relative to the performance of this universe. The actual benchmark will be the manager's expected return based on a multifactor APT-type model, but the factor loadings are estimated on the basis of the manager's peer group universe of investments.

Peter is troubled by the fourth quartile ranking for the management team. In the first place, quality-growth-type managers who aren't ranked currently in the fourth quartile are rare. The market hasn't been very kind to the type of issues that quality growth managers invest in as of late. Second, Peter and his staff have been impressed with this manager's team on the basis of numerous "on-site" visits and a detailed analysis of their trading history. This analysis takes into account, among other things, a consideration of value added to the portfolio as they moved from one transaction to another and from positions in one industry to another. They also feel that the team's trades were generally consistent with the overall objectives set by the portfolio.

Nevertheless, it's difficult to sell the virtues of a fourth quartile management team no matter how strongly you try to sell them on a qualitative basis.

Peter's *quantitative* evaluation of the management is quite sophisticated. He performs a statistical evaluation to determine whether the portfolio is positioned a statistically significant distance above or below the security market line. In the case of this particular management team, Peter can say with greater than 90 percent confidence that the portfolio is positioned below Peter's estimate of the security market line. However, based on his qualitative analysis of the situation, Peter feels that, for the most part, this is because the market has recently treated badly the type of stock favored by these managers.

In addition, Peter knows that this management team typically invests in the stocks of very large companies. Based on his own experience and what he has read in academic journals, the stocks of large companies are typically positioned below the security market line. Peter makes no specific quantitative adjustment for this. The phenomenon appears to be an inadequacy in the capital asset pricing model, and until a well-founded substitute becomes available, any adjustment made is qualitative rather than quantitative.

In any case, all these considerations and more go into the final report. In spite of the fourth quartile ranking, the overall assessment of the management team is favorable. However, Peter has his doubts whether the client is going to be able to overlook the ranking, itself, and recognize the other more favorable aspects of the team's performance.

cify the pricing structure. The Sharpe Index assumes the capital market line is straight, which it is under the standard form of the CAPM. However, if investors can't borrow at the risk-free rate, the capital market line bends back along the minimum variance set as it does in Figure 10.10. Recall that the Sharpe Index is equal to the slope of a straight line connecting the position of the fund or portfolio with the risk-free rate. Consider various portfolios all of which are positioned on the capital market line. Since anyone can achieve a position on the capital market line, the managers of none of the portfolios have exhibited any real skill. In spite of this, all the funds positioned between r_F and P' in Figure 10.10 will have the same Sharpe Index, and it will be greater than that of the market. As we move from P' to M on the graph, the Sharpe Index becomes smaller, gradually approaching that of the market. As we move beyond M on the capital market line, the Sharpe Index continues to grow smaller, and it is now less than that of the market. Under these conditions, the index gives an upward-biased indication of the performance of low-risk portfolios and a downward-biased indication of the performance of high-risk portfolios.

There is no easy way to correct the measure for this problem, as there was with the Jensen and Treynor indices. A simple measure really requires a linear benchmark. The capital market line is only linear under the standard form of the CAPM. In other versions, expected return is a rather complicated function of standard deviation, which doesn't lend itself to the application of a simple index.

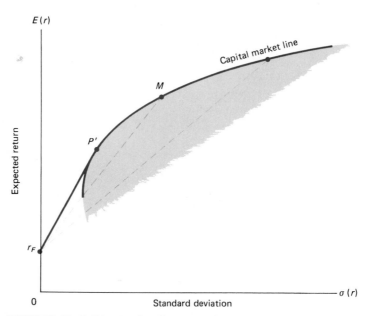

FIGURE 10.10 Bias in the Sharpe Index due to misspecification of pricing structure.

Misspecification of the Market Index

In addition to his critique of empirical tests of the CAPM, Richard Roll (1978) also criticized the Jensen (and implicitly the Treynor) measure of portfolio performance. It can be argued that your assessment of performance under the Jensen Index is related more to the character of your market index and its position relative to the efficient set than it is to the quality of the managers running the portfolio.

To see this, consider Figures 10.11 and 10.12. Figure 10.11 presents the minimum variance set for a population of assets. Points A and B denote the positions of two mutual funds having the same expected rate of return but different standard deviations. Suppose portfolio M is selected as the market index. Since it is on the efficient set, based on property II (Chapter 5), all portfolios and securities will be positioned on the security market line of Figure 10.12. Since funds A and B have the same expected rate of return as the market portfolio, they must both have a beta of 1.00, and they are positioned at the point labeled AMB. The Jensen Index for both funds is, of course, zero.

Suppose instead, we had selected portfolio M' in Figure 10.11 as the market

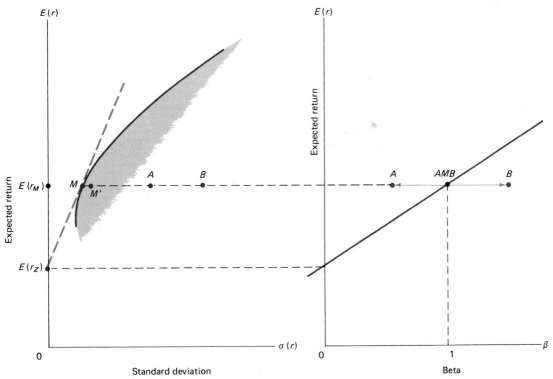

FIGURE 10.11 Positions of two different market indices.

FIGURE 10.12 Effect of changing indices on beta.

index. This portfolio is slightly inside the bullet, so we know on the basis of property AIV (Appendix 8) that individual securities and portfolios will be positioned *off* the security market line of Figure 10.12. Positions will change in Figure 10.12, not because of changes in expected return (expected return will not change just because we go from one index to another), but rather, because of changes in *beta* factors. It can be shown that under some conditions dramatic changes in beta can result from slight changes in the composition of the market index selected. Consequently, in going from M to M', the beta of fund A can decrease dramatically, moving the fund to point A in Figure 10.12 and the beta for fund B can, at the same time, increase, moving the fund to point B.

If we select M as our market index, we conclude that neither fund outperformed the market. If we select M' instead, we give high marks to A and low marks to B. We could easily reverse our rankings if we select still another index. Performance evaluation seems to be highly dependent on the choice of a market index. How are we to decide which index is the most appropriate?

From property AIV (Appendix 8), we know the deviation of a stock or portfolio from the security market line, or the Jensen Index, is given by the following expression:[2]

$$\underbrace{[E(r_P) - E(r_Z)]\sigma^2(\varepsilon_{M'})}_{\substack{\text{Portfolio} \\ \text{risk premium}}} - \underbrace{[E(r_{M'}) - E(r_Z)]}_{\substack{\text{Market index} \\ \text{risk premium}}} \mathrm{Cov}(\varepsilon_{M'}, \varepsilon_P) \over \sigma^2(r_{M'})} = J_P$$

Note if the risk premium on the portfolio is greater than the risk premium on the market index, there is a *propensity* for the portfolio to be positioned above the security market line. Much depends, however, on the risk characteristics of the index. If the index is highly inefficient, its residual variance $\sigma^2(\varepsilon_{M'})$ is likely to be large. This by itself increases the expected size of the first term in the numerator, but it also increases the expected size of the covariance between the residuals on the portfolio and the index, $\mathrm{Cov}(\varepsilon_P, \varepsilon_{M'})$, in the second term. The sign of the Jensen Index

---

[2]See Green (1984) for a proof of this. As we note in Appendix 8 at the end of the book, in the equation for the Jensen Index or the deviation from the security market line, the expected rate of return to the zero beta portfolio is that which is consistent with property AVI (Appendix 8). Also, the residuals in the residual variance and covariance terms are those obtained from a regression of security returns on any two different portfolios taken from the bullet. Residual variance, in this sense, will always be zero for portfolios that are themselves on the bullet. This is true because, based on property I, Chapter 5, bullet portfolios can always be viewed as simple, linear combinations of other bullet portfolios (say, portfolios A and B). As such their returns in any period can be written as follows:

$$r_P = x_A r_A + (1 - x_A)r_B$$

The returns on portfolio P are, thus, fully explained by the returns on minimum variance portfolios A and B. As such the coefficient of multiple correlation is 1.00, and the residual variance is zero. Thus, the Jensen Index for any efficient portfolio can be written as

$$[E(r_P) - E(r_Z)]\frac{\sigma^2(\varepsilon_{M'})}{\sigma^2(r_{M'})}$$

will depend on the relative magnitudes of the risk premiums, the residual variance of the index, and the covariance between the residuals on the portfolio and the index.

Note that in the case of Figure 10.11, the residual variance of the inefficient market index must be very small because the index is close to the efficient set. Given this, the covariance between the residuals on the index and the residuals on the portfolio must also be very small. However, if the market index has an expected return in the vicinity of the minimum variance portfolio, the difference between $E(r_{M'})$ and $E(r_Z)$ will be very large, and there will also be substantial differences between $E(r_P)$ and $E(r_Z)$ for the various portfolios. In this case, in moving from an efficient portfolio such as M to a slightly inefficient portfolio such as M', we move from a perfect fit to a considerable scattering of observations about the security market line.

Ambiguity of ranking based on choice of market index is really the same as the problem we had in testing the CAPM. In choosing the Jensen Index, we have assumed securities are priced in accord with the CAPM. The CAPM tells us betas should be computed with reference to the true market portfolio. Our choice of a market index with respect to measuring performance is *unambiguous*. We should use the index that most closely approximates the true market portfolio. Ambiguity in performance measurement is not the real problem. The real problem is, once again, that we can never employ a market index which comes even close to the true market portfolio. As a consequence, we can never know whether our relative performance indices are due to relative skill, or are due instead to the fact that our index, even though it's the best available, is still a poor approximation for the market portfolio.

Finally, the problem results from the sensitivity of *beta* to the choice of a market index. Thus, rankings under the Sharpe Index (which employs standard deviation as opposed to beta) are insensitive to this problem. The problem works its way in through the back door, however, when you select a market proxy as a basis of comparison.

MEASURING PERFORMANCE USING THE ARBITRAGE PRICING THEORY

The Jensen Index uses the linear relationship of the security market line as a benchmark to measure performance. In the arbitrage pricing theory there is a similar linear relationship between the factor betas and the expected rates of return on securities and portfolios. The relationship for any given portfolio, P, is given by

$$E(r_P) = E(r_Z) + \lambda_1\beta_{1,P} + \lambda_2\beta_{2,P} + \cdots + \lambda_n\beta_{n,P}$$

Expected portfolio return	=	Risk-free rate	+	sum of factor risk premiums

Once we have estimates of $E(r_Z)$ and the various factor prices, λ, we can use this relationship as a benchmark, measuring performance as the difference between a portfolio's rate of return in a given period and what we would expect it to be, based on the APT equation for expected return. Although there are several ways to do this, we might proceed as follows. The first step is to decide on the number of factors needed to account for the covariances between stocks. Suppose your prior opinion with respect to this question is that there are two, and the factors are unexpected changes in the rate of inflation and the real rate of interest.

The next step is to estimate the factor betas for a cross section of securities. This is done by relating the returns on each security to the unexpected percentage changes in each of the two factors. We are dealing with a three-dimensional space, where we are plotting the security's rates of return on the vertical axis and the unexpected percentage changes in each of the two factors on the two horizontal axes. We slide a plane of best fit through the scatter of points, as in Figure 10.13, each point representing the rates of return to the security and the unexpected percentage changes in each of the two factors in a particular period of time, say a month. The slopes of the plane going down each axis represent the sensitivity of the security's return to changes in the two factors. These slopes serve as estimates of the two factor betas.

The next step is to estimate the factor prices. This can be done cross sectionally by relating the estimated factor betas to the average rates of return on each stock for the total period examined, in the manner of Black, Jensen, and Scholes. Here, again, we are sliding a plane of best fit through a scatter of points in three dimensions. On the vertical axis we have average return, and on the two horizontal axes we have the factor betas for each stock. Each point in the scatter represents one of the stocks in

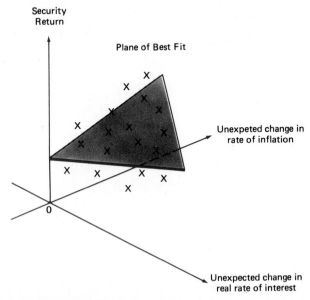

FIGURE 10.13 Relationship between security return and portfolio return.

the population. The plane is depicted in Figure 10.14. The point where the plane intercepts the vertical axis is our estimate of the average rate of return to a stock or portfolio with zero factor risk, r_Z. The slope of the plane relative to each horizontal axis serves as the estimates of the two factor prices.

We now have a benchmark to measure performance. The risk-adjusted performance measure is the difference between the portfolio's actual average rate of return for the period and the rate of return given by the position of the portfolio on the plane, given estimates of its factor betas. In Figure 10.14, point X represents a portfolio with superior performance relative to this benchmark. Given the estimated factor betas for the portfolio and the portfolio's average rate of return, it is positioned above the plane.

Note that this performance measure is subject to one of the criticisms leveled at the Jensen Index. It reflects only depth and not breadth of performance. Performance measures based on the APT are also subject to the same types of criticisms

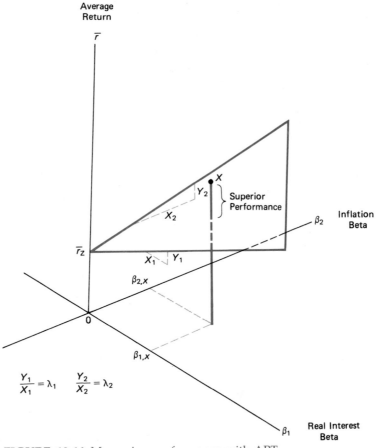

FIGURE 10.14 Measuring performance with APT.

that are levied at CAPM-based performance measures. As we know, the APT really makes no predictions about what the factors are. Given the freedom to select factors (or, alternatively, portfolios that represent factors) without restriction, it can be argued that you can literally make the performance of a portfolio anything you want it to be. In the case of the CAPM, you can never know whether portfolio performance is due to management skill or to the fact that you have an inaccurate index of the true market portfolio. In the case of APT-based measures, you have similar questions with regard to the selection of the appropriate factors.

SUMMARY

A portfolio's rate of return is an inadequate measure of performance. It is more dependent on the risk of the portfolio and the performance of the market than it is on the quality of the portfolio's managers. Because of this, we move to risk-adjusted measures of performance which remove the component due to relative risk, given market performance, from the portfolio's return.

Three risk-adjusted measures of performance have been suggested which are based on the CAPM. The Jensen and Treynor indices use the security market line as a benchmark. Both focus on management's ability to generate excess returns (depth of performance) and ignore its ability to generate excess returns on more than one security (breadth of performance). The Treynor Index recognizes the opportunity for portfolio investors to lever excess returns. It is in that sense a better measure of the attractiveness of a given portfolio as an investment opportunity. The Sharpe Index uses the capital market line as a benchmark. It is a composite measure of the depth and breadth of performance.

All three measures suffer from potential problems. If in estimating the measures you assume the wrong form of the CAPM holds in the marketplace, you get biased measures of performance, usually in favor of low-risk portfolios. This problem is easily corrected in the case of the Jensen and Treynor measures, but the problem is not so easily handled in the case of Sharpe. The Jensen and Treynor measures also suffer from the problem of possible misspecification of the market portfolio. In constructing the measures, you clearly want to use the broadest market indices which most closely approximate the market portfolio. However, since even the broadest market indices are very distant cousins of the true market portfolio, you never know whether the number you get for the index is related to the quality of the portfolio's management or the inadequacy of the index you used.

This problem is overcome when you measure performance based on the APT. However, since we know very little about the factor structure at this point, we also know very little about the accuracy of performance measurement based on the APT.

Adding to our concerns about performance measurement, a recent study by Lehmann and Modest (1987) of the performance of 130 mutual funds indicates that rankings are heavily dependent on the choice of APT versus CAPM benchmarks.

The choice of benchmark seems to be important to evaluation, and we have no unambiguously preferred benchmark!

To sum up, based on the current state of the art, you may well have a right to scream and yell if you ever get fired on the basis of poor portfolio performance. It is hoped that what you have learned in this chapter will provide you with some effective arguments to enable you to retain your job.

QUESTION SET 1

1. In selecting a measure of performance, why do we want a measure that is insensitive to the risk of the investment?

   Refer to the following information for Problems 2 through 4. Suppose the returns and corresponding beta values for two assets (*A* and *B*) were as indicated on the following graph:

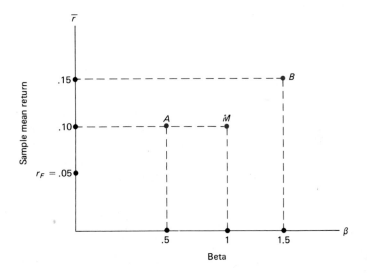

2. a. Compute the Treynor Index for *A* and *B*.
   b. Interpret the results.
3. a. Compute the Jensen Index for *A* and *B*.
   b. Interpret the results.
4. Suppose one manager had selected a portfolio represented by *A* and another manager had selected a portfolio represented by *B*. Would you feel confident in evaluating the manager's relative performance with the Treynor or Jensen results? Explain.

Refer to the following graph for Problems 5 through 8:

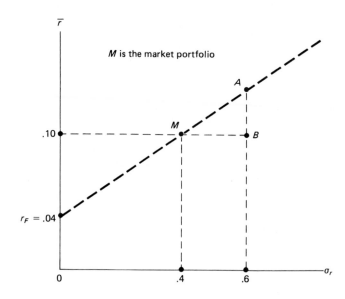

5. Compute the Sharpe Index for *B*. How would you interpret this result?
6. Compute the Sharpe Index for *A*. How would you interpret this result?
7. Suppose you decided that the "no-borrowing" version of the CAPM was the appropriate model. How would your interpretation of *A*'s performance (Problem 6) be affected?
8. Suppose you were presented with an asset having a beta of .5 and an expected return of 7.5 percent. What could you conclude about the Jensen Index of this asset?

Refer to the following information for Problems 9 through 12:

	Observed $\bar{r}$	Beta	Residual Variance
Portfolio 1	.15	1.3	0
Portfolio 2	.09	.9	.04

$$\bar{r}_F = .05.$$
$$\bar{r}_M = .10.$$

Standard deviation of market = .3.

9. Compute the Jensen Index for portfolios 1 and 2. Interpret the results.
10. Compute the Treynor Index for portfolios 1 and 2. Interpret the results.
11. Compute the Sharpe Index for the market portfolio.
12. Compute the Sharpe Index for portfolios 1 and 2. Interpret the results.

QUESTION SET 2

1. You begin a job with a medium-sized financial firm. Your firm has a number of clients who are risk averse, but in a tremendous bull market, the firm pulls in a whopping 33 percent on the portfolio for the pension fund of the local tractor-drivers. You are assigned to present the "great" news to the head of the local tractor-drivers, but when you arrive and present the news, his face looks grim and he tells you the return signals too much risk. What should be your plan of attack to your client?

2. How can two funds have the same expected rate of return, and yet nearly always have different realized rates of return?

3. Two managers both are awarded Jensen indices of 3 percent on their performances.
   a. Does this indicate a good performance or a poor performance?
   b. What line is used as the benchmark for this index?
   c. If you were a portfolio manager who was sure your performance was superior to the other manager's, what shortfalls would you point out in this index?

4. The Treynor Index adds what factor into its measure of management performance? If you are comparing a levered low-beta portfolio fund to a high-beta portfolio fund, what do you think that you, in general, will find—that the low-beta fund or the high-beta fund has the greater Treynor Index?

5. You plot the performance of two portfolios in expected return–beta space in relation to your estimated security market line. You are delighted to find they line up perfectly equidistant above the line and proudly announce to your clientele that you have two well-managed funds and they can be placed in either, depending on their attitudes toward risk. At a later date you discover your estimate of the security market line had too great a slope because you used the wrong risk-free rate; that in fact, the true SML had a very mild incline. What does this do to your evaluations of your two managers?

ANSWERS TO QUESTION SET 2

1. You should tell the head of the tractor-drivers that the risk of a portfolio must be considered in relation to the market portfolio, similar to the Dow Jones Index he keeps hearing on radio and television. When the market goes up, his portfolio also goes up. Then compare his portfolio's return to the return on the market portfolio, which should also show a significant gain in a bull market. A riskier portfolio that was well managed probably went up much more than your more modest portfolio, and you should show him such a portfolio, and the gains it made. Make sure to point out to him how he will be right to be worried about his return if the market portfolio were only earning 10 percent, but since the market itself went up quite a bit, his portfolio, even with low risk, showed a pleasing return.

2. Under risk neutrality two funds can have the same expected rates of return and yet different realized rates of return when their betas are sharply contrasting, or one is sharply high beta and the other low beta. The characteristic lines of each might intersect at the coordinates equal to the expected return to the market portfolio, or $E(r_M)$, but the high-beta fund would have a steeper slope for its characteristic line.

3. a. A positive Jensen Index indicates superior performance.
   b. The security market line is used as a benchmark for the Jensen Index.

c. A major problem with the Jensen Index is that it is only sensitive to depth, or distance from the security market line, and not breadth, or the number of different securities that have captured excess returns. In effect a "lucky" manager who invested all his funds in one stock and was thus not diversified against risk could have gotten a great return for one year on his investment and be ranked the same as a superior manager who diversified against risk and captured great returns on many securities in his portfolio.

4. The Treynor Index adds into its account the leverage factor, or the risk premium per unit of risk taken. In effect, a lower-beta portfolio can be leveraged out, giving it a higher-beta factor (and higher ranking) than a higher-beta portfolio with the same positive Jensen Index. In the case where the Jensen Index gives the same or lower rankings for the higher-beta portfolio, the Treynor Index will give the lower-beta fund the higher ranking.

5. Depicting this graphically, suppose you estimated the security market line as the solid line below, with both the low-beta portfolio (A) and the high-beta portfolio (B) positioned on the estimated security market line. The true security market line was less upward sloping, positioned at the broken line. Note that the portfolio at A has performed below the true security market line, giving it a negative Jensen Index, while the portfolio at B has performed better than the true security market line, thus giving it a positive Jensen Index. Your evaluations of the managers would also change accordingly, with the manager at B, all other things being equal, having outperformed the manager at A.

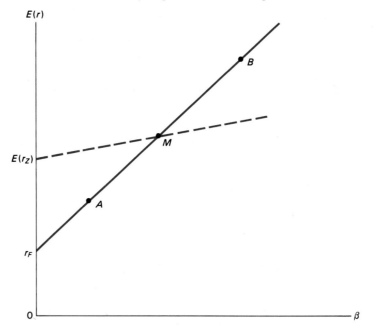

PROBLEM SET

1. You are presented by a new, feisty client with the following: "I've lived through many a time you'd never see, you young whippersnapper, and if there is one thing I've learned,

it's that anyone can have luck now and then. But MANAGEMENT! now that's the key to real success. I've selected two assets for you to assess, my young pup, and I'll take the risky one or the nonrisky, makes no matter. But MANAGEMENT! Find me the one that there's some real talent behind, and you'll have the entire clan's account next week!'' You take the paper he hands you, and read the names of the two funds. Doing research into the wee hours of the night, you find that fund A has a sample mean of .13 and fund B has a sample mean of .18, with the riskier fund B having double the beta at 2.0 as fund A. The respective standard deviations are 15 percent and 19 percent. The mean return for your market index is .12, while the risk-free rate on the bond market is 8 percent.

    a.   Compute the Jensen Index for each of the funds. What does it indicate to you?

    b.   Compute the Treynor Index for the funds. Interpret the results and compare it to the Jensen Index.

    c.   Compute the Sharpe Index for the funds and the market.

    d.   What did you say to the client to get the entire clan's account?

2. With a risk-free rate of 5 percent, and with the market portfolio having an expected return of 10 percent with a standard deviation of 5 percent, what is the Sharpe Index for portfolio A, with a return of 8 percent and a standard deviation of 10 percent? For portfolio B, having a return of 12 percent and a standard deviation of 8 percent? Would you rather be in the market portfolio or one of the other two portfolios?

3. Suppose you are asked to analyze two portfolios having the following characteristics:

	Observed r	Beta	Residual Variance
Portfolio 1	.15	1.5	.02
Portfolio 2	.10	.5	.00

The risk-free rate is .05.

The return on the market portfolio is .12.

The standard deviation of the market is .04.

a. Compute the Jensen Index for portfolios 1 and 2.

b. Compute the Treynor Index for portfolios 1 and 2.

c. Compute the Sharpe Index for the market portfolio.

d. Compute the Sharpe Index for portfolios 1 and 2.

ANSWERS TO PROBLEM SET

1. a. Fund B has twice the Jensen Index as fund A:

$$\text{Fund } A: \quad J = \bar{r}_P - [\bar{r}_F + (\bar{r}_M - \bar{r}_F)]\beta_P$$

$$= 13\% - [8\% + (12\% - 8\%)\ 1.0]$$

$$= 1\%$$

$$\text{Fund } B: \quad J = 18\% - [8\% + (12\% - 8\%)\ 2.0]$$

$$= 2\%$$

b. The Treynor Index shows the securities performing at the same level:

$$\text{Fund } A: \quad T = \frac{\bar{r}_P - \bar{r}_F}{\beta_P}$$

$$= \frac{13\% - 8\%}{1.0} = 5$$

$$\text{Fund } B: \quad T = \frac{18\% - 8\%}{2.0} = 5$$

c. The Sharpe Index places fund B ahead of fund A, but by a lesser margin than the Jensen Index:

$$\text{Fund } A: \quad S = \frac{\bar{r}_P - \bar{r}_F}{\sigma_{r_P}}$$

$$= \frac{13\% - 8\%}{15\%} = .333$$

$$\text{Fund } B: \quad S = \frac{18\% - 8\%}{19\%} = .526$$

$$\text{Market:} \quad S = \frac{12\% - 8\%}{8\%} = .500$$

d. Both funds appear to be able to identify undervalued securities because they have positive Jensen indices. Fund B's Jensen is larger, but when considering the investors' ability to lever Fund A 1 percent excess return, they both look pretty much the same in this respect as indicated by their equal Treynor indices. Fund B, however, clearly has the better management because it can capture the excess return while diversifying over many individual issues, as indicated by its superior Sharpe Index. Fund B gets the nod!

2. $\quad$ Portfolio $A: \quad S = \dfrac{\bar{r}_P - \bar{r}_F}{\sigma_{r_P}} = \dfrac{8\% - 5\%}{10\%} = .3$

$\quad$ Portfolio $B: \quad S = \dfrac{12\% - 5\%}{8\%} = .875$

$\quad$ Market: $\quad S = \dfrac{10\% - 5\%}{5\%} = 1.0$

The market is superior to either A or B.

3. a. Jensen Index:

$$\text{Portfolio 1:} \quad J = \bar{r}_P - [\bar{r}_F + (\bar{r}_M - \bar{r}_F)\beta_P]$$

$$= 15\% - [5\% + (12\% - 5\%)1.5]$$

$$= -.5\%$$

$$\text{Portfolio 2:} \quad J = 10\% - [5\% + (12\% - 5\%).5]$$

$$= 1.5\%$$

b. Treynor Index

$$\text{Portfolio 1:} \quad T = \frac{\bar{r}_P - \bar{r}_F}{\beta_P} = \frac{15\% - 5\%}{1.5} = 6.67$$

$$\text{Portfolio 2:} \quad T = \frac{10\% - 5\%}{.5} = 10.00$$

c. Sharpe Index for the market:

$$S = \frac{\bar{r}_M - \bar{r}_F}{\sigma_{r_M}} = \frac{12\% - 5\%}{4\%} = 1.75$$

d. Sharpe Index for portfolios:
Standard deviation portfolio 1:

$$\sigma_{r_P} = [\beta_P^2 \, \sigma_{r_M}^2 + \sigma_{\varepsilon_P}^2]^{1/2}$$

$$= [1.5^2(.0016 + .02)]^{1/2} = 15.36\%$$

Sharpe Index for portfolio 1:

$$S = \frac{15\% - 5\%}{15.36\%} = .651$$

Standard deviation for portfolio 2:

$$\sigma_{r_P} = [.5^2(.0016 + .00)]^{1/2} = 2\%$$

Sharpe Index for Portfolio 2:

$$S = \frac{10\% - 5\%}{2\%} = 2.5$$

COMPUTER PROBLEM SET

The accompanying table lists the annual rates of return (in percent) to the S&P 500 and three mutual funds for the nine years 1976 to 1984.

Year	S&P 500	Fund 1	Fund 2	Fund 3
1976	23.64	− 28.5	34.5	23.4
1977	− 7.16	32.8	1.8	− 4.4
1978	6.39	9.5	11.1	5.3
1979	18.16	176.7	27.6	13.5
1980	31.48	64.6	26.8	22.6
1981	− 4.85	− 19.8	16.2	2.9
1982	20.37	51.9	29.9	24.5
1983	22.30	8.8	6.7	23.6
1984	5.97	− 22.9	2.6	10.7

The average annual rate of return to a portfolio of short-term U.S. treasury securities during the period was 8.92 percent.

Based on the information given:

1. Rank the three mutual funds using the Jensen, Treynor, and Sharpe indices. Use the single-index model program to compute the beta factors for the three funds and use the returns to the S&P 500 as a proxy for the returns to the market portfolio.

2. Rerank the three mutual funds by the Jensen and Treynor indices, but this time use the NYSE in the single-index model program (1976–84) as a proxy for the market portfolio.

REFERENCES

ANG, J. S., and CHUA, J. H., "Composite Measures for the Evaluation of Investment Performance," *Journal of Financial and Quantitative Analysis* (June 1979).

ARDITTI, F. D., "Another Look at Mutual Fund Performance," *Journal of Financial and Quantitative Analysis* (June 1971).

BLACK, F., JENSEN, M. C., and SCHOLES, M., "The Capital Asset Pricing Model: Some Empirical Tests,"in *Studies in Theory of Capital Markets,* ed. M. C. Jensen. New York: Praeger, 1972.

BOWER, R. S., and WIPPERN, R. F., "Risk-Return Measurement in Portfolio Selection and Performance Appraisal Models: Progress Report," *Journal of Financial and Quantitative Analysis* (December 1969).

CARLSON, S., "Aggregate Performance of Mutual Funds: 1948–1967," *Journal of Financial and Quantitative Analysis* (March 1970).

CHEN, N. F., COPELAND, T. E., and MAYERS, D., "A Comparison of APM, CAPM and Market-Model Portfolio Performance Methodologies: The Value Line Case (1965–1978)," working paper, University of Chicago, University of California, Los Angeles, 1983.

DIETS, P. O., "Components of a Measurement Model, Rate of Return, Risk and Timing," *Journal of Finance* (May 1968).

FAMA, E. F., "Components of Investment Performance," *Journal of Finance* (June 1970).

FRIEND, I., and BLUME, M., "Measurement of Portfolio Performance Under Uncertainty," *American Economic Review* (September 1970).

GREEN, R. C., "Benchmark Portfolio Inefficiency and Deviations from the Security Market Line," unpublished manuscript, Carnegie-Mellon University, Pittsburgh, June 1984.

HENDRIKSSON, R. D., and MERTON, R. C., "On Market Timing and Investment Performance. II. Statistical Procedures for Evaluating Forecasting Skills," *Journal of Business* (October 1981).

JENSEN, M. C., "Problems in Selection of Security Portfolios: The Performance of Mutual Funds in the Period 1945–1964," *Journal of Business* (May 1968).

JENSEN, M. C., "Risk, the Pricing of Capital Assets, and the Evaluation of Investment Portfolios," *Journal of Finance* (April 1969).

JOY, M. O., and PORTER, R. B., "Stochastic Dominance and Mutual Fund Performance," *Journal of Financial and Quantitative Analysis* (January 1974).

KLEMKOSKY, R. C., "The Bias in Composite Performance Measures," *Journal of Financial and Quantitative Analysis* (June 1973).

KON, S. J., and JEN, F. C., "Estimation of Time-Varying Systematic Risk and Performance for Mutual Fund Portfolios: An Application of Switching Regression," *Journal of Finance* (May 1978).

KON, S. J., and JEN, F. C., "The Investment Performance of Mutual Funds: An Empirical Investigation of Timing, Selectivity and Market Efficiency," *Journal of Business* (April 1979).

LEHMANN, B. N., and MODEST, D. M., "Mutual Fund Performance Evaluation: A Comparison of Benchmarks and Benchmark Comparisons," *Journal of Finance* (June 1987).

MERTON, R. C., "On Market Timing and Investment Performance. I. An Equilibrium Theory of Value for Market Forecasts," *Journal of Business* (July 1981).

ROLL, R., "Ambiguity When Performance is Measured by the Security Market Line," *Journal of Finance* (September 1978).

SCHLARBAUM, G. G., "The Investment Performance of the Common Stock Portfolios of Property-Liability Insurance Companies," *Journal of Financial and Quantitative Analysis* (January 1974).

SCHLARBAUM, G. G., LEWELLEN, W. G., and LEASE, R. C., "The Common Stock Portfolio Performance Record of Individual Investors: 1964–1970," *Journal of Finance* (May 1978).

SHARPE, W. F., "Mutual Fund Performance," *Journal of Business* (January 1966).

TREYNOR, J. L., "How to Rate Management Investment Funds," *Harvard Business Review* (January–February 1965).

TREYNOR, J. L., and MAZUY, K., "Can Mutual Funds Outguess the Market?" *Harvard Business Review* (July–August 1966).

WILLIAMSON, P. F., "Measuring Mutual Fund Performance," *Financial Analysts Journal* (November–December 1972).

CHAPTER

11

THE LEVEL OF INTEREST RATES

When we discussed the capital asset pricing model, we *assumed* a level for the risk-free rate. This assumed rate serves as a foundation for the expected returns on all the other securities in the economy. In this chapter we will examine some of the forces that push the general level of interest rates up and down over time.

In recent years, interest rates have been much more volatile. This may be due, in part, to the fact that in October 1979 the Federal Reserve changed its main target from the level of interest rates to the rate of growth in the money supply. Prior to October, the Fed adjusted the rate of growth in the money supply to achieve a targeted level for the rate of interest. After October, the money supply was adjusted so as to achieve target levels in *its* rate of growth. The Fed selected a range of acceptable growth rates in the money supply for the quarter or the year and then tried to adjust the money supply to keep its growth rate in the acceptable range.

As you can see from Figure 11.1, the probable result of the shift in policy was to increase the volatility of interest rates. Interest rates have now become an extremely important factor not only in the management of portfolios of fixed income securities, but for portfolios of common stocks as well. As a result, it's important for you to understand why interest rates move up and down over time. Once you understand this, it will help you not only to forecast the future direction of rates, but it will also help you to explain intelligently to your clients and superiors why your forecasts went wrong.

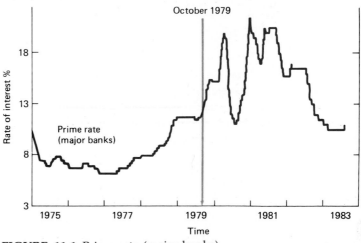

FIGURE 11.1 Prime rate (major banks).

THE REAL AND NOMINAL RATES OF INTEREST

If you looked up the rate of interest on 30-day treasury bills in the financial section of the newspaper, you would find the nominal, 30-day, risk-free interest rate. The *nominal interest rate* can be divided into two parts, the real rate of interest and the inflation premium.

The *real rate of interest* compensates investors for delaying consumption for the next 30 days. Most people want to fulfill their desires now rather than later. If they invest in treasury bills, they have to wait. To induce them to wait, investing in a treasury bill must offer the prospect of greater consumption in the future. If there was only a single commodity produced in the economy, the real rate of interest would be the percentage increase in the amount of the commodity that you could buy as a result of investing in treasury bills. In a world with multiple commodities and services, things are more complicated. In such a world, the real rate of interest is the percentage increase in your desired bundle of goods and services that results from investing in the treasury bill.

The *inflation premium* compensates investors for the loss in the purchasing power of the dollar that is expected to occur over the life of the security. With a 30-day treasury bill, the inflation premium is the expected rate of inflation over the next 30 days. The inflation premium in a 10-year government bond is the average, expected rate of inflation over the next 10 years.

The nominal rate of interest in the financial news is, therefore, the sum of the real rate of interest plus the inflation premium.

INTEREST RATES AND THE SUPPLY AND DEMAND FOR MONEY

The money supply is a crucial determinant of the level of interest rates in the economy. The equilibrium interest rate is determined when the quantity of money demanded is equal to the quantity of money supplied. The supply of money is determined by the Federal Reserve. We shall segment the demand for money into two parts, the transactions demand and the speculative demand.[1]

The Transactions Demand for Money

Transactions demand is the demand for money as a medium of exchange. Money serves as an efficient alternative to barter. We need it to trade goods and services. If you assume money can be held in two forms, checking accounts and saving-accounts, the transactions demand for money is that which we hold in checking accounts, so we can buy things when we need to.

What determines the total demand for checking account balances? To answer this question, think about what determines the amount of money you keep in your checking account. Suppose you get paid $1000 once a month. You take your check, deposit it in your checking account at the beginning of the month, and spend it at a uniform rate throughout the month. This being the case, your average checking account balance for the month as a whole is obviously $500.

Now suppose your income increases to $1500 per month. If you continue to spend all of your money at a stable rate each month, your average checking account balance increases to $750. Since the aggregate transactions demand for money is found by summing across all in the economy, we can say the overall demand for checking accounts increases with the aggregate level of income in the economy. One possible relationship between the level of income and transactions demand for money is depicted in Figure 11.2. The relationship is assumed to be linear, but it need not be.

The slope of the relationship of Figure 11.2 is equal to .50. If we take the inverse of this number, we get the *velocity of money* or the number of dollars of income supported by each dollar of money (in checking accounts) in the economy. The velocity of money in the example given is 2.00.

The velocity of money can change over time. Suppose your monthly income was $1000, but you were paid twice rather than once per month. In this case, your required average checking account balance falls from $500 to $250. If this happens to many people in the economy, the slope of the relationship between transactions demand and income falls, and the velocity of money rises. As Figure 11.3 indicates, the actual velocity of money in the U.S. economy has, until recently, been steadily rising over time.

---

[1]A third component of the demand for money is sometimes referred to as precautionary demand. To simplify the discussion, we will assume that is part of the speculative demand for money.

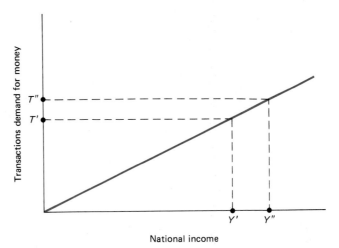

FIGURE 11.2 Transactions demand for money.

To summarize, the transactions demand for money is assumed to increase with the level of national income, and the relationship between income and transactions demand can change with changes in the payments system in the economy. Over time the payments system has become more efficient, generally increasing the velocity of money.

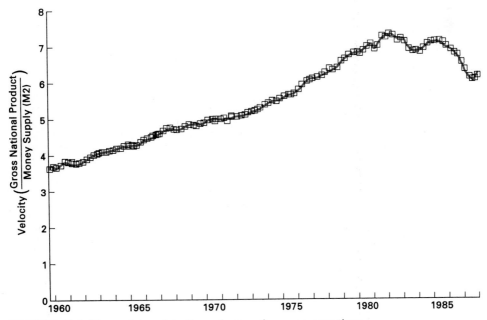

FIGURE 11.3 Upward trend in the velocity of money over time.

The Speculative Demand for Money

Money is also demanded as an alternative form of investment. We shall assume a very simple economy with two forms of investments, savings accounts and a perpetual bond, or **consol,** the payments on which are guaranteed by the government. The consols are issued by business firms to raise money to finance their investments on plant and equipment and by government to finance deficit spending. The consols represent the many different securities which are available in the actual economy. The rate of interest on the consols represents the average expected rate of return of all securities. We want to find the forces which determine that expected rate of return.

Assume all investors look forward over a common horizon period, say, a month. The nominal rate of interest on the savings accounts is assumed to be fixed over the month. On the other hand, in any given period, the realized nominal rate of return on the consols is given by

$$\frac{\text{Interest payment} + \text{change in market price}}{\text{Current market price}} \tag{11.4}$$

The realized real rate of return on the consol or the savings account can be obtained by subtracting the rate of inflation for the period from the realized nominal rate of return. The dollar interest payments on both the consol and the savings account are assumed to be guaranteed by the government, but the market price of the consol at the end of the month is given by the present value of its future interest payments, discounted at rates expected to prevail in the future. As interest rates go up, the

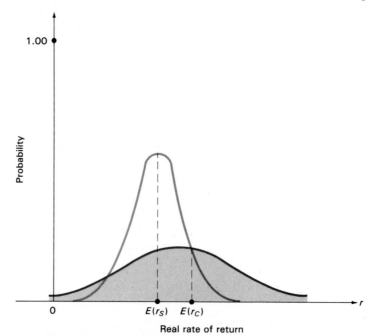

FIGURE 11.4 Probability distributions for the consol and the savings account.

market value of the consol falls; as rates go down, the market value rises. In short, even though the interest payments are guaranteed, the monthly nominal and real rates of return for the consol are uncertain because both the future level of interest rates and the rate of inflation are uncertain. There is an interest rate risk and an inflation risk associated with investing in the consol. In the case of the savings account, there is only an inflation risk, and the overall risk associated with the savings account is presumed to be less than that of the consol.

The probability distributions for the monthly real rates of return on the consol and the savings account are given in Figure 11.4. If we assume investors are risk averse, the expected rate of return on the consol will be higher than that on the savings account. This is because the variance of the rate of return on the consol is greater than that of the savings account.

The consol and the savings account are plotted on an $E(r)$, $\sigma(r)$ graph in Figure 11.5 at points C and S, respectively. Since the returns to the consol are normally distributed, we can draw the indifference curves of investors in the graph. Each investor, of course, has a different set of indifference curves. As an investor, you can position yourself anywhere on the solid combination line between points C and S. Your ideal portfolio can be found where the indifference curve is tangent to the

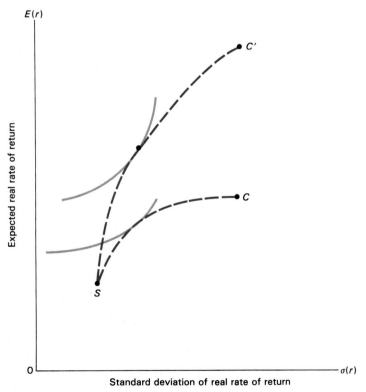

FIGURE 11.5 Effect of an increase in the real rate of interest on the optimal portfolio position.

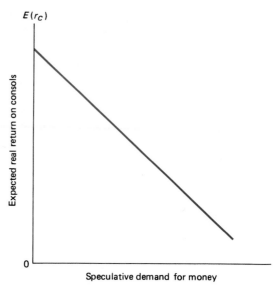

FIGURE 11.6 Speculative demand for money.

combination line, such as at point 1. In this case you're investing about 60 percent of your money in the savings account and 40 percent in the consol. Each investor is assumed to take an ideal portfolio position, investing some of his or her wealth in the savings account and the remainder in the consol.

When we speak of the real rate of interest in the economy, we are referring to the expected, real rate of return to the consol over the next month. Given this, if the real rate of interest increases, what will happen to the speculative demand for money or the demand for savings accounts? In Figure 11.5 we have increased the expected real rate of return on consols, moving the position of the consol to C'. In doing so, we move to a new point of tangency between the new combination line and your indifference curves. Whereas before you were investing 60 percent of your wealth in the savings account, now this percentage has fallen to roughly 50 percent. An increase in the real rate of interest on consols has reduced your demand for the other form of investment, savings accounts.[2]

Other investors will react in the same way. The total demand for savings accounts will fall as the real rate of interest on consols goes up. In Figure 11.6 we have drawn the **speculative demand for money** as a decreasing function (the solid line) of the real rate of interest on the other form of investment, *consols*.

The Total Demand for Money

Given a level for national income and the real rate of interest, we can find the total demand for money by summing the two component demands, transactions demand and speculative demand. In Figure 11.7 we have drawn the two components and the

---

[2]This treatment of speculative demand was first discussed by Tobin (1958).

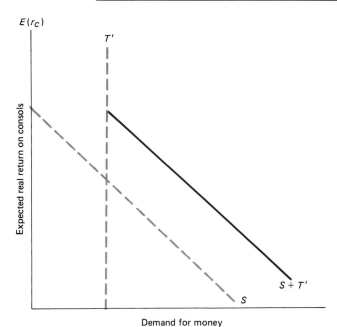

FIGURE 11.7 Total demand for money.

total demand as they relate to the level of the real rate of interest. We have assumed a given level of national income in Figure 11.2 of Y' which gives us a transactions demand for money of T'. The transactions demand for money is drawn as a constant at a level equal to T' in Figure 11.7 because it is assumed to be unrelated to the real rate of interest. The speculative demand for money schedule is merely repeated from Figure 11.6. To get the total demand at each rate of interest, we merely add T' to the speculative demand at each interest rate. This produces the schedule $S + T'$.

It should be obvious that if we change the level of national income, we change T and move to a new total demand for money schedule.

The Supply of Money and the Equilibrium Interest Rate

The supply of money is determined by the Federal Reserve System. The Fed can change the money supply by changing the interest rate on the loans it makes to the banking system or by changing the amount of required reserves. However, the Fed's principal tool to change the money supply is ***open market operations.***

When the Fed engages in open market operations, it buys and sells government bonds (in our simple economy, consols) from its own account. If it buys consols, there are fewer consols in the system and more money. If it sells consols, there are more consols but less money.

We will assume the Fed is not using an interest rate target, so the quantity of money in the system is not causally related to the level of the real rate of interest. Thus, the schedule relating the supply of money to the real rate of interest is perfectly inelastic, as in Figure 11.8.

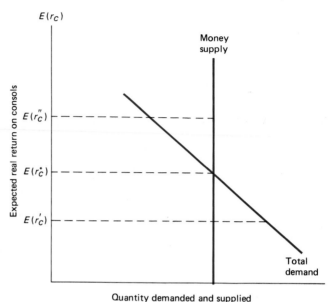

FIGURE 11.8 Equilibrium real interest rate.

We have equilibrium in the economy when the interest rate is such that the quantity of money supplied by the Fed is equal to the quantity of money demanded. This will be true in Figure 11.8 when the interest rate is equal to $E(r_C^*)$. To show this, suppose we are in a state of *disequilibrium*, and the rate of interest is too high, at $E(r_C'')$. In this case, the total demand for money is less than the supply. There is surplus liquidity. Individuals will "attempt" to get rid of it by buying consols in the securities market. I say attempt, because only the Fed can really get rid of money in the economy. Individuals can merely pass it from one to another. However, in the process of attempting to get rid of it by buying consols, they will raise the current price of consols and lower the expected, real rate of interest. This will continue to happen until the interest rate has reached its equilibrium level. At the equilibrium level, the supply of money is the same as it was before. However, the demand for money has now increased to equal the supply because the demand for savings accounts has increased due to the lower rate of interest on consols.

In the same sense, if the rate of interest were below its equilibrium level, at $E(r_C')$, the supply of money would be less than the demand. There would be a shortage of liquidity. People would attempt to increase liquidity by selling consols in the security market. This would drive the current market price of consols down and the expected, real rate of interest up to the equilibrium level.

Thus, the real interest rate settles at the intersection of supply and demand. Interest rates may change with a change in the supply of money. They may change with a change in the perceived risk of consols, which would shift the schedules for the speculative and total demand for money. They may also change with a change in the level of *national income,* which would change transactions demand and the schedule for the total demand for money. To gain a deeper understanding of the forces controlling interest rates, we move now to an examination of the forces controlling the level of national income.

INVESTMENT, SAVING, AND NATIONAL INCOME

Business firms are on the other side of the consol market. They issue consols to finance their investments. The consols, of course, are perpetual bonds and therefore don't mature. To retire them, the firm must repurchase them in the securities market at prevailing market prices. Over the planning horizon, the real cost of capital to the firm is equal to the expected real rate of return to the consol. In making its investment decisions, the firm compares its estimates of the real rates of return on its capital investment projects with the real cost of capital. If the project return is greater than the cost of acquiring capital to finance, the project is profitable and will increase the value of the firm if taken on.

Given the profitability of the firm's investment opportunities, if the real rate of interest falls, the firm will find that more projects can be profitably undertaken. Now, as all firms attempt to increase their spending on plant and equipment, the relative prices of capital goods should begin to rise. This will curb, to some extent, the increase in capital spending because it brings down estimates of the rates of return on these investments. Nevertheless, a reduction in the real rate of interest should be accompanied by a net increase in the level of investment spending on plant and equipment by business firms. Conversely, an increase in the real rate should be accompanied by a reduction in the level of spending on plant and equipment.

Thus, there is a connection between the level of interest rates and the level of economic investment on the part of business firms. Noting this, we now move to the link between economic investment and the level of national income.

Consider Figure 11.9. We start at the top with a given level of national income ($10 billion). We will initially assume a simple economy, with no government. Consumers divide the income up between consumption and saving. We assume that for each dollar earned $.20 is saved and $.80 is spent on consumption goods.

In the next year, business firms make their production and investment decisions. Production of consumption goods in year $t + 1$ is assumed to be determined by the following rule of thumb: The amount produced this year is equal to total domestic consumption last year, less that which was spent on foreign goods (imports) plus the amount spent on domestic goods by foreigners (exports). In Figure 11.9, exports are assumed to be equal to imports.

Investment decisions are based on the estimated profitability of individual projects and the level of the cost of capital, or the real rate of interest. In Figure 11.9 it is assumed that the level of investment spending in $t + 1$ is equal to the level of saving in the previous year. This need not always be the case, however.

The amounts spent by business firms on production for consumption and in-

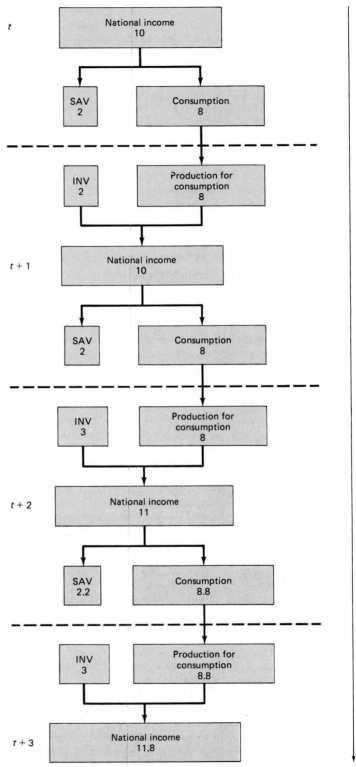

FIGURE 11.9 Savings, investment, and national income.

vestment in plant and equipment are paid to the factors of production, land, labor, and capital. These payments become the income for year $t + 1$. With exports equal to imports and saving equal to investment, the level of income in $t + 1$ is the same as in t. Indeed, unless something happens to change the level of investment or to cause an imbalance between exports and imports, income will remain indefinitely at $10 billion.

However, suppose something happens to cause investment spending to increase from $2 billion to $3 billion in period $t + 2$. This might be caused by a reduction in interest rates or by the receipt of new information that causes business firms to revise upward their estimates of the expected rates of return on their investment projects. The effect of this will be to increase the level of income to $11 billion in $t + 2$. If the split between saving and consumption remains the same, $8.8 billion will be spent on consumption in $t + 2$. This means that if the international balance of trade stays even, production for consumption will rise to $8.8 billion in $t + 3$. If investment spending stays constant at $3 billion, the level of $t + 3$ income will grow to $11.8 billion. This will lead to a further increase in consumption, followed by more production for consumption and more income. Each successive yearly increase in income is smaller than the last, however, and we gradually move toward a new, higher equilibrium level of national income.

An increase in the level of exports relative to imports will have a similar effect. This results in an increase in production for consumption, which increases the level of national income, which increases domestic consumption, which increases production for consumption again. Once again, we move in progressively smaller steps toward a higher equilibrium level of national income.

In general the following events will tend to push income upward:

1. An increase in the fraction of income consumed
2. An increase in the level of exports
3. An increase in investment spending

In the same sense, the following events will tend to push income downward:

1. A decrease in the fraction of income consumed
2. An increase in the level of imports
3. A decrease in investment spending

A change in the level of national income may lead to a change in the levels of real and nominal interest rates. Suppose, for example, national income should increase. If production in the economy is near capacity, increase in aggregate demand may be inflationary. If there is an increase in the current rate of inflation, this may lead to an increase in the expected rate of inflation for future periods. Given this, there will be an accompanying increase in the ***inflation premium*** in interest rates.

The increase in national income may also affect the real rate of interest as well. As you know, the real rate of interest is determined at the intersection of the supply and demand for money. An increase in national income may increase the transactions demand for money because, unless the pattern of transacting changes, people will want to carry larger checking account balances to support the larger volume of spending. If the Fed doesn't support the increase in national income by expanding the money supply, people will attempt to generate their own increment in liquidity by selling securities (consols). This will drive down the price of securities and drive up the real rate of interest.

You see, there is an interconnection between interest rates and national income. Given the preceding discussion, we know that income can affect interest rates, but interest rates can affect income as well. An increase in the level of interest rates means a higher cost of capital and, therefore, a lower volume of spending on plant and equipment by business firms. An increase in the real rate of interest in the United States also means that the U.S. financial markets are more attractive to foreign investors. Foreign investors will buy dollars in order to purchase securities in the United States. This drives up the value of the dollar. A strong dollar makes U.S. goods more expensive to foreigners and makes foreign goods less expensive to our domestic consumers. Thus, we would expect exports to decrease and imports to increase. Given the flows of Figure 11.9, we would expect U.S. firms to react by producing fewer consumption goods. This means a reduction in national income.

As we shall see in the next section, to understand fully the impact of various "shocks" to the economic system, we must keep in mind these interrelationships between interest rates and national income.

THE EFFECT OF A CHANGE IN THE MONEY SUPPLY ON REAL AND NOMINAL INTEREST RATES

What will be the ultimate impact on interest rates if the Fed increases the supply of money in the economy? The initial effect will be to create an imbalance in the portfolio positions of investors. People now have too much money in savings and checking accounts relative to their investments in securities or consols. Presumably, before the injection of funds, they had struck an ideal balance in their portfolios. Now the balance is upset. They respond by attempting to restore it by buying consols in the financial markets. This drives up the market price of consols and drives down the real rate of interest. Since portfolio adjustments can be made very rapidly, this first adjustment of interest rates to the change in the money supply is almost instantaneous. When the money supply goes up, we expect interest rates to immediately fall in response to portfolio adjustments. This first adjustment is called the *liquidity effect.*

The liquidity effect can be seen in Figure 11.10. As the money supply increases from S to S^*, at the old real rate $E(r_C)$ the supply of money is greater than the demand. As people attempt to get rid of the surplus money by buying consols, bond prices rise and the rate of interest falls to $E(r_C^*)$, closing the gap between supply and demand.

The lower rate of interest has two implications for the real (as opposed to the financial) sector of the economy. First, lower interest rates mean a lower cost of capital, which means that spending on plant and equipment by business firms will

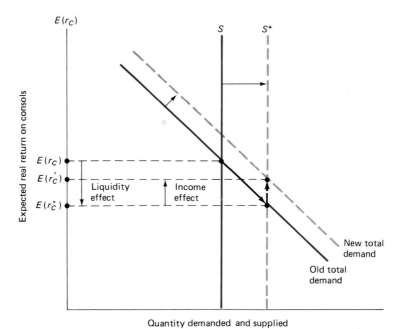

FIGURE 11.10 Liquidity and income effects of an increase in the money supply.

increase. The increase in investment spending by firms will force income upward in the coming year.

Second, the lower real rate of interest makes the U.S. financial markets less attractive to foreign investors. The demand for dollars to buy U.S. securities falls, and the value of the dollar falls as well. This makes it cheaper for foreigners to buy U.S. goods and more expensive for U.S. citizens to buy foreign goods. Exports will rise, and imports will fall. This stimulates the production of consumption goods by U.S. firms. More spending on production means more income, so income is on the rise, propelled by a lower cost of capital and a more favorable balance of trade. Of course, the increase in national income will stimulate domestic consumption, which leads to further increases in production and still more income in periods to come. Income, in any case, will be on the increase.

In response, individuals will want to maintain larger checking account balances to support their larger levels of spending. If the Fed doesn't meet this demand with a second increase in the money supply, people will attempt to generate their own liquidity by selling off securities in the financial markets. As a result, the market price of consols falls, and the real rate of interest rises. At the higher rate of interest, they will be willing to hold a larger fraction of their portfolio in consols and a smaller fraction in savings accounts. Thus, while the total money supply (savings plus checking) remains the same, a larger fraction is held in the form of checking account balances.

This second adjustment in interest rates is depicted in Figures 11.2 and 11.10.

In Figure 11.2, the increase in the level of national income to Y'' increases the transactions demand for money to T''. The increase in transactions demand shifts the total demand for money to the right in Figure 11.10. The result is a movement in interest rates from $E(\tilde{r_C})$ back up to $E(r_C')$. This second interest rate adjustment is called the **income effect** of a change in the money supply. The income effect comes after the liquidity effect, and moves in the opposite direction.

A third effect may reinforce the income effect. The **price effect** results from a change in expectations relating to the future rate of inflation. If the economy is operating near capacity, the increase in national income discussed earlier may be inflationary. If so, it may increase the expected *future* rate of inflation which results in an increase in the inflation premium in the nominal interest rate. If this happens, while the real rate of interest may be lower than it was before the monetary increase, the nominal rate may well end up at a higher level. You may remember reading articles in the financial news about exchanges between congressional committees and the chairman of the Federal Reserve Board relating to whether the Fed should expand the money supply to reduce interest rates. In the past, the chairman has argued that monetary expansion may well result in *higher* as opposed to *lower* interest rates. In assessing these exchanges, it may be said that Congress is thinking in terms of the liquidity effect, while the Fed is thinking ahead to the income and price effects.

The links in the chain of events connecting the initial increase in the money supply with the final increases in interest rates are given in Figure 11.11. It's interesting to think about the timing of the liquidity, income, and price effects. The liquidity effect should appear very rapidly, because portfolio adjustments can be made very rapidly. On the other hand, the effect of the change in monetary policy on the real economy should take place more slowly. Firms must adjust their capital budgeting decisions to the change in the cost of capital resulting from the liquidity effect. Plans must be changed and projects initiated. These things all take time, so the upward pressure on interest rates, stemming from the resulting increase in national income, will take time as well. At first thought, we might expect the income and price effects to appear many months after the appearance of the liquidity effect.

However, suppose you are an intelligent investor who knows the whole process from beginning to end. The Fed has injected money into the system, and interest rates have fallen with the liquidity effect. Are you going to sit around holding consols waiting for the income and price effects to come a few months later? Why wait for the fall in bond prices when you can get out now? That's exactly what you would expect people to do: anticipate the income and price effects and sell before they come. If this happens, we will see the income and price effects well before we see the increases in national income and inflation. Empirical evidence seems to indicate that the financial markets are indeed acting in advance of the real economy. While the lag between the liquidity and the income and price effects was as long as six months a few decades ago, more recent studies have indicated that the lag has now shortened to a month or two.[3]

---

[3]See Gibson and Kaufman (1968), Gibson (1970), Melvin (1983), Mishkin (1981, 1982), and Brown and Santoni (1983).

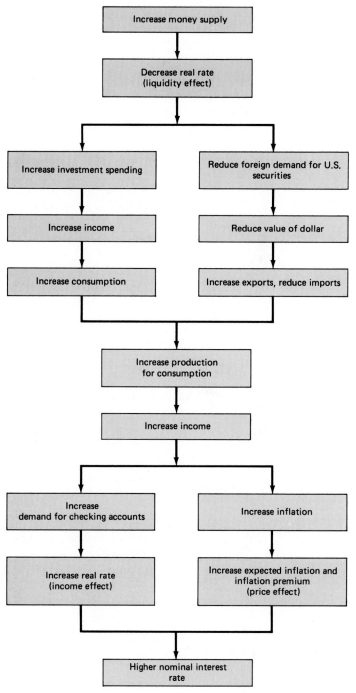

FIGURE 11.11 The effect of an increase in the money supply.

THE EFFECT OF A CHANGE IN FISCAL POLICY

A Tax Cut

In Figure 11.12 we have added government to our simple model of the economy. We have assumed that 20 percent of income is taxed and that consumers save 20 percent of their after-tax income and consume the rest. We also assume, initially, that desired saving is equal to desired investment, that exports are equal to imports,

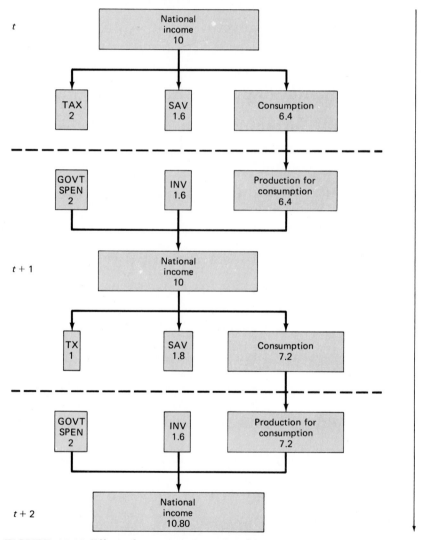

FIGURE 11.12 Effect of a tax cut on national income.

and that government spending is equal to government revenue. In this case income in $t + 1$ is equal to income in t.

We have assumed there is a 50 percent tax cut in period $t + 1$. Government revenue falls from \$2 billion to \$1 billion. Government spending remains at \$2 billion, so there is a deficit in the budget of \$1 billion. What will be the impact of the tax cut on interest rates? Once again there will be liquidity, income, and price effects.

The liquidity effect comes from the financing of the deficit. In our simple economy the deficit is financed by selling consols in the financial markets. To see the impact of this, consider the schedule for the speculative demand for money in Figure 11.13. The initial speculative demand for money schedule is labeled S. It shows the dollar demand for savings accounts, given particular interest rates on consols. It is based on Figure 11.5, where investors assign portfolio weights to consols and savings accounts based on the consol's expected interest rate and standard deviation. Given a dollar volume of consols outstanding, these portfolio *weights* imply the desired *dollar* investments in savings accounts plotted in Figure 11.13 as the speculative demand schedule. That is, if all investors desired to invest 40 percent of their portfolios in savings accounts, this would imply a \$2 billion demand for savings accounts if there were \$3 billion in consols outstanding. If there were, instead, \$6 billion in consols outstanding, the demand for savings accounts would be \$4 billion.

Given the preceding discussion, we would expect that an increase in the supply of consols in the market will shift the speculative demand for money schedule to the

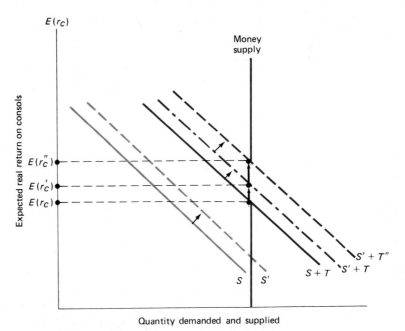

FIGURE 11.13 Effect of a tax cut on the real rate of interest.

OUT ON THE STREET

FORECASTING A TURNAROUND

It's 9:00 P.M. Streams of busy shoppers are making their way home through the streets of Chicago down below. Sy Lotsoff leans back in his chair on the thirty-second floor of the Civic Opera Building contemplating the future—not his future, but the future of the economy and interest rates in particular.

Sy is the managing director of Lotsoff Capital Management, an investment management firm that runs the portfolios of pension plans and life insurance companies nationwide. He specializes in the management of fixed income securities, and because of this, he watches the movement in interest rates very closely.

Rather than forecast what the *level* of rates is going to be in the future, Sy concentrates on direction. If you can get a jump on direction, you can make excess returns for your client, even if you're only accurate to within six months of forecasting the peak or trough.

To help him forecast the future direction on rates Sy tries to identify the stages of the business cycle. He follows several macroeconomic series such as new claims for unemployment insurance, actual and estimated capital expenditures, department store sales, auto sales, durable goods orders, and various price change indexes. He utilizes contracts throughout the economy for confirming microeconomic inputs. These people are his own clients and other relationships that he has developed over the years in diverse walks of economic life.

In the past few weeks, Sy watched as things began falling into place. The economy was nearing the tail end of the "boom" part of the business cycle and entering the early "slowdown" phase. Retail sales were beginning to falter, and corporations were being forced to borrow to finance expanding inventory. Firms were finding that internally generated cash flows were inadequate to finance spending commitments made earlier in the boom, again forcing them into the markets for capital. Although not a particular problem this time around the cycle, inflation was reaching its peak. Sy could feel it. This was the time of maximum upward pressure on interest rates.

To Sy this meant two things. He would begin to move his portfolios long, and he should begin to move them low. Long means long maturity, concentrating on those bonds with lower coupons selling at discounts under their face values. These are the bonds least likely to be called after the coming fall in interest rates.

right. At each real rate of interest on the consol, given their desired portfolio *weights*, investors will desire a larger dollar amount of savings accounts.

The impact of this is to shift the total demand for money schedule to the right in Figure 11.13, increasing the real rate of interest from $E(r_C)$ to $E(r_C')$. This is the liquidity effect of the tax cut on interest rates, and it should be coincident with the

These are the bonds that will enjoy the greatest appreciation in their market prices. Sy does not use bonds rated below investment grade (BBB).

Sy moves low because, in addition to being the time of the interest rate peak, this is the time of the greatest spreads between the yields on the highest-quality issues and the bonds of lesser quality. To a great extent this market anticipates the coming recession, lowering the prices of medium-grade issues relative to those of the highest quality. This is also the time of greatest financial stress. Lines of credit are being stretched, and commercial banks are forcing companies, especially those without unquestioned financial strength, to go out into the financial markets to obtain permanent financing. This not only helps to force rates up in general, but it forces the rates on medium-grade issues up in particular, widening the spreads.

By moving low and long, Sy maximizes the potential return that will come as the general level of rates begins to fall in the coming months and as the spreads begin to narrow into their normal range.

Perhaps 6 months, perhaps 18 months after the coming recession has ended, the growth in loan demand will once again begin to accelerate after an extended flat or down period. Sy calls this the inflection point in the cycle. All the forces now signaling downturn will be reversed. Rates will have fallen and spreads will have narrowed as internal sources of financing open up and financial markets anticipate substantial corporate profit improvement. This is the time that Sy shifts his posture from long and low to short and high.

Sy is seldom one to go to extremes. Even now he doesn't *know* that rates are reaching their peak. Because of this, his shifts in posture are often made slowly, prudently, depending on how confidently he feels he can locate himself in the business cycle.

Sy's approach has been successful in the past. The average returns on his portfolios have exceeded the Shearson Lehman index returns by about 2.5 percent per year over 15 years. Perhaps equally as important, the quarterly volatility of returns has been lower than that of the index!

If Sy's expectations prove correct, he may be able to improve on that record.

financing of the deficit.

The tax cut will also increase consumption because it increases after-tax income. Since 80 percent of after-tax income is consumed, consumption will increase by $.8 billion to $7.2 billion in $t + 1$; $.2 billion of the tax cut will be lost to savings. The increase in consumption will stimulate production for consumption in period $t + 2$. This will lead to a series of increases in income in $t + 2$ and beyond. The increases in income will be dampened somewhat by the increase in interest rates stemming from the liquidity effect. The increase in the cost of capital will reduce investment spending, and as foreign investors move into the U.S. security markets, the value of the dollar will rise, stimulating imports and reducing exports. However, there should be a net increase in the level of national income in any case.

As a result of the increase in income and spending, people will require larger balances in their checking accounts. The Fed isn't expanding the money supply, so people will "attempt" to generate the extra liquidity themselves by selling consols in the market. The price of consols will fall, and the real rate of interest will rise once again. This second increase in the real rate is again called an income effect.

The income effect is graphed in Figure 11.13 by the second shift in the total demand for money curve. This time the curve shifts as a result of a change in the transactions demand for money. The real rate of interest ends up at $E(r_C'')$.

We may again have a price effect that is coincident with the income effect. If the increase in income that results from the tax cut is inflationary, it may increase expectations regarding future inflation and the inflationary premium in interest rates. In this case, the nominal rate would go up by even more than the real rate.

Rather than cut taxes, we could have increased government spending. The effects on interest rates would have been very similar. We would have again seen the liquidity, income, and price effects. The main difference is that we would feel the full force of the increase in spending, while a fraction of the tax cut was lost to saving.

Monetizing the Deficit

In the previous example, it was assumed the deficit was financed by selling consols to the public. The result of this is an immediate increase in the real rate of interest through the liquidity effect.

The Treasury can avoid the liquidity effect if the Federal Reserve System simultaneously engages in open market purchases of securities.[4] In this case there will be no increase in the supply of consols held by the public and no shift to the right in the speculative demand for money schedule as we had in Figure 11.13. However, the Treasury will eventually spend the money it gets from "selling securities to the Fed." When it does, new money will flow into the economy, resulting in an increase in the money supply. Once the money supply goes up, we release liquidity, income, and price effects which have the net effect of putting upward pressure on the level of nominal interest rates. Thus, if the deficit is financed by "selling securities to the Fed" instead of to the public, we avoid the short-run problem of the liquidity effect putting upward pressure on the real rate but face the longer-run problem of income and price effects putting upward pressure on nominal rates.

---

[4]Technically speaking, the Treasury can't, under existing law, sell securities in unlimited amount directly to the Federal Reserve.

SUMMARY

The nominal rate of interest can be divided into two parts, the real rate and the inflation premium. The real rate compensates investors for delaying consumption; the inflation premium compensates them for erosion in the purchasing power of the dollar payments they get from investing in the security.

The real rate of interest equilibrates the supply and demand for money. The supply of money is determined by the monetary policy of the Federal Reserve. The demand for money can be divided into transactions demand and speculative demand. Transactions demand is the demand for money as a medium of exchange. We have represented it as the demand for checking accounts. Transactions demand increases with the level of national income. Speculative demand is the demand for money as an investment alternative to securities, which we have represented by a single consol bond. We take the speculative demand for money to be the demand for savings accounts. The speculative demand for money is inversely related to the expected real return on the alternative investment, the consol.

If the demand for money is greater than the supply, people will attempt to generate their own liquidity by selling off securities. This selling pressure reduces the price of securities, increases the real rate of interest, and lowers the demand for money to the point where it is equal to the supply. If supply is greater than demand people use the surplus liquidity to buy securities, and the opposite happens.

There is an interaction between the real rate of interest and the level of national income. An increase in the real rate of interest reduces the level of investment spending on plant and equipment by business firms and also creates an unfavorable balance of trade through its effect on the value of the dollar. Both factors exert downward pressure on the level of national income. On the other hand, an increase in national income exerts upward pressure on the real rate of interest, because higher levels of income mean greater demand for transactions balances. In attempting to get them, people will sell off securities, lowering their prices and increasing their real expected rates of return.

A change in the money supply changes the rate of interest through the liquidity, income, and price effects. The liquidity effect comes from portfolio adjustments in response to the change in the level of liquidity induced by the Fed. The income effect results from the link between interest rates, investment spending, the balance of trade, and the level of national income. A change in the level of national income means a change in the transactions demand for money and a resulting change in the real rate of interest. If the change in national income affects the rate of inflation, we may get a price effect. The price effect is caused by a change in the inflation premium. It affects the magnitude of the nominal rate but not the real rate.

Forces that exert upward pressure on interest rates include autonomous increases in investment spending, a reduction in the savings rate by consumers, increases in the level of exports, reductions in the level of imports, increases in government spending, and tax cuts. Movements in the opposite direction by these factors exert downward pressure on interest rates.

QUESTION SET 1

1. Contrast the nominal rate of interest with the real rate of interest.

2. Assume there is no inflation in an economy and that if you put aside $100 today in a consol bond, you will receive $105 back in one year. What are the real and nominal rates of interest? Next, assume the same information except that prices are expected to rise generally by 4 percent over the year. What are the real and nominal rates of interest?

3. Suppose the transactions demand for money was described by the following equation:

$$T = .3Y$$

where T = transactions demand
Y = national income

a. What is this equation telling us?

b. If we are experiencing a decreased velocity of money, what sort of change would we expect in the equation?

c. Improvements in the workings of the economy's mechanism for payments would lead to what sort of change in the equation?

4. If your holdings of money as an investment yield a return which is less than the return from consols, why would people want to hold *any* money as an investment?

5. Explain why a lower rate on consols would be associated with a larger quantity of speculative money being demanded.

Refer to the following graph for Questions 6 through 8:

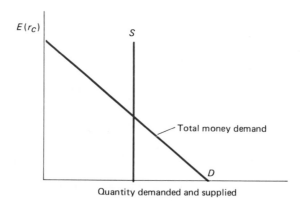

6. Indicate how the equilibrium interest rate on consols would be determined on the accompanying graph.

7. Indicate graphically the result of a decrease in the total demand for money. What is the implication for the interest rate on consols?

8. What would be a possible explanation for the decrease in total money demand indicated in Question 7?

9. Suppose the Federal Reserve decreased the money supply and immediately thereafter the demand and supply of money were in disequilibrium.
   a. What exactly do we mean by disequilibrium here?
   b. Explain the forces that would be set in motion in this market to bring it back to equilibrium.

10. Suppose the Federal Reserve has implemented a policy action which caused an increase in the real rate of interest.
    a. Discuss the manner in which national income and the real interest rate itself will respond.
    b. Differentiate between the income effect and the liquidity effect.
    c. Could there be a price effect as well?

11. Suppose the economy is in equilibrium with businesses producing a total of $75 billion for consumption and $25 billion for investment in plant, equipment, etc. The national income being generated is $100 billion. Individuals, in the aggregate, save one-fourth of their income. Assume there is no government and the economy is closed with no imports or exports. Suppose now, that businesses reduce investment to $20 billion.
    a. What is the implication for national income over the next three time periods? (Assume that the business investment remains at the $20 billion level.)
    b. Can you determine what the equilibrium level of national income would be if we followed the impact over a large number of time periods? (Business investment remains at $20 billion.)

12. Will the reduction in expenditures on investment posed in Question 11 (plant, equipment, etc.) ultimately have an impact on the real rate of interest?

13. Explain the impact of a tax increase on the real rate of interest and the level of national income.

QUESTION SET 2

1. In a period of inflation, is the real rate of interest or the nominal rate of interest higher? Can there be a time when it will not be to your advantage to postpone consumption, assuming that you are not on your death bed?

2. What is meant by the velocity of money, and which type of payment would increase it: monthly payments of income or weekly payments?

3. An increase in the real rate of interest on consols will have what type of effect on balances held in savings accounts?

4. The Federal Reserve System has determined that there is an oversupply of money in the system. What action do you expect that they will take? What effect will this action have on the price of consols currently in the system?

5. Which of the following would tend to push the equilibrium level of national income upward?
   a. Increased Japanese automobile exports to the United States.
   b. U.S. consumers' overly exuberant overspending at Christmas.
   c. An increased influx of investment dollars into savings accounts from their former places in innerspring mattresses.

6. Explain how the increase in the supply of money affects the real and nominal interest rates.

7. What is the liquidity effect?
8. What is the effect of a tax cut on the real rate of interest?
9. You invest $1000 on January 1 in a bond with a coupon rate of 20 percent. The expected rate of inflation is 7 percent. What is your expected real rate of interest at the end of the year? In light of the historic real rates of interest, if this were a quality bond and you did not know the price, but only the rate of inflation and the coupon rate, would you expect it to sell at a premium or a discount on January 1?

ANSWERS TO QUESTION SET 2

1. The nominal rate of interest is higher since

$$\text{Nominal rate} = \text{Real rate of interest} + \text{inflation premium}$$

   In a time where inflation is greater than the nominal rate of interest (hence you have a negative real rate of interest), it is in your interest to immediately consume your dollars, since tomorrow's dollar will buy less than today's dollar.

2. The velocity of money refers to how quickly money turns over in a system. Hence, the more often money is received, the more quickly it can be spent. Weekly payments would thus increase the velocity of money.

3. An increase in the real rate of interest on consols will have consumers shifting their portfolios from savings to consols.

4. If the Fed decides there is an oversupply of money, they will sell treasury bonds (consols) to reduce the oversupply. Since there will be more consols in the system, they will have to compete more rigorously for the investment dollar, and the rate of return on all consols, all other things being equal, will increase somewhat.

5. National income tends to be pushed upward when there are increases in the fraction of income consumed, an increase in the level of exports, or an increase in the money supply. Both (b) and (c) fall in these categories. An increase in the level of Japanese exports is an increase in *imports* to the United States (which will have an effect on domestic production and consumption) which tends to push national income downward.

6. An increase in the money supply initially drives down nominal and real interest rates because people are buying consols. This affects other areas of the economy, with businesses increasing investment spending, and exports rising. With income thus increasing, investment spending and domestic consumption increases, resulting in an increased transactions demand for money, which raises the nominal and real interest rates. If the economy is operating near capacity, then there is an increase in the inflation premium in the nominal interest rate, with the effect of a lower relative real rate of interest as part of the nominal rate.

7. The liquidity effect is the term given to the initial change in interest rates which result from changing the money supply, investment spending, or the federal deficit.

8. If the tax cut is financed by government borrowing, the liquidity effect initially forces the real rate upward. In addition, a tax cut has the effect of increasing disposable income which individuals may either save or consume. As consumption increases, the transactions demand for money increases the real rate of interest.

9. The real rate of interest = the nominal rate of interest − inflation premium, so the real rate on the bond selling at $1000 with a coupon of 20 percent and inflation at 7 percent is equal to

$$13\% \ = \ 20\% \ - \ 7\%$$

Since historical real rates of interest have been in the 2–3 percent range, you would expect the bond to sell at a premium (more than $1000) so that the yield to maturity was in the 10 percent range:

$$3\% \ = \ 10\% \ - \ 7\%$$

REFERENCES

BROWN, W. W., and SANTONI, G. J., "Monetary Growth and the Timing of Interest Rate Movements," *Federal Reserve Bank of St. Louis Review* (August–September 1983).

CAGAN, P., *The Channels of Monetary Effects on Interest Rates*. Washington, D.C.: National Bureau of Economic Research, 1972.

FRIEDMAN, M., "Factors Affecting the Level of Interest Rates," in *Money Supply, Money Demand, and Macroeconomic Models*. Boston: Allyn & Bacon, 1972.

GIBSON, W. E., "Interest Rates and Monetary Policy," *Journal of Political Economy* (May–June 1970).

GIBSON, W. E., and KAUFMAN, G. E., "The Sensitivity of Interest Rates to Changes in Money and Income," *Journal of Political Economy* (May–June 1968).

IBBOTSON, R. G., and SINQUEFIELD, R. A., *Stocks, Bonds, Bills, and Inflation: The Past and the Future*. Charlottesville, Va.: The Financial Analysts Research Foundation. 1982.

MELVIN, M., "The Vanishing Liquidity Effect of Money on Interest: Analysis and Implications for Policy," *Economics Inquiry* (April 1983.)

MISHKIN, F. S., "Monetary Policy and Long-Term Interest Rates: An Efficient Markets Approach, *Journal of Monetary Economics* (January 1981).

MISHKIN, F. S., "Monetary Policy and Short-Term Interest Rates: An Efficient Markets-Rational Expectations Approach," *Journal of Finance* (March 1982).

TOBIN, J. "Liquidity Preference as Behavior Towards Risk," *The Review of Economic Studies* (February 1958).

WALSH, C. E., "Interest Rate Volatility and Monetary Policy," *Journal of Money, Credit and Banking* (May 1984).

C H A P T E R

12

THE TERM STRUCTURE OF INTEREST RATES

When we studied the capital asset pricing model and the arbitrage pricing theory, we were interested in the relationship between the *risk* of a security and the rate of return it produces for investors. You could call this relationship the *risk structure of interest rates*. In this chapter, we are interested in the **term structure of interest rates**, or the relationship between the *term* to maturity of a bond and its *yield* to maturity. Yield to maturity is the average rate of return you would earn on a bond investment if you held the bond from the current time until its maturity date and if there was no default on any of the promised payments. The term to maturity is the number of years until the last promised payment.

THE NATURE AND HISTORY
OF THE TERM STRUCTURE

The term structure of interest rates is usually drawn for bonds of a uniform quality with respect to the probability of default and for bonds with a uniform degree of tax exposure. Thus, you might examine the term structure for U.S. Treasury bonds, all of which are default-free, are taxable at the federal level, and are tax exempt at the state level. The term structure is drawn for a given point in time; each point on the plot shows the yield to maturity and term to maturity for a given bond.

Figure 12.1 represents the term structure of interest rates for U.S. Treasury bonds as of January 1, 1979. Each point on the graph represents one treasury bond. The smoothed curve which has been drawn through the points represents the term structure, or the relationship between yield to maturity and term to maturity. At this point in time, the term structure was downward sloping in the sense that short-term yields were higher than long-term yields.

The shape of the term structure changes dramatically as time goes by. This is readily apparent in the three-dimensional diagram of Figure 12.2. In this figure, we are plotting yield to maturity vertically. Time is plotted horizontally going from the

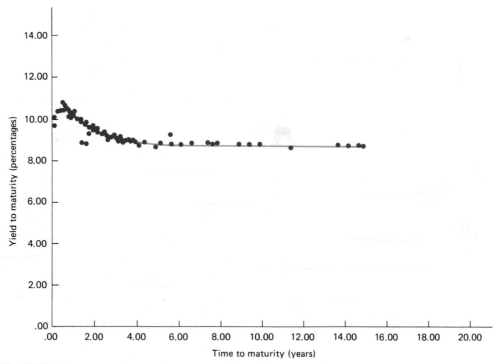

FIGURE 12.1 Term structure, January 1, 1979, U.S. Treasury bonds.

OUT ON THE STREET

RIDING THE YIELD CURVE

The room is in the shape of a square, roughly the size of a baseball diamond. The 80 people who fill the room don't seem very active, but the atmosphere is electric. Literally millions are being made or lost through trading in securities related to the government bond market. On any given day, more is usually made than lost.

We are at a Chicago-based division of a major government security dealer. This company trades for its own account in U.S. government bonds, government agency securities, and option and futures contracts on these securities.

The floor rises on two sides from the middle of the room as a "V." Four rows of desks move up the "V" on each side. Eight traders are positioned along each row. Before each trader is an array of monitors, some green, some black. Flashed on the monitors are prices for foreign currency futures, mortgage-backed securities, Government National Mortgage Association securities, treasury bonds, and other option and futures contracts. Some of the data on these monitors are quotations from one or more of the 41 primary government bond dealers in the United States. Each of these dealers is required to make a bid on all outstanding treasury securities. These dealers support the secondary market in government and agency securities. Approximately $120 billion is traded in this market daily, as compared to the approximately $2 billion that is traded in the stock market each day. Only the dealers themselves have access to the quotations on the screen. None of the individual dealers knows which dealer actually stands behind the quote. This firm is 1 of the 41 dealers.

Rob Schumacher sits before one of the panels of monitors. Rob graduated with an MBA in finance from Northwestern University in 1976. He now rides the yield curve every day, trading in long- and short-term government securities.

right to the left, and term to maturity increases as you move toward the rear of the diagram. Thus, the blue line, in the lower right portion of the diagram, is the term structure for the month of January 1955. This term structure is upward sloping, with long-term yields above short-term yields. As is evident from the figure, upward-sloping term structures are more common than downward-sloping term structures. As we shall see later, this may reflect the presence of what we shall call *liquidity premiums* in expected bond returns, or it may simply reflect the fact that the market, to some extent, anticipated the upward trend in the general level of interest rates that occurred over the period. In any case, it is obvious that the term structure undergoes dramatic changes in shape over time.

If you go to work for a major bank and you end up managing the bank's portfolio of government bonds, the term structure of interest rates will be a crucial piece of information you will be dealing with each day. In fact, your major objective will be to place the bank's bond portfolio on an optimal point on the term structure.

Among other things, he tries to forecast movements in the term structure of interest rates and then trades on the basis of his forecasts. The yield curve is currently upward sloping, and Rob expects it to flatten over the next day or so. One of the positions he has taken today is to go long in $26 million of 5-year treasury bonds to notes. He has financed the position by going short in $22 million 3-year treasury notes and $16 million 4-year treasury notes. If short rates go up and long rates go down, the rates of return on the notes he is short in will be less than the rate associated with his long position, and the difference will belong to his company.

Rob makes his prediction based on his own past economic training, the past history of spreads between securities such as treasury and government agencies and movement of issues *relative* to the yield curve, and areas of supply, such as the treasury financing schedule. He is trading the company's money, and this trade alone, though large in relative dollars, is not a major commitment of the Chicago-based division's equity base. This aside, it is not a job for a timid soul.

Prices begin to move on screens everywhere. A voice from the center of the room cries out, "Something is happening." People attempt to guess at what, but no one knows for sure. Rob studies his monitors steadily and intently.

A bell rings, announcing the close of the market. The head trader of this division begins announcing the closing prices of several key issues. As prices are read off one by one, Rob breaks into a broad smile. He turns to his colleague and beams, "We got a great close." This and other positions have netted the firm several hundred thousand for the day.

Suppose, for example, that you were dealing with the term structure of Figure 12.1. Given the general policy of a typical bank, you will confine your bond investments to bonds with terms to maturity no longer than five years. The main question at issue for you here is, "Should you shorten the average maturity of the bank's portfolio to pick up the additional increment in yield offered by the shortest-term bonds?"

While it appears from Figure 12.1 that as you move to shorter terms to maturity you increase your expected return, this is not necessarily true, at least for a given period of time into the future. As we shall see, a downward-sloping term structure, such as the one in Figure 12.1, is usually consistent with a market expectation of a decline in interest rates. If interest rates decline, the prices of long-term bonds will rise. While long-term bonds are priced to produce an *average* return to investors of approximately 9 percent over the entire life of the bond, this is not necessarily the rate of return expected on the bonds in the next year. A one-year bond may be priced to yield a rate of return of 10 percent in the coming year, but, given the expected

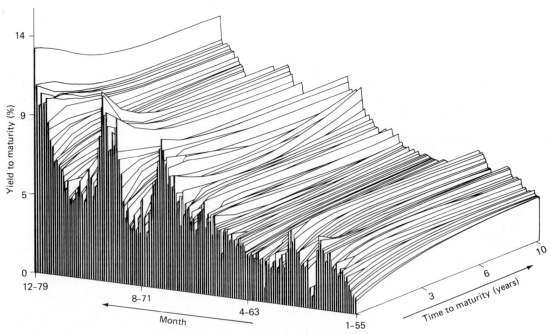

FIGURE 12.2 History of the term structure, January 1955–December 1979.

SOURCE: P. Lau, ''An Empirical Examination of Alternative Interest Rate Immunization Strategies,'' unpublished Ph.D. dissertation (Madison: University of Wisconsin, 1983).

decline in interest rates and the accompanying capital gains, long-term bonds may be expected to produce a rate of return in excess of 10 percent, at least in the coming year.

To answer the question of where to position yourself on the term structure intelligently, you must first understand the forces which bend and twist the term structure into the various shapes that we see over time.

DRAWING THE TERM STRUCTURE

As indicated, in drawing the term structure, you deal with bonds of a given investment quality and tax exposure. In Table 12.1 we have a listing of a group of such bonds, U.S. Treasury bonds, taken from *The Wall Street Journal*. The listing is for March 13, 1984. The first column labeled ''Rate'' shows you each bond's annual interest, or coupon, payment divided by the bond's principal, to be paid at maturity. The principal for these bonds is $1000.00, so a rate of 9 percent indicates an annual interest payment of $90.00. Actually the interest is paid every six months in $45.00 increments. Interest is paid each year on the fifteenth day of the month in which the bond matures and on the fifteenth day of the month falling six months earlier.

TABLE 12.1 Price Listing for U.S. Treasury Securities

Treasury Bonds and Notes

Rate	Mat.	Date	Bid	Asked	Bid Chg.	Yld.	Rate	Mat.	Date	Bid	Asked	Bid Chg.	Yld.
14s,	1985	Jun n.............	100.7	100.11+	.1	12.51	13¾s,	1986	May n.............	105.14	105.18+	.1	7.30
10s,	1985	Jun n.............	100.2	100.6	.....	3.65	13s,	1986	Jun n.............	105.2	105.6	.....	7.67
10⅝s,	1985	Jul n.............	100.12	100.16	.....	6.04	14⅞s,	1986	Jun n.............	106.29	107.1	+ .1	7.65
8¼s,	1985	Aug n.............	100.5	100.9	+ .1	6.27	12⅝s,	1986	Jul p.............	104.31	105.3	− .2	7.78
9⅜s,	1985	Aug n.............	100.12	100.16+	.1	6.21	8s,	1986	Aug n.............	100.8	100.12	− .4	7.66
10⅝s,	1985	Aug n.............	100.18	100.22	.....	6.89	11⅜s,	1986	Aug n.............	103.24	103.28	− .3	7.81
13⅛s,	1985	Aug n.............	100.29	101.1	.....	6.23	12⅜s,	1986	Aug p.............	104.27	104.31	− .5	7.95
10⅞s,	1985	Sep n.............	100.31	101.3	.....	6.75	11⅞s,	1986	Sep p.............	104.18	104.22	− .3	7.96
15⅞s,	1985	Sep n.............	102.11	102.15−	.1	6.70	12¼s,	1986	Sep n.............	104.31	105.3	− .3	8.00
10½s,	1985	Oct n.............	101.3	101.7	+ .1	6.97	11⅝s,	1986	Oct p.............	104.15	104.19−	.3	8.01
9¾s,	1985	Nov n.............	100.30	101.2	+ .1	6.99	6⅛s,	1986	Nov.............	97.28	98.28−	.2	6.98
10½s,	1985	Nov n.............	101.9	101.13	.....	7.24	10⅜s,	1986	Nov p.............	102.27	102.31−	.4	8.16
11¾s,	1985	Nov n.............	101.23	101.27+	.2	6.99	11s,	1986	Nov n.............	103.23	103.27	− .3	8.05
10⅞s,	1985	Dec n.............	101.25	101.29+	.2	7.15	13⅞s,	1986	Nov n.............	107.22	107.26	− .2	7.90
14⅛s,	1985	Dec n.............	103.17	103.21+	.2	6.99	16⅛s,	1986	Nov n.............	110.21	110.25	− .3	7.88
10⅝s,	1986	Jan n.............	101.26	101.30+	.1	7.36	9⅞s,	1986	Dec p.............	102.10	102.14	.....	8.15
10⅞s,	1986	Feb n.............	102.5	102.9	+ .1	7.47	10s,	1986	Dec n.............	102.16	102.20+	.1	8.14
13½s,	1986	Feb n.............	103.26	103.30	.....	7.28	9¾s,	1987	Jan p.............	102.3	102.7	.....	8.26
9⅞s,	1986	Feb n.............	101.11	101.15+	.1	7.55	9s,	1987	Feb n.............	101.1	101.5	.....	8.24
14s,	1986	Mar n.............	104.26	104.30+	.1	7.40	10s,	1987	Feb p.............	102.13	102.17−	.2	8.37
11½s,	1986	Mar n.............	102.28	103	+ .2	7.49	10⅞s,	1987	Feb n.............	103.25	103.29+	.1	8.31
11¾s,	1986	Apr n.............	103.10	103.14+	.3	7.57	12¾s,	1987	Feb n.............	106.20	106.24−	.1	8.31
7⅞s,	1986	May n.............	100.5	100.9	+ .4	7.55	10¼s,	1987	Mar n.............	102.30	103.2	+ .1	8.37
9⅜s,	1986	May n.............	101.13	101.17+	.4	7.59	10¾s,	1987	Mar p.............	103.24	103.28+	.1	8.37
12⅝s,	1986	May n.............	104.11	104.15+	.4	7.65							

The next two columns show the maturity date for each bond. First we have the year in which the bond matures. If a range of years is given, this means the bond matures on the last year but is callable as of the first year. After the year, we have the month in which the bond matures. The symbol ''n'' after the month indicates that the issue is a treasury note as opposed to a treasury bond. Aside from the maturity when originally issued, there is really no important investment difference between notes and bonds.

In the fourth and fifth columns we have the bid and asked prices for the bonds. Treasury bonds are bought and sold through dealers, who carry an inventory of each issue. The bid price is the price they are willing to pay in order to add bonds to their inventory. The asked price is the price you must pay them in order to induce them to sell you a block of bonds from their inventory. The price is expressed as a percentage of the principal amount of the bond ($1000). It's important to note that the number following the decimal point in the quote isn't a decimal. The price is quoted in thirty-seconds, so a bid price of 80.30 indicates that the price of the bond is 80 and 30/32 percent of $1000.00, or $809.375. The number in the sixth column is the change in the bid price from the previous day.

The number in the final column is the yield to maturity for each bond. As we indicated, the yield to maturity is the average annual rate of return you will get on the bond if you hold it until maturity.

The bonds in Table 12.1 are arranged in order of term to maturity. In Figure 12.3, we have plotted the yields and terms to maturity of treasury bonds taken from a different point in time, July 1, 1976. We have plotted yield to maturity on the vertical axis and term to maturity on the horizontal axis. The curve running through

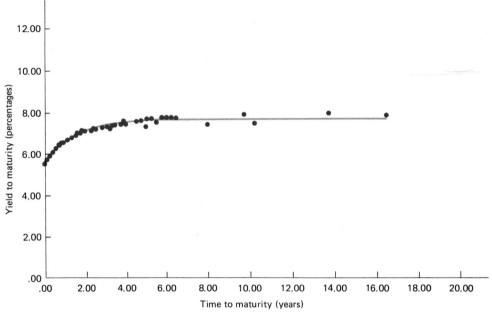

FIGURE 12.3 Term structure, July 1, 1976.

SOURCE: P. Lau, "An Empirical Examination of Alternative Interest Rate Risk Immunization Strategies," unpublished Ph.D dissertation (Madison: University of Wisconsin, 1983).

the scatter is our estimate of the term structure, and it conforms to the following equation:

$$Y_J = (a_1 + a_2 t_J)e^{-a\alpha 3 t_J} + a_4 \tag{12.1}$$

In the equation, Y_J is the yield to maturity on bond J, and t_J is the term to maturity of bond J. The symbol e is the natural antilog of 1.00, or 2.718. The coefficients a_1 through a_4 are to be estimated with a computer.

The estimated values for the term structure of July 1, 1976 are given as follows:

$$a_1 = -.022736$$

$$a_2 = .000026$$

$$a_3 = .621600$$

$$a_4 = .076393$$

The coefficient a_1 can be regarded as the difference between the yield on a bond with the shortest terms to maturity and the yield on bonds with the longest terms to maturity. The coefficient a_4 is an estimate of the yield on bonds with the longest terms

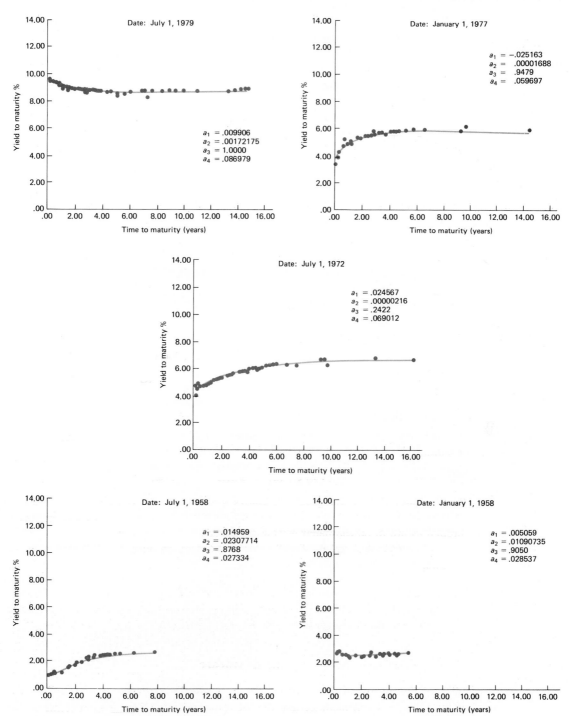

FIGURE 12.4 Example term structures.

to maturity. The other two coefficients control the shape of the curve between the longest and shortest maturities.

 In fitting the curve through the data, a computer finds those values for the four coefficients which minimize the sum of the squared vertical distances from the curve. Thus, the curve is analogous to what we have called the line of best fit in previous chapters. You will find that Equation (12.1) is a comparatively simple, yet powerful, tool for fitting a term structure of interest rates. It requires the use of a nonlinear regression routine, but this type of software is readily available. Some examples of term structures that have been fit with the equation are provided in the graphs of Figure 12.4.

METHODS OF COMPUTING THE YIELD TO MATURITY

The yield to maturity is the average annual rate of return promised over the life of a bond. As discussed in Appendix 5 at the end of this chapter, there are three accepted methods of computing the average rate of return. Each method carries its own assumption about what you do with profits you earn on the investment along the way.

The Arithmetic Mean Yield to Maturity

The most straightforward method is to compute the arithmetic mean of the expected periodic future returns. With this method, you first estimate the rates of return you expect the bond to produce in each of the years of its life. If interest is paid at the end of each year, the rate of return in any given year is equal to the sum of the annual interest payment and the change in the price of the bond in the course of the year, divided by the market price of the bond at the beginning of the year. To get the arithmetic mean yield to maturity, you sum up the expected returns on the bond in each of the coming years of its life and divide the sum by its term to maturity. The arithmetic mean yield to maturity assumes that you keep the dollar investment in the bond constant over time. That is, at the end of each year, you set any profits aside. If you have a loss for the year, you restore the investment to its original dollar value by adding new funds. Given this assumption regarding the reinvestment of funds, the arithmetic mean yield to maturity gives you the expected average annual percentage increase in your (constant) capital investment in the bond. In their test of the capital asset pricing model, Black, Jensen, and Scholes employed the arithmetic mean to measure the returns on their 10 stock portfolios.

The Geometric Mean Yield to Maturity

The second method is called the geometric mean yield to maturity. To compute the geometric mean, you add 1.00 to each of the expected future annual returns on the bond. Thus, if you expected the bond to produce a rate of return of 15 percent in

1988, you would convert that number to 1.15. Then you multiply all the converted returns together and take the nth root of the product, where n is the term to maturity for the bond. After subtracting 1.00 from the root, you have the bond's geometric mean yield to maturity. The geometric mean yield assumes that you reinvest all profits back into the bond. That is, as interest is paid, you reinvest the interest payments by buying more of the bond. Moreover, you do not realize capital gains or restore capital losses. Under these assumptions, the geometric mean yield to maturity gives you your average percentage increase in your wealth over the life of the bond.

The Internal Yield to Maturity

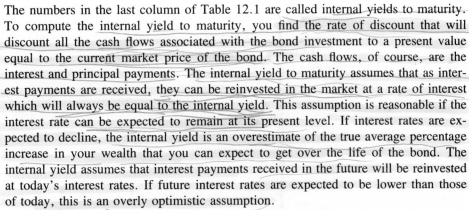

The numbers in the last column of Table 12.1 are called internal yields to maturity. To compute the internal yield to maturity, you find the rate of discount that will discount all the cash flows associated with the bond investment to a present value equal to the current market price of the bond. The cash flows, of course, are the interest and principal payments. The internal yield to maturity assumes that as interest payments are received, they can be reinvested in the market at a rate of interest which will always be equal to the internal yield. This assumption is reasonable if the interest rate can be expected to remain at its present level. If interest rates are expected to decline, the internal yield is an overestimate of the true average percentage increase in your wealth that you can expect to get over the life of the bond. The internal yield assumes that interest payments received in the future will be reinvested at today's interest rates. If future interest rates are expected to be lower than those of today, this is an overly optimistic assumption.

In spite of the fact that it makes an assumption, which at times can be unrealistic, the internal yield to maturity is the accepted standard of the industry. Nevertheless, you should recognize that other methods for computing the yield of a bond are available, and at times their assumptions may be more acceptable to you.

Because of its relative simplicity, in the discussion of the theories of the term structure that follows, we shall be working with a term structure of *arithmetic mean yields to maturity*.

A BRIEF OVERVIEW OF THE THREE THEORIES OF THE TERM STRUCTURE

At any given point in time, there are three possible factors influencing the shape of the term structure:

1. The market's *expectations* regarding the future direction of interest rates
2. The possible presence of *liquidity premiums* in expected bond returns
3. Market *inefficiency* or possible impediments to the flow of funds from the long- (or short-) term end of the market to the short- (or long-) term end

There are three main theories of the term structure. In each of the theories, one of the three factors takes center stage.

The *market expectations theory* contends that the term structure is influenced exclusively by the first factor. In this theory the yield to maturity of a 5-year bond is simply the average of the yields expected on 1-year bonds over the next 5 years.

The *liquidity preference theory* contends that the shape of the term structure is also affected by the presence of liquidity premiums. A liquidity premium is a type of risk premium. If investors don't regard long-term bonds and short-term bonds as perfect substitutes, they may require different returns from them over common intervals of time, much as they require different returns from high- and low-beta stocks. The liquidity preference theory contends the shape of the term structure is affected not only by the market's expectations regarding future interest rates but also by the nature of the liquidity premiums between long- and short-term bonds.

The third theory is called the *market segmentation theory*. This theory is consistent with the notion of market inefficiency in the pricing of bonds. The theory contends that each maturity sector of the bond market can be viewed as being segmented from the others. It is segmented in the sense that there are impediments to the free flow of capital from one segment to another. Each segment of the market is said to be inhabited by a distinct group of investors who feels that they absolutely must invest in bonds of a given maturity, irrespective of opportunities for higher returns outside their preferred maturity range. If money happens to flow to the inhabitants of the long-term segment, they will buy long-term bonds, bidding their prices up and their yields down. The term structure will tend to be downward sloping not because of market expectations or risk premiums but merely because of the direction in which funds happen to be flowing.

THE MARKET EXPECTATIONS THEORY
OF THE TERM STRUCTURE

Under the market expectations theory,[1] the term structure is determined solely by the market's expectations regarding future interest rates. When we speak of future interest rates, we will be referring to the future expected yields to maturity on 1-year bonds. The choice of a year as the basic interval of time is arbitrary; we could as easily discuss the theories in terms of monthly returns.

The numbers in the first six rows of the table in Figure 12.5 are expected yearly returns on bonds of various maturities. These are the returns we expect to get by investing in the bonds in the years indicated. The returns are computed by summing the interest payment and capital gain or loss for the year and dividing this sum by the market price of the bond at the beginning of the year.

As we move across the rows toward the right, we move to different bonds, each having a longer maturity than the last. As we move down the columns, we move farther into the future. The first row represents the rates of return expected on

---

[1]Fisher (1896) was the first to suggest that market expectations influence the shape of the term structure. The theory was later refined by Hicks (1939) and Lutz (1940).

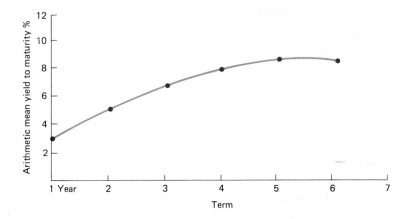

	1–yr bond	2–yr bond	3–yr bond	4–yr bond	5–yr bond	6–yr bond	
Now	3%	3	3	3	3	3	
1 year from now	7%	7	7	7	7	7	
2 years from now	10%	10	10	10	10	10	Expected annual rates of return
3 years from now	12%	12	12	12	12	12	
4 years from now	10%	10	10	10	10	10	
5 years from now	8%	8	8	8	8	8	
Arithmetic mean yield to maturity	3%	5	6.67	8	8.4	8.33	Yields to maturity
Geometric mean yield to maturity	3%	4.98	6.63	7.95	8.35	8.29	

FIGURE 12.5 Market expectations theory.

the bonds in the current year. The second row represents the rates of return expected next year, and so on. The first column of numbers represents the market's expectation of future yearly rates of return on 1-year bonds. Since the bonds mature at the end of each year, these are also the market's expectation of the yields to maturity on these bonds. Thus, when we speak of the market's expectation for future interest rates, we are speaking of the numbers going down the first column of the table. In this particular case, the market expects 1-year interest rates to rise from their current level of 3 percent to 12 percent in 3 years and then fall back to 8 percent at the end of 5 years. These numbers, of course, have been arbitrarily assumed.

As years pass, each bond moves to a cell in the table to its immediate lower left. Thus, a bond that is a 2-year bond today will be a 1-year bond a year from now. Its expected yearly return moves, therefore, from the cell in the first row, second column, to the cell in the second row, first column. The paths taken by each of the bonds are given by the arrows in the table.

The arithmetic mean yield to maturity for any one of the bonds can be computed by averaging its expected future rates of return. To compute the yield to maturity for a 3-year bond, you simply average the three returns in the three cells moving diagonally from the first row, third column to the third row, first column. The current yield to maturity of a 3-year bond is, thus, the average of 3 percent, 7 percent, and 10 percent or 6.67 percent. The current arithmetic mean yields to maturity for each of the bonds is given in the seventh row of the table. The eighth row of the table provides the geometric mean yields to maturity. Note there is very little difference between the magnitude of the two types of yields.

The arithmetic mean yields to maturity are graphed in the term structure of Figure 12.5 above the table. For the most part, the shape of the term structure is upward sloping, reaching a peak for the yield to maturity of a 5-year bond. *Humped-shaped* term structures, like this one, are consistent with a market expectation of 1-year interest rates rising to a future peak and then falling.

The distinctive feature of the market expectations theory is that, for a given period of time, the market expects to get the same rate of return on all bonds, regardless of their term to maturity. Thus, in the table in Figure 12.5, the market expects a 3 percent rate of return on all of the bonds in the current year. Over the next 2 years, you can expect to get an average rate of return of 5 percent by buying a 1-year bond today at 3 percent, holding it until maturity, and then buying another 1-year bond a year from now at 7 percent. You can get the same 5 percent average return by holding a 2-year bond until maturity or by buying a 3-year bond and selling it after 2 years. Your average expected return on all these investments is 5 percent over the next 2 years. This is true for any combination of bond investments over any given period of time. Given this is true, we can say the yield to maturity on an n-year bond is equal to the average of the yields to maturity on 1-year bonds for the next n years. This is true because the numbers going across the rows are all identical. Given this, the numbers going down the first column (future yields on 1-year bonds) are identical to the diagonals (future rates of return expected on an n-year bond). However, this relation between the yield on an n-year bond and the future yields on 1-year bonds over the next n years holds only for the market expectations theory.

The market will require the same rate of return on a 3-year bond as it does on a 1-year bond if it regards them as perfect substitutes. This will be the case if there is perfect certainty regarding the future returns on the bonds, if investors are risk neutral, or if it is the case that the risk associated with uncertainty in future interest rates can be diversified away. These are the conditions under which there will be no term-related risk premiums in expected bond returns, and the market expectations theory of the term structure will hold. If these conditions don't hold, we may expect differentials in expected return, or risk premiums, to arise between bonds of different maturity. In the context of the term structure, these risk premiums are called liquidity premiums, and they are the focal point of the liquidity preference theory.

THE LIQUIDITY PREFERENCE THEORY OF THE TERM STRUCTURE

The market may not regard a 5-year bond as a perfect substitute for a 1-year bond. Consider the probability distributions for rates of return on the bonds for the next year, as given by Figure 12.6. If we are dealing with treasury bonds, where there is no probability of default, the rate of return on the 1-year bond is known with certainty. The distribution is drawn as a single spike with zero variance. In the course of the next year, however, the 5-year bond has an uncertain rate of return. If interest rates should fall, the price of the bond will rise by the end of the year, and based on both the interest payment and the capital gain, our return may be very large. On the other hand, if interest rates should rise, the price of the bond will fall. The capital loss may more than offset the interest payment, and the return for the year could well be negative. The probability distribution for the rate of return, thus, has a positive variance.

In Figure 12.6, both distributions have the same expected value, but if investors are risk averse, they may lower the current price of the 5-year bond relative to the 1-year bond to create a risk premium on the 5-year issue, as in Figure 12.7.

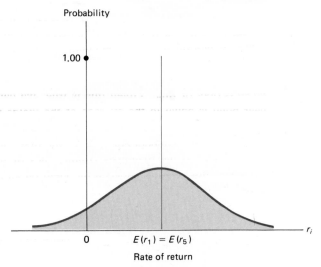

FIGURE 12.6 Probability distributions for 1- and 5-year bonds under market expectations theory.

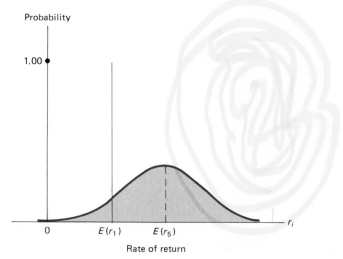

FIGURE 12.7 Probability distributions for 1- and 5-year bonds under liquidity preference theory.

Given the presence of the premium, they may now be willing to invest in the 5-year bond even though it is perceived to have a greater degree of risk.

The liquidity preference theory allows for the possible existence of risk, or liquidity, premiums such as these in the term structure.[2] To see the effect they may have, consider the table in Figure 12.8. The market's expectations regarding future interest rates on 1-year bonds are identical to those of Figure 12.5. However, now it is assumed investors require an additional 2 percent premium in their expected return to invest in a 2-year bond over what they require to invest in a 1-year bond. Thus, while they expect to get 3 percent by holding a 1-year bond for the current year, they expect to get 5 percent by holding a 2-year bond in the same year. A 3-year bond is assumed to command a 3 percent premium over the 1-year bond. This same premium is assumed to hold for bonds with maturities in excess of 3 years. The structure of liquidity premiums is assumed to remain constant in future years, although this is not a required assumption for the liquidity preference theory. A 2-year bond is assumed to command the same premium in expected return in 5 years as it does today. This, of course, is an arbitrary assumption of the table.

The effect of liquidity premiums which increase in size with term to maturity is to make the term structure more upward sloping (if rates are expected to rise) or less downward sloping (if rates are expected to fall). In the table in Figure 12.8, the yield to maturity for a 2-year bond is now the average of 5 percent and 7 percent (which is 6%) instead of the average of 3 percent and 7 percent (which is 5 percent). The broken curve of Figure 12.8 is reproduced from Figure 12.5. It shows the yield curve based on market expectations alone, without any liquidity premiums. The solid

---

[2]Hicks (1939) was the first to argue that the market expectations theory was incomplete.

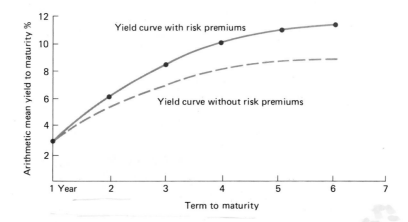

	1–yr bond	2–yr bond	3–yr bond	4–yr bond	5–yr bond	6–yr bond	
Now	3%	5	6	6	6	6	
1 year from now	7%	9	10	10	10	10	
2 years from now	10%	12	13	13	13	13	Expected annual rate of return
3 years from now	12%	14	15	15	15	15	
4 years from now	10%	12	13	13	13	13	
5 years from now	8%	10	11	11	11	11	
Arithmetic mean yield to maturity	3%	6	8.33	10	10.6	10.67	Yields to maturity
Geometric mean yield to maturity	3%	6	8.32	9.97	10.56	10.62	

FIGURE 12.8 Liquidity preference theory.

curve shows the term structure based on the expected interest rates in the table below, including the liquidity premiums. The term structure has changed from being hump shaped to being upward sloping through the 6-year bond.

Not much is known about the nature of the liquidity premiums in the term structure. It is even possible to argue that for some investors long-term bonds may be viewed as less risky than short-term bonds. The probability distributions of Figure 12.6 were drawn on the basis of a 1-year horizon. Suppose, however, you were concerned with how much money you were going to have at the end of 5 years instead of 1 year. Suppose also the 5-year bond is truly a 5-year bond in the sense that it is a pure discount issue with no interest payments until the payment in the fifth year. Over a 5-year horizon, the probability distribution for the 5-year bond is now a single spike with zero variance. However, the 1-year bond can now be viewed as being risky because we have a to buy new 1-year bonds at the end of each year. While we know the 1-year rate in effect now, we don't know what the 1-year rate will be a year from now, or the year after that, and so on. The probability distribution for investments in 1-year bonds now has a variance, and investors with long-term horizons may require a premium to invest in short-term bonds.

To complicate matters further, the bond market is dominated by financial institutions with widely differing time horizons. Commercial banks have short-term liabilities in the form of deposits. These institutions minimize risk by matching these liabilities with short-term investments. On the other hand, pension funds and life insurance companies have long-term liabilities. If they are concerned at all about their *survival*, they would view long-term bonds as less risky than short-term.

Furthermore, even if we agree that investors uniformly have short-term horizons and therefore long-term bond return distributions have bigger variances, it isn't clear that the bigger variance would be regarded as an undesirable property. Long-term government bonds produce their greatest rates of return when interest rates are falling. Interest rates tend to fall in time of economic adversity. Thus, long-term bonds tend to pay off the most when you are in greatest need of the funds. In this sense they may act as insurance, and when viewed in this light, their greater variance may be viewed as a desirable property.

Thus, we face ambiguity on two fronts. First, do long-term or short-term bonds have the largest variance of return? The answer to this question depends on the time horizons of investors. Second, if long-term bonds do indeed have the largest variance of return, do investors regard this as a desirable or undesirable property? The answer to this question depends on the perceived relationship between the level of interest rates and general economic activity.

The empirical evidence relating to the issue is also inconclusive. The best evidence (Fama, 1984) indicates that expected rates of return reach a *peak* at 8 to 10 months. Beyond 1 year there appears to be little evidence of additional liquidity premiums.

THE MARKET SEGMENTATION THEORY
OF THE TERM STRUCTURE

In essence, the market segmentation theory assumes the market is populated by individual investors who are extremely risk averse and corporations and financial institutions for whom survival is of paramount importance.[3] Everyone seeks to *immunize*

---

[3]A leading advocate of the market segmentation theory is Culbertson (1957).

his or her portfolio. As we shall learn in Chapter 14, your portfolio is immunized if the effective maturity of your assets is matched up with the effective maturity of your liabilities.

This means, if you run a commercial bank, you will always buy short-term bonds because your liabilities are deposits, and they are mostly short term. If you manage a pension fund, you will want to buy long-term bonds because you have contracted to pay long-term annuities over the retired lives of pensioners. If you were seeking to maximize the market value of the stock of the firm backing the pension fund, you might actively manage your bond portfolio, buying long-term bonds when you think interest rates are going to fall and moving short when you think a rise in rates is imminent. The market segmentation theory assumes, instead, that the survival of the institution is the objective function. To assume survival, you minimize risk, and this means matching the maturities of assets and liabilities, irrespective of the relatively attractive rates of return you may see in other maturities.

In Figure 12.9, we have broken the term structure into two parts, a short-term segment and a long-term segment. For each segment, there is a schedule of supply and demand for loanable funds. At the intersection of supply and demand, we establish the yield. The suppliers of loanable funds are those who invest in the securities. The demanders of loanable funds are those who issue the securities.

The suppliers in the short segment of the market are commercial banks and nonfinancial corporations. The nonfinancial corporations are investing their liquid balances until they need them to purchase raw materials, pay laborers, or make expenditures on plant and equipment. If you were working for the treasurers of these firms, you would invest these funds in the short-term end of the market. You may be thinking here of your own survival. If you invest these funds long and rates go up, what will happen to your job if your investment decision results in a liquidity crisis for your firm?

The suppliers in the long-term segment include life insurance companies and pension funds. Life insurance companies sell their product on the basis of the assertion that they are financially as sound as a rock. To assure their policyholders that this is true, they minimize the risk of their investments. This, of course, includes matching the maturities of their assets and liabilities.

The demanders of funds include the Treasury of the United States and nonfinancial corporations seeking financing for their investments. Once again the market segmentation theory assumes the financing strategies of the nonfinancial corporations are shaped by their desire to survive. Just as financial institutions seek to match the maturities of their investments with their liabilities, so do nonfinancial corporations match their liabilities with the maturities of their investments. If they are investing in an expansion of their inventory, they seek to finance their inventory expansion with short-term loans. On the other hand, if they are financing the construction of a major plant which is expected to produce cash flows for the corporation for many years to come, they can be expected to finance this type of investment with long-term debenture or mortgage bonds. In any case, the demand for long- and short-term loanable funds is said to be determined by the nature of the investment opportunities of corporations.

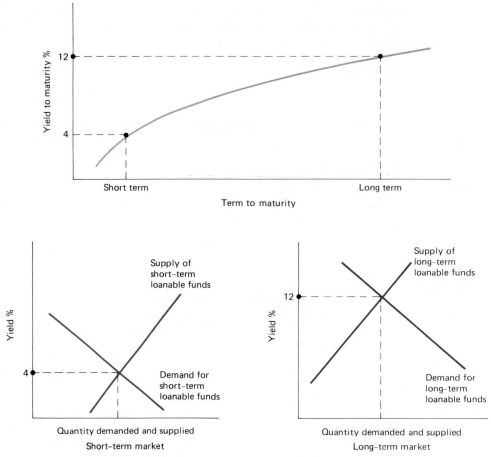

FIGURE 12.9 Market segmentation theory.

As we said, the yield in each segment of the market is determined by the intersection of supply and demand. The supply schedule in each market shifts back and forth with the flow of funds into and out of the various types of financial institutions. If funds flow out of pension funds and into commercial banks, this puts upward pressure on long rates and downward pressure on short rates. The demand schedules shift with changes in the nature of investments being financed by corporations. At the beginning of the upside of the business cycle, the demand for long-term funds should increase, putting upward pressure on long-term interest rates. As the cycle matures and inventories begin to accumulate, demands for short-term loans to finance inventory expansion should increase, putting upward pressure on short-term rates.

In this framework the term structure is shaped not by market expectations regarding the future direction of rates or by the structure of liquidity premiums, but rather by the direction of fund flows from one financial institution to another and by the intensity and nature of economic investment by business firms.

In assessing this theory, it must be said that immunization is, in fact, widely practiced by financial institutions. However, it is doubtful that survival is the paramount objective of corporations and financial institutions. If these firms sought survival without any regard to maximizing the market value of their stock, they would soon find themselves targets for takeover by other firms who would gladly maximize their stock value and realize the capital gain.

Moreover, there are many individual investors here, and all over the world, who reject immunization in favor of wealth maximization. The market segmentation theory is a theory of market inefficiency. If the term structure is shaped without regard to the best available estimate of the future course of interest rates, then huge profit opportunities arise for the speculator who is free to invest in either end of the market. Suppose for example, based on the best available information, it is highly likely that interest rates are going to fall. In spite of this, because of the nature of fund flows and investment demands, the term structure is upward sloping. In this case, the expected rates of return to long-term bonds are going to be much higher than for their short-term counterparts. Speculators will move into long-term bonds to capture these attractive returns. In the process, they will drive the prices of long-term bonds up and their yields down. This pressure will continue until the expected returns on long-term bonds return to reasonable levels. This, of course, will happen only when the shape of the term structure conforms to the market's expectations.

It is reasonable to conclude the term structure is shaped for the most part by the nature of the market's expectations regarding the future direction of interest rates. Liquidity premiums may play a role, but their role at this point has not been clearly defined. At times market imperfections and the pattern of capital flows through the market place may also play a role, causing the shape of the term structure to temporarily depart from that which is consistent with the best available estimate of the future direction of interest rates. When this happens, it is time for you, as a financial analyst, to act. In the process of acting, you may make a profit for your firm or your own portfolio and help force prices to conform to the best estimate of expected future interest rates.

DERIVING THE MARKET'S FORECAST OF FUTURE INTEREST RATES FROM THE TERM STRUCTURE

Finding the Market's Forecast from Arithmetic Mean Yields

To the extent that the bond market is efficient, the term structure of interest rates will reflect the best estimate of the future course of interest rates. If you make an assumption about the structure of liquidity premiums, it is possible to extract from the term structure the market's forecast of future interest rates.

To see how to do this, consider Figure 12.10. The current yields to maturity

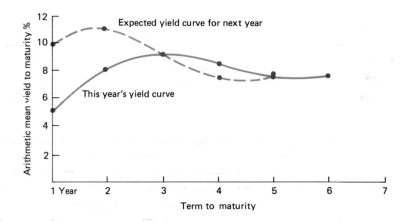

	1-yr bond	2-yr bond	3-yr bond	4-yr bond	5-yr bond	6-yr bond	
Now							Expected annual rates of return
1 year from now							
2 years from now							
3 years from now							
4 years from now							
5 years from now							
Arithmetic mean yield to maturity	5%	8%	9%	8%	7%	7%	Yields to maturity
Next years mean yield to maturity							

FIGURE 12.10 Extracting the market's forecast from arithmetic mean yields.

on bonds with maturities from 1 to 6 years are provided in the seventh row of the table in the figure, and the term structure itself is plotted in the figure. What we would like to find is the market's forecast of future 1-year interest rates going down the first column of the table.

One of these numbers is directly observable. The current yield to maturity of a

1-year bond is 5 percent. Thus, you can write 5 percent in the first row of the first column.

To get more numbers, we need to make an assumption about the structure of liquidity premiums. Let's assume that bonds with 2 or more years to maturity command a 1 percent premium in their yearly expected returns. This being the case, while investors expect to get a 5 percent return on a 1-year bond in the first year, they will expect 6 percent on all bonds with 2 or more years to maturity. Thus, you can write 6 percent in the remaining columns of the first row.

Now we can determine the numbers in the second row. The current yield to maturity of a 2-year bond is 8 percent. We know this is the arithmetic mean of the bond's expected returns in the first and second years. The bond is expected to produce a rate of return of 6 percent in the first year (first row, second column). Given an 8 percent mean, the market must be expecting a 10 percent rate of return in the second year (second row, first column). Given our assumption regarding the liquidity premiums, the market is expecting 1-year interest rates to climb to 10 percent next year.

If we assume the structure of liquidity premiums remains constant over time, we can now fill in the remaining numbers in the second row. Bonds with 2 or more years to maturity will command a 1 percent increment in their yearly expected return, so we can write in 11 percent for the remaining numbers.

We can now find the market's expectation for the 1-year rate of interest 2 years from now. The current yield to maturity on a 3-year bond is 9 percent. This is the arithmetic mean of 6 percent, 11 percent, and the number in the first column, third row. That number must therefore be 10 percent.

The three remaining numbers in the first column can be computed in the same way. If you make the computations, you will find the market expects 1-year interest rates to fall to 4 percent in 3 years, continue falling to 2 percent in 4 years, and rise back to 6 percent in 6 years. This rather strange forecast results from the peculiar humped shape that we have assumed for the yield curve.

You can also find the market's expectation for the *term structure* of interest rates for next year and years beyond. To do this, just move forward 1 year and drop off the first row of the table. We know the expected yield to maturity of a 1-year bond is 10 percent (first column, second row). You can write this number in the first column of the last row of the table. To find the yield to maturity of a 2-year bond next year, think of the remaining expected returns in its life. It is expected to produce an 11 percent return next year (second row, second column) and a 10 percent return in 2 years. The arithmetic mean of these two numbers is 10.5 percent, so this will be the yield to maturity of the bond next year. Write this number in the second column of the last row. Continuing in this fashion, you can compute the market's expectation for the yield to maturity for a 3-year bond to be 8.67 percent, for a 4-year bond to be 7.25 percent, and for a 5-year bond to be 7.2 percent. These numbers are plotted as the broken curve in Figure 12.10. The market expects short-term rates to rise, intermediate-term rates to settle somewhat, and long-term rates to rise a little.

Finding the Market's Forecast with Internal Yields

Unfortunately, you can't find arithmetic mean yields printed in the financial news. As we know, the yields published there are internal yields. The internal yield is found by solving for Y in the following formula:

$$V = \sum_{t=1}^{n} \frac{C}{(1 + Y)^t} + \frac{P}{(1 + Y)^n} \tag{12.2}$$

In the equation, V is the current market value of the bond, C is the annual coupon or interest payment, and P is the principal payment at maturity.

As we said, the internal yield assumes interest rates are expected to remain constant over time because it assumes future cash flows can be reinvested at the internal yield in effect for the bond today. We can generalize Expression (12.2) to allow for the possibility of changes in the level of rates over time as follows:

$$V = \frac{C}{1 + r_1} + \frac{C}{(1 + r_1)(1 + r_2)} + \cdots + \frac{C + P}{(1 + r_1)(1 + r_2) \cdots (1 + r_n)} \tag{12.3}$$

In this equation, the r's are 1-year interest rates expected in the years indicated by the subscripts. Thus, each interest payment is discounted by the product of the 1-year rates expected through the time of the payment.

The first step in computing the market's expectation of future rates[4] is to fit a smooth curve through the term structure of internal yields to maturity using a nonlinear function such as that of Equation (12.1). Assume you do this and you obtain a fit such as that of Figure 12.11.

Next, read yields from the curve at equally spaced intervals of time to maturity. Using yearly intervals, we would obtain the following schedule for Figure 12.11. The individual bonds scattered above and below the curve have different annual interest payments. When the ratio of a bond's annual interest payment to its principal exceeds its internal yield to maturity, the bond sells at a premium over its principal value. In the opposite case the bond sells at a discount. As we shall learn in Chapter 19, there is a tax advantage to investing in bonds selling at a discount below their principal value, because a fraction of the total yield is coming in the form of a capital gain as the price of the bond rises to approach its face value at maturity. Capital gains are sometimes taxed at lower rates and can be deferred until realized at maturity. Because of this tax advantage, discounted bonds typically sell at lower *pretax* yields. Because of this, their *after-tax* yields are competitive with the after-tax yields on the higher *pretax* yielding premium bonds.

Because of this tax factor, bonds positioned below the curve representing the term structure are typically those selling at discounts. The bonds selling above the curve are those selling at premiums, or at least lesser discounts than those below the curve. A bond positioned *on* the curve would be an intermediate case. Since the

---

[4]The procedure described below for computing future rates and geometric mean yields to maturity is identical to that employed in your software.

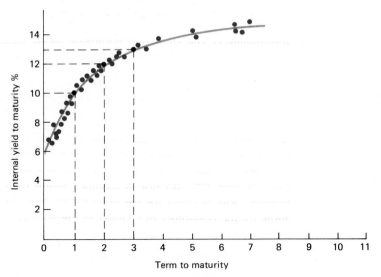

FIGURE 12.11 Fitting the term structure to extract the market's forecast of future interest rates.

internal yields represented in the schedule above are taken from the curve, you must decide the extent to which a bond taken from each part of the curve would be selling above or below its principal value. Your assumption regarding this may differ from one part of the curve to another, and it may change at different points in time.

Let's assume for simplicity, that it looks like bonds positioned on the curve would be selling at prices equal to their principal values, irrespective of their term to maturity. Given this assumption, the next step is to compute the annual interest payments consistent with the internal yields read from the curve. We know the internal yield to maturity for a 2-year bond is 12 percent. If the bond is assumed to sell at a market price of $1000.00, its interest payment must then be $120.00:

$$\$1000.00 = \frac{C}{1.12} + \frac{C + \$1000.00}{1.12^2}; \quad C = \$120.00$$

Now to find the market's expectation of the 1-year rate for next year, we use the more general formula for the value of a bond which allows for changes in interest rates over time.

Think of the bond as a portfolio of two pure discount bonds, one paying $120.00 at the end of 1 year and the other paying $1120.00 at the end of 2 years. We know the market requires a 10 percent rate of return on the first bond because, given the schedule taken from the term structure, the rate on 1-year bonds is currently 10 percent. A more puzzling question is: "What does the market require as a rate of return on the second bond in the current year?" This is where we must make an assumption regarding the liquidity premium. Let's again assume the market requires a premium of 1 percent to invest in a 2-year bond in the current year over what is expected as a return on a 1-year bond. Given this, we can express the value of the bond as follows:

$$\$1000.00 = \frac{\$120.00}{1.10} + \frac{\$120.00 + \$1000.00}{1.11(1 + r_2)}$$

We can now solve for r_2, the market's expected 1-year rate for next year, as 13.26 percent.

Term to Maturity	Internal Yield
1 year	10%
2 years	12%
3 years	13%

We can solve for r_3 in the same way. The annual interest rate consistent with a bond with an internal yield of 13 percent selling at a price equal to its principal value is $130.00. If we assume 3-year bonds command the same liquidity premium as 2-year bonds, we can solve for r_3 with the following equation:

$$\$1000.00 = \frac{\$130.00}{1.10} + \frac{\$130.00}{1.11(1.1326)} + \frac{\$130.00 + \$1000.00}{1.11(1.1426)(1 + r_3)}$$

Note that the second interest payment is treated as a 1-year bond in the next year, while the third interest and principal payment is treated as a 2-year bond next year and thus commands a 14.26 percent rate of return in the second year. Given this, we can solve for r_3 as 14.46 percent.

Of course, by extending this process to longer-term bonds, you can find the market's forecast for as many years in the future as desired. Once you have obtained the series of future expected interest rates, you can compute geometric mean yields to maturity for n-period bonds by taking the nth root of the products of one plus the rates of return. For example, the geometric mean yield to maturity for a 2-year bond is computed as

$$[(1.10 + .01)1.1326]^{1/2} - 1 = 12.12\%$$

and the geometric mean yield for a 3-year bond as

$$[(1.10 + .01)(1.1326 + .01)1.1446]^{1/3} - 1 = 13.23\%$$

Note that the geometric mean yields are greater than the internal yields. This is due to the difference in their assumption regarding the reinvestment of interest income. The internal yield assumes interest is to be reinvested at the bond's current internal yield to maturity. The geometric mean yield assumes interest income is reinvested in the bond and accumulates at the rates expected to be earned by the bond in the future. Since interest rates are expected to rise in this example, your terminal wealth will be greater based on the geometric mean assumption than under the internal yield assumption.

While your estimate of the market's forecast of the future series of 1-year bond rates is highly sensitive to the assumption you make regarding the structure of liquidity premiums, your estimate of the geometric mean yields to maturity is *insensitive* to the assumption. You can verify this by replacing our assumption of a 1 percent liquidity premium for bonds of 2 or more years to maturity with an assumption that liquidity premiums don't exist. Under either assumption, we get virtually the same schedule of geometric mean yields to maturity.

As we said before, the internal yield to maturity is the accepted standard of the industry. At times, however, the internal yield's assumption that interest will be reinvested when received at the internal yield may be either unduly conservative or optimistic. Given this, using it may either cause you to lose accounts or get you into deep trouble.

Let's suppose you and I are competitors. We are both trying to land the same account, the pension fund of an extremely large company. The company has supplied us with estimates of the cash payments it has promised to make to its pensioners throughout their expected lifetimes. They want to give us as much money now as is needed to make all the required payments, and they want us to manage the money and make the payments from the portfolio as needed.

We both decide to invest in 3-year bonds. You use an internal yield to compute the return on the bonds, and I use a geometric mean yield. The term structure is as given in the example, so the internal yield is 13 percent and the geometric mean yield is 13.23 percent. The present value of the stream of required pension payments is, of course, higher at 13 percent than it is at 13.23 percent. So I tell the company I can do the job for less money up front, and I land the account. You lost because you used an overly conservative assumption about the rate at which you are going to be able to reinvest interest in the future. You assumed future interest payments would be reinvested at 13 percent. I assumed future interest payments would be reinvested at interest rates which are expected to prevail in the future, and these rates are expected to be higher than those in effect today. My assumption was the more reasonable, and in making it, I won the account.

If the term structure is downward sloping, the internal yield will be greater than the geometric yield. Now the internal yield's reinvestment assumption is overly optimistic. Interest rates are expected to fall, and it assumes interest can be reinvested at today's yields. You may be winning accounts, but you are probably asking your clients for too little money to fund their pension funds. You will find, as interest rates fall and you have to reinvest interest at progressively lower rates, you will be running short of money. You will have to go to your clients and ask for more money, and they will not like that.

SUMMARY

The term structure of interest rates relates the yields to maturity of bonds of a given quality to their terms to maturity.

There are three theories concerning the forces that cause the term structure to change its shape as time goes by. The *market expectations theory* contends the term structure is shaped exclusively by the market's expectations regarding the future yields on 1-year bonds. The market expectations theory is consistent with a world of certainty or a world populated by risk-neutral investors. If investors are risk averse, they may not regard bonds of different maturities as perfect substitutes. In this case, risk (or liquidity) premiums may arise in the expected rates of return on bonds of different maturities. This is the case of the *liquidity preference theory*. Both the market expectations theory and the liquidity preference theory assume a relatively efficient and integrated market. On the other hand, the *market segmentation theory* assumes the market can be divided into segmented or contained submarkets on the basis of maturity. The investors that populate each market are assumed to be unwilling to venture into other markets, irrespective of how attractive they perceive returns to be there. In this environment, the term structure is shaped by the flows of funds from one segmented market to another and not on the basis of market expectations about future interest rates or on the basis of the structure of liquidity premiums. In truth, the term structure is probably affected by all three forces, with market expectations the probable dominant force.

APPENDIX 5

AVERAGING MULTIPLE RATES OF RETURN

A rate of return expresses the percentage change in your wealth from one period to another. An average annual rate of return over several years expresses the annual percentage change in invested wealth from the beginning of the first year to the end of the last. For example, you might ask, "If you start out with $100 and you end up with $220 after 3 years, then what's been your rate of return?" This is the same as asking, "What constant annual percentage change would increase your initial investment of $100 to $220 in the time of 3 years?" The answer to this question is 30 percent:

$$\$100 \times 1.30 = \$130; \quad \$130 \times 1.30 = \$169; \quad \$169 \times 1.30 = \$220$$

Over a single period, the meaning of a rate of return is clear, but over multiple periods of time where you're getting amounts of money along the way, the concept of a rate of return becomes ambiguous.

First consider a single period of time. Suppose we're dealing with the cash flows of the investments given by the graph of Figure A.5.1. Presume that we're talking about a stock and that you're investing $100 in the stock at the beginning of the period, so you have a negative cash flow of $100 at the beginning of the first year. At the end of the first year, the stock is worth $110, and you get a $40 dividend. Let's suppose you sell the stock at the end of the year. The total amount you receive is $150. You compute the rate of return by the formula given in the figure caption. The r is the rate of return, and it is equal to the dividend you get

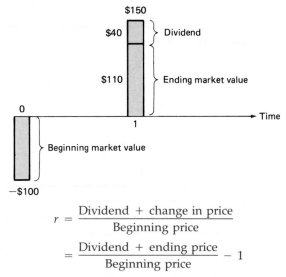

$$r = \frac{\text{Dividend } + \text{ change in price}}{\text{Beginning price}}$$

$$= \frac{\text{Dividend } + \text{ ending price}}{\text{Beginning price}} - 1$$

FIGURE A.5.1 Single-period cash flows.

on the stock plus any change of price, or capital gain or loss, divided by the market price of the stock at the beginning of the year—the price at which you bought the stock. It's also equal to the dividend plus the ending stock value divided by the beginning value, less 1.

Now consider the example of Figure A.5.2. This is the case of a stock with a beginning market value of $100. At the end of one period you get a dividend of $30 from the stock. At the end of the second period you get another dividend of $20, and at the end of this period the stock is worth $120. So you've got an interim cash flow of $30, an ending value of $120, and an ending dividend of $20. Now what is the rate of return on this investment? The problem here is what are we going to assume we do with the $30 that we get at the end of the first period. The average rate of return that you get on the investment will depend on

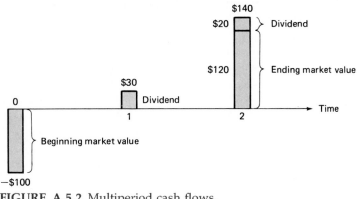

FIGURE A.5.2 Multiperiod cash flows.

the nature of that assumption. There are three different ways of computing the average rate of return, each carrying a different assumption with respect to what we do with the money received along the way. They are the arithmetic mean, the geometric mean, and the internal rate of return.

The arithmetic mean assumes you keep the dollar amount invested constant; so if you invest $100 in the beginning, you always keep $100 invested in your portfolio. The geometric mean assumes you reinvest all profits back into the stock and that those reinvestments earn the rates of return the stock earns in subsequent periods. The internal rate of return assumes you take any interim cash flows that are generated by the investment and that you reinvest those cash flows at the internal rate of return. Let's go through an illustration of each.

Consider the stock we were dealing with in Figure A.5.2. We didn't discuss what the market price of the stock was at the end of the period, but let's assume it was $120. The price of the stock goes from $100 to $120, and then it remains at $120 through the end of the second period. The stock distributes a dividend of $30 at the end of period 1 and then $20 at the end of the second period.

If we compute the rate of return in each of the 2 years, we find them to be 50 percent and 16.7 percent, respectively:

$$\frac{\$30 + \$20}{\$100} = 50\%$$

$$\frac{\$20 + \$0}{\$120} = 16.7\%$$

Now, how do you compute the average rate of return going across both periods? Keep in mind this return should express the average percentage of increase in our wealth, going from the beginning of the first period to the end of the second. You have three choices in computing the average return.

The Arithmetic Mean

In computing the arithmetic mean, we take individual rates of return in each year, add them up, and divide by the number of years. Or in the case of the example,

$$\frac{50\% + 16.7\%}{2} = 33.3\%$$

Remember, this computation assumes that the dollar amount invested is kept constant—in this case, at $100. You start with a $100 investment, and you assume you keep $100 invested at the beginning of each year. So at the end of the first year, you have a stock worth $120, and you have a dividend of $30. You're going to have to put the dividend aside, and you're going to have to sell off $20 worth of stock and put that aside as well. So you set aside $50, and you leave invested in the stock your initial $100 capital commitment. The stock earns a 16.67 percent rate of return in the second period. So if you've got $100 invested at the beginning of the second period, you're going to end up with $116.67 at the end of the period. You'll also have the $50 set aside. Your total income across the two periods will be $66.67. If you divide that by 2, your average annual income is $33.33. And since you've invested at all times $100, the average annual income represents an annual percentage increase in the amount invested of 33.3 percent.

Consider now a stock that doesn't pay any dividends. It starts out at the beginning of the first year at $100, doubles in price to $200, and then halves in price to $100. What's the rate of return? At first glance it appears to be zero, but that's only because you're used to thinking in terms of reinvesting your money in the security. If this is true, you will end up with as much money as when you started. But with the arithmetic mean formula, you assume that you set aside profits and keep the dollar amount invested constant, and if you do that, your wealth will increase at an average annual rate of 25 percent. The rate of return in the first year is 100 percent. In the second it's -50 percent. So the average rate is 25 percent. Under what conditions will that represent your return? It will if you set aside your profits at the end of each period. You leave $100 invested, and you take the $100 gain at the end of the first year and set it aside. Now you've got $100 left invested in the stock. The stock produces a -50 percent rate of return for the second period, leaving you with $50. But you still have your $100 set aside. That gives you a total of $150 at the end of the second period, a total profit of $50 or $25 per year. This represents a rate of return on the amount you had invested ($100) of 25 percent per year.

The Geometric Mean

The second method of computing the average rate of return is called the geometric mean. As I said before, the geometric mean assumes you let your profits ride and reinvest everything in the security. The formula for the geometric mean rate of return is

$$G_r = [(1 + r_1)(1 + r_2) \cdot \cdot \cdot (1 + r_N)]^{1/N} - 1$$

$$G_r = [1.5(1.167)]^{1/2} - 1 = 32.29\%$$

The geometric mean rate of return also represents your average percentage increase in wealth but under different assumptions relating to what you do with income produced during the life of the investment. If you've got a capital gain, you leave it alone. If you get any dividends, you buy more stock. In this case you've got a $30 dividend at the end of the first period. At that time, the stock is selling for $120, so you can buy a quarter of a share for $30. Thus, going into the second period, you would own 1.25 shares. Each share produces $140 at the end of the second period. Each share will be worth $120, and each will distribute a dividend of $20. You own 1.25 shares, so your ending wealth will be equal to 1.25 times $140 or $175. What kind of an average percentage increase does that represent? That is, for what rate could you increase $100 twice in a row to get $175. The answer in this case is 32.29 percent:

$$\$100 \times 1.3229 = \$132.29; \quad \$132.29 \times 1.3229 = \$175$$

The Internal Rate of Return

The final rate of return concept is the internal rate of return. The internal rate of return can be defined as the rate of return that discounts the cash flows coming from an investment to a present value equal to the amount initially invested. In the example we are working with, you invest $100 at the beginning of the first period when you buy the stock. At the end of the first period, you get a $30 dividend, and at the end of the last period, if you sell the stock and keep the dividends, you have $140. So you have two positive cash flows, $30 and $140, following your initial negative cash flow which was $100:

Time	0	1	2
Cash flow	− $100	$30	$140

To compute the internal rate of return, you find the rate of discount that will discount the positive cash flows equal to a present value that is equal to $100:

Time	0	1	2
Present value	$100 =	$\dfrac{\$30}{1 +}$ +	$\dfrac{\$140}{(1 + r)^2}$

The rate of discount can be found through a trial and error process. That is, you try an r and see what kind of present value you get and then compare it to the amount on the left-hand side of the preceding equation. If it's not equal, you try a different r until you converge to the value on the left. In this case, the rate of discount that will discount those two flows to $100 is 34.27 percent:

$$\$100 = \frac{\$30}{1.3427} + \frac{\$140}{1.3427^2}$$

Again, this assumes that you take any interim money that you get along the way and reinvest it at this particular rate of return. It assumes that there's some investment available that always yields that return. In the example, we get $30 at the end of the first period. If we put that in the investment and earn 34.27 percent on it, we would end up at the end of the last period with $40.28. If we add that to our $140 which we get as a holder of the stock at the end of the last period, that gives us an ending wealth of $180.28. Again, if $100 increases twice by a percentage amount equal to 34.27, it grows to $180.28:

$$\$100 \times 1.3427 = \$134.27; \quad \$134.27 \times 1.3427 = \$180.28$$

So if we follow the assumption of reinvesting interim cash flows at the internal rate of return, we will have an ending wealth level that is consistent with the internal rate of return value.

QUESTION SET 1

Assume the following information for Questions 1 through 3:

Year	0	1	2	3
Bond price	$970	$975	$985	$1000

Assume that the bond pays an annual coupon at the end of each year of $60. Assume that to receive the end-of-year coupon you must have purchased the bond at the beginning of the year.

1. Compute the 1-year rates of return on the bond for each of the periods represented in the data.

2. Compute the average multiperiod rate of return if you had purchased the bond at time 0 and sold it at time 2. Do this for each of the following methods of computing such a return:
   a. Arithmetic mean yield
   b. Geometric mean yield
   c. Internal yield

3. Compute the average multiperiod rate of return if you had purchased the bond at time 0 and held it until maturity (at time 3). Do this for each of the following methods of computing such a return:
   a. Arithmetic mean yield
   b. Geometric mean yield
   c. Internal yield

4. a. Which of the multiperiod methods for computing return is the one that has become the standard in bond markets?
   b. In what sense could the standard method (from part (a)) be misleading to an investor?

5. Suppose you purchased a stock at year-end 1986 and held it to year-end 1988. The year-end stock prices are shown next. The stock paid no dividends.

1986	1987	1988
$100	$112	$100

   a. Compute the average annual return according to the arithmetic mean method.
   b. Compute the average annual return according to the geometric mean method.
   c. Compute the average annual return according to the internal yield method.
   d. Compare the results and indicate which is more intuitively appealing in assessing the performance of your investment.

6. The text presented an equation used to fit a yield curve to a set of yield data as well as parameter estimates for this equation at July 1, 1976. Given this information, compute the approximate yields on 1- and 5-year U.S. government securities at July 1, 1976.

Refer to the following information for Questions 7 through 10. Assume that the following represent points on the currently observed yield curve (assume these are arithmetic mean yields).

1-year bond: 9.62%
2-year bond: 9.12%
3-year bond: 8.72%
4-year bond: 8.42%
5-year bond: 8.17%

7. Assuming the market expectations theory of the term structure, compute the market's expectations of 1-year yields to occur
   a. One year in the future
   b. Two years in the future
   c. Three years in the future
   d. Four years in the future

8. Assuming the market expectations theory of the term structure, compute the market's expectations of
   a. The expected 1-year return on a 2-year bond 1 year in the future
   b. The expected 1-year return on a 3-year bond 1 year in the future

9. Assuming the market expectations theory of the term structure, compute the market's expectation of the term structure that will exist in 1 year.

10. Suppose that we assume there are liquidity premiums embedded in bonds with maturities greater than 1 year. In particular, suppose there is a uniform 1 percent liquidity premium in all bonds with maturity greater than 1 year. Compute the market's expectations of 1-year yields to occur
    a. One year in the future
    b. Two years in the future
    c. Three years in the future
    d. Four years in the future

Refer to the following data for Questions 11 and 12. Assume the expectations theory of the term structure and that the yields you observe are internal yields to maturity. Suppose the following points on the yield curve are observed currently:

1-year bond: 8%
2-year bond: 10%
3-year bond: 11%

11. Compute the market's expectation of 1-year bond yields to occur
    a. One year in the future
    b. Two years in the future

12. Compute the geometric mean yield and compare it with the given internal yields for
    a. The 2-year bond
    b. The 3-year bond
    What accounts for the difference between the internal yield and the geometric mean yield?

13. Assume the market expectations theory of the term structure and that the observed yields are geometric mean yields to maturity. Suppose the following points on the yield curve are observed currently:
    1-year bond: 9%
    2-year bond: 10%
    3-year bond: 10.5%

Compute the market's expectation of 1-year bond yields expected to occur
a. One year in the future
b. Two years in the future

14. Why would a belief in the segmented markets theory of the term structure imply a belief in market inefficiency?

15. When you look at the yields to maturity on U.S. government securities plotted against time to maturity, the data do not plot exactly on a smooth curve. What would account for departures of the actual yields from a smooth curve?

QUESTION SET 2

1. What is meant by the term structure of interest rates? Who would be more interested in it, the investor who buys 10-year bonds at 10 percent in order to later make a balloon payment of $5000 at the end of 10 years, or a pension fund manager who has a series of pensioners retiring within the next 10 years?

2. You are a bank's portfolio manager. You purchase 1-year bonds to match the 1-year obligations of the bank, 2-year bonds to match the 2-year obligations of the bank, and so on. You purchase all bonds at the best return possible, and the bank is always able to meet its obligations. Is there anything wrong with this strategy?

3. How does the liquidity preference theory differ from the market expectations theory? What effect does this have on the term structure under the liquidity preference theory?

4. What does the market segmentation theory maintain? What would this theory presume about the individual investor in Question 1, and the bank portfolio manager in Question 2?

ANSWERS TO QUESTION SET 2

1. The term structure of interest rates refers to the relationship between the *term* to maturity of a bond and its *yield* to maturity. The investor who purchases bonds which mature simultaneously with the investor's liability would probably be less interested in the term structure, since it is guaranteed that the liability can be met. The pension fund manager, on the other hand, may have to plan to meet pension liabilities as they appear, and, unless the liabilities are cash-matched with the maturity of the bonds, will have to absorb the effects that changes in interest rates may have on the value of his assets and the future rates of interest at which he reinvests the income from those assets. If the pension fund manager's planning and forecasts are not correct, he or she may be unable to meet the pension liabilities if the market value of bonds he has purchased has dropped significantly, or in the opposite case, if he or she is unable to earn sufficient returns on reinvested income.

2. The strategy of matching asset maturities to liabilities forgoes the opportunities to place the bank's portfolio on an optimal point on the term structure based on your forecast for the changes in interest rates. For example, if you expect rates to go up sharply, shorter maturities will give the greater return to your portfolio, whereas if you forecast lower rates,

longer maturities would have a greater value. So, although meeting obligations is certainly one function of the portfolio manager of a bank, most certainly that person will also be judged on the overall performance of his or her portfolio.

3. Under the market expectations theory, the term structure is determined solely by the market's expectations regarding future interest rates. The liquidity preference theory asserts that, in addition to the market expectations of future interest rates, the term structure is also affected by liquidity, or risk premiums. This means that investors do not necessarily regard long- and short-term bonds as perfect substitutes. Liquidity premiums that increase in size with term to maturity have the effect of making the term structure more upward sloping if interest rates are expected to rise, or less downward sloping if rates are expected to fall.

4. The market segmentation theory contends that each maturity sector of the bond market can be segmented from the others, with each segment of the market inhabited by a distinct group of investors who feel that they must invest in bonds of a given maturity. Under this theory, both the individual investor and the bank portfolio manager would, once they had matched their bond maturities to their liabilities, have no compunction to move to another bond maturity, irrespective of opportunities for higher returns outside their maturity range.

PROBLEM SET

1. In the following table, the expected yearly returns on bonds of various maturities are given.

Expected Returns to Bonds

Time	Bond Maturity				
	1 yr	2 yr	3 yr	4 yr	5 yr
Now	10	11	11	11	11
1 yr from now	8	9	9	9	9
2 yr from now	7	8	8	8	8
3 yr from now	7	8	8	8	8
4 yr from now	7	8	8	8	8

   a. Compute the arithmetic mean to maturity for each bond.
   b. Graph the arithmetic mean yield to maturity. What does the shape of the curve indicate to you?

2. Find the market's forecast of future one year interest rates for the next 3 years from the arithmetic mean yields, utilizing the following table and assuming bonds with 2 or more years to maturity require a 1 percent premium on their yearly expected returns.

Arithmetic	1 yr	2 yr	3 yr	4 yr
Mean yield	8%	11%	13%	14%

3. Assume the following internal yields to maturity:

Term to maturity	1 yr	2 yr	3 yr	4 yr
Internal mean yield	8%	11%	13%	14%

What is the expected yield on 1-year bonds for next year if the bonds are selling at par ($1000) and the liquidity premium is again assumed to be 1 percent as in Problem 2?

4. Assume you purchased a stock on January 1, 1984 and held it until December 31, 1986. The stock paid no dividends and had the following prices at the end of each of the years as follows:

1984	1985	1986
$50	$60	$75

a. Compute the average annual return using the arithmetic mean method.
b. Compute the average annual return using the geometric mean method.
c. Compute the average annual return using the internal mean method.

5. Assuming the market expectations theory of the term structure, and given that a 1-year bond has an arithmetic mean yield of 8 percent, a 2-year bond has an arithmetic mean yield of 9 percent, and a 3-year bond has an arithmetic mean yield of 10 percent, compute the market's expectation of the arithmetic mean yield to maturity for
a. A 1-year bond one year in the future.
b. A 2-year bond one year in the future.

6. Given the same data, only now assuming that the observed yields are internal yields to maturity (versus the arithmetic mean yield). Compute the market's expectation of the internal yield to maturity for a 2-year bond next year. Assume that the bonds are selling at face values.

ANSWERS TO PROBLEM SET

1. a. 1-year bond: $= 10.0\%$

   2-year bond: $\dfrac{11 + 8}{2}$ $= 9.5\%$

   3-year bond: $\dfrac{11 + 9 + 7}{2}$ $= 9.0\%$

   4-year bond: $\dfrac{11 + 9 + 8 + 7}{4}$ $= 8.75\%$

   5-year bond: $\dfrac{11 + 9 + 8 + 8 + 7}{5}$ $= 8.60\%$

   b. The downward-sloping term structure indicates that interest rates are expected to fall. The positive liquidity premium makes the curve less downward sloping than it would be otherwise.

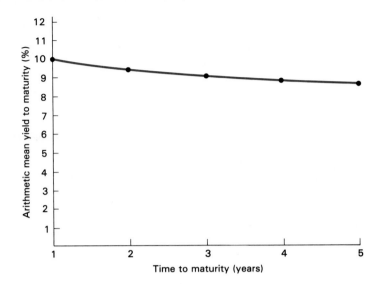

2.

	1 yr	2 yr	3 yr	4 yr
Now	8	9	9	9
1 year from now	13	14	14	14
2 years from now	16	17	17	17
3 years from now	16	17	17	17

3. Coupon rate for a 2-year bond consistent with an 11 percent internal yield and $1000 market price is $110:

$$\$1000 = \frac{\$110}{1.11} + \frac{\$1110}{(1.11)^2}$$

Recognizing that the market wants an additional 1 percent on the second payment during the first year:

$$\$1000 = \frac{\$110}{1.08} + \frac{\$1110}{1.09 \times (1 + r_2)}$$

$$r_2 = 13.38 \text{ percent}$$

4. a. Yearly rates of return:

$$\text{Year 1:} \quad \frac{60}{50} - 1 = 20\%$$

$$\text{Year 2:} \quad \frac{75}{60} - 1 = 25\%$$

$$\text{Arithmetic mean:} \quad \frac{20 + 25}{2} = 22.50\%$$

b. Geometric mean: $[(1.20)(1.25)]^{1/2} - 1 = 22.47\%$

c. Internal yield (no interim payments):

$$\frac{75}{(1 + Y)^2} = 50$$

$$Y = 22.47\%$$

5. Now:

	1-yr bond	2-yr bond	3-yr bond
Now	8	8	8
1 yr from now	10	10	10
2 yr from now	12	12	12
Current arithmetic mean yield	8	9	10

One year from now:

	1-yr bond	2-yr bond
Now	10	10
1 yr from now	12	12
Arithmetic mean yield	10	11

6. Coupon rate for 2-year bond:

$$\$1000 = \frac{\$90}{1.09} + \frac{\$1090}{(1.09)^2}$$

Coupon rate for 3-year bond:

$$\$1000 = \frac{\$100}{1.10} + \frac{\$100}{(1.10)^2} + \frac{\$1100}{(1.10)^3}$$

Calculation of r_2:

$$\$1000 = \frac{\$90}{1.08} + \frac{\$1090}{1.08(1 + r_2)}$$

$$r_2 = 10.10\%$$

Calculation of r_3:

$$\$1000 = \frac{\$100}{1.08} + \frac{\$100}{(1.08)(1.1010)} + \frac{\$1100}{(1.08)(1.1010)(1 + r_3)}$$

$$r_3 = 12.36\%$$

Market price of a 2-year bond next year:

$$\$980.01 = \frac{\$100}{1.101} + \frac{\$1100}{(1.101)(1.1236)}$$

Internal Yield of a 2-year bond next year:

$$\$980.01 = \frac{\$100}{1 + Y} + \frac{\$1100}{(1 + Y)^2}$$

$$Y = 11.17\%$$

COMPUTER PROBLEM SET

Refer to the following information for Problems 1 through 4. Bond prices are quoted in thirty-seconds.

Today's date: October 6, 1988

Coupon Rate	Maturity Date	Asked Price
7⅛	Apr 1989	99.17
11⅞	Oct 1989	103.17
7⅝	Apr 1990	99
11½	Oct 1990	105.21
12⅜	Apr 1991	108.23
9⅛	Oct 1991	101.21
11¾	Apr 1992	109.16
9¾	Oct 1992	103.30
7⅜	Apr 1993	95.14
7⅛	Oct 1993	93.30

1. Using the bond yield program, calculate the yields to maturity of the 10 bonds listed. Draw a graph of the term structure and interpret your findings.
2. Assuming the market expectations theory of the term structure, use the forward interest rate program to compute the six-month forward rates of interest over the next 5 years. Note the geometric mean rates of return to the 10 stocks.
3. Based on your answer to Problem 3, compute the market expectations of
   a. The geometric mean yield to maturity on a 2-year bond 1 year from now.
   b. The geometric mean yield to maturity on a 3-year bond 2 years from now.
4. Assume there is a uniform 1 percent liquidity premium for all bonds with maturities of 1 year or more. Calculate the 6-month forward rates for the 10 bonds listed. Also, note the geometric mean yields for the 10 stocks and compare them to the geometric yields calculated in your answer to Problem 3.

REFERENCES

BENNINGA, S., and PROTOPAPADAKIS, A., "Real and Nominal Interest Rates Under Uncertainty: The Fisher Theorem and the Term Structure," *Journal of Political Economy* (October 1983).

BENNINGA, S., and PROTOPAPADAKIS, A., "General Equilibrium Properties of the Term Structure of Interest Rates," *Journal of Financial Economics* (July 1986).

CAMPBELL, J. W., "A Defense of Traditional Hypotheses About the Term Structure of Interest Rates," *Journal of Finance* (March 1986).

COX, J., INGERSOLL, J., and ROSS, S., "A Re-examination of Traditional Hypotheses About the Term Structure of Interest Rates," *Journal of Finance* (September 1981).

CULBERTSON, J. M., "The Term Structure of Interest Rates," *The Quarterly Journal of Economics* (November 1957).

FAMA, E. F., "Term Premiums in Bond Returns," *Journal of Financial Economics* (December 1984).

FISHER, I., "Appreciation and Interest," *Publications of the American Economic Association* (August 1896).

HICKS, J. R., *Value and Capital*. London: Oxford at the Clarendon Press, 1939.

LONG, J. B., "Stock Prices, Inflation and the Term Structure of Interest Rates," *Journal of Financial Economics* (July 1974).

LUTZ, F. A., "The Structure of Interest Rates," *Quarterly Journal of Economics* (November 1940).

MANKIW, G. N., and MIRON, J. A., "The Changing Behavior of the Term Structure of Interest Rates," *Quarterly Journal of Economics* (May 1986).

MCCOLLOCH, J. H., "An Estimate of the Liquidity Premium," *Journal of Political Economy* (January–February 1975).

MEISELMAN, D., *The Term Structure of Interest Rates*. Englewood Cliffs, N.J.: Prentice-Hall, 1962.

MURPHY, R. G., "The Expectations Theory of the Term Structure: Evidence from Inflation Forecasts," *Journal of Macroeconomics* (Fall 1986).

OLDFIELD, G. S. and ROGLASKI, R. J., "The Stochastic Properties of Term Structure Movements," *Journal of Monetary Economics* (March 1988).

ROWE, T. D., LAWNER, T. A., and COOK, T. Q., "Treasury Bill versus Private Money Market Yield Curves," *Economic Review* (Federal Reserve Bank of Richmond) (July–August 1986).

SCOTT, T., "An Arbitrage Model of the Term Structure of Interest Rates," *Journal of Financial Economics* (January 1978).

STIGLITZ, J., "A Consumption-Oriented Theory of the Demand for Financial Assets and the Term Structure of Interest Rates," *Review of Economic Studies* (July 1970).

13

BOND PORTFOLIO MANAGEMENT

In the chapters on portfolio management, we learned how to construct the efficient set. The efficient set contains portfolios of securities—not merely common stocks but bonds and other types of securities as well. In this chapter, we shall talk about some issues and problems relating to the management of bonds in your portfolio.

We shall spend most of our time discussing some techniques which may be used to estimate the expected return and risk of a bond investment. As you shall see, bonds present some unique problems in this regard. As with previous chapters, we will assume that our investment horizon is relatively short, perhaps a month or a year. Our assumption will again be that, given the level of risk, you seek to maximize the expected rate of return on your portfolio.

ESTIMATING THE EXPECTED RETURN
OF A BOND FOR PORTFOLIO ANALYSIS

Throughout our discussion, we will assume we are dealing with relatively high-quality bonds. Speculative bonds, where default is a real factor are priced by the market and can be treated by the portfolio investor much like common stock. Higher-grade issues, on the other hand, are priced for the most part, on the basis of the term structure of interest rates. Your estimate of the bond's expected rate of return, therefore, is based largely on your forecast of the term structure of interest rates at your horizon point, say a month or a year from now.

Forecasting Expected Returns on Treasury Bonds

As portfolio managers we're faced with the task of estimating the expected returns on treasury bonds over the course of the next year. Our first step is to examine the current shape of the term structure. Suppose we fit the term structure using Equation (12.1), and it turns out to be "humped"-shaped as in the colored curve of Figure 13.1. The values for the coefficients a_1 through a_4 are given as follows:

$$\text{Short rate minus long rate: } a_1 = -.0100$$

$$\text{Shape parameters: } \begin{bmatrix} a_2 = .0100 \\ a_3 = .5000 \end{bmatrix}$$

$$\text{Long rate: } a_4 = .1000$$

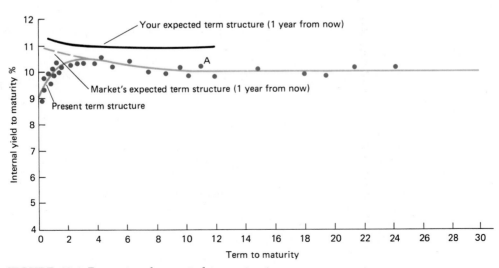

FIGURE 13.1 Present and expected term structures.

Notice the individual treasury bonds are positioned above and below the colored curve. As discussed in the previous chapter, the bonds positioned above the curve have relatively large semiannual interest payments and are selling at prices at or above their principal values. Those positioned below the curve have smaller interest payments and usually sell at discounts below their principal values. We shall refer to the ratio of the actual yield of each bond to the yield of a bond with the same maturity taken from the fitted curve, as its *relative yield differential* or *RYD*. The relative yield differential of any one of the bonds is given by the following equation:

$$RYD_J = \frac{Y_J}{(a_1 + a_2 t_J)e^{-a_3 t_J} + a_4}$$

or

$$RYD_J = \frac{Y_J}{Y_J^*}$$

where Y_J^* is the yield from the term structure for a bond with t_J years to maturity.

Our objective is to compute each bond's expected rate of return in the course of the next year. In general, the expected rate of return on a bond can be defined as

$$E(r) = \frac{E(\text{interest payment} + \text{ending price})}{\text{Current market price}} - 1$$

In the case of a treasury bond, we know the interest payment with certainty, so the formula can be written as

$$E(r) = \frac{\text{Interest payment} + E(\text{ending price})}{\text{Current market price}} - 1$$

Our task is to estimate each bond's ending market price. The key to estimating the bond's ending market price is estimating its yield to maturity at the horizon point. Once we estimate the bond's ending yield to maturity, we can estimate the bond's ending price through the following equation. In the equation, the current time is assumed to be zero, and the bond is assumed to have currently n years to maturity. For simplicity we have assumed that the bond's interest payments are paid annually, at the end of each year.

$$\text{Ending price} = \sum_{t=1}^{n-1} \frac{\text{interest payment}}{(1 + Y_1)^t} + \frac{\text{principal payment}}{(1 + Y_1)^{n-1}} \qquad (13.1)$$

In this equation Y_1 is your estimate of the bond's internal yield to maturity at the end of the year.

Thus, our problem is one of estimating the bond's yield to maturity at the end of the year. This, in turn, requires a forecast of (1) the term structure and (2) the bond's position relative to the term structure, or its relative yield differential.

Let's begin with our forecast of the term structure. We might start by asking what the market thinks the term structure of interest rates will look like next year. To extract the market's expectations from the term structure, we need to go through the process discussed in Chapter 12. Suppose we assume that there are no liquidity premiums in the term structure and that all bonds which are positioned exactly on the curve are selling at prices which equal their principal values. Reading from the curve of Figure 13.1, we can develop the following schedule of internal yields to maturity:

Bond	Internal Yield
1 year	10.00%
2 years	10.37
3 years	10.45
4 years	10.41
5 years	10.33

Based on this schedule and the procedure developed in the last chapter, we can find that the market expects the following series of 1-year bond rates:

Time	1-Year Rate
Now	10.00%
Next year	10.78
2 years from now	10.64
3 years from now	10.26
4 years from now	9.92

To find the market's expectation for next year's term structure of *internal* yields to maturity, we need to compute the expected market prices for bonds positioned on the yield curve with various maturities. To see how this is done, consider a bond positioned *on* the curve of Figure 13.1 which is a 3-year bond today. Based on its internal yield of 10.45 percent and the assumption that it is selling at a price equal to its principal value, it must carry an annual interest payment of $104.50. Given the market's expectation of future 1-year rates, the market price of this bond will be $995.47 at the *end* of the year, at which time it will be a 2-year bond:

$$\$995.47 = \frac{\$104.50}{1.1078} + \frac{\$104.50 + \$1000.00}{1.1078(1.1064)}$$

Given this price, the internal yield to maturity is expected to be 10.71 percent, as we can see from the following equation:

$$\$995.47 = \frac{\$104.50}{1.1071} + \frac{\$104.50 + \$1000.00}{1.1071^2}$$

Similar calculations can be made for bonds of other maturities. Based on these calculations, the market's expectation for the term structure of internal yields to maturity is given by the broken curve of Figure 13.1. The market expects short-term rates to rise substantially and long-term rates to remain relatively constant.

You have to ask yourself whether this forecast is reasonable. If the forecast turns out to be accurate, all the bonds on the term structure will produce about the same rate of return in the course of the coming year. Of course, equality in rates of return over given periods of time is consistent with the market expectations theory, and we have assumed away liquidity premiums in constructing the market's expectation of the term structure.

Suppose you have noticed the Fed has dramatically increased its rate of growth in the money supply in recent months, and you have decided this is consistent with a permanent change in policy toward monetary expansion. Surveys have also indicated intentions on the part of consumers to lower their savings rate and on the part of business firms to increase their spending on plant and equipment later in the year. You anticipate the year-end incidence of income and price effects associated with the lower savings rate and monetary expansion and the liquidity effect of business firms attempting to finance their investments in the long-term market. You more or less agree with the market in terms of its forecast of short-term rates, but you believe long-term rates will rise to 11 percent. Your personal forecast of the term structure is given by the solid black curve of Figure 13.1.

Having made your forecast of the term structure, to obtain consistent forecasts of the expected rate of return on each bond, you need to forecast the relative yield differential of each bond with respect to your term structure estimate. If you are willing to assume these yield differentials remain constant over time, you can estimate each bond's year-end yield by multiplying the yield consistent with your personal forecast of the term structure by the bond's current relative yield differential.

For example, the bond labeled *A* in Figure 13.1 has a relative yield differential of 1.02. The bond is currently an 11-year bond, but at the end of the year it will be a 10-year bond, and you have forecasted the general level of 10-year bond rates to be 11.0 percent. The forecast of the yield on this particular bond is thus 11.22 percent:

$$1.02 \times .11 = .1122$$

You can obtain forecasts for each of the bonds on the term structure in the same fashion. Once you have estimates of each bond's individual yield to maturity, you can turn these into estimates of their year-end market prices by employing Equation (13.1). The year-end prices can then be used to estimate the expected returns for the year.

Forecasting Expected Returns on Corporate Bonds

It's a little more difficult to estimate the expected returns on corporate bonds. First, there is usually some probability of default on the bonds. If you assume the probability of partial payments is zero, the expected value of the interest payment can be found as follows:

$$\text{Expected interest payment} = \text{Promised interest payment} \times (1 - \text{default probability})$$

Thus, if the promised payment is $100.00 and the probability of default is 2 percent, the expected interest payment is $98.00.

In estimating expected returns, you will be dealing with corporate bonds of a given quality, as estimated by the rating agencies. Thus, your estimates of AA utility bonds will be conducted separately from your estimates of BBB industrial bonds. For the higher-quality issues, you can probably assign the same (small) probability of default to all the issues in the class. For lower-quality issues, you may want to assign differential probabilities because, even though every bond in the class has the same rating, there is still a considerable range of quality within the rating class. After allowing for the tax effect of the size of the promised interest payment, you may want to accept the market's assessment of the chances for default and assign higher probabilities of default to bonds that are positioned above the term structure and lower probabilities to those positioned below.

Another difficulty associated with corporate bonds comes from the fact that the maturity of the bonds is, in the majority of cases, ambiguous. The firm usually holds an option to call the bond at a fixed price (or, more likely, prices which vary through time). If the market value of the bond rises above this call price, it is likely the firm will exercise its option and retire the bond. The firm can usually exercise its option any time after a period of call protection, which begins immediately after the bond is originally issued.

In addition to call provisions, corporate bonds may have sinking fund provisions mandating stated portions of the bond issue be retired each year. The corporate treasurer has the option of buying the bond in the market at prevailing market prices or calling some of the bonds in at a predetermined price. The identity of the specific bonds called in is determined by lottery. In any case, a corporate bond with 10 years until maturity isn't really *expected* to be "alive" for 10 years, the longest possible period of its life. Given the nature of its sinking fund and call provisions, the corporate bond's expected life may be considerably less than 10 years.

The ambiguity regarding the life of corporate bonds causes potential problems. First, if you plot the bonds in terms of yield against their longest possible maturity, you're not going to get as good a fit as with treasury bonds because corporate bonds may be priced in terms of the time they are expected to be called, as opposed to the time they mature. Consider, for example a corporate bond carrying a $150 coupon, originally issued when interest rates were at 15 percent. The bond has 20 years until maturity, but it is callable by the firm in 2 years at a price of $1150. Interest rates are currently at 10 percent, and if they stay there, the firm will certainly exercise its option to call. It is likely that the market will be pricing this bond as a 2-year issue with a "principal" payment of $1150 (the call price). If the term structure is flat at 10 percent, the market price of the bond will be

$$\$1210.74 = \frac{\$150.00}{(1.10)} + \frac{\$150.00 + \$1150.00}{(1.10)^2}$$

Based on this price, the bond's internal yield to *maturity* is 12.4 percent. Plotted on this basis relative to its term to maturity, it would be positioned well above the curve fitting the term structure.

In fitting the term structure, you must take situations like this into account. Of course, not every case will be so clear-cut. Unless you can obtain perfectly accurate assessments of the market's *expected* maturity and yield to expected maturity, the fit you obtain will not be nearly as good as the one obtained for treasury bonds.

It's best to think of a callable bond as a portfolio of two securities. The portfolio consists of a positive position in the straight bond, without the call option attached, and a negative position in the call option, which is held by the firm that issued the bond. The market price of the bond you read in the financial news is really the net value of these two individual securities. Consequently, if you compute the bond's yield to maturity based on this net value, you will get a confused picture of the straight bond's true yield.

The yield to maturity can be accurately computed by estimating the market value of the call option, and then adding this to the net value of the straight bond and the call option to find the value of the straight bond. The yield to maturity on the straight bond can then be found as the rate that will discount the stream of interest and principal payments to a present value equal to this estimated value.

We will be learning how to value options that are similar to those attached to corporate bonds in Chapters 15 and 16.

In estimating the bond's expected rate of return, you must estimate the net market value of the straight bond and the call option at the end of your planning period. The market value of the straight bond can be estimated using essentially the same procedure that you followed in estimating the ending market value for a treasury bond. The details involved in estimating the ending value for the call option are best saved for the next two chapters, but we can say at this point that the estimated value of the call will crucially depend on (1) your estimate of the ending value for the straight bond and (2) your estimate of the variance of the daily rate of return to the straight bond.

A DURATION-BASED APPROACH TO ESTIMATING THE RISK OF A BOND PORTFOLIO

One of the most popular measures of the risk of a bond investment is called **duration**. To a great extent bond duration has replaced bond maturity as a measure of the length of the stream of payments associated with a bond investment. Duration will be discussed more fully in the next chapter, but the formula for the duration of a bond paying interest annually is given by

$$D_1 = 1 \times \frac{C_1/(1 + Y)^1}{V} + 2 \times \frac{C_2/(1 + Y)^2}{V} + \cdots + n\frac{(C_n + P_n)/(1 + Y)^n}{V}$$

(13.2)

In this expression V represents the market value of the bond, C the annual coupon or interest payments, and P the principal payment. To get the duration, you multiply the maturity of each payment by the fraction of the total value of the bond accounted for by each of the payments. Duration is, therefore, the weighted average maturity of the stream of payments, where the maturity of each payment is weighted by the fraction of the total value of the bond accounted for by the payment. In computing duration, we're considering the bond as a portfolio of individual payments. Just as the expected rate of return on a portfolio is a weighted average of the expected rates of return on the stocks in the portfolio, the maturity of the portfolio of payments is a weighted average of maturities of the payments in the portfolio.

It is easy to see why duration has replaced maturity as a measure of the length of the payments stream. Maturity tells us about the timing of the very last payment in the stream. It completely ignores the timing and magnitude of all the other payments to be received between now and then. For example, a bond with a large semiannual interest payment has a lower duration than a zero coupon bond, even though they may have identical maturities. Duration is quite simply a more accurate descriptor of the average length of time you must wait to get your money in a bond investment.

But duration is also a more accurate indicator of something else, and herein lies its use in bond risk management. As we shall discover in the next chapter, duration is also a good indicator of the response of the value of a portfolio to changes in interest rates.

There are, however, at least four limitations to duration as a measure of the risk of a bond portfolio. First, duration addresses only the risk associated with changes in interest rates. In particular, it does not address changes in the market value of bond investments that result from changes in the bond's projected income stream. These changes may result from changes in the market's assessment of the probability of default or from changes in the probability of early retirement of the bond issue due to exercise of the corporate call option, the sinking fund requirement, or the investor's conversion option, if the issue is convertible. Second, all measures of duration are limited in terms of the type of changes in yield to maturity they relate to. For example, the measure set forth in equation 13.2 will rank bonds correctly in terms of the percentage change in price that will occur if we move from one perfectly flat term structure of interest rates to another at a higher or lower rate level. This point will also be discussed in more detail in the next chapter. Third, duration only tells half the story. True enough, long-duration bonds are more price sensitive to a given change in yield to maturity than are short-duration bonds. But it is also true that short-duration *yields to maturity* are more volatile than are long-duration yields. In assessing the ultimate risk of a bond investment, both factors must be considered together. Finally, it is relatively easy to measure the duration of bonds, but very difficult to measure the duration of other investments like common stocks. What if the investor has a mixed portfolio of stocks as well as bonds? Duration is of very limited use in describing the overall risk of the combined portfolio.

Given these limitations of duration-based risk, it may be worthwhile to consider applying more traditional techniques of risk management to bond and bond-stock portfolios.

A MARKOWITZ APPROACH TO BOND RISK MANAGEMENT

Until recently, accurate records of bond prices based on actual trades were very difficult to obtain. Estimates of bond prices called "matrix prices" *were* available, but these estimates were based on a few bonds with either similar or bridging characteristics that were actually traded on a given day. The errors associated with matrix pricing were sufficiently large to render a time series of matrix returns to a particular bond issue of little value in estimating the variances and covariances needed for Markowitz portfolio analysis. A more accurate history of bond pricing, based on actual trades for large populations of bonds, is now becoming generally available. Given a reliable history of bond returns, we can now think about employing Markowitz portfolio analysis to bond investments.

To compute the Markowitz efficient set, you need to eliminate the covariance between the periodic returns on each bond and the rest of the securities in your population. In making the estimates, you can follow the same procedures you used for common stocks, but you need to keep one additional factor in mind. As time passes, the time to maturity of a bond becomes shorter and shorter. This is of little consequence if you are taking sample estimates of covariances over relatively short time intervals. However, if your sample extends over a considerable period, the nature of the bond may change dramatically from the beginning of the period to the end. Your covariance estimate reflects a composite picture of the risk of the bond as it goes from a relatively long-term bond at the beginning of the period to a relatively short-term bond at the end of the period.

To get more accurate estimates of the covariances, you may have to construct index bonds of various maturities. Suppose your investment horizon is 1 month long. To construct an index bond representing a 10-year treasury issue, you might fit the term structure using Equation (12.1) for a series of months. You are interested in the series of rates of return produced by a bond that is a 10-year bond at the beginning of each month and a 9-year, 11-month bond at the end of each month. Suppose, in the first month of your sample, your fitted curve indicates that a 10-year bond should have an internal yield of 12 percent. At the end of the month (or the beginning of the next), the curve indicates that a 9-year, 11-month bond should have an internal yield of 11.5 percent. The following equation provides for an *extremely* good approximation for the rate of return on the bond for the month.[1] In the equation, Y_1 represents the yield at the beginning of the month and Y_2 represents the yield at the end of the month.

$$r_t = Y_1 + \left(1 - \frac{D_1}{t}\right)(Y_2 - Y_1) \tag{13.3}$$

The symbol t represents the length of the time interval over which the rate of return is computed, in this case one-twelfth of a year. The symbol D_1 refers to the bond's *duration* at the beginning of the month.

---

[1] This equation was developed by Babcock (1984).

Again, assuming that bonds taken from the curve fitting the term structure sell at market prices equal to their principal value, the duration of a 10-year bond with an internal yield of 12 percent and annual interest payment of $120.00 is 6.328 years. Substituting this number into Equation (15.2) for the rate of return, we get an annualized rate of return equal to

$$.4947 = .12 + \left(1 - \frac{6.328}{1/12}\right)(.115 - .12)$$

By performing this same operation for each of the months of the series in your sample, you can produce a series of rates of return on a bond that is a 10-year bond at the beginning of each of the months in the sample period. These rates of return can then be used to compute sample covariances with other bond returns (constructed in the same way) and stock investments.

DIVIDING THE PORTFOLIO BETWEEN BONDS AND STOCK

The division of the portfolio between bonds and stock should come naturally in the process of finding the efficient set. You input your estimates of expected returns on both stock and bond investments. Both estimates reflect your expectations of what will be happening to the general level of interest rates and the term structure in the various parts of the bond market (AAA industrial, AA utility, etc.). You also input your estimates of the covariances that exist between the different investments, bonds as well as stocks.

With these estimates, the computer can find the efficient set. If you forecast that the economy is recession bound, with business firms experiencing falling interest rates and deteriorating profitability, you will find the efficient portfolios are weighted heavily in high-quality bonds. If instead, you forecast that the economy will be emerging from a recession, with interest rates and corporate profits rising, your efficient portfolios may be more heavily invested in stock and lower-quality bonds.

In other words, the character of the efficient set reflects the character of your forecast of the economy, interest rates, the profitability of firms in general, and the relative performance of different companies. The optimal mix of bonds and stocks in your portfolio is then determined by the point of tangency between your indifference curve and the efficient set.

SUMMARY

You can determine the ratio of bond to stock investments in your portfolio by finding the portfolios in the efficient set. The portfolios in the efficient set specify not only how many bonds and stocks to buy but which individual bonds and stocks.

Bonds present some unique problems in estimating expected return and risk for purposes of portfolio analysis. Relatively high-quality bonds are priced relative to the term structure for other bonds in their risk and tax classification. To estimate their expected return, you must first forecast the term structure and then estimate the position of the bond relative to the term structure. This is a comparatively simple problem for treasury bonds. However, there are additional complications for corporate bonds. Corporate bonds are usually callable, and they have sinking fund provisions. This makes estimating their expected life problematic. It is, therefore, difficult to position the bonds relative to both today's term structure and your forecasted term structure at the horizon point.

It is also difficult to estimate the covariance between a bond and other investments in the portfolio. Covariances are usually estimated by sampling from a series of past returns. If the series of past returns is long, the bond will slowly mature during the series, and its nature will change from the beginning to the end. This problem can be overcome by estimating the returns on *indexed* bonds taken from points on the term structure of interest rates.

QUESTION SET 1

1. Suppose that a yield curve was fitted to yields on U.S. government securities using the equation for the curve of best fit presented in Chapter 12. The estimated coefficients are $a_1 = -.0100$, $a_2 = .0100$, $a_3 = .5000$, and $a_4 = .1000$. What would the relative yield differential be for a bond with 2 years left to maturity and having a yield of 10.7 percent?

2. What does it mean to say that a bond has a value less than one for its relative yield differential? What might account for such a differential?

   Refer to the following information for Questions 3 through 5: Suppose that today's annual yield on a 1-year U.S. government security is 10 percent. Given the internal yields on today's yield curve and assuming the market expectations theory of the term structure, you have solved for the expected future 1-year yields as follows:

	Expected 1-Year Yield
1 year from now	9.5%
2 years from now	8.5
3 years from now	8.0

Suppose you are looking at a government security which pays annual coupons of $75 and which currently has 4 years left until maturity. Assume for simplicity, that the bond pays its coupon in one payment at the end of each time period. It also returns its face value of $1000 at maturity.

3. Under the market expectations theory, what is the market's anticipated price of this bond
   a. One year from now
   b. Two years from now

4. Under the market expectations theory, set up the equation that would be used to solve for the market's anticipated internal yield to maturity for the bond

a. One year from now

b. Two years from now

Try to solve the equation from (b) for the internal yield.

5. Suppose there also exists a government bond with 2 years left until maturity which you knew to have a relative yield differential of .98. What would be your forecast for this bond's internal yield 1 year from now?

Refer to the following information for Questions 6 and 7: Early in this chapter, five internal yields were taken from the initial term structure presented in Figure 13.1. Assuming the market expectations theory, these internal yields were used to derive the following current and expected 1-year yields:

Time	1-Year Yield
Now	10.00%
Next year	10.78
2 years from now	10.64
3 years from now	10.26
4 years from now	9.92

6. Try to derive the preceding expectations from the yield curve information given in the text.

7. Show how you would use the preceding information to derive the market's forecast of the price and internal yield to maturity on a particular bond 2 years from now. The bond in question currently has 5 years left until maturity. It pays annual (end-of-year) coupons of $90 and will return its face value of $1000 at maturity.

8. Why is the maturity of some bonds ambiguous?

9. What problems would there be in trying to derive information about the term structure of interest rates from data on *corporate* bond yields?

10. Suppose a bond with a face value of $1000 pays an annual coupon of $100. Interest rates are currently at 7 percent for all maturities of the same default risk. The bond has 10 years until maturity but is callable in 2 years at a price of $1075.

    a. If interest rates are expected to stay at 7 percent, would you expect the institution that issued the bond to call it in 2 years?

    b. Given your answer to (a), what would be the current market price of the bond?

    c. How would you compute the internal yield of this bond?

11. Refer to the example of the 20-year bond presented in the chapter in the section entitled "Forecasting Expected Returns on Corporate Bonds." The text first derived a price of $1210.74 and then an internal yield to maturity of 12.4 percent. How would one proceed to get the 12.4 percent result for the internal yield?

12. In view of discussion in earlier chapters about selecting optimal portfolios of securities, how should you reach a decision about the relative importance of bonds in a portfolio of various securities?

QUESTION SET 2

1. Although you and your friend use exactly the same formulas and personal computers, you each have estimated different expected rates of return on the same bond. For the next year, your 20-year bond is estimated to have a higher expected return than your friend's. What

causes this difference, and what do you know about your outlook for interest rates and economic activity?

2. What is a relative yield differential?

3. In estimating a bond's yield to maturity, what two forecasts are necessary?

4. Corporate bonds have two features which makes forecasting expected returns to them more difficult than government bonds. What are these features? Which affects the position of the bond in relation to your forecast of the term structure?

5. How are bonds unique in terms of managing a portfolio of securities? Under what economic conditions might they be more important to some investors?

ANSWERS TO QUESTION SET 2

1. The estimate of a bond's expected rate of return is based largely on a forecast of the term structure of interest rates. Since your estimate of expected return on your bond is higher than your friend's, you probably have forecasted a term structure that is lower, and your outlook for the pace of the economy is probably less optimistic.

2. The relative yield differential is the ratio of the actual yield of a bond to the yield of a bond with the same maturity taken from the fitted curve of the term structure.

3. To estimate a bond's yield to maturity at the end of a year, you need to forecast the term structure and its relative yield differential with respect to the term structure.

4. First, there is usually some probability of default on corporate bonds. Secondly, the maturity of the bonds, due to call options and sinking fund provisions, is in most cases ambiguous. The ambiguity of the life of the bond may affect the pricing of the bond because they may be priced in relation to the time they are expected to be called versus their maturity. Hence a longer-term bond may be positioned as a shorter bond in relationship to the term structure.

5. Bonds are unique to a portfolio of securities because, in the case of U.S. Treasury bonds, the principal payment is certain, as well as the interest payment. This allows the portfolio manager to be able to calculate the return to his portfolio with increased certainty. It may be advantageous to those portfolio managers who have definite liabilities to meet. Under adverse, or recessionary economic conditions, bonds might take on heavy weights in efficient portfolios for those with high degrees of risk aversion or for those investors forecasting low expected returns to variable income securities like common stocks.

PROBLEM SET

1. A new 1-year treasury bond has a semiannual coupon of 9.5 percent, a current market price of $1050, and an expected ending price for 6 months of $1075.
   a. Compute the expected 6-month rate of return.
   b. If you hold the bond until its maturity 1 year from now, what is the expected internal yield to maturity?

2. What is the expected return on a corporate bond with an annual coupon of 12 percent, a current market price of $1050, and a probability of default on the interest of .05? The bond matures at the end of the year at par ($1000).

3. You have forecasted the year-end term structure of interest rates to be flat at 12 percent, and have estimated the relative yield differentials for your three bond portfolio to be 1.10, 1.01, and 1.05. All your bonds are 3-year bonds and carry a $100 annual interest payment and a face value of $1000.
    a. What is the expected year-end yield to maturity for each of your bonds?
    b. What is the expected market price for for each of the bonds at the end of the first year?

4. Suppose the yield to maturity on a bond with a duration of 10 years is 11 percent at the beginning of the month and a 10.9 percent at the end of the month. What is the annualized rate of return on the bond during the course of the month?

ANSWERS TO PROBLEM SET

1. a. $E(r) = \dfrac{\$95 + \$1075}{\$1050} - 1 = 11.43\%$

   b. $\$1050 = \dfrac{\$95}{(1 + Y)^{1/2}} + \dfrac{\$1095}{(1 + Y)}$

   $Y = 13.94$

2. $E(r) = \dfrac{(1 - .05)\$120 + \$1000}{\$1050} = 6.095\%$

3. a. $12\% \times 1.10 = 13.20\%$

   $12\% \times 1.01 = 12.12\%$

   $12\% \times 1.05 = 12.60\%$

   b. $\dfrac{100}{1.1320} + \dfrac{1100}{(1.1320)^2} = 88.34 + 828.42 = \$946.76$

   $\dfrac{100}{1.1212} + \dfrac{1100}{(1.1212)^2} = 89.19 + 875.04 = \$964.23$

   $\dfrac{100}{1.126} + \dfrac{1100}{(1.126)^2} = 88.81 + 867.59 = \$956.40$

4. Use the following formula to get the annual return:

$$r_t = Y_1 + \left(1 - \frac{D_1}{t}\right)(Y_2 - Y_1)$$

$$r_t = .11 + \left(1 - \frac{10}{1/12}\right)(.109 - .11)$$

$$= 22.9\%$$

REFERENCES

BABCOCK, G., "Duration as a Link Between Yield and Value," *Journal of Portfolio Management* (Summer and Fall 1984).

BRENNAN, M. J., and SCHWARTZ, E. S., "Conditional Predictions of Bond Prices and Returns," *Journal of Finance* (May 1980).

COOK, T. Q., "Some Factors Affecting Long-Term Yield Spreads in Recent Years," *Monthly Review,* Federal Reserve Bank of Richmond (September 1973).

DARST, D. M., *The Complete Bond Book.* New York: McGraw-Hill, 1981.

HO, T. S. Y., and SINGER, R. F., "Bond Indenture Provisions and the Risk of Corporate Debt," *Journal of Financial Economics* (December 1982).

JAFFE, J. F., and MANDELKER, G., "Inflation and the Holding Period Returns on Bonds," *Journal of Financial and Quantitative Analysis* (December 1979).

PINCHES, G., and SINGLETON, J. C., "The Adjustment of Stock Prices to Bond Rating Changes," *Journal of Finance* (March 1978).

VAN HORNE, J. C., *Financial Market Rates and Flows.* Englewood Cliffs, N.J.: Prentice Hall, 1978.

C H A P T E R

14

INTEREST IMMUNIZATION

In the previous chapter, we talked about making forecasts of future interest rates and then positioning portfolios to take best advantage of our forecast. This might be called *aggressive* bond portfolio management. In this chapter, we will discuss *defensive* bond portfolio management. In managing the portfolio defensively, our objective is to reduce the interest rate risk of the portfolio to zero. A portfolio with zero interest rate risk is said to be *immunized*.

CASH MATCHING AND INTEREST IMMUNIZATION

Immunization is gaining increasing popularity with pension funds. At the present time, more than $100 billion in pension assets is immunized, in one form or another, against changes in the rate of interest. Pension funds promise to pay annuities to retired employees over their remaining lifetimes. A change in interest rates may threaten the fund's ability to fulfill its promise. If interest rates fall, interest income must be reinvested at lower rates. The wealth of the fund may not accumulate as fast as anticipated, and the fund may run short of money while it has remaining liabilities outstanding. The fund can protect against this risk by investing in very long-term bonds that produce most of their cash flows at points in time beyond the required payments to the pensioners. However, in doing this the fund faces another risk. To make its promised payments, the fund must sell its bond investments in the market. If interest rates go up, the market value of its bonds may not be sufficient to produce the funds required to make the required payments. Thus, if you invest too short, you run the risk of having to reinvest the proceeds of your investments at inadequate rates. On the other hand, if you invest too long, you run the risk of having to liquidate your portfolio at inadequate market prices.

To understand the concept of immunization, consider the case of the pension fund of Figure 14.1 which has promised to pay the retired employees of the firm it represents annuities for the remainder of their lives. As time goes by, the employees gradually pass away, and the total amount of the payments becomes smaller, finally reaching zero after 23 years.

If the pension fund is fully funded, it has sufficient invested assets to enable it to pay the liabilities in full at the current level of interest rates. Assume that interest rates are currently 10 percent and the present value of the stream of payments at this rate is $10 million. Also assume, you invest this amount of money in short-term

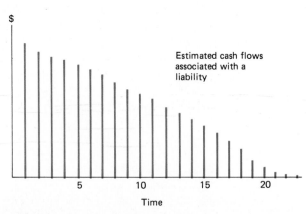

FIGURE 14.1 Cash flows associated with the liabilities of a pension fund.

treasury bills. Suppose interest rates should fall. In this case, the present value of the stream of payments goes up. The amount of money you need to have invested at the lower rate of interest is higher than it was before. However, the market value of your portfolio of treasury bills will have changed very little. The market prices of very short-term bonds are insensitive to changes in interest rates. You are in trouble. As portfolio manager, you have less money in your portfolio than you need to make all the expected payments to the retired workers.

Now assume, that you invested the money in a 23-year treasury bond. To make the payments along the way, you plan to sell off some of your holdings in the bond each year. Interest rates now go up. Being highly sensitive to changes in interest rates, the market value of your treasury bond falls dramatically in price. The present value of your liabilities falls also, but not as much as the fall in the value of your bond portfolio. The amount of money you have invested is once again less than the amount you need to make all the payments. You must sell many more of the bonds than expected to make the relatively large payments at the beginning of the stream. You are again in trouble. You will run out of funds while you still have more payments to make.

Your portfolio isn't immunized. There is no risk of default because you have invested in treasury bonds. There is no inflation risk because we have assumed the pension isn't indexed with respect to inflation, so your liabilities are written in fixed dollar amounts. You still, however, are subject to *interest rate risk,* and this is what keeps getting you in trouble.

To immunize the portfolio, you must invest so that its value fluctuates in accord with the present value of your liabilities. Conceptually, the easiest way to achieve this state is by **cash matching**. A cash-matched portfolio produces a stream of cash flows which match up exactly with the stream of liabilities. One way to cash-match the liabilities of Figure 14.1 is to buy treasury bonds which have been stripped of their coupons or interest payments. You would buy enough 1-year treasury bonds so that their total principal payments would equal your first pension payment coming at the end of 1 year. You would receive the money from the Treasury and pay it out to the retired workers on the same day. If you did the same thing with all the other payments in your liability stream, you would have cash-matched your portfolio, and you would now be immunized.

Cash matching is conceptually simple, but it has a major disadvantage. The problem is, to cash-match you have to invest in many different bonds, some of which may be unattractive to you for tax reasons. As we discussed in the previous chapter, bonds sell at differential pretax yields to maturity based on the size of their annual interest payments. Bonds with relatively large coupons are typically positioned above the term structure, and those with small coupons are typically positioned below. Pension funds pay no income taxes. For a pension fund, the pretax yield is also the after-tax yield. As a pension fund portfolio manager, it is in your interest to invest in the bonds with the largest interest payments. These have the greatest tax exposure and the greatest pretax yields. Since you pay no taxes, you keep the entire yield.

If you cash-match, you must spread your investments over many different bonds, and you give up the opportunity to concentrate your investments in the two or three bonds on the term structure with the greatest tax exposure. This means cash matching may cost you a great deal of money.

What we need is a means to achieve immunization while concentrating our investments in a few securities. The total market value of these securities must rise or fall in step with the present value of our liabilities. Thus, we need a measure of the sensitivity of the values of our liabilities and assets to a change in interest rates. Duration is such a measure.

ALTERNATIVE MEASURES OF DURATION

Macaulay's Duration

Macaulay's duration measure (1938) is the most simple. The formula for Macaulay's duration for the case of a bond investment is as follows:

$$D_1 = 1 \times \frac{C_1/(1 + Y)^1}{V} + 2 \times \frac{C_2/(1 + Y)^2}{V} + \cdots + n \times \frac{(C_n + P_n)/(1 + Y)^n}{V}$$

In the equation, Y is the bond's internal yield, C_1 is the annual coupon or interest payment to be paid in year 1, P_n is the principal payment, n is the number of years until maturity, and V is the current market value of the bond. The formula assumes interest is paid annually, with the first payment coming at the end of the first year. Each maturity date $(1, 2, \ldots, n)$ is multiplied by the ratio of the present value of the payment to be received to the total present value of all the payments.

Suppose we were dealing with a bond that carried a $100 annual coupon and had 2 years to maturity. The internal yield to maturity of the bond is 10 percent, and its market value is $1000;

$$\$1000 = \frac{\$100}{1.10} + \frac{\$100 + \$1000}{1.10^2}$$

The Macaulay duration for this bond is 1.909 years:

$$1.909 = 1 \times \frac{\$100/1.1}{\$1000} + 2 \times \frac{\$1100/1.1^2}{\$1000}$$

Thus the formula provides the weighted average maturity of the payments stream, where the maturity of each payment is weighted by the fraction of the total value of the bond accounted for by the payment. In the formula you will note that the present value of any one of the coupons is given by

$$\frac{C_t}{(1 + Y)^t}$$

where Y is the bond's internal yield to maturity and t is the number of years until the coupon is paid. This will be the present value of the interest payment if the rate of interest is expected to remain constant through time.

If we allow for expected changes in rates, the present value of the coupon coming at year t is given by

$$\frac{C_t}{(1 + r_1)(1 + r_2) \cdots (1 + r_t)}$$

Fisher-Weil Duration

Allowing for future rates to change, a more general formula for the weighted average maturity of the payments stream is given by

$$D_2 = 1 \times \frac{C_1/(1 + r_1)}{V} + 2 \times \frac{C_2/[(1 + r_1)(1 + r_2)]}{V} + \cdots$$

$$+ n \times \frac{(C_n + P_n)/[(1 + r_1)(1 + r_2) \cdots (1 + r_n)]}{V}$$

This measure of the duration of the stream is called the Fisher-Weil duration (1971), named after the two people who revived duration after Macaulay first introduced it. To compute Fisher-Weil duration, you need estimates of the future interest rates r_1, r_2, and so on. These can be obtained from the term structure using the procedures discussed in Chapter 12.

For the example of the bond just described, the Fisher-Weil duration can be found to be 1.907 if the first-year interest rate is assumed to be 8 percent and the second-year rate is assumed to be 12.24%. Under these conditions, the value of the bond is calculated as

$$\$1000 = \frac{\$100}{1.08} + \frac{\$1100}{1.08(1.1224)}$$

and the Fisher-Weil duration as

$$1.907 = 1 \times \frac{\$100/1.08}{\$1000} + 2 \times \frac{\$1100/[1.08(1.1224)]}{\$1000}$$

Duration and Yield Elasticity

Duration not only measures the average length of the payment stream, it also approximates the elasticity of the value of the bond with respect to a change in one plus the bond's yield to maturity. Macaulay's duration is approximately equal to the negative of the elasticity with respect to a change in one plus the internal yield to maturity, and Fisher-Weil duration has the same relationship with respect to a change in one plus the geometric mean yield to maturity. Thus, in the case of Macaulay duration,

$$D_1 \approx \frac{(V_2 - V_1)/[(V_1 + V_2)/2]}{(Y_2 - Y_1)/[1 + (Y_1 + Y_2)/2]} = -\frac{\text{Percentage change in value}}{\text{Percentage change in one} + \text{internal yield}}$$

OUT ON THE STREET

STALKING THE BIG ONE

The decor of the room is absolutely impeccable. It reflects wealth, power. We are in the offices of National Investment Services of America (NISA), based in Milwaukee, Wisconsin.

Seven people sit around an oval dining table, drinking coffee from fine china. Four of the six represent NISA. The remaining two are potential clients. NISA has been immunizing pension fund portfolios for several years now. They use Macaulay duration and the techniques discussed in this chapter. The techniques have worked effectively. At this point, in addition to extensive management of conventional stock and bond portfolios, they currently have approximately $500 million under immunization for several clients.

But this account is the big one.

The client is one of the biggest firms in America. Its pension fund is approximately *$7 billion!* The portion of this that is being considered for immunization is approximately $2.5 billion. Five of those at the table are very tense; two are quite relaxed.

Each representative from NISA speaks in turn. Joe Gorman, president of the company, introduces his four colleagues. Mary Jo Dempsey runs the immunization program and trades in the bonds when reimmunization is required. Tom Tuschen markets the program on a nationwide basis. Jeff Bryden also manages the portfolio. Professor Leif Grando works for the company as a consultant. He designed the program and has introduced modifications when required by NISA.

These five have been through this many times before, but this time is clearly different. The stakes are high, so high that when you open your mouth to speak, you wonder if it will be a lucid train of logic or garbled nonsense?

Gorman begins, and it is a lucid train of logic. The client already has an existing bond portfolio that is so large that moving completely out of it into an immunized portfolio is infeasible. The size of the required trades would be so large as to upset prices in the market. To attack this problem, NISA proposes the following solution. They would sell from existing bond holdings those issues for which the cash flows couldn't be forecast with precision. These would be callable bonds with large coupons, similar bonds with sinking funds, and bonds of doubtful quality.

Gorman explains they are dealing with two types of risk. First, there is the risk that the cash flows associated with the liabilities and the assets of the pension fund will not actually be as expected. This is an actuarial risk for the liabilities and a default or call risk for the bonds. This risk will be minimized by retaining the proper investments in the bond portfolio—high-quality bonds for which there is little danger of premature retirement through call or execution of the sinking fund. Second, there is the risk of a change in interest rates. This will be eliminated through immunization.

After retaining the investments with relatively certain cash flows, these cash flows will be netted against the cash flows associated with the liabilities of the fund. The remaining net cash flow stream will have cash outflows in most months, but it can also have cash *inflows* in months where the cash inflows associated with the bonds retained are greater than the cash outflows associated with expected pension fund payments.

This *net* cash flow stream is to be immunized using NISA's conventional immunization techniques, using government bonds as a *cap* for the rest of the portfolio. If on the basis of relative yield spreads or other considerations part of the underlying corporate bond portfolio can be traded at a profit, the composition of the government bonds in the cap will be adjusted to keep the overall portfolio immunized.

Gorman goes into some of the more technical aspects of the program until both sides agree that the plan is a sound one.

Then the client voices the first challenge to the presentation.

"But why immunize in the first place? The $2.5 billion will be completely riskless, but the rest of the portfolio will be invested in risky securities like common stock. On an overall basis, it will be as though we hadn't considered immunization."

NISA is ready for this question. Gorman's eyes lock with Grando's, and Grando begins the response.

The beneficiaries of the pension fund can be divided into two groups, those who are still working and those who have already retired. It's difficult to estimate the benefits associated with the active workers, because they will be based on wages paid at retirement. If retirement comes in prosperity, the benefits will be large; if it comes in adversity, they will be small. To reduce the risk associated with the fund, the assets supporting these benefits should be invested in variable income securities such as common stock. To invest these funds in bonds would be to increase the risk of the fund rather than reduce it. The benefits for those who have already retired can be estimated much more precisely. These liabilities can be considered as fixed, and they can be either immunized or matched up with fixed income securities. By dividing up the liabilities of the fund in this way, you address the problem of risk reduction in the fund in a more systematic, precise fashion.

"But why should we act to reduce the risk associated with the fund at all? Why shouldn't we manage the fund actively to squeeze out some extra profit?"

That's a good question. Your stockholders won't care if you reduce the risk associated with your pension fund. They can readily change the risk of their portfolios in the capital market by buying or selling additional amounts of stocks or bonds. But management operates for the benefit of more than one constituent. In making decisions, for example, management must also consider the welfare of its employees. These people are interested in the firm's survival, because they want to keep their jobs.

Because of this, firms generally make decisions that will extend the expected life of the firm when they can do so without penalizing the market value of their common stock. In making their investment decisions in the real sector of the economy, the firm can't hide from risk because the most risky projects may be those that will increase the price of their common stock. If management doesn't adopt these projects, someone else will buy up the stock of the firm and invest in them for them. But prices in the capital market are set on a highly competitive basis. There are no clearly profitable or unprofitable investments in the securities market. Thus, management can take low-risk positions there without materially affecting the price of their common stock. They can extend the expected life of the firm and so benefit their employees without penalizing their common stock-holders. Immunization can be viewed as a precise way of reducing the risk associated with the pension fund.

The tension in the room begins to ease. Some good points have been made. Doubts have been eliminated. NISA clearly has a long road to go on this account, but today it has taken a very big step toward landing the big one. NISA would eventually end up successfully managing the biggest single immunized bond portfolio in the world.

Suppose the internal yield of the 2-year bond increased from 10 percent to 12 percent. In this case, the market value of the bond would fall from $1000 to $966.20:

$$\$966.20 = \frac{\$100}{1.12} + \frac{\$1100}{1.12^2}$$

The elasticity of the value of the bond with respect to the change in one plus the internal yield could then be computed as

$$\frac{(\$966.20 - \$1000.00)/[(\$966.20 + \$1000.00)/2]}{(1.12 - 1.10)/[(1.12 + 1.10)/2]} = -1.908$$

The elasticity is the percentage change in value accompanying each percentage change in one plus the yield. In computing an elasticity, the base used for computing the percentage change is the average of the beginning and ending values rather than the beginning value alone. The negative sign in front of the elasticity indicates there is an inverse relationship between value and yield.

Thus, given that a bond has a duration of 9 years, if there is an increase in one plus its yield to maturity of 1 percent, there will be a decrease in its market value of approximately 9 percent. The approximation becomes better the smaller the change in the yield. For infinitesimally small changes in yield, it is an exact relationship. Thus, duration is *approximately* equal to the negative of the *arc* elasticity and *exactly* equal to the negative of the *point* elasticity.

Duration and the Response of the Value of a Stream of Payments or Receipts to a Change in Discount Rates

We can think of our liabilities as a portfolio of required payments and our investments as another portfolio of anticipated receipts. To be immunized, we want the value of the two portfolios to respond identically to changes in interest rates.

The value of either portfolio is given by the following general expression:

$$V = \frac{I_1}{1 + r_1} + \frac{I_2}{(1 + r_1)(1 + r_2)} + \cdots + \frac{I_n}{(1 + r_1)(1 + r_2) \cdots (1 + r_n)}$$

In the expression, I_1 is the cash flow associated with the portfolio in year 1 and n is the number of years until the last cash flow. When we speak of a change in interest rates, we are referring to some change in the rates used to discount the cash flows, that is, r_1, r_2 and so on. You can think of these rates as the numbers going diagonally down the matrix of Figure 12.8 in Chapter 12 on the term structure of interest rates. For example, in the context of Figure 12.8, we would discount a cash flow expected in the third year (analogous to a 3-year bond) by the product of

$$1.06(1.09)(1.10)$$

If two portfolios have the same duration but they are not cash matched and there is a small change in these discount rates, will the market value of both portfolios respond to the same degree? This depends on the way interest rates change. Since Macaulay's duration is based on the internal yield, which assumes interest rates will be constant through time, the portfolios will respond identically if the term structure is initially flat and remains flat at the new yield level. This means that, initially all the numbers in the matrix like Figure 12.8 must be equal (resulting in a flat term structure), and they must still be equal after the change in interest rates.

If the portfolios have the same Fisher-Weil duration, the response of the two portfolios to a small change in interest will be the same if the change in rates is of the form of a parallel shift in a term structure of any shape. This means the shape of the term structure at the new level of rates is the same as the shape at the old level of rates. In other words, initially we can have any pattern of numbers in a matrix like that of Figure 12.8, but the change in rates must be such that we add or subtract a constant amount to each one of the expected future discount rates.

Thus, if we match up the duration of our assets and liabilities, we are fully protected from *these types* of interest rate changes.

Cox, Ingersoll, Ross Duration

These types of changes are highly restrictive, however. In light of this, a third duration measure has been suggested by Cox, Ingersoll, and Ross (CIR) (1979). This measure allows for more complicated changes in interest rates. CIR assumes that the interest rate on the shortest-term bond changes over time in the following fashion:

$$r_t - r_{t-1} = E(r_t - r_{t-1}) + \sigma \times r_{t-1}^{1/2} \times z_t \tag{14.1}$$

In this formula, the change in rates which takes place today is equal to the expected change in rates plus an unexpected change. The unexpected change is equal to the product of a random shock z (which, itself, has an expected value of zero and a variance and standard deviation equal to 1) and two terms which together determine the response of the interest rate to the factor and through this the variability of the interest rate over time. The first term, σ, denotes the underlying standard deviation of interest rates. The second term is the square root of the current level of interest rates. In the presence of this term, the variance will tend to become larger as interest rates become higher, a tendency which has been demonstrated empirically.

The *expected* change in interest rates today is assumed to be given by the following expression:

$$E(r_t - r_{t-1}) = a(\bar{r} - r_{t-1})$$

In this expression $\bar{r}$ is the long-run average level of interest rates. It is assumed that when interest rates are below their long-run level, they will be expected to return to it (the expected change in rates will be positive). The strength of the expected propensity to return is given by the coefficient a.

Based on this assumed process for interest rate changes over time, CIR develop an alternative duration measure. In employing the measure, you have to estimate values for $\bar{r}$, σ, and the coefficient a. These are simultaneously estimated using sampling procedures using a past series of daily interest rates on short-term treasury bills. The CIR duration measure is quite complex. A complete description can be found in their article which introduces the measure.

We can say that two portfolios, which are not cash matched, will experience the same change in value if they have identical CIR duration and if interest rates change according to the process described in Equation (14.1). This means, that initially the numbers in the matrix of Figure 12.8 must reflect the expected propensity for interest rates to revert to the long-run expected level of r in future periods. The change in the one-period rate must correspond to Equation (14.1), and after the change, the numbers in the rest of the matrix must again reflect the assumed propensity for rates to revert to the long-run expected level in the future.

Of the three duration measures Macaulay's is clearly the most simple, and as we shall see, it is at least as effective as any of the three. Moreover, it is the measure most commonly employed in practice. Consequently, we will concentrate on it in learning how to immunize a stream of liabilities.[1]

IMMUNIZING WITH MACAULAY'S DURATION: THE CASE OF A SINGLE-PAYMENT LIABILITY

Suppose you have a liability where you must make a single payment of $1931.00 in 10 years. The rate of interest is currently 10 percent, and the term structure is flat. The present value of the liability is $745.00, as given by

[1]There are other measures of duration that are consistent with still other forms of interest rate changes. See, for example, Brennan and Schwartz (1983) and Khang (1979).

$$\text{Present value of liability} = \frac{\$1931.00}{(1 + Y)^{10}} \qquad (14.2)$$

$$\$745.00 = \frac{\$1931.00}{1.10^{10}} \qquad (14.3a)$$

Thus, you must invest $745.00 now to accumulate enough cash to pay off the liability in 10 years. If interest rates remain at 10 percent, you will have enough cash to pay it off no matter what kind of bond you invest in now as long as it is default-free. However, unless you immunize, if interest rates should change between now and the time the liability is due, you may not have enough to pay the bill.

Since it is a single payment, the liability has a Macaulay duration equal to its maturity, 10 years. To immunize you must invest in a bond that also has a duration of 10 years. At a 10 percent interest rate, a 20-year bond carrying a $70.00 annual interest payment has a current market value of $745.00 and a duration of 10 years. That is,

$$\$745 = \frac{\$70.00}{1.10^1} + \frac{\$70.00}{1.10^2} + \cdots + \frac{\$70.00 + \$1000.00}{1.10^{20}} \qquad (14.3b)$$

$$10 = 1 \times \frac{\$70.00/1.10^1}{\$745.00} + 2 \times \frac{\$70.00/1.10^2}{\$745.00} + \cdots$$

$$+ 20 \times \frac{(\$70.00 + \$1000.00)/1.10^{20}}{\$745.00}$$

The Effect of Interest Rate Changes on Present Values

If you invest in the bond represented by Equation (14.3b), you are immunized against a change in interest rates. To understand this, consider what happens to the present value of your required payment and the market value of the bond [as determined by substituting different interest rates into Equations (14.3a) and (14.3b)] if interest rates either go up or down. The present value of the liability and the market value of the bond are given in the following table:

Interest Rate (Y)	Bond Value	Liability Value	
4%	$1409	$1305	
6	1115	1078	
8	902	895	
10	745	745	Present levels
12	627	622	
14	536	521	
16	466	438	

Note that at the current interest rate of 10 percent, the liability and the bond have the same value. However, if interest rates should either rise or fall, the value of the bond becomes larger than the value of the liability. This means you have more funds invested in your bond portfolio than you need in order to pay off the liability at each interest rate.[2]

The Effect of Interest Rate Changes on Terminal Values

Moving from present values to terminal values, consider how much your bond investment will be worth in 10 years when you have to pay off the liability. Table 14.1 shows the total value of your bond investment at the end of the tenth year under three assumed scenarios for interest rates. The first set of numbers assumes interest rates remain constant at 10 percent. If they do, you will be able to invest each interest payment, when received, at 10 percent. The first payment received after 1 year, for example, can be reinvested for 9 years at 10 percent, accumulating to a terminal value of $165 at the end of the tenth year. The second, reinvested for 8 years, accumulates to $150, and so on. The total value of the accumulated interest payments is $1115. In addition to the interest payments, of course, you will have a bond in your portfolio with 10 years remaining until maturity. The market value of the bond at the end of the tenth year is given by the formula at the bottom of the table. At a 10 percent interest rate, the market value is $816. Thus, if you sell the bond and add the proceeds to your accumulated interest, you will have a total of $1931, exactly enough to pay off the liability.

[2] It's important to remember that these calculations assume that the shape of the term structure remains flat at all levels of the interest rate.

TABLE 14.1 Effect of Interest Rate Changes on Terminal Values

	Rates Stay at 10%	Rates Fall to 4%	Rates Rise to 16%
Accumulated value of interest payments received and reinvested at indicated interest rates	$70 × 1.10^9 = $ 165	$70 × 1.04^9 = $100	$70 × 1.16^9 = $ 266
	70 × 1.10^8 = 150	70 × 1.04^8 = 96	70 × 1.16^8 = 229
	70 × 1.10^7 = 136	70 × 1.04^7 = 92	70 × 1.16^7 = 198
	70 × 1.10^6 = 124	70 × 1.04^6 = 89	70 × 1.16^6 = 171
	70 × 1.10^5 = 113	70 × 1.04^5 = 85	70 × 1.16^5 = 147
	70 × 1.10^4 = 102	70 × 1.04^4 = 82	70 × 1.16^4 = 127
	70 × 1.10^3 = 93	70 × 1.04^3 = 79	70 × 1.16^3 = 109
	70 × 1.10^2 = 85	70 × 1.04^2 = 76	70 × 1.16^2 = 94
	70 × 1.10 = 77	70 × 1.04 = 73	70 × 1.16 = 81
	70 × 1 = 70	70 × 1 = 70	70 × 1 = 70
	Total = $1115	Total = $842	Total = $1492
Market value of bond in the 10th year at indicated interest rate	$ 816	$1243	$ 565
Grand total	$1931	$2085	$2057
Less required payment	$1931	$1931	$1931
Surplus	0	$ 154	$ 126

$$\text{Market value of bond in 10th year} = \frac{\$70}{1 + Y} + \frac{\$70}{(1 + Y)^2} + \cdots + \frac{\$70}{(1 + Y)^{10}} + \frac{\$1000}{(1 + Y)^{10}}$$

Now suppose instead of remaining constant, interest rates fall in the first year to 4 percent and remain at that level through the tenth year. In this case, something good and something bad happens. You're happy because the bond is worth more in the tenth year than before ($1243). It's worth more because interest rates are lower and consequently market values are higher. On the other hand, you're sad because the annual interest payments must be reinvested at a lower rate, and they accumulate to only $842. However, when you net out the good and bad, you find you have more money than needed to make the payment. You have $154 remaining.

The same thing happens if interest rates rise to 16 percent, instead of fall. You're happy because the annual interest payments can be reinvested at the higher 16 percent rate, accumulating to a sum of $1492. On the other hand, you're sad because at the higher interest rate, the market value of your bond in the tenth year is *lower,* only $565. Again, however, when you net the good and the bad, you find you have more money than you need to make the payment. You now have $126 remaining. You're protected against a swing in rates in either direction.

You may be thinking, "This works if interest rates rise or fall in the first year and then stay there, but what if rates go down to 4 percent, stay there until the tenth year, and then rise to 16 percent just before you have to sell the bond. If this happens you're sad twice, and you lose!"

If you lost, you lost because you didn't stay immunized. When interest rates fell, the duration of your bond became longer. Remember, duration is the weighted average maturity of the stream of payments, where you are weighting by the relative contribution of each payment to the total present value. When interest rates fall, the present values of all the individual payments go up. However, the present values of the more distant payments go up by a greater percentage amount than do the present values of the payments coming soon. This means the fraction of the total present value accounted for by the distant payments increases. Given this, the weighted average maturity becomes longer and so does the duration.

While the duration of the bond became longer, the duration of the liability remained at 10 years because the liability consists of a single payment. Thus, its duration is always equal to its maturity, irrespective of the level of interest rates.

At 10 percent interest, your durations were matched. At 4 percent interest, the duration of your bond is too long. To remain immunized, you must sell the bond and reinvest the proceeds of sale in another bond that has a duration of 10 years. This means, you have to invest in a bond which has a maturity shorter than 20 years or an annual interest payment greater than $70. Given maturity, bonds with larger annual interest payments have shorter durations because these bonds pay out more money in a shorter time period.

If you reimmunize with each change in interest rates, you can be assured you will have more than enough money to make the payment, provided you are willing to make one assumption. On the days you must reimmunize, in moving from one bond or bond portfolio to another, you must be able to *maintain* the internal yield on your portfolio. That is, the new portfolio you're getting into must have an internal yield to maturity which is at least as large as the current internal yield of the old portfolio you're getting out of. This, of course, will be the case if the term structure is flat, which is the inherent assumption of the Macaulay duration. If the term structure isn't flat, you may have to slide down the term structure to a portfolio with a lower yield. If you consistently lose yield when you reimmunize your portfolio, you may run short of money when it comes time to pay the liability.

Fortunately, as we shall see later, it turns out that more often than not, you gain yield, as opposed to lose, upon reimmunization because there are differentials in bond yields caused by taxes and other market imperfections. More often than not, you can put together a portfolio of bonds with the duration you need to be immunized and still maintain, or increase, the internal yield on your portfolio.

COMPUTING THE MACAULAY DURATION AND INTERNAL YIELD OF A BOND PORTFOLIO

The expected return and beta of a stock portfolio are simply weighted averages of the expected returns and betas of the stocks you put in the portfolio because the expected returns for all the stocks are computed with reference to a common horizon interval. In our examples, this interval was usually a month.

In the case of bond investments, each bond has a different maturity date, and you can't simply average up the internal yields to get the internal yield of the portfolio. If you did, you'd be averaging apples and oranges. A 10 percent yield on a 30-year treasury bond isn't comparable to a 20 percent yield on a 30-day treasury bill. If you invested half your money in each, the yield on your portfolio wouldn't be 15 percent.

To understand this, consider two pure discount bonds, both of which pay no interest until maturity. Bond A pays $1100 and matures in 1 year. Bond B pays $1407 and matures in 7 years. Both bonds are selling for the same market price, $1000.

The yields on each portfolio can be computed as

$$Y_A = 10\% = \frac{\$1100}{\$1000} - 1.00$$

$$Y_B = 5\% = \left(\frac{\$1407}{\$1000}\right)^{1/7} - 1.00$$

Suppose you bought both bonds, investing half your money in each bond. Would the yield on your portfolio be 7.5 percent, the weighted average of the two yields?

The cash flows for your portfolio are pictured in Figure 14.2. You have an immediate outflow of $2000 associated with buying the bonds. Then you get two positive cash flows, $1100 from bond A at the end of the first year and $1407 from bond B at the end of the seventh year. What is the internal rate of return to this portfolio?

The internal rate of return is the rate of discount which will discount the stream

Cash inflows and outflows:

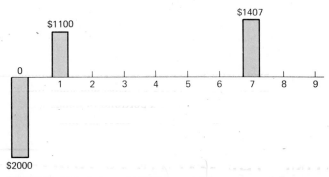

FIGURE 14.2 Internal yields cannot be averaged.

of payments associated with the portfolio to a present value equal to its market value. In the case of this portfolio, the internal yield is 5.634 percent:

$$\$2000.00 = \frac{\$1100.00}{1.05634} + \frac{\$1407.00}{1.05634^7}$$

Pure discount bonds (paying no coupons):

	Face payment	Maturity	Market Value	Yield
Bond A	1100	1 yr	1000	10%
Bond B	1407	7 yr	1000	5%

To compute the internal yield to a portfolio, you must first set forth the cash flows associated with investing in the portfolio and then find the rate of discount which will equate the present value of the cash flows to the market value of the portfolio. In Figure 14.3 we have the cash flows associated with a 2-year bond paying a $100 coupon and a 4-year bond paying a $200 coupon. The cash flows associated with a portfolio of the two bonds are depicted in the lower portion of the figure. In the first year you receive $300 worth of interest payments. In the second year you receive $300 in interest plus $1000 in principal. In the third year you receive $200 in interest and finally in the fourth year $1200 in interest and principal. Once the cash flows have been set forth, it is an easy matter for a computer to calculate the portfolio's internal yield.

Once you have an internal yield, you can then compute the Macaulay duration, weighting the maturity of each payment by the fraction of the portfolio's total value accounted for by the present value of the payment given the internal yield.

You should remember from Chapter 13 that neither the internal yield nor the

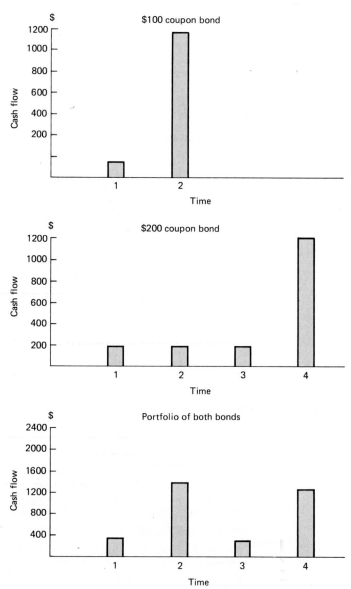

FIGURE 14.3 Cash flows associated with two bonds and a portfolio.

Macaulay duration can be found by taking a simple weighted average of the components in the bond portfolio. This is a mistake commonly made by bond portfolio managers in the real world. They nearly all use internal yields on individual bonds, and quite often you will find them averaging internal yields and durations to obtain portfolio yields and durations.

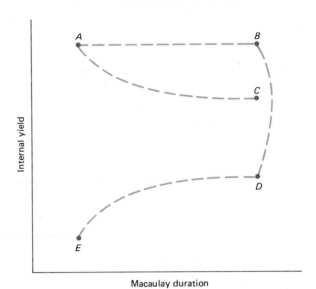

FIGURE 14.4 How bonds combine into portfolios.

Combination Lines for Internal Yield and Duration

Figure 14.4 shows the combination lines relating internal yield to duration for portfolios of five different bonds. Note that the combination line is concave when the bond with the shorter duration has the lower internal yield, as with the case of combining bonds E and D. The combination line is convex when the bond with the shorter duration has the higher yield, as with A and C. Sometimes it is the case that when you combine two bonds with the same duration but with different yields, the duration of the portfolio may be longer than that of either bond, as with bonds B and D. Only when the bonds have the same yield, as with A and B, do both duration and internal yield combine as a weighted average.

IMMUNIZING WITH THE MACAULAY DURATION: THE CASE OF A MULTIPLE-PAYMENT LIABILITY

Suppose you are managing a pension fund, and you face the stream of required cash payments that is depicted in Figure 14.5. The Macaulay duration of this stream depends on the rate of interest used to compute its present value. The higher the rate of interest, the lower the duration because with higher rates the more distant payments account for a smaller fraction of the total present value. Thus, as depicted in Figure 14.6, at an interest rate of 10 percent the duration might be 7 years, and at an interest rate of 4 percent, the duration might be as high as 10 years. The curve drawn in Figure 14.6 is called the immunization curve. It shows the duration of this

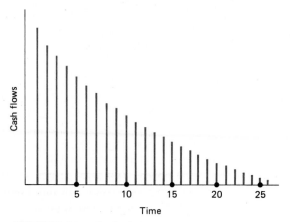

FIGURE 14.5 Cash flows associated with liability.

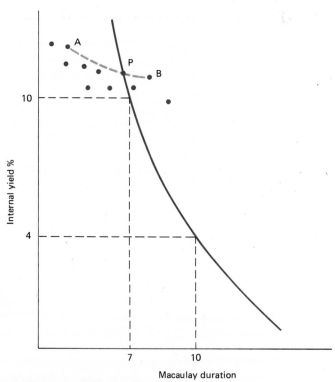

FIGURE 14.6 Immunizing with a multiple-payment liability.

particular stream of liabilities at various values for the interest rate. Each stream of liabilities has its own associated immunization curve.

To immunize your portfolio, you need to take a position on the immunization curve. In the case of Figure 14.6, if you invest in a bond with an internal yield of 10 percent and a duration of 7 years, you are immunized. You are also immunized if you invest in a bond with a 4 percent yield and a 10-year duration. Naturally, the present value of the liabilities is smaller at 10 percent than it is at 5 percent, so you would prefer 10 percent because you have to invest less.

As portfolio manager, your objective is to climb as high on the immunization curve as you can. The scattered points plotted in Figure 14.6 represent the positions of individual bonds. You want to find the portfolio of bonds which will put you as high on the curve as possible. In this example, you can achieve this by combining bonds A and B into a portfolio at point P.

Finding the highest-yielding immunized portfolio must be done through a process of trial and error by a computer. Immunizing a single-payment liability can be done in the same way. The immunization curve for a single-payment liability is, of course, a vertical line at a duration equal to the maturity of the liability.

A TEST OF THE RELATIVE EFFECTIVENESS OF THE THREE DURATION MEASURES

A test of the effectiveness of the Macaulay, Fisher-Weil, and Cox-Ingersoll-Ross duration measures has been completed by Patrick Lau (1983). Lau looks at the time period January 1955 through December 1979. He assumes that you face a single-payment liability of $1 million due in 8 years. You are allowed to invest in treasury bonds of various maturities. He begins his first experiment in January 1955. In this month, he combines the two highest-yielding bonds on either side of the immunization curve (a vertical line at an 8-year duration) into a portfolio with an 8-year Macaulay duration. He then computes the present value of $1 million at the yield of the portfolio and invests this amount in the portfolio. The market value of the portfolio is, thus, initially equal to the present value of the liability.

At the beginning of February 1955, he again finds the two highest-yielding bonds on either side of the immunization curve, and he reimmunizes the portfolio. At the new portfolio yield, the market value of the portfolio may now be different from the present value of the liabilities. In any case, the process is continued through December 1963. At this point, he compares the market value of the portfolio with the required payment for the liability ($1 million).

The differences between the market value of the portfolio and the present value of the liability for each of the months between January 1955 and December 1963 are plotted in Figure 14.7. At the end of the 8-year period, you obviously have more money than is necessary to meet the payment.

Lau now repeats the experiment, this time beginning the whole process in February 1955. He keeps repeating until the end of his horizon date coincides with the

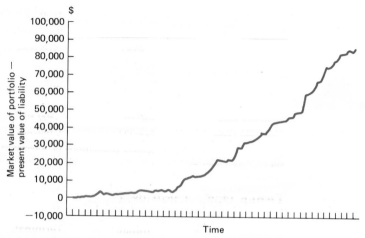

FIGURE 14.7 Difference between portfolio value and liability value through time.

last date of his study, December 1979. In all, he conducts 204 overlapping simulation experiments.

Table 14.2A shows the results for all the experiments. The first and second columns indicate the mean values for the beginning and ending values of the portfolio. Surprisingly, in every one of the experiments, the ending portfolio value exceeds the value of the liability payment ($1 million). The third and fourth columns show the result in terms of the expected internal yield to maturity on the initial portfolio and the actual realized yield over the course of each experiment. Note that, on average, the realized yield is higher than the expected yield by approximately 1.33 percentage points.

Lau also conducts his experiments using Fisher-Weil and Cox-Ingersoll-Ross durations. The FW duration measure requires estimates of future one-period interest rates. Lau extracts these estimates from the term structure. At the beginning of each month, he fits the term structure using Equation (12.1). He then computes the future one-period rates using the methodology described at the end of Chapter 12. He again immunizes by building a portfolio of the highest-yielding bonds on either side of the

TABLE 14.2A   Macaulay Strategy Results
(Investment Horizon = 8 Years)

	Initial Investment Value ($)	Terminal Investment Value ($)	Realized Rate of Return (%)	Expected Rate of Return (%)
Mean	703,420	1,106,600	5.90	4.57
Standard deviation	69,073	43,490	1.67	1.34
Minimum value	536,240	1,038,000	3.41	2.46
Maximum value	823,030	1,220,400	9.59	8.10

SOURCE: W. P. Lau, "An Empirical Examination of Alternative Interest Rate Immunization Strategies," unpublished Ph.D. dissertation (Madison: University of Wisconsin, 1983).

TABLE 14.2B Fisher and Weil Strategy Results
(Investment Horizon = 8 Years)

	Initial Investment Value ($)	Terminal Investment Value ($)	Realized Rate of Return (%)	Expected Rate of Return (%)
Mean	701,770	1,008,100	4.71	4.61
Standard deviation	72,655	37,477	1.34	1.44
Minimum value	496,697	800,806	2.49	2.53
Maximum value	818,955	1,103,900	7.94	9.14

SOURCE: W. P. Lau, ''An Empirical Examination of Alternative Interest Rate Immunization Strategies,'' unpublished Ph.D. dissertation (Madison: University of Wisconsin, 1983).

TABLE 14.2C CIR (Cox, Ingersoll, and Ross) Strategy Results
(Investment Horizon = 8 Years)

	Initial Investment Value ($)	Terminal Investment Value (%)	Realized Rate of Return (%)	Expected Rate of Return (%)
Mean	703,360	1,092,400	5.73	4.57
Standard deviation	69,119	46,301	1.66	1.34
Minimum value	536,240	1,025,200	3.25	2.46
Maximum value	823,030	1,208,400	9.36	8.10

SOURCE: W. P. Lau, ''An Empirical Examination of Alternative Interest Rate Immunization Strategies,'' unpublished Ph.D. dissertation (Madison: University of Wisconsin, 1983).

immunization curve and reimmunizes monthly as with the Macaulay duration experiments. The results are presented in Table 14.2B. The performance of the FW duration is inferior to that of the Macaulay measure.

The CIR duration measure requires estimates of a, σ, and $\bar{r}$ in Equation (14.1). Lau estimates these parameters simultaneously using a maximum likelihood procedure. He estimates each of the parameters in each of the months of the study using a 1-month treasury bill rate as r. For each set of estimates, he uses the previous 60 months as data. The performance of the CIR duration measure is given in Table 14.2C. As indicated, the performance of CIR duration seems comparable to that of Macaulay. In light of its relative simplicity, Macaulay duration seems to be the preferable alternative.[3]

SUMMARY

A portfolio is immunized if it is devoid of interest rate risk. Investors who interest immunize seek a guaranteed return over their horizon interval. One way to accomplish this is to cash match, that is, invest in a pure discount bond (or bonds) that

[3]Immunization using the techniques described in this book have been consistently employed over the past 10 years by National Investment Services of America, Milwaukee, WI. In more than thirty applications, they have never missed a target.

matures at your horizon point (or points). The disadvantage of cash matching is that you are constrained to invest in bonds that might otherwise be unattractive to you, given your tax status. If you immunize using some measure of duration, on the other hand, you can invest in one or two of the bonds that are the most attractive to you in terms of after-tax return.

The three duration measures discussed in this chapter are Macaulay, Fisher-Weil, and Cox-Ingersoll-Ross. The Macaulay and Fisher-Weil durations are approximately equal to the negative of the elasticity of the value of a stream of payments (or receipts) with respect to a change in one plus the internal yield and geometric yield, respectively. Two portfolios (say, a portfolio of investments and a portfolio of liabilities) that are not cash matched but have the same durations will respond equally to small changes in interest rates if these changes take certain forms. If the portfolios have the same Macaulay duration, they will respond identically if the change in rates takes the form of a parallel shift in a flat term structure. If they have the same Fisher-Weil duration, they will respond identically if the change takes the form of a shift in the term structure of any shape, where the ending shape of the term structure is identical to the beginning shape. If they have the same Cox-Ingersoll-Ross duration, they will respond identically if the change in rates is consistent with a process where the interest rate has a propensity to revert to some long-run mean level and where interest rates also have a propensity to increase in variability as the level of rates go up.

To immunize, you construct your portfolio of bonds such that its duration is equal to the duration of your liabilities. You must reimmunize with each change in interest rates, because as interest rates change, durations change as well. In immunizing with the Macaulay duration, you can be assured of meeting your required payments if when you reimmunize from one portfolio to another, the new portfolio has an internal yield at least as large as the yield of the old portfolio.

In comparing the performance of the three duration measures, the Macaulay and Cox-Ingersoll-Ross duration measures appear to perform the best. In view of its relative simplicity, the Macaulay duration seems to be preferable.

QUESTION SET 1

1. a. What does it mean to adopt a cash-matching management strategy?
   b. What is the objective of a cash-matching management strategy?
2. Assume the following characteristics for a particular bond:

$$\text{Face value} = \$1000$$

$$\text{Annual coupon payment} = \$60 \quad \text{(first payment due in 1 year)}$$

$$\text{Internal yield to maturity} = 7\%$$

$$\text{Term} = 3 \text{ years}$$

   a. Compute the Macaulay duration of the bond.

b. Given your answer to (a), compute the approximate change in the bond's value if the internal yield fell to 6.5 percent. (You should use the duration in (a) for this computation.)

c. Now compute the actual change in the bond's value.

d. Suppose the yield curve was flat at an interest rate of 7 percent. How would Fisher-Weil duration compare with the Macaulay duration computed in (a)?

3. Compute the Fisher-Weil duration of the following payment stream:

Year		
1	2	3
$1000	$1200	$2000

Assume that the following are the current and expected 1-year yields you have already derived:

	Yield
Now	6.0%
1 year from now	6.5
2 years from now	7.0

4. Indicate how you would compute the Fisher-Weil duration of a single-payment liability due 3 years from now? Would this differ from the Macaulay duration?

5. Consider a pure discount bond (no coupon payments) with a maturity of 4 years. The current internal yield to maturity is 9 percent. If the internal yield suddenly changes to 8.5 percent, how would the Macaulay duration respond to such a change?

6. You are faced with a liability requiring payment of $2000 1 year from now and $2000 2 years from now. You can invest in bonds with internal yields to maturity of 9 percent.

a. Compute the Macaulay duration of this liability.

b. Suppose the yield suddenly changes to 10 percent. Use the duration computed in (a) to approximate the dollar change in the present value of the liability.

7. What is immunization intended to accomplish? What is meant by the term reimmunization?

8. Explain the elasticity interpretation of Macaulay duration.

9. Suppose we have matched the maturity and present value of a single-payment liability with the same characteristics of a coupon bond. When we make the match, the yield curve is flat at 7 percent. Immediately after making the match, the yield curve shifts to 8 percent (still flat).

a. What would be the result of such a change?

b. Was the strategy appropriate to help you achieve an immunized position?

10. Assume that although the level of interest rates may change, the yield curve remains flat. You attempt to immunize at the beginning of some time horizon by matching the value and Macaulay duration of a single-payment liability with the value and Macaulay duration of a bond portfolio. Will this match at the beginning of the horizon to be sufficient to keep your portfolio immunized as time passes?

11. Suppose you purchase one of each of the following bonds:

	Annual Coupon	Face Value	Internal Yield	Year to Maturity
Bond 1	$85	$1000	10%	2
Bond 2	0	$1000	9%	1

  a. Compute the internal yield of the portfolio of bonds.
  b. Show how you would proceed to get the Macaulay duration of this portfolio.

12. The following are values for the indicated internal yields on a particular bond:

Present Value	Internal Yield (Y)
$979	8.0%
$950	9.0%

Compute the arc elasticity of the bond's value with respect to $1 + Y$. Define the term *arc elasticity*.

13. Suppose you put together the following portfolio:
  a. Purchase one pure discount bond (no coupons) with a 20-year maturity. Face value to be received at maturity is $1000.
  b. Sell short 1.92 pure discount bonds having 5 years until maturity. Face value at maturity is $1000. Assume your short sale allows you the full use of the proceeds.
  c. Invest $1127.49 in very short-term bonds (zero duration).

  Assume the internal yield on all issues is 5 percent to start.
  a. How much of your own money was required to put this portfolio together?
  b. Compute the Macaulay duration of the assets in the portfolio and then of the liability.
  c. Suppose that the internal yield on all maturities rises to 6 percent. What is the value of the portfolio (asset value less liability value)?
  d. Suppose that the internal yield on all maturities falls to 4 percent. What is the value of the portfolio (asset value less liability value)?

QUESTION SET 2

1. What is meant by cash matching? Why is this not the most preferable method for immunization?
2. What does duration measure?
3. What does immunization mean?
4. As a portfolio manager, you have a portfolio with one liability of a single payment 5 years from now of $7500 and five bonds which mature 10 years from now at par ($1000 each) with annual interest payments of $100 each. Assuming that the bonds sold at par, and the nominal interest rate remains at about 10 percent, you should be able to make the balloon payment with the interest on the bonds for 5 years ($500 × 5 = $2500, not including the

interest from reinvesting the interest) plus redeeming the bonds ($1000 $\times$ 5 = $5000). Your calculations are simple, and you sleep in blissful ignorance. What is the fallacy in this calculation?

5. If interest rates fall, what happens to the present values of individual payments? To the duration? To remain immunized, what action must be taken?

6. Why would you prefer a position on the immunization curve which has a shorter duration?

ANSWERS TO QUESTION SET 2

1. Cash matching is the process of matching up a stream of cash flows so that it exactly matches a stream of liabilities. It has the major disadvantage that you must invest in many different bonds, some of which may be unattractive to you for tax or other reasons.

2. Duration measures the average length of time you have to wait to receive the cash receipts for an investment. It also measures the sensitivity of the values of the investment to changes in interest rates.

3. Immunization is the process through which a portfolio is constructed so as to reduce its interest rate risk to zero. It does this through constructing portfolios of liabilities and receipts in such a way so that the value of the two portfolios respond, as identically as possible, to changes in interest rates.

4. You have not taken into account what will happen if interest rates rise. If this happens, the value of the 10-year bond 5 years into its term will drop significantly below its par value of $1000, and thus you will find yourself short of the money to pay the $7500 liability. How short you will be depends on how much the interest rates rise. For example, if interest rates rise to 20 percent, you could easily lose a substantial fraction of the bond price.

5. If interest rates fall, the present value of all the individual payments go up, but the present values of the more distant payments go up by a greater percentage amount than do the present value of the payments coming soon. Hence, the fraction of the total present value accounted for by the distant payment increases. The weighted average maturity thus becomes longer and so does the duration. To remain immunized, the duration of the bond must equal the duration of the liability. Hence the bond must be sold and the proceeds reinvested in another bond with the same duration as the weighted average maturity.

6. Higher yielding positions on the immunization curve are associated with lower durations. Since the present value of liabilities at a higher rate of return is less, at the higher yield you have to invest less in order to meet them.

PROBLEM SET

1. Assume you have a liability with three required payments:
   $3000 due in 1 year
   $2000 due in 2 years
   $1000 due in 3 years
   a. What is the Macaulay duration of this liability at a 20 percent rate of interest?
   b. At a 5 percent rate of interest?

2. Assume the internal yields to maturity for current coupon bonds selling at market prices equal to their face values of $1000 are 10 percent and 14 percent for 1- and 2-year issues, respectively.

a. Compute the Macaulay and Fisher-Weil durations for the 1- and 2-year bonds assuming the market expectations theory for the term structure.

b. Account for the difference in the two duration numbers.

3. You invest in zero coupon bonds. One matures in 1 year paying $100. Its price is $56.93. The other matures in 2 years paying $1100. Its price is $943.07.

a. Compute the yield on each bond.

b. Compute the duration for each bond.

c. Compute the weighted average yield for the portfolio of the two bonds.

d. Compute the weighted average duration for the portfolio of the two bonds.

e. Compute the true yield on the portfolio of the two bonds.

f. Compute the true duration of the portfolio of the two bonds.

ANSWERS TO PROBLEM SET

1. a. Present value of the liability at 20 percent:

$$\$4467.59 = \frac{\$3000}{1.20} + \frac{\$2000}{(1.20)^2} + \frac{\$1000}{(1.20)^3}$$

Macaulay duration of liability at 20 percent:

$$D_1 = 1 \times \frac{\$3000/1.20}{\$4467.59} + 2 \times \frac{\$2000/(1.20)^2}{\$4467.59} + 3 \times \frac{\$1000/(1.20)^3}{\$4467.59}$$

$$= (1 \times .5596) + (2 \times .3109) + (3 \times .1295)$$

$$= 1.57 \text{ years}$$

b. Present value of the liability at 5 percent:

$$\$5535.04 = \frac{\$3000}{1.05} + \frac{\$2000}{(1.05)^2} + \frac{\$1000}{(1.50)^3}$$

Macaulay duration of liability at 5 percent:

$$D_1 = 1 \times \frac{\$3000/1.05}{\$5535.04} + 2 \times \frac{\$2000/(1.05)^2}{\$5535.04} + 3 \times \frac{\$1000/(1.05)^3}{\$5535.04}$$

$$= (1 \times .5162) + (2 \times .3277) + (3 \times .1561)$$

$$= 1.64 \text{ years}$$

2. One-year bond: Assuming interest paid annually at the end of the year, the Macaulay and Fisher-Weil durations are both equal to 1.00 years.

Two-year bond: First, compute the expected one-year rates for the next year. Since the two-year bond is selling at a market price equal to $1000, its annual interest payment must be $140.

$$\$1000 = \frac{\$140}{1.14} + \frac{\$1140}{(1.14)^2}$$

Allowing for changes in rates and assuming no liquidity premiums;

$$\$1000 = \frac{\$140}{1.10} + \frac{\$1140}{1.10(1 + r_2)}$$

$$r_2 = 18.75\%$$

We can now compute the Fisher-Weil duration as

$$D_2 = 1 \times \frac{140/1.10}{1000} + 2 \times \frac{1140/(1.10)(1.1875)}{1000}$$

$$= (1 \times .1273) + (2 \times .8727)$$

$$= 1.8727$$

The Macaulay duration is computed as:

$$D_1 = 1 \times \frac{140/1.14}{1000} + 2 \times \frac{1140/(1.14)^2}{1000}$$

$$= (1 \times .1228) + (2 \times .8772)$$

$$= 1.8772$$

The Macaulay duration is larger because with rising expected interest rates, the Fisher-Weil duration formula applies higher discount factors to more distant payments.

3. a. Yield on 1-year bond:

$$\frac{\$100}{\$56.93} - 1 = 75.65\%$$

Yield on a 2-year bond:

$$\left(\frac{\$1100}{\$943.07}\right)^{1/2} - 1 = 8.00\%$$

b. Duration for 1-year bond: 1 year (single payment)
Duration for 2-year bond: 2 years (single payment)

c. Weighted average yield for the portfolio:
Total portfolio value = $56.93 + $943.07 = $1000.00

$$75.66\% \times \frac{56.93}{1000.00} + 8.00\% \times \frac{943.07}{1000.00} = 11.85\%$$

d. Weighted average duration for portfolio:

$$1 \times \frac{56.93}{1000.00} + 2 \times \frac{943.07}{1000.00} = 1.943 \text{ years}$$

e. True internal yield for portfolio is 10 percent.

$$\$1000 = \frac{\$100}{1.10} + \frac{\$1100}{(1.10)^2}$$

f. True Macaulay duration for portfolio is

$$1 \times \frac{100/1.10}{1000} + 2 \times \frac{1100/(1.10)^2}{1000} = .090909 + (2 \times .90909) = 1.909$$

COMPUTER PROBLEM SET

Refer to the following information for Problems 1 through 3.

Bond No.	Coupon Rate	Maturity Date	Asked Price 11/15/85	Asked Price 2/14/86
1	8¼	May 1988	99.13	100.27
2	8¾	Nov. 1988	100.8	101.30
3	9¼	May 1989	101.2	103.18
4	10¾	Nov. 1989	105.2	107.19
5	8¼	May 1990	99.9	102.14

1. Today's date is November 15, 1985. Suppose you are faced with a liability requiring payment of $10,000 exactly three years from now. Construct an immunized portfolio consisting of one or more of the bonds listed using the immunization program. How much must you invest today to make the required payments three years from now?

2. Three months have passed. Today's date is February 14, 1986. Is your portfolio still immunized?

3. If your answer to Problem 2 was "no," reimmunize your portfolio. What is the net value of your portion (present value of assets less present value of liabilities)?

4. Consider the following three riskless bonds, 1, 2, and 3. Each carries an annual coupon payment of $40. The maturity dates and market prices of the bonds are as follows:

	Maturity Date	Market Price
Bond 1	Jan. 1, 1992	$704
Bond 2	Jan. 1, 2005	415
Bond 3	Jan. 1, 2050	333

Each bond carries approximately the same yield to maturity (12 percent). Therefore, the bonds are identical save for their respective maturities. Assume the current date is January 1, 1987.

a. Compute the duration of each bond. You may use the computer program "Duration on Bonds and Bond Portfolios."

b. How do you explain the relative durations for the bonds?

c. Would the relative order (in terms of duration) change if the yields for the bonds were increased or decreased? If so, how?

REFERENCES

BIERWAG, G. O., "Immunization, Duration and the Term Structure of Interest Rates," *Journal of Financial and Quantitative Analysis* (December 1977).

BIERWAG, G. O., and KAUFMAN, G., "Coping with the Risk of Interest Rate Fluctuations: A Note," *Journal of Business* (July 1977).

BRENNAN, M. J., and SCHWARTZ, E. S., "Duration, Bond Pricing and Portfolio Management," in G. KAUFMAN, ed. *Innovations in Bond Portfolio Management: Duration Analysis and Immunization.* Greenwich, Conn.: JAI Press, 1983.

COOPER, I., "Asset Values, Interest Rate Changes and Duration," *Journal of Financial and Quantitative Analysis* (December 1977).

COX, J. C., INGERSOLL, J. E., and ROSS, S., "Duration and the Measurement of Basis Risk," *Journal of Business* (January 1979).

FISHER, I., and WEIL, R. L., "Coping with the Risk of Interest Rate Fluctuations," *Journal of Business* (January 1971).

INGERSOLL, J. E., SKELTON, J., and WEIL, R. L., "Duration Forty Years Later," *Journal of Financial and Quantitative Analysis* (November 1978).

KHANG, C., "Bond Immunization When Short-Term Rates Fluctuate More than Long-Term Rates," *Journal of Financial and Quantitative Analysis* (December 1979).

LAU, P. W. P., "An Empirical Examination of Alternative Interest Rate Risk Immunization Strategies," unpublished Ph.D. dissertation, University of Wisconsin, Madison, 1983.

MACAULAY, F. R., *Some Theoretical Problems Suggested by the Movements of Interest Rates, Bond Yields, and Stock Prices in the United States Since 1856.* New York: National Bureau of Economic Research, 1983.

REDINGTON, F. M., "Review of the Principles of Life-Office Valuations," *Journal of the Institute of Actuaries,* No. 3 (1952).

15

EUROPEAN OPTION PRICING

A stock call option is a contract giving its owner the right to buy shares of a stock at a stated *exercise price* on (and sometimes before) a stated *expiration date*. A put option is basically the same thing, but it gives its owner the right to *sell* the shares of stock at the exercise price. These contracts are truly *options* in the sense that they do not obligate you to buy or sell. You *may* transact at the stated prices if it's in your interest to. It *is* in your interest to exercise a call option if, at expiration, the market price of the stock is greater than the exercise price in the option contract. It's in your interest to exercise a put option if the market price is below the exercise price at expiration.

There are two types of call and put options. *European options* give their owners the right to exercise only on the expiration date. *American options* give their owners the right to exercise at any time on or before the expiration date.

An understanding of option pricing is extremely important. This is true because options can be used in many imaginative ways to create many attractive investment opportunities. In addition, as we shall learn in Chapter 17, securities that are commonly observed such as callable bonds can be viewed in principle as portfolios of options. In this sense options are the building blocks of many financial securities, and an understanding of the pricing of options is vital to an understanding of the pricing of nearly all securities.

In this chapter, we will learn how to estimate the value of European options and how their prices behave in relation to the prices of the assets they are written on. In the next chapter, we will learn how to estimate the value of American options. Then, in Chapter 17, we will talk about some issues in option pricing and the development of investment strategies employing options.

Our discussion of the pricing of European options proceeds in three stages. In each stage, the assumptions we make become progressively more realistic. First, we will assume investors are risk neutral and there is an equal probability of getting any stock value between two extremes at the expiration date. In this setting it is very easy to value an option. You can also get an intuitive feel for the basis of option pricing and the behavior of option prices relative to stock prices. In the second stage, we will admit risk-averse investors into the market but assume there are only two possible prices for the stock at the expiration date. In this setting, it is easy to understand the important principle that an option must be priced so that if you use it to construct a risk-free investment strategy, you earn the risk-free rate of return on your investment. We then take this important principle to the final stage where we make the more realistic assumption that rates of return on the stock are normally distributed, and we value options under the Black-Scholes option pricing framework.

PRICING OPTIONS UNDER RISK NEUTRALITY AND UNIFORM PROBABILITY DISTRIBUTIONS

Valuing a Call Option

Consider a European call option written on a stock that pays no dividends and that expires at the end of one year. The probability distribution for the value of the stock at the end of the year is given in Figure 15.1. The distribution is assumed to be

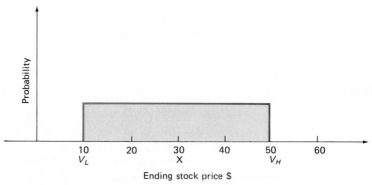

FIGURE 15.1 Probability distribution for stock.

shaped like a rectangle, with equal probabilities for all stock values between an extreme low value, V_L (which is $10) and an extreme high value V_H (which is $50).

Under risk neutrality, the market value of the stock at the beginning of the year is equal to its expected value at the end of the year discounted at the risk-free rate r_F. It's easy to compute the expected value for a rectangular, uniform distribution such as that of Figure 15.1. You simply add the extreme high and low values and divide by 2. Thus, if we assume the risk-free rate is 10 percent, the current market price for the stock is given by

$$V_{S,0} = \frac{E(V_{S,1})}{1 + r_F} = \frac{(V_L + V_H)/2}{1 + r_F} \tag{15.1}$$

The market value for the stock is therefore $27.27:

$$\frac{(\$10 + \$50)/2}{1.10} = \$27.27$$

The current market value for the call option is also equal to its expected value at the end of the year discounted at the risk-free rate. If the exercise price for the call option is X, the value of the call at the end of the year is equal to

$$V_{S,1} - X \qquad \text{or} \qquad .00$$

whichever is greater. Remember, we are dealing with an option, so if the ending stock price is less than the exercise price, you can always throw the contract away. You don't have to exercise it.

The probability distribution for the ending value of the call option is given in Figure 15.2. We have assumed in drawing the figure that the exercise price is $30. Given this, if the year-end stock price is less than $30, the option will be worthless. In Figure 15.1, we see that half the rectangle for the stock lies to the left of a $30 stock price. This means the probability that the call option will be worthless at the end of the year is equal to .5. This probability is represented by the spike in Figure

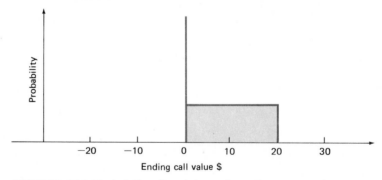

FIGURE 15.2 Probability distribution for call option with exercise price = $30.

15.2. It is also the case that the probability the option will be worth $1 is the same as the probability the stock will be worth $31. The probability for a $2 option value is the same as for a $32 stock value and so on. Thus, the probabilities in the part of the rectangle lying to the right of $30 in Figure 15.1 are the same as those lying to the right of the spike in Figure 15.2.

It was very easy to find the expected value of the ending *stock* price. It is only slightly more difficult to find the expected value of the year-end value of the *call option*. To compute the expected value, first calculate the expected value as though 100 percent of the probability was in the rectangle lying to the right of the spike. If this were true, the expected value would be the midpoint of the rectangle, which can be computed as

$$E(V_H - X) = \frac{V_H - X}{2} = \frac{\$50 - \$30}{2} = \$10$$

Next, multiply this *conditional* expected value by the fraction of the total probability that is actually in the rectangle. We know that half the probability is represented by the spike, so the other half is in the rectangle. The fraction of the probability that is in the rectangle can be found by

$$\frac{V_H - X}{V_H - V_L} = \frac{\$20}{\$40} = .50$$

The product of this fraction and the conditional expected value is given by

$$\left[\frac{V_H - X}{2}\right]\left[\frac{V_H - X}{V_H - V_L}\right] = \frac{(V_H - X)^2}{2(V_H - V_L)} = E(V_{C,1}) \qquad (15.2a)$$

Equation (15.2a) gives the expected year-end value for the option when the exercise price is greater than the lowest possible value for the stock. For those cases where the lowest possible value for the stock is greater than the exercise price, the expected year-end value for the option is computed as

$$E(V_{C,1}) = \frac{V_L - X + V_H - X}{2} = \frac{V_L + V_H}{2} - \frac{2X}{2} = E(V_{S,1}) - X \qquad (15.2b)$$

The market value of the CALL option at the beginning of the year is equal to its expected year-end value discounted at the risk-free rate. Employing Equation (15.2a) or (15.2b) when appropriate, we obtain

$$V_{C,0} = \frac{E(V_{C,1})}{1 + r_F}$$

In the case of the probability distributions of Figures 15.1 and 15.2, the market value of the call is $4.55 if the risk-free rate is 10 percent:

$$\$4.55 = \frac{\$5.00}{1.10}$$

Valuing a Put Option

A put option is valued in nearly the same way. The only difference is that a put option takes on value when the year-end value of the stock falls *below* the exercise price. Thus, the year-end value for the put is given by

$$X - V_{S,1} \quad \text{or} \quad .00$$

whichever is greater.

The probability distribution for the value of the put at the end of the year is given in Figure 15.3. Except for the fact that the horizontal axis is reversed, it is identical to the distribution for the value of the call because the exercise price is again assumed to be equal to the expected value of the stock price.

The formula for the expected year-end value for the put is nearly the same as the formula for the year-end expected value for the call. For the case where the highest possible value for the stock is greater than the exercise price, it is given by

$$\frac{X - V_L}{2} \frac{X - V_L}{V_H - V_L} = \frac{(X - V_L)^2}{2(V_H - V_L)} = E(V_{P,1}) \tag{15.4a}$$

If the probability distribution for the stock is given by Figure 15.1 the expected year-end value for the put is

$$\frac{(\$30 - \$10)^2}{2(\$50 - \$10)} = \$5$$

Similar to the call, for the case where the exercise price is greater than the highest possible value for the stock, the expected value for the put is given by

$$E(V_{P,1}) = \frac{X - V_H + X - V_H}{2} = \frac{2X}{2} - \frac{V_L + V_H}{2} = X - E(V_{S,1}) \tag{15.4b}$$

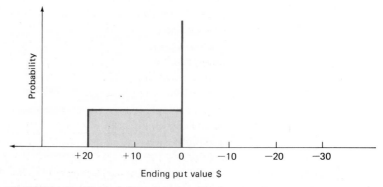

FIGURE 15.3 Probability distribution for put option with exercise price = $30.

The market value for the put at the beginning of the year is thus

$$V_{P,0} = \frac{E(V_{P,1})}{1 + r_F} \tag{15.5}$$

which, for the distribution of Figure 15.1, is equal to

$$\$4.55 = \frac{\$5.00}{1.10}$$

The Relationship Between Option Values and Stock Values

Suppose we change the market value of the stock that the options are written on. The market value will change if we change expectations about possible ending market prices for the stock. Assume the market receives some good news about the stock, causing the probability distribution for ending stock values to shift to the right as in Figure 15.4. The expected value for the stock is now $40,

$$\frac{\$60 + \$20}{2} = \$40$$

and the market value is now $36.36:

$$\frac{\$40.00}{1.10} = \$36.36$$

The change in the probability distribution for the stock induces changes in the probability distributions for the call and the put, as in Figures 15.5 and 15.6. Given the exercise price remains the same at $30, the expected ending value for the call can again be found by first finding the conditional expected value of the rectangular distribution lying to the right of the spike. The midpoint, or expected value of this distribution is $15. To find the expected value, multiply this conditional expected value by .75, which is the fraction of the total probability actually included in the

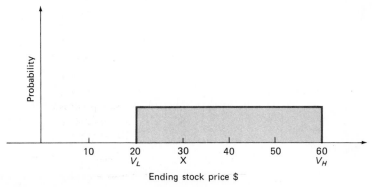

FIGURE 15.4 Probability distribution for stock.

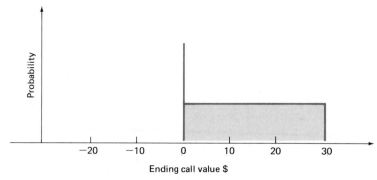

FIGURE 15.5 Probability distribution for call option.

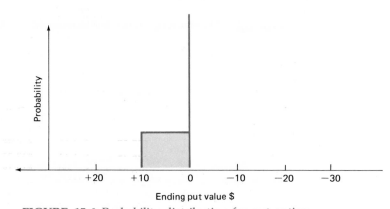

FIGURE 15.6 Probability distribution for put option.

rectangular part of the distribution. The expected ending value for the call is thus $11.25,

$$\$15 \times .75 = \$11.25$$

and the market value of the call is $10.23:

$$\frac{\$11.25}{1.10} = \$10.23$$

The market value of the put is found in the same way. The put takes on value at the end of the year if the value of the stock falls *below* $30. In this case, a contract giving you the right to sell someone a share for $30 is valuable. The probability of the stock being worth $30 or more is .75. This is the probability of the put being worth nothing at the end of the year. The lowest possible value for the stock is now $20. This means the highest possible value for the put is now $10. To find the expected ending value for the put, again find the conditional expected value for the rectangular part of the distribution and multiply it by the fraction of the total probability actually in the rectangle. The conditional expected value, or midpoint of the rectangle, is $5. The fraction of the total probability in the rectangle is .25, so the expected value is $1.25,

$$\$5 \times .25 = \$1.25$$

and the market value is $1.14:

$$\frac{\$1.25}{1.10} = \$1.14$$

Thus, the increase in the price of the stock produces an increase in the price of the call and a decrease in the price of the put.

Other pairs of values for the put and the call can be found by shifting the expected value and market price of the stock to other values. In each case, we change only the midpoint of the rectangle and not the spread between the highest and lowest possible values. Put and call values corresponding to various stock values are given by the following schedule:

	Market Value	
Stock	Put	Call
$18.18	$10.23	$ 1.14
$27.27	$ 4.55	$ 4.55
$36.36	$ 1.14	$10.23
$45.45	$ .00	$18.18
$54.55	$ .00	$27.27
$63.64	$ .00	$36.36

This schedule is graphed for the call and the put in Figures 15.7 and 15.8, respectively. Notice as the stock price increases, the value of the call approaches a line with a slope equal to 1.00 emanating from the present value of the exercise price. The value of the call reaches the line when the distribution shifts to the right to such an extent that the lowest possible stock value V_L exceeds the exercise price of $30.

In Figure 15.8, we see that as the stock price decreases, the value of the put approaches a line with a slope equal to -1.00 emanating from the present value of the exercise price ($27.27). The put reaches the line when the highest possible value of the stock V_H is less than the exercise price.

Based on Figures 15.7 and 15.8, we can draw the following conclusions about the behavior of the options relative to the behavior of the stock:

1. The value of the call increases with the value of the stock, while the value of the put decreases with the value of the stock.
2. Unless the option is certain to be exercised ($V_L > X$ for the call, and $X > V_H$ for the put), the absolute dollar change in the stock value is greater than the accompanying absolute dollar change in the option value.

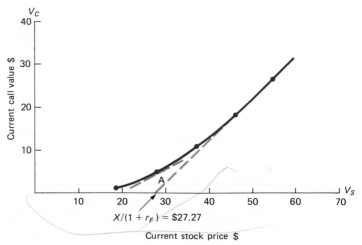

FIGURE 15.7 Relationship between prices for stock and call options.

3. The *difference* between the absolute dollar changes for the stock and for the options becomes smaller as the options move from **out of the money** to **in the money.** (A call option is said to be out of the money if the stock price is less than the present value of the exercise price. It is said to be in the money if the stock price is greater than the present value of the exercise price. The opposite relationship holds for a put option.)

4. The absolute *percentage* changes in the option prices are greater than the accompanying absolute percentage changes in the stock price. (Looking at the schedule,

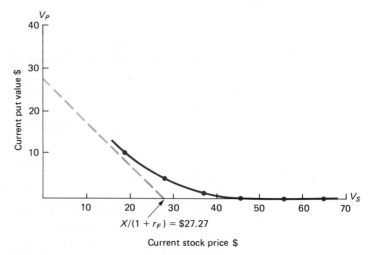

FIGURE 15.8 Relationship between prices for stock and put options.

we see in going from $18.18 to $27.27, the stock price increased in value by 50 percent. This change induces a reduction in the value of the put of approximately 56 percent and an increase in the value of the call of almost 300 percent.)

5. The *difference* in the absolute percentage changes between the stock and the options again becomes smaller as the options move from being out of the money to being in the money. Thus, out-of-the-money options are inherently more volatile than their in-the-money counterparts.

Now consider the slope of a line drawn tangent to the curves of Figures 15.7 and 15.8 at any point, such as point *A* in Figure 15.7. The slope of the line is the ratio of the change in the value of the option accompanying a very small change in the value of the stock. As we show in Appendix 6 at the end of this chapter, when the lowest possible stock price is less than the exercise price, this ratio is equal to the probability of exercising the option at maturity.

As the stock price goes up, the slope of the line approaches 1.00, as does the probability of exercising the option. Finally, when the lowest possible value for the stock price climbs above the exercise price, the probability of exercising the option is 100 percent, and the slope of the relationship between the value of the stock and the value of the option is 1.00.

It can also be shown that the absolute value of the slope of the relationship between the put value and the stock value is also equal to the probability of exercising at maturity.

The Effect of a Change in Stock Variance on Option Values

Suppose the ending value for the stock is distributed as in Figure 15.4. In this case, we found the market value for the stock was $36.36, the market value for the put was $1.14, and the market value for the call was $10.23. Now assume something happens to increase the uncertainty about the ending price of the stock. While before the price at the end of the year was believed to fall somewhere between $20 and $60, now it is believed to fall between $10 and $70. The new distribution for the value of the stock and the call and put options are drawn in Figures 15.9, 15.10, and

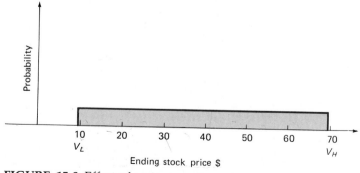

FIGURE 15.9 Effect of an increase in variance on the stock.

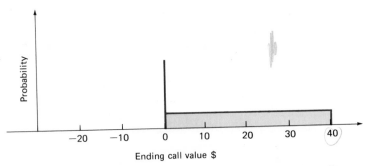

FIGURE 15.10 Effect of an increase in variance on the call.

15.11. The expected value is still $40 and, given our assumption of investor risk neutrality, the market value will still be $36.36.

While the price of the stock stays the same, the price of the put and the call will both go up. Consider the probability distribution for the ending value for the call. The conditional expected value for the rectangle is now $20. Two-thirds of the total probability is actually in the rectangle, so the expected value of the call is now $13.33. Therefore, the market value is $12.12, an increase in price of more than 18 percent. Why does the price of the call rise? The stock can go as high as $70 now. This means the option can go as high as $40, whereas before its highest possible ending value was $30. While it is true the lowest possible stock price is now $10, as a holder of the call option, you don't really care because as soon as the stock falls below $30, your option is worthless. The increase in the variance of the stock price has increased the upside potential for your investment, while leaving the downside potential unaffected. Granted, the *probability* of a zero value for the option is now greater (33.3 percent instead of 25 percent); however, this is more than offset by the increase in the conditional expected value for the rectangle.

Now consider the probability distribution for the put. The conditional expected value for the rectangle is $10. One-third of the total probability is actually in the rectangle, so the expected value of the put is $3.33, and its market value is $3.03,

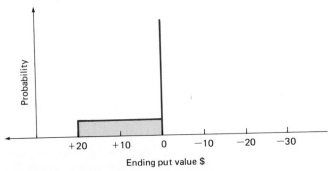

FIGURE 15.11 Effect of an increase in variance on the put.

an increase of nearly 200 percent. Again the increase in variance has increased the upside potential for the investment.

Based on our analysis thus far, we can draw two more conclusions about the behavior of stock options:

1. An increase in the variance of the stock will increase the market value of put and call options written on the stock.
2. Given a change in the variance of the underlying stock, the absolute percentage change in the price of out-of-the-money options will be greater than the absolute percentage change in the price of in-the-money options.

The variance of the stock price is actually a key factor in pricing options and developing investment strategies based on options. While the variance of the price of a stock sometimes remains stationary for periods as long as months or even years, the variance can undergo abrupt, dramatic changes. When this happens, the value of the options written on the stock will change. Thus, recognizing changes in variance shortly after they occur, and understanding the implications of these changes for the valuation of options, is an important facet of developing option investment strategies.

Summarizing what we have learned so far, as the stock price increases, the value of a call will rise, and the value of a put will fall. The absolute value of the slope of the relationship between the stock and option values tells you the probability of exercising the option. Options are more volatile in terms of percentage changes in market value than are stock investments, and out-of-the-money options are more volatile than in-the-money options. An increase in the variance of the underlying stock price will drive up the price of an option written on the stock. The resulting percentage change in the values of in-the-money options will be less than that for out-of-the-money options. While these relationships were derived in the context of a very simplistic framework, they hold under more complex pricing structures and actually characterize the way real options are priced.

We have obtained these relationships under the very special assumption that the distribution of the ending value for the stock is uniform, or rectangular. However, it's important to realize these relationships generalize to a wide variety of different assumed shapes for the ending stock value. For example, as we shall later see, in the case of the Black-Scholes model, a log-normal distribution is assumed for the ending value for the stock price. It is still the case that all of the relationships just discussed hold for Black-Scholes option prices.

So far we have also assumed investors are risk neutral. In the next section, we relax this assumption and discuss how to price an option to produce a risk-free return for someone who constructs a risk-free portfolio with it.

BINOMIAL OPTION PRICING

In this section, we will change our assumption concerning the nature of the distribution for the ending value for the stock. Rather than assume a uniform distribution, we will assume in the course of each period that there are two possible percentage changes in the stock price. If the options expire at the end of one period, then there are also two possible ending values for the stock price. At first, this may seem unrealistic to you, but remember that the length of the period can be made arbitrarily small. Given this, there can be an arbitrarily large number of periods before expiration. As the number of periods grows large, the probability distribution for the final value of the stock at the end of the last period approaches the shape of a log-normal distribution. There is evidence that an assumption of log-normality is reasonable for the ending stock value.

As the analysis of the previous section might indicate, options are among the most risky securities in existence. If risk and risk premiums affect the values of any securities, risk will play a substantial role in the pricing of these securities.

Researchers on option pricing were stymied for many years because they couldn't resolve the riddle of how options would be priced in the presence of risk-averse investors. One of the problems was the shape of the probability distribution for the ending value of the option. As you can infer from Figures 15.1, 15.2, and 15.3 even if the probability distribution for the ending value of the stock is normally distributed, the distribution for the ending value of the option is going to be skewed toward large positive values. This means that, unless we put unrealistic constraints on investor utility, it may be inappropriate to price options on the basis of models such as the capital asset pricing model.

In 1973, Fisher Black and Myron Scholes published a paper which resolved the riddle. Their insight was that options, used in combination with the stocks they are written on, can be used to construct investments that are riskless. Given this is the case, the options must sell at prices such that when you construct such a riskless portfolio, you earn the risk-free rate of return on your own investment in the portfolio.

Consider, for example, the relationship between the put option and the stock graphed in Figure 15.8. If the stock is priced at $27.27 (the present value of the exercise price), the slope of the relationship between the value of the put and the value of the stock will be $-.50$. This means, if the stock rises in price by $1.00, the value of the put option will fall by approximately $.50. You can create a riskless portfolio by buying one share of stock and two put options. In this case, the fall in the price of the put options will completely offset the rise in the price of the stock. Of course, with each change in the price of the stock, you move to a new point on the relationship, with a new slope, so you have to slightly adjust the number of puts you buy in relation to the number of shares of stock you hold. In any case, by adjusting your portfolio, you can maintain its riskless status over time (much in the manner of reimmunization discussed in the previous chapter). If the portfolio is riskless, it should produce the same rate of return as other riskless investments. Thus, the put options should sell at a price to make this the case.

Binomial Call Option Pricing over a Single Period

Suppose we have a European call option with one year to expiration and an exercise price of $110. The current market price of the stock it is written on is $100. In the course of the next year, two rates of return on the stock are possible, -10 percent and +20 percent. Thus, the price of the stock can either fall to $90 or rise to $120. No dividends are expected to be paid on the stock. The risk-free rate of interest available in the bond market is 10 percent.

How can you hedge an investment in this option? There are two possible ways to make a hedged investment. Since the values of the call and the stock move in the same direction, you must buy one and sell the other. Thus, you can hedge by buying the stock and selling some options or by selling short the stock and buying some options.

Suppose you do the former. How many options must you sell for each share of stock you buy? To find out, consider the two possible ending values for the stock and the corresponding ending values for the option. If the stock turns out to have a market price of $120, based on its exercise price of $110, the option will be worth $10 at the end of the year. If instead, the stock falls to $90, the option will be worthless. There is a $30 difference between the possible high and low values for the stock and a $10 difference for the option. Since the spread for the stock is three times as great as for the option, to create an exact offset in the value of your two positions, you must sell three options for every share of stock you buy. To compute the number of options sold for each share of stock bought, you use the following formula:

$$\text{Number of call options sold for each stock bought} = \frac{\text{High-low spread for stock}}{\text{High-low spread for option}}$$

$$3.00 = \frac{\$120 - \$90}{\$10 - \$00}$$

Consider the year-end value of your portfolio if you buy one share of stock and sell three options which obligate you to sell three shares of stock to the buyers of the options at a price of $110.

If the stock falls to $90, you will have one share of stock worth $90. The holders of the options you sold will choose to throw them away at expiration because the price of the stock is below the exercise price. Thus, the total value of your portfolio will be $90.

On the other hand, if the stock rises to $120, you will have one share of stock worth $120, but the three people holding your options will choose to exercise them because the market price is now above the exercise price at expiration. Each will come with $110, asking for a share of stock. You will have to go into the market three times to buy three shares for $120 each. You will lose $10 each time for a total loss of $30. The net value of your portfolio is $90:

One share of stock:	$120
Loss associated with exercise of three options:	−$30
Net portfolio value:	$90

Thus, your portfolio is worth $90 irrespective of whether the stock goes up or down. Since we have assumed these are the only two things that can happen, the portfolio is a riskless investment, and as such, it should be expected to yield the riskless rate of return of 10 percent for the year. The portfolio's rate of return can be computed as follows:

$$r_P = \frac{\text{Year-end portfolio value}}{\text{Price of 1 share of stock} - 3 \times \text{call option price}} - 1.00$$

$$10\% = \frac{\$90}{\$100 - 3 \times \text{option price}} - 1.00$$

We can now solve for the option price which will yield the risk-free rate to someone who follows this hedging strategy. If the options sell at a price of $6.06, the hedged portfolio requires an initial investment of $81.82 = $100 − 3 × $6.06. Since the ending value for the portfolio is known to be $90, this is consistent with a portfolio return of 10 percent.

$$\frac{\$90.00}{\$81.82} - 1.00 = 10\%$$

You can also hedge by selling the stock short and buying options. Again, based on the relative spreads on the two investments, you must buy three options for each share of stock you sell short. Three options will cost you $18.18 at the price indicated above. You will receive $100 from short selling the stock, so you can invest the remaining $81.82 in risk-free bonds. Note that you don't have to invest any of *your* money in this portfolio. Since you don't invest any money and since it's a riskless investment, the fair value for the payoff should be zero. If it's not, you could get something for nothing. If the options sell at $6.06, the ending value of this portfolio will be zero whether the stock goes up or down.

If the stock rises to $120, you will own three options worth a total of $30. It will cost you $120 to buy the stock to cover the short sale, and the $81.82 you invest in the risk-free bonds at the beginning of the year will be worth $90 at the end of the year. The total value of the portfolio is $90 + $30 − $120 = $00. You invest nothing in the portfolio, you take no risk, and you get nothing back. What could be more fair?

If the stock falls to $90, the options will be worthless, and you can use the $90 from investing in the risk-free bonds to cover the short sale. Again the portfolio is worthless. You put nothing in, and you take nothing out.

Consider, however, what happens if the options sell at a price different from $6.06. What if they sold at a price of $10 instead? In this case, the rate of return on the first hedged portfolio where you bought the stock and sold the options would be 28.57% = $90/($100 − $30). If this were true, the bottom would drop out from the bond market. Why invest in risk-free bonds for a return of 10 percent when you can hedge risklessly with options for a return of 28.57 percent? Investors would move into the option market, attempt to hedge by selling options, and force the price back down to $6.06. In fact, if we could sell riskless bonds to raise funds, we all could become infinitely wealthy without taking any risk, by selling the bonds at an interest rate of 10 percent and using the funds to invest in the hedged option portfolio at 28.57 percent.

What would happen if the option sold at a price below $6.06, say, at $5.00? Now we can make money from nothing by using another hedge. Sell the stock short, raising $100. Buy three options for a total cost of $15 and invest the remaining $85 in risk-free bonds. If the stock goes up, it will cost you $120 to cover the short sale, the options you own will be worth $30, and your investment in risk-free bonds will produce $93.50 at the end of the year. The portfolio will have a net value of $3.50, and it didn't cost you anything to get into it. On the other hand, if the stock goes down, it will cost you $90 to cover the short sale, the options will be worthless, and your bond investment will produce $93.50, a net gain of $3.50, again for no investment. Since this strategy requires no investment, you can make the net gain as large as you want, simply by selling more stock and buying more options. This is a very similar operation to constructing the arbitrage portfolios in the arbitrage pricing theory.

There are strong economic forces keeping the price of the option at $6.06. If the price goes above or below this, we can all become infinitely wealthy through arbitrage. In the face of these forces, $6.06 must be the only possible equilibrium price.

It can be argued that we, as individual investors, can't take advantage of these arbitrage opportunities, because we aren't free to invest the proceeds of short sales. As a matter of fact, we must commit an amount of money as a margin to guarantee that we will be able to cover the short sale when necessary. There is also a margin required to sell puts and calls.

However, it takes only *one* powerful investor to force the option to its equilibrium value. Large financial institutions employ arbitragers to hunt for opportunities to make money while making no commitment of capital and taking no risk. These large institutions can invest the proceeds of short sales in other investments, especially when they are riskless, and they are not restricted by margin requirements. These institutions can effectively police the options market, forcing the market value of the option to conform to the value which eliminates arbitrage opportunities.

Binomial Put Option Pricing over a Single Period

A put option can be priced in the same way. Since the value of the put and the value of the stock move in opposite directions, we need to either buy or sell them both in order to hedge.

Our relative positions in the put and the stock are still determined on the basis of the relative spread between their high and low values. In the example, if the stock goes to $120, the put (an option to sell the stock at a price of $110) is worthless. If the stock falls to $90, the put is worth $20.

The number of puts you must buy for each share of stock you hold is given by the following equation:

$$\text{Number of put options bought for each stock bought} = \frac{\text{High-low spread for stock}}{\text{High-low spread for put}}$$

$$1.50 = \frac{\$120 - \$90}{\$20 - \$00}$$

If you buy two shares of stock, you need to buy three puts to hedge. If the stock goes to $120, you have two shares of stock worth a total of $240 and three puts which are worth nothing. If the stock falls to $90, you have two shares of stock worth a total of $180 and three puts worth $20 each, for a total portfolio value of $240. Your portfolio is worth $240 in either case. It is riskless. As such, it should offer investors the risk-free rate of return. The rate of return on this portfolio is given by

$$r_P = \frac{\text{Year-end portfolio value}}{\text{Price of 2 shares of stock} + 3 \times \text{put option price}} - 1.00$$

$$10\% = \frac{\$240}{\$100 \times 2 + 3 \times \text{put option price}} - 1.00$$

In this example, the equilibrium value for the put option is also $6.06. With this value, it will cost us a total of $218.18 to invest in the portfolio. We know the portfolio will pay off $240 if either rate of return on the stock appears. Given this, the rate of return to the portfolio is known to be 10 percent.

Once again, if the put sells at a price below $6.06, we can obtain a riskless rate of return in excess of 10 percent by buying puts in combination with an investment in the stock. If the put sells at a price above $6.06, we can all become infinitely wealthy with no required investment, by selling puts and the stock short and using the proceeds of those sales to invest in riskless bonds. Strong economic forces are again present to keep the price of the put at its equilibrium level of $6.06.

Binomial Option Pricing over Multiple Periods

We can use this valuation principle (pricing to give a hedged investment the risk-free rate) to value an option that expires in 2 years instead of 1 year. Suppose, in each of the 2 years, the stock can either increase in value by 20% or decrease by 10 percent. This means, that after 1 year the stock can move from its current price of $100 to either $120 or $90. If it goes to $120, it can move in the second year to either $144 (with another 20 percent increase) or to $108 (with a 10 percent decrease). If, on the other hand, the stock drops to $90 at the end of the first year, it can rise in the second year to $108 (with a 20 percent increase) or fall again to $81 (a second 10 percent decrease). These possible values are indicated by the event tree of Figure 15.12.

Now assume we have a call option with an exercise price of $110 which expires at the end of the second year. The option values that correspond with the stock values are also given by the tree of Figure 15.12. Consider first, the possible values for the option at expiration at the end of the second year. Since the exercise price is $110, the option is worthless if the stock is priced at $108 or $81. It is worth $34 if the stock is priced at $144, however.

Next, consider the possible values for the option at the end of the *first* year. If the stock has fallen to $90, it can rise in the second year to $108 or fall to $81. In either case, it will be below the call option's exercise price. Thus, if the stock falls to $90 in the first year, the option is dead and its market value will be zero.

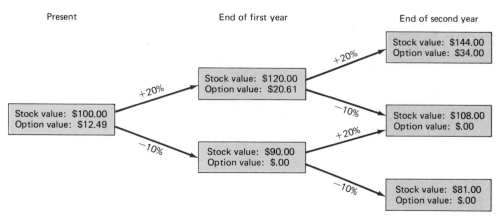

Present   End of first year   End of second year

FIGURE 15.12 Binomial option pricing over two periods (exercise price = $110.00, $r_F = 10\%$).

If instead, the stock rises to $120 in the first year, the option has a positive value, based on the chance that the stock will rise again to $144. We can compute the market value for the option in the same way we did for a 1-year option. The spread between the high and low values for the stock is $36. The corresponding spread for the option is $34. This means, for each share of stock we buy, we must sell 1.0588 options ($36/$34 = 1.0588). Let's operate on a big scale, buying 10,000 shares of stock and selling 10,588 options.

If the stock price rises at the end of the second year, our stock holdings will be worth $1,440,000. The options we sold will be exercised, and this will cost us $360,000. Thus, our portfolio will be worth the difference, or $1,080.00. This is also what our portfolio will be worth if the stock falls to $108 because, in this case, the options will not be exercised. We have a riskless portfolio which we know will be worth $1,080,000 at the end of the second year.

To build this portfolio at the beginning of the second year, we will have to pay $1,200,000 for the 10,000 shares of stock less what we can raise by selling the 10,588 call options. The call options must sell at a price to give us the riskless rate of return on this investment, which we will assume is still 10 percent. This equilibrium price is $20.61:

$$10\% = \frac{\$1,080,000}{\$1,200,000 - \$10,588 \times \$20.61} - 1.00$$

Now let's move to the beginning of the first year. Based on our analysis thus far, we know there are two possible values for the option at the end of the first period, $20.61 (if the stock rises to $120) and $.00 (if the stock falls to $90). We can again create a riskless portfolio which has a known and certain value at the end of the first period by hedging. The spread between the high and low possible values for the stock is $30. The corresponding spread for the option is $20.61. To hedge, we must sell 1.4556 options for each share of stock we buy ($30.00/$20.61 = 1.4556). Let's buy 10,000 shares of stock and sell 14,556 options. If we do this and the stock goes up, we have a portfolio worth $900,000. Our long position in the stock is worth $1,200,000, and our short position in the options is worth $300,000 ($20.61 × 14,556). Our portfolio is also worth $900,000 if the stock falls to $90 because, in this case, the options are dead and our short position has no value.

Since the portfolio is riskless, again it should produce the riskless rate of return. To build the portfolio at the beginning of the first period, we must invest an amount equal to $1 million worth of stock less what we can get by selling 14,556 options. If we sell the options at a price of $12.49, building the portfolio will require an investment of $818,196, and the portfolio will produce a 10 percent rate of return in the first period:

$$10\% = \frac{\$900,000}{\$1,000,000 - 14,556 \times \$12.49} - 1.00$$

Thus, the equilibrium value for the 2-year option is $12.49. Note, the only difference between this option and the 1-year call option priced in the preceding section is the term to expiration. The 1-year option was based on the same stock and had the same exercise price. Yet the value of the 1-year option was only $6.06. Just as with the variance of the underlying probability distribution for the stock, as you increase the time to expiration for an option, if you hold all other factors constant, you increase the market value for the option. The reason for this is that you increase the upside potential for the stock. The fact that the downside potential increases as well is unimportant because, once an option is dead, it is dead, and it makes no difference if the stock goes to $108, to $81, or for that matter to $0.

If we extended the analysis to a 3-year case and beyond, we would find that the option again increases in value. Each successive increase would be smaller than the last, however. And as the term to expiration approached perpetuity, the value of the option would approach the value of the common stock, of $100.

In Figure 15.13, we move to a different example. Here we are dealing with a 1-year call option, but we have reduced the period for the percentage changes on the stock to one quarter. In each quarter there are two possible percentage changes on the stock, + 17.5 percent and − 15 percent. To value the option, we need not specify the probabilities of getting either percentage change, but let's assume they are equal, and the distribution for the rate of return on the stock in any quarter is given in Figure 15.14(a). As you can see in Figure 15.13, with this distribution for the quarterly return, there are five possible year-end values for the common stock. There are 16 ending branches on the tree. There is an equal probability of reaching each branch. A stock value of $190.61 is represented on only one of the branches. The probability of getting this value, therefore, is one-sixteenth. A stock price of $137.89 is represented on four of the branches. The probability of getting this price, therefore, is one-fourth. The probability distribution for the ending value of the stock is given in Figure 15.14(b). Note the distribution for the year-end value for the stock looks much different from the distribution for the quarterly return. While the distribution for the quarterly rate of return is symmetric, the distribution for the ending value for the stock is skewed to the right.

The corresponding values for a call option on the stock with an exercise price

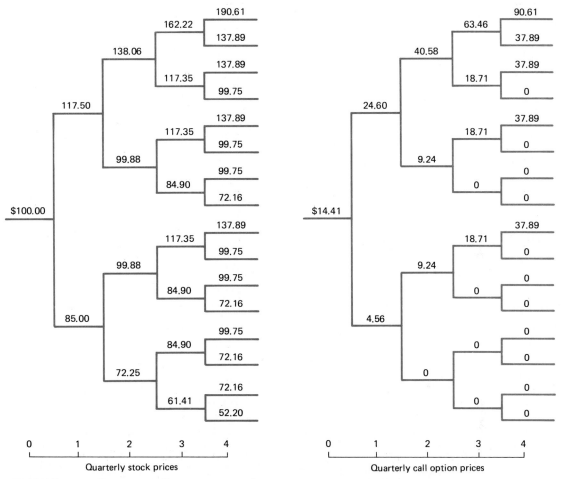

FIGURE 15.13 Pricing a call option over a four-quarter horizon.

SOURCE: R. J. Rendleman, Jr., and B. J. Bartter, "Two State Option Pricing," *Journal of Finance* (December 1979).

of $100 and which expires at the end of the year are given in Figure 15.13. The option prices are computed using the same technique employed in the preceding sections. You start at the end of the tree, valuing the option at expiration, and work backward. In each case, you value the option so that a riskless portfolio produces the riskless rate of return, which, in the case of this example, is assumed to be 1.25 percent per quarter.

Note that to maintain your hedged position from quarter to quarter, you must keep adjusting your relative position in the stock and in the call. At the beginning of the first quarter, the spread for the stock is $32.50 and $20.04 for the option. Thus, you must sell 1.622 options for each share of stock you buy. If the stock goes up, its spread in the second quarter is $38.18. The option's spread is $31.34, so you

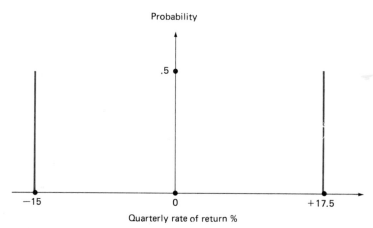

FIGURE 15.14(a) Probability distribution for quarterly rates of return on stock.

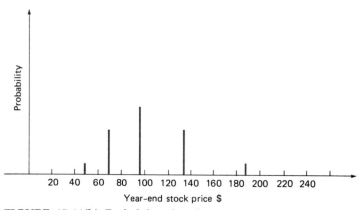

FIGURE 15.14(b) Probability distribution for year-end stock value.

must now sell 1.218 options for each share of stock you buy. And so, as you move along in time, you must keep adjusting your positions in the option and the stock to remain hedged.

We are now very close to the framework assumed in the option pricing model of Black and Scholes (1973). In the example we're considering, we have assumed the distribution of rates of return to the stock is constant through time and binomial (two-point) in form, which implies a distribution for the ending value of the stock of the form in Figure 15.14(b). We have assumed that, in hedging, you adjust your position at the end of each quarter. And we value the option to give you the riskless rate of return on your hedged position.

Black and Scholes make two slightly different assumptions. First they assume the distribution for rates of return on the stock is normal or *bell shaped*. Second, they reduce the time interval for the percentage changes from a quarter to an instant. Except for these changes, the principle for valuing the options is the same.

Before moving to the Black-Scholes model, we should note that computer programs are available in your software that value options based on the binomial frame-work. Programs like these are currently used by professional traders to help formulate their investment strategies.

VALUING OPTIONS USING THE BLACK-SCHOLES FRAMEWORK

As discussed already, Black and Scholes assume the probability distribution for rates of return on the stock over an instant of time is normal, as in Figure 15.15(a). Just as the distribution of rates of return in Figure 15.14(a) implied the distribution for ending stock values of Figure 15.14(b), so the normal distribution of Figure 15.15(a) implies the log-normal distribution of stock prices at the expiration of the option of Figure 15.15(b). The nature of a log-normal distribution is such that if you plotted

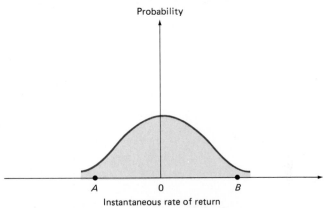

FIGURE 15.15(a) Normal probability distribution for stock rates of return.

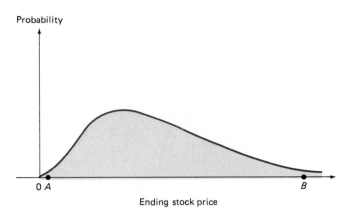

FIGURE 15.15(b) Log-normal probability distribution for ending stock values.

OUT ON THE STREET

A RUN FOR HIS MONEY

In a split second the computer's evaluation of the spread flashes on the screen. Again, the implied market value of the spread, and the return based on the current value, is simply incredible!

Jack Reynoldson is sitting in the offices of First Options of Chicago, a clearing firm on the Chicago Board Options Exchange (CBOE). Jack is a market maker on the CBOE. In the parlance of market makers, he is known as a neutral spreader. Neutral spreaders acquire options that are mispriced relative to theoretical values and hedge these options against other puts, calls, or stock. Jack's game is to buy the theoretically underpriced options and sell the theoretically overpriced options to create a position that is insensitive to small changes in the stock price. He then waits until the options revalue themselves. When the options become properly priced, Jack closes out his positions and takes his profits.

Jack is viewing a TV monitor furnished him by the clearing firm. He holds a seat on the exchange and works for himself. Each time he makes a trade on the floor, he pays a small commission to the clearing firm. In return the firm provides him with accounting and other services like this computer.

The computer is programmed to value options based on several option pricing models, including the Black-Scholes model. The system provides model value estimates, including the expected variance of the underlying stock, the forecast for interest rates, and dividends that are expected to be paid out over the life of the option.

Over the 4 years he has been trading options, Jack has found that the Black-Scholes model provides him with the best indicator of mispricing in the options market. In his opinion, the biases which exist in the model are small and 99.9 percent of the time have no impact on the spreads he designs and executes. In any case any bias presents no problem to him as long as it's consistent over time and he's aware of it. At times, though, he knows he has to be careful about the appropriateness of the assumptions of the model to the particular situation.

For instance, one of the assumptions of the model is that the distribution of returns of the stock is normal. At times it's clearly not. This is particularly true in a takeover situation. During these instances Jack knows that the options slip away from their Black-Scholes values not because they are "mispriced" but because the model's assumptions are inappropriate for the situation. A good example of this would be the case of Superior Oil. Superior was rumored to be a takeover candidate on several occasions. Each time the call options on the stock appeared to be overpriced on the basis of the Black-Scholes model. The options, however, were discounting the possibility of a huge one-time return on the stock, assuming the takeover went through. For those who bet that the rumors were inaccurate and that the model assumptions were correct, losses on short positions in calls appeared when the stock price jumped on the news that Mobil was indeed buying out Superior Oil. On an overall basis, however, the normality assumption is a reasonable one.

Jack can feel his adrenalin building with each response from the terminal. He was attracted to this particular stock because of an unfavorable announcement regarding negotiations with their labor union. A strike seemed imminent. The announcement was made at 9:30 A.M., and the options promptly began changing in price, perhaps by too much. The out-of-the-money calls really took a dive. Upon seeing this, Jack thought he'd better check the situation out on the machine.

The computer is telling him that the market for the options is completely out of kilter. The puts are overpriced while the out-of-the-money calls are greatly underpriced. The only way you could justify the call prices is with an extremely low estimate of the stock's variance, far below the estimates provided him by the services. A strike seemed like a sure thing at this point, but the *length* of the strike was another matter. If the strike is settled more quickly than expected, these call options could be worth more money. Factoring in uncertainty regarding the length of the strike into the variance estimate, the call options were clearly underpriced. The question now becomes how to best take advantage of the situation.

Jack now goes through the familiar process of designing the best spread through a sensitivity analysis. A key element in designing a spread is the option *delta*. Delta is equivalent to 100 multiplied by $N(d_1)$ in the Black-Scholes equation. Each option contract (to buy or sell 100 shares of stock) can be thought of as the equivalent to holding a certain number of shares of stock. If a call option contract has a delta of 50, that means if the stock goes up by $1.00, the option contract will rise in value by $50.00. To hedge, you must buy 50 shares of stock for each contract you sell.

The deltas on the deeply out-of-the-money options approximate 10. Since Jack feels these are the most underpriced, he will want to buy these. The question is how to match them up to create the spread.

One candidate is the stock. Jack enters a spread into the computer in which he sells short 1000 shares of stock and buys 100 option contracts. Now he inputs estimates for the risk-free rate (in this case it's the 90-day treasury bill rate) and the variance for the stock. The computer displays the theoretical price for the spread that is justified on the basis of the Black-Scholes model. The current market value is much less than what is generated on the basis of the theoretical values for the options. A good sign.

Now Jack tries to find out how sensitive the value of the spread is to changes in the values of the model's parameters. Suppose the stock's variance declines substantially from what the services are now estimating. If Jack exits from the spread under these conditions, he will have to buy the stock and sell the call options. The computer indicates, however, that even if the variance decline is substantial, the spread will still be profitable because of the relative cheapness of the calls. Similar analysis also indicates that its potential profitability is also insensitive to changes in interest rates.

Jack has never seen the market this far out of line. He now tries an alternative spread. This time he simultaneously buys the puts and the calls. Then he tries one where he buys 50 deeply out-of-the-money calls and sells 20 offsetting in-the-money calls. The process is repeated until Jack has tried *nearly* all possible combinations. He can't try everything, because he simply can't afford the time. He's not the only one looking at a screen like this one. Other spreaders are becoming aware of the situation. He's got to move fast. There are others who are looking to execute similar neutral spreads, acting to drive option prices closer in line with theoretical values.

While Jack still makes money on 70 percent of his spreads, the business isn't as profitable as it was 2 years ago and certainly not as profitable as it was 4 years ago. Part of the problem is machines like this one and the prevalence of all the option pricing services. To make money these days, you've got to become faster on your feet and increasingly more sophisticated.

As it turns out, the first spread is the best one. Jack curses the waste of time under his breath. He turns off the machine and races down to the street below. The CBOE is just next door. After dodging a few cars, Jack races through the doors and into the pit where the options are bought and sold.

Several other traders have preceded Jack in discovering that the market is out of whack. Fortunately they haven't as yet had an impact on the deeply out-of-the-money call options.

Jack executes his buy order and prepares to set up his short position. This one's going to be a winner for sure!

the stock values on a log scale on the horizontal axis of the graph, the distribution would then take the shape of a normal distribution. That the normal distribution of rates of return implies the log-normal distribution of ending stock prices can be better understood if you think of the following. Suppose the stock undergoes a long series of negative percentage changes such as that represented by point A in the normal distribution. This would imply the stock price would approach a value near zero, such as point A in the log-normal distribution. If, on the other hand, the stock has a long series of positive percentage changes, such as that of point B in the normal distribution, its ending value would become extremely large, falling well to the right of point B in the log-normal distribution. Thus, even though the distribution for the percentage changes is symmetric, the distribution for the ending values is skewed to the right.

Black-Scholes value the option to give you the risk-free rate of return if you attempt to hedge with the option. As a hedger, you must continuously adjust your relative positions in the stock and the option, just as the hedger did on a quarterly basis in the example of Figure 15.13. In this example, your relative position is based on the relative spreads between the high and low values for the stock and the option.

With a normal distribution for the rates of return, we can no longer base our position on these spreads. Instead our position is based on the ratio of the dollar change in the value of the option that will accompany each dollar change in the value of the stock, much in the manner of the hedge we discussed in relation to Figure 15.7. If a $.02 change in the stock price induces a $.01 change in the option price, we hedge by selling two options for each share of stock we buy.

The Black-Scholes Value for a Call Option

Based on this framework, the value of a European call option written on a stock that pays no dividends is given by the following equation:

$$V_C = V_S N(d_1) - \frac{X}{e^{r_F t}} N(d_2) \tag{15.6}$$

In the formula, V_S is the current market price for the stock, X is the exercise price for the option, r_F is the continuously compounded riskless interest rate, and t is the number of years to expiration. We have seen e before. It is the natural antilog of 1.00 or 2.718. When we raise this number to a power equal to the product of r_F and t, we convert it to a discount factor that discounts the exercise price to a present value, using continuous compounding. The term multiplied by $N(d_2)$ is, thus, the present value of the exercise price.

The numbers d_1 and d_2 are determined by the following formulas:

$$d_1 = \frac{\ln(V_S/X) + (r_F + (1/2)\sigma^2(r)]t}{\sigma(r)\sqrt{t}} \tag{15.7}$$

$$d_2 = d_1 - \sigma(r)\sqrt{t} \tag{15.8}$$

In the formula, $\ln(\ )$ is the natural logarithm of the number in parentheses.

The numbers d_1 and d_2 can be taken to be deviations from the expected value of a unit normal distribution. A unit normal distribution is a special case of the normal distribution. It has an expected value of zero and a standard deviation of 1.00. Thus, a value for d of -1.5 would imply a deviation equal to 1.5 standard deviations below the expected value.

$N(d)$ is a probability operator. It tells you the probability of getting a deviation that is below d. In Figure 15.16, d is taken to be -1.00. We are thus one standard deviation below the expected value of a normal distribution. $N(d)$ is the probability remaining in the shaded area of the distribution. It is roughly 16 percent.

Table 15.1 shows the values for $N(d)$ corresponding to various values for d. To illustrate the table, if d_1, computed on the basis of Equation (15.7), is .00, then $N(d_1)$ is equal to .50. We are right on the unit normal distribution's expected value. The probability of falling below the expected value is 50 percent.

To compute the value of a call option using the Black-Scholes formula, first compute the values for d_1 and d_2 using Equations (15.7) and (15.8). Then find the

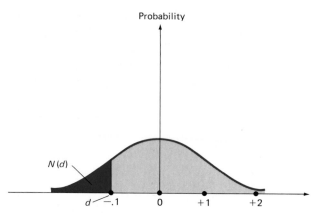

FIGURE 15.16 Unit normal probability distributions.

values for $N(d_1)$ and $N(d_2)$ using Table 15.1. Finally multiply $N(d_1)$ by the current stock price and $N(d_2)$ by the present value of the exercise price and net the two products.

Suppose we have a call option written on a stock with 6 months (.5 year) to expiration. The current stock price is $100, the annualized standard deviation of the stock's instantaneous rate of return is 50 percent, and the riskless rate is 10 percent. The value for d_1 is given by

$$d_1 = .318 = \frac{\ln(\$100/\$100) + (.10 + \frac{1}{2} \times .25).5}{.5 \times .707}$$

Interpolating from Table 15.1, $N(d_1)$ is seen to be .6236.

The value for d_2 is given by

$$d_2 = -.0355 = .318 - .50 \times .707$$

We can see from the table that the corresponding value for $N(d_2)$ is .4859.

The value for the call option is now computed using Equation (17.6):

$$V_C = \$100 \times .6236 - \frac{\$100}{2.718^{.10 \times .5}} \times .4859 = \$16.14$$

Don't try to make intuitive sense of the formula. It is in a final, simplified mathematical form, and the economic intuition behind the formula can't be seen in this final form. Just remember in the case of this example, if the option sells at a price of $16.14 and you hedge with it, continually adjusting your portfolio position over time, the rate of return on your hedged investment will be 10 percent, which is the assumed riskless rate of return in the bond market.

The Black-Scholes option pricing formula has become the most widely used benchmark for pricing options in the industry. Prices based on the formula are published by financial services, and routines for computing the Black-Scholes value are readily available in modules for hand-held calculators.

TABLE 15.1 Values for d and $N(d)$

d	$N(d)$	d	$N(d)$	d	$N(d)$
		−1.00	.1587	1.00	.8413
−2.95	.0016	−.95	.1711	1.05	.8531
−2.90	.0019	−.90	.1841	1.10	.8643
−2.85	.0022	−.85	.1977	1.15	.8749
−2.80	.0026	−.80	.2119	1.20	.8849
−2.75	.0030	−.75	.2266	1.25	.8944
−2.70	.0035	−.70	.2420	1.30	.9032
−2.65	.0040	−.65	.2578	1.35	.9115
−2.60	.0047	−.60	.2743	1.40	.9192
−2.55	.0054	−.55	.2912	1.45	.9265
−2.50	.0062	−.50	.3085	1.50	.9332
−2.45	.0071	−.45	.3264	1.55	.9394
−2.40	.0082	−.40	.3446	1.60	.9452
−2.35	.0094	−.35	.3632	1.65	.9505
−2.30	.0107	−.30	.3821	1.70	.9554
−2.25	.0122	−.25	.4013	1.75	.9599
−2.20	.0139	−.20	.4207	1.80	.9641
−2.15	.0158	−.15	.4404	1.85	.9678
−2.10	.0179	−.10	.4602	1.90	.9713
−2.05	.0202	−.05	.4801	1.95	.9744
−2.00	.0228	.00	.5000	2.00	.9773
−1.95	.0256	.05	.5199	2.05	.9798
−1.90	.0287	.10	.5398	2.10	.9821
−1.85	.0322	.15	.5596	2.15	.9842
−1.80	.0359	.20	.5793	2.20	.9861
−1.75	.0401	.25	.5987	2.25	.9878
−1.70	.0446	.30	.6179	2.30	.9893
−1.65	.0495	.35	.6368	2.35	.9906
−1.60	.0548	.40	.6554	2.40	.9918
−1.55	.0606	.45	.6736	2.45	.9929
−1.50	.0668	.50	.6915	2.50	.9938
−1.45	.0735	.55	.7088	2.55	.9946
−1.40	.0808	.60	.7257	2.60	.9953
−1.35	.0885	.65	.7422	2.65	.9960
−1.30	.0968	.70	.7580	2.70	.9965
−1.25	.1057	.75	.7734	2.75	.9970
−1.20	.1151	.80	.7881	2.80	.9974
−1.15	1251	.85	.8023	2.85	.9978
−1.10	.1357	.90	.8159	2.90	.9981
−1.05	.1469	.95	.8289	2.95	.9984

One reason for the model's popularity is that it isn't very demanding in terms of the estimates required to compute the value of an option. The current stock price and the yield on a treasury bill with a maturity date equal to the expiration date can be read from the financial news. The exercise price and term to expiration can be read from the option contract. The only challenging estimate is that of the variance or standard deviation of the instantaneous rate of return on the stock.

Estimating the Variance of the Stock's Return

Technically, the variance is that of the instantaneous rate of return on the stock. However, most people estimate the variance on the basis of sampling the stock's daily rate of return. You are trying to estimate the variance of the stock's return over the remaining life of the option. Thus, your sample should be over a period that immediately precedes the current date. If the variance remains constant over time, the longer the sample period, the more accurate the sample estimate. However, a stock's variance typically undergoes changes from time to time. In view of this, you will want to extend the sample period as far back as you are confident that there was no change in the underlying variance. Consider Figure 15.17. On the horizontal axis we are plotting time. As you move to the right, you are moving farther into the past. On the vertical axis, we are plotting the daily rate of return on the stock. Based on the plot connecting daily rates of return, it appears there was a reduction in the stock's underlying variance that occurred approximately 60 trading days ago. Given this, you will want to estimate the variance using a sample of returns taken over the preceding 60 days.

The variance you get from this sample will be an estimate of the stock's daily variance. If you are using annualized numbers for t and r_F in the Black-Scholes formula, you will have to annualize your variance estimate as well. If you are willing to make the reasonable assumptions that successive changes in stock prices are uncorrelated and that stock values continue to fluctuate even on days that we can't see the fluctuations because they aren't traded, the annualized variance can be obtained by multiplying the daily variance by 365.

After obtaining your annualized sample variance, you now have to ask yourself whether the future period, covering the remaining life of the option, is comparable to your sample period. Stock prices usually become more variable around earnings and dividend announcements, so if there was an announcement date in your sample period but none in the remaining period to expiration, you may have to adjust down-

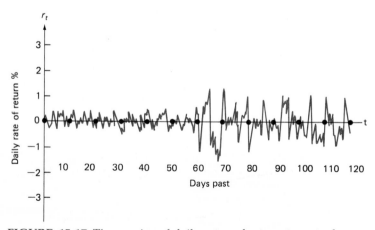

FIGURE 15.17 Time series of daily rates of return to a stock.

ward your estimate of the sample variance. Perhaps there is some ambiguity regarding the characteristics of a new product, the outcome of a serious litigation involving the firm, or the possibility of a takeover bid that will be resolved sometime during the life of the option. In these cases, the stock will make a significant move up or down when the ambiguity is resolved. In such situations you may want to adjust upward your sample estimate of the variance.

The Black-Scholes Value for a Put Option

The Black-Scholes formula for the value for a put option is deceptively simple:

$$V_P = V_C + \frac{X}{e^{rFt}} - V_S \tag{15.9}$$

The reason I say "deceptively" is because V_C is the Black-Scholes value of an identical call option written on the same stock. You add the present value of the exercise price to this value and then subtract the current stock price.

The Relationship Between Black-Scholes Put and Call Values and Underlying Stock Prices

In Figures 15.18(a) and (b), we have plotted the relationship between the value of a call and put, respectively, and the value of the stock options. Note, once again, the values of the options approach a line with slope $+1.00$ (for a call) and -1.00 (for a put) emanating from the present value of the exercise price. Now the call option value approaches but never reaches the line because the probability distribution isn't truncated on the left side as it was in the case of the rectangular, uniform distribution. As a consequence, there is always some small probability of not exercising the option no matter how large the present price of the stock becomes.

The (negative of the) slope of the line at any point, such as point A, reflects the probability of exercising the (put) call option. As the stock price becomes larger, so does the probability of exercise at maturity. The slope of the line also reflects the number of shares of stock you must buy for each call (put) option you sell (buy) in order to hedge at the current price of the stock. As the stock price changes, you move to a new point on the curve, with a new slope, and you must adjust your hedge position. The slope of the line is also equal to $N(d_1)$ in the option pricing formula.

If we increase the stock's variance, we move to a curve higher than the solid curve of Figure 15.18(b). Increasing the time to expiration also moves us to a higher curve.

Using the Black-Scholes Framework to Value Options on Stocks that Pay Dividends

The model of Equations (15.6) and (15.9) can be used to value European options on stocks which aren't expected to pay a dividend during the life of the option. If the stock is going to go ex-dividend before the expiration date, and if you are sure of

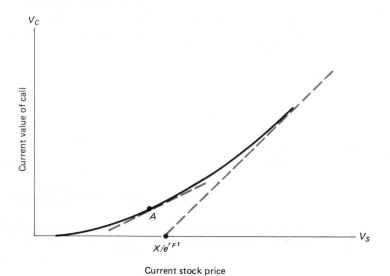

FIGURE 15.18(a) Black-Scholes relationship between stock value and call value.

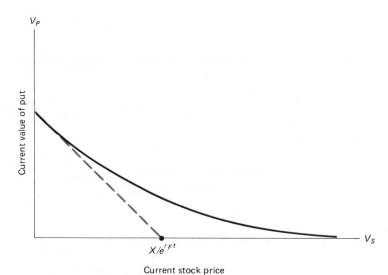

FIGURE 15.18(b) Black-Scholes relationship between stock value and put value.

what the dividend D is going to be, you can use the following modified form of the Black-Scholes formula to account for the dividend:

$$V_C^* = \left(V_S - \frac{D}{e^{r_F t}} \right) N(d_1) - \left(\frac{X}{e^{r_F t}} \right) N(d_2) \qquad (15.10)$$

The formula is basically the same, but you subtract the present value of the dividend from the current stock price. In the equation, t is the number of years until the dividend is expected to be paid.

The corresponding equation for the value of a put is given by

$$V_P^* = V_C^* + \frac{X}{e^{r_F t}} - V_S - \frac{D}{e^{r_F t}} \tag{15.11}$$

PUT-CALL PARITY

If there exists a European put and call option written on the same stock with the same exercise price and expiring at the same time t, the difference between the prices on the put and the call must take on a specific value, or opportunities for unlimited arbitrage profit once again open up.

If the options are in parity with respect to one another, the difference in their prices must be equal to the difference between the present value of their exercise price and the current market price of the stock:[1]

$$V_P - V_C = \frac{X}{(1 + r_F)^t} - V_S \tag{15.12}$$

In this equation, V_P is the current market value of the put, V_C is the current market value of the call, X is the exercise price of both the put and the call, r_F is the risk-free rate of interest, and V_S is the current stock price.

Suppose first, the difference between the put and call prices is greater than that of parity. In that case, we can manipulate Equation (15.12) to form the following inequality:

$$(1 + r_F)^t [V_S + V_P - V_C] > X$$

This inequality implies there is an investment strategy we can use to make money while taking no risk and making no investment of our own funds. We will sell the stock short, sell the put, and buy the call. The net proceeds of this transaction are in the bracketed expression on the left-hand side of the inequality. If we invest these net proceeds in a riskless bond, the ending value of the investment will be greater than the exercise price of the options.

This is important, because we are obligated under the short sale to return a share of stock to our broker. Since we own a call option, if at expiration, the stock

---

[1]Equation (15.12) is applicable when no dividends are to be paid before the option expires. If a dividend is known to be paid, the equation should be modified as follows,

$$V_P = V_C = \frac{X + D(1 + r_F)^{t^*}}{(1 + r_F)^t} - V_S$$

where D is the dividend expected to be paid, assumed known with certainty, and t^* is the length of time between payment of the dividend and the expiration of the options.

is selling above the exercise price, we can acquire a share at X using the call option. If the stock is selling at a price less than the exercise price, we will throw our call option away, but the person to whom we sold the put option will exercise and sell us a share of stock at a price equal to X. Consequently, no matter what happens to the price of the stock at time t, we are set to cover the short sale at a cost of X dollars.

Thus, we can get out of the transaction for X dollars, but based on the inequality, this will be less than the ending value of our bond investment that we made with the initial net proceeds of the transaction. We have invested no money of our own, we have taken no risk, yet we have made money. The amount of money we can make is limited only by the number of shares we can find to sell short.[2]

Once again, there are strong economic forces present to keep the prices of puts and calls in parity with one another. There are special times, however, when these forces are blocked, allowing the prices to move out of parity. One example of such a case was in March 1981. A takeover bid was announced, directed by Brunswick Corporation. Prior to the bid, the price of the stock was at $20. The takeover bid price was approximately $30. Put and call options existed on the stock which had approximately 2 months to expiration. No dividend was expected to be paid over these 2 months. The exercise price on both these options was $30. Based on the takeover bid, the stock price rose to approximately $29. The put was selling at a price of about $9 and the call at a price near $1. The risk-free rate of interest, at the time, was approximately 15 percent, so the present value of the exercise price was $29.31. Thus, the put and call were out of parity:

$$\$9.00 - 1.00 > \$29.31 - \$29.00$$

You would generate net proceeds of $37 by selling the put, buying the call, and short-selling the stock. You could have invested these proceeds at 15 percent in the bond market for 2 months, producing a terminal value of $37.87. You know that at the end of 2 months you will be able to cover your short sale at a price of $30 through either the put or the call option. Therefore, you make a profit of $7.87.

Now, as individual investors, you and I aren't free to invest the proceeds of short sales in the bond market, and there are also margin requirements for both the short sale and the sale of the put option. Even in the face of these problems, however, the transaction offers an extremely attractive rate of return and no risk. Moreover, large financial institutions face no constraints on short selling and have no margin requirements on a riskless transaction such as this. Yet the prices of the put and call remained out of parity for several weeks.

The explanation lies in a blockage that occurred to the arbitrage. Because there was a bid outstanding for the common stock, it became impossible to find anyone willing to lend their shares to sell short. If you had shares and lent them to someone for purposes of a short sale, you wouldn't be able to tender them to the acquiring

---

[2]This can be considered truly riskless arbitrage only for European options. In the case of American options, they can be exercised prior to maturity, in which case the proceeds from the riskless bond investment may be insufficient to cover the short sale.

company at the premium price. Thus, the supply of shares available to short sellers dried up completely. In the absence of this form of discipline by the market, the prices of the put and the call drifted out of parity.

Now assume, the difference between the prices of the put and the call becomes *less* than that of the parity relationship. In this case, the inequality goes in the opposite direction:

$$(1 + r_F)^t(V_S + V_P - V_C) < X$$

We can now reverse the transaction just discussed. We buy the stock and the put, and we sell the call. We raise the net proceeds required to do this by borrowing money in the bond market. The total amount on the left-hand side of the inequality is the amount we must pay off on our loan at t. Given our position in the put and the call, we know that we will be able to sell the stock at t at an amount equal to X, which is greater than the required payment on our loan. The difference is our profit on the transaction. We make no investment of our own; we take no risk, yet once again, we make a profit which is limited only by the number of shares and options we can buy and sell at the disequilibrium prices. In the process of buying the put and selling the call, we will widen the gap between them until it conforms to the parity relationship. At that point, the profit from the arbitrage transactions is zero.

Technically, the put-call parity relationship given above is for European options. In the case of American options the hedge isn't completely riskless, because the options may be exercised early. To illustrate, in the case of the first transaction discussed above, if the holders of the put option exercise early, we might not have sufficient funds in our bond investment to cover the transaction at a profit.

SUMMARY

A European option gives you the right either to buy or sell a stock at a specified exercise price on a specified expiration date. A call option gives you the right to buy the stock, and a put option gives you the right to sell it.

The value of a call (put) option increases (decreases) with increases in the price of the stock. For both types of options, the dollar changes in the options are less than the corresponding dollar changes in the price of the stock, but the percentage changes are greater. In terms of percentage changes, out-of-the-money options are more variable than in-the-money options. The value of both the put and the call will increase with the variance of the stock they are written on.

In the presence of risk-averse investors, options can be valued to provide the risk-free rate of return to an investor who hedges with them. If the value of the option deviates from this equilibrium price, investors can become infinitely wealthy through riskless arbitrage portfolios that require no investment. Thus, there are strong economic forces that keep the option price in line with that which will produce a risk-free rate of return to a hedged investor.

The Black-Scholes model assumes that the probability distribution for the instantaneous rate of return to the stock that underlies the option is constant over time and normally distributed. This implies that the probability distribution for the ending price of the stock at the expiration of the option is log-normal in shape. The model prices the option to provide the risk-free rate of return to hedgers that continually adjust their positions as the stock price changes over time.

The Black-Scholes model is technically a model for European options. However, as we will see in the next chapter, it can be used in some cases to value American options as well.

The difference between the market values of identical put and call options written on the same stock must be equal to the difference between the present value of the exercise price on the options and the market value of the common stock. If the put and call prices fail to have this parity relationship, arbitrage opportunities present themselves which offer unlimited wealth at no risk. Thus, there are very strong economic forces keeping put and call prices in parity.

APPENDIX 6

PROOF THAT $\partial V_C / \partial V_S$ IS THE PROBABILITY OF EXERCISE FOR A CALL OPTION ON A STOCK WITH A UNIFORM DISTRIBUTION

The equation for the value of the call is given by

$$V_C = \frac{(V_H - X)^2 / [2(V_H - V_L)]}{1 + r_F}$$

Multiplying and dividing V_H by 2 in the squared term at the top of the equation and then adding and subtracting V_L, we get

$$V_C = \frac{\{[(2V_H + V_L - V_L)/2] - X\}^2}{2(V_H - V_L)(1 + r_F)}$$

The equation can now be manipulated as follows:

$$V_C = \frac{\{[(V_H + V_L)/2] + [(V_H - V_L)/2] - X\}^2}{2(V_H - V_L)(1 + r_F)}$$

Recognize that

$$\frac{V_H + V_L}{2} = (1 + r_F)V_S$$

so that by substitution,

$$V_C = \frac{\{[1 + r_F]V_S + [(V_H - V_L)/2] - X\}^2}{2(V_H - V_L)(1 + r_F)}$$

Taking the derivative of the option with respect to the price of the stock, we get

$$\frac{\partial V_C}{\partial V_S} =$$

$$\frac{2(1 + r_F)(V_H - V_L)\{2V_S(1 + r_F)^2 + 2(1 + r_F)[(V_H - V_L)/2] - 2X(1 + r_F)\}}{(1 + r_F)4(V_H - V_L)^2}$$

which simplifies to

$$\frac{\partial V_C}{\partial V_S} = \frac{(1 + r_F)V_S + [(V_H - V_L)/2] - X}{V_H - V_L}$$

Recognizing that $(1 + r_F)V_S = (V_H + V_L)/2$, we obtain

$$\frac{\partial V_C}{\partial V_S} = \frac{V_H - X}{V_H - V_L} = \text{Probability of exercise}$$

QUESTION SET 1

1. Suppose that the end-of-year price on a stock is uniformly distributed from a low of $0 to a high of $100. Assume that investors are risk neutral and that the rate of interest is zero. A call option exists on this stock with an exercise price of $60.
   a. Sketch the probability distribution of the ending stock price.
   b. Sketch the probability distribution of the ending call option value.
   c. What is the expected value of the ending call option value, conditional on the assumption that you know the ending stock price will be such that the option will not be worthless?
   d. What should the current market value of the option be?
2. What does the assumption of risk neutrality imply about determination of current market value of some risky asset (such as a stock)?

   Refer to the following information for Questions 3 through 7: A given stock's end-of-year price is uniformly distributed from a low price of $75 to a high price of $175. Investors are risk neutral. The 1-year interest rate is 6 percent.
3. What should be the current market price of the stock?
4. Assume a call option exists with an exercise price of $150 and 1 year to expiration.
   a. What should be the current market price of the call?
   b. What is the probability that the call will be exercised?
5. Assume a put option exists with an exercise price of $75 and 1 year to expiration.
   a. What should be the current market price of the put?
   b. What is the probability that the put will be exercised?
6. Suppose the stock price distribution now changes so it is uniformly distributed from a low of $65 to a high of $165.
   a. What would be the current price of the stock?

  b. Compute the current price of the call from Question 4 and note the change.

  c. Compute the current price of the put from Question 5 and note the change.

7. Starting from the original stock price distribution ($75 to $175), suppose the distribution "spreads out," now ranging from a low of $65 to a high of $185. The distribution is still uniform.

  a. How would the current stock price compare with the price computed in Question 3?

  b. Compute the current price of the call from Question 4 and note the change.

  c. Compute the current price of the put from Question 5 and note the change.

8. Consider the following statement: "When we are modeling the ending stock price with a uniform distribution and assuming risk neutrality, a change in the variance of the stock price should be irrelevant in determining the value of a call or a put option." Is this statement true or false? Explain.

  Refer to the following information for Questions 9 and 10: A stock's current price is $160, and there are two possible prices that may occur next period: $150 or $175. No dividends will be paid. The interest rate on risk-free investments is 6 percent per period.

9. Assume that a European call option exists on this stock having an exercise price of $155.

  a. How could you form a portfolio based on the stock and the call so as to achieve a risk-free hedge?

  b. Compute the equilibrium market price of the call.

10. Assume that a European put option exists on this stock having an exercise price of $180.

  a. How could you form a portfolio based on the stock and the put so as to achieve a risk-free hedge?

  b. Compute the equilibrium market price of the put.

11. Assume the following information for a stock and a call option written on the stock:

Exercise price $= \$40$.
Current stock price $= \$30$.
$\sigma^2 = .25$.
Time to expiration, $t = .25$ year.
Risk-free rate $= .05$.

  a. Use the Black-Scholes procedure to determine the value of the call option.

  b. Change the time to expiration, t, to .5 and compute the call value again.

12. In using the Black-Scholes call option formula, what would be the impact on the call option value in each of the following situations?

  a. If σ rises, other things remaining the same

  b. If t falls, other things remaining the same

  c. If the current stock price rises, other things remaining the same

13. Consider the Black-Scholes call option formula and suppose that the price of the underlying stock gets very large relative to the option's exercise price. As the stock price gets larger, what value would the option be approaching?

14. Suppose a put and a call exist on the same stock, each having an exercise price of $75 and each having the same expiration date. The current price of the stock is $68. The put's current price is $6.50 higher than the call's price. A riskless investment over the time until expiration will yield 3 percent. Given this information, are there any riskless profit opportunities available? Are the put and the call priced in an equilibrium relationship with one another?

QUESTION SET 2

1. Suppose you were holding 10 out-of-the-money European calls on June 29 that were to expire on June 30. The exercise price is $25 and the stock price is currently $24. What are your calls worth?

2. Due to the recent tornadoes abounding over the grain belt, there is increased uncertainty about the stock in a grain company which is a large cattle grain feed supplier. However, the initial prediction of the crop has remained good due to other weather factors. The ending price of the stock is more uncertain, yet the current price is unchanged. What effect will this have on the value of the option written on the stock?

3. According to Black and Scholes, in the presence of risk-averse investors, options should be used in combination with the stocks they are written on to construct riskless investments. Given this, how should options be priced?

4. What does the slope of the relationship between the value of the option and the value of the stock indicate?

5. A stock has a price of $30. A put exists that at this price has a 50 percent probability of being exercised.
   a. How would you create a riskless portfolio combining these two securities?
   b. How will the portfolio be readjusted if the stock price changed to $32 where the probability of exercise was 45 percent?

6. How would you hedge an investment in call options?

7. Describe the Black-Scholes framework.

8. The normal distribution of rates of return implies a log-normal distribution of ending stock prices. What is a log-normal distribution?

9. Strong economic forces keep an option at its equilibrium price, in which case you are indifferent as to what hedge to choose. However, if the option is priced above or below equilibrium, you can set up a hedge that can make you infinitely wealthy, sometimes with no investment. Explain how you would hedge in call or in puts when the option is over-priced and when it is underpriced.

ANSWERS TO QUESTION SET 2

1. Your call is currently worth very little. An option is "out-of-the-money" when, if the expiration date were moved up to the present day, $t = 0$, it would have no value.

2. An increase in the variance on the underlying stock will increase the market value of the option written on it, since this increases the upside potential of investment in the option, while leaving the downside less affected.

3. Since the portfolio is riskless, it should produce the riskless rate of return. Options should be priced so that, when combined with stocks in a hedged portfolio, the total initial invest-ment will be expected to earn the risk-free rate of return.

4. The slope indicates the probability of exercising the option, and the hedge ratio (e.g., the number of shares of stock you must buy for each call you sell or for each put you buy). This slope is also $N(d_1)$ in the Black-Scholes pricing formula.

5. a. At \$30.00, a \$1.00 increase in the price of the stock means that the put will fall in price by \$0.50. Buy one share of the stock for every two put options to completely offset changes in the prices of both.
   b. With each change in the prices of stocks and options, the probability that the option will be exercised changes and the portfolio must be adjusted to maintain its riskless status. At \$32.00, the number of options that will offset the increase of \$1.00 in stock price is $1/.45 = 2.22$. So you would buy 2.22 puts for every stock purchased.

6. Since the values of call options and stocks move in the same direction, hedge by buying one and selling the other. Either buy stock and sell some calls, or sell short the stock and use the proceeds to buy enough calls to hedge, investing the remainder in risk-free bonds.

7. Black-Scholes framework assumes that
   a. The probability distribution for rates or return on stock are normal.
   b. The time interval on which hedged positions are based is reduced to an instant.
   c. A hedged position is based on the ratio of the dollar change in the value of the stock and the resulting dollar change in the value of the option.
   d. To maintain a hedged position, you must continuously readjust your relative positions in stocks and options.

8. If a distribution of ending stock values is skewed to the right on a standard scale but normally distributed on a log scale, it is log-normal.

9. If an option is underpriced you want to buy it; if it is overpriced, you want to sell it. When a call is underpriced, sell short the stock and with the proceeds buy calls and invest in risk-free bonds. When a call is overpriced, hedge by selling it and buying stock puts and shares of stock. When a put option is underpriced, buy both. Sell both when the option is over-priced, investing the proceeds in risk-free bonds.

PROBLEM SET

1. A stock has two possible ending prices: \$150 or \$90. A call option written on it has an exercise price of \$110. The option expires in one year. You choose to make a hedged investment by buying stock and selling calls.
   a. How would you create an exact offset in the value of your two positions?
   b. Suppose you hedge a portfolio of 1000 shares of stock with the sale of options. What is the value of this portfolio in one year?
   c. Given that the initial price of this stock was \$95, how would the option be priced so that your hedged investment would yield a risk-free rate of return of 10 percent?

2. A stock has two possible ending values—\$150 or \$90. A put option written on it has an exercise price of \$110. The stock initially sells for \$95.
   a. How would you hedge an investment in puts?
   b. What is the ending value of this portfolio if you buy only one share of stock and hedge with puts?
   c. What put option price would produce a portfolio return of 10 percent?

3. A stock has an initial price of \$150. In one year it is expected to be worth \$175 or \$125. A call option with one year to expiration has an exercise price of \$150. The risk-free rate of return is 8 percent. What is the return on a hedged portfolio if the option sells at \$18? What if the option sells at \$16?

Use the following information for Problems 4 through 8.

A stock has a beginning market value of $95. It can either increase in value each year by 10 percent or decrease in value by 20 percent. A 3-year European put option written on it has an exercise price of $85. The risk-free rate of return is 5 percent. Assume that you always have only one share of stock in your portfolio.

4. What is the current equilibrium price of the put if you maintain a riskless portfolio by readjusting your relative positions in stocks and puts at the end of each year?

5. What if the exercise price is changed to $130, all other things the same, what is the current market value of the put?

6. Is the option initially in-the-money?

ANSWERS TO PROBLEM SET

1. a.
$$\frac{\text{No. of call options sold}}{\text{for each stock bought}} = \frac{\text{High-low spread for stock}}{\text{High-low spread for option}}$$

$$1.5 = \frac{\$150 - \$90}{\$40 - \$0}$$

Sell 1.5 call options for each stock you buy.

b. To hedge an investment in 1000 stocks, 1500 call options must be sold. If the stock price is $150, at expiration the portfolio value is $90,000.

1000 shares	$150,000
Loss from options [(150-110) × 1500]	−60,000
	$ 90,000

If the ending stock price is $90, the options will not be exercised and you have 1000 shares of stock worth $90,000.

c.
$$1 + r_P = \frac{\text{Year-end portfolio value}}{\text{Initial net investment}}$$

$$= \frac{\text{Year-end portfolio value}}{\text{Stock investment} - \text{proceeds from sale of options}}$$

$$1.10 = \frac{\$90,000}{(1000 \times \$95) - (1500 \times \text{call option price})}$$

Solving for the option price $V_{C,0}$

$$V_{C,0} = \frac{(1 + r_F)(\text{stock investment}) - (\text{year-end portfolio value})}{(1 + r_F)(\text{number of call options sold})}$$

$$= \frac{(1.10)(\$95,000) - \$90,000}{(1.10)(1500)} = \$8.79$$

2. a. Since the prices of the stock and the put move in opposite directions, you must either buy both or sell short the stock and sell puts in order to hedge.

b. $\dfrac{\text{No. of put options}}{\text{bought per stock}} = \dfrac{\text{High-low spread for stock}}{\text{High-low spread for put}}$

$$3 = \frac{\$150 - \$90}{\$20 - 0}$$

If the stock falls to \$90, you have one stock worth \$90 and three options worth (\$20 × 3) \$60 for a portfolio value of \$150.

The year-end portfolio value if the stock goes to \$150 is \$150 since the options are worthless.

c. $r_P = \dfrac{\text{Year-end portfolio value}}{\text{Stock investment} + \text{put investment}} - 1.00$

$$.10 = \frac{\$150}{(1 \times \$95) + (3 \times V_{P,0})} - 1.00$$

$$V_{P,0} = \frac{\$150 - (1.10)(\$95)}{(1.10)(3)} = \$13.79$$

3. Hedge ratio: $\dfrac{\$175 - \$125}{\$25 - 0} = 2$

This means that you sell two call options for each stock bought. At an ending value of \$175, you have one stock worth \$175 and there will be two options exercised by you for a cost of \$50 each for a net portfolio value of \$125. If the ending price is \$125, the options will not be exercised by you, and you have only stock worth \$125.

$$r_P = \frac{\text{Ending portfolio value}}{\text{Stock investment} - \text{sale of calls}}$$

$$1.08 = \frac{\$125}{\$150 - (2)(V_{P,0})}$$

When the beginning value of the call options is \$18.00, the rate of return on the portfolio is 9.65 percent, which is greater than the risk-free rate. When the initial value is \$16.00, you have a net gain of \$2.44 with no investment of your initial funds.

Sell one stock short	+150
Buy two call options	−32
Invest in risk-free bonds	−118

If the stock goes to \$175, you must cover the short sale at a cost of \$175. Your options are worth \$50 and your investment in risk-free bonds will return (\$118)(1.08) = \$127.44 at the end of the year. You have a net gain of \$2.44. Remember, your initial investment in this hedged portfolio was zero.

If the stock goes to \$125, your options are worthless. You can cover the short sale at a cost of \$125 and your investment in risk-free bonds will return \$127.44. Again, the net gain is \$2.44 with no investment.

4. Possible stock prices:

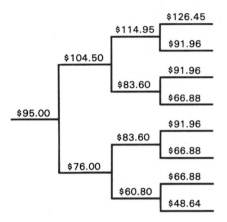

Because the hedged portfolio is riskless, you could justify requiring the risk-free rate of return on your investment.

When the risk-free rate of return is 5 percent and the exercise price of this option is $85.00, the possible market values of the option today and at the end of each year are

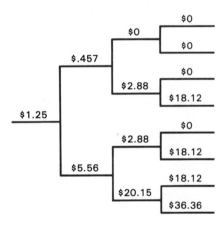

The values for the end of year 3 are obtained by subtracting the end of the year 3 value of the stock from the exercise price of the option. The values are, then, $X - V_{S,3}$ or 0, whichever is greater.

If you require only a 5 percent return on your investment, the current market value of the put is $1.25.

5. The current market value for the put is $2.67.

   The event tree for the option now looks like this:

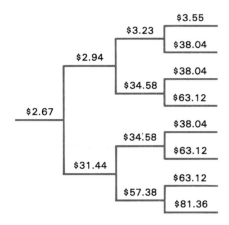

6. No. The present value of the exercise price less the stock price is less than zero.

COMPUTER PROBLEM SET

Refer to the following information for Problems 1 and 2

Stock price	$40.00
Exercise price	$40.00
Standard deviation of returns	30.00%
Day to expiration	182
Risk-free rate	5.00%

1. Using the Black-Scholes model, construct a graph similar to Figure 15.7 showing the relationship between the value of the call and the price of the underlying stock. If you change the number of days to maturity from 182 to 30, how does this affect the shape of the curve?

2. Assuming the current price of the non-dividend paying stock in problem 1 is $40, use the binomial approximation method to estimate the value of the call option. For your first estimate, set the number of iteration periods to 5 and note the call value. Obtain additional estimates of the value of the call where the number of periods are 10, 20, 30, 40, and 50. Compare your answers with the value of the call using the Black-Scholes model.

REFERENCES

BLACK, F., "Fact and Fantasy in the Use of Options," *Financial Analysts Journal* (July–August 1975).

BLACK, F., and SCHOLES M., "The Pricing of Options and Corporate Liabilities," *Journal of Political Economy* (May–June 1973).

COX, J. C., ROSS, S. A., and RUBINSTEIN, M., "Option Pricing: A Simplified Approach," *Journal of Financial Economics* (March 1979).

GESKE, R., "The Valuation of Compound Options," *Journal of Financial Economics* (March 1979).

LATANÉ, H. and RENDLEMAN, R. "Standard Deviations of Stock Price Ratios Implied in Option Prices," *Journal of Finance,* (May 1976).

MERTON, R., "The Theory of Rational Option Pricing," *Bell Journal of Economics and Management Science* (Spring 1973).

RUBINSTEIN, M., "The Valuation of Uncertain Income Streams and the Pricing of Options," *The Bell Journal of Economics* (Autumn 1976).

RUBINSTEIN, M., and COX, J. C., *Option Markets,* Englewood Cliffs, N.J.: Prentice Hall, 1985.

SMITH, C. W., "Option Pricing: A Review," *Journal of Financial Economics* (December 1976).

C H A P T E R

16

AMERICAN OPTION PRICING

In the previous chapter we discussed the characteristics and pricing of *European options,* which can be exercised only at maturity. In this chapter, we will discuss the pricing of **American options** which can be exercised *before* maturity. In some cases this right to exercise early has value. This is true in general for put options, and it is true for many call options on stocks which pay dividends. Thus, the value of an American option may be greater than an otherwise identical European option.

On the one hand, the Black-Scholes model is exclusively an European option pricing model. It should be used with caution in pricing American options where the right to exercise early has value. On the other hand, the binomial option pricing model can be used to value American, as well as European options.

THE LOWER LIMITS TO THE VALUE
OF AMERICAN OPTIONS

Floors Supporting American Call Options

There are two floors which underlie the market value of any *American* call option. We will call one of these floors the **soft floor**. When the call option drops below the soft floor, the option dominates the stock it is written on, as an investment. Thus, the market for the common stock evaporates. The value of an American call option is supported by a **hard floor** as well as a soft floor. The hard floor is positioned below the soft floor. The consequences of an option dropping below the hard floor are even more dramatic; it becomes easy to create unlimited wealth through arbitrage.

We should emphasize here that the soft floor is only applicable to options on stocks that are not expected to pay dividends during the life of the option.

The hard and soft floors are drawn in Figure 16.1 as the solid and broken 45-degree lines, respectively, emanating from the horizontal axis. The hard floor emanates from the exercise price and the soft floor from the present value of the exercise price. The hard floor is equal to

$$V_S - X \qquad \text{or} \qquad 0, \qquad \text{whichever is greater}$$

and the soft floor is equal to

$$V_S - \frac{X}{(1 + r_F)^t} \qquad \text{or} \qquad 0, \qquad \text{whichever is greater}$$

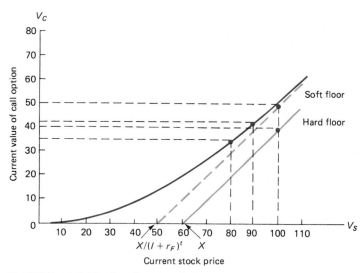

FIGURE 16.1 The hard and soft floors.

OUT ON THE STREET

SLIDING DOWN THE CML

"But that's the point. Bonds have shown as much volatility as stocks in recent years. If you're going to reduce the risk of your portfolio, we think you've got to begin thinking about other markets. And we think the option market provides a viable alternative."

Peter Thayer is executive vice president of Gateway Investment Advisers, a money management firm located in Cincinnati, Ohio. Gateway specializes in the application of options to investment strategies.

Pete is on the phone to a potential investor in Gateway Option Income Fund, which was first established in December 1977. The fund is designed to provide its investors with high yield and low risk. They hope to attain superior investment results to that which an investor can attain by combining investments in the overall market with investments in fixed income securities.

Suppose you want your portfolio to have a beta of .5. Unless you want to go into the bond market or can short-sell without restriction, you have to invest in common stocks with extremely low betas. This means concentrating your investments in regulated utility-type stocks and exposing yourself to the residual variance associated with a portfolio with high industry concentration.

The Option Index Fund provides an alternative. Gateway invests in the population of nearly 400 optionable stocks. For each 100 shares of stock they buy, they sell one option contract, at the money, on the same stock. The dollar movement in an *at-the-money option* is approximately half the dollar movement in the stock, so the beta of this partially hedged position will be approximately half the beta of the underlying common stock. Since the betas for the stocks in the overall portfolio are distributed around 1.00, the overall portfolio is usually between .4 and .6. This is accomplished for a widely diversified portfolio without the need to invest in fixed income securities. This is particularly attractive to corporate

Market Forces Supporting the Hard Floor

In Figure 16.1 the exercise price of the option is $60, the present value of the exercise price is $50, and the current price of the stock is $100. Thus, given the present price of the stock, the hard floor is $40, and the soft floor is $50.

Suppose the option sells below the hard floor at $38. You can now make money if you buy the option at $38 and then exercise and acquire a share of stock with it for an additional $60. The total cost of acquiring a share in this way is $98. Now you can turn around and sell the stock immediately for $100, making a profit of $2.

Why stop now when you can do it again?

You can repeat this transaction as many times as you want, making $2 each

investors, because while they are taxed on interest income in its entirety, they get to exclude 85 percent of the dividend income from common stock investments for tax purposes.

Up until passage of the new tax law in July 1984, there has been an additional tax advantage to investing in the fund for corporations. In selling the call options, Gateway, of course, raised money. The old law allowed it to distribute these as ordinary dividends to corporations which could then take advantage of the 85 percent exclusion. Moreover, the biggest premiums are on at-the-money options.

As the prices of the individual common stocks move up and down, Gateway rolls out of its old out-of- or in-the-money positions and into a new at-the-money option. As the option moves away from being at the money, the beta for the combined position with the stock changes. For example, suppose the exercise price on the option was $100. If the stock price was $110, the beta for the combined position would be virtually .00 because the dollar change in each option contract would be approximately the same as the dollar change in each 100 shares of common stock. On the other hand, if the price of the stock moved to an out-of-the-money position, say at $90, the beta would move toward the beta of the stock because the dollar changes in the option would now be small relative to the dollar changes in the stock. Thus, Gateway must actively manage its positions to keep the betas halved. Considering the great liquidity in the option market, however, this presents no problem.

Gateway's mutual fund appeals to pension funds and corporate money managers who are looking for bond substitutes. It provides an effective way to slide down the capital market line for those who disdain making bond investments and paying taxes.

time, and as you accumulate capital, you can increase the scale of the transaction so you make more money each time around. In a short period of time, you and people like you, will drive the price of the option above the hard floor.

When the option is below the hard floor, it makes sense to exercise it. You will exercise any options you own, and you will buy all the options you can in order to exercise them. However, once the option is above the hard floor, except under special circumstances, no one will exercise unless the options are about to expire. Suppose for example, that the option was priced at $42. If you exercise, it will cost you an additional $60 to buy the stock. If instead, you sell the option, you can acquire the stock in the market at $100 by adding an additional $58 to the investment. Thus, if the option is above the hard floor, if you want to invest in the stock, you sell the option and buy the stock rather than exercise the option.

Market Forces Supporting the Soft Floor

It can be shown, that at least for call options, the hard floor is really redundant because the market will not permit the stock to fall below the soft floor. Once the option falls below the soft floor, everyone will invest in the option rather than the stock. For example, the option were selling at $42, you could construct a portfolio with the option which would dominate an investment in the stock. The portfolio would consist of one option, purchased at a price of $42, and $50 invested in riskless bonds.

Since the present value of the exercise price of $60 is $50, we know the $50 bond investment which matures at expiration will produce $60 at that time. You can use the $60 to exercise the option, should you choose to do so. If the stock is above $60 at expiration, you will exercise, and you will own a share of stock. If the stock is below $60 at expiration, you will throw your option away, but you will still have the $60 from your bond investment. Consequently, the lower limit on the value of your investment is $60.

If you bought the stock instead of this portfolio, there would be no lower limit on the value of your investment. Assuming there are no dividends paid on the stock, you are equally well off as the option investor if the price of the stock is above $60, but you are worse off if the price of the stock turns out to be below $60. The option investors have the $60 from their bond investment; all you have is a share of stock worth less than $60.

The option portfolio is clearly the better investment, but if the option is selling at a price below the soft floor, it is also cheaper to buy. At a $42 option price, it costs $92 to set up the portfolio of the option and bonds but $100 to buy a share of stock. The option is clearly the better buy. Everyone will recognize this, the market for the stock will evaporate, and everyone will move into the option, eventually driving its price above the soft floor. Since the portfolio of the option and the bonds is clearly the better investment, it commands a higher total price. This will be the case when the option sells at a price on the option pricing curve, *above* the soft floor.

Floors Supporting American Put Options

We have discussed the hard and soft floors in terms of a call option. These floors also exist for put options. The hard floor is given by

$$X - V_S \quad \text{or} \quad 0, \quad \text{whichever is greater}$$

and the soft floor by

$$\frac{X}{(1 + r_F)^t} - V_S \quad \text{or} \quad 0, \quad \text{whichever is greater}$$

The soft and hard floors for a put option are depicted in Figure 16.2. In the case of an American put, the hard floor is above the soft floor, making it the only floor of consequence. As soon as the value of the put ''alive'' falls below its value ''dead'' (the hard floor), the put may be exercised.[1]

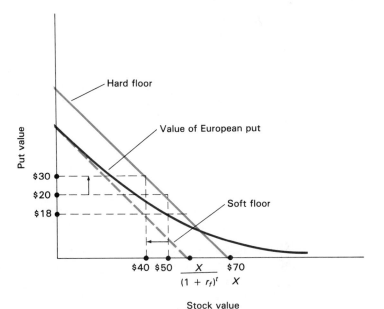

FIGURE 16.2 Early exercise of put option.

THE VALUE OF EARLY EXERCISE

When the Right to Exercise Early Has No Value

Based on the foregoing discussion, we know that

1. An option will not be exercised prior to expiration unless it is priced below the hard floor.
2. The market will not permit the price of the option to fall below the hard floor (or even the soft floor in the case of a call option).

The obvious conclusion, based on these facts, is that some American call options will never be exercised before maturity. While, as we will soon see, this conclusion doesn't hold for all American call options, it does hold for American call options on stocks that are not expected to pay dividends during the life of the option. For these options, since there is never an incentive to exercise prior to expiration, the right to

---

[1]An expectation of a forthcoming dividend payment and an accompanying decline in the stock price as it goes ex-dividend may prevent early exercise.

exercise before expiration has no value. This means that, in these cases, identical American and European options written on the same stocks will have the same market value.

The Black-Scholes equation is technically valid only for the valuation of European options. However, given that for these stocks, the right to exercise early has no value, it can also be used to value American call options that pay no dividends in the exercise period.

The payment of a dividend in the exercise period complicates matters, however. As we shall see, the expected payment of a dividend may trigger early exercise of a call option.

How Dividend Payments May Induce Early Exercise of American Call Options

What if the stock of Figure 16.1 is going to pay a dividend of $20 to all stockholders of record at the end of trading today? The price of the stock today is $100 because if you buy it today, you get the dividend of $20. However, if you wait until tomorrow to buy, you don't get the dividend. Consequently, tomorrow's price is expected to drop to $80.

The curved line approaching the soft floor from above is the relationship that is expected to exist between the value of the option and the value of the stock. Thus, if the price of the stock is going to be $80 tomorrow, we can expect that the option will be priced at $35. Note that if you exercise the option today, it is worth $40 to you because you can use it to buy a share of stock at $60. Also if you buy the stock today, you get the dividend, which is worth $100 along with the stock. Under these conditions, it makes sense for you to exercise your option prior to its expiration date because you are $5 better off if you do. On the day the stock goes ex-dividend, the market value of the option will be priced at $40 and, except for those held by a few unfortunate investors who are unaware of the situation, they will nearly all disappear by the end of the day.

Note that if the dividend were smaller, say $10 instead of $20, it wouldn't trigger early exercise in the case of Figure 16.1 because we can expect the stock to be priced at $90 and the option to be priced at $42 tomorrow. So it makes no sense for us to exercise the option for $40 today. The price of the option today will be approximately equal to $42, its expected price tomorrow.

However, even a $10 dividend can trigger early exercise if the time between the ex-dividend day and expiration was shorter. In this case, the present value of the exercise price would be closer to the exercise price; the soft floor would be closer to the hard floor. Early exercise is triggered as soon as the expected value of the option tomorrow falls below the hard floor of the option today. This is more likely to happen the

1. Larger is the dividend.
2. Shorter is the time between the ex-dividend date and the expiration date.

3. Smaller is the variance of the stock price. (The larger the variance, the greater is the distance between the curve and the soft floor.)

If you are valuing an option where early exercise is a distinct possibility, you must be very cautious about using the Black-Scholes framework. This framework should be used for valuing European options or for valuing American options where early exercise is unlikely. If early exercise is a distinct possibility, the right to exercise early has value, and the value of an American option rises above the value of a Black-Scholes European option, as given by Equations (15.10) and (15.11) in the previous chapter. In this case you may want to consider using an alternative option pricing model for American options such as the binomial model or the model presented in Appendix 7, at the end of this chapter.

Early Exercise of American Put Options

We saw in the preceding section that the prospect of the payment of a dividend can induce early exercise of an American call option. The *prospect* of dividend payments has the opposite effect on American put options. This is because the expected drop in the stock price on the ex-dividend day will increase the value of the put. Thus, the presence of an ex-dividend day between now and the expiration day may induce holders of the option to delay exercise until after the stock has gone ex-dividend.

To see why, consider Figure 16.2. The broken line emanating from the present value of the exercise price is the put's soft floor. The solid line emanating from the exercise price itself is the hard floor. The curved line shows the market value of the put *if it were a European as opposed to an American option*. If the stock paid no dividends, this American put would be exercised as soon as it is worth more dead than alive. This is the case when the curved line falls below the hard floor. If the stock is priced at $50, the put is worth $18, if it is to be kept alive until maturity. If exercised today, it gives you the right to sell someone the stock at $70. Since you can buy the stock for $50 and immediately sell it with the option for $70, the put is worth $20 dead. The put is worth $2 more dead than alive. If this is all there is to the story, it will die.

But what if the stock is expected to pay a dividend of $10? If nothing else happens between now and the time the stock goes ex-dividend, the value of the stock will fall to $40, and the option will be worth $30 dead. If the expected dividend is large enough, and the time between now and the ex-dividend date is small enough, put options may remain alive even if they are currently worth more dead than alive.

It should be obvious from the graph that early exercise is a potentially bigger factor in the valuation of American puts than it is in the valuation of American calls. For this reason you should take great caution in using the Black-Scholes model in valuing put options. Because the Black-Scholes model assigns no value to the right to exercise early, (it would value the put of Figure 16.2 at $18 when the stock price is at $50), it is likely to undervalue many American put options significantly.

Fortunately, we have at our disposal several alternative American option pricing models. One of these is discussed in the appendix to this chapter. Another is a model we've already discussed—the binomial option pricing model.

THE BINOMIAL MODEL AS AN AMERICAN OPTION PRICING MODEL

To see the value of the binomial model as an American option pricing model, consider the following situation. Suppose that the risk-free rate is 5 percent, and there are two possible rates of return on the stock, +10 percent and −10 percent. The current price of the stock is $100. The stock is expected to pay a dividend of $10 at the end of one year. We are valuing an American call option on the stock with two years to expiration. The exercise price for the option is also $100.

The event trees for the stock and the call option (valued as a European option) are as follows. (The expected prices for the stock ex-dividend at the end of the first year are given in parentheses.)

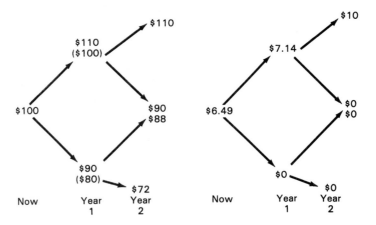

Note that the stock price can go to either $110 or $90 in the course of the first year. At the end of the year either of these prices is reduced to $100 or $80 as the stock goes ex-dividend. From there, the stock can go to $110, $90, $88, or $72 depending on which of the two possible returns comes up next.

We value the call option as a European option just as we did in Chapter 15. We first go to the end of the event tree at expiration and determine the value of the option at each branch. Since the call option has an exercise price of $100, it has value ($10) only at the top branch, where the stock is worth $110. So if the stock price goes down in the first year, we may as well discard the option because it can never have any value in the future. If the stock goes up in the first year, however, the option will be worth $7.14 at the beginning of the second. We know this because we can form a hedge portfolio by buying one share of stock and selling two options. This portfolio will be worth $90 at the end of the second year no matter what happens to the stock. If the options sell at a price of $7.14 at the beginning of the second year, we will get a 5 percent rate of return on this hedge portfolio. Since this portfolio is riskless, and since the risk-free rate is 5 percent, this is a fair deal and $7.14 is the fair price. We can find the value of the option at the beginning of the *first* year in the same way. We know that, at the end of the second year, the option will be worth either $7.14 or nothing, and the stock (with the dividend) will be worth $110 or $90. Now we can form a hedge portfolio by buying one share of stock and selling 2.2 options. The value of this portfolio must be worth $90 at year-end, and if the option currently sells at a price of $6.49, we will get a 5 percent return on our investment—another fair deal.

Thus, the value of the call option as a European option is $6.49. How will the option be valued if it is an American option instead? If the option is American, and if the stock goes up in price in the first year, we will exercise early, right before it goes ex-dividend at the end of the first year. With the stock at a cum-dividend price of $110, the option is worth $10 if we exercise it immediately. We know that if we wait until the stock goes ex-dividend (and falls to a price of $100), the option will only be worth $7.14. Thus, we're better off if we exercise early, so we will. Now, how do we value this option at the beginning of the first year? We know the option will never make it to the end of the second year, so we don't even have to consider those branches. At the end of the first year the option will be worth either $10 (exercised) or $0, if the stock falls in price. We can again create a riskless hedge portfolio by selling two options and buying one share of stock. This portfolio will produce the risk-free rate of return if the option sells at a price of $7.14 *at the beginning of the first year*. The difference between this price and the price we obtained for the European option is the value of the right to exercise early.

Thus the binomial model can be used in this way to value American as well as European options. In valuing an American option, the model checks to see if the option is worth more dead than alive at each branch of the tree. If it is, the particular branch ends at that point, and we work our way back, as before, to find the current value of the American option.

Because the European, binomial valuation converges to the Black-Scholes valuation when the number of branching periods is reasonably extensive, and because the binomial model values American as well as European options, it is a relatively valuable model, particularly in the pricing of American put options.

SUMMARY

There are two floors below which the value of American options cannot fall. The floors differ with respect to the strength of the economic forces supporting them. The hard floor is the difference between the stock price and the exercise price, or zero, whichever is greater. If the option drops below this floor, we all gain unlimited wealth by repeatedly buying the option, exercising it, and selling the stock. The soft floor is the difference between the stock price and the present value of the exercise price or zero, whichever is greater. If the option drops below this floor, an investment in the option dominates an investment in the stock, and the market for the stock evaporates. Since an option won't be exercised until it falls below the hard floor, call options won't be exercised prematurely unless there is an expected, sudden drop in the stock's price associated with the dividend payment. This implies equal value for European and American call options on stocks which don't pay dividends.

However, the right to exercise early may be potentially valuable for call options on stocks that pay dividends, and for put options, especially those which don't pay dividends. For these options, a European option pricing model like the Black-Scholes model will tend to underestimate the true value of the options. The binomial model, however, can be used to value both American as well as European options.

APPENDIX 7

THE GESKE-ROLL-WHALEY AMERICAN OPTION PRICING MODEL

Roll (1977) developed a model for the pricing of American options on stocks that are expected to pay a dividend before expiration that is known with certainty. This model differs from the binomial American option model in that it is derived in the context of continuous time, and it has the advantage of a closed form, as opposed to a numerical solution. Geske (1979) later simplified the model, and Whaley (1981) later corrected an error in both derivations. The market value for such an option is given by the following equation:

$$V_C = V_S W_1 - \frac{X}{e^{r_F t}} W_2 + a \frac{D}{e^{r_F t}} W_3$$

In this equation, D is the dividend, t is the time to expiration of the option, T is the time until the ex-dividend day, and a is the expected decline in the stock price at the ex-dividend date as a fraction of the dividend. For example, if the dividend is $1.00 and the stock is expected to fall by $.80 when it goes ex-dividend, a is equal to .80. The values for the W's are given by the following equations:

$$W_1 = N^*(k_1, - m_1, - \sqrt{T/t}) + N(m_1)$$

$$W_2 = N^*(k_2, - m_2, - \sqrt{T/t}) + N(m_2)e^{r_F(t-T)}$$

$$W_3 = N(m_2)$$

In these equations the operator $N(\ )$ is the same as the Black-Scholes model. The $N^*(\ )$ operator is similar, but it operates in terms of a unit normal, *joint* distribution. The numbers k and m refer to the deviations from the mean (or zero) on each horizontal axis of the joint distribution. The value for $\sqrt{T/t}$ is the correlation coefficient assumed for the distribution. The value $N*(\ )$ is the sum of the probabilities of simultaneously falling below the two deviations. The values for the deviations are determined as follows:

$$k_1 = \frac{\ln(V_S/X) + \left[r_F + \frac{1}{2}\sigma^2(r)\right]t}{\sigma(r)\sqrt{t}}, \qquad k_2 = k_1 - \sigma(r)\sqrt{t}$$

$$m_1 = \frac{\ln(V_S/V_S') + \left[r_F + \frac{1}{2}\sigma^2(r)\right]T}{\sigma(r)\sqrt{T}}, \qquad m_2 = m_1 - \sigma(r)\sqrt{T}$$

In the formulas for the deviations, V_S' is the ex-dividend stock price that will trigger early exercise of the option. In the case of Figure 16.1 that value would be approximately $87.

QUESTION SET 1

1. Suppose a put and a call exist on the same stock, each having an exercise price of $75 and each having the same expiration date. The current price of the stock is $68. The put's current price if $6.50 higher than the call's price. A riskless investment over the time until expiration will yield 3 percent. Given this information, are there any riskless profit opportunities available? Are the put and the call priced in an equilibrium relationship with one another?

   Refer to the following information for Questions 2 through 5. Suppose an American call option exists on a particular stock. The exercise price is $105. The present value of the exercise price is $100.

2. What is the hard floor price of the option if the underlying stock is priced at $160? Sketch a graph of the hard floor option prices against several stock prices.

3. Sketch a graph of soft floor prices against several stock prices.

4. At a stock price of $125, you notice the option selling for $18. Would this option price be an equilibrium price? Explain.

5. Suppose the stock price is $135. You notice the option is selling for $32. Would this option price be an equilibrium price? Explain.

6. Although the Black-Scholes call option formula was developed for European call options, could it be legitimately used to value American calls?

7. A stock is selling today for $150. If you are holding the stock today, you will receive a $15 dividend. Holding the stock tomorrow will no longer entitle you to the dividend. You are holding an American call option on the stock having an exercise price of $130. Suppose the anticipated option price is $12 when the stock price is $135. Would you hold on to your option or exercise it? Why?

QUESTION SET 2

1. A call option should never sell below either the hard floor or the soft floor. Why?

2. If a call option is priced below the hard floor, what investment strategy can be used to create instant wealth?

3. When a put option is priced below its hard floor, what investment strategy materializes? Demonstrate this with the current stock price equal to $25.00 and an American put option with an exercise price of $30.00 priced at $4.50.

4. Suppose you hold a call option that is priced above the hard floor and you wish to acquire a share of stock. What is the best strategy to pursue?

5. What portfolio dominates an investment in shares of stock when a call option is priced below the soft floor? Explain. Compare this portfolio to a direct investment in stocks.

6. According to Black and Scholes, the relationship between the value of a call and the value of the stock is such that, as the price of the stock increases, the option approaches but never reaches the soft floor value. If the curve indicating this relationship were to shift higher, away from the soft floor, what is implied?

7. How can an expected dividend payment trigger the early exercise of an option?

8. A short time period between the ex-dividend day and the expiration date for an option can lead to an increased probability of the early exercise of an American option. Why?

9. Should an otherwise identical American option be priced higher than a European option?

ANSWERS TO QUESTION SET 2

1. If the option falls below the soft floor, portfolios involving options dominate investment in the stock itself. If the option falls below the hard floor, you make money by buying options, exercising them, and then selling the acquired stock. In a competitive market, demand for options keeps their prices in equilibrium at the highest price floor.

2. If a call option is priced less that the value of the stock less the exercise price, buy the option and exercise it to acquire a share of stock for a total of less than the value of the stock. You can then profit by selling the stock immediately. Continue by repeating the strategy.

3. If a put is priced less than the exercise price less the value of the stock, buy the option and a stock and then exercise the put to profit on the sale of the stock. If the current price is $25.00 and an American put option having an exercise price of $30.00 is priced at $4.50, the following will dominate purchase of the stock:

Buy put option	$(4.50)
Exercise put by selling short	30.00
Buy stock to cover the short sale profit	(25.00)
	+$ 0.50

You can do this as many times as you like, making $.50 on each transaction with no investment on your own.

4. If the call is priced above $V_S - X$, sell the option and use the proceeds for the stock purchase.

5. A portfolio consisting of one option priced below the soft floor and riskless bonds in the amount of the present value of the exercise price completely dominates an investment in one share of stock in which the investment is written. At expiration you would hold one option giving you the right to purchase a share of stock at X, and proceeds equal to X from the risk-free bonds. If the stock price at expiration is less than X, you can acquire a share of stock and keep the difference. If you had initially purchased stock, there would be no lower limit to the value of your investment at the expiration date; while a portfolio of options and riskless bonds has a lower limit value of X.

When the option is priced below the soft floor, the market for the stock would evaporate, because the cost of constructing the above strategy is less than the cost of a share of stock. Ultimately, at equilibrium, the portfolio of one option and riskless bonds in the amount of should cost more than an investment in one stock. The demand for options will push their price above the current soft floor.

6. An upward shift in the curve indicating the relationship between the values of an option and the stock on which it is written implies an increase in the value of the option given the value of the underlying stock. This can be caused by an increase in the variance of the underlying stock or possibly by a negotiated increase in the term to expiration of the option.

7. An expected dividend payment can trigger early exercise when it is large enough to cause the ex-dividend option price to fall below the current hard floor price. That is, the ex-dividend stock price will be lower by an increment approximately equal to the dividend. The call will be priced correspondingly lower. If this expected future call price is below today's hard floor value, it makes sense to exercise the option now to acquire a share of stock.

8. Early exercise of an option is more likely the shorter time between the ex-dividend date and the expiration date. This means that the soft floor moves closer to the hard floor because the exercise price approaches

$$\frac{X}{(1 + r_F)^t}$$

as the option approaches maturity.

The ex-dividend stock price will be lower by an increment approximately equal to the dividend. Tomorrow's ex-dividend option will be priced correspondingly lower. The dividend amount that will trigger early exercise need not be as great as the option approaches maturity, because the amount by which the ex-dividend expected value of the option tomorrow must fall to break the hard floor is smaller.

9. If there is a possibility that it may be profitable to exercise an American option before maturity, the market should recognize this and price the American option higher than the European option.

COMPUTER PROBLEM SET

Refer to the following information for Problems 1 and 2.

Stock price	$40.00
Exercise price	$40.00
Standard deviation of returns	30.00%
Days to expiration	182
Risk-free rate	5.00%

1. Assume that the underlying stock pays a quarterly dividend of $1.00 in 90 days.
   a. What is the value of the call option using the Black-Scholes model?
   b. What is the value of the call option using the binomial approximation method?
   c. Compare the two values and explain your finding.

2. Now suppose the stock does not pay a dividend and adjust the inputs in the option pricing program accordingly.
   a. Value the put and call options using the Black-Scholes and binomial approximation models.
   b. Compare these two values for both the call and the put.
   c. Explain the difference in the pricing of the options compared with the results in Problem 1.

REFERENCES

BLACK, F., and SCHOLES, M., "The Valuation of Option Contracts and a Test of Market Efficiency," *Journal of Finance* (May 1972).

GESKE, R., "A Note on an Analytic Valuation Formula for Unprotected American Call Options on Stocks with Known Dividends," *Journal of Financial Economics* (December 1979).

ROLL, R., "An Analytic Valuation Formula for Unprotected American Call Options on Stocks with Known Dividends," *Journal of Financial Economics* (November 1977).

RUBINSTEIN, M., "Non-Parametric Tests of Alternative Option Pricing Models Using All Reported Quotes and Trades on the 30 Most Active CBOE Option Classes from August 23, 1976 Through August 31, 1978," Berkeley Working Paper No. 117, October 1981.

STERK, W., "Tests of Two Models for Valuing Call Options on Stocks with Dividends," *Journal of Finance* (December 1982).

STERK, W., "Comparative Performance of the Black-Scholes and the Roll-Geske-Whaley Option Pricing Models," *Journal of Financial and Quantitative-Analysis* (September 1983).

WHALEY, R., "On the Valuation of American Call Options on Stocks with Known Dividends," *Journal of Financial Economics* (June 1981).

WHALEY, R., "Valuation of American Call Options on Dividend Paying Stocks," *Journal of Financial Economics* (March 1982).

C H A P T E R

17

ADDITIONAL ISSUES IN OPTION PRICING

In the previous two chapters we discussed the characteristics and pricing of European and American options. In this chapter, we will discuss some additional topics related to options. These topics include using option pricing models to calculate the market's estimate of the variance of the returns on a stock, some bias problems in option models pricing, and the usefulness of options in formulating investment strategies to take advantage of special situations. We shall also discover that conventional securities, like corporate bonds, can be viewed as portfolios of options, or optionlike securities. In this sense, options can be viewed as the building blocks of complex financial contracts.

USING THE OPTION PRICING FORMULAS
TO FIND THE MARKET'S ESTIMATE
OF THE STOCK'S VARIANCE

If you substitute the current market price of the option into Equations (15.6) and (15.7) of the Black-Scholes option pricing model, along with the specifics of the option contract and the risk-free rate, you can solve for the remaining unknown value in the equation, the variance of the rate of return on the stock. This value can't be solved for directly, but there are computer routines which can be used to solve for the implied variance through an iterative process. Thus, you can find the variance that is consistent with the current price of the option and the Black-Scholes option pricing framework. Given the validity of the framework, the implied variance serves as an estimate of the variance that the market has in mind for the stock in setting the price for the option.

As we discuss later in this chapter, because there is a problem of bias in the model, in pricing options that are significantly in or out of the money, it is best to compute the implied variance using an option where the underlying stock price is approximately equal to the present value of the exercise price.

Figure 17.1 plots the implied variance on such an option over time. Superimposed on the diagram are the percentage changes in the price of the security underlying the option. Notice as the variability of this series becomes smaller, the implied variance associated with the option becomes smaller as well. The market is apparently reassessing its estimate of the security's variance as it experiences lower variability in the return from day to day.

Keep in mind that the Black-Scholes model is for European options. It does not value the right to exercise prior to the option's expiration. As discussed in Chapter 16, this right can have significant value for put options and for call options on stocks that pay dividends. For these options the Black-Scholes estimated price will be less than the actual market price even if the best available estimate of the stock's volatility is used in the Black-Scholes equation. Conversely, if you insert the option's market price into the equation, the estimate of stock volatility that you solve for will be larger than the best available estimate. Thus, the implied volatility estimates derived from the Black-Scholes equation should be considered upward biased in general. The bias increases with the probability of early exercise for the option. It will be greatest for put options and American call options on stocks which pay significant dividends.

You can avoid *this* bias problem if you use an American option pricing model, like the binomial model, to iterate to the implied volatility number. Your software provides a program for this procedure. There are, as we discuss later in this chapter, potential remaining bias problems in American models that still must be contended with. These problems create errors in *pricing* the option, given a volatility estimate, and errors in *implied volatility,* given a market price for the option.

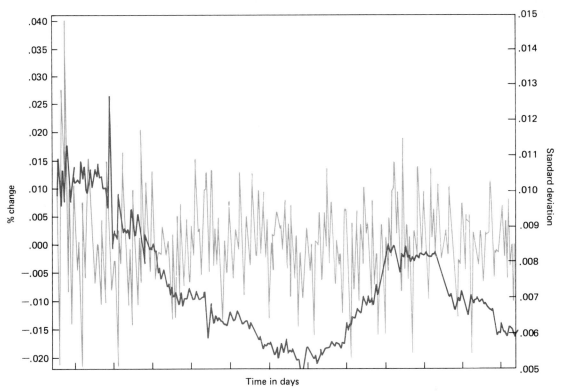

FIGURE 17.1 Implied variance and percentage change in value of underlying asset.

BIAS PROBLEMS IN OPTION PRICING MODELS

The Black-Scholes model has an apparent propensity to overvalue out-of-the-money options and undervalue in-the-money options. This can be seen in the results of a study by MacBeth and Merville (1980), presented in Figure 17.2. On the vertical axis of the graph, we are plotting the percentage difference between the actual market price of each option and the Black-Scholes price. On the horizontal axis, we are plotting the percentage difference between the stock price and present value of the exercise price. Each observation in the figure represents an option written on International Business Machines stock. To be represented on the graph, the options must have at least 90 days to expiration. The variance estimate used in computing the Black-Scholes price is the implied variance for the IBM option that is closest to being in—the—money at the time the option value is computed.

For the option labeled *A*, the actual market price of the option was approximately 23 percent greater than the Black-Scholes value at a time when the market

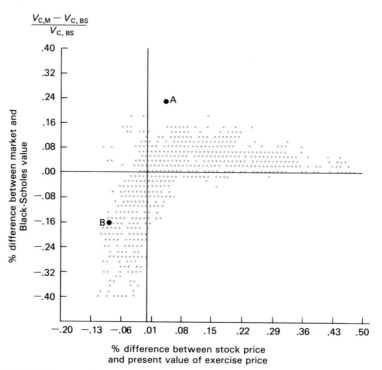

FIGURE 17.2 Bias in the Black-Scholes model.

SOURCE: J. MacBeth and L. Merville, "Tests of the Black-Scholes and Cox Option Valuation Models," *Journal of Finance* (May 1980).

price for IBM stock was 4 percent greater than the exercise price of this particular option.

Out-of-the-money options are positioned to the left of the vertical axis, and in-the-money options are positioned to the right. Note that the in-the-money options tend to be positioned above the horizontal axis, while the out-of-the-money options are positioned below. If you compute the Black-Scholes values for an out-of-the-money option, the actual market price will likely be lower. The opposite will be true for an in-the-money option.[1]

We aren't detecting errors in pricing by the *market*. That is, there's no propensity for the out-of-the-money options to rise to their "equilibrium" Black-Scholes values, and we also see no tendency for in-the-money options to fall back toward their "equilibrium" Black-Scholes values because the Black-Scholes model is in error and not the market. The Black-Scholes value simply isn't the true equilibrium value for the option. Some aspect of the framework assumed in deriving the model

[1]This bias was also reported by Rubinstein (1981). However, the reverse bias was found in studies by Black (1975) and Emanuel and MacBeth (1981).

apparently is misspecified, resulting in an error that is systematically related to the extent to which the option is in or out of the money.

Thus, while the option positioned at point B is selling at a market price which is 16 percent below the value implied by the Black-Scholes equation, it would be wrong to conclude this option was selling at a price below its true equilibrium value. In fact, given the extent to which other options, which are similarly out-of-the money, are overvalued by the Black-Scholes model, we might even conclude this particular option is selling at a price that is *above* its true equilibrium value.

Others have found additional biases in the model. Using over-the-counter option data, Black and Scholes (1972) found that their model underpriced call options on low-variance stocks and overpriced call options on high-variance stocks. Geske and Roll (1984) found that the Black-Scholes model tended to underprice near-maturity American call options.

If you are going to use an option pricing model, such as the Black-Scholes model, as a yardstick to determine whether the market has over- or undervalued a particular option, you must do one of two things to allow for possible biases in your model:

1. You recognize the bias in your model and allow for it in determining the extent to which an option is mispriced.
2. You can revise your model, correcting the misspecification to eliminate the bias.

Changing Volatility as a Source of Bias in Option Pricing Models

The Black-Scholes model and the binomial model assume that the variance of the rates of return to the underlying stock is constant throughout the life of the option. There are a number of empirical tests, however, which indicate there is a tendency for the variance of the rates of return to increase as the market value of a stock becomes smaller. This tendency makes some sense on a theoretical level because a reduction in the market value of the common stock reflects an erosion in the firm's equity base. A reduction in the value of equity relative to the value of the firm's debt means an increase in stockholder risk.

We can allow for this tendency by assuming the returns to a stock are produced by the following process:

$$r_t = E(r) + b_t z_t \tag{17.1}$$

where

$$b_t = a_1 V_{S,t}^{(a_2 - 2)/2} \tag{17.2}$$

In Equation (17.2), the rate of return to the stock in any day t is assumed to be equal to the stock's expected daily rate of return plus a random increment which can be positive or negative. The increment is equal to the product of (1) a factor z_t associated with the individual stock (z_t is normally distributed, has an expected value of zero, and a variance *and* standard deviation of 1.00) and (2) a beta coefficient b_t

which relates the returns on the stock to the factor. The factors associated with different stocks may be correlated, but the number that appears for a given factor on any given day is assumed to be completely independent of the numbers which appeared for the factor on previous days.

The formula for the stock's b_t coefficient is given in Equation (17.2). In the formula, the coefficient a_1 can be interpreted as the number representing what the underlying standard deviation of the stock's return would be if there were no relationship between the variance and the stock price level. The coefficient a_2 specifies the nature of the relationship between the variance and the level of the stock price. To illustrate how a_2 operates, consider the following special cases:

1. If $a_2 = 2.00$, then $b = a_1$, and $\sigma^2(r) = b^2\sigma^2(z) = a_1^2$.
2. If $a_2 = 4.00$, then $b = a_1V_S$, and $\sigma^2(r) = b^2\sigma^2(z) = a_1^2V_S^2$.
3. If $a_2 = .00$, then $b = a_1/V_S$, and $\sigma^2(r) = b^2\sigma^2(z) = a_1^2/V_S^2$.

Note that the variance of the stock's rate of return is computed as the square of the stock's b coefficient multiplied by the variance of the factor (which is assumed to be 1.00). This is analogous to the case of the single-index model where the systematic component of the stock's variance is equal to the product of the stock's squared beta and the variance of the index. In this case, there's no residual component to the variance because there's no residual component to the rate of return in Equation (17.1). If the z's are, in fact, correlated between stocks, we could, split them into an index-related term and a residual term. However, there isn't any need for that here.

When a_2 is equal to 2.00, the variance of the stock is a constant equal to a_1^2, and it is related to the level of the stock price. This is the special case assumed in the Black-Scholes framework. When a_2 takes on a value greater than 2.00, the variance of the rate of return becomes larger as the stock price becomes larger, as in the case where a_2 is equal to 4.00, and $\sigma^2(r)$ is equal to $a_1^2 V_S^2$. A positive relationship between variance and stock price level is contrary to theory and empirical evidence, but the formula allows for this special case in any event. When a_2 is less than 2.00, the variance becomes larger as the stock price becomes smaller, as when a_2 is .00 and $\sigma^2(r)$ is equal to a_1^2/V_S^2.

Cox (1975) has derived an alternative formula to that of Black and Scholes which assumes that stock returns are generated according to Equations (17.1) and (17.2). Once again, the model derives the option value required to produce a risk-free rate of return to an investor that hedges with the option. The Cox model simplifies into the Black-Scholes model when a_2 is given a value of 2.00. To use the Black-Scholes model, you must estimate the standard deviation of the stock's return (which is equal to a_1 in that framework). To use the Cox model, you must estimate the coefficients a_1 and a_2 simultaneously, using samples of the stock's past returns.

From available evidence, it appears the Cox model is free of some of the bias problem which plagues the Black-Scholes model. However, the Cox model is much more computationally complex than the Black-Scholes model. If you are interested in learning more about the model, you will find a complete description in the paper by MacBeth and Merville (1980).

How might this propensity for volatility to become larger when the stock price becomes smaller account for the tendency of the Black-Scholes model to overvalue out-of-the-money options? To see how, consider an option with an exercise price of $50. The stock price is currently $40, and the option is selling at a price of $2. The value of the option, as estimated by the Black-Scholes model, is $3. The difference might be accounted for by the fact that (1) the only way for the option to pay off is for the stock price to rise above $50, (2) the Black-Scholes model assumes the stock's volatility will remain intact at its present level should this occur, and (3) the market, in setting the price at $2, recognizes that the stock's volatility is likely to become smaller if this occurs—a negative for the option.

The Black-Scholes model may undervalue in-the-money options for exactly the same reason. The market may recognize that should these options fall out-of-the-money, there will be an accompanying increase in stock volatility—a positive for the option which will cushion the impact on their market price. In its assumption of constant stock volatility, the Black-Scholes model fails to recognize this tendency and therefore, undervalues the option.

This particular problem also holds for the binomial model because it also assumes stock volatility is a constant throughout the life of the option. The binomial model, however, can easily be adapted to account for any tendency for volatility to change as we move to higher and lower branches on the event tree.

Bias from Using European Models to Value American Options

We know that a European option pricing model, like the Black-Scholes model does not place any value on the right to exercise early.[2] Thus, the Black-Scholes model will generally place a lower value on an option than the market. We also know that the extent of the underpricing will be different for different options. It should be expected to be greater for puts than for calls because there is a greater probability for early exercise on put options. It should also be greater for call options on stocks which pay dividends than on stocks which don't. In fact, this particular source of bias in pricing should be of no problem whatsoever for call options on stocks which do not pay dividends because the probability (and, therefore, the value) of early exercise is zero for these options.

But should we expect the magnitude of the American-European bias will be related to the extent that an option is in or out of the money, as in Figure 17.2? The answer to this question is yes. As we see in Figure 16.3, from the previous chapter, the probability for early exercise on a put option increases as the stock price goes down and the put moves deeper into the money. The same thing is true for call options on stocks which pay dividends. Holding all other factors constant, the prob-

---

[2]Geske and Roll (1984) argue that the bias problems in the Black-Scholes model may result from the fact that a European model is being used to value American options. Roll (1977) and Geske (1979b) have developed an American option pricing model for stocks with dividend payments that are known with certainty. Although less complex than the Cox model, this model is somewhat more complex than the Black-Scholes model. The model was presented in Appendix 7 at the end of Chapter 16.

ability of a given dividend payment inducing early exercise increases as the option moves deeper into the money.

Consequently, the pricing bias for the Black-Scholes European option model is likely to be strongest for in-the-money options. You might ask, if this problem is the only source of pricing bias in the model, what accounts for the apparent *overvaluation* by the model for out-of-the-money options in Figure 17.2? First, you must remember that there are other problems, like nonstationary volatility, to contend with. More important, the numbers represented in Figure 17.2 required an estimate of volatility to be used in the Black-Scholes equation. The volatility numbers used to construct Figure 17.2 were the implied volatilities computed from *at-the-money* IBM options for the particular days in which the options were priced. This procedure forces *the appearance* of unbiased pricing for at-the-money options. (If we insert the implied volatility back into the Black-Scholes model, we must get an estimated Black-Scholes price which is equal to the market price because the market price was used to obtain the implied volatility.) Thus, even if all the options were undervalued, the procedure will give the appearance of overvaluation and undervaluation for out-of- and in-the-money options, respectively.

Pricing Bias Resulting from Error in the Model's Inputs

Bias problems, like that apparent in Figure 17.2, may appear even if we were pricing European options on stocks which had constant volatility, and even if all the other assumptions of the Black-Scholes model were accurate descriptions of reality.

This is true because the model requires that we input the following numbers in order to obtain a Black-Scholes price:

1. An estimate of the stock's volatility
2. An estimate of the number of *effective* days until maturity
3. An estimate of the appropriate risk-free rate

What if it is the case that our estimates are biased? Are out-of- and in-the-money options equally sensitive to bias in the estimates to the model? They are not. Errors in the estimates will result in much larger *percentage* pricing errors for out-of-the-money options than for in-the-money options. For example, suppose your estimates of stock volatility are, in general, larger than those employed by the market. Generally you will overvalue options, but the extent of your percentage overvaluation will be greater for those which are out of the money. If, on the other hand, your volatility estimates are on the low side, you will undervalue options in general, but the degree of undervaluation will be most pronounced for options that are out of the money.

Perhaps this accounts for the fact that others (Fisher Black in 1975) have reported relationships reversed from that of Figure 17.2, where it is out-of-the-money options that are undervalued.

Errors can be made in other inputs to the model as well. How many days are left before the option expires? At first glance, the answer to this question seems unambiguous. However, all calendar days are not the same. Some of these days may be holidays and some may fall on weekends. The stock market is not open on these days. Trading may not take place on these days, but the value of the stock moves nonetheless. Still, you must remember that the generation of new and relevant information undoubtedly slows down considerably.

Stock price volatility on weekends and holidays can be inferred by observing the relationship between the closing price on the day before the weekend or holiday and the opening price on the following trading day. Based on these observations we know on days where the market is closed the volatility is a small fraction of the volatility on days when the market is open. Most option pricing models treat every day as though it had the same volatility as any other. To allow for the fact that volatility differs from day to day, you may either adjust your estimate of volatility accordingly or reduce the number of effective days to expiration. The fact that most of those who have documented bias problems in option pricing models failed to make these adjustments may partially account for their findings of bias.

We may also be facing bias problems in terms of the risk-free rate. Most analysts use the rate of return promised on a treasury bill with a maturity equal to the number of days until the expiration of the option. However, if the term structure of interest rates isn't flat, and since there are potential problems with the number of effective days until the option's maturity, these problems carry over to the risk-free rate itself.

The use of treasury bill rates may also be questioned. Since, in creating a "riskless" hedge with options, your position can't be continuously adjusted to keep you unaffected by changes in (1) the price of the stock, (2) the volatility of the stock, or (3) the level of the risk-free rate, there is a residual level of risk associated with your position. This residual risk may call for a risk premium in the return to the hedge strategy. There may also be an additional premium related to the transactions costs consumed in the changes in your position that you do make from day to day. Thus, the treasury rate may underestimate the true rate required on the hedge, causing an additional element of undervaluation by the option pricing model. (The greater the risk-free rate, the greater the value for the option.) Again, the degree of undervaluation will be more pronounced for out-of-the money options, although for relatively short-term options, changes in the risk-free rate have a minimal impact on the option price.

OPTION STRATEGIES

The Straddle

Options can be put together into packages to take advantage of special situations. Suppose a firm is involved in antitrust litigation. The suit is to be settled in the next month, but the direction of the decision is completely unclear. If the firm wins the suit, the price of the stock is likely to be worth $40; if it loses, the value will be $20. There is a 50 percent chance of the suit going either way, and the current market price of the stock is poised halfway between the two possible outcomes at $30.

If you use options, it *may* be possible to construct a strategy whereby you make money regardless of the outcome of the case. The strategy that is suitable for this particular situation is called a straddle. To construct a straddle, you buy an equal number of put and call options on the same stock that have the same exercise price and mature on the same date. In this case, you'll want the expiration date on the options to be after the date the case is expected to be decided. The market value of the straddle as function of the market value of the stock is graphed in Figure 17.3. In drawing the figure, we have presumed the rate of interest is equal to zero, so the exercise prices *and* their present values are all equal to the current stock price, $30. The solid curves show the relationships between the put and call and the stock price. The broken curve shows the relationship between the value of the straddle and the stock price. Based on the Black-Scholes framework, when the term to expiration for the put and call are equal, and when the present value of both exercise prices are equal to the current stock price, the put and call will have identical market values, in this case $4.00. Thus, the total value of the straddle is $8.00.

It seems the value of the straddle will increase if the stock moves in either direction from its present position. This is true if the move takes place immediately. However, as time goes by and the expiration date for the options approaches, the value of the put will approach $X - V_S$ or 0, whichever is greater, and the value of the call will approach $V_S - X$ or 0, whichever is greater. Thus at expiration, the value of the straddle will be positioned on one of the two 45-degree lines emanating from the exercise price. If the firm wins the case, the stock rises to $40, and the straddle is worth $10 at expiration (the value of the call). If the firm loses, the stock falls to $20, and the straddle is worth $10 at expiration (the value of the put). Since you paid $8 for the straddle initially, you win in either case.

There are two problems, however.

First, there is always the possibility of the trial lingering on without a decision. If no decision is reached until after the expiration date, the price of the stock will

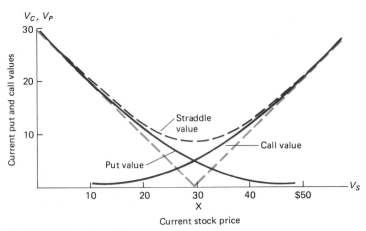

FIGURE 17.3 Straddle.

remain at $30 at expiration, and the straddle will be worthless, resulting in the loss of your initial $8 investment.

Second, the market may fully recognize the firm's high-variance situation in pricing the options. It may derive the price of the put and the call to $5, in which case you break even if the trial is decided before expiration. To make money, the price of the stock would have to move outside the $20 to $40 range. If it falls inside the range instead, you lose money on the straddle. Falling in or out of this range may well be an even bet. In determining whether this is a good strategy, you must assess the extent to which the market has taken the firm's situation into account in pricing the options.

The Butterfly Spread

Another example of an option strategy is the butterfly spread. You would want to construct a butterfly spread when you believe the possible outcomes for the stock price are in a more narrow range than is implied in the pricing of the options by the market.

A butterfly spread can be constructed with call options written on the same stock, expiring at the same date, but having three different exercise prices. Suppose the present price of the stock is $60. You buy one call option with an exercise price of $50 for a price we will assume is $13. You sell two calls with an exercise price of $60 for a market price of $5 each, and you buy one call with an exercise price of $70 for $1. The total cost of this investment is $4 = \$13 - 2 \times \$5 + \$1$.

The value of the butterfly spread at the expiration date for the options, as a function of the value of the stock at that time, is given in Figure 17.4. If the stock is worth $50 or less, all the options are worthless. As the stock price goes from $50 to $60, the option with the $50 exercise price takes on value, rising from $0 to $10. Once the stock price increases in value beyond $60, the two options you sold with exercise prices of $60 take on value. Their value must be subtracted from the value of the $50 option, because your position in them is negative. Thus, if the stock price is at $70, the $50 call you bought is worth $20, but the two $60 calls you sold are worth $10 each, so the total value of the package is $0. Once the stock price moves

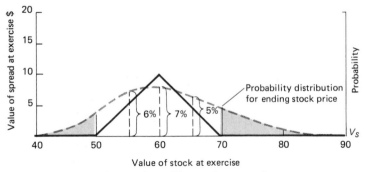

FIGURE 17.4 Ending value of butterfly spread.

beyond $70, the $70 option you bought adds to the value of the package. Thus, at an $80 stock price, the $50 call is worth $30, the two $60 calls are worth a total of $40, and the $70 call is worth $10. Adding up the positive and negative positions, we again get a total value for the package of $0. No matter how far the stock price climbs above $70, the value of the butterfly spread will be $0.

This butterfly spread is a good investment if you believe the price of the stock will remain near its present value. If the stock price doesn't move, the ending value of the spread will be $10, and it cost you only $4 to set it up.

Computing the Expected Return on an Option Strategy

To compute the expected rate of return on a strategy like the butterfly spread, you need to estimate the shape of the probability distribution for the value of the stock at the expiration date for the options. In Figure 17.4, we have superimposed a probability distribution for the ending stock value. We assume the distribution for the rates of return to the stock is normal, so the resulting distribution for the ending value of the firm will be log-normal in shape.

From the distribution of the ending stock value and the relationship between the ending spread value and stock value, we can construct the probability distribution for the ending spread value.

First, consider the probability that the ending spread value will be $0. This is equal to the total probability in the shaded tails of the distribution for stock prices less than $50 and greater than $70. The sum of these probabilities is assumed to be equal to 20 percent, and this is graphed in Figure 17.5, which shows the probability distribution for the butterfly spread.

Other points in the distribution of Figure 17.5 can be obtained as follows. The

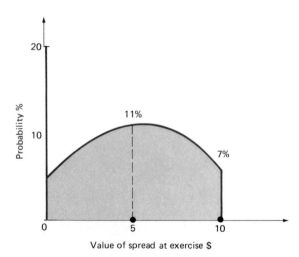

FIGURE 17.5 Probability distribution for ending value of butterfly spread.

probability of the stock being worth $60 is 7 percent. This is also the probability of the spread being worth its maximum value of $10. If the stock is worth either $55 or $65, the spread is worth $5. The probability of the stock being worth $55 is 6 percent, and the probability of its being worth $65 is 5 percent. The probability of the spread being worth $5 is the sum of these two probabilities or 11 percent.

We can repeat the same process for all other possible stock values and corresponding spread values and construct the probability distribution for the spread, as drawn in Figure 17.4. Given the distribution, we can compute its expected value, which we will assume to be $5. The expected rate of return on the spread can now be found by dividing this expected value by the spread's cost or $4:

$$25\% = \frac{\$5.00}{\$4.00} - 1.00$$

This entire process can be easily computerized. If you supply the computer with estimates of the variance of each stock's return, then based on an assumption of normality in the return distribution, it is easy to compute the probability distribution for the ending value for the stock. If desired, implied variance estimates can be computed using an option pricing model, in conjunction with market prices of at-the-money options. You can also supply the computer with information on outstanding options on the stock, including their current market values. Based on this information, the computer can estimate the probability distributions for the ending values of every possible combination of options conceivable. Given the current prices for the options, it can find combinations that offer high expected rates of return at low risks and print out the most attractive stategies.

Delta, Gamma, and Theta

In establishing their positions, options traders like to keep an eye on three numbers called delta, gamma, and theta. In the software which accompanies this book you will notice that these numbers are among those provided in the position analysis program. Delta and gamma provide information about the relationship between the price of the underlying stock and the total market value of the position. Theta, on the other hand, provides information about what will happen to your position if (1) the risk-free rate remains constant and nothing happens to the price or volatility of the underlying stock and (2) time passes and you get one day closer to the expiration date.

Figure 17.6 shows the relationship between the market value of a particular position (perhaps a straddle) and the value of the underlying stock. The stock is currently priced at $50.

Gamma is the expected change in delta that will accompany a change in the stock price. It is the expected change (second derivative) in the slope of the relationship—between the option value and the stock price as the stock price changes. In Figure 17.6, at a $50 stock price, gamma is positive, while in Figure 17.7 gamma is negative. Delta is zero in both figures. Gamma is valuable because it tells you the extent to which you're going to have to readjust your position (sell more options and

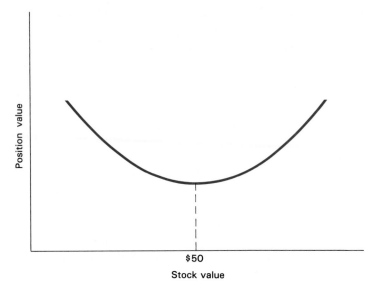

FIGURE 17.6 Delta zero, gamma positive.

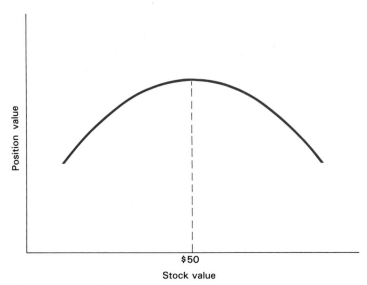

FIGURE 17.7 Delta zero, gamma negative.

buy less stock, for example) as the stock price changes. In Figure 17.8, both delta and gamma are zero, so no adjustment in the position is required until the stock price reaches $45 or $55, where gamma becomes negative and positive, respectively.

Option traders usually are betting, on the basis of option pricing models, that particular options are under or overvalued. They don't generally bet that the under-

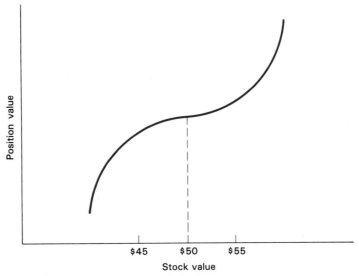

FIGURE 17.8 Delta zero, gamma zero.

lying stock itself will be going up or down. This is why they prefer their positions to be "delta neutral" (delta = 0). They package positions such that they are selling options they believe to be overvalued and buying options which are undervalued. As the prices of the *options* return to their equilibrium values, they should make money irrespective of what happens to the price of the underlying stock—so long as they remain delta neutral. Gamma is an indicator of how much readjustment or trading is required to remain delta neutral.

Theta provides the expected change in the value of your position if nothing else happens and a day goes by. If you construct a straddle by buying a put and a call, theta is negative. If nothing happens to the price of the stock, you expect the market value of both options to fall as they approach expiration. On the other hand, if you construct a reverse straddle, where you *sell* a put and a call (Figure 17.7 might represent such a position), theta is positive. You expect the value of your position to increase as the options approach expiration.

Getting Delta Neutral

You can use $N(d_1)$ to help you create a delta-neutral position. For example, suppose you had a nondividend-paying stock selling at a price of $100. The volatility of the stock is 20 percent, and the risk-free rate is 10 percent. You are dealing with an American put and a call that both have an exercise price of $100 and 60 days to expiration. The put and the call are selling at their Black-Scholes values of $2.49 and $4.05, respectively.

Suppose you want to create a delta-neutral straddle position because you feel that the put option is undervalued due to the fact that the Black-Scholes model does

OUT ON THE STREET

MELTING DOWN

It's 8:00 A.M. Central Standard Time on Monday, October 19, 1987.

Mac Conway reached his desk early today. He was expecting some real action—and little of it good. The market had closed down more than 100 points the preceding Friday. Mac had been on the phone and reading and watching the media for much of the weekend trying to gauge what was in store for him today.

Mac is a quantitative analyst at Centerre Bank in St. Louis. He joined the firm in 1981 and now spends his time managing the bank's equities under its dividend discount model as well as its indexed equity applications. But these duties aren't his chief concern today. All things point to a turbulent day for the market. Prices could continue to slide or even reverse Friday's dramatic decline with a powerful correction. One thing for sure. Mac would have to keep on his toes.

He was in charge of approximately $400 million in assets covered by portfolio insurance. Centerre ran the money with a computer program licensed to it by the firm of Leland, O'Brien and Rubenstein (L.O.R.). The bank moved its clients in and out of the equity market with financial futures. Selling more stock index futures eased the clients further out of the market. Closing the futures positions moved the clients deeper in. The computer program tells how many futures contracts it should buy or sell, exiting the stock market by selling futures in downturns like Friday's and deepening its position in the market by closing futures positions in upturns, hopefully like the one it would see today.

Centerre had two clients under portfolio insurance, each application supporting approximately $200 million in equities. One client came on board in August, while the other reinstalled insurance a week earlier this October after being out of it for a period of several months. The rather conservative "August" application was already substantially hedged with futures contracts. The hedge position on the more recently placed application wasn't nearly so substantial.

It's 8:16. The XMI futures market opened on the Chicago Board of Trade a minute ago, 15 minutes before the Mercantile Exchange opens in Chicago. S & P 500 futures are traded on the "Merc," and these will be used to implement the portfolio insurance strategies.

Mac brings up the prices of XMI stock index futures on his Quotron. The XMI is an index of 20 common stocks.

Unbelievable! The contracts are selling at a 10 percent discount under the cash value of the index. Mac had never seen anything like this before.

There would be no powerful correction today!

Sensing a real problem, Mac calls the "August" client. Does it want to sell additional futures at these extreme discounts to deepen the hedge even further? The answer is no. It is comfortable with the existing size of the hedge. Abandon the dynamics of the insurance system temporarily until the futures and cash markets reach an equilibrium. Now for the "October" client. This time the answer is yes. Obey the commands of the L.O.R. software and take additional positions in futures as trigger points are reached.

Mac pulls the plug on "August" and braces for the inevitable moves with "October."

First, however, the market volatility estimate carried in the L.O.R. program had to be upgraded. Today's market was clearly a more violent animal than the one experienced over the past few months. Based on what he is seeing, Mac increases the volatility estimate in his machine from 18 percent to 25 percent.

The computer's response is immediate. Deepen the futures position accordingly. Get further out of the market. If the volatility has, in fact increased, you must get further out to avoid crashing through the clients' established floor for the net value of the portfolio.

Mac picked up the phone and dialed the "Merc." He placed an order to sell the first batch of 1100 futures contracts that he would eventually position for "October" throughout the biggest trading day in history. Each of the contracts controlled $100,000 worth of index equities. As the market plummeted downward past trigger point after trigger point in his insurance program, the hedge position for "October" deepened and deepened. Although he had to sell each successive block of contracts at agonizingly deep discounts, he was able to conduct the series transactions with little difficulty. The market was in chaos, but the liquidity was there—at least in the futures pits.

By the end of the afternoon, "October" was down only 8.5 percent, this in the face of more than a 20 percent decline for the market as a whole. "October's" cash positions in stock took a real beating, but the gains made on the futures contracts buffered the impact on the client. If the discounts relative to cash on the futures contracts looked big in the morning, they paled by comparison to what was there at the end of the day. In fact, the discounts were so large that "October" decided to liquidate its futures positions on October 20 and lift its portfolio insurance strategy. This move was based in part on the unprecedented size of the discounts and in part on the fact that the lower level for stock prices seemed to lessen the need for an insurance program. Thus, Centerre, at least for the insurance application, said farewell to a happy client. During October 19 and 20, its position was down only 5 percent.

As agreed, no positions were taken for "August." However, given the relatively deep hedge already in place before October 19, it experienced only a 5 percent decline in the net value of their portfolio during Monday's debacle. "August" was well within range of its floor as of the close of trading.

Admittedly, the insurance strategy had not worked perfectly, but it worked well enough to preserve the goodwill of both "August" and "October" during the most traumatizing day in the history of Wall Street.

not value the right to early exercise. You feel the call is priced correctly (no dividends), but you're buying it anyway to get delta neutral.

How many puts and calls should you buy to get delta neutral? According to the Black-Scholes model, the following relationships hold:

$$\frac{1}{N(d_1)} \text{ for the put} = 2.44$$

$$\frac{1}{N(d_1)} \text{ for the call} = 1.69$$

This means you must buy 244 puts and 169 calls to get delta neutral. Given that you do, and the stock price goes up by a dollar, the dollar change in your put position should nearly exactly offset the dollar change in your call position. (You are buying more puts because the value of the put is less sensitive to changes in the value of the stock.) The total value of your position is given by

$$
\begin{aligned}
244 \text{ puts @ \$2.49} &= \$\ 607.56 \\
169 \text{ calls @ \$4.05} &= \underline{\quad 684.45} \\
\text{Total value} &= \$1292.01
\end{aligned}
$$

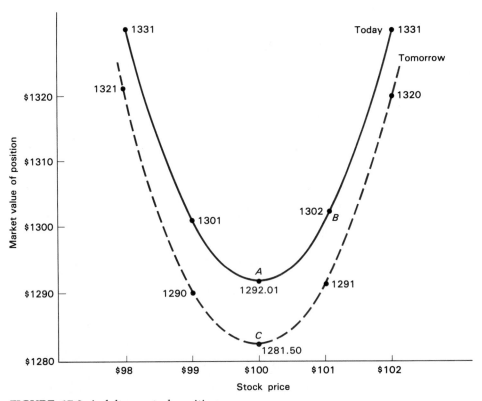

FIGURE 17.9 A delta-neutral position.

The current value of our position as it relates to the value of the stock is plotted by the solid curve in Figure 17.9. The broken curve shows the same relationship as we expected it to be tomorrow (with the passing of one day). The values of delta, gamma, and theta for the current position are as follows:

$$
\begin{aligned}
\text{Delta} &= \quad \$.67 \\
\text{Gamma} &= \quad 19.77 \\
\text{Theta} &= \ -\$10.51
\end{aligned}
$$

The value for delta tells us that if the price of the stock should immediately increase by $1 to $101, the value of our *position* can be expected to increase by $.67. This isn't zero, but it's a small amount relative to the total position value nonetheless. If you could buy fractions of put and call contracts, you could make delta as close to zero as you wished.

The value for gamma tells us that as the stock price goes up, delta will become a larger positive number, as it would if we moved from position A to position B in Figure 17.9.

The value for theta tells us that, if a single day passes and nothing else relevant happens, we should expect the value of our position to fall by $10.51, as it would if we moved from point A to point C.

Portfolio Insurance

Options and option pricing models can be used to construct an interesting strategy called portfolio insurance. Portfolio insurance has become very popular in recent years, reaching as much as $60 billion in "insured" assets at the time of the stock market crash of October 1987.

To see how portfolio insurance works, look at Figures 17.10, 17.11, and 17.12. Suppose you are holding a portfolio of stocks and you wanted to put a floor or lower limit on the value of the portfolio. In each of the figures, we are plotting the market value of your portfolio on the horizontal axis. The value of your net position is being plotted on the vertical axis.

Let's take Figure 17.10 first. Here we are assuming you simply invest in the portfolio itself. The relationship between the value of your net position and the value of the portfolio is simply a 45-degree line emanating from the origin. The current value of the portfolio is assumed to be $10 million, and the value of your net position is $10 million as well.

In Figure 17.11 we assume a European put option exists which gives you the right to sell your portfolio to someone at an exercise price of $10 million in T years. The market value of the put is plotted on the vertical axis. This would be the net value of your position if you only invested in the put option.

Now suppose you invest in both the put and your portfolio. The current value of your total position is plotted on the vertical axis of Figure 17.12. Your total position (the solid curve in Figure 17.12) is the sum of the value of the put in 17.11 and your portfolio in 17.10. You now have a floor or lower limit ($10 million, or

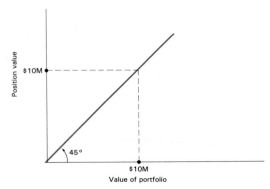

FIGURE 17.10 Portfolio only.

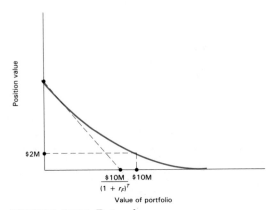

FIGURE 17.11 Put only.

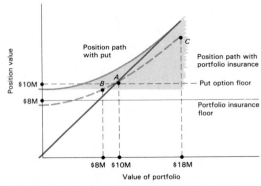

FIGURE 17.12 Portfolio with put and with portfolio insurance.

the exercise price of the put) to the value of your portfolio as of T years into the future. The *current* value of your position can fall below this floor, but the value of your position at your "T-year horizon" can't fall below $10 million. In this sense, your position is insured. The insurance premium, or the cost of the insurance, is the current market value of the put, or $2 million.

In effect portfolio insurance has made the returns to your net position more positively skewed than the returns to the portfolio itself. Apparently, many people have a distinct preference for positive skewness, because portfolio insurance had until the October 1987 experience become a very popular strategy.

The problem is: How can you find a put option on *your* portfolio? They may exist on some portfolios like the S & P 500, but you're not likely to find one on the particular portfolio that you have chosen to own.

This is where option pricing models come into play. The option pricing model will tell you how much you should invest in your portfolio (referred to now as the "risk asset") and how much should you invest in treasury bills (referred to now as the "safe asset"). If you look at the shaded portion of Figure 17.12, you will note that it takes the form of a call option. This shouldn't come as too much of a surprise, since we used an option as part of the total position. The option pricing model will help you to adjust the allocation of your funds between the safe asset and the risk asset so that your path follows the broken curve of Figure 17.12. This curve is identical to the solid curve, less a constant equal to the dollar value of the put.

Imagine yourself at point A. If you invest all your funds in the risk asset (your portfolio), your net position will move up and down the 45-degree line. To find out how much you should be investing in the safe asset, you input the following into an option pricing model (perhaps the Black-Scholes model):

1. An estimate of the volatility of your portfolio
2. The number of years to your horizon (t)
3. The risk-free rate
4. The lower limit to the value of your portfolio t years into the future
5. The current market value of your portfolio ($10 million)

The option pricing model will provide $N(d_1)$. We know this is the slope of the call option pricing curve at a $10 million value for the risk asset (your portfolio). Suppose $N(d_1)$ turns out to be .40. This means that if there is a $1 reduction in the value of the risk asset, your net position should fall by only $.40. It *will* if you currently have 60 percent of your funds in the safe asset (treasury bills).

Now suppose the value of your portfolio falls to $8 million. Suppose also, when you input $8 million into the option pricing model, it outputs a value of .30 for $N(d_1)$. This means you should now have 70 percent of your funds in treasury bills. If you have continuously made adjustments in your position as the value of your portfolio fell, you should now be at point B in Figure 17.12.

Similarly, as the value of the risk asset goes up, you gradually reduce your position in treasury bills, until by the time you get to point C, with a value for $N(d_1)$ of .99, your position in treasury bills is minimal.

Continuous position adjustments are not practical, so adjustments are actually made at "trigger points" defined in terms of the current value of the portfolio which are related to the level of the floor, the underlying volatility of the portfolio being insured, and the length of the investor's horizon.

In many portfolio insurance applications, changes in positions are done through futures markets (buying and selling stock index futures and treasury bill futures). Futures are used to economize on transactions costs and to avoid disruption in the management of the actual cash positions in the portfolio.

Recent market history has revealed some real problems with the portfolio insurance strategy. The basic problem is that when a sufficient number of investors are employing the strategy, it may be impossible to make the required adjustments as quickly as you need to. In the stock market crash of October 19, 1987, many investors found it impossible to make changes in their positions as quickly as they needed or at reasonable prices. They also found that the volatility of their portfolios had increased dramatically. Consequently, the crucial volatility (through the horizon period) estimates to the model became extremely difficult to estimate.

We can safely conclude, at this point, that portfolio insurance provides an effective one-way hedge against some, but not all, market declines.

COMPLEX SECURITIES AS PORTFOLIOS OF OPTIONS

Common Stock as an Option

Toward the end of their paper on the valuation of options, Black and Scholes made the insightful point that the common stock of a levered firm is, itself, an optionlike security. To see this, consider the simple case of a firm that has one bond issue outstanding. The bond issue is very simple in form. It matures in 1 year, calling for a single payment of principal and interest at that time which totals $50,000. There are no interim interest payments during the year.

Now consider the position of the stockholders. At the end of the year they have the choice of either paying $50,000 to the bondholders to retain control of the firm, or by not paying the $50,000, go into default and surrender ownership of the firm to the bondholders. In this sense, we can consider the stockholders as really owning an option to buy the firm from the bondholders at an exercise price of $50,000. The time to expiration for the option is equal to the time to maturity of the debt. Since the stockholders' claim is identical to that of an option holder, the stock should be priced in the market as though it was an option, with an exercise price of $50,000 and 1 year to expiration.

If the stock is priced as an option, it should be priced as in Figure 17.13. In the figure, we are plotting the total market value of all the assets of the firm on the horizontal axis. The 45-degree line emanating from the present value of the principal

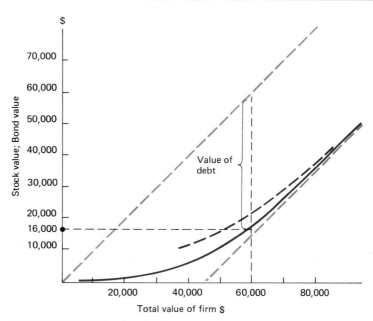

FIGURE 17.13 Stock priced as an option.

payment on the debt (which is $45,454, assuming a risk-free rate of 10 percent) is the same as the option's soft floor, emanating from the present value of the exercise price. The curved solid line shows the value of the common stock (the option) as it relates to the value of the firm. The slope of this line, once again, reflects the probability of exercising the option, which, of course, is the probability of making the payment on the debt. As the value of the firm rises above the promised debt payment, the probability of paying off the debt approaches 100 percent.

The 45-degree line emanating from the *origin* of the graph represents the total value of both the bonds and the stock. The total market value of both the bonds and the stock must sum to the total market value of the firm. Since this is true, the value of the bonds can be found by subtracting the value of the stock from this total value. Thus, if the total value of the firm is equal to $60,000, the value of the stock will be equal to $16,000, and the value of the bonds will be equal to $44,000. The bonds are selling at a price that is less than the present value of their promised payment, discounted at the risk-free rate, because there is some probability of default on the payment. As the total value of the firm's assets increases, however, the market value of the bonds approaches that of risk-free debt, $45,454.

Just as the common stock can be thought of as an option, the bonds can be thought of as the complement of an option. From this insight, we can gain a deeper understanding about the valuation of bonds. For example, it should be true, holding all other factors constant, that the default premium in the yield on a long-term bond should be greater than that of a short-term bond. We know if you increase the term to expiration of an option, you increase its market value. Since you increase the market value of the option, you should decrease the market value of the option's complement, the bond. In Figure 17.13, if we increased the term to expiration or maturity for the bond, we move to the broken curve which is positioned higher relative to its soft floor. This increases the percentage difference between the market value of the bond and corresponding risk-free debt.

Looking at bonds and stocks in this way also reveals some interesting conflicts of interest between bondholders and stockholders. Since stockholders have voting control, it's in the interest of management to maximize stockholder wealth. If the stock is priced as an option, management can increase its value by making investment and production decisions that increase the risk of the firm while maintaining its total market value. Thus, if the broken curve of Figure 17.13 reflects an increased level of variance for the firm, rather than an increased term to maturity, increasing risk can increase the market value of the stock from $16,000 to $20,000. This increase in stock value comes at the expense of the bondholders. There is now a greater probability of default on their debt, and there has been a transfer of wealth from bondholders to stockholders.

There is also an incentive for management to pay out large amounts of funds as dividends to stockholders. As you can see from the graph, since the slope of the option pricing curve is less than 1.00, paying $1.00 in dividends to the stockholders will reduce the total value of the firm by $1.00, but the value of the stock will fall by less than $1.00. The difference between the $1.00 payment and the reduction of the value of their stock again is reflected in a reduction in the value of the bonds. The payment of dividends results in a transfer of wealth from bondholders to stockholders.

Bondholders attempt to protect themselves from these tactics by including protective covenants in the bond indenture agreement. These provisions limit the amount of dividends paid to stockholders and attempt to control to some extent the investment and production decisions of management by at least specifying the purpose for which the proceeds of the bond issue will be used.

Bonds as Portfolios of Options and Option Complements

The foregoing discussion related to a very simple debt security. Let's make the bond a little more complicated and see what this does to our conclusions.

Suppose we were dealing with a 2-year bond that has an interest payment due at the end of the first year. The stockholders can now be viewed as holding an option to acquire *another* option to buy the firm from the bondholders at the maturity of the debt. If the stockholders pay the first interest payment, they acquire the option to buy the firm from the bondholders by making the final interest and principal payments at maturity. It they don't make the first interest payment, they lose all rights to the firm, and the bondholders take over. The stock can be viewed, in this context, as a compound option and the bond as the complement of a compound option. If we talk about a longer-term bond, with a string of required interest payments, the option is merely compounded many times over.

Now consider a *callable* bond. The call provision gives the stockholders the option of buying at a specific exercise, or call, price. The callable bond is a portfolio where you have taken a positive position in the complement of a compound option (this is the bond as a noncallable issue) and a negative position in a call option which is held by the stockholders. The market value of the callable bond is the net of its value as a noncallable issue and the market value of the call privilege held by the stockholders.

If we make the callable bond convertible, we simply add another option to the portfolio. Now the bond can be viewed as a portfolio of three securities: (1) a positive position in the complement of a compound option, (2) a negative position in the call option to buy the bond held by the stockholders, and (3) a positive in another option to buy the stock of the firm at the conversion price. The market value of the bond will reflect the net value of this portfolio.

In this sense, options can be viewed as the structural building blocks of nearly all financial securities. The securities we see traded in the marketplace are really portfolios of options and option complements. Thus, an understanding of the behavior of option prices is crucial to a deep understanding of the behavior of the prices of all securities.

SUMMARY

The Black-Scholes model is subject to a bias problem in that the model tends to overvalue options that are out of the money and undervalue options that are in the money. This problem can be resolved by either allowing for the bias or by moving to a more general option pricing model which is free of the bias.

Options can be used to construct many interesting strategies which you can use to take advantage of special situations. For example, if you think a stock is going to make a significant move but you aren't sure of the direction, you may want to buy a straddle, which is a put and call with the same exercise price and time to maturity. A butterfly spread may be a good investment for a stock you think is locked in its current position.

Three numbers to follow closely when building option strategies are delta, gamma, and theta. Delta is the expected change in the position value with a small change in the price of the underlying stock. Gamma is the expected change in delta with a small change in the price of the underlying stock. Finally, theta is the expected change in the value of the position with the passage of time.

Option pricing models can also be used to allocate funds between aggressive investments like stock and defensive investments like bonds to provide a lower limit to the value of the portfolio. This strategy is called portfolio insurance.

Many of the securities we see traded in the marketplace can be thought of as portfolios of options. Levered common stock, for example, can be thought of as an option to acquire the firm from the bondholders by making the required payments at maturity. Bonds can be viewed as the complements of options with other options attached.

QUESTION SET 1

1. What was the nature of the bias in Black-Scholes option pricing discovered empirically by MacBeth and Merville?
2. Contrast the assumption of the Black-Scholes model and the Cox model on the variance of the return on a stock.
3. Suppose you construct a strategy based on options on a stock which is currently selling for $100. The strategy is as follows:

   Buy one call option having an exercise price of $95.
   Sell two calls having an exercise price of $100.
   Buy one call option having an exercise price of $105.

   (All these options are written on the same stock, and all have the same expiration date.)
   a. Compute the payoff (the dollars you receive) from this strategy at the expiration date for each of the following alternative stock prices: $90, $95, $98, $100, $102, $105, and $110.
   b. What additional information would be required to determine whether your strategy had been profitable?
   c. What is the name given to this strategy?
4. a. What constitutes the price of a straddle?
   b. Suppose you *sold* a straddle. What would cause your sale to be a profitable one?
5. If you view common stockholders as if they are holding a call option on the firm, what bias might the stockholders have in selecting projects for the firm to undertake? Explain.
6. Consider a callable bond and view it (as in the text) as a portfolio of optionlike instruments.
   a. In what sense have the bondholders sold a call option to the stockholders?
   b. Can you speculate on what impact the call provision of the bond might have on desire by the stockholders to select risky investment projects?

QUESTION SET 2

1. Suppose you are an energetic investor and you like to see action in any stock you pursue. After following closely a particular issue, you suspect an opportunity in that stock using a straddle strategy.
   a. What is likely to be your expectation of the stock price?
   b. What can go wrong with your strategy?

2. What apparent bias did MacBeth and Merville (1980) find in the Black-Scholes option pricing framework?

3. The bias in the Black-Scholes model was shown to be a systematic error implying there will be no propensity for in or out-of-the-money options to revert to their Black-Scholes values. How might you correct for this bias?

4. Explain what delta, gamma, and theta tell you about your position in an options strategy.

5. What is the rationale behind getting a delta-neutral position?

6. Explain why portfolio insurance proved to be a very popular strategy.

7. Why might portfolio insurance be called a dynamic strategy, and how might this be a problem?

ANSWERS TO QUESTION SET 2

1. A straddle strategy is adopted where it is felt that the price of the stock will move, either up or down, in a short period of time. The straddle strategy can be unprofitable if
   a. The stock price doesn't change enough to allow a profit, or changes not at all, in which case you lose your entire initial investment in the options, or
   b. The market recognizes the chance of the future stock price change and bids up the price of the options, so as to make the expected rate of return on the investment unattractive.

2. Using data on IBM stock, MacBeth and Merville found that the Black-Scholes model for an out-of-the-money stock was likely to be higher than the actual market value and that the Black-Scholes value for an in-the-money option is likely to be lower than the actual market value.

3. To allow for the bias in the BS model you could
   a. Use a different option pricing model to correct for the bias problem, or
   b. Estimate empirically the bias in your model to determine the extent to which the stock is mispriced. You might use a regression model relating the percentage difference between the stock price and the present value of the exercise price (as the independent variable) to the percentage difference between the actual option price and the BS value (the dependent variable). (An option is then considered over- or undervalued if its price is significantly below or above the curve of best fit.)

4. Delta is (approximately) the expected dollar change in the value of the position for a dollar change in the price of the stock. Gamma is the expected change in delta given a change in the stock price. Theta is the expected change in the value of the position holding everything constant except that one day goes by.

5. Getting delta neutral is desirable when you believe that the options you are taking positions in are currently mispriced, but will revert to their true prices, thus yielding you a profit. Being delta neutral makes your position insensitive to changes in the underlying security.

6. Portfolio insurance makes returns more positively skewed; that is, the upside potential is nearly as great, but the downside risk is substantially reduced when compared to a noninsured portfolio.

7. Portfolio insurance can be called a dynamic strategy because it requires adjustments to be made to maintain its effectiveness. This can be a problem when there are many investors

using this strategy, all trying to make similar adjustments at the same time, thus the required adjustments may be impossible, or at least very unprofitable, to make.

PROBLEM SET

1. Suppose that a stock is equally likely to be worth either $30 or $50 in two years. No other values are possible. A put and a call written on the stock have an exercise price of $40 and mature in two years. The market price of the call is $5.00. Assume that the discount rate is 0 percent and investors are risk neutral.
   a. What is the current market value of the stock?
   b. What is the current value of the put option?
   c. What is the dollar payoff on a straddle investment in the options and the percent expected return on this strategy?
2. Suppose that the price of a certain stock has remained stable in the past. It is priced at $40.00, and there are five possible ending values at time $t = 1$: $30.00, $35.00, $40.00, $45.00, and $50.00. Their probabilities of occurrence are, respectively, 5, 15, 65, 10, and 5 percent.
   a. Set up a butterfly spread in calls with exercise prices of $35, $40, and $45, assuming their current market values are $8, $3, and $1, respectively. Note any necessary characteristics of these calls.
   b. What is the maximum value that this spread can take on?
   c. When will the payoff on this investment be $0?
   d. What is the expected value of the investment at $t = 1$?
   e. What is the expected return on the spread?

ANSWERS TO PROBLEM SET

1. a. In equilibrium, the stock will be priced at

$$(.5 \times \$30) + (.5 \times \$50) = \$40$$

   b. When the price of the stock is the same as the exercise price of both the call and the put, and the options are in all other respects identical, their current market values should be in parity. With a zero interest rate, this implies

$$V_P - V_C = X - V_S$$

   Thus, the put option is priced at $5.00.
   c. A straddle will break even whether the stock price ends up at $30.00 or $50.00. You can construct a straddle with a purchase of a put and a call. If the stock goes up to $50.00, your call is worth $50.00 − $40.00 = $10.00. If the stock price falls to $30.00, your put option is worth $10.00. In either case you break even on your initial investment of $10.00 in one put and one call for a rate of return of 0 percent. This makes sense since the investment is riskless and the risk-free rate is zero.
2. a. To create a butterfly spread, you would buy one call with an exercise price of $35, sell two calls having an exercise price of $40.00 and buy one call that has an exercise price of $45.00.

b. This investment in calls will have a maximum value of $5.00 if the stock price remains unchanged at $40.00. When the value of the stock is $40.00, the two options you sold and the call with an exercise price of $45.00 are worthless. The call with exercise price of $35.00 is worth $5.00.

c. All the options will be worth zero if the ending value of the stock is less than or equal to $35.00. In addition, if the ending stock price is $45.00, the options you hold are worth $7.50 + $2.50 = $10.00, and the two options you sold will be exercised, costing you $10.00. Again, a net value of zero for any stock value of $45.00 or more.

d. At $t = 1$, the stock can take on five possible values. The portfolio value at each possible stock price and their probability of occurring are

V_S	V_P	Probability
$30.00	$0	.5
35.00	0	.15
40.00	5.00	.65
45.00	0	.15
50.00	0	.5

The expected value of the ending portfolio is:

$$.65 \times \$5.00 = \$3.25$$

e. The expected rate of return is the expected dollar return divided by the amount of your initial investment, less one. You bought two calls for a total of $8.00 + $1.00 = $9.00 and sold two for a total of $3.00 × 2.00 = $6.00. Your net investment is $3.00. The expected return on this investment is $3.25/$3.00 − 1 = 8.33%.

REFERENCES

BLACK, F., "Fact and Fantasy in the Use of Options," *Financial Analysts Journal* (July–August 1975).

BLACK, F., and SCHOLES, M., "The Valuation of Option Contracts and a Test of Market Efficiency," *Journal of Finance* (May 1972).

COX, J., "Notes on Option Pricing I: Constant Elasticity of Diffusions," unpublished draft, Stanford University, Stanford, Calif., September 1975.

COX, J., and ROSS, S., "The Valuation of Options Under Alternative Stochastic Processes," *Journal of Financial Economics* (January–March 1976).

EMANUEL, D., and MACBETH, J., "Further Results on Constant Elasticity of Variance Call Option Models," *Journal of Financial and Quantitative Analysis* (November 1981).

GESKE, R., "The Valuation of Compound Options," *Journal of Financial Economics* (March 1979). (a)

GESKE, R., "A Note on an Analytic Valuation Formula for Unprotected American Call Options on Stocks with Known Dividends," *Journal of Financial Economics* (Dec. 1979).

GESKE, R., and ROLL, R., "On American Call Options with the Black-Scholes European Formula", *Journal of Finance* (June 1984).

GESKE, R., ROLL, R., and SHASTRI, K., "Over-the-Counter Option Market Dividend Protection and 'Biases' in the Black-Scholes Model—A Note," *Journal of Finance* (September 1983).

MACBETH, J., and MERVILLE, L., "An Empirical Examination of the Black-Scholes Call Option Pricing Model," *Journal of Finance* (December 1979).

MACBETH, J., and MERVILLE, L., "Tests of the Black-Scholes and Cox Option Valuation Models," *Journal of Finance* (May 1980).

ROLL, R., "An Analytic Valuation Formula for Unprotected American Call Options on Stocks with Known Dividends," *Journal of Financial Economics* (November 1977).

RUBINSTEIN, M., "Non-Parametric Tests of Alternative Option Pricing Models Using All Reported Quotes and Trades on the 30 Most Active CBOE Option Classes from August 23, 1976 Through August 31, 1978," Berkeley Working Paper No. 117, October 1981.

STERK, W., "Tests of Two Models for Valuing Call Options on Stocks with Dividends," *Journal of Finance* (December 1982).

STERK, W., "Comparative Performance of the Black-Scholes and the Roll-Geske-Whaley Option Pricing Models," *Journal of Financial and Quantitative Analysis* (Sept. 1983).

WHALEY, R., "On the Valuation of American Call Options on Stocks with Known Dividends," *Journal of Financial Economics* (June 1981).

WHALEY, R., "Valuation of American Call Options on Dividend Paying Stocks," *Journal of Financial Economics* (March 1982).

C H A P T E R

18

FINANCIAL FORWARD AND FUTURES CONTRACTS

Forward and futures contracts have generated a great deal of interest in the last decade. The volume of futures contracts has increased dramatically. Moreover, in recent years the most popular futures contracts have been *financial* futures, which are contracts to buy or sell financial securities, with treasury bond futures leading the way in terms of volume.

A forward or futures contract *obligates* you to buy or sell a specific commodity at a specific price on a specific delivery date. If you buy such a contract, you must buy the commodity at the stated time and price. If you sell the contract, you must sell the commodity at the stated time and price. If I sell you a contract, I must sell and you must buy according to the terms of the contract. As an example, you typically initiate the purchase of a residence by exchanging a forward contract with the seller. The buyer and the seller obligate themselves to purchase and sell the house at the closing date and at the stated price.

An *options* contract, on the other hand, gives you the *right* to buy or sell. With a *forward* or *futures* contract, you *must* buy or sell according to the terms of the contract, unless you liquidate the contract in the marketplace prior to expiration. The lower limit to the value of an options contract is zero because you always have the right to throw it away. A forward contract, on the other hand, can have a negative value. If you have obligated yourself to buy a commodity at a price of $20, and the current price of the commodity has dropped to $10, the contract has a negative value of $10, if today is the expiration date.

CHARACTERISTICS OF FORWARD
AND FUTURES CONTRACTS

In the discussion of options, our attention focused on the market value of the contract itself, given a fixed value for the exercise price. In the pricing of forward and futures contracts, the situation is turned around. By tradition, the *exercise price* (which is called the forward or futures price) is initially set so that the current market value of the contract is equal to zero. Thus, with respect to these contracts, given a fixed (zero) market value for the contract, we attempt to find the forward or futures price (the exercise price) which is consistent with this zero market value.

One significant difference between a forward and a futures contract is in the way your account is handled. With a forward contract, you obligate yourself to buy or sell a commodity, some time in the future at a particular price. As we said, initially the forward price is set so the current market value of the contract is zero, but this value can become positive or negative as time goes by. Suppose expectations about the future commodity price are revised upward so new forward contracts issued today are issued at a higher forward price than yesterday. If you hold a contract to buy at the previous, lower forward price, the market value of your contract becomes positive. Forward contracts are always designed initially to have a zero value, but as expectations change their value can become positive or negative.

The terms of a futures contract, on the other hand, are revised every day to maintain a zero market value for the contract. The aspect of the contract that is revised is the futures price. Suppose, you initially entered into a futures contract to sell a commodity for $10 in 30 days. The next day the futures price of identical contracts for sale in 29 days is being negotiated at a futures price of $9. If your contract were a forward contract, it would take on a positive market value. As a futures contract, however, the futures price of your contract would be revised to $9, and you would have added to your account the difference between the futures prices yesterday and today, multiplied by the number of commodities controlled by the futures contracts you have outstanding.

This process of revising the terms of the contract, and crediting or debiting your account accordingly, is called *marking to market*. The process of marking to market is an important difference between a forward and a futures contract. Obviously, it does create a difference in the cash flows to investors in forward and futures contracts. There are no cash flows to an investor in a forward contract until the settlement date. There are positive or negative cash flows from day to day associated with investing in a futures contract, as you mark to market in correspondence with changes in the prevailing futures price.

This subtle difference in the way your account is handled, and the associated differences in the cash flows, differentiates the two types of contracts in terms of the way they are priced. As we shall see, this difference may be especially important in the pricing of financial futures.

Futures contracts are also standardized in terms of their specifications, such as maturity date and the price at which the commodity is to be exchanged. In addition, a clearing house stands between the buyer and seller of the contract, guaranteeing to each that the commodity can be purchased or sold on the terms specified in the contract. Futures contracts are traded on organized exchanges, and the futures price is determined in a market setting. Consequently, positions in futures contracts can be easily liquidated prior to the maturity date of the contract. For example, if you have purchased futures contracts to sell a given amount of a commodity at a certain date, you can later relieve yourself of the obligation by selling futures contracts to sell the same amount of the commodity at the same date. This is an important relative advantage of futures contracts over forward contracts.

Forward contracts may not be standardized in their specifications. The terms of the contracts, including the forward price, are set by the parties to the contracts through negotiation. In some cases, as in the sale of a house, one or both of the parties may be required to put up funds or securities as a guarantee that they will meet the obligation of the forward contract. If you want to terminate the agreement prior to maturity, you must seek relief through negotiation from the other party to the contract. In this sense, forward contracts are less liquid than are futures contracts. On the other hand, the terms of the contract (the forward price, the maturity date, the grade or type of commodity acceptable for delivery, the place of delivery) can be more precisely tailored to the needs of the buyer and seller.

Remember, when we talk about the pricing of forward and futures contracts, we are talking about determining the "exercise prices" for the contracts. We are trying to determine the values for the forward or futures prices which will make the current value of the contract equal to zero. Table 18.1 shows the open, high, low, and settling (closing) futures prices for U.S. Treasury bonds. Also included in the table are the change in the futures price for the day, the yield to maturity based on the settling price, the change in the yield from the previous settling price, and the number of contracts currently outstanding. The prices are expressed as a percentage of principal value ($1000), with 65–13 indicating a price equal to 65 and 13/32 percent of $1000, or $654.06.

TABLE 18.1 Futures Prices for Treasury Bonds

Treasury Bonds (CBT)—$100,000; pts. 32nds of 100%

Mar	....	....	....	....		....	....		....	15,585
June	65–25	67–01	66–21	66–30	+	6	12.547	–	.036	116,569
Sept	66–07	66–15	66–03	66–12	+	6	12.655	–	.037	16,405
Dec	65–21	65–29	65–20	65–28	+	6	12.753	–	.037	6,578
Mar85	65–05	65–14	65–05	65–14	+	7	12.839	–	.044	6,079
June	64–24	65–02	64–24	65–01	+	5	12.920	–	.044	4,143
Sept	64–14	64–21	64–14	64–21	+	7	12.996	–	.044	1,130
Dec	64–08	64–11	64–06	64–11	+	7	13.059	–	.045	918
Mar86	64–02	64–02	64–02	64–02	+	7	13.117	–	.045	1,201
June	63–19	63–26	63–19	63–29	+	7	13.169	–	.045	1,909
Sept	63–14	63–19	63–13	63–19	+	7	13.214	–	.046	326
Dec	63–08	63–13	63–08	63–13	+	7	13.253	–	.046	2

Each contract obligates you to buy or sell 100 U.S. Treasury bonds at the stated price. If you buy or sell a contract, you must put up a margin of $2000. This isn't really an investment, as the margin can be put up in the form of U.S. treasury bills. As you mark to market, money will be added or subtracted from this account. Thus, you can control a portfolio of $100,000 in U.S. Treasury bonds (in principal amount) with an initial "investment" of only $2000! The high degree of possible leverage helps to explain why forward and futures contracts have gained such a wide following.

THE DETERMINATION OF FORWARD PRICES

As explained, a forward contract obligates you to buy or sell a specific commodity at a specific time and at a specific price. It is fundamentally different from an options contract which gives you the right to buy or sell. The difference between the two contracts is easily seen in Figure 18.1, which shows the values of forward contracts to buy or sell a commodity and the values of call and put options as they relate to the value of the commodity at the expiration date of each of the contracts. The lower limit to the value of the options is zero, and the forward contracts can take on a negative value. If you have contracted to buy a commodity at a price of $50, and at expiration the prevailing market price of the commodity is $30, you would be willing to pay someone $20 to assume the burden of the contract for you.

Note, at expiration the value of a forward contract to buy a commodity is equal to

$$\text{Commodity price} - \text{forward price}$$

whereas the value of a forward contract to sell is equal to

$$\text{Forward price} - \text{commodity price}$$

The Relationship Between the Forward Price and the Current Commodity Price

The forward price can be easily expressed in terms of the current commodity price and the risk-free rate of interest across the time period to expiration. If you sell a forward contract, you are assuring yourself of a dollar payment equal to the forward price at the expiration date. You can buy the commodity at its present market value, and you can receive the forward price for the commodity when you sell it at expiration. Because this is a riskless transaction, the following relationship must hold in the absence of carrying costs for the commodity:

$$\text{Current commodity price} = \frac{\text{Forward price}}{(1 + Y)^T}$$

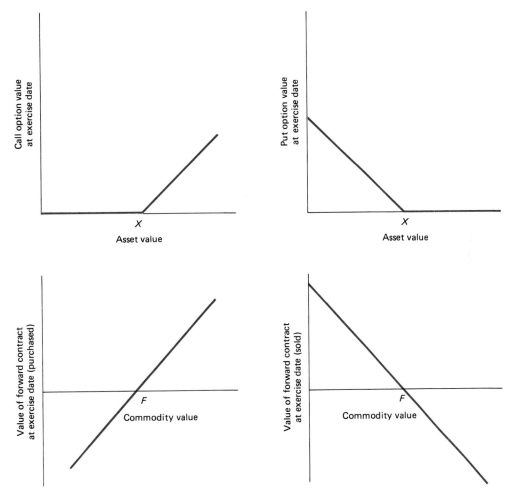

FIGURE 18.1 Relation between option and future values and commodity values at expiration.

where Y is the yield to maturity for a risk-free bond with a maturity equal to the term of the forward contract, T. Thus

$$\text{Forward price} = \text{Current commodity price} \times (1 + Y)^T$$

That is, the forward price is also equal to the *future value* of the current commodity price invested at the risk-free yield to maturity for the term of the contract.

To illustrate, consider a forward contract to sell risk-free bonds with 15 years to maturity and annual interest payments of $150. The forward contract expires in 1 month. The 15-year bonds are currently selling at $1000 to yield 15 percent until maturity. Comparable risk-free bonds with 1 month until maturity are selling at prices

OUT ON THE STREET

SPREADING FUTURES

Gregg Silver raises five fingers into the air and as quickly as that, sells five contracts obligating him to sell $500,000 in U.S. Treasury bonds in four months. Gregg is a floor trader on the Chicago Board of Trade. He trades from his own personal capital. This particular trade requires a margin of $10,000, $2000 for each $100,000 of U.S. Treasury bonds controlled.

Gregg is standing in the U.S. Treasury bond futures pit. The pit rises on all sides as a series of steps, similar to the amphitheaters in Greek times. The room is huge, approximately the size of a small city block. Other pits for other securities like U.S. Treasury note futures are arranged in the room by rule and tradition at points to make the process of price discovery as smooth and orderly as possible. To an outsider, the milling about of the 1200 to 1500 traders seems like chaos. An experienced trader sees through the chaotic activity to the trading process refined through the years to facilitate the exchange of money for contracts and to make possible rapid price adjustments to new information.

Gregg wears a badge on his jacket with the letters "IYO" identifying him. Some of those around him wear loud ties or trading jackets with wild designs in an effort to attract attention, so that they may get their trades processed a little more quickly. In the pit a few seconds can mean thousands of dollars. Some of the largest traders have made or lost in excess of $1 million in a single day!

Trading can be tough on the nerves. Many believe that in most cases a trader's "life span" on the floor is limited to six years before he or she becomes emotionally burned out. Gregg knows that this is a misnomer, however. It is the losers who burn out. Successful traders trade well into their sixties and many into their seventies. As a matter of fact, Gregg's great uncle traded until he was 82 years old, when it finally became too physically taxing.

Good traders have to have enough self-confidence to take risk, when warranted, in whatever form necessary. Yet they must have sufficient flexibility to admit quickly mistakes in judgment. They must take losses quickly rather than become intellectually wedded to an idea that can ultimately become very expensive. The pit is no place for the insecure.

to yield a 1 percent monthly rate of return. The current forward price for the 15-year bonds must then be $1010:

$$\text{Forward price} = \text{Current commodity price} \times (1 + Y)^{1/12}$$

$$\$1010.00 \quad = \quad \$1000.00 \quad \times \quad 1.01$$

Suppose we extend the maturity of the contract to 2 years. The forward price must now reflect the existing yield to maturity on risk-free, 2-year bonds such that

Gregg's trading horizon usually ranges from one to five days. His trading decisions are based on his knowledge of the domestic and international economy, Federal Reserve policy, and political events shaping up in Washington. Over the years he has also developed a sensitive feel for historical relationships between the yields on securities of different term and risk. When these relationships move out of line, he moves in to make money with a spread position.

A spread consists of a long and a short position in two different issues. For example, today Gregg is going short in treasury bill futures and long in treasury bond futures. His position is based on his feeling that the economic outlook doesn't justify the extreme spread between the yields on long- and short-term securities. He feels that the yields on treasury bills will rise and that the yields on treasury bonds will fall over the next day or so. If so, he will make money on his position.

Gregg recalls a similar position taken earlier in the year. The first rumblings were coming out about problems with respect to payments on loans by third world countries. The spread between the yield on treasury bill futures and Euro-dollar futures was then 75 basis points. (A basis point is 1/100th of 1 percent.) Typically, the spread hovers around 50 basis points. At the time, Gregg had a sinking feeling that this was going to become more serious and that all the information relating to the problem hadn't been fully disclosed.

If he was wrong, Gregg estimated that he would lose 25 basis points on his spread position. On the other hand, if he was right, the spread could widen to as much as 150 basis points. As it turned out, the spread widened by 75 basis points in a single week, eventually reaching as much as 220 basis points.

Unfortunately, not every position is as profitable as that one. On any given workday, traders never know whether they will pay or get paid. You can only make your decisions, execute them with confidence, and hope for the best. With this in mind, Gregg climbs from the treasury bond futures pit and makes his way toward the bond options pit.

$$\text{Current commodity price} = \frac{C}{(1 + Y)^1} + \frac{C + \text{forward price}}{(1 + Y)^2}$$

where Y is now the existing yield to maturity on risk-free, 2-year bonds, and C is the annual interest payment on these bonds. The forward price must therefore be equal to

$$\text{Forward price} = \text{Current commodity price} \times (1 + Y)^2 - C \times (1 + Y) - C$$

Thus, in our example, if the annualized yield on 2-year bonds is 13 percent, with a $150 annual interest payment and a $1000 current market price for the 15-year bonds, the forward price must be equal to

$$\$957.40 = \$1000 \times (1.13)^2 - \$150 \times (1.13) - \$150$$

The Relationship Between the Forward Price and the Expected Commodity Price

If you enter into a forward contract to buy a commodity at a stated price, you know for certain the price at which you are going to be able to buy the commodity. If the commodity is a treasury bond, you know you will be able to buy the bond at the forward price, irrespective of what happens to interest rates between now and the time the contract matures. In effect, you have eliminated the risk of fluctuations in interest rates.

Suppose initially, you don't care about risk; you are risk neutral. The relationship between your utility, or well-being, and the total value of your portfolio of wealth at the time the contract expires is presented in Figure 18.2. Note that if you are risk neutral, the relationship is linear. The additional increment in utility associated with an additional increment in wealth is the same, irrespective of the total amount of your wealth.

If you are risk neutral and don't care about risk, you won't care about the fact that the contract eliminates the risk of interest rate fluctuations. If the sellers of the contract are also risk neutral, they won't care about the fact that the contract assures them of the price for which they will sell the bond. In this situation, both the buyers and sellers of the contract will be willing to enter into the agreement to buy and sell, at expiration, at a forward price equal to their expectation for the value of the commodity at the time the contract expires.

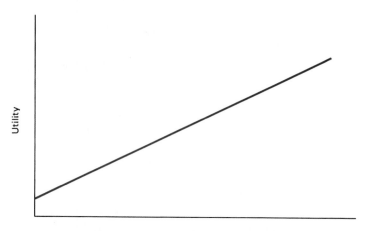

Consumption at Expiration of Forward Contract

FIGURE 18.2 Utility function for risk-neutral investor.

Under these conditions, the equation for the forward price is

Forward price = Expected commodity price

It is important to realize, however, this relationship holds only for risk neutrality. If instead, investors are risk averse, the relationship between their utility and the level of their total consumption of goods and services looks something like Figure 18.3. In this case, as the market value of your portfolio of assets goes up, utility goes up, but at a decreasing rate. Suppose at the time of expiration of the contract, we are in a recession and the value of your portfolio is low, as in the case labeled *R*. In this situation, you need money badly, and an additional payoff by one of the securities in your portfolio brings a substantial increase in your well-being or utility. In states like these, your *marginal utility* is high. On the other hand, suppose we are in economic prosperity or boom when the contract expires. This might be a case like the one labeled *B* in Figure 18.3. In this case you've already got a lot of money, you're driving a new car, and although it might be nice to have a little more money, you don't really need it very much. In boom periods, the additional utility (marginal utility) gained from additional payoffs is low.

If you are risk averse, you will care about whether a securities or financial contract pays off most in booms or recessions because your need for additional increments of wealth is different in prosperity and hard times. Recall that at expiration, the value of a forward contract can be positive or negative. You will like it if the contract tends to pay off the most when times are hard because this is when you need the money the most. Although losses are never welcome, you will prefer it if the value of the contract tends to be negative in boom periods rather than in recessions because a drainage of cash in times of prosperity isn't going to present you with a lot of problems. If the contract tends to pay off in this way, it acts like an insurance

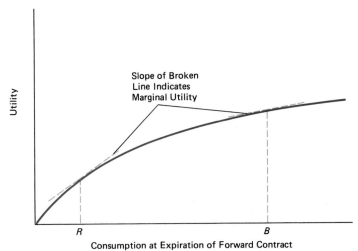

FIGURE 18.3 Utility function for risk-averse investor.

policy, stabilizing the return on your overall investment portfolio and reducing your risk. If, on the other hand, the contract pays off the most in booms and the least in recessions, it increases the uncertainty of your overall portfolio return and generates risk in the same way a security with positive covariance generated risk in the market portfolio in the capital asset pricing model.

Because the payoff to the buyer of a forward contract is equal to the difference between the commodity price and the forward price (which is fixed), the relationship between the commodity price and the value of the market portfolio will determine whether the contract is insurance or risk generating to the buyer. In Figure 18.4, the relationship between the commodity price and the value of the market portfolio is plotted. Each point in the plot represents the value of the market portfolio and the commodity price that exists at a given point in time. If, as in Figure 18.4, the commodity price tends to go up and down with aggregate wealth, the contract will pay off the most in booms and the least in recessions, and it will be risk generating to the buyer. If, as in Figure 18.5, the commodity price tends to move in the opposite direction from the market portfolio, the contract will act as insurance to the buyer. Because the payoffs to the seller of the contract are the opposite of those to the buyer, the opposite will be true for the seller.

In the presence of risk-averse investors, the value for the forward price that the buyers and sellers will be willing to negotiate into the contract is given by

$$\text{Forward price} = \text{Expected commodity price} - \text{risk premium}$$

The sign and magnitude of the risk premium is determined by the sign and magnitude of the covariance between the commodity price and the aggregate level of wealth. For most commodities the covariance is positive. Because the risk premium is subtracted from the forward price, for most commodities the forward price will be less than the expected commodity price. Viewed from the buyers' prospective, the contract generates risk in their portfolios, and they will be willing to enter the contract only at a forward price which is less than their expectation for the commodity price. Remember, the *lower* the forward price, the better for the *buyer* of the contract.

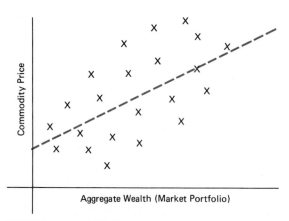

FIGURE 18.4 Positive correlation between commodity price and aggregate wealth.

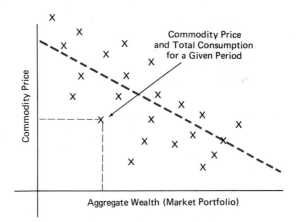

FIGURE 18.5 Negative correlation between commodity price and aggregate wealth.

Because the payoffs to the sellers are the opposite of those for the buyers, the contract *reduces* risk in *their* portfolios. Because they view the contract as insurance, they will be willing to enter the contract at a forward price which is lower than their expected commodity price. Remember, the *higher* the forward price, the better for the *seller* of the contract.

If the commodity happens to move in the *opposite* direction from the aggregate level of wealth, as in Figure 18.5, the contracts act as insurance for the buyer and generate risk for the seller. In this case the forward price would be expected to be above the expected commodity price. If there is no relationship between the commodity price and the aggregate level of consumption, any risk in the contract is presumably diversifiable, and therefore, inconsequential, and the forward price is then equal to the expected commodity price.

If the forward price is less than the expected commodity price, we are said to be in a situation called "normal backwardation." If, on the other hand, the forward price is greater than the expected commodity price, we are in a situation called "contango." Whether we are in normal backwardation or contango depends on the properties of the commodity we are dealing with. Because the values of most commodities are positively correlated with the value of wealth in general, normal backwardation is the typical situation.

If investors are risk neutral, they have linear utility functions. This means that marginal utility is a constant and does not decrease as consumption increases. This also means their need for money doesn't vary from recessions to booms. Thus, here we have the case where the forward price is equal to the expected commodity price.

The Consistency of the Two Expressions for the Forward Price

We now have two equations for the forward price, one in terms of the *current* commodity price and one in terms of the *expected* commodity price. It is easy to show the two equations are mutually consistent because if we equate them we can solve for an expression for the current commodity price that is quite reasonable. By equating our two equations for the forward price, we can solve for the following expression for the current commodity price:

$$\text{Current commodity price} = \frac{\text{Expected commodity price} - \text{risk premium}}{(1 + Y)^T}$$

Thus, if we are dealing with a forward contract to buy a common stock, we can express the current stock price as the discounted (at the risk-free rate) value of the expected stock price at time T, less the risk premium associated with the stock investment.

Market Value of Previously Issued Forward Contracts

Although the forward price is initially set to make the market value of the contract equal to zero, as time passes and the forward prices for contemporary contracts change, the market value of the previously issued contract may become greater or less than zero. In Figure 18.6 the solid line represents the value at expiration of a

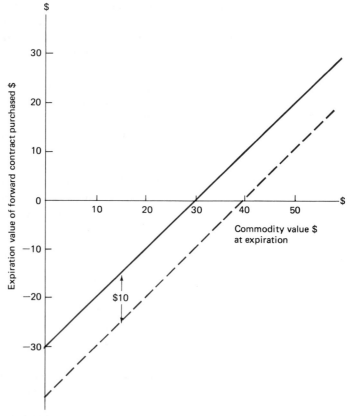

FIGURE 18.6 The difference between the expiration value of two forward contracts.

contract previously purchased for a forward price of $30. The broken line represents the value at expiration for a contract purchased for the current forward price of $40. Both contracts expire at the same time. Note, the difference in the payoffs for the two contracts is a constant, $10, across all possible values for the ending commodity price.

Because the value of a contract written with the current forward price is zero, and because the difference in the payoffs between the two contracts is a known constant, the market value of the previously issued contract is equal to the discounted value of the constant difference in the payoffs. The difference is a known constant, so we discount at the risk-free rate. The value of the contract is given by

$$\frac{\text{Contemporary forward price } - \text{ original forward price}}{(1 + Y)^t} = \begin{array}{l}\text{Market value} \\ \text{of previous} \\ \text{forward} \\ \text{contract}\end{array}$$

where Y is the yield to maturity of a bond that matures at the expiration date of both forward contracts and t is the time remaining to expiration of both contracts.

DETERMINATION OF FUTURES PRICES

As we learned, a major difference between a forward and a futures contract is in the way an account is handled. With a futures contract, the futures price is revised each day to make the current market price of the contract equal to zero. If you bought the contract, and the futures price today is greater than the futures price yesterday, your account is credited with the difference multiplied by the number of commodities controlled by the contracts you have open. If the price is less, your account is debited in the same way.

Table 18.2 sets forth an assumed series of commodity, forward, and futures prices and the associated market values and cash flows accruing to the contracts in the course of a year. Both the forward and futures contracts are assumed to have one year to expiration at the beginning of the year. It is assumed the futures account is marked to market at the end of each quarter rather than on a daily basis, which is actually the case. The market value of the forward contract originally issued at the beginning of the year is computed using the equation for the market value of a previously issued forward contract, at an assumed interest rate of 10 percent. Notice the market value of the futures contract is always equal to zero because the futures price is adjusted to keep it that way.

The four rows at the bottom of the table show the cash flows accruing to buyers and sellers in each of the contracts. The cash flows associated with the two types of contracts are markedly different. If you bought a futures contract to buy one unit of the commodity, at the end of the first quarter $1 is credited to your account because the prevailing futures price has increased by $1. You are free to take this money and reinvest it at prevailing interest rates. If, on the other hand, you sold a futures contract, your account is debited by $1. To maintain the balance in your account, you may have to borrow money at current interest rates.

TABLE 18.2 Cash Flows from Forward and Futures Contracts

Time	Beginning of Year	End of First Quarter	End of Second Quarter	End of Third Quarter	End of Fourth Quarter
Commodity price	10	12	8	10	11
Current forward price	11	12. 9	8.4	10.2	11
Current futures price	10.3	12.2	8.1	10.1	11
Market value of forward contract issued at beginning of year ($r_F = 10\%$)	0	1.77	−2.48	−.78	2
Market value of futures contract issued at beginning of year	0	0	0	0	0
Cash flow to buyer of forward contract at beginning of year	0	0	0	0	0
Cash flow to seller of forward contract at beginning of year	0	0	0	0	0
Cash flow to buyer of futures contract at beginning of year	0	+1.9	−4.1	+2	+.9
Cash flow to seller of futures contract at beginning of year	0	−1.9	+4.1	−2	−.9

The differences in the cash flows associated with investing in a forward or futures contract create a meaningful economic difference between the two contracts. This difference results in a divergence between the forward and futures price. The formula for the futures price contains (1) an additional term reinvestment premium that is related to the profit or loss that can be expected to be generated from reinvestment of the cash flows from marking to market and (2) a second additional term (delivery premium) that is present because a futures contract sometimes give the seller of the contract options with respect to the exact nature of the commodity that can be delivered to the buyer.

$$\text{Futures price} = \text{Expected commodity price} - \text{risk premium} + \text{reinvestment premium} - \text{delivery premium}$$

The nature of the *risk premium* is the same as that of the forward contract. The sign of the *reinvestment premium* depends on the relationship of the covariance between the commodity price and the level of interest rates. If the relationship is positive, as in Figure 18.7, the contract tends to pay off the most to a buyer when interest rates are high. This means buyers will tend to have money added to their accounts when interest rates are high. Thus, they will be able to reinvest the profits from the contract at attractive terms. On the other hand, they will have money taken from their account when rates are low. They will also be able to borrow money to replace these amounts at favorable terms. This is an attractive feature of the contract to buyers, and it

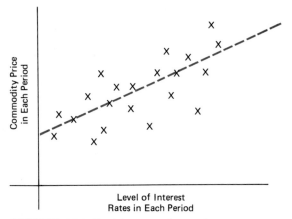

FIGURE 18.7 Positive correlation between commodity price and interest rates.

increases the expected value of the payoff to them. The reinvestment premium is positive when the covariance is positive, and buyers of the contract are willing to negotiate for a higher futures price. What is good for the buyer of the contract is, of course, bad for the seller. Therefore, sellers will refuse to enter into the contract unless the futures price is also above their expectation for the commodity price.

As we said, the sign of the reinvestment premium depends on the relationship between the commodity price and the level of interest rates. If the relationship is positive, the reinvestment premium is positive. In the case of a futures contract to buy treasury bonds, the relationship is almost certainly negative. When interest rates go up, treasury bond prices go down. Thus, the sign of the reinvestment premium for treasury bonds is probably negative, driving down treasury bond futures prices relative to expectations about the future value of treasury bonds. On the other hand, the reinvestment premium for a futures contract to buy gold can be argued to be positive. Gold prices are high in periods of inflation because gold acts as a reasonably good inflation hedge. Interest rates also tend to be high in periods of inflation. Thus, the buyers of a gold futures contract can expect to reinvest positive payoffs from the contract at high rates, and they can borrow to finance negative payoffs at low interest rates. Given this, the buyers would be willing to enter the contract at futures prices which are high relative to their expectations about the future price of gold.

As you will see in one of the following sections, the treasury bond futures contract gives the seller of the contract latitude with respect to the exact treasury bond to be delivered. This is like an option held by the seller of the contract. Thus, it reduces the value of the contract to the buyer. To induce the buyer to enter into the contract with no side payment, the futures price must be lowered. Thus, the delivery premium has a negative sign. The magnitude of the premium depends on the degree of latitude the seller has in terms of delivery and the extent to which the futures price can be adjusted on delivery to fit the character of the specific commodity delivered.

OUT ON THE STREET

A FORWARD OR A FUTURE?

Professor Leif Grando peers intently. He is seated directly across the table from Joe Gorman, the president of National Investment Services of America, Inc., an investment management firm based in Milwaukee, Wisconsin. The firm has grown rapidly to become one of the largest (based on total assets managed) investment management firms in the nation. Most of this growth has been based on the strength of the firm's interest immunization programs. The two are having lunch at the University Club on Lake Michigan in downtown Milwaukee. Gorman is studying a series of charts and tables that are before him on the table.

"Leif, I've asked you to lunch today because we've got a slight problem. As you know, for most of our pension fund clients we immunize their liability streams on the basis of a "core and cap" strategy. The client comes to us with a stream of required payments to be made to its retired employees and a portfolio of existing securities that it expects to produce investment income to make the required payments. Our job is to reconstruct the portfolio so as to be able to guarantee effectively that the income will always be sufficient to make the payments as required.

"With the core and cap strategy, the first thing we do is sell from the client's investment portfolio those securities we feel are inappropriate for immunization. Basically, these are the securities that have payment streams which are risky in terms of their timing and magnitude. These would include variable income securities such as common stocks, low-quality bond issues, and bond issues where the call provision plays a significant role in their pricing. Once these issues have been removed, we are left with what we call the "core portfolio." When we plot the payments expected to be received from the core portfolio as a function of time into the future, they may look like the pattern I have drawn in Figure A.

"The client's required liability payments usually take the pattern of Figure B. The client promises to pay each retired employee a constant dollar annuity for his or her remaining lifetime. Based on actuarial estimates of expected remaining lifetimes, the stream of payments is expected to become smaller as we move farther into the future.

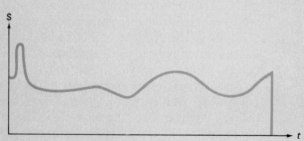

FIGURE A The payments associated with the core portfolio.

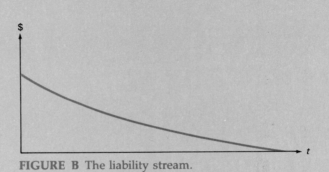

FIGURE B The liability stream.

"To get what we call "the cap," we subtract the payments in the core from the liability stream. For example, if in the first year we expect to receive $1 million from the core portfolio, and we have a $1.5 million required payment in the liability stream, we have a net required payment of $.5 million in the cap. The stream of payments associated with the cap are plotted in Figure C.

"After determining the best available yield, we compute the present value of the cap and invest this amount of money in a portfolio of government bonds that has a duration equal to the duration of the stream of payments in the cap. In this way, the client's total portfolio is immunized."

Grando responds, "Yes, I'm very familiar with this strategy, but I don't see your problem."

"Well, take a close look at that large negative payment in the second year of Figure C. This results because the income produced by the core portfolio happens to be much larger in that year than the required payment to the pensioners. Now think of what happens to the duration of the portfolio as we enter the second year, receive the net payment, and reinvest it in the government bond portfolio. A dramatic change will occur in the pattern and the duration of the remain-

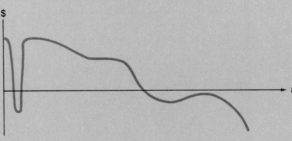

FIGURE C The payments associated with the cap.

ing payments in the cap. This means that we must make a dramatic readjustment in the government bond portfolio to reimmunize. We like to avoid dramatic changes of this type whenever possible, because at times they can work
against us."

Grando ponders the problem and then begins to smile. "I think I may have
an answer to your problem. If you buy a forward or futures contract to buy, let's
say 10-year bonds, for a total value equal to the amount of the negative payment,
in effect you can exchange the negative payment in the second year for payments
associated with the bonds you buy that come in the following 10 years. The effect
of this will be to change the nature of the cap to that in Figure D."

Gorman responds, "I see. You mean the cash flow coming in the second
year disappears because it is used to buy the 10-year bonds under the forward or
futures contract, and the payments received from the bond investment reduce the
magnitude of the positive payments required in each of the next 10 years."

"Exactly, and now you immunize the new cap in accord with your standard
procedures with no dramatic changes in required duration expected along the
way."

"This sounds like the answer I've been looking for, but should we use a
forward or futures contract to execute the strategy?"

"Well," replies Grando, "each contract has its own advantages and disad-

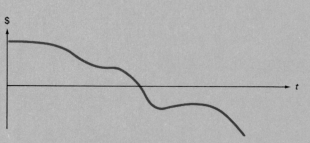

FIGURE D The cap reflecting the effect of the forward or
futures strategy.

Under the special case of risk neutrality, the equation for the futures price
simplifies to

Futures price = Expected commodity price + reinvestment premium

− delivery premium

The risk premium disappears because risk-neutral investors don't care whether the

vantages. If you buy a futures contract, you will have to buy contracts that have fixed maturity dates that extend in 3-month intervals for a limited time into the future. You will also be marked to market every day, and that will create an uncertain pattern of cash flows during the next year in which you hold the contract. This, of course, will create uncertainty in the duration of your bond portfolio. Moreover, in a futures contract there is considerable uncertainty in the bond that you will ultimately receive for delivery. The seller of the futures contract that you buy can deliver a number of different qualifying bond issues. In fact, you may end up taking delivery on an issue that doesn't even exist at the present time but that may be issued by the Treasury during the coming year."

Grando adds, "On the other hand, if you decide to go with a forward contract, you will have to find someone who is willing to sell the contract to you on the terms that you want. I can give you a pretty good idea of what the forward price should be, but you and the party on the other side of the contract, perhaps your government bond dealer, are going to have to provide some assurances that each will ultimately be able to meet the obligation specified in the contract. The seller has to be sure that you will buy the bonds at the stated price, and you have to be sure that he or she will sell the bonds to you. With a futures contract a clearing house stands between you and the seller, assuring the both of you that you will be able to complete the contract at the stated terms, if you desire."

Gorman responds, "Based on what you're saying, it appears that it's going to be much easier to get into, and for that matter, out of the transaction with the futures contract, but the strategy can be executed with much more precision, which is very important to us, with the forward contract. The forward contract can be tailored exactly to our needs, if we can find someone with complementary needs on the sell side."

"That's right. It's a matter of weighing the advantages against the disadvantages and selecting the contract that most fits your needs. I would suggest first trying to negotiate a forward contract that meets your particular needs, and if you find that infeasible, then go to the futures market."

Gorman's eyes shift to the waiter who has been patiently waiting to take their order. He quickly returns to Grando and asks, "The usual?" As Grando nods, Gorman responds, "I think we're both going to have the buffet today."

contract acts as insurance or a risk-bearing security. The effect of entering into the contract on the risk of their overall portfolios is immaterial. The reinvestment premium remains because the relationship between the commodity price and interest rates does affect the *expected value* of the payoffs for the contract. Risk-neutral investors may not care about the risk of the contract, but they do care about its expected value. The same is true with respect to the delivery premium.

The Sign of the Premiums for Various Financial Futures

The sign of the delivery premium (if the premium is nonzero) is the same for all commodities. The sign of the reinvestment and risk premiums, however, may be expected to differ from commodity to commodity. Although there is little in the way of empirical evidence on this matter, we may conjecture about the signs of the two premiums for the various financial futures contracts.

Futures Contract	Sign of Reinvestment Premium	Sign of Risk Premium
Treasury bonds	$(-)$	$(-)$
Treasury bills	$(-)$	$(-)$
Stock indices	$(-)$	$(-)$

For future contracts on high-quality fixed income securities like treasury bonds and bills, the sign of the reinvestment premium is undeniably negative. There is an identity relationship between the prices of these securities and the level of interest rates which forces a negative covariance between interest rates and long-term bond prices. The covariance between the returns to all these securities and the returns to the market portfolio is likely to be positive, making the risk premium a negative number reducing the futures price. The risk premiums should be largest for stocks and larger for bonds than for bills because of the relative volatility of their prices.

The Significance of the Premiums to Investors and Financial Managers

As an investor, you have to take the three premiums into account in making your investment decisions. First, it obviously would be foolish to take the futures price as an estimate of the market's expected commodity price. The fact that the adjusted futures price for bonds is below the current level of bond prices doesn't necessarily imply that the market expects bond prices to fall. In fact, the premiums may mask an expectation for a fall in interest rates. Second, you must recognize that the expected return on buying a futures contract may be negative for some commodities. This is the case because the contract has a propensity to reduce risk, but you still must weigh this propensity against the price you must pay for it, the risk premium, in making your investment decision.

There has been an explosive growth in the use of financial futures by financial institutions. These institutions typically use the futures market to hedge. If the expected commodity price is different from the futures price, there may be a cost or even a profit associated with hedging. If the securities markets are fully integrated, and risk is priced uniformly everywhere, the institution will not affect the market value of its stock by hedging (or speculating) with futures. If hedging with the futures contract truly reduces the risk of the institution's common stock, hedging will come at a commensurate cost that will reduce the expected return on the stock to the exact extent required to maintain its market value. Your institution may be interested in other things besides maximizing stock value, however. If it is interested in survival or maximizing profits, a knowledge of the costs and benefits of hedging with futures contracts will give you a crucial edge in helping your company to achieve its objectives.

THE SECURITY UNDERLYING A FUTURES CONTRACT TO BUY TREASURY BONDS

On March 21, 1984, the futures price on U.S. treasury bond contracts expiring in June closed at 66.08. If you bought such a contract, you agreed to buy 100 treasury bonds at 66.25 percent of their principal value ($1000 each). The person on the other side of the contract can actually deliver to you any one of a number of different treasury bonds. To be eligible for delivery, a bond must have at least 15 years remaining until maturity or earliest call date. The price of 66.08 actually only applies to a bond that has a coupon rate of 8 percent. If a bond with a coupon rate different from 8 percent is delivered, you must buy the bond at an adjusted futures price. The adjusted futures price is determined on the basis of the following formula:

$$\text{Adjusted futures price} = \text{Unadjusted futures price} \times \frac{\sum_{t=1}^{n} C/(1.04)^t + \$1000/(1.04)^n}{\$1000.00}$$

where C is the semiannual coupon on the bond being delivered and n is the number of semiannual interest payments until maturity. In choosing which bond to make delivery, the seller of the contract will compare the adjusted futures price with the current market price for the bonds. The seller will want to deliver the bond with the highest adjusted futures price relative to the prevailing market price.

In March 1984, the most popular bond for delivery was the U.S. treasury maturing on August 15, 2013, with a 12 percent coupon. The adjusted futures price for this bond is 94.11, and on March 21 the bond closed at a price of 95.31 in the cash market.

Can we say the market expected interest rates to rise and the price of the bond to fall by June? We cannot. Given the presence of the various premiums in the equation for the futures price, the fact that the futures price is below today's bond price doesn't necessarily indicate that the expected bond price is lower than today's bond price. It may well be that the reinvestment premium is negative and is large (in absolute value) relative to the size of the other premiums, and interest rates were really expected to fall. The futures price doesn't give an unbiased estimate of the market's expected price even in the presence of risk neutrality.

Similar flexibility and corresponding adjustments in the futures price are present in the terms of delivery for other financial futures contracts. The buyers of such contracts should be aware of the terms and should anticipate delivery of the securities that are least favorable to them.

HEDGING WITH BOND FUTURES CONTRACTS

Suppose you are carrying a portfolio of long-term government bonds. You want to liquidate the portfolio at the end of the year, and you are concerned about possible fluctuations in the value of the portfolio between now and the end of the year. You can reduce the interest rate risk associated with the portfolio by entering into a contract to sell treasury bonds at a specific price through a treasury bond futures contract.

One problem with reducing risk in this way is, given the terms of the futures contract, the bond to be delivered under the contract may not correspond to the bonds that you have in your portfolio. However, you can adjust for this by adjusting your position in the futures contract relative to the total market value of your bond portfolio.

To be completely hedged, you want the dollar change in the market value of your bond portfolio to be the negative of the dollar change in your futures position. Because you are selling the futures contract, the changes will be of opposite signs, but you want them to be equal in absolute magnitude. Thus, you want the following relationship to hold:

Dollar change in bond portfolio = Dollar change in futures position

The dollar change in your bond portfolio accompanying a change in its average yield to maturity can be approximated by

$$
\begin{array}{c}
\text{Dollar change} \\
\text{in bond} \\
\text{portfolio}
\end{array}
\approx
\underbrace{
\begin{array}{c}
\text{Portfolio} \\
\text{duration}
\end{array}
\times
\begin{array}{c}
\text{change in one} \\
\text{plus portfolio} \\
\text{yield}
\end{array}
}_{\substack{\text{Percentage change in} \\ \text{bond portfolio}}}
\times
\begin{array}{c}
\text{market value} \\
\text{of bond} \\
\text{portfolio}
\end{array}
$$

The portfolio's duration is roughly equal to the absolute value of the ratio of the percentage change in the portfolio value relative to the percentage change in one plus the portfolio's yield to maturity. Thus, multiplying duration by the change in one plus the portfolio's yield, we get the percentage change in the portfolio's value.

Similarly, the dollar change in the futures position can be approximated by

$$
\begin{array}{c}
\text{Dollar change} \\
\text{in futures} \\
\text{position}
\end{array}
\approx
\underbrace{
\begin{array}{c}
\text{Duration of} \\
\text{bond underlying} \\
\text{contract}
\end{array}
\times
\begin{array}{c}
\text{change in one} \\
\text{plus underlying} \\
\text{bond yield}
\end{array}
}_{\substack{\text{Percentage change in market value} \\ \text{of bonds controlled by futures contract}}}
\times
\begin{array}{c}
\text{futures position}
\end{array}
$$

By equating the right-hand sides of both approximations and solving for the futures position, we get

$$
\begin{array}{c}
\text{Futures} \\
\text{position}
\end{array}
\approx \text{Duration ratio} \times \text{yield change ratio} \times \text{portfolio value}
$$

The duration ratio is the ratio of the duration of the bond portfolio to the duration of the bond controlled by the futures contract. The yield change ratio is your expectation for the ratio of the change in one plus the yield on the portfolio to the change in one plus the yield for the bond controlled by the futures contract. Short-term bond yields are usually more volatile than are long-term bond yields. Thus, if the portfolio has a shorter duration than the bond expected to be delivered under the futures contract, the yield change ratio would be greater than one. The yield change ratio must be estimated by observing the relationship between the yield of your bond portfolio and the yield of the bond underlying the futures contract over past periods.

To illustrate, suppose the duration of your bond portfolio is 3 years. The duration of the bond underlying the futures contract is 5 years, and your estimate of the yield change ratio is 1.30. (You estimate that fluctuations in one plus your portfolio yield are 30 percent greater than are fluctuations in one plus the yield of the bond underlying the futures contract.) The sudden value of your bond portfolio is $30,000,000. Your futures position should then be

$$\$23,400,000 \ = \ .60 \ \times \ 1.30 \ \times \ \$30,000,000$$

That is, you should sell a sufficient number of futures contracts such that you control $23,400,000 in bonds at market value.

USES OF STOCK INDEX FUTURES

Stock index futures contracts are written on major stock indices such as the New York Stock Exchange Index, the Standard & Poor's 500 Index, or the Value Line Index. These futures contracts can be used to manage the risk of any given stock portfolio. The first step in managing risk with futures contracts is to estimate the beta of your stock portfolio. The beta must be estimated with reference to the index that the futures contract is written on. For example, if you are going to be dealing with futures contracts written on the New York Stock Exchange Index, you would estimate your portfolio beta by relating its returns to the NYSE Index.

The beta will help you determine the position you should take in the index futures. Your position is measured in index units. A unit of the NYSE Index is equal to 500 multiplied by the value of the index. Let's suppose the index is at $50. Then an index unit is $25,000. If your portfolio is currently worth $250,000, then we can say it is worth 10 index units. We will now define the value H as

$$H \ = \ \frac{\text{Number of index units sold}}{\text{Current value of portfolio in index units}}$$

If you sold six index units, H would be equal to .6.

The effective beta factor of your portfolio, taking into account your position in the index futures, can be computed as

$$\beta_P^* \ = \ \beta_P \ - \ H$$

where β_P is the beta of your stock portfolio as computed with reference to the index. Based on this relationship, it is obvious you can make the beta of your portfolio anything you want by adjusting your position in the index.

This method of adjusting risk may be desirable if you want to change the risk of your portfolio without changing the composition of your stock investments. You might, for example, be forecasting a low return for the market as a whole but also the appearance of positive-residuals for some of the high-beta stocks currently in the portfolio. By increasing the value of H, you can reduce the effective beta of your portfolio while maintaining your position in the high-beta stocks.

Suppose you feel you can earn excess rates of return by making better than average forecasts of company-specific events. You are good at doing this, but you feel you have no particular ability to forecast the market. You don't want swings in the market to have an influence on your investment performance. If this is the case, you can render your portfolio insensitive to overall market movement by adjusting your position in index futures such that $H = \beta_P$.

FULL COVARIANCE APPROACH TO CONSTRUCTING A FUTURES OVERLAY

Suppose you had a team of asset managers who knew how to pick stocks with extraordinarily high expected rates of return. The problem was that these managers knew nothing about managing risk. The risk of the portfolio of stocks that they picked was extremely high—so high that it is scaring clients away. You are afraid to go to the managers and tell them to try to bring the risk of the portfolio down for two reasons. First, they don't know how to do it. Second, you are afraid any attempt to manage risk will impair the ability of the managers to concentrate their investments in undervalued stocks.

You can solve your problem by building a portfolio of futures contracts that you will overlay on top of the portfolio of stocks built by the managers. To do this, you can use the standard Markowitz model. First, constrain the program to assign a portfolio weight of 100 percent to the portfolio of stocks picked by the analysts. Then provide it with a covariance matrix or at least a history of the periodic percentage changes in the futures prices for the futures contracts you want to make available for possible inclusion in the overlay portfolio. These might include contracts of different maturities for the various stock index futures as well as contracts on treasury bonds, notes, and bills and others. Next, instruct the computer that the weights it assigns to the various contracts may be positive or negative. (You are willing to be a buyer or a seller of the contracts.) A weight of +30 percent assigned to a particular contract tells you to buy a sufficient number of the futures contracts such that the amount of the commodity controlled by the contract is equal to 30 percent of the total market value of the stock portfolio selected by the analysts.

Now assign expected percentage changes in the futures prices for each of the contracts. To do this you might want to go back and review the previous discussion about the relationship between the current commodity price, the current futures price,

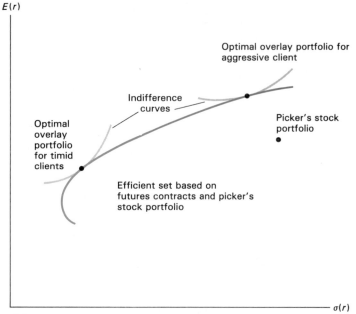

FIGURE 18.8 Optimal futures overlay portfolios.

and the expected commodity price. (The relationship between the futures price and the commodity price should hold at the end of your horizon as well as currently.)

Given the expected returns to the futures contracts and the covariances between the various contracts themselves and between them and the stock portfolio selected by the analysts, you should easily be able to construct an efficient set, as in Figure 18.8. Each point on the efficient set will represent a different overlay portfolio of futures contracts. If you are managing money for clients, each client will select a different overlay portfolio depending on their risk aversion.

Clients need no longer live in fear of your aggressive stock pickers. Moreover, the stock selection activities of the pickers themselves will be totally unaffected by this strategy. In fact, if they are sensitive pickers, you don't even have to tell them what you are doing. They must keep you informed, however, about changes they are making in their portfolio, so that you can counter these changes with changes in the futures overlays.[1]

SUMMARY

Forward and futures contracts obligate you to buy or sell a specific commodity at a specific time at a specific price. The difference between the two contracts is in the way your account is handled. There are no cash flows associated with a forward

[1]For a detailed discussion of risk management with futures contracts, see Figlewski and Kon (1982).

contract until the expiration date, when the contract is worth (to a buyer) the difference between the market value of the commodity and the originally contracted forward price. A futures contract is revised each day, so the market value of the contract itself remains at zero through time. The futures price is revised each day to the contemporary futures price, which is set at a level to make the market value of the contract zero. Your account is credited each day with the difference between the futures price today and the futures price yesterday. Thus, you have positive or negative cash flows accruing to your account throughout the life of the contract.

The difference in the cash flows creates a difference in the value of the forward and futures price. With risk neutrality, the forward price is equal to the expected commodity price. With risk aversion, it is equal to the expected commodity price plus a premium that is dependent on the relationship between the price of the commodity and the aggregate level of consumption. If the relationship is negative, the contract pays off the most in times of economic adversity, when you need the money the most. In this case the contract is useful as a hedge, and you would be willing to buy the contract at a futures price that is higher than your expected commodity price.

With risk neutrality, the futures price is equal to the expected commodity price plus a premium that depends on the relationship between the commodity price and interest rates. If the commodity price tends to be high when interest rates are high, your account will be credited when rates are high, and you can reinvest the credits on favorable items. Thus, a positive covariance between the commodity price and interest rates increases the expected value of the contract to you, and you would be willing to buy it at a futures price that is higher than your expected commodity price, even if you are risk neutral.

Under risk aversion, the futures price differs from the expected commodity price because of the two additional premiums. The delivery premium is negative if the seller of the futures contract had options regarding the exact nature of the commodity to be delivered. The reinvestment premium is related to the relationship between the commodity price and interest rates. Again, a positive relationship increases the expected value of the contract to a buyer. The risk premium in a forward contract is similar to the premium in the forward price under risk aversion.

QUESTION SET 1

1. Suppose the following prices represent the time series of futures prices for various months for wheat to be delivered in August of the same year (in price per bushel).

Month	Feb.	Mar.	Apr.	May	June	July	Aug.
Futures price	$3.20	$3.25	$3.35	$3.25	$3.25	$3.30	$3.40

Suppose that in February you sold a contract for 1000 bushels of August wheat.
a. What was the value of your contract at its inception?
b. If you are marked to market at the end of each month, what would your cash flow be for each of the months?

2. What is the basic difference between a forward contract and a futures contract? Of what importance is this difference in determining the contract prices?

3. Is the "forward price" the same thing as the "value of the forward contract"? Explain.

Refer to the following information for Questions 4 through 6. A forward contract exists for a unit of 2-year government securities with delivery to take place 3 years from now. Suppose the price of these securities 3 years from now is uniformly distributed from a low of $800 to a high of $1400. The 1-year expected riskless rate of interest is 5 percent for all periods under consideration.

4. If investors are risk neutral, what should be the current forward price?

5. Suppose now that investors are risk averse and that the forward price is $1200. What do you know about the relationship between the market value of 2-year government securities and aggregate consumption?

6. Continue to assume (as in Question 5) that the current forward price (at time 0) is $1200. One year from now (at time 1) the forward price for the same item and same delivery date is $1000. Determine the time 1 value (to the buyer) of the contract that was agreed upon at time 0.

7. Explain why a long-term treasury bond might possess a hedging property that would be of value to individuals. What implication would this have for the relationship of long-term to short-term interest rates?

8. Suppose that utility is a linear function of consumption.
   a. What does this imply about forward prices?
   b. What does this imply about future prices?

9. Suppose a particular commodity's price tends to be negatively correlated with consumption. What does this imply about the forward price for the commodity?

10. Suppose that the reinvestment premium from the formula for the futures price is positive. What impact does this have on the futures price? Explain the intuition behind this influence.

11. Suppose the pure expectations theory of the term structure is correct. Which of the "premiums" in the futures price is affected, and in what way?

QUESTION SET 2

1. What is the major difference between an option and a forward and a futures contract?

2. Forward contracts are priced so that their initial value is zero and no cash changes hands between buyer and seller. Compare the relationship between the forward price and the expected commodity price and the relationship between the forward price and the current commodity price. Assume you are risk averse.

3. Compare the cash flows for otherwise identical forward and futures contracts to buy a commodity. How would the cash flows differ on forward and futures contracts to sell the same commodity?

4. In general, what characterizes the type of commodity on which forward or futures contracts can be written?

5. Suppose you want to sell a futures contract to ensure that you will have money in the event that there is a terrible tumble in the stock market so you can continue your practice of taking 3-month vacations away from Bismark, North Dakota, in the winter. What type of contract should you buy?

6. How is a forward price determined if
   a. You are risk neutral?
   b. You are risk averse?

7. What is meant by the terms ''normal backwardation'' and ''contango''?

8. Explain the concept of the reinvestment premium.

9. Describe a hedged position in government bonds and futures.

10. In the formula $\beta_P^* = \beta - H$, the effective level of portfolio risk represented by β_P^* is the net of your stock portfolio beta, β_P, and H, which depends on the number of futures index units you sell and the current value of your stock portfolio in terms of index units.
    a. How must β_P be calculated?
    b. Define an index unit for the NYSE Index.
    c. If you feel that the high-beta stocks in your portfolio are underpriced but feel that the general performance of the market will be poor, how can you effectively reduce the beta of your portfolio without selling the undervalued stocks?
    d. If you are good at predicting company specific risk and wish to make your portfolio insensitive to overall market movement by investing also in index futures, what do you want β_P^* to equal?

ANSWERS TO QUESTION SET 2

1. The purchase of an option gives you the right to buy or sell a commodity on or before a specified date at a specified price. A forward or futures contract *obligates* you to buy or sell a commodity at a specified price and place at expiration unless you have liquidated the contract prior to expiration. since you may have to deliver on a contract even if it is unprofitable, the forward or future contract can have a negative value at expiration. An option, however, has a lower limit of zero because you can always throw it away if the exercise would be unprofitable.

2. a. If you negotiate a forward contract as a risk-averse investor, making no dollar investment, you would agree to a futures price that is equal to the expected commodity price plus premium that accounts for the risk associated with being obligated to buy or sell according to the terms of the contract.
   b. If you invest in a portfolio consisting of a forward contract and the long-term bond covered by the contract, the forward price you negotiate should be related to the current commodity price such that

$$\text{Current value of the commodity} = \frac{\text{Expected value of the commodity} + \text{risk premium}}{(1 + Y)^T}$$

   Having made a dollar investment in the portfolio at $T = 0$, you require a rate of return Y, equal to the yield to maturity on a bond that matures at the same time your contract expires. In either relationship, buyer and seller negotiate a price that reflects not only the expected commodity price but the costs or benefits of being locked into the contract—risks relating to the volatility of commodity prices and aggregate consumption.

3. There are no interim cash flows to the holder of a forward contract to buy or sell until the settlement date unless the contract is liquidated prior to expiration.

A futures contract is marked to market on a daily basis to maintain current contract value. For example, if you bought a 30-day contract to buy a commodity and on day 10 the contemporary futures price is $1 higher, your contract would be worth $1 more. Your account is credited by $1, and you are free to withdraw this amount and invest it elsewhere. Had the futures price declined $1, your account would have been debited $1, and you would have to add that amount to your account, perhaps borrowing at prevailing interest rates to do so.

4. Two characteristics delineate the type of commodity on which a forward or futures contract can be written. The commodity must (a) be graded and standardized and (b) be widely used so that the price is determined in a competitive market. Examples include U.S. Treasury bonds, No. 2 winter wheat, currencies, and stock indices.

5. You need to sell a futures contract to sell a stock market index, one that pays off when the market goes down.

6. a. If you are risk neutral, the forward price is equal to the expected commodity price at settlement date.

   b. If you are risk averse, you might agree to a less favorable price in order (a) to reduce risk in your portfolio or (b) to negotiate a sale on a contract that is insurance to you but risk generating to the person buying it. You might demand a more favorable price on a contract that is risk generating to you. Both buyer and seller will agree to a forward price equal to the expected commodity price plus or minus a risk premium, the sign of which is the same as that of the correlation between the commodity price and the aggregate level of consumption.

7. In the state of "normal backwardation," the forward price is less than the expected commodity price. The value of such a commodity would be positively correlated with the value of wealth in general. Less typical, the state of "contango" is where the forward price is greater than the expected commodity. The value of such a commodity varies inversely with the value of the wealth in general.

8. The reinvestment premium is related to the profit or loss that is expected to be generated from reinvestment of cash flows created in the process of marking to market. Its sign is the same as that of the correlation between the commodity price and the level of interest rates. It can be generally argued that interest rates are generally high in periods of inflation and low in recessions. Given this is true, if a contract on a commodity pays off more in economic highs than lows, you can reinvest credited amounts at high prevailing rates and borrow to maintain the balance in your account when rates are low. When the payoff promises to be favorable, you would be willing to negotiate a somewhat less favorable futures price—higher if you are buying, lower if you are selling—into this contract. The opposite would be true if the correlation between changes in the commodity price and aggregate consumption (and, hence, interest rates) was negative. Note that any payoffs favorable to the buyer are unfavorable to the seller. When the buyer will accept a higher (less favorable) price, the seller will demand a higher (more favorable) price, so they will always agree.

9. If you hold a portfolio of long-term government bonds that you wish to sell on a particular date, you can hedge by taking an offset position in futures maturing on that date. This would eliminate much of the risk of interest rate fluctuations at the cost of reducing your portfolio rate of return. To construct a hedged portfolio, sell futures in an amount such that the dollar change in your futures position is the same as the dollar change in your bond portfolio, but of opposite sign. Continually readjust your position in futures as interest rates change.

10. a. β_p must be estimated with respect to the stock index used.
   b. An index unit for the NYSE is 500 multiplied by the value of the index.
   c. You can reduce the market sensitivity of your portfolio by investing both in stocks and index futures. Sell index futures in an amount that will counter the risk of your stock portfolio to the extent that a particular effective portfolio risk is achieved. Adjust your position in futures, varying H so that a desired β_p^* is maintained.
   d. When $\beta_p^* = 0$, a portfolio of both stocks and index futures is totally insensitive to market movement. Adjust your position in units of index futures so that H is equal to the beta of your portfolio.

PROBLEM SET

1. Suppose you hold a 30-day forward contract on a stock purchased at a price of $25. Ten days later, a 20-day contract with the same settlement date is written on the commodity and purchased at a forward price of $35.00. At what price could you liquidate your contract at the time the 20-day contract was written? Assume the yield to maturity on a 20-day treasury bill at day 10 is .10.

2. The market value of a riskless 10-year zero coupon bond promising $1000 with a 10 percent yield to maturity is currently $385.54. Yields on one-year zeros are currently 9 percent. You wish to enter into a forward contract to sell the 10-year zeros in one year at the forward price. What should the forward price be on your contract?

ANSWERS TO PROBLEM SET

1. The current value of your forward contract is the discounted difference between the contemporary forward price and your original forward price.

$$\begin{array}{c} \text{Market value} \\ \text{of} \\ \text{previous forward contract} \end{array} = \frac{\text{Contemporary price} - \text{original price}}{(1 + Y)^t}$$

$$= \frac{\$35 - \$25}{(1.10)^{20/365}}$$

$$= \$9.948$$

2. If you buy the 10-year zeros and sell a forward contract that obligates you to sell them in 1 year at the forward price, you have created a 1-year riskless investment which should yield the 1-year riskless return of 9 percent.

$$\frac{\text{Current price of}}{\text{10-year zeros}} = \frac{\text{Forward Price}}{1 + Y}$$

where Y is the current yield to maturity on the 1-year bonds. Therefore the forward price should be

$$\text{Forward Price} = \$385.54 \times (1.09) = \$420.24$$

REFERENCES

BLACK, F., "The Pricing of Commodity Contracts," *Journal of Financial Economics* (September 1976).

CORNELL, B., and REINGANUM, M., "Forward and Futures Prices: Evidence from the Forward Exchange Markets," *Journal of Finance* (December 1981).

COX, J. C., INGERSOLL, J. E., and ROSS, S. A., "The Relation Between Forward and Futures Prices," *Journal of Financial Economics* (December 1981).

FIGLEWSKI, S., and KON, S., "Portfolio Management with Stock Index Futures," *Financial Analysts Journal* (January–February 1982).

GARBADE, K., and SILBER, W., "Futures Contracts on Commodities with Multiple Varieties: An Analysis of Premiums and Discounts," *Journal of Business* (July 1983).

GRAUER, F. L. A., and LITZENBERGER, R. H., "The Pricing of Commodity Futures Contracts, Nominal Bonds and Other Risky Assets Under Uncertainty," *Journal of Finance* (March 1979).

JARROW, R. A., and OLDFIELD, G. S., "Forward Contracts and Futures Contracts," *Journal of Financial Economics* (December 1981).

KILCOLLIN, T. E., "Differences Systems in Financial Futures Markets," *Journal of Finance* (December 1982).

LELAND, H., and RUBENSTEIN, M., "Replicating Options with Positions in Stock and Cash," *Financial Analysts Journal* (July–August 1981).

MORGAN, G. E., "Forward and Futures Pricing of Treasury Bills," *Journal of Banking and Finance* (December 1981).

RESNICK, B. C., and HENNIGAR, E., "The Relationship Between Futures and Cash Prices for U.S. Treasury Bonds," *Journal of Futures Markets,* Vol. 2, no. 3 (1983).

RICHARD, S. F., and SUNDARESAN, M., "A Continuous Time Equilibrium Model of Forward Prices and Futures Prices in a Multigood Economy," *Journal of Financial Economics* (December 1981).

STEVENSON, R., and BEAR, R., "Commodity Futures: Trends or Random Walks," *Journal of Finance* (March 1970).

TRAINER, F. H., "The Uses of Treasury Bond Futures in Fixed Income Portfolio Management," *Financial Analysts Journal* (January–February 1983).

CHAPTER

19

THE EFFECT OF TAXES ON INVESTMENT STRATEGY AND SECURITIES PRICES

The government usually takes a share of the returns from an investment through federal, state, and local income taxes. One of the things we're going to learn in this chapter is how to maximize your after-tax return from an investment while reducing the share of investment income going to government.

While trying to minimize the tax bite, investors trade and thereby affect the relative prices of securities with differing degrees of tax exposure. The prices of securities with the greatest exposure to taxation are lowered relative to the prices of securities with tax-sheltered income. In the end, the ideal strategy isn't necessarily one of investing in those securities with the least tax exposure. These investments are likely to be more "expensive" than others, and you must weigh the "price" of sheltering your investment income against the increase in taxes associated with exposing it.

In this chapter we will discuss the structure of the new tax law and how it affects your investment strategy. We will also discuss how taxes may affect the pricing of securities. Because of the wide diversity of the treatment of taxes at the state and municipal levels, we will center our attention on the federal income tax.

THE TAX STRUCTURE

In the United States, personal income is taxed progressively at graduated rates of 14 percent and 28 percent. However, it is still the case that different individuals with the same level of taxable income may pay income taxes at different rates. Given your level of income, your tax rate may depend on your tax status. For example, for each level of income, the tax rate for married couples may be less than for a single person.

What Investment Income Is Taxed?

Not all investment income is subject to taxation. The interest income from state and municipal bonds, for example, is exempt from the federal income tax. Income from capital gains on these bonds is not exempt, however. Although exempt from federal income taxation, state and municipal bond interest is subject to state and local income tax.

Interest income from bonds issued by the U.S. government is subject to taxation by the Internal Revenue Service, but it is exempt from taxation by state and local governments. Interest income from corporate bonds is subject to taxation at all levels by the federal, state, and local governments.

If you buy a bond that was *originally issued* at a price that is less than the principal payment, you must report as interest income each year the amortized difference between the principal and the original issue price. Suppose you buy a bond that promises a single principal payment with no annual interest payments. If the bond had 5 years to maturity when originally issued, had a principal value of $1000, and was sold for a price of $750 when originally issued, you must report interest income in an amount of $50 per year for each year that you own the bond. Thus, you must pay taxes on the interest even though you receive no cash payments from the bond.

The new tax law allows some individuals to invest a limited amount each year in an Individual Retirement Account (IRA). The amount invested can be deducted from your taxable income for the year. You can also defer taxation on any income earned on the investment until you withdraw the money at some future date. The funds can be invested in a wide variety of investments, including mutual funds, making the IRA an extremely attractive tax shelter for all investors.

Keogh retirement plans are similar to an IRA and many are available to those investors who have income from self-employment. You can invest annual amounts of 25 percent up to $30,000 of self-employment income in a Keogh plan. The investment amount itself is deductible from taxable income, and investment income earned in the plan isn't taxable until withdrawn.

Tax-sheltered annuities, or 401(K) plans, are also available to certain individuals whose employer sets up a plan. They can invest limited amounts in a tax-sheltered annuity usually a percentage of income up to $7500 per year. Again, the contribution is deductible, and income earned on the investment is deferred until withdrawn. Tax-deferred annuities, or 403(b) plans, are available to education and other nonprofit institutions. The amount that can be contributed is 20 percent of income up to a maximum of $9500. The contribution is not included in gross income, and the investments are not taxed until withdrawn.

These tax shelters are really doubly advantageous for the following reasons. First, income, which would normally be taxed away, can be successively reinvested to produce yet more income. This feature dramatically increases the earning power of the investment. Second, you will presumably withdraw funds from the account at retirement, when your annual income will be less than it is when you make the contributions. Thus, in addition to deferring payment of the tax, you eventually may be taxed at a lower rate.

Capital Gains and Losses

A capital gain or loss results from a change in the market value of your investment. Capital gains and losses are taxed in the year that they are realized.

There are tax advantages in taking your investment income in the form of capital gains, as opposed to regular interest or dividend income. Taxation of capital gains can be deferred until the gain is realized. This gives you the opportunity to earn more profits by reinvesting the income that would otherwise be taxed away. In effect, it's like getting an interest-free loan from the government in an amount equal to what would be the capital gains tax, if the gain were realized immediately. *Other things being equal,* if you pay taxes, you should have a preference for investments that produce their investment income in the form of capital gains, as opposed to periodic cash payments like interest or dividends, which may be exposed to the full force of the income tax.

TAXES AND INVESTMENT STRATEGY

Computing After-Tax Rates of Return

To compute the after-tax rate of return on an investment, you must first estimate the cash flows associated with the investment, determine the tax status of these cash flows, and then estimate your expected tax rate at the time the cash flows are received. For example, suppose you are considering purchasing a riskless bond with n years until maturity that pays interest annually. The after-tax internal yield to maturity on the bond can be found as the rate that will discount the after-tax cash flows on the bond to a present value equal to the bond's current market price. Thus, through a process of trial and error, you would solve for Y in the following formula,

$$V = \sum_{t=1}^{n} \frac{C - \tau_t C}{(1 + Y)^t} + \frac{P - \tau_n^*(P - V)}{(1 + Y)^n} \qquad (19.1)$$

where C is the annual interest payment, V is the current value of the bond, τ_t is your expected tax rate on marginal income at time t, and τ_t^* is your expected tax rate on capital gains or losses in the year that the bond matures. (τ_t and τ_t^* may be equal as they were in 1990, or, if you foresee changes in the tax law, you may presume them different.)

As you move into the future, your tax rate on investment income may be expected to change because of changes in the expected level of your total *taxable* income or because of anticipated changes in the tax law. In each year we subtract from the interest payment that amount of the payment that will be paid to the government in taxes. P represents the principal payment on the bond. For conventional bonds, the bond is originally issued at a price equal to the principal payment. If interest rates subsequently go up, and you buy the bond at a price, V, that is less than P, you will have realized a capital gain, equal to $P - V$, when the bond matures. Your capital gains tax, equal to the gain multiplied by the estimated effective tax rate on capital gains at maturity, is subtracted from the principal payment at maturity.

To illustrate the computation, consider the following example. Assume that you foresee a future tax structure whereby you are in the 28 percent tax bracket for regular income. Your capital gains are also expected to be taxed at a 28 percent rate. You are considering the purchase of either of two U.S. government bonds. Both have 2 years to maturity. We will assume for simplicity that interest is paid annually at the end of each year. One of the bonds carries a $50 annual interest payment and sells at a price of $823.42. Its pretax internal yield to maturity is therefore 16 percent.

$$\$823.42 = \frac{\$50.00}{(1.16)} + \frac{\$1000.00 + \$50.00}{(1.16)^2}$$

The other bond carries an annual interest payment of $160 and sells at a price of $1000. Its pretax internal yield is also 16 percent.

$$\$1000.00 = \frac{\$160.00}{(1.16)} + \frac{\$1000.00 + \$160.00}{(1.16)^2}$$

If you were a tax-exempt institution, and didn't pay taxes, you would be indifferent to either bond. However, because you are in the 28 percent bracket, you are attracted to the $50 bond because it produces its income in the form of capital gains as well as interest. As the bond approaches its maturity, the price of the bond will rise from its current value of $823.42 to its principal value of $1000. The fact that some of the income from this investment is in the form of price appreciation is advantageous to you because you can defer payment of the tax on the capital gain.

The after-tax yield to maturity on the $50 bond can be computed according to Equation (19.1). It is equal to 11.82 percent.

Thus, although the pretax yields on the two issues are the same, the after-tax yield is smaller on the high-coupon issue. Because the two investments are nearly identical in all other respects, it is in your interest to invest in the issue with the smaller interest payment. To determine the best investment, you would make your decision on the basis of a comparison of the *after-tax* yields.

$$
\$823.42 = \frac{\$50 - \overbrace{(.28 \times \$50)}^{\substack{\text{Tax} \\ \text{on} \\ \text{interest,} \\ \text{year 1}}}}{(1.1182)}
$$

$$
+ \frac{\$50 - \overbrace{(.28 \times \$50)}^{\substack{\text{Tax} \\ \text{on} \\ \text{interest,} \\ \text{year 2}}} + \$1000 - \overbrace{.28 \times (\$1000 - \$823.42)}^{\substack{\text{Tax} \\ \text{on} \\ \text{capital gain,} \\ \text{year 2}}}}{(1.1182)^2}
$$

On the other hand, the after-tax yield on the $160 bond is only 11.52 percent.

$$
\$1000 = \frac{\$160 - \overbrace{(.28 \times \$160)}^{\substack{\text{Tax} \\ \text{on} \\ \text{interest,} \\ \text{year 1}}}}{(1.1152)} + \frac{\$160 - \overbrace{(.28 \times \$160)}^{\substack{\text{Tax} \\ \text{on} \\ \text{interest,} \\ \text{year 2}}} + \$1000}{(1.1152)^2}
$$

The Locked-In Effect

As discussed, capital gains and losses are taxed and deducted, respectively, when realized rather than when accrued. Suppose you bought a bond some time in the past; interest rates have since fallen, and the bond is now selling at a price much higher than the price you originally paid. You are looking at an alternative bond that is selling at a very attractive yield. The problem is this. If you sell the bond that you own, you will realize the capital gain, and the government will take some of your invested funds. In other words, you won't be able to commit as much capital to the new bond as you now have invested in the old. Even if the new bond is more attractive than the old in terms of percentage yield, your total dollar return may be less. In effect, the accrued capital gain has "locked" you into the investment in the old bond in the sense that it has increased the propensity for you to stay with it.

Accrued capital losses do the opposite. They provide an incentive to sell and move into other investments, because if you sell, you can realize the capital loss and take it as a tax deduction.

How can you tell when it is in your interest to realize a capital loss by switching from one bond to another? When is it best to remain in a bond with an accrued gain, even though there are other, alternative bonds with more attractive yields?

In computing the after-tax yield in Equation (19.1), we found the rate that would discount the after-tax cash flows, that we would get if we bought the bond, to a present value equal to what we would have to give up in order to get the bond, its current market price. To compute the after-tax yield on a bond you already own, you make a similar computation. However, Equation (19.1) must be modified in two respects.

First, the capital gain or loss at maturity is computed on the basis of the *price that you paid for the bond when you bought it* rather than the bond's current market price. Second, in the original equation, we related the after-tax cash flows associated with buying the bond to what we had to give up in order to buy it. If you don't already own the bond, you have to give up the market price in order to acquire it. If you already own the bond, you relate the after-tax cash flows associated with keeping the bond to what you have to give up to keep it. To keep the bond, you're giving up the net proceeds associated with selling it. The proceeds are equal to the bond's current market value less any capital gains tax you must pay if you sell now, or if you have an accrued capital loss, any taxes you would save by deducting the loss immediately.

Thus, the after-tax yield to maturity for a bond you already own is computed by solving for Y in the following equation:

$$V - \tau_0^* (V - V_K) = \sum_{t=1}^{n} \frac{C - \tau_t C}{(1 + Y)^t} + \frac{P - \tau_n^*(P - V_K)}{(1 + Y)^n} \qquad (19.2)$$

where V_K is the price you originally paid for the bond. The second term on the left side of the equation represents the capital gains tax you must pay if you sell the bond now. The capital gain is computed as the difference between the current price of the bond and your original cost. There is a similar term in the numerator of the last term on the right side. This represents the capital gains tax you must pay if you hold the bond to maturity. The capital gain in this case is computed as the difference between the principal payment and your original cost.

If you have an accrued capital loss, you can use the same equation. In this case by holding the bond you are giving up, in addition to its value in the market, the tax deduction associated with realizing the accrued capital loss. We relate the sum of these two to the after-tax cash flows associated with keeping the bond in calculating the after-tax yield to maturity.

To illustrate the formula, suppose that there are two bonds that have two years to maturity and $100 annual interest payments. You bought one of the bonds many years ago at a price of $600. The price of this bond is now $918.71. The price of the other bond, which you don't own, is being offered to you at the seemingly attractive price of $910.00. In this example, assume that you feel that there will be future upward revisions in tax rates and that capital gains will be taxed at a preferred rate in the future. Assume now that you *expect* in the *future* to be in a 28 percent tax bracket, and will also be taxed in the *future* at the rate of only 28 percent on capital gains and losses, and that the after-tax internal yield on the bond you don't own is equal to 11.24 percent.

$$\$910 = \frac{\$100 - (.28 \times \$100)}{(1.1124)}$$

$$+ \frac{\$100 - (.28 \times \$100) + \$1000 - .28(\$1000 - \$910)}{(1.1124)^2}$$

OUT ON THE STREET

STRIPPING DIVIDENDS

"What's your pleasure, Buddy?"

Peter Thayer slammed the taxi door and responded, "La Guardia, and push it. I've got 45 minutes to make a flight."

This was the tail end of a business trip on which Pete landed two new corporate accounts, both for the investment management service that specialized in providing dividend income in concentrated doses to corporate investors.

This was still another specialized service of Gateway Investment Advisers, the money management firm located in Cincinnati, Ohio. Gateway specializes in the creative use of options in investment management. In this case, they were using options to provide corporations with concentrated doses of dividend income from common stocks without exposing them to the risks associated with the fluctuations in the prices of the common stocks.

Corporations typically have liquid funds which they must invest prior to making financial commitments, such as the payment of interest on their bond issues. Since the funds move in and out of the market rather quickly, the investments must be highly liquid. The problem is that most corporations are in the 36 percent bracket for marginal income, and this takes a big bite on anything they can earn on their financial investments.

However, the tax law allows them to deduct 70 percent of their dividend income from their taxable income. This creates a major incentive for them to invest in any security that distributes what the IRS will recognize as dividends. After all, the effective tax rate for them on this type of investment income is only $10.8\% = .36 \times (1 - .70)$. Five or six years ago corporations had big preferred stock portfolios. However, many preferred stocks lacked real liquidity. Moreover, since they were the only investments around with low risk and dividend income, the corporate demand forced their prices up and expected returns down relative to other securities.

The after-tax yield on the bond you do own is 12.01 percent.

$$\underbrace{\$918.71 - .28(\$918.71 - \$600.00)}_{\text{What you give up to keep the bond}}$$

$$= \underbrace{\frac{\$100 - (.28 \times \$100)}{(1.1201)} + \frac{\$100 - (.28 \times \$100) + \$1000 - .28(\$1000 - \$600)}{(1.1201)^2}}_{\text{What you get if you keep the bond}}$$

Thus, even though someone who doesn't own either bond would prefer the bond with the lower price, because in all other respects the two bonds are identical,

With Gateway's service, their corporate clients can capture common stock dividends without worrying about capital gains or losses.

Gateway's strategy is to buy common stocks that are about to go ex-dividend. At the same time they sell relatively deep in-the-money call options on the same stock. They also buy positions in put options in the Standard & Poor's 100 Index to provide additional protection against a downward slide in stock market prices that may force their call options out of the money. After the stock goes "ex," they hold it for the length of time required under the law to enable their corporate clients to avail themselves of the 70 percent exclusion. Then they sell the stock, buy back their options, and move into another stock that is about to go ex-dividend.

Prior to July 16, 1984, corporations were required to hold stocks for more than 16 days to get the exclusion. Now they must hold them for 46 days. This, however, was approximately the average length of the holding period for Gateway's dividend investments anyway. Even with the extended holding period Gateway can produce up to eight quarterly dividends a year for the invested dollar instead of the normal four.

The market for this strategy has been huge! It is low risk. The beta factor for these portfolios is typically around .2. If the companies invest in Euro dollars or certificates of deposit, they can expect to earn $1 - 36$ percent of whatever these securities are yielding. The dividend strategy produces a higher pretax return, and they get to keep 89.2 percent of it. This adds up to double or triple the after-tax return for their corporate cash. While it may sound odd for dividends to be moving from one corporation to another to be taxed again before final receipt by investors, they've got to invest their idle cash in something, and this minimizes the tax bite going to government.

Peter notices the red blur of what might have been a traffic light outside the window. "I know I said push it, but not all the way to the floor. Please!"

it is in your interest to hold on to the bond you already own. If you sell it to move into the other issue, you must pay tax on the gain that you have accrued. Thus, you must give to the government money that you could otherwise keep invested on your own account. By comparing after-tax yields computed in this way, you can determine when it is to your advantage to realize a gain or loss and move into another issue.

Dividend Clienteles

As you know, bonds that sell at discounted prices below their principal values have a tax advantage. Part of the return that these bonds produce for investors comes in the form of a capital gain, as the value of the bonds approaches the principal at maturity. Because capital gains can be deferred, the income from these types of bonds is, to some extent, tax sheltered.

A similar phenomenon exists in the stock market. A stock's total expected return can be broken down into two parts,

$$E(r) = \frac{E(D) + E(\Delta V)}{V} = \frac{E(D)}{V} + \frac{E(\Delta V)}{V} = \frac{\text{Dividend}}{\text{yield}} + \frac{\text{expected}}{\text{growth}}$$

where ΔV is the change in the value of the stock during the period that you hold it.

In general, as stocks pay out a larger fraction of their earnings as dividends, and thereby retain less for future investments, they reduce the expected growth in their stock price. Thus, by changing the fraction of earnings paid out as dividends, they alter the mix of return to their investors between dividends and capital gains. As we will see in the next section, just as discounted bonds sell at lower pretax yields than bonds that sell at premiums, investors may require higher rates of return on stocks that pay larger dividends and therefore have greater tax exposure.

There is some question as to whether this is really true, but if it is, it has been suggested that stocks may then have particular investor clienteles, where low-bracket investors invest in stocks with high dividend payouts, and high-bracket investors invest in stocks with low dividend payouts. This is directly parallel to the clienteles that exist in the bond market. High-bracket investors generally invest in municipal bonds, and low-bracket investors, like pension funds, which pay no income taxes at all, generally avoid municipals and invest in corporates and U.S. government issues.

The existence of clienteles in the stock market can be questioned, however, because there are mechanisms for investors to separate the dividend and capital gains components of a stock's total return and then invest exclusively in either one. If you want to invest exclusively in the dividend of a given stock, you need only do the following:

1. Buy a share of stock.
2. Buy a put option on the stock, with any arbitrary exercise price, X, that expires shortly after the ex-dividend date.
3. Sell a call option on the stock with an exercise price and expiration date equal to that of the put.
4. Borrow the present value of X and use the money to help finance the purchase of the share.

Now consider the proceeds of this strategy on the expiration date of the options. First, if the stock price, V_S, is greater than X

Stock value	V_S + dividend
Put value	0
Call value	$-(V_S - X)$
Debt value	$-X$
Total value	Dividend

On the other hand, if the stock value turns out to be less than X

Stock value	V_S + dividend
Put value	$X - V_S$
Call value	0
Debt value	$-X$
Total value	Dividend

As you can see, no matter what happens to the stock, you get the dividend as the only payoff from the strategy. If you want to invest in dividends, you need not restrict your investments to stocks with high dividend payouts. You can easily invest in low payout companies and strip the dividends from the stocks with the strategy. There is no need for any particular type of clientele in certain companies.

Although the transactions costs associated with adopting such a strategy may be large for the individual investor, financial institutions such as Gateway Investment Advisors, can employ the strategy on a large scale and then market the dividend fund to investors.

THE EFFECT OF TAXES ON SECURITIES PRICES

Because taxes may alter the trading strategies of individual investors, they may have an impact on the way securities are priced in the market. In this section we will look at the way taxes affect the pricing of dividends versus capital gains in the stock market, and the pricing of securities that are taxable, such as corporate bonds, relative to the pricing of securities that are tax exempt, such as municipal bonds.

The Effect of Dividends on Expected Stock Returns

Brennan (1973) introduced personal income taxes into the capital asset pricing model. He assumed that capital gains were taxed at a lower rate than dividends, investors could borrow and lend at a risk-free rate of interest, and dividends were known with certainty. Under these assumptions, Brennan derived the following analog to the securities market line in the no-tax CAPM:

$$E(r_J) = \underset{\substack{\text{Risk-free} \\ \text{rate}}}{r_F} + \underset{\substack{\text{Risk} \\ \text{premium}}}{a_1\beta_J} + \underset{\substack{\text{Tax exposure} \\ \text{premium}}}{a_2\,(d_J - r_F)}$$

In the equation, you can interpret a_1 as the slope of the relationship between risk and expected rates of return, and a_2 as a coefficient relating the firm's dividend yield, d_J, to its expected rate of return. Firms with dividend yields (the ratio of the dividend to the market price) greater than the risk-free rate sell at a premium in their expected return, and firms with lower dividend yields sell at a discount in their return. In the Brennan model, the coefficient a_2 is a weighted average of the marginal tax rates of investors in the market, and it is a positive number.

Miller and Scholes (1978) have presented a counterargument to show that the fraction of its earnings a firm pays out as dividends should have no impact on the expected return of its common stock. Essentially, they argue that there are many ways investors can shelter dividends from taxes. We discussed some tax shelters at the beginning of this chapter. In addition to these, Miller and Scholes suggest the following.

If you have some taxable dividends from your stock investments, all you need is a tax deduction to shelter them. To get one, you need only borrow money and invest it in something like a tax deferred annuity. You won't be taxed on the income from the annuity, and you won't increase your risk if the income from the annuity is derived from risk-free investments. If you borrow (and invest) enough money so the interest on the debt is equal to the amount of your dividends, you can use the dividends to pay the interest and use the interest as a tax deduction to cover the dividends. In effect, you have transformed the dividends into a tax-deferred annuity. Because you can do this with any form of investment income, the tax exposure of investment income should matter little to you. If tax-exposed investments sell at lower prices, you can take advantage of these discounted prices while paying no taxes on the associated investment income.

In a more recent paper Litzenberger and Ramaswamy (LR) (1982) empirically tested a slightly modified version of Brennan's model. They looked at a large sample of stocks in the period 1940 through 1980. In the 60 months prior to any given month of their test, they estimated the beta factors for all the stocks in their sample by relating the returns on each stock to the returns on their New York Stock Exchange market index. They then estimated the dividend for each stock for the month, using a statistical model which employs information that was available at the beginning of the month. Having estimated the dividend, they then computed each stock's dividend yield.

At this point, LR examined the relationship between the dividend yields for different stocks and the returns produced in each month, after allowing for the effect of differences in beta on differences in security return. Do the stocks that have large dividend yields, and therefore great tax exposure, tend to be priced so as to produce larger returns before taxes? To answer this question, LR examined the relationship between pretax return and dividend yield in each of the months covered in their study by fitting a linear line through the cross section of stocks in their sample. The slopes of each of these lines were then averaged, and the average turned out to be a positive number that is statistically significant. Thus, their study supports the view that stocks, like bonds, with greater tax exposure tend to sell at lower prices and greater expected pretax rates of return. Thus, their results support Brennan and are inconsistent with the tax avoidance argument of Miller and Scholes.

There remains a puzzling question: If dividends do affect the expected rate of return on stocks, why don't all firms act to reduce their costs of capital by lowering the amount of their dividends? Why, in fact, do dividends exist at all when you can deter payments with capital gains? Researchers in finance are actively seeking the answer to this question.

Relative Expected Returns on Taxable and Tax-Exempt Securities

It is clear that there is a differential expected return between securities that are fully exposed to taxes, such as corporate bonds, and securities that are exempt from taxes, such as municipal bonds. In his presidential address to the American Finance Association, Merton Miller (1977) introduced a model that helped to predict how large a differential should be expected. In the most simple form of his model, he assumes that investors can escape taxation on common stock returns through the various tax-avoidance mechanisms discussed earlier. Given that they can, common stock should sell at the same (risk-adjusted) expected rate of return as fully tax-exempt securities, such as municipal bonds. He assumes that corporate bonds are fully exposed to personal income taxes and that the interest on these bonds is deductible for purposes of computing the corporate income tax.

Corporations can finance their investments by either selling common stock or corporate debt. The payments on the debt are deductible; the dividends on the stock are not. Given this, if the stock and the debt sell at the same (risk-adjusted) rate of return, firms will prefer to finance with debt. If τ_C is the corporate income tax rate, the firm can save $\tau_C r_C V_D$ dollars in taxes for each year the debt is outstanding, where r_C is the interest rate on the corporate debt. If the debt is perpetual, the present value

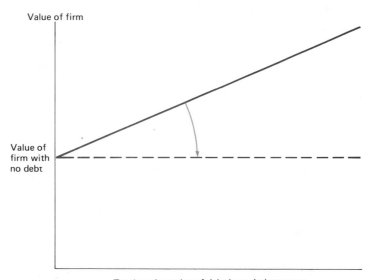

FIGURE 19.1 Debt and firm value: Miller.

of these tax savings is equal to $\tau_C \, r_C V_D / r_C$, or $\tau_C V_D$. Thus, for each dollar in debt issued by the firm, the market value of the firm goes up by τ_C cents.

The relationship between the value of the firm and the amount of debt outstanding under these assumptions is given in Figure 19.1. Note that it is in the interest of the firm to issue as much debt as possible, if it wishes to maximize its market value. In other words, if corporate debt sells at the same (risk-adjusted) expected rate of return as common stock and municipal bonds, corporations will flood the market with debt. Suppose debt sells at a higher (risk-adjusted) expected rate of return. In this case, the firm gets the benefit of the tax deduction but pays a penalty through the premium in the cost of debt. In this case the slope of the function in Figure 19.1 is reduced. Suppose that the differential in the (risk-adjusted) expected returns between corporate debt and stock and municipal bonds becomes large enough to equate the after-tax returns for someone in the same bracket as the corporate tax rate. This will be the case when $r_C = r_S / (1 - \tau_C)$ where r_S is the (risk-adjusted) expected return on stock investments. Now the penalty through the differential premium exactly offsets the benefit of the tax deduction. In Figure 19.1 the slope of the function is now zero, as given by the broken line. If the differential in return becomes any bigger, the slope becomes negative.

Thus, if the (risk-adjusted) expected return on debt is greater than $r_S / (1 - \tau_C)$, the firm will want to issue no debt, because debt drives down the value of the firm. If it is less than $r_S / (1 - \tau_C)$, all firms will want to finance with all debt, because debt drives up the value of the firm. The supply curve for corporate debt is, therefore, perfectly horizontal at a (risk-adjusted) interest rate of $r_S / (1 - \tau_C)$, as given in Figure 19.2.

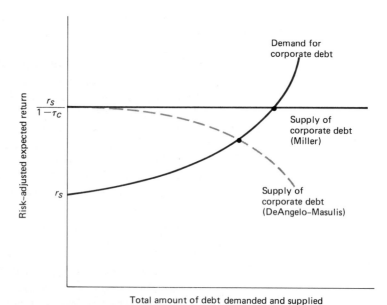

FIGURE 19.2 Equilibrium in the market for corporate debt.

The equilibrium interest rate on corporate debt will be determined by the intersection of supply and demand. The demand curve is based on the needs of individual investors. Miller assumes that these investors are taxed at graduated rates including taxes at the federal, state and municipal levels. Because the interest payments on debt are taxable, investors will prefer municipal bonds and common stock, unless there is a (risk-adjusted) differential in the pretax expected return on corporate debt. If this differential is very small, only those investors in the very lowest brackets will prefer corporate debt as an investment. As the differential is increased, investors in the higher brackets will be enticed into the market for corporate debt. The demand curve is thus upward sloping, reflecting the fact that there will be a greater demand for corporate debt as its pretax interest rate is increased. (Most demand curves are *downward* sloping, because prices, and not interest rates, are plotted on the vertical axis.)

In Figure 19.2 the rising demand curve intersects the horizontal supply curve at a risk-adjusted interest rate that fully reflects the corporate tax rate. Miller *assumes* that the marginal corporate rate is less than the highest marginal personal tax rate. Firms will be indifferent to issuing debt or equity to finance their investments, because the amount of debt outstanding has no impact on the value of the firm, as can be seen by the broken line in Figure 19.1.

The Miller equilibrium has been modified by DeAngelo and Masulis (1980). DeAngelo and Masulis introduce other tax deductions, such as depreciation charges, into the model. In the presence of these, the firm may find that in any given year the interest payment is in whole or in part unnecessary, because earnings are small enough that depreciation charges are sufficient to reduce the tax liability to zero. As additional units of debt are issued by the firm, the probability increases that the earnings will be small enough to make the additional interest payments redundant as a tax deduction. Their expected value as a tax shelter decreases. As additional units of debt are issued, the value of the firm increases, but at a decreasing rate, as with the solid curve of Figure 19.3.

If we introduce a differential between the (risk-adjusted) expected return on debt and equity, each firm will issue debt until, for the last unit of debt issued, the diminishing benefit associated with the tax deduction is exactly equal to the penalty associated with the yield differential. As the yield differential becomes smaller, each firm will issue additional amounts of debt. Thus, in the context of this model, the supply curve for debt is downward sloping, as with the broken curve of Figure 19.2. The differential (risk-adjusted) expected return on corporate debt now reflects a break-even tax rate that is less than the corporate rate. The differential does bring down the curve of Figure 19.3, however. In the presence of the differential, the relationship between firm value and the amount of debt issued is given by the broken curve, and the optimal amount of debt for the firm is given by V_D^*.

DeAngelo and Masulis have assumed, of course, that redundant tax shelters can't be transferred from firm to firm through takeover or through some other mechanism allowed by law. They have also assumed that the mechanism for carrying over shelters to successive years is either limited or imperfect. In the actual tax law, it is

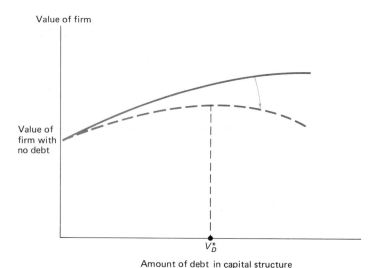

FIGURE 19.3 Debt and firm value: DeAngelo-Masulis.

both. No credit is given for interest that could have been earned on the money and the amount of the carryover is limited.

We can contrast the theories of Miller and DeAngelo-Masulis. In Miller, the tax rate that will make you indifferent between investing in municipal and corporate bonds is the *corporate* tax rate. Moreover, we would expect that this rate should be a constant over time. In DeAngelo-Masulis, the break-even rate is less than the corporate rate, and we would expect it to be variable over time, as the expected profits and available depreciation charges fluctuate. The evidence on which theory is correct is inconclusive. You will usually find the rate that equates the after-tax, promised yields to maturity on corporate bonds and municipal bonds, to be less than the corporate tax rate. On the other hand, you must be very cautious about drawing a conclusion from this, because of the following points:

1. There may be differential default probabilities between the corporate and municipal bonds, and the relative promised yields to maturity may not be a good indicator of relative expected yields.
2. There may be differential provisions related to callability and sinking funds.
3. The market may not expect the differential tax treatment between corporate and municipal bonds to persist indefinitely in the tax law. If they see a real possibility that all interest will become tax exempt in the next year, the prices of long-term corporate and municipal bonds will be very close, even if corporates are *currently* taxable.

Skelton (1979) has examined the differential between realized rates of return on corporate and municipal bonds and has found that the differential is close to the corporate rate, at least for short-term issues. This is consistent with the Miller model, but the available evidence on the issue, thus far, is incomplete.

SUMMARY

Taxes have an impact on investment strategy and securities prices. You can avoid taxes on your investments by investing in tax-exempt securities, bonds that are selling at deep discounts, stocks that pay small dividends, or tax-deferred to tax-sheltered retirement plans. You can determine which investments will give you the most lucrative returns after taxes by computing their after-tax rates of return. In computing these returns, you must relate what you have to give up to get or keep the investments to what you expect to get after tax payments if you buy or keep them. In general, it is in your interest to realize capital losses for tax purposes and defer capital gains.

Taxes may affect the relative prices of common stocks. Capital gains are tax sheltered because they can be deferred. As a result, the stocks of firms that pay out large dividends may be viewed as less desirable by investors, and their pretax expected rates of return may be higher. Some have argued against this possibility because of the ease of sheltering dividends from taxes. The best available empirical evidence, however, indicates the possible presence of a dividend effect in expected stock returns.

Taxes affect the relative yield differential between tax-exempt securities like municipal bonds and fully taxable securities like corporate bonds. In the presence of perfect capital markets, where redundant tax shelters like depreciation charges can't be marketed from firm to firm by takeover or other mechanisms allowed in the tax law, the differential between the rates on municipal and corporate bonds will reflect the corporate tax rate. In a less than perfect capital market where the interest tax shelter may go unused by anyone, the break-even rate may be less than the corporate rate.

QUESTION SET 1

1. In what sense could a capital gain on an investment you have made in the past effectively "lock" you into that investment, even though other investments appear to have better prospects for the commitment of new money?

Assume the following information for Questions 2 and 3. The data are for three bonds, each having 1 year until maturity and each having a principal payment due at maturity in the amount of $1000.

You purchased bond 1 several years ago for $850. Assume that you *foresee* your marginal tax rate on ordinary income will be 40 percent and your tax rate on capital gains will be 20 percent. Suppose you view the three bonds as having the same default risk.

	Annual Coupon Payment	Current Market Price
Bond 1	$50	$970
Bond 2	80	960
Bond 3	40	960

2. Would it be advantageous to sell bond 1 and reinvest the proceeds in one or both of the other bonds?

3. What if you were considering the investment of additional funds in one or more of the three bonds. Which would offer the best after-tax return?

Assume the following data for Questions 4 through 6. Both bonds have 2 years until maturity and both have a principal payment at maturity of $1000. Assume that your marginal tax rate on ordinary income is expected to be 50 percent and the tax rate on capital gains is expected to be 28 percent.

	Annual Coupon Payment	Pretax Internal Yield
Bond A	$200	10%
Bond B	100	13

4. What are the current prices of the two bonds?

5. Suppose you were considering an investment of new funds in one of these bonds. Which one would give the better rate of return on an after-tax basis?

6. Suppose that you already owned bond A and had purchased it for 1000. You were now contemplating whether you should have your funds in that bond or direct them toward the purchase of bond B. Which one would bring a better return? (Assume capital gains are currently taxed at 28 percent.)

7. Suppose that you want to invest in just the dividend portion of a stock. A stock, a put, and a call exist with the following characteristics:

$$\text{Current stock price} = \$100$$
$$\text{Expected dividend} = \$\ 2$$
$$\text{Exercise price (on both the put and call)} = \$\ 95$$

Both the put and call options expire on the same date, immediately after the dividend is paid. The rate of interest for the period until the options' expiration date is 3 percent.
   a. Indicate what portfolio would ensure an ending payoff equal to the dividend payment.
   b. Demonstrate that the portfolio indicated in part a would give the dividend as a payoff under two alternative price assumptions for the stock at the expiration date: $90 or $110.

8. Suppose you have $1000 invested in a stock and, during the course of the year, you are paid $50 in dividends on the stock. If you can borrow at 8 percent, and if there is a tax-deferred annuity available for purchase, which pays 8 percent, can you contrive a way to shield your dividend payments from taxes?

9. What would be the logic in support of the idea that stocks paying higher dividend yields would also have an extra premium incorporated in their equilibrium returns? Why would some (like Miller and Scholes) argue that the dividend payout should have no bearing on the expected return?

10. Suppose a firm happened to be financed entirely with $200,000 of stock. The dividends it pays to stockholders represent the same risk-adjusted return as the firm would have to pay on debt. Suppose that this rate is 8 percent. Also, assume that the corporate income tax rate is a flat 50 percent.

    a. What would you recommend to the firm in terms of possible changes in its debt-equity structure?

    b. How much would the company save each year by implementing the strategy suggested in (a)?

11. Suppose that the rates of return paid by firms on debt and equity have adjusted so that, from the firm's viewpoint, neither security is preferred to the other as a means of raising funds.

    a. If income from stock is considered to be tax exempt, what would be the relationship between the rate paid on debt and the rate paid on stock?

    b. What market scenario might account for this kind of relationship?

QUESTION SET 2

1. What is the difference between a tax-deferred investment and a tax-exempt investment?

2. What type of investor is most likely to desire municipal bonds in a portfolio?

    a. An individual earning $75,000 a year in the 28 percent marginal tax bracket who has a mortgage interest deduction of $15,000

    b. A pension fund manager, who is managing assets of 10 million dollars

    c. A business with sales of $500,000, accelerated depreciation credits of $400,000, operating expenses of $50,000, but a net cash flow of $450,000 in 25 percent tax bracket

3. What is meant by the locked-in effect?

4. Why might you want to separate capital gains from dividends in a stock? What type of client might be interested in the dividends of such a separation?

ANSWERS TO QUESTION SET 2

1. A tax-deferred investment does not avoid taxes, it simply delays them until a future time, usually retirement. A tax-exempt investment, on the other hand, misses the tax entirely.

2. The most likely person among this group is the individual earning $75,000 per year. Even with the $15,000 deduction, he will be taxed on $60,000 at the current 28 percent marginal rate. (Note, however, that the *marginal rate* is greater than the *effective rate,* which is the rate you pay as a percent of your total income.) The pension fund manager pays no taxes, since all of his investment have a tax-exempt status until they are paid out. The business has effectively reduced its income to $50,000, which is taxed at the 25 percent rate, or a lower rate than the individual.

3. The locked-in effect is the term given to the situation in which an investor finds himself or herself when he or she has accrued unrealized gains in an investment and desires to switch into a more profitable investment. To do so, the investor must realize the gain and pay taxes on it, thereby reducing the amount of capital available to place in the other investment, and making it, in effect less attractive.

4. There are two principal reasons to separate the capital gains component from the dividend component of a stock: (a) to separate the tax treatment given to each for different investors and (b) to take out the risk element of a stock for the investor who is only interested in the

dividend commponent of the equity. Typical investors who might be interested in the dividend component include retired persons who desire a steady income and a client who needs cash at a specific date to meet an obligation. This situation is somewhat analogous to the separation of the interest component in a bond security.

PROBLEM SET

1. Suppose you are advising a friend who expects to be in a 35 percent tax bracket when she/he receives the investment income. She asks you whether she should invest in a 12.5 percent 1-year taxable corporate bond or a 7.9 percent 1-year tax-exempt bond on a new tin-can recycling facility. Both sell at par. Which do you recommend, and why?

2. It is possible to separate the capital gain or loss feature from a stock and invest exclusively in the stock's dividends? You are a pension fund manager who wants to take life a bit easy while pacifying your pensioners, who are extremely suspicious of any stock whose name isn't recognized by second-graders. You invest in IBM, AT&T, and GM. All have for the current year guaranteed dividend payments of 5 percent and are selling at $100 per share. You purchase 1000 shares of each. The price of puts and calls with an exercise price of $100 is $10. Explain your strategy to strip the dividends, and show how the numbers work out if the price of the stock remains at $100 or drops to $80.

3. Assume you have your choice to invest in the following two bonds:

	Annual Coupon	Pretax Internal Yield
Bond 1	$250	12%
Bond 2	$150	9%

Assume these are 1-year bonds with a principal payment of $1000 and in this *hypothetical* tax environment you are taxed at the 50 percent marginal rate on the interest income and 20 percent on capital gains.
a. What are the current prices for the two bonds?
b. Which would give you the better after-tax return?
c. If you were in the 30 percent tax bracket paying 12 percent on capital gains, which bond is the preferable one, given that they are of the same quality?

ANSWERS TO PROBLEM SET

1. To make a decision on the bonds, you need to compute the after-tax yield to maturity on each bond. For the 12.5 percent taxable bond, you compute

$$\text{Yield} = \frac{C - (\text{tax rate} \times C) + \$1000}{\text{Market value}} - 1$$

$$= \frac{\$125 - (.35 \times \$125) + \$1000}{\$1000} - 1$$

$$= 8.125\%$$

For the nontaxable bond, the yield is $1079/$1000 − 1 or 7.9 percent. Hence, you should choose the taxable issue, all others things being equal.

2. First, you have purchased 3000 shares at $100 a share, or $300,000 worth, with a 5 percent dividend, or $15,000. To strip the dividend from the capital gain (or loss), you buy put options and sell call options. You borrow the present value of $90 for each share of stock or $270,000, so that at exercise time you have the money to purchase the shares as obligated under the options. Suppose the price of the stock remains at $100. Your position looks like this:

Stock value	$300,000 + $15,000
Put value	0
Call value	− ($300,000 − $270,000) or − $30,000
Debt value	− $270,000
Net value	$15,000

If the stock decreased in price to $80, your strategy would have worked out as follows:

Stock value	$240,000 + $15,000
Put value	$270,000 − $240,000
Call value	0
Debt value	− $270,000
Net value	$15,000

3. a Bond prices:

no. 1: $\dfrac{1250}{1.12} = 1116.07$

no. 2: $\dfrac{1150}{1.09} = 1055.05$

b. After-tax return:

no. 1: $\dfrac{250 \times (1 - .5) + 1000 - .2(1000 - 1116.07)}{1116.07} = 2.88\%$

no. 2: $\dfrac{150 \times (1 - .5) + 1000 - .2(1000 - 1055.05)}{1055.05} = 2.93\%$

Bond no. 2 gives the better after-tax return.

c. With the changed tax situation:

no. 1: $\dfrac{150(1 - .30) + 1000 - .12(1000 - 1116.07)}{1116.07} = 6.53\%$

no. 2: $\dfrac{150(1 - .30) + 1000 - .12(1000 - 1055.05)}{1055.05} = 5.36\%$

Bond no. 1 gives the better after-tax return in this situation.

REFERENCES

BARNEA, A., HAUGEN, R., and SENBET, L., "An Equilibrium Analysis of Debt Financing Under Costly Tax Arbitrage and Agency Problems," *Journal of Finance* (June 1981).

BLACK, F., and SCHOLES, M., "The Effects of Dividend Yield and Dividend Policy on Common Stock Prices and Returns," *Journal of Financial Economics* (March 1974).

BRENNAN, M. J., "Taxes, Market Valuation and Corporate Financial Policy," *National Tax Journal* (December 1973).

CONSTANTINIDES, G. M., "Optimal Stock Trading with Personal Taxes: Implications for Prices and Abnormal January Returns," *Journal of Financial Economics* (March 1984).

CONSTANTINIDES, G. M., and INGERSOLL, J. E., "Optimal Bond Trading with Personal Taxes: Implications for Bond Prices, and Estimated Tax Brackets and Yield Curves," *Working Paper No.* 70, Center for Research in Security Prices, Graduate School of Business, University of Chicago, 1983.

CONSTANTINIDES, G. M., and SCHOLES, M. S., "Optimal Liquidation of Assets in the Presence of Personal Taxes: Implications for Asset Pricing," *Journal of Finance* (May 1980).

DEANGELO, H., and MASULIS, R. W., "Optimal Capital Structure Under Corporate and Personal Taxation," *Journal of Financial Economics* (March 1980).

DYL, E. A., "Capital Gains Taxation and Year-end Stock Price Behavior," *Journal of Finance* (March 1977).

EADES, K. M., HESS, P. J., and KIM, E. H., "On Interpreting Security Returns During the Ex-Dividend Period," *Journal of Financial Economics* (March 1984).

HESS, P., "The Ex-Dividend Behavior of Stock Returns: Further Evidence on Tax Effects," *Journal of Finance* (May 1982).

JORDAN, J. V., "Tax Effects in Term Structure Estimation," *Journal of Finance* (June 1984).

LITZENBERGER, R. H., and RAMASWAMY, K., "The Effects of Dividends on Common Stock Prices: Tax Effects or Information Effects," *Journal of Finance* (May 1982).

MILLER, M., "Debt and Taxes," *Journal of Finance* (May 1977).

MILLER, M., and SCHOLES, M., "Dividends and Taxes," *Journal of Financial Economics* (December 1978).

SKELTON, J. F., "The Relative Pricing of Tax-Exempt and Taxable Debt," mimeo, University of California, Berkeley, November 1979.

TRZCINKA, C., "The Pricing of Tax-Exempt Bonds and the Miller Hypothesis," *Journal of Finance* (September 1982).

C H A P T E R

20

STOCK VALUATION

In this chapter, you will learn to estimate the intrinsic value of common stocks. In the chapters on asset pricing, our attention centered on the appropriate rate of return to require from a common stock investment. How does one go about measuring risk, and, given risk, what is the appropriate rate of return? This, however, is only one side of the coin in valuing a security. In addition to determining the appropriate capitalization rate, you must also estimate the investment income to be capitalized. In the case of common stocks, the income payments to be capitalized are dividends. In this chapter, we will derive some models that can be used to value stocks, based on the expected flow of future dividends.

A FRAMEWORK FOR VALUING COMMON STOCKS

The only way a corporation can transfer wealth to its stockholders is through the payment of dividends. Because dividends are the only source of cash payments to a common stock investor, it follows that dividends are the single source of value for common stocks.

At this point you might object and point to the fact that most investors are far more concerned with capital gains than they are with dividends. After all, the principal determinant of the variability in a stock's return from year to year is the magnitude of the capital gains or losses. However, the changes that occur in the stock price can be attributed to changes in the market's expectations regarding the magnitude of dividends to be received beyond the current year.

The current market price for the stock can be written as a function of the market's expectation of the dividend to be received at the end of the year and the market price to be in effect at the end of the year,

$$V_0 = \frac{E(D_1) + E(V_1)}{1 + E(r)} \tag{20.1}$$

where V_0 is the current stock price, $E(D_1)$ is the expected year-end dividend per share, $E(V_1)$ is the expected year-end price, and $E(r)$ is the market's required or expected rate of return on the stock. The expected rate of return is equal to the sum of the rate of return available on risk-free securities and the risk premium that is appropriate, given the risk of the individual stock.

However, if the expected rate of return on the stock is not expected to change, the expected price at the end of the year can similarly be written as

$$E(V_1) = \frac{E(D_2) + E(V_2)}{1 + E(r)} \tag{20.2}$$

Substituting Equation (20.2) into (20.1), we get

$$V_0 = \frac{E(D_1)}{1 + E(r)} + \frac{E(D_2) + E(V_2)}{[1 + E(r)]^2}$$

Now the stock value is seen to be determined by the dividend payments expected in the first two years. This same process can, of course, be continued through years 3, 4, and so on, resulting finally in

$$V_0 = \frac{E(D_1)}{1 + E(r)} + \frac{E(D_2)}{[1 + E(r)]^2} + \cdots + \frac{E(D_N)}{[1 + E(r)]^N} \tag{20.3}$$

where N is the number of years remaining in the life of the firm.

Thus, even if investors are primarily concerned with capital gains because the source of the capital gains is expected future dividends (or changes in expected future dividends), the current market price of the stock is based on the expected flow of dividends throughout the life of the firm.

Dividends Versus Earnings

It might seem more logical to capitalize the expected series of cash earnings per share to obtain a stock value. After all, stockholders have a claim on these cash earnings after payment of bond interest and other expenses. However, it must be remembered that the magnitude of future dividends is due, in part, to the reinvestment of some fraction of the current earnings. Thus, you can't have the one without reinvestment of a part of the other.

We can write Equation (20.3) in terms of earnings by making the following substitution for the expected dividend in any given year, t:

$$E(D_t) = E(\text{earnings}_t - \text{retained earnings}_t)$$

Once the role of retained earnings is recognized, the earnings and dividend approaches to stock valuation are completely equivalent.

The Constant Growth Model

If you are willing to assume the dividend payments on a stock are going to grow at a constant rate in perpetuity, the stock valuation equation collapses to a very simple form. Suppose the dividend paid yesterday is given by D_0. The value of the stock can be written as

$$V_0 = \frac{D_0[1 + E(g)]}{1 + E(r)} + \frac{D_0[1 + E(g)]^2}{[1 + E(r)]^2} + \cdots \text{ and so on}$$

Although this is a perpetual sum, it does reach a limit if the expected rate of growth is less than the required rate of return. The limit is equal to

$$V = \frac{D_0[1 + E(g)]}{E(r) - E(g)} = \frac{E(D_1)}{E(r) - E(g)}$$

To illustrate, consider a stock that paid a dividend of a dollar yesterday, the expected growth in the dividend is a constant 10 percent, and the required rate of return is 20 percent. The expected series of dividends is

$$E(D_1) = \$1.00 \times 1.10 = \$1.10$$

$$E(D_2) = \$1.10 \times 1.10 = \$1.21$$

$$E(D_3) = \$1.21 \times 1.10 = \$1.33$$

and so on. The market value for the stock is given by

$$\frac{\$1.10}{.20 - .10} = \$11.00$$

Under the constant growth model, both price and dividends per share grow at the same rate through time. For example, in the case of the stock just considered, because the dividend expected to be paid at the end of the second year is equal to $1.21, the market price of the stock is expected to be equal to

$$\frac{\$1.21}{.20 - .10} = \$12.10$$

The change in price from $11.00 to $12.10 represents a rate of growth of 10 percent

$$\frac{\$12.10 - \$11.00}{\$11.00} = 10\%$$

which, of course, is consistent with the rate of growth in the dividend.

We should also note, that in the context of this model, the investor's expected return is equal to (1) the ratio of the next expected dividend to the market price plus (2) the constant expected growth rate in dividends and market price.

$$E(r) = \frac{\text{Expected year-end dividend}}{\text{Beginning of year market price}} + \text{expected growth rate}$$

In the context of our example, this would be

$$20\% = \frac{\$1.10}{\$11.00} + 10\%$$

Although the constant growth model is conceptually very simple, the assumption of a constant rate of growth in perpetuity is unacceptable, however, because a company growing at a constant, but above-average rate can be expected eventually to grow to encompass the entire economy. Thus, we need to make a more realistic assumption regarding future growth.

The Multistage Growth Model

Analysts frequently make the assumption that a firm's growth rate will change in a series of stages. The most simple variant is the two-stage growth model. Here we assume the dividend will initially grow at an above or a below average rate for a number of years. At the end of this period, which is called the *growth horizon,* the growth rate reverts to that of an average or standard share. The length of the growth horizon depends on the length of time into the future you feel comfortable with your forecast of abnormal growth for the stock. Obviously, at some point in the future, things will seem so uncertain that you have no reason to believe that the stock can be distinguished in terms of its growth rate. Beyond this point the best assumption will be that the stock will grow at an average rate.

The *growth profile* for a two-stage model is presented in Figures 20.1 and 20.2.

In both figures time into the future is plotted on the horizontal axis. However, in Figure 20.1 the expected growth rate for the dividend is plotted on the vertical axis, and in Figure 20.2 the dividend itself is plotted. In this example, the dividend is initially expected to grow at an above-average rate and then revert to the average rate at the end of the growth horizon (the end of year *n*).

The market value of the stock can be expressed as the present value of the dividend stream of Figure 20.2.

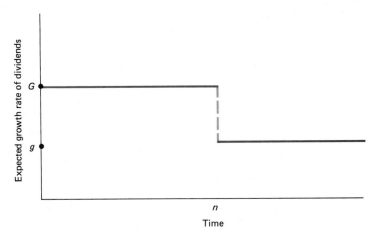

FIGURE 20.1 Expected rate of growth in dividends.

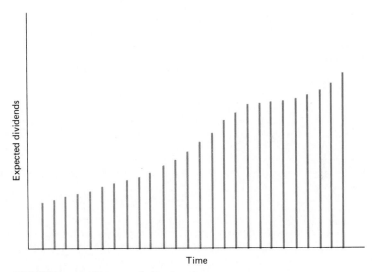

FIGURE 20.2 Expected dividends.

$$V = \frac{D_0[1 + E(G)]}{1 + E(r)} + \frac{D_0[1 + E(G)]^2}{[1 + E(r)]^2} + \cdots + \frac{D_0[1 + E(G)]^n}{[1 + E(r)]^n}$$

$$+ \frac{D_0[1 + E(G)]^n[1 + E(g)]}{[1 + E(r)]^{n+1}} + \cdots \text{ and so on} \tag{20.4}$$

where $E(G)$ is the initial above or below average rate of growth and $E(g)$ is the average or standard rate of growth. Although this is again a perpetual sum, if $E(g)$ is less than $E(r)$, the sum approaches a finite limit.

As was the case in ''Hunting for Bargains Out on the Street'' in Chapter 7, the required rate of return can be estimated using an asset pricing model such as the

CAPM. The average growth rate can be estimated by observing the past growth rate for earnings and dividends per share associated with some broad stock market index such as the Standard & Poor's 500. The average historic growth rate for the index can then be subjectively modified to account for any differences in the economic environment between the past and the future.

One important difference to consider is the rate of inflation. If you think the rate of inflation in the future is going to be greater than it was in the past period over which you measured the historic growth rate for the index, you may want to adjust upward your estimate for the average future rate of growth to account for this.

To illustrate the two-stage growth model, consider the following example. A stock has just paid a dividend of $1 per share. The dividend is expected to grow at a rate of 30 percent for the next 6 years. Thereafter the growth rate is expected to revert to the standard or average rate of 6 percent. The required expected rate of return on the stock is assumed to be 15 percent.

The following stream of dividends is expected to be paid from the stock at the end of each year:

Year 1: $D_0[1 + E(G)]^1$ = $1.30

Year 2: $D_0[1 + E(G)]^2$ = $1.69

Year 3: $D_0[1 + E(G)]^3$ = $2.20

Year 4: $D_0[1 + E(G)]^4$ = $2.86

Year 5: $D_0[1 + E(G)]^5$ = $3.71

Year 6: $D_0[1 + E(G)]^6$ = $4.83

Year 7: $D_0[1 + E(G)]^6[1 + E(g)]^1$ = $5.12

Year 8: $D[1 + E(G)]^6[1 + E(g)]^2$ = $5.42

and so on

With a 15 percent discount rate, the present value of this stream of dividends is

$$\$1.30/1.15^1 = \$1.13$$

$$\$1.69/1.15^2 = \$1.28$$

$$\$2.20/1.15^3 = \$1.45$$

$$\$2.86/1.15^4 = \$1.64$$

$$\$3.72/1.15^5 = \$1.85$$

$$\$4.83/1.15^6 = \$2.09$$

$$\$5.12/1.15^7 = \$1.92$$

$$\$5.43/1.15^8 = \$1.78$$

Total present value (including dividends received after year 8) = $\overline{\$34.00}$

As we learned in the context of the constant growth model, dividends and price per share can be expected to grow at identical constant rates. In the two-stage model, however, the growth rates in dividends and market price will differ until we reach the end of the growth horizon, when the growth in the dividend is expected to revert to that of an average share. In the period of the growth horizon, the growth rate in the stock price will fall between the initial expected growth in the dividend and the growth rate of an average share. The longer the period of the growth horizon, the closer will be the growth rate in the stock price relative to the initial growth rate in the dividend.

To illustrate this point, we can use Equation (20.4) to calculate the present value of the expected dividend stream for the stock in the foregoing example, as we move forward in time through the growth horizon. To compute each future market price for the stock, we compute the present value of the remaining dividends at the assumed capitalization rate of 15 percent.

Beginning of Year	Present Value of Remaining Dividends	Growth Rate in Present Value
1	$34.00	—
2	37.79	11.15%
3	41.77	10.53
4	45.85	9.77
5	49.87	8.76
6	53.61	7.52
7	56.86	6.05
8	60.27	6.00

The general pattern of expected growth in market price and dividends per share is given in Figure 20.3. The solid lines depict the relative growth pattern for a stock that is initially expected to grow at a relatively fast rate for a relatively long period. The broken lines depict the pattern for a stock that is initially expected to grow at a below average rate for a relatively short period.

Even when the growth rate in expected dividends is not constant through time, it will still be the case that we can break the expected return into two parts: (1) the ratio of the next expected dividend to current market price and (2) the expected growth in the market price during the year. For example, in the case of the stock considered, at the beginning of year 1

$$\text{Expected return} = \frac{\text{Year-end dividend}}{\text{Beginning price}} + \text{growth in price}$$

$$15\% = \frac{\$1.30}{\$34.00} + 11.5\%$$

Equation (20.4) and Figures 20.1 and 20.2 relate to a two-stage valuation model. When desirable, you can also employ three-stage models and beyond. These

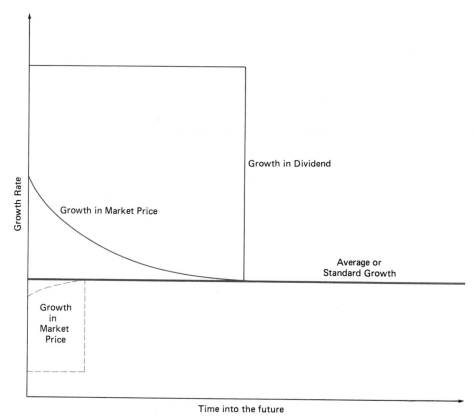

FIGURE 20.3 Relative growth rates in dividends and market price.

models are computationally easy to use, are readily available, and are widely employed in computer software packages. In fact, as we discuss in the next section, the software which accompanies this book includes a three-stage stock valuation model.

COMPUTERIZED THREE-STAGE STOCK VALUATION

The software that accompanies this book includes a three-stage growth stock valuation model. The three stages of growth include an initial stage in which dividends are assumed to grow at a firm-specific rate that is above or below the rate for an average stock. In the second stage, the growth in the dividend is assumed to decline gradually (if $G > g$) or increase (if $G < g$) to the growth rate for an average stock in even, or equal, annual steps. (The model can easily be converted to a two-stage model by setting the length of the transitional period equal to zero.) In the final stage, the dividend is presumed to grow at the average rate in perpetuity.

To see how the program works, consider the following example. Assume, as required by the program, that the stock pays quarterly dividends. The initial dividend is expected to be $.25. To use the program, you must specify the number of days until the expected receipt of this first dividend, and assume, for purposes of this example, that the period is 90 days. Also assume that you want a 10 percent rate of return on your investment in this stock. You believe that the dividend will grow at a rate of 10 percent for 5 years (20 quarters) and then decline to the average rate of 5 percent during a 5-year transitional period.

After entering these numbers into the program, you will see the following display:

Stock Valuation

INPUT PARAMETERS:	
1) Initial dividend	$0.25
2) Number of days until first dividend payment	90.00 days
3) Duration of initial growth rate	20.00 quarters
4) Duration of linearly decreasing growth rate	20.00 quarters
5) Initial growth rate	10.00 percent
6) Terminal growth rate	5.00 percent
7) Discount rate	10.00 percent
STOCK PRICE (present value method)	$26.91

The indicated market value of the stock is $26.91. If you pay this price, and if your forecast of the dividends turns out to be correct, you will earn your desired, 10 percent rate of return on your investment.

An expected future for dividends, market value, dividend/price ratio, and annual growth in dividends and market price is also displayed as follows:

Stock's Growth Forecast

Year	Dividends	Div Growth	Stock Price	Stock Growth	Div/Price
0.00			$26.91		
1.00	$1.04	10.00%	$28.63	6.38%	3.63%
2.00	$1.15	10.00%	$30.42	6.23%	3.77%
3.00	$1.26	10.00%	$32.26	6.07%	3.92%
4.00	$1.40	10.00%	$34.16	5.89%	4.09%
5.00	$1.54	10.00%	$36.11	5.70%	4.27%
6.00	$1.70	9.00%	$38.10	5.51%	4.45%
7.00	$1.85	8.00%	$40.13	5.34%	4.61%
8.00	$2.00	7.00%	$42.23	5.22%	4.73%
9.00	$2.13	6.00%	$44.40	5.13%	4.81%
10.00	$2.26	5.00%	$46.66	5.10%	4.84%

Dividend Flows Capitalized at 10.00%

OUT ON THE STREET

USING A THREE-STAGE MODEL

The sun slipped slowly behind the southern leg, and Dan Coggin was cast in the shadow of the Gateway Arch. The other end of the shadow was about 30 feet away, and sunlight would be at least 5 minutes in returning to the park bench situated on the eastern side of the Mississippi River.

Dan had walked the three blocks to the park from Centerre Trust Company in St. Louis, where he formerly worked as the head of the quantitative analysis department of the investment division. Dan was back in St. Louis to visit old friends, including Mac Conway, the new department head. Through the years he has watched the firm progressively become more quantitative and systematic in its stock selection.

There's no question about when the move began. It started when Jim Wright was hired as research director in 1979. Before Jim's arrival, the analysts at Centerre pretty much picked stock subjectively. After hearing a story about some stock, they might decide that it would be a good idea to put some of it in the portfolio, and in it would go. One of the first things Jim decided to do was to develop a systematic approach for ranking stocks for possible purchase. Dan worked with Jim in getting the system running and in selling its merits to the rest of the firm.

The system they developed for valuing stocks is based on a *dividend discount model* (*DDM*) that forecasts dividend growth in three stages or phases. The first is called the *growth phase.* In this initial phase the firm behind the stock is introducing new products, gaining market share, and growing off a relatively small capital base. Eventually, however, the rate of product introduction begins to subside, the firm begins to stabilize its market share, and the rate of growth in earnings and dividends begins to slow. When this begins to happen, the stock moves into what is called the *transitional phase.* In the transitional phase the rate of growth in dividend income declines in a linear fashion to the basic level of growth for the general economy. When the growth rate actually reaches the basic level, the stock is then said to be in the *maturity phase* of its growth profile. The assumed growth profile for a given company might look like the accompanying figure.

Thus, in using the model, the analyst must estimate (1) the initial growth rate for the growth phase, (2) the length of the growth phase, and (3) the length of the transitional phase. The growth rate for the maturity phase is the same for all companies and isn't changed very often.

The length of the phases is determined by the individual analyst, on the basis of fundamental security analysis. Centerre has six security analysts, each assigned to follow about 50 stocks in a few industries. Firms like Genetech might be considered to be rather early in their growth phase, whereas firms like Kellogg might be considered more transitional. The length of the growth phase does vary from stock to stock, but it averages about 5 or 6 years. The transitional phase might be 10 years for a stock with low estimated growth in the growth phase to 20 years for a stock with high estimated growth in the growth phase.

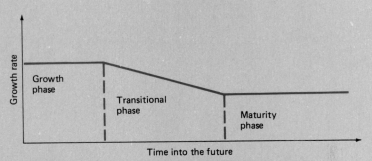

FIGURE A Growth profile for the three-phase model.

The expected rate of growth in the growth phase is estimated on the basis of a standardized procedure. The analysts at Centerre use a variation of a standard security analytic model called the *Du Pont model*. They fill in formalized input sheets with their forecasts of net sales, total assets, and pretax profits, and these, as well as other estimates, are funneled through the model to obtain an estimate of the net rate of return on equity capital. This net rate of return is then multiplied by an estimate of the fraction of earnings per share retained in the firm each year to come up with the final estimated rate of growth for the growth phase. In coming up with their estimates for the inputs to the model, Centerre's analysts examine the nature of the firm's product line, its competition, and the firm's history.

Dan feels that it is the quality control of the inputs to the model that differentiates Centerre's success with dividend discounting from that of other investment management firms. In addition to using the Du Pont model on a formal basis, the analysts' inputs are checked for consistency and accuracy of assumptions. They must also justify any changes made in these inputs in terms of changes in the fundamental outlook for the company. Other firms may use DDMs, but their analysts frequently "game" them and inevitably destroy their effectiveness. For example, if the analyst thinks for some reason that IBM is a good buy, he or she may simply increase the initial expected growth rate to 40 percent so that it comes out well under the DDM. In Dan's opinion, this is deadly. If you're going to use a DDM, you've got to use it systematically, with quality control, and not merely pay lip service to it.

Centerre's success in using the three-phase model is evident in the numbers provided in the accompanying table. In the table, each number represents the total rate of return on an equally weighted portfolio of common stocks. The returns include both dividends and capital gains, but do not incorporate taxes or transactions costs.

Starting with a population of roughly 250 large capitalization firms that Centerre believes to be of high quality and good growth potential, the analysts at

Results of Stock Selection Based on the Three-Phase Model

Quintile	1979	1980	1981	Year 1982	1983
1	35.07%	41.21%	12.12%	19.12%	34.18%
2	25.92	29.19	10.89	12.81	21.27
3	18.49	27.41	1.25	26.72	25.00
4	17.55	38.43	−5.59	28.41	24.55
5	20.06	26.44	−8.51	35.54	14.35
250 stocks	23.21	31.86	1.41	24.53	24.10
S&P 500 Index	18.57	32.55	−4.97	21.61	22.54

1984	1985	1986	1987	1988
15.26%	38.91%	14.33%	.42%	39.61%
5.50	32.22	11.87	4.34	31.31
6.03	35.83	19.49	8.15	17.78
−4.20	29.29	12.00	4.64	8.18
−7.84	23.43	20.82	−2.41	6.76
3.24	33.80	15.78	2.71	20.62
6.12	31.59	18.47	5.23	16.48

Centerre ranked the firms on the basis of their betas, as estimated using historical returns over the 5-year period previous to each individual month. The firms were then grouped by beta into five quintiles.

Then the expected rate of return was computed on each stock using the three-phase DDM and the market price of the stock at the beginning of the month. The expected return is computed as the rate that will discount the expected flow of dividends to a present value equal to the current market price for the stock. The stocks in each beta quintile were then ranked by expected rate of return and then grouped into expected return quintiles. The stocks in the highest expected return quintile from each beta grouping were assembled into an equally weighted portfolio. The same thing was done for the next highest quintile and so on down to the lowest quintile. Thus, quintile 1 in the table is an equally weighted portfolio of the 20 percent of the stocks with the highest expected returns from each of the beta quintiles. Quintile 2 contains the 20 percent of the stocks with the next highest expected return and so on through quintile 5.

By following this procedure, we can expect that at the beginning of each month, each of the portfolios has approximately the same beta factor. Some firms adjust the percentages in each quintile, allowing fewer stocks in quintiles 1, 2, 4,

Wealth Accumulation Based on
the Three-Phase Model (1979-88)

Quintile	Ratio Ending to Beginning Investment Value
1	7.77
2	4.28
3	4.31
4	2.86
5	2.08
250 stocks	4.05
S&P 500 Index	3.51

and 5 and more in 3. This reflects a belief that most stocks are fairly valued by the market, with any under or over valuation falling in the extreme quintiles.

In any case, Centerre followed strict quintile ranking. The procedure of ranking into quintiles was repeated on the first business day of each month from January 1979 through December 1988.

It should be stressed that each portfolio was actually constructed at the time of the beginning of the first business day of each month using estimates of the initial growth rate, the length of the growth phase, and the length of the transition phase for each company. At the beginning of the next month the portfolios were rebalanced on the basis of new estimates turned in by the analysts. Thus, it actually took 10 years to produce the numbers in the table.

The ratios of ending to beginning values of an investment made in each quintile for the 10 year period are given in the accompanying table.

The results are impressive. Even though it initially started as an experiment with no actual commitment of invested funds, the success of the strategy over the years attracted the attention of Centerre's portfolio managers. These managers increasingly began to rely on the dividend discount model. By 1984, most of the managers were heavily into the model, and Centerre had constructed the P1 Fund, which was an actual equally weighted fund invested exactly according to the rules of the strategy.

It is interesting to consider the 1982 experience. In this year performance was *perversely* related to the quintile rankings. This can be attributed to a significant error in the general economic forecast made by Centerre for the year. At the beginning of the year, it was looking for a resurgence in the rate of inflation that never materialized. Normally errors made in a macroeconomic forecast tend to have a uniform effect on different stocks. Inflation, however, has a different impact on different companies. Oil and energy stocks, for example, are highly sensitive to inflation. Consequently, the error in the inflation forecast led the model to favor stocks that would be expected to respond well to increased inflation. When inflation failed to increase, these stocks failed to respond. By the end of the year, however, this error had been corrected. The years 1986 and 1987 represent the last two years of the bull market which began in August 1982. In hindsight, the bull was fading into a speculative "bubble" which burst in October 1987. Value-oriented models such as the DDM did not fare well in these two years. However, 1988 was another good year for the DDM as value returned to favor.

Dan is well aware of the fact that the success of a DDM depends crucially on the ability of analysts to predict *relative* growth rates among companies. He is also well aware of the literature that purports that the pattern of earnings changes for companies as a random walk. Dan feels that the demonstrated success of properly formulated DDMs makes that research irrelevant to the practice of stock selection.

Dan looked back towards downtown St. Louis and smiled. It was good to see an old friend.

The number listed for dividends is the total of the four quarterly dividends expected to be paid in each year. The value of $1.04 for the first year is computed as:

	Value	No. Days Until Receipt
Received		
First dividend	$ .2500	90
Second dividend	$ .2562 = $.2500*(1.025)	180
Third dividend	$ .2627 = $.2562*(1.025)	270
Fourth dividend	$ .2693 = $.2627*(1.025)	360
Total dividends	$1.0382 or $1.04	

The number in parentheses (1.025) reflects a quarterly compounding of the assumed 10 percent annual rate of growth in the dividends in the initial stage of growth.

The dividend/price ratios displayed by the software are computed by dividing the previous years total dividends by the expected market price of the stock at the beginning of each year. The expected future stock prices are calculated as the discounted value of the remaining future dividends, much as we did with the two-stage model.

PRICE-EARNINGS RATIOS

An indicator widely followed by investors in common stocks is the ratio of the current market price per share to the current earnings per share. The price-earnings ratio is computed on the basis of earnings available for distribution to common stockholders, that is, after deducting operating expenses, depreciation, taxes, and interest from net revenue.

What Determines the Level of the Price-Earnings Ratio?

In the context of a two-stage growth valuation model, we can say that the current price-earnings ratio becomes larger, (1) the smaller is the stock's expected rate of return, $E(r)$, and (2) the larger is the stock's initial expected rate of growth, $E(G)$. It is also true that the price-earnings ratio becomes larger as the growth horizon becomes longer, when $E(G) > E(g)$, and the growth horizon becomes shorter, when $E(G) < E(g)$.

Given the expected stream of earnings and dividends, the lower the expected return required from the investment, the more investors will be willing to pay for the investment in terms of the current market price for the stock. Thus, holding other things constant, the lower the expected return, the greater the ratio of the current price to the current level of earnings per share.

If future earnings and dividends are expected to be larger than their current levels, the present value of these future dividends, the current market price, will also be large relative to the current dividend and earnings per share. Thus, given the *length* of the period of abnormal growth expected by the market, the larger the abnormal *growth rate* expected, the larger will be future dividends (and their present value, the market price) relative to the current levels of dividends and earnings per share.

If the market expects the initial growth rate to be above average, the longer this growth rate is expected to persist, the larger will be future dividends (and their present value, the market price) relative to current earnings per share. Similarly, if the initial growth rate is expected to be below average, the smaller will be the level of future dividends relative to those of an average stock, and the smaller will be the price-earnings ratio relative to that of an average stock.

Changes That Can Be Expected in the Price-Earnings Ratio over Time

If both the growth of earnings and dividends and the stock's expected rate of return are expected to remain constant over time, the price-earnings ratio should also be expected to remain constant. If, instead, the growth rate is expected to change in a series of stages, the price-earnings ratio can be expected to change as time goes by, eventually ending up at the level of the price-earnings ratio for an average (growth rate) stock in the same risk class.

The pattern of change that can be expected in the case of a two-stage growth stock is presented in Figure 20.4. In the figure, the price-earnings ratio is plotted on the vertical axis and time into the future on the horizontal axis. The expected price-earnings ratios for three firms are plotted. In the case of the upper curve, the initial expected rate of growth is presumed to be 12 percent for 6 years. In the case of the stock represented by the lower curve, it is presumed to be 0 percent for 3 years. The horizontal line represents a stock that is expected to grow perpetually at the average rate, which is presumed to be 6 percent. For all three stocks, we have also presumed that 50 percent of earnings is paid out as dividends, and the expected rate of return is expected to be constant at 15 percent.

To obtain the curves in the figure, we begin with an initial value for the dividend, determine its future values based on the assumed growth rates, and double each value to obtain the corresponding future values for earnings per share. Then we determine the future values for the stock price using Equation (20.4). It is then easy to find the future values for the price-earnings ratios by dividing the future stock prices by the future earnings per share in each year.

Note that we can expect the price-earnings ratio to decline for the stock with abnormally high initial growth and rise for its abnormally low growth counterpart. The change in the price-earnings ratio isn't induced by changes that are occurring in investor expectations but merely by the evolution of each stock toward the status of that of an average share as time passes.

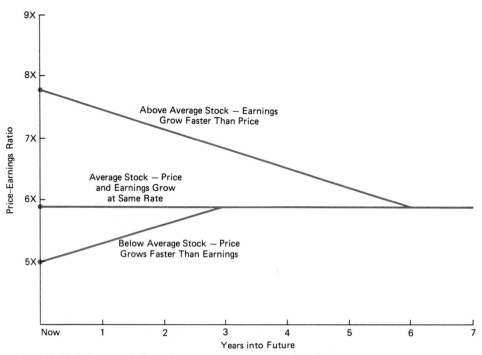

FIGURE 20.4 Expected future price-earnings ratios for three stocks.

SUMMARY

The market value of any corporate security must be based on the expected flow of cash from the firm to the investor. In the case of common stock, this transfer is always in the form of dividends. Thus, the market value of a common stock is based on the discounted value of expected dividends throughout the life of the firm.

A multistage growth model provides a convenient way to model the flow of future dividends. The model makes the assumption that the dividend will grow at above or below normal rates for assumed periods and then revert to the rate of growth of an average share after this growth horizon. Obviously, in using the model, you have to make a decision concerning the length of the growth horizon. For how long a period into the future do you want to forecast an above- or below-average rate of growth for the stock? We address this question in Chapter 21.

QUESTION SET 1

1. Why would an investor, concerned primarily with capital gains, estimate a stock's current market price on the basis of expected future dividends?
2. Explain how the earnings and dividends approaches to stock valuation are equivalent.
3. Assume a stock has a current market price of $26.25 and is expected to grow at a perpetually constant rate of 5 percent. Current dividend is $1. What is the capitalization rate that justifies this price? State any necessary assumptions.
4. Explain what is meant by growth horizon in terms of the two-stage growth model.
5. In years 1 through n, a dividend is expected to grow to an annual rate of G. In years $n + 1$ and beyond, the dividends are expected to grow at an annual rate of g. The current dividend is D_0. In terms of D_0, $E(G)$, $E(g)$, and n, what is the expression for the expected dividend in year $n + 2$ [or $E(D_{n+2})$]?
6. What could cause a higher than average ratio of current stock value to current dividend, V_0/D_0? Will this ratio for a given stock persist as a permanent characteristic of that stock?
7. Consider the price-earnings ratio where the earnings are known and invariant (constant for the period under consideration) and the numerator, V_0, depends on the extent to which higher or lower future growth is discounted into the current price of the stock. What market forces can cause changes in the current market price of the stock?

QUESTION SET 2

1. When using a three-stage growth model, what must an analyst estimate for each security he is valuing?
2. If a stock is currently selling at $50 per share, is expected to grow at a rate of 9 percent and is expected to pay a year-end dividend of $3, what is the stock's expected rate of return?

3. Now suppose that you know the expected return on the stock in Question 2 is only 12 percent. Given that its dividend and price per share are unchanged, what is its expected growth rate?

4. In the context of a two-stage growth model, what is the relationship between a stock's price-earnings ratio and
   a. Its initial rate of growth, $E(G)$?
   b. Its expected rate of return?

5. Why do the price-earnings ratios for stocks with above- or below-average growth outlooks change over time?

ANSWERS TO QUESTION SET 2

1. The analyst must come up with the following estimates: (a) the initial and terminal (g) growth rate for the growth phase (G), (b) the length of the growth phase, (c) the length of the transitional phase, and (d) the required return $[E(r)]$.

2. $E(r) = \dfrac{\text{Expected year-end dividend}}{\text{Market Price}} + \text{expected growth rate}$

   $= \dfrac{\$3.00}{\$50.00} + .09$

   $= 15 \text{ or } 15\%$

3. From the equation in Question 2, we know that

   $$12\% = \frac{\$3.00}{\$50.00} + \text{expected growth rate}, E(G)$$

   $$E(G) = 12\% - \frac{\$3.00}{\$50.00}$$

   $$E(G) = 6\%$$

4. A stock's price-earnings ratio is positively related to its initial expected rate of growth and inversely related to its expected rate of return.

5. The price-earnings ratios of such stocks will change over time because of the stocks' reversion over time to the status (i.e., the growth rate) of an average share.

REFERENCES

BAYLIS, R., and BHIRUD, S., "Growth Stock Analysis: A New Approach," *Financial Analysts Journal* (July–August 1973).

BEAVER, W., and MORSE, D., "What Determines Price-Earnings Ratios," *Financial Analysts Journal* (July–August 1978).

BERNSTEIN, P., "Growth Companies vs. Growth Stocks," *Harvard Business Review* (September–October 1956).

BIERMAN, H., DOWNES, D., and HASS, J., "Closed Form Price Models," *Journal of Financial and Quantitative Analysis* (June 1972).

BING, R., "Survey of Practitioners' Stock Evaluation Methods," *Financial Analysts Journal* (May–June 1971).

GOOD, W., "Valuation of Quality-Growth Stocks," *Financial Analysts Journal* (September–October 1972).

HOLT, C., "Influence of Growth Duration on Share Prices," *Journal of Finance* (September 1962).

KEENAN, M., "Models of Equity Valuation: The Great Serm Bubble," *Journal of Finance* (May 1970).

MALKIEL, B., "Equity Yields, Growth, and the Structure of Share Prices," *American Economic Review* (September 1970).

WILLIAMS, J., *The Theory of Investment Value*. Cambridge, Mass.: Harvard University Press, 1938.

C H A P T E R

21

ISSUES IN ESTIMATING FUTURE EARNINGS AND DIVIDENDS

Unlike bond investments, which have payments that are fixed in time and magnitude, the dividends from stocks may become larger or smaller as time goes by. One of the jobs of the security analyst is to estimate the propensity for growth or decline in the expected dividend stream. In doing their jobs, analysts must come to grips with an important issue: How far into the future can the relative growth in earnings and dividends be forecast with any reasonable degree of accuracy? Can a prudent analyst really say that a given stock is going to grow at a faster or slower than average rate over the next decade or so? How much confidence can we place in such forecasts? How do the answers to these questions affect the way we value stocks or the development of our investment strategy? In this chapter we will seek the answers to these questions.

PAYING IN ADVANCE FOR GROWTH

The market's expectations for the future relative rates of growth in earnings and dividends per share are discounted into current market prices per share. If investors think a stock's dividends are going to grow at a faster than average rate for a prolonged period of time, they will bid up the current price of the stock relative to the *current* level of dividends per share. The ratio of the stock's current market price to its current dividend per share will be greater than that for an average stock.

Thinking in terms of Equation (20.4), suppose we have two stocks with the same expected or required rate of return, $E(r)$. One of the stocks is expected to grow indefinitely at the average rate, $E(g)$, and the second stock is expected to grow at a rate, $E(G)$, that is higher than average over some growth horizon, n. In this case, if the initial dividend is the same for both stocks, the present value of the dividend stream for the second stock will be greater than that of the first. The ratio of the present value to its current dividend will also be greater. It is also true that if you buy the stock at a price equal to this higher present value, the higher than average expected growth must materialize in order for you to earn your minimum required rate of return, $E(r)$, on the investment. If instead, it turns out that the stock grows at the average rate, the rate of return earned will be less than the minimum requirement.

In this sense you are *paying in advance* for the higher than average rate of growth which is expected to occur. The stock must achieve this greater than average level of performance just to provide you with a reasonable rate of return. If the stock's performance, in terms of dividend growth, turns out to be merely average, its rate of return to you as an investor is likely to be below average. This is true, because the dividends you receive will be small relative to the price you paid, and investors are likely to revise downward their expectations for future growth in the dividend stream, resulting in possible capital losses for your shares.

To illustrate the principle of paying in advance for growth, and the market's willingness to discount liberal expectations of future growth into current share prices, let's go back in time to the year 1960 and take a look at two stocks, Florida Power & Light and New England Electric System. Both stocks are regulated electric utilities and have similar risk characteristics, so they are likely to have similar expected or required rates of return. Their stock price histories are graphed in Figure 21.1. Each bar in the figure represents the range between the high and the low price for the month. The records for each company, in terms of earnings and dividends per share, are given in the accompanying table.

Note that Florida Power & Light was distributing a smaller fraction of its earnings as dividends. The remaining earnings were retained and reinvested in the firm to provide a base for larger future earnings and dividends. This may account for the superior record of Florida Power & Light in terms of earnings and dividend growth through the year 1960.

Recognizing the greater potential for future growth, the market bid the current market price of Florida Power & Light up, relative to its current dividend. In 1960, the price reached $68 per share, which was approximately seventy times the current

Year	Florida Power & Light		New England Electric System	
	Earnings	Dividends	Earnings	Dividends
1953	.77	.40	1.18	.90
1954	.88	.44	1.16	.90
1955	1.03	.50	1.24	.90
1956	1.30	.61	1.23	1.00
1957	1.49	.66	1.19	1.00
1958	1.76	.76	1.26	1.00
1959	1.93	.87	1.31	1.02
1960	2.11	.97	1.35	1.08
Growth rate, 1953–1960	15%	13%	2%	3%

dividend. The market price of New England Electric System was as low as $20 per share in 1960, a multiple of only 19 times its current dividend.

If we make assumptions about the expected rate of growth for an average or standard share and the market's expected or required rate of return for these two stocks, we can determine the future growth performance that will justify these prices.

The late 1950s was a period of little or no inflation. Extrapolating the rates of growth in earnings and dividends per share for the aggregate market indices which were occurring then into the future, a conservative estimate for the rate of growth in dividends for an average stock might be 2 percent.

In 1960, the yield to maturity on AAA public utility bonds was only 4.6 percent. The average rate of return to the market in general, over the period 1926 through 1960, was approximately 9 percent. We will take 8 percent as a reasonable estimate of the minimal required expected return for an investment in these two relatively low-risk common stocks. If we substitute into Equation (20.4) 8 percent for $E(r)$, 2 percent for $E(g)$, and $20 and $48 for the market prices of New England Electric and Florida Power & Light, respectively, we can find values for $E(G)$ and n that will make the present value of the future dividend stream equal to the two stock prices.

For example, in the case of Florida Power & Light, if you were to assume that the dividend was going to grow at a rate of 12 percent over the next 25 years, through 1985, the current market price for the stock could be justified. If the dividend were to grow at this rate, and you paid $48 for the stock, you would indeed get an 8 percent rate of return on your investment. If the rate of growth turned out to be more modest, your rate of return would also be more modest. Thus, the growth profile in Figure 21.2 would produce an 8 percent rate of return for an investor in the stock. Different combinations of $E(G)$ and n would also suffice. For example, a 20 percent rate of growth for 10 years would also generate 8 percent.

The picture for New England Electric is much different. The growth rate in dividends needs only be slightly greater than the assumed average rate of 2 percent to justify the current price. For example, if the dividend were to grow at 3 percent for 25 years, the rate of return produced for investors in the stock would be greater

Florida Power & Light Company
Stock price

New England Electric System
Stock price

FIGURE 21.1 Stock price history of Florida Power & Light and New England Electric System.

SOURCE: *Moody's Handbook of Widely Held Common Stocks,* 3rd ed. (Moody's Investor's Services, Inc., 1969), pp. 214 and 388.

OUT ON THE STREET

IN FIRST PLACE

It was well beyond time to leave for work, but going through the article one more time seemed irresistible. After all, it's not every day that you get favorable press in the *New York Post*. The *Post* had surveyed 20 professional security analysts, asking them which industries would outperform the market over the next 6- to 12-month period. Elaine Garzarelli was one of those analysts. As it turned out, the industries that she selected produced a 25 percent return for the period in the face of a 9 percent return for the market as a whole.

Elaine is the director of sector analysis at Shearson-Lehman Brothers in New York City. While working on her Ph.D. at New York University, she became interested in building econometric models to forecast industry earnings. Over the last 10 years she progressively refined her techniques, steadily increasing the accuracy of her projections. At this point, Elaine can document the fact that her quantitative, econometric-based projections are considerably more accurate than the more subjective estimates of earnings per share made by the typical security analyst. For one thing, analysts usually go directly to the company and ask management about what it thinks about the future prospects for the firm. These opinions are usually biased upward. Analysts can also become emotionally committed or opposed to a firm or industry, adding a further element of bias to their forecasts.

Elaine's approach is more objective. She forecasts earnings per share by industry for a period of up to 12 to 18 months into the future. The reliability of forecasts beyond this point depends on your confidence in your general economic outlook, and beyond 2 to 3 years your confidence usually isn't very good.

Elaine makes forecasts for 60 industries as defined by Standard & Poor's. The forecast for each industry is based on a set of approximately 14 statistical models. One of the models, for example, might be the product of a correlation, or regression, analysis where she is trying to explain the movement in sales for the steel industry over the last 15 years. She might be correlating percentage changes in steel sales with factors like percentage changes in nonresidential construction, domestic auto sales, and producer durable equipment spending.

The correlation analysis reveals the relationship between changes in each of these variables, or factors, and changes in steel industry sales. Elaine has found that she can explain up to 90 percent of the changes in steel sales on the basis of the changes in her factors. Having identified the relationship, if she herself supplies or is given forecasts for each of the determining factors, she can calculate a forecast for future steel sales.

Similar relationships are modeled for other elements of the income statement, like labor and fixed costs. The models provide estimates of each element of the income statement, and after all costs have been subtracted from revenue,

Elaine has a forecast of earnings in the steel industry. Elaine revises her models annually to account for any changes that may occur between the factors and the income statement element she is trying to forecast. She has found that, although the nature of the relationships may change, the identity of the factors themselves is relatively stable. For example, the prime interest rate was an important factor in explaining changes in auto sales back in 1974, when it was 8 percent, and it still was an important factor in 1979, when she was using an 18 percent prime.

The models tell her the relationship between the factors and the various elements of the income statement for the industry. However, to implement each model, she needs forecasts of the future values of the factors themselves. She begins with the outlook for the general economy, moving then to an element like consumer durables, and gradually filtering down to the factors required for the forecast. In part, she relies on her own training as an economist, but she also looks to Shearson's economists and published surveys, such as for expected capital spending, from McGraw-Hill and the Commerce Department.

Elaine's basic, final product is a booklet entitled "Sector Analysis," published by Shearson and released to its clients once each month. In the booklet, Elaine classifies the 60 different industries into three categories: (1) those that will outperform the market in the next six to 12 months, (2) those that will move with the market, and (3) those that will underperform. To be placed in the "outperform" classification, an industry must meet two qualifications. First, Elaine's forecast for the industry's earnings growth must exceed that which she is forecasting for the earnings growth for the Standard & Poor's 500 Stock Index. Second, the Industry's average price-earnings ratio must be 5 percent under its normal relationship to the price-earnings ratio for the 500 index. Meeting both above average prospects and undervaluation, the industry gets on the outperformance list.

In each of the last 8 years, Elaine's forecasts have proved to be more accurate than *Zack's Consensus* published out of Chicago. Zack surveys 80 brokerage firms to get individual company forecasts. The individual company forecasts are then aggregated by industry, as defined by Standard & Poor's.

The accuracy of Elaine's forecasts is paying off. Recently *Institutional Investor* magazine surveyed approximately 3000 institutional clients asking them to vote on which professional analyst had given them the most reliable information over the last year. Based on the survey, the top analysts were named to the magazine's "All America Team." Elaine was not only named to this team, she placed first in the balloting.

Enough. Time is Money. Looking through the window of her Greenwich Village apartment, she can see the window of her office at 2 World Trade Center. With luck, in 5 minutes she would be back in the thick of things.

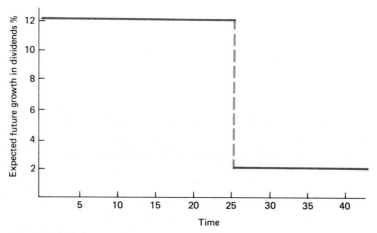

FIGURE 21.2 Future growth required to produce an 8% return for Florida Power & Light.

than 8 percent. Thus, the price is justified with the relatively modest growth profile in Figure 21.3.

As things turned out, Florida Power & Light did grow at a faster rate than New England Electric during the next 25 years. However, the difference wasn't nearly as great as would be implied by their relative stock prices in 1960. The earnings per share of Florida Power grew at approximately 7 percent annually compounded rate, whereas the earnings of New England Electric grew at a 6 percent rate.

The cases of New England Electric and Florida Power & Light illustrate the point that the market has at times exhibited a willingness to discount growth rates in

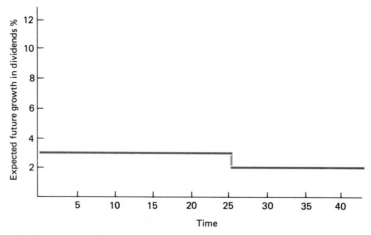

FIGURE 21.3 Future growth required to produce an 8% return for New England Electric System.

dividends which are *much* different from average, for *prolonged* periods of time, into the current prices for common shares. However, it can be argued, as we do shortly, that the attitude of professional security analysts toward growth and their willingness to capitalize expected future growth into current stock prices have undergone evolutionary changes over time.

GROWTH AND STOCK VALUATION: AN HISTORICAL PERSPECTIVE

In the early part of this century, security analysts were concerned with estimating the value of a company's earnings per share under "normalized" conditions. They tried to make adjustments in earnings numbers to account for differences in accounting techniques among companies, and they tried to allow for the presence of unusual or extraordinary conditions which might make the current number different from what might be expected in a "normal" year. Present-day analysts do this as well, but they also tend to spend a great deal of time trying to estimate the growth potential for different stocks.

In contrast, early financial analysts regarded growth as a "speculative," as opposed to an "investment," consideration in security valuation. Prudent analysts estimated as carefully as possible the level of current, normal earnings, and then they computed the intrinsic value of the stock through the product of earnings and a value-earnings multiple that was based, for the most part, on the quality of the issue. Quality, it should be said, had little or nothing to do with the potential for growth. This practice is consistent with the hypothesis that expected growth is completely unpredictable; the growth profile for all stocks should be identical with $n = 0$. No stock could be predicted to grow at a below- or above-average rate for any period of time into the future.

This philosophy was challenged with the publication of a book in 1926 by Edgar Lawrence Smith entitled *Common Stocks as Long Term Investments*. Smith presented some numbers which showed the historical rates of return on common stock investments had been much greater than returns to bond investments. The differential could be argued to be too large to be attributable to the greater relative risk of common stocks. Instead, Smith argued it was due to an error being made in stock valuation. Stocks were clearly different from bonds in that the income from a stock can be expected to grow. The analysts of the time were missing half the picture. Much of their effort should have been spent determining which stocks had the greatest potential for growth. These stocks should be assessed at greater intrinsic values.

Smith's book gained wide attention, and the race was on to find "growth stocks." Growth stock prices were bid up to extremely large multiples of current income. The valuation of common stocks had entered a new era, and appropriately enough the new valuation philosophy was called the "New Era Theory." The New Era Theory ended abruptly with the great stock market crash of October 1929.

In the midst of the Great Depression (1934) Benjamin Graham and David Dodd published a book, *Security Analysis*. In their book they attacked the New Era Theory and growth stock valuation. They argued for a return to former practice and continued to maintain their position in later years:

> . . . the analyst's philosophy must still compel him to base his investment valuation on an assumed earning power no larger than the company has already achieved in some year of normal business. Investment values can be related only to demonstrated performance.[1]

Graham and Dodd felt that future growth was largely, if not completely, unpredictable. Stock valuation could be founded only on *demonstrated,* as opposed to *anticipated,* earning power. They were particularly opposed to estimating future earnings by extrapolating from historical trends: "Value based on a satisfactory trend must be wholly arbitrary and hence speculative, and hence inevitably subject to exaggeration and later collapse."[2]

But they also regarded estimates of relative growth which were based on factors other than simple trend, such as the relative amount of earnings retained as dividends (as in New England Electric and Florida Power & Light), as undependable.

> if a business paid out only a small part of its earnings in dividends, the value of its stock should increase over a period of years; but it is by no means so certain that this increase will compensate the stockholders for the dividends withheld from them. An inductive study would undoubtedly show that the earning power of corporations does not in general expand proportionately with increases in accumulated surplus. *Assuming that the reported earnings were actually available for distribution,* then stockholders would certainly fare better in dollars and cents if they drew out practically all these earnings in dividends.[3]

In the years after the publication of Graham and Dodd's book, analysts seemed to discard the emphasis on factoring growth into stock valuation. *Security Analysis* was a highly successful text and went through many editions. However, it began to fall out of favor in the late 1950s as the previously questioned theory purporting growth as a significant factor in the valuation of common stocks was dusted off and revived. This time a paper was published by Fisher and Lorie (1964) showing that common stocks had far outstripped bonds in producing high rates of return. Sophisticated stock valuation models were developed by Myron Gordon (1962) and others in which future growth in earnings and dividends played a central role.

Coincident with these developments, however, the work of I. M. D. Little was

---

[1]Graham, Dodd, and Tatham (1951, pp. 422–423).

[2]Graham, and Dodd (1934, p. 314).

[3]Graham and Dodd (1934, p. 330). The inductive study suggested by Graham and Dodd was actually conducted 36 years later by Baumol, Heim, Malkiel, and Quandt (1970). In this study the authors concluded:

> Ploughback does generally appear to yield a positive return. . . . Nevertheless, as we have seen, the rate of return to firms relying on ploughback for their new investment is typically uncomfortably small. . . . All this raises serious questions about the workings of the economy and the efficiency of the investment process. Is it really true that earnings retention serves the interests of the stockholder? (pp. 354–355)

published supporting the view that growth in earnings per share for the largest manufacturing firms in the United Kingdom was random and therefore unpredictable. This work would later lead to further studies in the United States that were largely consistent with this point of view.

Thus, we have two opposing views. One states that relative growth rates between stocks are largely predictable. If this is true, stocks which are expected to grow at faster than average rates for prolonged periods of time should be assigned higher prices by the market. The other states that relative growth rates are largely unpredictable. If this is true, differences in ratios of market price to current normalized earnings per share should be due only to differences in risk. As time has passed, those who value stocks in the market seem to have favored one view and then the other. If the nature of the economy is reasonably stable over time, it is likely that only one view is correct. In the following section we examine the evidence relating to this issue and its implications for investment strategy.

THE ACCURACY OF PREDICTIONS OF GROWTH IN EARNINGS AND DIVIDENDS

Is Past Growth a Reliable Guide to Future Growth?

In 1962, a British professor named I. M. D. Little published the results of a study investigating the relationship between past and future rates of growth in earnings per share for British companies. Alluding to the resurgence of analysts' emphasizes on growth in stock valuation that had occurred at the end of the 1950s, Little stated:

> My impression is that many stockholders, financial journalists, economists, and investors believe that past growth behavior is some sort of guide to future growth. This belief seems to have developed especially in the last few years.[4]

To test whether past growth was an indication of future growth, Little related the rate of growth in earnings per share for a given period to the rate of growth in a subsequent period, as in Figure 21.4. Each observation in the figure represents a particular firm. The firm's rate of growth in one period is plotted on the horizontal axis, and its rate of growth in the next period is plotted vertically.

If growth rates were perfectly stable, replicating themselves from one period to the next, the points would plot as a 45-degree line emanating from the origin. Instead, in this example, the points plot as a scatter. The broken line of best fit has a slightly positive slope, indicating that a relatively high rate of growth in the first period would lead you to believe the same firm has a better than even chance of growing at an above-average rate in the second period. The goodness of fit about the line, or the correlation coefficient, provides an indication of the accuracy of a prediction of growth in the second period, based on a knowledge of growth in the first

---

[4]I. M. D. Little (1962, p. 391).

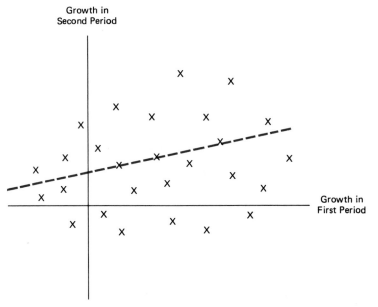

FIGURE 21.4 Possible relationship between past and future growth.

period. In this particular case, the correlation coefficient is rather low, so a prediction of future growth, based on growth in the first period, would not be very reliable.

Little ran a number of correlations of this type covering the decade of the 1950s. The correlations can be classified by the industry of the firms in the study and by the number of years in the first and second periods over which growth is measured. To illustrate the nature of the results, consider the group of correlation studies in which four years are included in both the first and second periods. A total of 18 such correlations are run covering different industries and different years. Out of the 18, 9 correlations are significantly negative, 5 are significantly positive, and 4 are not significantly different from zero. The average value for the correlation is .02.

Similar results are found when Little changed the number of years included in the first and second periods. Overall, if there was any relationship to be found at all between past and future growth, it was slightly *negative*. The firms that grew at a faster than average rate in the first period had a *slight* propensity to grow at a slower than average rate in the second period. Little also found little relationship between the rate of retention of earnings in one period and growth in future periods. Company size also appeared to have little to do with future growth.

Little's findings were disturbing. They drew much attention, and soon others attempted to see if the same conditions were true in the United States. Surprisingly, these early studies came to similar conclusions. The firms which grew at a faster than average rate in one period seemed to have only an even chance of growing faster than average in the next period.

Researchers pressed on, applying increasingly sophisticated procedures to model the time series of earnings per share. By analyzing the behavior of quarterly earnings per share over some past period, they tried to develop models which could predict the future value of earnings per share based on its past behavior. Although the models were reasonably successful in predicting for short periods, forecasts of the growth in earnings became highly inaccurate when the time horizon was extended beyond a single year.

Thus, in making a forecast of the long-term rate of growth in earnings and dividends per share, analysts would be ill-advised to base their forecasts on the historical record. In spite of this survey, studies (Cragg and Malkiel, 1968) have shown that in making their forecasts, analysts started with the historical record and then made subjective modifications. The actual forecasts of growth made by professional analysts tend to be positively correlated with the past growth records of the same companies.

Given that the amount of useful information in the past record of growth is meager, the growth forecasts of analysts are likely to be inaccurate, unless the subjective modifications they make are based on more useful information. In the next section we determine whether this is, in fact, true.

The Accuracy of Growth Forecasts Made by Professional Analysts

In making their forecasts, analysts look to other information in addition to that contained in the past time series of earnings per share numbers. This includes information pertaining to the firm's industry, the outlook for interest rates, inflation, the value of the dollar, and innovations in products and techniques of production. They attempt to assess how each of these factors will affect the firm's profitability. In addition, during the course of the year, management often makes announcements regarding the outlook for the year-end profits for the firm. This information, and more, are factored into the analyst's forecasts for growth in the firm's earnings per share.

One would expect that, given their access to all this additional information, the forecasts of professional analysts should be considerably more accurate than those based on a statistical analysis of the past time series of earnings alone.

The Accuracy of Short-Term Professional Forecasts

The question of short-term accuracy was addressed in a study by Collins and Hopwood (1980), in which the accuracy of earnings forecasts made by the *Value Line Investment Survey* and by statistical models were compared. The *Value Line Investment Survey* is a well-known investment service that provides information, analysis, and forecasts of earnings and other numbers for their subscribers.

Value Line's sample consists of 50 firms with quarterly earnings data available from 1951 through 1974. Annual forecasts were obtained for the period 1970 through 1974. Several statistical models were employed as a basis of comparison. To assess the relative accuracy of the forecasts, the absolute value of the percentage difference between the forecast and the actual value for the earnings number reported at the end of the year is computed. This value is averaged for all the forecasts made by Value

Line and by the statistical models. To adjust for the influence of extreme errors (such as a forecast of $1 when actual earnings turn out to be $.01), Collins and Hopwood make an adjusted comparison where they assign a percentage error of 300 percent to all errors greater than this value.

The results are given in the accompanying table by the quarter during the year in which the forecast of earnings per share for the same year is made. The results indicate that Value Line's forecasts are more accurate than the statistical models, although they are nearly identical when extreme outliers are eliminated from consideration. Much of the superiority is apparently due to the inability of the models to respond to economic events such as strikes that will have a known effect on earnings per share. Note also, that the accuracy of Value Line's predictions begins to fade rapidly as the length of the period of the forecast is extended to a year.

	Unadjusted Average Absolute % Error	Adjusted Average Absolute % Error
First quarter		
Value Line	34	32
Statistical models	60	32
Second quarter		
Value Line	28	26
Statistical models	47	25
Third quarter		
Value Line	22	18
Statistical models	33	20
Fourth quarter		
Value Line	10	10
Statistical models	18	11

Another study, by Crichfield, Dyckman, and Lakonishok (1978), covers a more representative group of analysts. They assess the relative accuracy of forecasts published in the *Earnings Forecaster,* a biweekly publication of Standard & Poor's which collects the forecasts of more than 50 investment firms. In any given issue, there may be up to 10 forecasts for any given single firm. The study covers forecasts for 46 firms during the 113 months of January 1967 through May 1976.

As a basis of comparison, they use forecasts from five models, such as a prediction that next year's earnings will be identical to this year's. In each case they compute the difference between the forecast and the actual earnings number reported at the end of the year. In the case of the analysts, their individual forecasts are averaged, and the accuracy of the average is assessed. The errors are then squared and summed by month, relative to the actual report month. For example, the errors for all the average forecasts of the analysts, or a particular model, made three months prior to the month in which the actual earnings were reported would be summed together. To assess the accuracy of the analysts relative to any given model, they compute a ratio of the sum of the model's squared errors to the sum of the analysts' squared errors. If the ratio is greater than 1, the analysts' forecasts are more accurate.

The analysts' forecasts *are* more accurate when compared to four of the five forecasting models. However, with the exception of the model forecasting that next year's earnings will be the same as this year's, none of these models allows for seasonal patterns in earnings. The fifth model allows for such patterns. Predictions under this model are based on the following rules. Remember that we are trying to predict earnings for the current year, *during* the current year.

1. Predictions made during April, May, and June: This year's earnings will be equal to four times the earnings reported for this year's first quarter plus or minus the error you would have made using such a rule last year.
2. Predictions made during July, August, and September: Same as for April, May, and June, except you use the second quarter's earnings.
3. Predictions made in October, November, December, and the following January (earnings aren't usually reported until February or March of the following year): Same as for April, May, or June, except you use the third quarter's earnings.

The ratios of the model's squared errors to the analysts' squared errors are as follows:

Month	Ratio
April	.62
May	.68
June	.75
July	.85
August	.81
September	1.10
October	1.22
November	1.44
December	1.55
January	1.67

Early in the year, the simple model actually makes better forecasts than the average of the analysts. Only later in the year, when announcements are being made by management about expectations for the earnings numbers, do the forecasts made by the analysts become relatively more accurate.

The most recent study of the short-term accuracy of professional forecasts was conducted by Patricia O'Brien (1988). O'Brien studied professional forecasts collected by the Institutional Brokers Estimate System during the period 1969 through 1975. The forecasts were made for earnings per share for the current year for 184 firms. O'Brien measures the accuracy of the forecasts made during the first, second, third, and fourth quarters. The accuracy of the forecasts are compared to that for a statistical time series model. The median average absolute error for the professionals and the statistical model is as follows:

	Quarter			
	I	II	III	IV
Statistical model	$.97	$.78	$.59	$.35
Professionals	$.79	$.68	$.55	$.43

Note once again, accuracy decreases rapidly with the time horizon for the forecast. The professionals, in this study, perform at a superior level early in the forecast year. However, the magnitude of these errors are quite large relative to a typical earnings per share number, making the errors in terms of *percentage earnings growth* even larger.

The Accuracy of Long-Term Professional Forecasts

Little is known about the accuracy of longer-term forecasts of earnings and earnings growth. Cragg and Malkiel published a study in 1968 which looked at the accuracy across a three-year period of long-term forecasts of earnings growth by five professional investment management firms. Two were large New York banks heavily involved in trust management, one was an investment banking firm, another was a mutual fund, and the final member of the group was involved in investment advising and brokerage.

The forecasts for as many as 185 individual companies were made in 1962 and 1963. Cragg and Malkiel then compared the forecasts with the historical rates of growth for the individual companies over the preceding 10 years and with the actual rates of growth over the *next* 3 years. The bars in the back of Figure 21.5 show the percentage of the differences between the historic rates of growth for the 185 companies that can be explained by differences in the analysts forecasts. These numbers are the square of the correlation coefficients between the forecasts and the 10-year growth history. Obviously, at least three of the analysts were relying heavily on past trends to make their forecasts. We know, of course, that past trend and future growth have very little to do with one another.

The bars in the front of Figure 21.5 show the percentage of the differences in actual future growth for the 185 companies that can be explained by differences in the analysts forecasts. These bars tell us about the actual accuracy of the forecasts. Only one of the five analysts seems to be doing a reasonably good job of forecasting future growth. Cragg and Malkiel point out that this particular analyst tended to supply forecasts for the study which concentrated on stable companies for which there was an a priori reason to believe the forecasts would be reliable. The authors noted also that forecasts based on past growth alone did not perform much differently from the predictions.

Overall, we seem to be able to draw the following conclusion. It is very difficult to forecast the future growth in earnings based on a statistical analysis of the past earnings series. The accuracy of these forecasts diminishes rapidly as the term of the forecast extends beyond one year. Professional forecasters can rely on a wealth

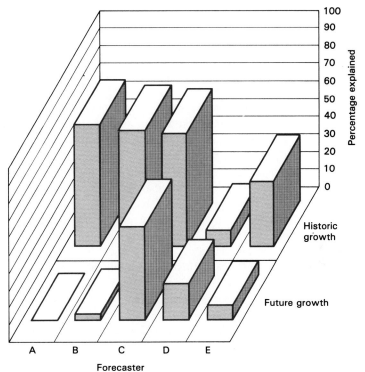

FIGURE 21.5 Cragg and Malkiel study of long-term forecasts.

of additional information besides the past series of earnings numbers. In spite of this, the accuracy of their forecasts seems to be only marginally better. It seems that forecasting the relative rate of growth for a particular stock beyond one year is hazardous.

IMPLICATIONS FOR INVESTMENT STRATEGY

If forecasts for the long-term relative rates of growth for earning and dividends are inherently inaccurate, then you should be hesitant to make them. You should also be hesitant to pay for them in advance if they are discounted into the current price of a stock.

The price-earnings ratio offers a rough indication of the extent to which a prolonged period of abnormal growth is discounted into the current market price of a stock. If the market price is large relative to an estimate of current normalized earnings, then either of the following is likely to be true: (1) The market expects earnings in the future to be considerably larger than it is today, or (2) the market is capitalizing the income stream at an unusually low rate. If a case cannot be made that the stock is of unusually low risk, then the former, and not the latter, is likely to be true. If you buy the stock, you are paying in advance for a prolonged above average record of growth. If this above-average performance materializes, the rate of return on your investment will not be above average but only reasonable. Instead, if the stock grows at an average rate, then the return on your investment will be less than sufficient.

Available evidence points to the conclusion that forecasts of prolonged above- or below-average growth are highly unreliable. If you believe this is true, you should approach a stock with a large ratio of price to normalized earnings with great caution. The price may be based on an optimistic forecast for growth, and there is good reason to believe this forecast is unreliable. On the other hand, you should be attracted to stocks with small ratios of price to normalized earnings. These stocks are priced on a pessimistic forecast which is also unreliable. If both stocks have approximately an equal chance of growing at an above- or below-normal rate in the long run, the high price-earnings stock is overpriced, and its low price-earnings counterpart is a bargain.

If (1) high (low) price-earnings ratios are attributable to optimistic (pessimistic) forecasts of growth rather than to low (high) risk, and if (2) these forecasts tend to be overly optimistic (pessimistic), this leads to the following prediction: *After adjusting for differences in risk, stocks with high (low) price-earnings ratios should earn lower (higher) than average rates of return.* If these stocks truly have no better than an even chance of performing at an above- or below-average level over the long term, the market will show a tendency to revise both its expectations and the market prices for the shares as the optimistic or pessimistic forecasts fail to materialize in the earnings numbers. In fact, as we will learn in Chapter 23, available evidence supports this prediction.

SUMMARY

The appropriate answer to the question of the extent to which future growth in earnings and dividends should play a role in stock valuation isn't completely clear, and the issue is controversial. The prevailing philosophy of financial analysts regarding the issue has vacillated. At times the attention of analysts has centered on estimating the current level of normalized earnings. Stocks with similar current earnings and similar risks were assigned similar values. At other times attention has shifted to the future and to the expected rate of growth in normalized earnings. Then the stock with the larger expected growth in normalized earnings would be assigned a significantly larger value.

What should be the role of expected future growth in the valuation of common stocks? The answer to this question depends on the length of the period over which we can say that one stock will grow at a faster rate than another with any degree of accuracy. Based on presently available evidence, it appears that this period is relatively short, not much more than a year for a representative pair of stocks. If you believe that this is true, *and* that the market is pricing stocks on the basis of a longer forecasting period, then you should be inclined to move against the market's forecasts and, other factors being equal, invest in stocks with relatively low price-earnings ratios.

QUESTION SET 1

1. An investor considers a stock undervalued. He or she buys it at a price higher than can be justified by current average expected growth, g, because the investor expects a higher future growth rate, G. Several other investors do the same, bidding up the market price of the stock, V_0. What can happen if the market turns out to be wrong in its evaluation of the stock?

2. In the text, two regulated utilities companies are used in an illustration of the application of a two-stage growth model. If the expected rate of growth for an average or standard share, $E(g)$, and the market's expected or required rate of return for the stocks, $E(r)$, can be estimated, and the market prices of the stocks, V_0, are given, an abnormal rate of growth, $E(G)$, for a number of years, n, that will justify the stock prices can be found. Set up an equation that a computer could use to solve for $E(G)$ and n, given $E(g)$, $E(r)$, and V_0. Assume that the abnormal rate of growth occurs over the years 1 through n, and thereafter the stocks growth reverts to the market average rate, $E(g)$.

3. What is meant by normalized earnings?

4. In the 1960s there were two opposing views regarding stock valuation. State these and their basic implications.

5. What comparisons did Little make to test his theory of stock valuation, and what were his overall findings?

6. How accurate are models of the time series of earnings per share in predicting the future value of earnings per share based on past information?

7. What are some subjective modifications used in an analyst's forecasts (as opposed to a statistician's) of growth in earnings per share?

8. Collins and Hopwood (1980) compared the accuracy in earnings forecasts made by *Value Line Investment Survey* with that of forecasts made by statistical models. What were their findings?

9. Crichfield, Dyckman, and Lakonishok (1978) compared the accuracy of analysts' forecasts with those of five forecasting models. What were their findings?

10. Comment on the following statement: "Forecasting the relative rate of growth for a particular stock beyond one year is hazardous at best."

11. Would it be appropriate investment strategy always to buy growth stocks that have high price-earnings ratios? If not, suggest an alternative strategy.

QUESTION SET 2

1. If two otherwise identical stocks that are paying identical dividends are selling at different multiples, why can we not determine the exact difference in the market's estimation of the two companies' growth patterns (both magnitude and length of growth)?

2. What was the error, according to Edgar Lawrence Smith, in stock valuation by the market analysts of his era?

3. What consequences did Little's findings have regarding the techniques of market analysts during the 1960s?

4. What rationale might an investor have in buying high P–E stocks? Why might it be better to buy low P–E stocks instead?

5. According to the empirical evidence presented in the chapter, which are more accurate in growth forecasts, quantitative forecasting models or professional analysts?

ANSWERS TO QUESTION SET 2

1. The problem arises because the market price is a composite of all the investors' estimates of both the magnitude and length of stock growth. Hence we have one equation and two unknowns, which cannot be solved.

2. Smith thought that, since the income from stocks can be expected to grow, stocks should be valued according to not only normalized earnings, but also according to their potential for future growth.

3. Little found that a stock's past growth is not significantly related to future growth. This finding contradicted the predominant forecasting technique in the 1960s.

4. An investor might choose stocks with high P–E ratios if he or she sees this ratio as a proxy for demand for the stock by other investors, or possibly in the mistaken belief that the company has a low cost of capital. Low P–E stocks have historically shown greater price appreciation than high P–E stocks.

5. The empirical evidence in the chapter supports the notion that quantitative models work better in the very short run, and beyond that (up to about one year), professional forecasters are more accurate, if only slightly more so.

COMPUTER PROBLEM SET

1. a. Using the stock valuation model in your software, determine at what price stock X should sell, given the following information:

Initial dividend	$0.80
Number of days until first dividend payment	35
Duration of initial growth rate	24
Duration of linearly decreasing growth rate	16
Initial growth rate	10%
Terminal growth rate	6%
Discount rate	14%

b. Suppose that stock X is selling for $50. On the basis of this, you decide to tell a client to buy the stock. If it turns out that the stock grows at 10 percent for only 12 quarters instead of 24, is the stock still a good buy?

c. Now assume that all the foregoing estimates are correct except that the appropriate discount rate for stock X is only 12 percent. How does this affect the stock's estimated price?

d. If stock X sells for $50, what is the stock's expected return, assuming all other information on stock X is correct?

e. Now suppose that you decide the stock's dividend growth of 10 percent can only be predicted for four quarters. Also, the linearly decreasing growth rate is likewise four quarters. If you are correct, is it accurate to assume that investors have compounded too long a growth period into the stock's present price of $50?

REFERENCES

BAUMOL, W., HEIM, P., MALKIEL, B., and QUANDT, R., "Earnings Retention, New Capital, and the Growth of the Firm," *Review of Economics and Statistics* (November 1970).

COLLINS, W., and HOPWOOD, W., "A Multivariate Analysis of Annual Earnings Forecasts Generated from Quarterly Forecasts of Financial Analysts and Univariate Time Series Models," *Journal of Accoaunting Research* (Autumn 1980).

CRAGG, D., and MALKIEL, B., "Consensus and Accuracy of the Predictions of the Growth of Corporate Earnings," *Journal of Finance* (March 1968).

CRICHFIELD, T., DYCKMAN, T., and LAKONISHOK, J., "An Evaluation of Security Analysts Forecasts," *Accounting Review* (July 1978).

FISHER, L., and LORIE, J., "Rates of Return on Investments in Common Stock," *Journal of Business* (January 1964).

GORDON, M., *The Investment, Financing and Valuation of the Corporation.* Homewood, Ill.: Irwin, 1962.

GRAHAM, B., and DODD, D., *Security Analysis.* New York: McGraw-Hill, 1934.

GRAHAM, B., and DODD, D., with TATHAM, C., *Security Analysis.* New York: McGraw-Hill, 1951.

LITTLE, I. M. D., "Higgledy Piggledy Growth," *Institute of Statistics Oxford* (November 1962).

LINTER, J., and GLAUBER, M., "Higgledy Piggledy Growth in America," in *Modern Developments in Investment Management,* ed. J. Lorie and R. Brealey. New York: Praeger, 1972.

O'BRIEN, P., "Analyst's forecasts as earnings expectation," Journal of Accounting and Economics (January 1988).

22

MARKET EFFICIENCY: THE CONCEPT

The capital asset pricing model and the arbitrage pricing theory are theories which allegedly describe the *structure* of the prices of financial assets. They tell us how we can expect prices and expected rates of return on securities to differ when the securities differ with respect to their risk characteristics.

In contrast, when we talk about market efficiency, we are interested not in the form of the structural relationship between risk and expected return but rather in the precision with which the market prices securities in relation to its structure, whatever that structure may be. If new information becomes known about a particular company, how quickly do market participants find out about the information and buy or sell the securities of the company on the basis of the information? How quickly do the prices of the securities adjust to reflect the new information? If prices respond to all relevant new information in a rapid fashion, we can say the market is relatively efficient. If, instead, the information disseminates rather slowly throughout the market, and if investors take time in analyzing the information and reacting, and possibly overreacting to it, prices may deviate from values based on a careful analysis of all available relevant information. Such a market could be characterized as being relatively inefficient.

You might ask, since on average investors are clearly not fully informed about all securities and perhaps not about even a single security, how could the market reach a state where the prices of all securities fully reflect all information that is both relevant and available? The answer to this question is that prices are not established by the *consensus* of all investors. Prices are set by those marginal investors who actively trade in the stock. An advocate of the notion that the stock market is relatively efficient would argue that there exists an "army" of intelligent, well-informed security analysts, arbitragers, and traders, who literally spend their lives hunting for securities which are mispriced based on currently available information. These professionals are armed with computers, and they subscribe to data base management services which are tied into their computers. They have at their fingertips up-to-date information on thousands of companies, and they process this information using state of the art analytical techniques. These people can access, assimilate, and act on information very quickly. In their intense search for mispriced securities, professional investors may police the market so efficiently that they drive the prices of all issues to fully reflect all information that is "knowable" about a company, its industry, or the general economy.

Whether or not this is the case, is a controversial issue. Until recently, the weight of the evidence supported the notion that the market was relatively efficient in pricing securities. However, studies recently released have cast some doubt on the validity of the efficient market hypothesis. In this chapter, we will discuss the concept of market efficiency, its importance as an issue, and the characteristics of an efficient market. In the next chapter, we will examine some of the evidence on both sides of the issue.

FORMS OF THE EFFICIENT MARKET HYPOTHESIS

The issue is not merely black or white. The market is neither strictly efficient nor strictly inefficient. The question is one of degree. Just how efficient is the market?

One way to measure the efficiency of the market is to ask what types of information, encompassed by the total set of all available information, are reflected in securities prices. The outer circle of Figure 22.1 represents all information relevant to the valuation of a particular stock which is currently "knowable." This includes publicly available information about the company, its industry, and the domestic and world economy. It also includes information which is privately held by select groups of individuals. Within the outer circle, is a second circle which represents that part of the information set that has been publicly announced and is therefore publicly available. The information outside of this set, therefore, is inside or private information. Within the second circle, there is yet a third circle which represents a subset of the information that is publicly available. This third circle represents any information relevant to the valuation of the stock which can be learned by analyzing the history of the market price of the stock. For example, has the stock been rising or falling and does this have any implications for the future?

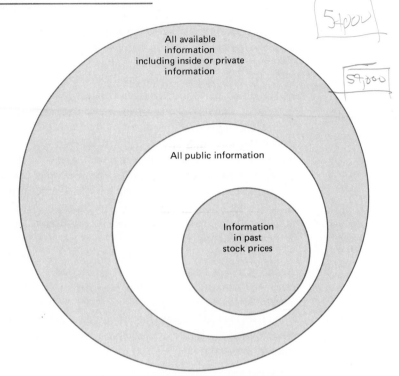

FIGURE 22.1 Subsets of available information for a given stock.

There are three forms of the efficient market hypothesis. Under each, different types of information are assumed to be reflected in securities' prices.[1]

Under the ***weak form of the efficient market hypothesis,*** stock prices are assumed to reflect any information that may be contained in the *past history of the stock price* itself. For example, suppose there exists a seasonal pattern in stock prices such that stock prices fall on the last trading day of the year and then rise on the first trading day of the following year. Under the weak form of the hypothesis, the market will come to recognize this and price the phenomenon away. Anticipating the rise in price on the first day of the year, traders will attempt to get in at the very start of trading on the first day. Their attempts to get in will cause the increase in price to occur in the first minutes of the first day. Intelligent traders will then recognize that to beat the rest of the market, they will have to get in late on the last day of the previous year when stock prices have historically fallen. Their attempts to buy late in the day will act to support prices and reduce the extent of the fall on the last trading day of the year. This process of attempting to get in earlier and earlier will, of course, continue until the entire year-end pattern of a dip and rally is eliminated from the price series. Other, more complex patterns in the price series will be de-

---

[1]The three forms of the efficient market hypothesis were first suggested by Fama (1970).

tected and eliminated in similar fashion until it becomes impossible to predict the future course of the series by analyzing its past behavior. Once we have reached this state, the weaker form of the efficient market hypothesis will be satisfied.

Under the ***semistrong form of the efficient market hypothesis,*** *all publicly available information* is presumed to be reflected in securities' prices. This includes information in the stock price series as well as information in the firm's accounting reports, the reports of competing firms, announced information relating to the state of the economy, and any other publicly available information relevant to the valuation of the firm.

The ***strong form of the efficient market hypothesis*** takes the notion of market efficiency to the ultimate extreme. If you believe in this form, you believe *all information* is reflected in stock prices. This includes private, or inside information as well as that which is publicly available. Under this form, those who acquire inside information act on it, buying or selling the stock. Their actions affect the price of the stock, and the price quickly adjusts to reflect the inside information.

As you move from the weak form of the hypothesis to the strong form, various types of investment analysis become ineffective in discriminating between profitable and unprofitable investments.

If the weak form is valid, technical analysis or charting becomes ineffective. A chartist plots movements in the price of the stock over time. When the stock price movements take certain patterns, this implies to the chartist that the stock may take off in a particular direction in the future. In effect, the chartist is using various techniques to analyze the past series of stock prices in order to predict the future of the series. If the weak form is in effect, there is no information in the past series which is useful in predicting the future. Any information that was there has been analyzed by thousands of watchful chartists everywhere. They have acted on what they found, and the stock price has settled to a level which reflects all the useful information embedded in past stock prices. To find under- or overvalued stocks, you have to resort to some other form of analysis which is based on information other than the past price series.

If the semistrong form of the efficient market hypothesis is in effect, no form of analysis will help you attain superior returns as long as the analysis is based on publicly available information. This means, for example, an analysis of the firm's accounting statements is now ineffective in discriminating between profitable and unprofitable investments. These statements have already been analyzed by thousands of other analysts before you. The other analysts have acted on what they found, and the current price of the stock now reflects all the relevant information which can be found in the accounting statements. The same is true for all other sources of public information. Traditional security analysis as well as technical analysis is now useless as a weapon to "beat the market." You have to resort to attempts to uncover, or purchase, private information if you are going to distinguish yourself as an investor.

All is lost if the market is strong form efficient. Under this form those who acquire inside information act on it and quickly force the price to reflect the information. Allegedly, the initial acquisition of new pieces of this information is largely a matter of chance, and since stock prices already reflect the existing inventory of inside information, efforts to seek out inside information to beat the market are ill-advised. Under this ultimate form of the hypothesis, the professional investor truly has a zero market value because no form of search or processing of information will consistently produce superior returns.

THE SIGNIFICANCE OF THE EFFICIENT MARKET HYPOTHESIS

Why should you care if the market is efficient?

If you are going to take a job in the securities industry, this is a crucial issue for you. If your fellow analysts have been so proficient at doing their jobs that mispriced securities are, for all intents and purposes nonexistent, it may be impossible for you to be effective in doing what you are hired to do. You may well be hired to find mispriced securities so you can produce an additional increment of return on the portfolios that you are managing. If the market is truly efficient, in making it that way, professional investors have performed a valuable service for society.

The investment decisions of the managers of business firms are based to a large extent on signals they get from the capital market. If the market is efficient, the cost of obtaining capital will accurately reflect the prospects for each firm. This means the firms with the most attractive investment opportunities will be able to obtain capital at a fair price which reflects their true potential. The "right" investments will be made, and society will be better off. To the extent that professional security analysts played a role in making it this way, they have served society well, and the total benefit of their services may be very large.

The *marginal* benefit of any one analyst is another matter, however. If the market is efficient, any one financial institution can fire all their analysts without affecting its expected investment performance. Rather than doing analysis, they can select their investments at random, knowing each security selected has been priced correctly by the remaining analysts. In an efficient market, the *total* product of professional investors may be positive, but the *marginal* product of any one analyst is close to zero. Unfortunately, the amount any one firm is willing to pay an analyst is based on the marginal product. Thus, unless you can convince people the market is inefficient, you will make very little money as a security analyst. If the market is truly efficient and you happen to land a job as an analyst, your success in your profession will be a matter of chance. Your expected probability of "beating" the market in any 1 year will be 50 percent, and there is nothing you, personally, can do to improve these odds.

Suppose instead, you take a job as a corporate financial manager. Of what significance is market efficiency to you then?

Companies frequently repurchase their own stock because they feel it has been undervalued by the market. If the market is strong form efficient, this rationale is untenable. The stock is never undervalued by the market. If you, as a manager, disagree with the valuation, it may be because your estimate of the company's prospects are overly optimistic. Perhaps you have neglected to consider carefully the implications of some macroeconomic variable, such as the future course of interest rates, on the future prospects and valuation of your firm.

Frequently, investment projects are postponed or financing is done with debt rather than with equity because management feels the entire stock market is depressed. If by the term *depressed* they mean stock prices have fallen below their intrinsic value based on available public information, this rationale is also inappropriate if the market is semistrong form efficient. In a semistrong form efficient market stocks are never "depressed" in the sense their values are less than the present value of the best estimate, based on publicly available information, of the future stream of dividends. In an efficient market, the cost of equity capital to the firm is both fair and reasonable in bear as well as bull markets. Future prospects may not appear as good in bear markets, but in an efficient market the prospects upon which stock prices are set are based on rational analysis of all publicly available information.

In an efficient market, you can also question the rationale for including complexities, such as call provisions in bond indentures. A call provision gives the firm a call option to buy the bonds back from the bondholders at a specific price. This call option held by the stockholders has an implicit market value. The market value of a callable bond will be less than the market value of a comparable noncallable bond by the market value of this call option. If the only rationale for including the call provision is to provide the firm with the opportunity to reissue the bond at a lower interest cost should interest rates fall, this rationale should be questioned if the market is taken to be efficient. In an efficient market, the callable bond will be priced as the difference between the market value of an identical noncallable issue and the market value of the call option held by the stockholders. Both market values will be based on the best available forecast of the future course of interest rates. Given the firm's forecast can't be better than the best forecast available, the firm is no better off by including the call provision in the bond indenture than it would be by selling the bond as a noncallable issue. You can look at it this way; if the call option is priced correctly by the market, the firm should be indifferent toward buying it (including it in the bond indenture) or not buying it.

You will frequently see advertisements by firms announcing that the firm has achieved a remarkable growth record in earnings and dividends. These advertisements frequently appear in financial publications such as *The Wall Street Journal*. If these advertisements were placed to cast a favorable light on the firm's common stock so as to support its market price, the money to purchase the ad was unwisely spent, given that the market is semistrong form efficient. The information contained in the ad has already been publicly disclosed, fully analyzed by the army of professional analysts, and is also reflected in the stock price. If the market is efficient, the ad will have absolutely no impact on the market value of the common stock.

Managers sometimes express concern over the effect that a change in accounting procedure will have on reported earnings per share. If the market is semistrong form efficient, they should not be concerned. Informed, rational analysts will adjust for different accounting procedures used by different firms and assess prospects based on standardized numbers. The adjustment in accounting technique will have no effect on the opinions of those analysts or on the price of the firm's common stock.

As you can see, the issue of market efficiency has some important practical implications for you even if you don't become one of the members of the army of professionals who allegedly enforce market efficiency. Many important business decisions are based on rationales which implicitly assume that the securities markets price inefficiently. In this chapter and the next, we will investigate the accuracy of this assumption.

RISK AND EXPECTED RETURN IN AN EFFICIENT MARKET

As we said, the efficient market hypothesis doesn't assume or imply any particular theory relating to the structure of stock prices. However, since we are familiar with it, in this particular discussion we will assume all investors invest in mean variance–efficient portfolios, and the structure of stock prices is that of the simple form of the capital asset pricing model.

Let's assume first that the strong form of the efficient market hypothesis is in effect, which means security prices reflect all the information available and relevant to valuation. Suppose you are Super Analyst and you gather all the relevant information to the valuation of the securities of each firm. For each firm you process and analyze the information using state of the art techniques to estimate the expected return and the beta factor for each security in the market. If you did this and the market were strong form efficient, your plot might look like Figure 22.2. Note that

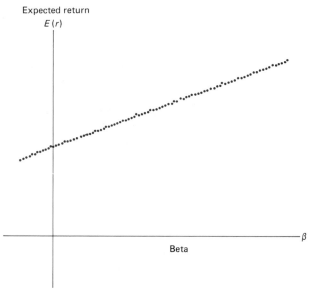

FIGURE 22.2 Risk and return in an efficient market.

securities are priced so that each, based on an analysis of all available information, has an expected rate of return which is consistent with its risk level and the CAPM. Viewed from the perspective of the total information set, the risk-return relationship is perfectly crisp and clean. Given the CAPM structure of security prices, the market is pricing efficiently with respect to that structure.

Now suppose you make the same estimates of risk and expected return, but this time you confine your analysis to publicly available information. Your estimates of beta, for example, are based on sampling from the past series of rates of return to the securities and the market index as well as company characteristics such as leverage, size, and earnings stability. Again, you employ state of the art techniques of analysis, but the information you feed into the techniques is all publicly available information. Your plot may now look something like Figure 22.3. The relationship between your estimates of risk and expected return is no longer crisp and clean. Securities are positioned above and below the security market line. If you were an analyst who did a creditable job of estimating risk and expected return based on publicly available information, it would appear to you that securities like the one labeled A were undervalued; their expected rates of return are excessive, given their level of risk. Securities like B appear overvalued; their expected rates of return are inadequate. The market appears to be inefficient to you. Given the results of your analysis, you might even think that you deserve to be paid an impressive salary,

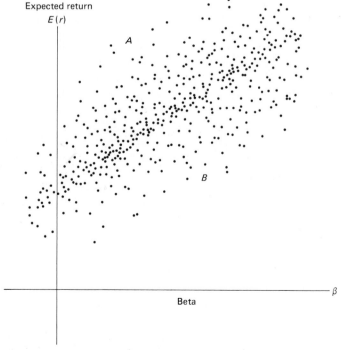

FIGURE 22.3 Risk and return in an inefficient market.

because it seems obvious that you can easily discriminate between profitable and unprofitable investments.

In reality, however, securities *A* and *B* are not mispriced. You are the one that is inefficient, not the market. The reason you think the market is inefficient is because you are basing your analysis on an incomplete set of information. In fact, both *A* and *B* have expected returns which are fair and reasonable if you examine them from the perspective of both private as well as public information. You might be surprised to discover that if you put together a portfolio of "undervalued" securities like *A*, the average realized returns on this portfolio are no more likely to be greater than average than a portfolio of "overvalued" securities like *B*. If your salary is based on your realized performance, it is not likely to remain impressive for long.

Now let's shift gears and assume the market is only semistrong form efficient. In this case, if you do your analysis based on publicly available information alone, your plot will look like Figure 22.2. However, if you are able to acquire private or inside information, your plot will appear as in Figure 22.3. Now you really have identified over- and undervalued securities, and you do deserve to make a lot of money as an analyst. Portfolios of stocks like *A* are, in fact, likely to outperform other portfolios in their risk class.

If we could locate Super Analyst, we could obtain plots like these and resolve the issue of how efficient the market is. Unfortunately, he or she doesn't exist, so we have to settle the issue some other way.

As it turns out, an efficient market exhibits certain behavioral traits or characteristics. We can examine the behavior of the real market to see if it conforms to these characteristics. If it doesn't, we can conclude that the market is inefficient.

If the market is efficient, it should exhibit the following characteristics:

1. Security prices should respond quickly and accurately to the receipt of new information that is relevant to valuation.

2. The change in security prices from one period to the next should be random in the sense that the change in price which takes place today should be unrelated to the change in price that occurred yesterday or any other day in the past.[2]

3. It should be impossible to discriminate between profitable (in the sense that the returns are greater than what you would normally expect to see, given the risk) and unprofitable investments in a future period based on any of the characteristics of these investments which can be known in the current period. It should be

---

[2] That random movements in stock prices are consistent with an efficient market was proven by Samuelson (1965). It should be noted that this is only *strictly* true in a market where equilibrium expected rates of return are also serially uncorrelated. In most multiperiod equilibrium models, you would expect to find some serial correlation in equilibrium prices and expected rates of return. Within the context of these models, it is technically correct to say that market efficiency is consistent with the case where future *deviations* from equilibrium rates of return can't be predicted on the basis of past *deviations* from equilibrium rates of return. Moreover, in a more general context, an increase in the value of a levered firm today will reduce its debt-to-equity ratio. This may result in a lower required and expected rate of return tomorrow. Thus we may have a slight tendency for negative correlation in stock returns even in an efficient market.

impossible, for example, for us to construct a trading rule that utilizes information available at time t which enables us to predict the most profitable investments of $t + 1$.

4. If we separate investors who are knowledgeable from those who are not, we should discover we are unable to find a significant difference between the average investment performance of the two groups. Moreover, it should be the case that differences in the performance of individual investors within each group should be insignificant. In other words, differences in performance between groups and within groups should be due to chance, and not something systematic and permanent like differences in ability to find information not already reflected in stock prices.

QUICK AND ACCURATE RESPONSE
TO NEW INFORMATION

Every day a rich flow of bits and pieces of information pours into the market. The information pertains to general economic conditions, weather, strikes, shortages of raw materials, international tension, and product demand. This information is relevant to security valuation, and it affects the prices of securities.

If the market is efficient, security prices should respond to the information as soon as it is received. Naturally, the response can't be instantaneous, but the gap between the receipt of the information and the reaction of the price should reflect the best available procedures and techniques for receiving and processing the information.

The reaction of market prices should also be unbiased. The initial reaction should accurately reflect the true implications of the information on the value of the security. There should be no need for a subsequent correction, for example, of an overreaction to a piece of information.

Figure 22.4 presents three possible scenarios for the reaction of a stock market price to the receipt of a single piece of information. This is an idealized example, since we assume that in all the days plotted on the horizontal axis, only a single piece of information is received which is relevant to the valuation of the stock. The information is received on the day labeled 0. The information is positive and increases the best available estimate of the value of the stock from $30 to $33.

First, consider the solid line. This represents the path taken by the stock in an efficient market. In this case, there is an immediate increase in the value of the stock to $33 on the day the information is received. No further changes take place in the value of the stock because we have assumed no additional new information is received by the market.

Now consider the broken line. This line depicts the path that the stock might take in an inefficient market. The story behind the path might go as follows. The information is released. It is acquired by the national offices of several large broker-

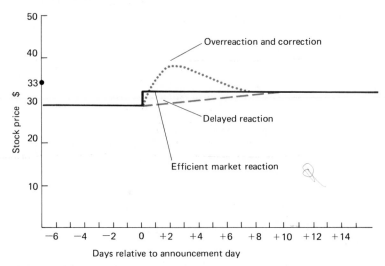

FIGURE 22.4 Stock price reaction to new information in an efficient and inefficient market.

age houses. They wire the information to their local offices and begin analyzing the implications of the information for the companies and the stocks affected. Local brokers receive the information and begin making their own, less sophisticated analyses. They may inform their more important clients about the information without drawing grounded conclusions. A few people might initiate trading the stock, driving the price up slightly in the first day. After a lag of one or more days, the analysts employed by the investment institutions release reports showing the information warrants a significant upward revision in the intrinsic value of the stock. Brokers inform their clients that the stock is undervalued at its current price. Decisions are made as to whether the stock should be purchased and if so, how the money should be raised. Orders flow into the market in the course of the next several days, causing the stock to rise gradually to its new intrinsic value of $33.

The dotted line represents still another scenario which is consistent with an inefficient market. In this case those investors who are the most optimistic about the implications of the information on the value of the stock either get the information first or are prepared to act on its first. They are of the impression that the new intrinsic value of the stock is above $33, and their buying activity begins driving the stock above that level. The best estimate of the new value is, of course, $33, and eventually this view prevails. More sophisticated investors begin selling the stock causing a correction in the price back down to the $33 level.

If the market is truly efficient, neither of the last two scenarios should be evident in the real market. If we were to observe the reaction of stock prices to the release of quarterly earnings reports, for example, there should be no evidence of a lag in the reaction or a tendency to overreact and then subsequently correct.

RANDOM CHANGES IN STOCK PRICES

If the market is efficient, the change in the price of a security which is taking place today should be completely unrelated to the change in price that took place yesterday or any other day in the past. The crucial condition that must hold is the *expected* change in the price on any given day must be unrelated to the past series of changes that have already taken place.

Momentum, for example, is a characteristic inconsistent with an efficient market. If once started on a downward slide, stock prices develop a propensity to continue sliding, the expected change in price today would, in fact, be related to the price changes that have occurred in the past. Given a series of past negative price changes, we would lower our expectation for the price change that we are going to see for today.

Why should security prices move randomly from one day to the next in an efficient market?

If the market is efficient, today's stock price should already reflect all the information that is both relevant to the valuation of the stock and "knowable." By knowable we mean all information that has been announced and can be predicted based on past announcements. The only information not reflected in the stock price is that which hasn't been received and can't be predicted to be received. This kind of information, by its very nature, must come into the market in an unpredictable, random fashion. As the market price responds instantly and accurately to its receipt, the price itself changes in a random, unpredictable fashion over time.

You might think, at this point, some important economic series have definite seasonal or cyclical patterns. Gross national product is an example of such a series. If GNP exhibits a cyclical pattern and stock prices instantly respond to announced changes in GNP, why don't stock prices exhibit a mimicking cyclical pattern? The answer is that stock prices don't respond to *changes* in GNP; they respond to errors in the market's *forecast* of the change in GNP. In an efficient market, the cyclical pattern will be recognized, identified, and modeled. Stock prices are set on the basis of the best possible forecast of the next GNP number. Suppose that the best available estimate of the next change in GNP is +$10 billion. There will be no reaction to the announced change in GNP unless it turns out to be different from the forecast of +$10 billion implicit in stock prices. The market will react only to errors in its forecast. These errors, themselves, must be random. If they are not, they can be modeled statistically and incorporated into an improved forecast. If the market is employing the best available forecast in setting the prices, the errors will be random, and the response of prices to the errors will be random as well.

Consider the three scenarios of Figure 22.4. In the case of the broken curve, the change in price that is occurring on day +2 can be functionally related to the change in price that took place the day before. The stock price is rising on day +2, *because* the stock price reaction was incomplete on day +1. The two changes are connected. If it takes a matter of days for the market to complete its reaction to new information, a positive price change today should increase our expected value for the price change that will take place tomorrow. Tomorrow we will expect to see a continuation of the reaction that began today.

In the same sense, in the case of the dotted curve, the stock price is falling in days $+3$, $+4$, and $+5$ *because* it overreacted in days $+1$ and $+2$. These changes are not independent; they are, in fact, connected causally. In the presence of such reversal pattens, a series of large positive price changes should cause us to lower our expectation for the price change that will take place tomorrow.

Now consider the solid path which is consistent with market efficiency. A single impulse of information induces a single instantaneous price change in the stock. No further changes will take place until the next unpredictable impulse of information. The next change is totally unrelated to the change that took place at day 0. Prices change in a series of unrelated, unpredictable steps.

FAILURE OF SIMULATED TRADING STRATEGIES

If the market is efficient, there should be no way to discriminate between profitable and unprofitable investments based on information that is currently available. A *profitable* investment is one that is expected to produce a rate of return that is higher than it should be, given an appropriate benchmark.

One way to test for market efficiency is to test whether a specific trading rule, or investment strategy, would have produced profitable rates of return in the past. Suppose, for example, you think the market is slow to react to the announcement of new information, such as the release of the firm's earnings reports. In this case, your investment strategy might be to always invest in the top 10 companies that have reported the highest dollar increases in earnings per share for the year. To test your hypothesis, you go back to a past period of time and try to simulate the results of investing on the basis of this trading rule. The question is: "Would this strategy have produced profitable returns in the past?" If the market is truly efficient, all strategies should fail in this regard.

Your first problem in testing any strategy is defining what you mean by a profitable rate of return. By profitable you must mean that the expected, or realized, rate of return is greater than what the investment should have, given some benchmark. If you chose the capital asset pricing model as a benchmark, the expected rate of return should be the rate given by the beta factor of the investment and the security market line. If you chose the arbitrage pricing theory as a benchmark, the expected rate of return should be that given the risk-free rate and the sum of the products of the factor betas of the investment and the factor prices. Your test of the performance of the trading rule, in this sense, can be viewed as a joint test of two hypotheses:

1. You have chosen the correct benchmark to measure profitability.
2. The market is efficient relative to the information employed by your trading rule.

In constructing your simulation experiment, you have to be careful about a number of other potential pitfalls.

First, you must be sure you are formulating your investment strategy on the basis of information which is actually available at the time you buy or sell the securities. If your strategy is to invest in the stocks that have the greatest dollar increases in earnings per share for the previous year, in simulating the results of executing this strategy in the past, you must be sure you have the earnings number for the year at the time you assume you buy the stock. If you "buy" the stock at the beginning of 1976 on the basis of the difference in the 1975 and 1974 earnings numbers, you are biasing your test in favor of the trading rule because the final quarter of 1975 earnings typically is not reported until February 1976. Since you are investing in the 10 firms with the greatest growth in earnings per share, the final quarter for each of the firms was probably unexpectedly good. Even in an efficient market, the reaction to the final quarter wouldn't occur until after the beginning of the year. By buying all the stocks at the beginning of 1976, your simulated portfolio will enjoy the increase in market value that you know is coming in the vicinity of the earnings release date. Your trading rule will show profitable returns not because of a lag in market reaction to new information but rather because your simulation assumed you had access to information (the final quarter's earnings) that may have been available to no one at the time you executed your strategy. The appropriate way to test this rule would be to buy the stocks only after you could determine which 10 actually had the greatest earnings growth. This is when the *last* candidate actually reports its earnings number.

In testing the profitability of your investment strategy, it's also important to consider the costs involved in finding and processing the required information as well as the differential costs involved in transacting in the market. In a passive investment strategy, you would invest at the very beginning of the period and hold on to your instruments until the very end. In the strategy discussed, you would completely reconstruct the portfolio at the end of every year or at the end of every quarter. In selling your investments of the previous period and buying your investments of the next period, you would not only incur round trip commissions, but you would also be subject to the capital gains tax, possibly the short-term capital gains tax. The extra commissions and extra taxes may serve to neutralize completely the performance of your trading rule.

You also have to determine whether any extra return produced by your strategy is due to chance or due to your having successfully exploited some systematic inefficiency in pricing by the market. To do this, you must determine whether the magnitude of the extra return is significant in a statistical sense.

The issue of whether the extra return is merely compensation for bearing extra risk must also be addressed. This gets back to the question of selecting the appropriate benchmark. Even if you have employed information that was actually available at the time you made your investments, even if you have factored in the additional costs associated with transacting and taxes, and even if you still find a statistically significant increment of extra return associated with your trading rule, you must be prepared to defend what you mean by *extra*. Have you selected the right pricing model? Have you selected the proper indices? Have you measured risk correctly?

After allowing for all these factors, if you can find trading rules that are capable of producing superior returns, you have found evidence that the market is inefficient with respect to the information employed by those trading rules.

MEDIOCRITY IN THE PERFORMANCE OF INFORMED INVESTORS

If security prices don't reflect all available information, those investors who are fully informed should be able to construct portfolios that produce superior returns. If the true market pricing structure is that of the capital asset pricing model and if security prices reflect publicly available information alone, traders who possess private information should see investments positioned relative to the security market line as in Figure 22.3. They should be able to construct portfolios that are also positioned above the security market line. If we use the CAPM-based risk-adjusted performance measures to assess their performance, we should find their performance is superior relative to that of other investors.

If, on the other hand, the market is efficient, no investment is truly positioned above or below the security market line. If you see an investment in such a position, it is because you are estimating its expected return and risk on the basis of less than the complete set of available information. You may construct a portfolio composed of securities that you *think* are above the security market line, but since their true expected returns are all positioned on the line, your risk adjusted investment performance will be indistinguishable from that of any other investor. It should also be true that, within the group of professional investors, there should be no significant differences in their performance. Even if some are more intelligent, or have more resources, than others, if security prices reflect all relevant information, intelligence and capital will be ineffective in searching for undervalued securities.

Thus, we can assess the efficiency of the market by first separating those investors who are likely to be most informed and then measuring their investment performance. If these investors exhibit records of superior performance, they must be investing on the basis of information that is both relevant and not reflected in security prices.

Professional investors are likely to be most informed. They are trained in security and portfolio analysis, and they spend their working days searching for, and analyzing, information. Thus, in attempting to resolve the question of market efficiency, we should determine whether professionals as a group are distinguished in terms of their performance and whether we can find significant differences in the performance of individual professional investors.

Once again our test is based on a joint hypothesis. We must first select the appropriate benchmark. This means we must make a hypothesis about the nature of the pricing structure. If we assume the CAPM, we may measure performance relative to an estimate of the security market line. Having made this assumption, we can then test the hypothesis that the market is efficient.

You may already have a prior opinion about this aspect of the investigation. You may have listened to many professional investors on "talk shows" on television or have read books written by investors who have amazing records of performance. If we take these records as being accurate, how can the market possibly be efficient?

Literally millions of people invest in the securities markets. Suppose we take all these people, put them in a gigantic stadium, and have them flip coins. We will declare flipping a head as winning and flipping a tail as losing. Even if each is flipping a fair coin, we will find individual "flippers" with unbelievable records of success and failure. There will be some who flip more that 20 heads in a row. These individuals, convinced of their superior flipping ability will go on television to tell others of their amazing success. Those who flip 20 *tails* in a row will hide in shame. Since all the head flippers will surface to expose themselves, it will appear as though winning is not a mere matter of chance. To determine whether it is, we would have to do a careful statistical analysis of the performance of the flippers. This is what we intend to do with respect to the performance of professional investors.

SUMMARY

In a perfectly efficient market, security prices reflect all information that is knowable and relevant. There are no undervalued or overvalued securities. Whatever the pricing structure of the market may be, the market is priced perfectly with respect to that structure.

There are degrees of market efficiency, each specifying the type of information that is reflected in security prices. If the market is *weak form* efficient, then security prices reflect any information pertaining to the security's future expected return that can be obtained by examining the security's past price history. If the weak form holds, technical analysis, or charting, will be ineffective. If the market is *semistrong form* efficient, security prices reflect all publicly available information. Among other things, this includes the firm's accounting statements and announced statistics pertaining to the general economy. If the semistrong form holds, both technical and fundamental security analyses are ineffective. To beat the market, the analyst must seek out private information. The extreme case is the *strong form* of the efficient market hypothesis. Here all information that is knowable is reflected in security prices. If this is true, no form of analysis will be effective in discriminating profitable from unprofitable investments.

To determine whether the market is, in fact, efficient, we must examine its behavior. An efficient market will exhibit the following behavioral characteristics:

1. Security prices should respond quickly and accurately to the receipt of new information that is relevant to valuation.
2. The change in security prices from one period to the next should be random.
3. It should be impossible to discriminate between profitable and unprofitable investments in a future period based on any of the characteristics of these investments that can be known in the current period.

4. If we separate investors who are knowledgeable from those who are not, we should discover that we are unable to find a significant difference between the average investment performance of the two groups. Moreover, it should be the case that differences in the performance of individual investors within each group would be insignificant.

In the next chapter, we shall examine the extent to which the real market exhibits these characteristics.

QUESTION SET 1

1. A rationale that is frequently given for the issuance of callable debt by a firm is that the firm would like to be able to save money if interest rates should fall. The call provision in the debt allows the firm to call in the debt and then issue new debt at a lower interest rate. If markets are efficient, what is the fallacy in this argument?

2. Suppose you discovered a systematic relationship between the price-earnings ratios of stocks and the performance of stocks. In other words, knowledge of a firm's price-earnings ratio proved helpful in predicting which stocks would show superior performance. Would this evidence be consistent with any of three versions of the efficient markets hypothesis?

3. If the market adheres to the strong form of the efficient markets hypothesis, what is the implication for the usefulness of the activities of gathering and analyzing data about companies? What sort of logical paradox seems to result?

4. If you believe that the market is efficient with respect to one of the information sets mentioned in the chapter, does this necessarily imply that you believe the market is inefficient with respect to one of the other information sets? Explain.

5. For each of the following kinds of information, indicate which form of the efficient markets hypothesis is supported *if* that information *is* reflected in security prices:
   a. Government-released data on the money supply
   b. A corporate quarterly earnings report
   c. A public release of information from the Securities and Exchange Commissions on insider trading
   d. Confidential discussions of a corporate board of directors on dividend policy
   e. A history of a bond's prices

6. Suppose there is a consistent seasonal movement in stock prices. Why might this be inconsistent with the efficient markets hypothesis?

7. Consider the following statement: "In an efficient market, today's price will have no systematic relationship to tomorrow's price." Is this true or false? Explain.

8. Refer to Figure 22.4 and the solid line on the graph depicting the efficient market scenario. Plots of actual stock prices show substantially more variability than this idealized plot. What is being assumed in Figure 22.4 which accounts for this difference?

9. What does it mean to use the capital asset pricing model as a benchmark to test a trading strategy?

10. Suppose you follow and compare two recommended trading strategies over several years. Does this necessarily imply that the higher-return strategy is a superior strategy? Explain.

11. Can you think of any readily available sources of data on the investment performance of professional investment analysts?

12. Tests of market efficiency are often referred to as *joint tests* of two hypotheses. Explain the meaning of this. Further, try to speculate on the difficulty this poses for tests of market efficiency.

13. Suppose you know several individuals who devised and implemented several trading rules or strategies based on publicly available information. They show you their returns, which are much higher than what would have been obtainable by investing in a broad market index. Would this information alone cast doubt on the efficiency of the market?

QUESTION SET 2

1. You are a new portfolio manager who, after your first successful trading day on the job, goes out with your new boss for a celebratory drink. At the tavern, you argue strongly for the strong form of the efficient market hypothesis. Your boss's eyes narrow, and you begin to get nervous. What is strange about your argument?

2. Rule 10b-5 in the securities law forbids insider trading. There has been regular prosecution against individuals who have traded with inside information about their firms. What conclusion can you draw from this, and how does this information affect which form of the efficient theory hypothesis you might adopt?

3. You know the net asset value of your firm is $2.5 million. The market believes it is only worth $2 million. Given this situation, and assuming the debt/equity ratio in the firm is within normal limits, would the firm prefer to do financing with debt or equity, and why? Can you also explain your answer with the Figure below?

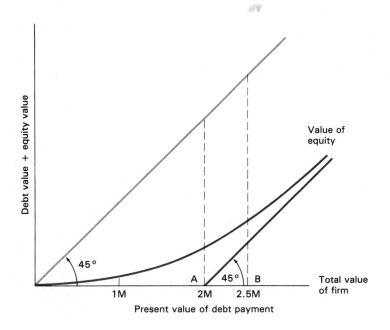

4. If the market is weak form efficient, what do the security prices reflect?

5. Assume that due to the explosion of computers and the expert training of security analysts, the market, as confirmed by unbiased studies, has been shown to be 95 percent efficient. Investment firms have thus decided to retire all the portfolio managers and let random choice govern the security selection process. What mistake is implicit in this action?

ANSWERS TO QUESTION SET 2

1. If you believe the strong form of the efficient market hypothesis, you believe that *all information* is reflected in stock prices, including inside private information. Under this form, those who acquire inside information quickly act on it and force the price to reflect the information. Hence efforts to seek out inside information and process it in order to "beat" the market are futile, and the professional investor has little value.

2. Insider trading occurs when people are trading based upon private information for personal gain in the security. The fact that this does occur quite regularly and that people do make money on inside deals would lead you to reject the strong form of the market hypothesis.

3. The current stock net asset value of $2.5 million when the market is valuing the stock at only $2 million indicates an undervalued firm. The stock price is *depressed,* meaning its price has fallen below its intrinsic value based on available public information. Since the market is not efficient in this case, the cost of equity capital is too great, because the stock is undervalued. The cost of debt would also be undervalued, but to a lesser extent.

   Depicted graphically, the market has valued the firm at point A, and the firm has an actual value at point B. The difference between the horizontal line and the curved line represents the value of equity in the total value of the firm. The difference between the curved line and the 45-degree line represents the value of the debt. In comparing the relative under-valuing of both the debt and equity from point A to point B, note that both debt and equity are undervalued, but, in percentage terms, the equity is more undervalued.

4. Under the weak form of the efficient market hypothesis, security price reflects the past history of the stock price itself.

5. The explosion of analyses has contributed to market efficiency, and the efficiency is thus predicated upon the continuing services of the force of analysts requires their employment to keep it efficient.

REFERENCES

BARON, D. P., "Information, Investment Behavior, and Efficient Portfolios," *Journal of Financial and Quantitative Analysis* (September 1974).

BLACK, F., "Random Walk and Portfolio Management," *Financial Analysts Journal* (March–April 1971).

BREALEY, R. A., *An Introduction to Risk and Return from Common Stocks.* Cambridge, Mass.: MIT Press, 1969.

FAMA, E. F., "Efficient Capital Markets: A Review of Theory and Empirical Work," *Journal of Finance* (May 1970).

GRANGER, C. W. J., "The Random Walk Misunderstood?" *Financial Analysts Journal* (May–June 1970).

GROSSMAN, S. J., "On the Efficiency of Competitive Stock Markets Where Trades Have Diverse Information," *Journal of Finance* (May 1976).

GROSSMAN, S. J., and STIGLITZ, J. E., "On the Impossibility of Informationally Efficient Markets," *American Economic Review* (June 1980).

JAFFE, J. F., and WINKLER, R. L., "Optimal Speculation Against an Efficient Market," *Journal of Finance* (March 1976).

LAFFER, A. B., and RANSON, R. D., "Some Practical Applications of the Efficient Market Concept," *Financial Management* (Summer 1979).

MALKIEL, B. G., and FINSTENBERG, P. B., "A Winning Strategy for an Efficient Market," *Journal of Portfolio Management* (Summer 1978).

PIPER, T. R., and FRUHAN, W. E., "Is Your Stock Worth Its Market Price?" *Harvard Business Review* (May–June 1981).

SAMUELSON, P. A., "Proof That Properly Anticipated Prices Fluctuate Randomly," *Industrial Management Review* (Spring 1965).

VERRECCHIA, R. E., "Consensus Beliefs, Information Acquisition and Market Information Efficiency," *American Economic Review* (December 1980).

C H A P T E R

23

MARKET EFFICIENCY: THE EVIDENCE

As discussed in the last chapter, the issue of market efficiency is important to you irrespective of whether you intend to become a practicing financial analyst or take a position in a nonfinancial corporation. The question of market efficiency is highly controversial. Recently published evidence has added more fuel to the unsettled debate. In this chapter we will take a balanced perspective, examining evidence on both sides of the issue. As we discussed in the last chapter, an efficient securities market exhibits four behavioral traits or characteristics:

1. Security prices respond rapidly and accurately to new information.
2. The changes in security prices should be random.
3. Trading rules fail to produce superior returns in simulation experiments.
4. Professional investors fail to produce superior returns individually or as a group.

The extent to which the real market exhibits these characteristics is an empirical question. In this chapter, we will examine some of the studies that have addressed the issue of market efficiency.

DO SECURITY PRICES RESPOND RAPIDLY AND ACCURATELY TO THE RECEIPT OF NEW INFORMATION?

Measuring Stock Price Response

A large number of studies have been directed at examining the nature of the market's reaction to events such as the announcement of earnings, dividends, and stock splits.

In most of these studies, an effort is made to estimate the stock's excess returns in the vicinity of the event. The excess return in a given period is defined as the difference between the stock's actual return for the period and what you would expect the stock to produce, given the stock's characteristic line and the performance of the market for the period.

The first step in the process is to estimate the stock's characteristic line. This is usually done by sampling in a period other than the one surrounding the event. If you are going to examine the stock price response to the event on a day-by-day basis, you would estimate the characteristic line using daily rates of return. For example, if we call the day of the event day 0 and we are going to examine the response of the stock from 10 days before to 10 days after the event (-10 to $+10$), we might estimate the characteristic line in the period from 70 days before to 11 days before (-70 to -11). Suppose we do this, and we fit the characteristic line as in Figure 23.1.

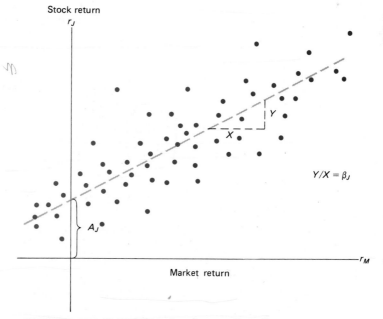

FIGURE 23.1 Estimating the characteristic line.

The characteristic line gives us an expectation of what the stock's return should be on a particular day, given that the market has produced a particular rate of return. The expected rate of return on the stock, conditional on the appearance of a particular rate of return to the market on day t, is given by

$$E(r_J|r_{M,t}) = \hat{A}_J + \hat{\beta}_J r_{M,t}$$

Since we are interested in the response of the stock to the event, we are interested in determining if the stock's returns in the vicinity of the event are above or below what we would expect to see in light of the performance of the market. Thus, our measure of response, $\varepsilon_{J,t}$, on a given day is the difference between the stock's actual rate of return and its conditional rate of return:

$E(R_B) = a_0 + a_1 E(R_B)$ $\qquad$ $\varepsilon_{J,t} = r_{J,t} - E(r_J|r_{M,t})$

To measure the stock's overall reaction to the event, we might accumulate the responses going from day -10 to day $+10$. In this case, the accumulated response in going from day -10 to day $+10$ would be given by

$$\sum_{t=-10}^{+10} \varepsilon_{J,t} = E_{J,+10}$$

Individual stocks are subject to the flow of a variety of types of information, some of which will push the stock up and some of which will push the stock down. Thus, the response to the particular event of interest may be masked by the responses to the other pieces of information. To handle this problem, we collect a large sample of stocks which have in common the incidence of a particular event, such as the announcement of a takeover bid on their common stock. The takeover bids may come at different calendar times for the different stocks, but for each stock we compute the accumulated response relative to day 0, the day the takeover bid is announced. For any given day t relative to day 0, the accumulated response is averaged over all M stocks in the sample as follows to obtain what is called the cumulative average excess return:

$$\bar{E}_t = \frac{\sum_{J=1}^{M} E_{J,t}}{M} = \text{Cumulative average excess return}$$

Since the only thing the stocks in the sample have in common is the event, the other factors which are influencing their prices should cancel out in the averaging. The movement in $\bar{E}_t$ as we approach the announcement of the event should give an indication of the average speed and accuracy of the response of stock prices to the particular event of interest.

Suppose the event is the announcement of information which should increase the market value of the stock. If the market is semistrong form efficient, $\bar{E}_t$ should exhibit the pattern depicted in Figure 23.2. It should have a value that is not significantly different from zero until we reach the day of the announcement. On that day most of the stocks in the sample should experience a positive value for ε_t. (Some

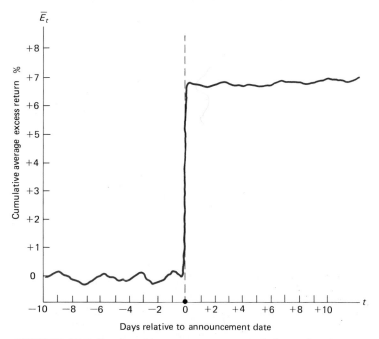

FIGURE 23.2 Stock price response to new information in a semistrong form–efficient market.

may not because of the incidence of a different negative piece of information on the day of the announcement.) The value for $\bar{E}_t$ should not change after the announcement. If the reaction to the event is completed on the announcement day and if the firms in the sample have nothing in common other than the event on any day after the announcement, approximately half the firms in the sample should have positive ε's and half should have negative ε's. If this is true, the value for the cumulative average excess return will not change from day to day.

If the market is strong form efficient and if information related to the event leaks out prior to the announcement, we should see a different pattern emerge. The pattern will be that of Figure 23.3. The value for $\bar{E}_t$ should gradually increase in the days prior to the announcement. There should be a substantial increase in $\bar{E}_t$ on the day of the announcement (reflecting the response of those stocks for which information didn't leak), and there should be no further change in $\bar{E}_t$ after the announcement. Don't misinterpret the gradual increase in $\bar{E}_t$ prior to the announcement. It doesn't necessarily reflect (1) a gradual response to the leakage of inside information for any one stock or (2) an incomplete response to the leakage of inside information. The only thing the stocks in the sample have in common is the announcement of the event at day 0. For any one stock the inside information could have leaked on any day prior to day 0. Since we are averaging the $E_{J,t}$'s to get $\bar{E}_t$, we should see a gradual rise in $\bar{E}_t$ even if each individual stock responds fully to the receipt of the inside information on the day that it is leaked.

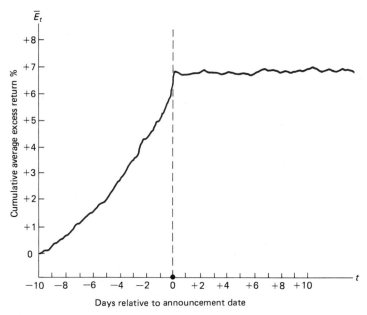

FIGURE 23.3 Stock price response to new information in a strong form–efficient market.

The Response of Stock Prices to the Announcement of a Stock Split

Fama, Fisher, Jensen, and Roll (1969) were the first to employ the methodology discussed above. They used monthly data to study the reaction of stock prices to the event of a stock split. They studied most of the splits that occurred on the New York Stock Exchange between 1929 and 1959.

Why should the stock price react to a split when the split does nothing more than divide the corporate pie up into more pieces? If the stock splits two for one, shouldn't the price of each share halve? Why should there be any effect on the rate of return, adjusted for the split?

As it turns out, splits act as a leading indicator of an increase in the dividend for the stock. In approximately 80 percent of the cases, a stock split is followed by an increase in the dividend. An increase in the dividend is of significance to the stockholders for the following reason. Management has a reluctance to cut dividends. Thus, they won't increase the dividend unless they are convinced there has been a permanent increase in the profitability of the firm to support the increased dividend payment. An increase in the dividend serves as a signal from management that they perceive the earning power of the firm has been permanently enhanced. Since a stock split serves as an indicator that there is an 80 percent chance for a dividend increase, it should induce a response in the stock price that reflects this probability.

Figures 23.4, 23.5, and 23.6 show the results of their study. The results for the entire sample are depicted in Figure 23.4. Note that the cumulative average ex-

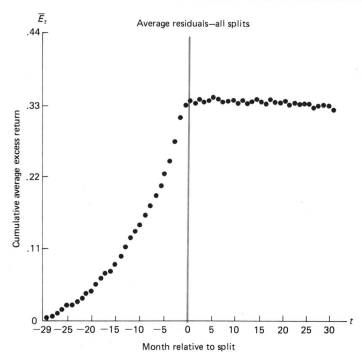

FIGURE 23.4 Price reaction for all splits.

SOURCE: C. F. Fama, L. Fisher, M. Jensen, and R. Roll, ''The Adjustment of Stock Prices to New Information,'' *International Economic Review* (February 1969).

cess return begins climbing as much as 29 months before the month of the split, which is month 0. The direction of causation here isn't running from the split to the stock price, however. Rather, it's more likely the case that the split itself results from the run-up in the stock price in the months prior to its occurrence. The sizable jump in the cumulative average excess return immediately before the split month may reflect a reaction to the split. The public announcement of the split may fall within these months for some stocks, and leakages of inside information may also be occurring here.

In any case, the reaction to the split seems to be complete by the month of its occurrence. There is no propensity for the split stocks to rise or fall, as a group, in the months after. There is no evidence of an incomplete reaction or overreaction to the event.

Figure 23.5 represents the 80 percent of the sample cases where the dividend increase actually occurs. When the split is announced, the stock prices rise to reflect the 80 percent probability of the dividend increase. When the increase occurs, the odds, of course, increase to 100 percent, and the stock price rises accordingly.

Figure 23.6 shows the results for the 20 percent of the cases where there was

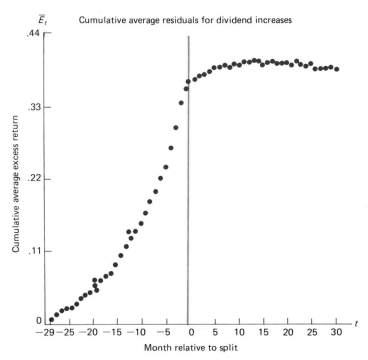

FIGURE 23.5 Price reaction for dividend increases.

SOURCE: C. F. Fama, L. Fisher, M. Jensen, and R. Roll, "The Adjustment of Stock Prices to New Information," *International Economic Review* (February 1969).

no accompanying dividend increase. Taking the split as a leading indicator, the prices of these stocks rose to reflect the 80 percent probability of a forthcoming dividend increase. When the dividend increase fails to appear, the cumulative average residual falls back to its presplit level.

Overall the pattern seems to be consistent with that of a rational, efficient market which reacts rapidly and correctly to the announcement of a stock split. Admittedly, it is difficult to measure the speed of the reaction here, because we are using monthly returns, and because the responses are lined up relative to the month split rather than the announcement month for the split. As mentioned, however, this is a pioneering study, and these shortcomings are addressed in later work, as we shall see below.

The Reaction of Stock Prices to Quarterly Earnings Reports

There have been many studies of the price reaction to the earnings announcement event. The most comprehensive is the study by Rendleman, Jones, and Latané (1982) (RJL).

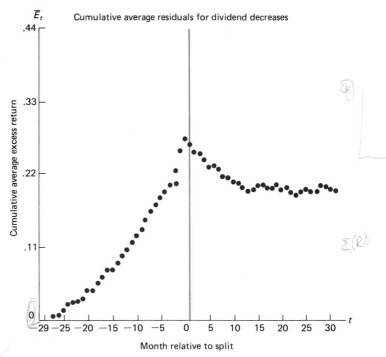

FIGURE 23.6 Price reaction for dividend decreases.

SOURCE: C. F. Fama, L. Fisher, M. Jensen, and R. Roll, "The Adjustment of Stock Prices to New Information," *International Economic Review* (February 1969).

RJL separate firms into 10 groups according to the nature of their earnings report in a given quarter. To group the firms, they first estimate what the earnings per share will be according to a statistical analysis of the firm's quarterly earnings' numbers in the past. They then compare the actual earnings reported with the statistical estimate. If actual earnings are more than two standard deviations above their estimate, the firm is put in group 10. If the actual number is between 1.50 and 2.00 standard deviations above the mean, the firm is put in group 9. This process continues through group 1, which is comprised of those firms that report earnings more than 2 standard deviations below the estimated value.

The cumulative average excess returns for each of the groups in the days surrounding the announcement of earnings are depicted in Figure 23.7. The stock prices appear to begin reacting to the earnings numbers up to 20 days before the announcement is made. This is probably accounted for by leakages of inside information. There is also evidence of a sizable reaction in the immediate vicinity of the event. So far, all this is consistent with market efficiency. However, in those cases where the earnings number is extremely good or extremely bad, there appears to be a de-

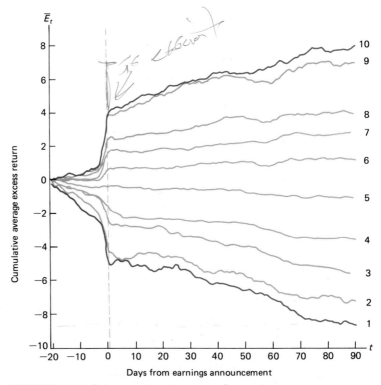

FIGURE 23.7 Price reaction to quarterly earnings report.

SOURCE: R. J. Rendleman, C. P. Jones, and H. A. Latané, "Empirical Anomalies Based on Unexpected Earnings and the Importance of Risk Adjustments," *Journal of Financial Economics* (November 1982).

layed reaction that continues up to 90 days after the announcement. Based on the figure, if you bought the stocks in group 10 on the day of the announcement, you would earn an additional increment in return of up to 8 percent that could be attributable to the earnings announcement. Group 1 shows a similar result in the opposite direction.

These results indicate that there appears to be *some* inside information impounded in stock prices. The stock price, however, doesn't fully react to the *public* announcement of the earnings report until a full 90 days after the report is released. The results are, therefore, inconsistent with even the semistrong form of the efficient markets hypothesis.

In fairness to the supporters of market efficiency, it must be said that most of the studies of market reaction to various events are consistent with market efficiency. However, since the RJL study is carefully done and the most comprehensive to date, it must be said that the best evidence indicates that the market's reaction, at least to the announcement of quarterly earnings, is less than efficient.

ARE CHANGES IN STOCK PRICES RANDOM?

If the securities markets are efficient, current prices should reflect all information, and they should change only in response to *new* information the receipt of which can't be predicted in advance. This type of information, by its very nature, comes to the market in a random, unpredictable manner. As security prices respond instantly and accurately to its receipt, they themselves should change randomly over time.

Studies of Serial Correlation

What do we mean by random? Technically speaking, if security prices followed a pure random walk, the probability distribution for the change in price would remain perfectly constant over time. All that is required for consistency with market efficiency, however, is that the best estimate of the expected change in the price for tomorrow be unrelated to the changes which have occurred in the price of the stock at any time in the past. This condition is violated in Figure 23.8 where we are plotting the percentage changes which occur on any one day in the price of a stock on the horizontal axis and the changes which occur on the next day on the vertical axis. Each point in the figure represents a single observation for a pair of days. The broken line running through the scatter is the line of best fit.

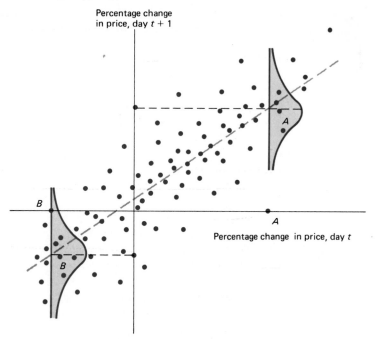

FIGURE 23.8 Correlation between successive price changes in an inefficient market.

Note that the scatter has a positive slope, indicating that when yesterday's change has been large, there is a propensity for today's change to be large as well. Thus, if yesterday's change were equal to that of point A, the probability distribution for today's change would be the one labeled A. If, on the other hand, yesterday's change were that of point B, the probability distribution for today's change would be the one labeled B. As you can see, the *expected* change for today is, in this case, positively related to the magnitude of yesterday's price change.

This can be contrasted with Figure 23.9. In this case successive changes in price are uncorrelated. The expected change for today is totally unrelated to what happened to the price yesterday.

If the market is efficient, we should obtain results like that of Figure 23.9 when we correlate percentage changes in any given stock. This should be true not only for successive percentage changes but also for changes lagged any number of periods. The change in price today should be unrelated to the change that took place yesterday, the day before, or any other day in the past.

Figure 23.10 depicts the relationship between successive percentage changes in a common stock index for the months of 1982 and 1983. Figure 23.11 shows a similar relationship where the percentage changes are separated by 1 month. In both cases, the correlation coefficient is not significantly different from zero. This result is typical of the results which have been found in many studies of many different stocks. Studies have been done on monthly, weekly, daily, and even interday returns on stocks that are both listed and traded on the over-the-counter exchange. In these studies, as the trading interval becomes smaller, the correlation coefficients for some stocks become significantly different from zero, usually for successive percentage changes. However, even when a statistically significant relationship is detected, it is seldom significant in an *economic* sense. That is, even if you were aware of it and

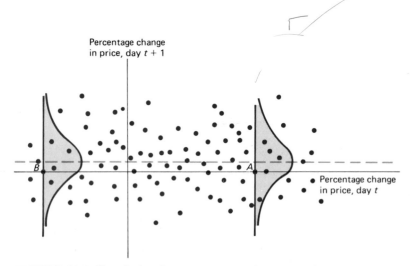

FIGURE 23.9 Correlation between successive price changes in an efficient market.

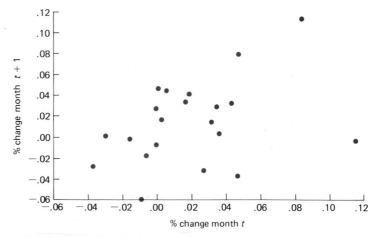

FIGURE 23.10 Relationship between successive monthly percentage changes in a stock index.

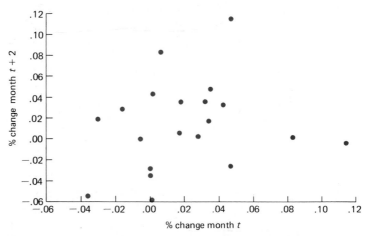

FIGURE 23.11 Relationship between lagged monthly changes in a stock index.

you attempted to trade on the basis of it, brokerage commissions would make your expected profits negative.

The evidence coming from studies which have attempted to model series of stock prices using standard statistical techniques seems to point in the direction that, unless you are a floor trader and pay no commissions, you would do well to look to sources other than the history of stock prices to make money in the market.

However, early research on the random character of stock prices may have made a mistake in concentrating on relatively small intervals (daily, weekly, or

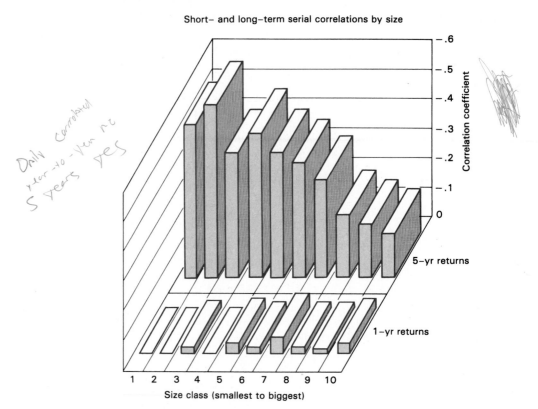

FIGURE 23.12 Short- and long-term serial correlations by size.

monthly) in which to measure the percentage changes in stock prices.[1] There is now rather significant evidence that, if percentage changes in stock prices are measured over long intervals, successive percentage changes in stock prices are highly negatively correlated. Figure 23.12, taken from a study by Fama and French (1988), shows the serial correlation coefficients for 10 equally weighted common stock portfolios, classified on the basis of size for overlapping periods in the interval 1926 through 1985. The figure shows the correlation coefficients for successive 1-year returns and for successive 5-year returns. Note that successive 1-year returns are largely uncorrelated. The 5-year returns, however, show pronounced negative correlation. If, over a given 5-year period, the return to a given size grouping has been above average, it is probable that average return in the next 5-year period will be below average. It also seems this rule works particularly well for small companies. If you believe this negative correlation is real, as opposed to some statistical artifact,

[1]Much of this discussion of systematic and seasonal patterns in stock returns is taken from an article by Haugen and Lakonishok (1988).

it is consistent with either (1) market efficiency in the context of a strange, and yet undiscovered form of capital asset pricing model, or (2) more conventional notions about asset pricing and *market inefficiency*.

To explain the finding in the context of market inefficiency, one can argue that the evidence is consistent with the notion that the market longitudinally *overreacts* to information—the prices of all stocks overreacting to a change in the nation's trade deficit. The long-term, negative correlation may result from the fact that the market corrects, in this 5-year period, the overreaction of the last 5-year period.

The Day of the Week Effect

Two independent studies conducted by French (1980) and Gibbons and Hess (1981) found evidence consistent with the hypothesis that there are significant differences in the expected percentage changes for stocks depending on the day of the week trading is conducted. The results for the Gibbons and Hess study are summarized in Figure 23.13.

Each bar in the figure represents the mean percentage change in the Standard & Poor's Index of 500 stocks for each of the 5 trading days of the week. The study covers more than 4000 trading days from 1962 through 1968. The expected percentage change on Mondays appears to be negative, and the expected percentage changes on Wednesdays and Fridays appear to be larger than on Tuesdays and Thursdays. While there appears to be a *statistically* significant difference between some of the mean returns for the different days, the differences again are not economically significant if you have to pay commissions. Unless you are a floor trader, if you attempted to buy stocks near the end of trading every Monday and then sell them near the end of trading every Friday, you would find your broker to be the only person making money from your efforts.

You may want to consider the day of the week effect, however, in timing your purchases and sales. If you are planning to buy some stock at the beginning of the week, you may want to postpone your purchases until the opening of the market on Tuesday and thereby take advantage of the expected decline in prices on Monday. Transactions costs are immaterial to this strategy, because they have to be paid on either day.

Studies of Seasonality

We also now have evidence on important *seasonal* patterns, and the evidence on seasonality is even more overwhelming than the evidence on long-term correlation and the day of the week effects.

The most compelling evidence on seasonality comes at the turn of the year. There is mounting evidence documenting unusual market activity at the end of the year.

You may well ask, "If this behavior is so unusual, why hasn't it been noticed until now?" The answer is, most of us watch the broad market averages, like the Standard & Poor's composite average of 500 stocks. These averages are weighted on

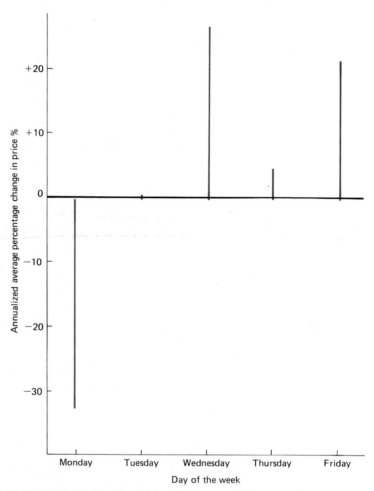

FIGURE 23.13 Results of the Gibbons and Hess study, 1962–1978.

the basis of total market value of the stock of each company. As such, they are dominated by the performance of the biggest firms. And, as it turns out, in the United States the turn-of-the-year effect is a *small-firm* phenomenon.

Something apparently causes upward pressure on the prices of small stocks at the turn of the year. Either (1) large, actively traded stocks aren't significantly affected by this pressure or (2) large stocks are not the targets of the source of the pressure.

To see the performance of the big market indices in January, look at Figure 23.14, which shows the average rate of return separated by month to the S & P 500 from 1926 to 1985. January doesn't stand out as being unusual. Its average return *is* relatively large, but it's not particularly special. In fact, there are other months with

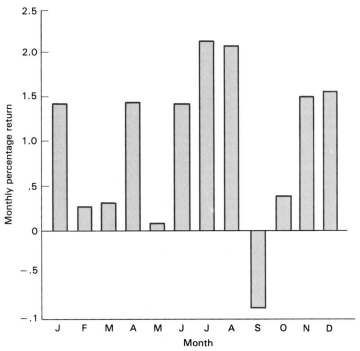

FIGURE 23.14 No January effect for the S & P 500.

SOURCE: R. Haugen and J. Lakonishok, *The Incredible January Effect* (Homewood, Ill.: Dow Jones-Irwin, 1988).

even bigger average rates of return. The S & P 500, you see, is dominated by big firms which don't feel the price pressure in January.

The January effect can be seen most clearly by looking at the average *difference* between the rates of return to small and large stocks. Figure 23.15, taken from Haugen and Lakonishok (1988), shows the differences, in successive Januaries, between the rates of return to the 10 percent of the firms on the combined New York and American stock exchanges which are the smallest and the rates of return to the S & P 500. Obviously, small stocks have a strong propensity to outperform large stocks in the first month of the year.

We also know most of this relative performance comes in first 5 trading days of the year. Figure 23.16 shows the results of a study by Donald Keim (1983). The period covered is 1963 through 1979. The total pie represents the total *annual* difference between the returns to small and large firms. Each slice represents the first 5 trading days of the year. Taken as a whole they account for more than a quarter of the annual difference between the returns to the smallest and largest firms.

Many people don't realize that the January effect is even stronger abroad than it is in the United States. Figure 23.17 is taken from a study by Gultekin and Gul-

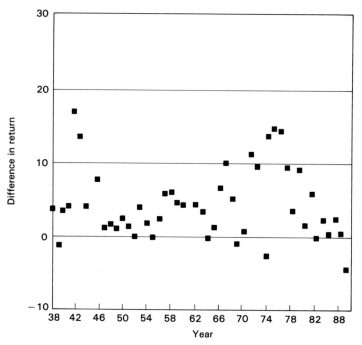

FIGURE 23.15 Small firm—S & P 500 return, January, last 50 years.

SOURCE: R. Haugen and J. Lakonishok, *The Incredible January Effect* (Homewood, Ill.: Dow Jones-Irwin, 1988).

tekin (1983) and shows the returns to market averages in January and the other months of the year for the following countries:

1. Australia
2. Austria
3. Belgium
4. Canada
5. Denmark
6. France
7. Germany
8. Italy
9. Japan
10. Netherlands
11. Norway
12. Singapore
13. Spain
14. Sweden
15. Switzerland
16. United Kingdom
17. United States

Small foreign firms also seem to be more pronouncedly influenced by the January effect than their large counterparts. Figure 23.18, from a study by Kato and Shallheim, shows the January effect on the Tokyo Stock Exchange. The magnitude of the first month's return increases, as it does in the United States, as we go from the largest-size decile to the smallest.

Annual extra difference by trading day.

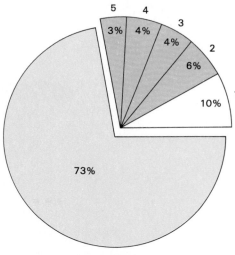

All other days

FIGURE 23.16 Annual extra difference by trading day.

SOURCE: R. Haugen and J. Lakonishok, *The Incredible January Effect* Dow-Jones Irwin Company (1988).

January also seems to be the only month in which there is a significant difference between the expected returns on bonds of the highest and lowest qualities. Figure 23.19 is from a study by Keim and Stambaugh (1986). It shows the difference between average rates of return (in the period 1926–1978) to bonds of various quality and the rates of return to U.S. Treasury bills. It seems the only time you can expect to get a premium return in the junk bond market is in January.

There is an even more surprising risk-reward pattern in the stock market. A recent study by Jay Ritter (1989) reports the results of Figures 23.20 and 23.21. Ritter first separates firms into 20 groupings based on size and beta. He then measures the average return (over the period 1935–1986) to each grouping in January and in the other months of the year. The results are startling to say the least! High-beta stock produce higher returns than low-beta stocks only in the month January and only for the smallest firms. He finds that the risk-return trade-off is actually negative for large firms during January. During the rest of the year all groupings produce about the same modest return, irrespective of size or beta.

Ritter also shows that, in January, small stocks with high betas outperform small stocks with low betas even when the performance of the overall market is relatively poor—an indication to him that what we're seeing in January is *not* a risk premium in the sense of the CAPM.

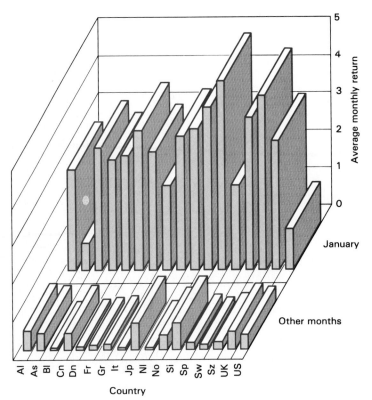

FIGURE 23.17 International January Effect.

SOURCE: R. Haugen and J. Lakonishok, *The Incredible January Effect* (Homewood, Ill.: Dow Jones-Irwin, 1988).

As we discussed in Chapter 19, stocks with high dividend yields may be expected to sell at discounted prices, and therefore offer relatively high pretax rates of return. This keeps their after-tax rates of return commensurate with other stocks with low dividend yields. Recall that stocks with low dividend yields produce most of their returns to investors in the form of tax-sheltered capital gains.

Keim (1985) examined the performance of stocks in different yield classes and found the surprising results of Figure 23.22. Apparently, if there is a tax premium in pretax expected rates of return, it is earned only in the month of January. There is also the puzzling result for stocks which pay *no* dividends. They earn an average return of 10 percent in January, but have the same average return as other stocks during the rest of the year.

Interestingly, Keim finds that, after controlling for size, risk, and month of the year, a 1 percent increase in a stock's dividend yield results in a 1.2 percent increase in expected return. There is, of course, no 120 percent bracket, so the differential

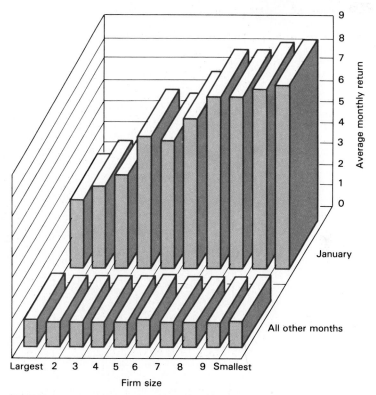

FIGURE 23.18 January—small firm in Japan.

SOURCE: R. Haugen and J. Lakonishok, *The Incredible January Effect* (Homewood, Ill.: Dow Jones-Irwin, 1988).

can only be partially tax-induced. Something else accounts for the relationship between dividend yield and realized return. It's interesting to speculate what that might be.

As with earnings-price ratios, discussed in a forthcoming section of this chapter, high dividend/price ratios can be an indicator of *over- or undervaluation*. High-dividend yield stocks may be the victims of negative, *cross-sectional* overreaction (the prices of General Motors and Ford overreacting to the news that one has increased its market share relative to the other) on the part of the stock market. Correction of the overreaction may account, in part, for the relatively high rates of return to these stocks in subsequent periods.

But, even if this is true, why would the correction of past mistakes come only in January?

If relative dividend yield is viewed as an indicator of relative value as well as relative tax exposure, Keim's results can be taken to be supported by another study by DeBondt and Thaler (1985).

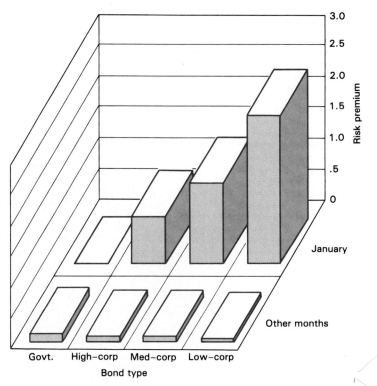

FIGURE 23.19 Risk premium in bond markets.

SOURCE: R. Haugen and J. Lakonishok, *The Incredible January Effect* (Homewood, Ill.: Dow Jones-Irwin, 1988).

DeBondt and Thaler took a large group of stocks and ranked them on the basis of market performance over a 60-month period. They examined stocks which were distinctive in terms of very good or very bad market performance. Then they examined the average cumulative between the returns for the stocks and the returns for a market index for both groups in the period after a 60-month evaluation period. For each stock the postevaluation period begins in January. Figure 23.23 plots the cumulative average excess return for both groups. It is easy to pick out January from the time series. In each subsequent January there is a jump in the cumulative average excess return. Note, also, that in the months of November and December there is a persistent decline in the cumulative average difference in return, at least for the stocks that performed poorly in the evaluation period.

The stocks in each group have only one thing in common, distinctive performance in the 60-month evaluation period. At the beginning of the postevaluation period, investors holding the stocks in the poor performing group are likely to have had accrued capital losses. It appears from the evidence that these stocks experienced year-end selling pressure as investors realized these losses for tax purposes. After

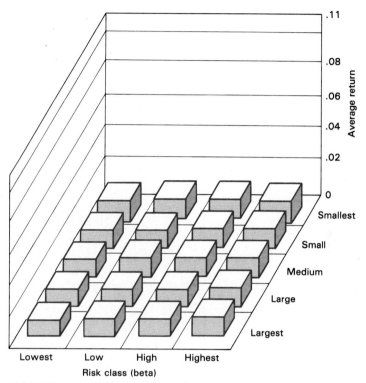

FIGURE 23.20 Risk return and size in other months, 1935–1986.

SOURCE: R. Haugen and J. Lakonishok, *The Incredible January Effect* (Homewood, Ill.: Dow Jones-Irwin, 1988).

this pressure the stocks then rallied in price in the month of January. This tendency persisted, although at a diminishing rate, over the next 5 years, as at the end of each year. The strength of the January rally following the November-December decline may suggest that the January effect may be attributed to tax loss selling. However, while tax-loss selling can't be dismissed as a contributing cause for the January effect, there are some problems with this explanation for the results just discussed.

In a recent paper in the *Journal of Finance,* Jones, Peace, and Wilson (1987) examined the period 1871–1917 (before the income tax) and found an effect at the beginning of the year that was not significantly different from that which existed after the introduction of the income tax. Moreover, the January effect has been shown to exist in countries like Japan and Belgium which don't tax capital gains and in a country like Australia which doesn't end its tax year in December. Unless one appeals to the tax-loss selling of international traders trying to escape taxes in other countries, it is difficult to see how *these* January disturbances are tax related.

There is another potential cause for the turmoil at the turn of the year which seems consistent with *all* we know about the January effect.

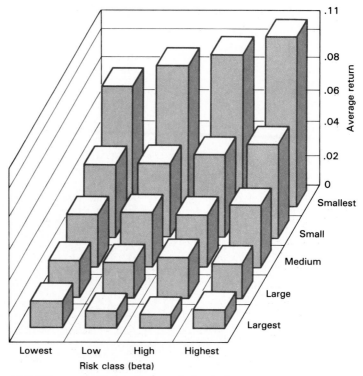

FIGURE 23.21 Risk return and size in January, 1935–1986.

SOURCE: R. Haugen and J. Lakonishok, *The Incredible January Effect* (Home-wood, Ill.: Dow Jones-Irwin, 1988).

Perhaps it is the case that a sufficient number of professional portfolio managers engage in extensive repositioning of their portfolios at the turn of the year to cause the January disturbance. At least two motives may induce the repositioning:

1. Managers may be reversing "year-end window dressing."
2. Managers may be positioning themselves to capture performance for the next calendar year.

Most professional managers are required to report the composition of their portfolios to their clients at the end of the year. It has been argued by many that some of them attempt to dress up their portfolios with stocks that have done well in the recent past. After the portfolio composition has been reported, these managers may want to reenter the market to invest in those stocks they perceive to be undervalued. The act of reentering may put pressure on the prices of small, risky stocks at the beginning of the year.

In addition to reverse window dressing, there may be an additional factor mo-

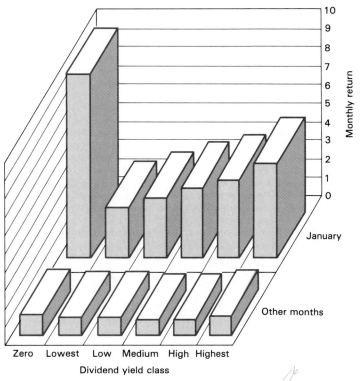

FIGURE 23.22 Tax premium in stock markets.

SOURCE: R. Haugen and J. Lakonishok, *The Incredible January Effect* (Homewood, Ill.: Dow Jones-Irwin, 1988).

tivating professionals to move into the backwaters of the market suddenly at the turn of the year.

Much of the compensation (raises, bonuses, etc.) of many individual professional managers is based on their performance for the calendar year. Performance is usually measured relative to a benchmark (the S & P 500 for equity managers and broad bond indices, such as the Shearson-Lehman Corporate-Government Bond Index, for fixed income managers). Suppose performance-related compensation increases at a decreasing rate in terms of performance, as in Figure 23.24. Given that this is true, managers may find it in their interests to lock in accrued performance when reductions in compensation associated with possible future performance losses outweigh increases associated with possible gains. *Exiting* from positions previously adopted early in the year can be expected to occur at different points during the year for managers of different portfolios. To lock in realized performance, managers can liquidate gains and move these positions into investments which more closely replicate the characteristics of the performance benchmark. This may happen gradually

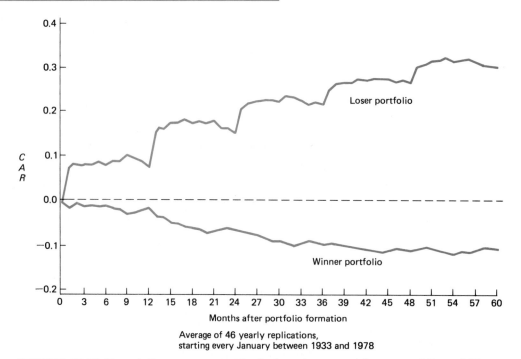

Average of 46 yearly replications,
starting every January between 1933 and 1978

FIGURE 23.23 Cumulative average residuals for winner and loser portfolios of 35 stocks, one to 60 months after portfolio formation; length of formation period: 5 years.

SOURCE: W. DeBondt, and R. Thaler, ''Does the Stock Market Overreact to New Information?'' *Journal of Finance* (July 1985), p. 803.

during the year even for a given manager, and it is almost certain to be a gradual process when viewed from the collective prospective of all managers.

Reentry should not be as gradual, however. For most managers, reentry will occur at a common time—at the turn of the year. In fact, since the measurement of annual performance is based on trade day, and some institutions, such as mutual funds, have the option to report holdings as of the day *prior* to year-end, managers can get a jump on the process by reentering early.

Reentry should not affect all stocks uniformly. As stated previously, price pressure has a greater effect on small, thinly traded stocks. To the extent professionals are reentering in an attempt to outperform their benchmark of the S & P 500 (which is dominated by large-capitalization stocks), small stocks may be among the *targets* of professional reentry. This being the case, the small firm effect will be exacerbated. We would suspect other targets of the reentry process would include the relatively risky, small stocks as well as risky bonds. In addition, to the extent some of these managers are value oriented, they will *bottom fish* in the backwaters of the market. Thus, another set of targets will be the losing stocks of the past.

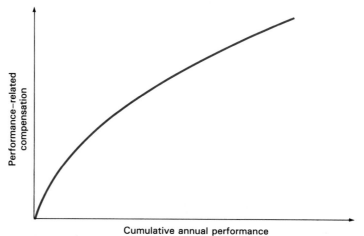

FIGURE 23.24 Hypothesized relationship between performance and compensation.

All these likely targets are the securities which have been found to be most pronouncedly affected by the January effect.

Human behavior can be generalized internationally, and it can be expected to change very slowly. Thus, the reentry process may explain the presence of the January effect in countries that do not tax capital gains as well as observations of the effect in distant times past when income was not taxed. The afternoon of the last day of the year, when the effect of these new positions on the current year's performance numbers is minimized, is an optimal time for reentry. This may explain why the biggest day for the January effect seems to be the last trading day in December!

Evidence supporting reentry into the more speculative areas of the market as a contributing cause of the January effect can be found in a recent paper by Chang and Pinegar (1988). Table 23.1 has been taken from the paper. The table plots monthly average risk premiums (portfolio returns less treasury bill returns) for portfolios grouped into deciles by size. Two months stand out. In January, the magnitudes of the average risk premiums are statistically greater than zero for 9 of the 10 size groupings. In addition, in July all 10 groupings show statistically significant, positive premiums.

These results were noted by the authors, but there is another interesting result which can be seen in the table. Figure 23.25 plots the magnitude of the risk premiums in relation to size grouping for December and January. Note that return increases with size in December, but it decreases with size in January. The same pattern is present in June and July, as is indicated in Figure 23.26. The June-July relationships aren't nearly as strong, but they are significant at about the same levels of confidence.

TABLE 23.1 Month-to-Month Holding-Period Return Spreads between Ten Stock Portfolios Ranked by Firm Size and T-Bills, 1927–1983 (Two-Tail p-Values in Parentheses)[a]

Portfolio	Jan	Feb	Mar	Apr	May	June	July	Aug	Sep	Oct	Nov	Dec
Smallest Stocks	0.1128	0.0138	−0.0024	0.0105	0.0029	0.0056	0.0253	0.0148	−0.0052	−0.0111	0.0112	−0.0063
	(0.000)*	(0.182)	(0.838)	(0.464)	(0.866)	(0.674)	(0.028)*	(0.366)	(0.760)	(0.344)	(0.401)	(0.580)
2	0.0781	0.0116	0.0001	0.0080	−0.0026	0.0025	0.0211	0.0144	−0.0174	−0.0076	0.0113	−0.0036
	(0.000)*	(0.127)	(0.995)	(0.582)	(0.879)	(0.838)	(0.078)*	(0.298)	(0.240)	(0.494)	(0.305)	(0.710)
3	0.0593	0.0095	−0.0031	0.0045	−0.0054	0.0024	0.0221	0.0121	−0.0173	−0.0081	0.0129	−0.0013
	(0.000)*	(0.184)	(0.774)	(0.703)	(0.737)	(0.829)	(0.064)*	(0.312)	(0.182)	(0.462)	(0.200)	(0.890)
4	0.0461	0.0067	−0.0011	0.0065	−0.0034	0.0027	0.0189	0.0145	−0.0130	−0.0065	0.0142	0.0040
	(0.000)*	(0.331)	(0.913)	(0.588)	(0.822)	(0.797)	(0.095)*	(0.217)	(0.311)	(0.512)	(0.135)	(0.633)
5	0.0408	0.0050	−0.0035	0.0043	−0.0048	0.0036	0.0189	0.0165	−0.0125	−0.0087	0.0153	0.0067
	(0.000)*	(0.411)	(0.738)	(0.713)	(0.706)	(0.733)	(0.084)*	(0.139)	(0.312)	(0.393)	(0.086)*	(0.363)
6	0.0347	0.0052	−0.0013	0.0051	−0.0075	0.0059	0.0185	0.0159	−0.0116	−0.0066	0.0128	0.0083
	(0.000)*	(0.424)	(0.895)	(0.663)	(0.555)	(0.540)	(0.095)*	(0.127)	(0.323)	(0.496)	(0.138)	(0.272)
7	0.0250	0.0046	−0.0005	0.0082	−0.0063	0.0062	0.0174	0.0153	−0.0109	−0.0051	0.0140	0.0096
	(0.003)*	(0.437)	(0.961)	(0.488)	(0.605)	(0.502)	(0.087)*	(0.108)	(0.337)	(0.589)	(0.099)*	(0.152)
8	0.0208	0.0026	0.0006	0.0053	−0.0089	0.0070	0.0161	0.0119	−0.0125	−0.0043	0.0124	0.0090
	(0.007)*	(0.655)	(0.943)	(0.635)	(0.409)	(0.459)	(0.096)*	(0.189)	(0.242)	(0.642)	(0.152)	(0.156)
9	0.0179	0.0031	−0.0005	0.0055	−0.0055	0.0087	0.0167	0.0149	−0.0144	−0.0023	0.0130	0.0113
	(0.011)*	(0.585)	(0.958)	(0.596)	(0.584)	(0.330)	(0.084)*	(0.125)	(0.159)	(0.790)	(0.088)*	(0.065)*
Largest Stocks	0.0071	0.0003	−0.0001	0.0070	−0.0056	0.0075	0.0147	0.0119	−0.0156	−0.0019	0.0105	0.0100
	(0.252)	(0.959)	(0.985)	(0.448)	(0.541)	(0.322)	(0.094)*	(0.150)	(0.083)*	(0.817)	(0.151)	(0.072)*
F-Statistic[b]	9.937	0.487	0.019	0.470	0.129	0.033	0.110	0.046	0.148	0.059	0.027	0.503
	(0.000)*	(0.884)	(1.000)	(0.895)	(0.999)	(1.000)	(0.999)	(1.000)	(0.998)	(1.000)	(1.000)	(0.873)

[a]The p-value is for a matched-paired t-test.

[b]The F-statistics have 9,560 degrees of freedom. The F-statistic tests the null hypothesis that mean spreads are jointly equal in every size-ranked portfolio.

*p-Value ≤ 0.100.

These similar patterns may be telling us something important because in Figure 23.25 the lines are separated by the end of the calendar year and in Figure 23.26 they are separated by midyear. There is no compelling reason to engage in tax-loss selling at midyear; however, midyear *is* significant to many professional investors. Nearly all professional managers report the composition of their portfolios to clients (1) quarterly, (2) semiannually, or (3) annually. Except for those operating on the basis of a fiscal year that ends in a month other than December, March, June, and September, all three groups will report at year-end. Those reporting at midyear will include the quarterly and semiannual reporters, as well as annual reporters with fiscal years ending in June. Thus, June will be a relatively popular month for reporting, perhaps second only to the month of December.

If some managers engage in window dressing during the report month and reentry during the month thereafter, we would expect to see the smaller, more speculative stocks underperforming the larger, more conservative stocks in the report month and outperforming them in the month thereafter. This seems to be what we see, but it should be stressed that this evidence is only suggestive. It would be much

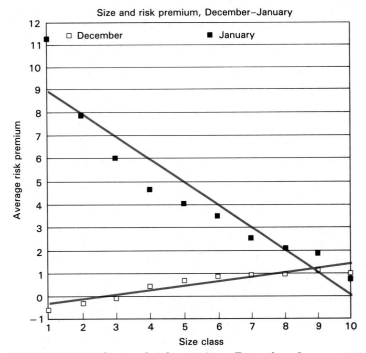

FIGURE 23.25 Size and risk premium, December–January.

more convincing if we could examine the actual trading behavior of professional investors around reporting dates. Unfortunately, this information is difficult to obtain, and very little direct evidence is available.

To sum up, do stock prices move randomly over time? The evidence seems to point conclusively to the conclusion that they do not.

DO TRADING RULES FAIL UNDER SIMULATION?

In an efficient market, each security sells at a price and an expected return that is reasonable and appropriate, given its risk, based on the *best* available estimate of the probability distribution of the future cash flows that will accrue to the firm. If your analysis leads you to conclude that the expected return is unreasonable, it is because you are either using an inappropriate benchmark for a ''reasonable'' return or you are basing your analysis on insufficient information and, therefore, you don't have the best estimates.

In such a market, all strategies or trading rules which attempt to separate profitable from unprofitable investments should fail because, based on the true underlying probability distributions, there are no such investments.

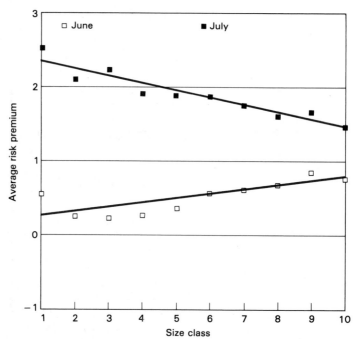

FIGURE 23.26 Size and risk premium, June–July.

This should be true now, and it should have been true for any arbitrary point in the past, so long as the trading rule is based on information which was available at the past point in time and the market was efficient then as well as now.

Have trading rules surfaced that seem capable of consistently "beating the market" in past periods of time? We have to be careful here because it's in the interest of those who find such rules to hide them rather than publicize them. With this caveat aside, it must be said that in the case of the vast majority of the trading rules which have been publicized as successful strategies, either the tests have been later shown to employ defective methodology, biasing the results in favor of the rule, or the superior performance fails to reappear when the rule is tested in alternative time periods.

However, at least one rule appears to have survived the test of time in this regard. The rule is based on the ratio of the market price of a stock to its earnings per share. In following this strategy, you buy stocks that have inordinately low price-earnings ratios, and you avoid stocks with inordinately high price-earnings ratios.

The idea behind the rule is, that there is a large body of empirical evidence pointing to the conclusion that earnings per share follow a random pattern over time. Evidence on this issue can be found in many studies, including Foster (1977). It seems that, even if you use the best available statistical techniques to model the time series of earnings per share numbers, the models are virtually useless in predicting the growth in earnings per share more than a few *quarters* into the future. In addition, studies by Brown and Rozeff (1978) and Cragg and Malkiel (1968) indicate that the forecasting ability of professional investors is questionable. Forecasting relative growth rates in earnings per share seems to be a hazardous business indeed.

In spite of this, the market seems to price stocks as though it can make useful forecasts of relative rates of growth in earnings per share for many years into the future. At times, stocks sell at prices which are more than 30 times what would be a reasonable estimate of the earnings-per-share number for the following year. Other stocks sell at prices which are less than two times current earnings. This is due to the price being set on the basis of the expectation that the growth rate in earnings for the high price-earnings stock will be well above the growth rate for the low price-earnings stock for a long time to come. On the basis of the evidence discussed earlier, pricing the stocks on the basis of such an expectation would seem to be a mistake.

If the market has a propensity to make such a mistake, the way to exploit it is to buy those stocks that the market is most pessimistic about and avoid those issues which are most favorably regarded. This *contrarian* view has been exposed for some time by many people, but it has been popularized in a book written by Dreman (1982).

If you are a contrarian, you are attracted to stocks with low price-earnings ratios. Have portfolios with low price-earnings ratios tended to produce abnormally high rates of return in the past? There have been many studies directed at answering this question, but most have suffered from fatal flaws, which have been pointed out by others.

The most conspicuous flaw in previous studies of the contrarian strategy is the method by which a sample of firms is chosen for the simulation. Typically a group of firms is chosen all of which have survived the entire period of the study. Can you see the problem in picking the sample in this way? If you actually invested in a portfolio of stocks, all of which had extremely low ratios of price to earnings, what would you be most concerned about? Since the market is apparently very pessimistic about the prospects for these companies, you probably would be concerned that the market might be right about some of them at least, and that they would go into bankruptcy. However, if in picking your sample, you choose firms for the study only if they survive the entire period, you have eliminated the major potential problem with the trading rule through the way you have constructed your sample. The test is now biased in favor of the rule.

There is one study which has overcome this problem as well as others associated with previous studies. Basu (1977) studied the performance of portfolios formed on the basis of price-earnings ratios during the period between April 1957 and March 1971. He begins with a representative sample of firms that were in existence in March 1957. No attempt is made to assure that the stocks in this sample survived the time period covered by the study. At the beginning of each month, he ranks the stocks on the basis of their price-earnings ratios. The 20 percent of the stocks with the highest price-earnings ratios go into group *A*, the 20 percent with the next highest go into group *B*, and so on through group *E* with the lowest price-earnings ratios. The portfolios are re-formed in this way at the beginning of each year. The perfor-

OUT ON THE STREET

PIECES GREATER THAN THE WHOLE

The ice was really beginning to build up now. Traffic was literally crawling. The usual 90-minute commute would probably double today.

Terry Langetieg was driving one of the several hundred thousand cars slowly making their way from New Jersey to Manhattan. The ice storm stood between him and the beginning of his working day at Salomon Brothers at One New York Plaza. It would have been great to get there on time today. The firm is conducting a major marketing operation of a new CMO (collateralized mortgage obligation). In this case the entire "Z Bond" piece was being marketed to Japanese investors in Tokyo. Increasingly, Salomon was finding international clientele with specialized investment needs. The firm met these needs, in some cases by splitting existing U.S. securities into component parts and marketing the parts to investors in the United States and throughout the world.

Take the CMO, for example—or collateralized mortgage obligation. Salomon, and later First Boston, were the first to enter the market for this new security, and in the past 2 years the volume of new issues has risen from literally nothing to $30 billion per year.

The CMO is basically a twist on the Ginnie Mae passthrough. The Ginnie Mae is notorious for uncertainty about the magnitude of its payments and the sensitivity of its market value to changes in interest rates. The Ginnie Mae is backed by a pool of conventional mortgages. The payments on these mortgages are passed through to the holder of the Ginnie Mae. If mortgage rates fall and prepayments on the underlying mortgages are greater than expected, the cash flows associated with the Ginnie Mae will also be greater than expected in the early years of the security's life. Because conventional mortgages are also relatively long term, the value of the Ginnie Mae will also be relatively sensitive to interest rate changes, a property that is undesirable to some investors.

With the CMO, the Ginnie Mae is effectively divided into pieces and then

mance of each of the portfolios is then evaluated over the time period covered by the study.

The basic results of the study are presented in Figure 23.27 through 23.30. The rates of return to each of the portfolios is presented in Figure 23.27. Note that the rates tend to become progressively larger as you move from the high price-earnings ratio portfolios to the low price-earnings ratio portfolios. The Jensen Index of performance is presented in Figure 23.28. Recall that the Jensen Index is the difference between the portfolio's return and the return you would expect it to have if it were positioned on the security market line. In the results of Figure 23.28 the security market line was estimated using the average risk-free rate in the bond market. Basu obtains similar results when he uses an estimate of the average rate of return on the zero beta portfolio. In any case, risk-adjusted performance improves as you move

marketed to separate segments of the market. To market a CMO, you acquire a pool of Ginnie Mae securities and typically divide the pool into four classes, based on priority of receipt of interest and principal payments. For example, the fast pay "A tranche" receives the highest priority. Its interest and principal payments will be entirely paid up within three years. No principle payments will be made to the "B tranche" until all payments to the A tranche have been fully paid. Then payments will begin on the second priority issue and so on through the lowest priority issue, which is called the Z Bond. The A tranche has some of the investment characteristics of a three-year treasury note, but it usually carries a fifty basis point premium in its yield over the treasury issue. The Z Bond is almost like a Zero coupon bond; no payments are made on this bond until all the payments are received on the pieces with greater priority.

The Z Bond is attractive to groups of investors like pension funds that have an aversion to buying corporate callable bonds, where the call option is a real threat in terms of the truncation of the cash flows associated with the investment. The Z Bond also seems to be attractive to many investors in Japan. That's what's behind today's major marketing operation.

Salomon initially found that the value of the pie's individual pieces was greater than the value of the pie as a whole. That is, the individual securities like the A tranche and the Z Bond could be marketed for a sum greater than the total value of the underlying pool of Ginnie Maes. This unexpected bonus disappeared, however, in the second year of the market history for the security. Now Salomon makes its money underwriting and market making in CMOs. Salomon and First Boston underwrite 80 percent of the new issues and make a secondary market for 100 percent of the trading in existing issues.

The traffic grinds to a complete stop. This is going to take even longer than he thought. Looks like a nerve-racking 2-hour trip to the island.

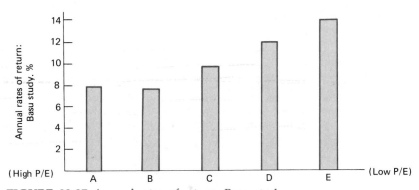

FIGURE 23.27 Annual rates of return: Basu study.

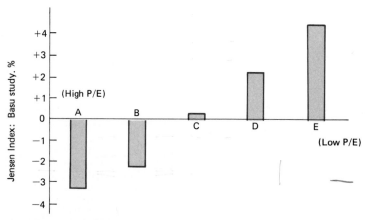

FIGURE 23.28 Jensen Index: Basu study.

from the left to the right. The Treynor and Sharpe indices for the portfolios are given in Figures 23.29 and 23.30. Recall that both are ratios of the risk premium earned on the portfolio to the risk of the portfolio. The Treynor Index uses beta to measure risk, while the Sharpe Index uses standard deviation of return. In the case of both indices, performance improves as the price-earnings ratio is reduced.

In other parts of his study, Basu allows for the differential transactions cost associated with re-forming the portfolios annually. He also allows for the differential tax payments associated with realizing capital gains annually. Even in the face of these adjustments he finds a statistically significant difference in the performance of an investor that holds a low price-earnings ratio portfolio from an investor that bought and then held the entire sample of stocks throughout the study period. Unless his results can be refuted, they seem to contradict the semistrong form of the efficient market hypothesis.

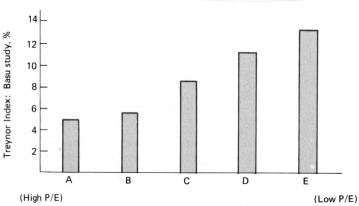

FIGURE 23.29 Treynor Index: Basu study.

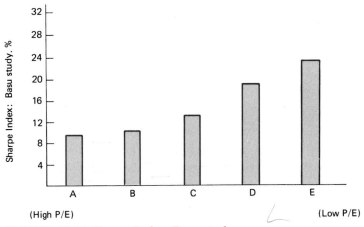

FIGURE 23.30 Sharpe Index: Basu study.

In two papers published from dissertations written at the University of Chicago, Banz (1981) and Reinganum (1981) argued that the price-earnings ratio anomaly analyzed by Basu is really masquerading for a size effect that itself is not inconsistent with market efficiency. They argued small firms have an element of risk that isn't captured by the risk measures in Basu's risk-adjusted performance ratings. There is less information known about small firms, and thus investors are likely to be less confident about their estimates of both risk and expected return. Thus, if a large company and a small company both have identical betas based on sample estimates of past returns, if you have additional information reinforcing your estimates for the large company, you may be more confident in your estimates of risk and expected return. Your lack of confidence in the estimates for the small company adds an extra dimension of risk which may increase the return you require to invest in the stock.

It also can be argued that on a percentage basis, it costs more to buy and sell the shares of small companies. Among other things, the market for the shares of small companies is thinner. If you buy the stock on a stock exchange or from a dealer in the over-the-counter market, the spread between the bid and the asked prices will be greater.

Based on the added dimension of risk and the higher costs of transacting, investors may require a higher rate of return on the stock of small companies. If this is true, it may explain why stocks with low price-earnings ratios produce abnormally large rates of return.

The stocks of small companies tend to have low price-earnings ratios. Given this, portfolios consisting of low price-earnings stocks will also consist of stocks issued by smaller than average companies. Is the price-earnings effect due to the market tending to be overly optimistic or pessimistic? Or is it because low price-earnings stocks tend to be small, and the market *requires* a higher rate of return on smaller firms?

In a subsequent paper, Basu (1983) attempted to address this question. Figure

23.31 plots the Jensen indices for 25 portfolios. The portfolios are formed by first ranking the stocks in the sample on the basis of the size of the firm and then on the basis of the total market value of the common stock. The firms are grouped into quintiles, where the 20 percent of the firms with the smallest total market value go into the first quintile, the next 20 percent into the second quintile, and so on through the fifth quintile. Then, within each quintile, the firms are ranked by price-earnings ratios and formed into 5 portfolios. The 20 percent of the firms with the smallest price-earnings ratio go into portfolio E, the next 20 percent into D, and so on through A. In all, we form 25 portfolios widely dissimilar with respect to both size and price-earnings ratio. By examining the performance of these firms, we can get some insight into whether we are observing a size or a price-earnings effect.

The Jensen indices in Figure 23.31 show that there appears to be both a price-earnings and a size effect present. As you move across the horizontal axis of the graph, you move from the smallest group of firms to the largest group. Notice, as size is increased, performance tends to deteriorate. An advocate of the size effect

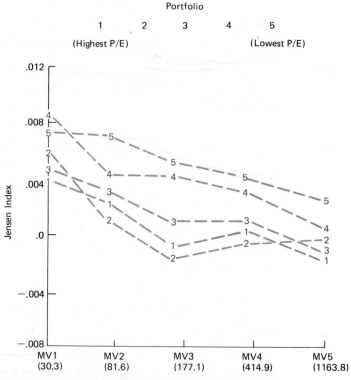

FIGURE 23.31 Size and price-earnings effect.

SOURCE: S. Basu, "The Relationship Between Earnings' Yield, Market Value and Return for NYSE Common Stocks," *Journal of Financial Economics* (June 1983).

would argue that *this* deterioration doesn't reflect market inefficiency but rather the fact that Basu is measuring risk on the basis of beta alone and that he is not adjusting for the differential costs of transaction in small and large companies.

Within each size grouping, however, the portfolios with the smallest price-earnings ratios have the highest risk-adjusted performance. Since the companies in the group are more or less uniform with respect to size, the differences in performance are likely to be attributable to differences in price-earnings ratio. This being the case, this evidence is inconsistent with the semistrong form of the efficient market hypothesis.

ARE PROFESSIONAL INVESTORS DISTINCTIVE IN TERMS OF THEIR PERFORMANCE?

In the presence of the capital asset pricing model and a strong form-efficient market, all securities would appear to be positioned on the security market line when estimates of beta and expected return are based on state of the art analysis of all knowable information. If a security appears to you to be positioned otherwise, it is only because you are basing your estimates on less than the full set of information. Since no security is truly positioned above or below the security market line, it is impossible to construct a portfolio which is so positioned, and if we take sample estimates of portfolio expected return and beta based on past returns, any deviation in the estimated position of the portfolio from the security market line should be statistically insignificant.

For any given group of investors, errors in our sample estimates of expected return and beta should produce a clustering of estimated portfolio positions above and below the security market line. However, on average, the portfolios should be positioned on the line, and the number of individual deviations from the line that is deemed to be statistically significant should be consistent with the level of confidence used in determining significance. For example, suppose we accept a deviation as being statistically significant if there is at most a 5 percent probability it is due to chance. Then, if all the deviations are actually due to chance (as they would be in an efficient market), you should find that approximately 5 percent of the portfolios have significant deviations.

Jensen (1969) examined the performance of 115 mutual funds in the period 1955 through 1964. The managers of these funds are usually highly trained and have access to broad sources of investment information. If the market is inefficient, we would expect this group of investors to capture abnormally high returns.

Jensen estimates the position of the security market line for the period using the Standard & Poor's Index of 500 stocks as a proxy for the market portfolio. The S&P is positioned in Figure 23.32 at point *M*. The beta factor for the S&P is, of course, 1.00, since its returns, when related to themselves, line up on a 45-degree line emanating from the origin of a graph like that of Figure 23.33, where we are plotting portfolio return vertically and market index return horizontally. The risk-free

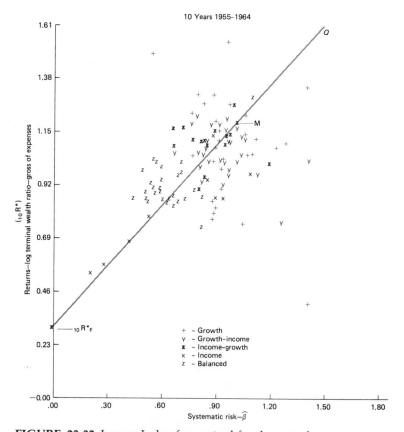

FIGURE 23.32 Jensen Index for mutual funds, net of expenses.

SOURCE: M. Jensen, "Risks, the Pricing of Capital Assets, and the Evaluation of Investment Performance," *Journal of Business* (April 1969).

investment is positioned at point $_{10}R^*$ in Figure 23.32. This is the rate of interest available in the U.S. government bond market during the period. The security market line is estimated as a straight line drawn through points $_{10}R^*$ and M.

Jensen measures the performance of each mutual fund by the vertical distance between the position of each fund in Figure 23.32 and the security market line. This analysis is based on the presumption that stocks are priced according to the version of the capital asset pricing model where investors are allowed to borrow and lend at the risk-free rate of interest. Note that you could have invested in the S&P 500 Index portfolio during this period without doing any security analysis whatsoever. By combining this portfolio with a positive or negative investment in the risk-free bond, you could have attained any of the positions on this security market line. Thus, the security market line represents those positions which were available to those of us who were investing on the basis of a knowledge of little or no information. In assessing the performance of the mutual funds, we compare these positions with the positions

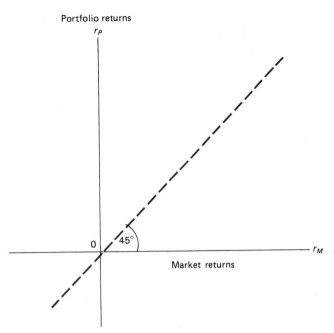

FIGURE 23.33 Graph for market returns and portfolio returns.

actually attained by managers who presumably had access to a considerable fraction of the full information set.

The individual points in Figure 23.32 represent the positions of individual mutual funds. Funds with different investment objectives are represented by different symbols explained in the key to the figure. In moving from the top to the bottom of the key, you move from funds that invest in growth-oriented stocks, to funds that invest in income-oriented stocks, to funds that balance their investments in stocks and fixed income securities. In Figure 23.32, the funds are positioned according to the actual rates of return received by the investors in the funds. That is, the returns are net of the expenses incurred by the funds. Jensen computes a beta factor for each fund by regressing its rates of return in the 10-year period on the returns to the S&P 500 Index portfolio. Each fund is then plotted on the graph according to its beta and its average return. Note there are more funds positioned below the security market line than above it. In fact, in averaging the Jensen Index across all the funds, you find that, as a group, the mutual funds are *underperforming* by approximately 1 percent per annum. That is, given the overall risk (beta) of the mutual funds, a naive investor, operating on the basis of little or no information, could have invested some money in the risk-free bond and the rest in the index portfolio and beaten the mutual funds by approximately 1 percent per year!

This finding is consistent with the hypothesis that all the efforts expended by mutual funds to find undervalued stocks were in vain. These efforts came at a cost.

Analysts and staff salaries had to be paid. Expenses associated with office space, advertising, data acquisition, and commissions also had to be paid. To determine whether these expenses were the source of the underperformance, Jensen adds the money spent on these items back into the fund's rate of return, and he recomputes the betas and average rates of return. The positions of the funds, gross of all expenses, are plotted in Figure 23.34. There are now an approximately equal number of funds above and below the line. If you were to average the positions of all the funds, you would find the group as a whole is now positioned almost exactly on the security market line. This is, of course, consistent with the hypothesis that the source of the underperformance is, indeed, the expenditures of funds associated with the management of the funds.

Jensen concludes that mutual funds, as a group, are not distinctive in their investment performance from investors who have little or no access to information. Are there, however, *individual* managers within the industry that have distinguished

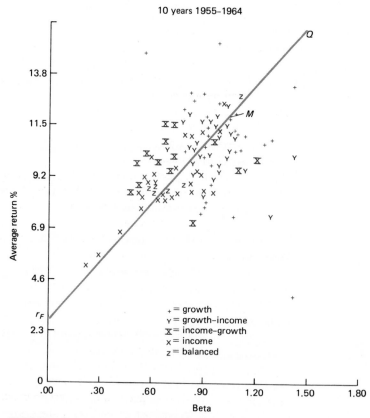

FIGURE 23.34 Jensen Index for mutual funds, gross of expenses.

SOURCE: M. Jensen, "Risks, the Pricing of Capital Assets, and the Evaluation of Investment Performance," *Journal of Business* (April 1969).

themselves in terms of their performance? Put another way, are the deviations from the security market line that we see in Figures 23.32 and 23.34 due to sampling error or to the funds' actual *expected* rates of return being positioned above (or below) the security market line? Perhaps there are managers who are consistently superior and others who are consistently inferior, and they are canceling each other in the averaging so that the group as a whole appears neutral.

In an effort to investigate this possibility, Jensen analyzes each fund individually to determine whether its Jensen Index is significantly different from zero in a statistical sense. To do this, he divides each index by its standard error to obtain a T statistic. Given the magnitude of the Jensen Index, the greater the *residual variance* in the fund's year-to-year return, the greater will be the standard error, and the lower will be the T statistic. Given the number of years of returns observed for each fund, if the T statistic has an absolute value greater than approximately 2.2, we can say there is less than a 5 percent probability the fund has achieved a nonzero Jensen Index on the basis of chance (or sampling error) alone.

The distribution of T statistics for the net returns for the funds is given in Figure 23.35. The observations in the shaded areas on each side of the distribution can be considered to be statistically significant. Jensen finds only one fund which comes close to having a statistically significant *positive* Jensen Index and a large number of funds for which the index is significantly negative. Apparently the negative funds are doing something consistently wrong so that, given their risk levels, their expected returns are positioned below the security market line. An advocate of market efficiency might argue that what they are doing wrong is expending large sums of money on security analysis. To determine whether this is true, Jensen again adds back to their returns the amounts spent to manage the portfolios and recalculates all the T statistics. The distribution of T values *gross* is present in Figure 23.36. Now there are only a few funds which exhibit T values that are significant in either the positive or negative direction. The number that *are* significant is, in fact, approximately equal to the number we would expect to see on the basis of chance alone. Since we are using a 5 percent test of significance, we would expect to see 5 percent of the sample of 115 funds showing significant T values even if relative investment performance is totally a matter of luck.[2]

Since these managers presumably have access to all forms of information, these results are consistent with the strong form of the efficient market hypothesis. This seems strange since we already have seen evidence which contradicts even the semistrong and weak forms.

There are at least two explanations for this apparent contradiction in the evidence. First, the mutual funds are rather large financial institutions. Even if the individual analysts are capable of discriminating between profitable and unprofitable investments, it may take a considerable period of time for these opinions to work their way down to actual changes in the portfolio position of the fund. The individual analysts may find themselves frustrated by the bureaucratic procedures involved in

---

[2]Technically speaking, Jensen's test assumes that mutual fund returns are independent. This is clearly not the case since most of the funds have securities in common.

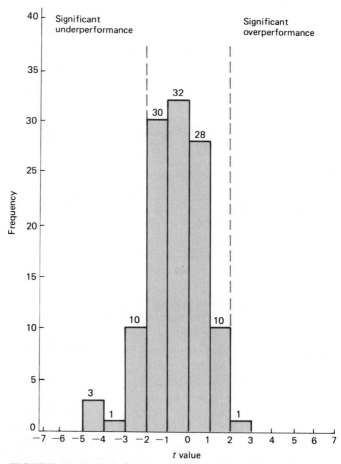

FIGURE 23.35 Distribution of T statistics: Net of expenses for mutual funds in Jensen study.

SOURCE: M. Jensen, ''The Performance of Mutual Funds in the Period 1945–1964,'' *Journal of Finance* (May 1968).

the funds' portfolio management process to the point where their analysis has little or no impact on the performance of the fund.

Second, it may be that mutual funds are distinctive in their performance but that our benchmark for measuring performance are too crude to detect their superiority. Several weaknesses in the various risk-adjusted performance measures were discussed in the chapter on portfolio performance. Additionally, another potential problem may explain why Jensen is unable to find many individual funds with statistically significant performance.

Most mutual funds try to forecast the future direction of the market. If they believe the return to the market is going to be high, they might take an aggressive

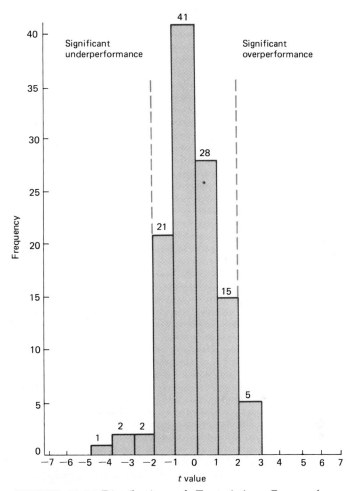

FIGURE 23.36 Distribution of T statistics: Gross of expenses for mutual funds in Jensen study.

SOURCE: M. Jensen, "The Performance of Mutual Funds in the Period 1945–1964," *Journal of Finance* (May 1968).

position and invest in stocks that will respond vigorously to the coming bull market. In taking such a position, they might plunge into the stock market such that the characteristic line of the portfolio looks like that of the solid line labeled "bull" in Figure 23.37. When they are in such a position, they might experience periodic returns like those labeled with circles in the figure. If, on the other hand, they believe the return to the market is going to be low, they might move their funds into low-beta stocks and fixed income securities such as bonds. When in this position the fund's characteristic line might look like the solid line labeled "bear" in

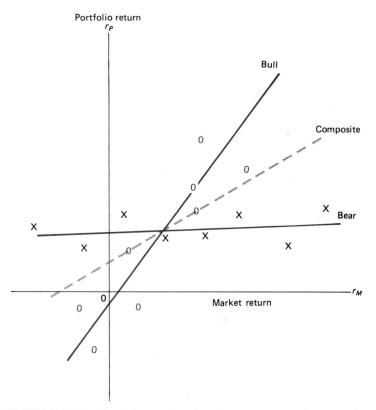

FIGURE 23.37 Obtaining a composite estimate of a portfolio's characteristic line.

Figure 23.37. The X's surrounding this line represent the fund's periodic return experience when it is in such a defensive position.

Now suppose you fail to recognize that the fund is actually shifting from one position to another. You simply regress all the fund's periodic returns on the returns to your market index. You will obtain a composite estimate of the fund's characteristic line that may look like the broken line of Figure 23.37. Note the fund will appear to have much more residual variance than it actually has when in either an aggressive or defensive position.

If you overestimate the fund's residual variance, you also will overestimate the standard error of its Jensen Index. Since the T statistic is the index itself divided by its standard error, you will obtain a downward-biased estimate of the T statistic. This may explain why Jensen found that most of the T values in his sample were very low.

A more recent paper by Kon and Jen (1979) attempts to correct this problem. They employ a statistical analysis which enables them to, first, determine whether a sample of observations was associated with one or more characteristic lines; second, estimate the characteristic line or lines; and third, separate the observations on the basis of their associated characteristic lines. They then can estimate the Jensen Index on the basis of each individual characteristic line to determine whether the managers of the funds are able to select investments with abnormal returns *when in a particular (aggressive or defensive) position.*

They find for most of the funds there is a high probability the returns can be associated with more than one characteristic line. After separating the observations coming from each characteristic line, they find that a large fraction of the Jensen indices are statistically significant. In computing the value for the index, they employ both the risk-free rate in the bond market and an estimate of the average rate of return on the zero beta portfolio. In both cases, they find many more significant T values than you would expect to see on the basis of chance. Their evidence is consistent with the hypothesis that some managers can be distinguished from others on the basis of talent or tendencies in selecting profitable investment. This can only be true if the market is less than perfectly efficient.

The Jensen result on neutral mutual fund performance can also be questioned on the grounds that measured performance can be sensitive to the choice of market proxy. As we learned in Chapter 10 on measuring portfolio performance, the Jensen Index can be sensitive to the characteristics of the proxy selected for the market portfolio and its position relative to the minimum variance set. Jensen estimated the security market line by connecting the positions of the Standard & Poor's 500 and the government bond rate in average return—beta space.

Suppose the 500 was positioned relative to a bullet constructed on the basis of the stocks in the 500 as well as those in the portfolios of the mutual funds as in Figure 23.38. The shaded cloud within the bullet represents the positions of the mutual funds. The risk-free bond rate is at r_F, and Jensen's estimated security market line is given by line $r_F A$ in Figure 23.39. Now consider the corresponding minimum variance portfolio M^* with the same average rate of return as the 500. If betas are computed with reference to this corresponding portfolio, all securities and portfolios will line up in Figure 23.39 along line $\bar{r}_Z C$. Since the 500 isn't minimum variance, we will not get a perfect alignment, and the mutual funds may be positioned within the cloud furthest to the east in Figure 23.39. In this case we see most of the mutual funds positioned *below* Jensen's security market line.

However, what if portfolio M is selected as a market proxy instead? Its corresponding minimum variance portfolio is M'. If betas are computed with reference to M', all securities will line up along line $\bar{r}'_Z D$. Again, since M is inefficient the positions will be scattered if betas are computed with reference to it, and the mutual funds may end up positioned within the western cloud. In the manner of Jensen, the security market line would be estimated by drawing a line connecting the riskless bond rate with the position of M in average return—beta space, as with line $r_F B$ in Figure 23.39. Note that now the mutual funds are positioned *above* the estimated security market line.

Errors in the measurement of the market portfolio and the risk of professionally managed portfolios aside, it remains the case that, in a typical year, roughly two-thirds of professional managers of stock portfolios produce returns that are below the

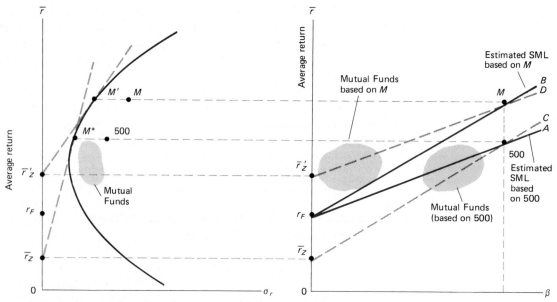

FIGURE 23.38 Position of mutual funds and market indices within minimum variance set.

FIGURE 23.39 Positioning of mutual funds relative to security market lines.

returns of broadly based stock market indices like the S&P 500. How can we account for this dismal performance in the face of the preponderance of evidence contradicting market efficiency presented in this chapter?

In a recent paper, Reinganum (1988) reports a marked doubling in institutional ownership in stocks which have experienced extraordinarily good performance in the past. Given the generally poor track record for institutional investors reported by Jensen and others, it is more likely than not that the institutional entry occurred during the latter stages of the extraordinary performance.

This tendency of professional managers to prefer to have the winning stocks *of the past* make appearances in their portfolios may itself account for their relatively poor performance. If there is cross-sectional overreaction in the market (winners of the past tend to become losers of the future), this may account for the relatively poor performance records of professional managers as a group—even in the presence of a relatively inefficient market. Because of their trading tendencies, institutions may, themselves, be the victims of market inefficiency!

SUMMARY

In this chapter we have examined some of the evidence on whether the actual market exhibits four behavioral traits that are consistent with market efficiency.

In an efficient market, security prices should respond instantly and accurately to the receipt of new information. There have been many studies of the response of stock prices to events such as stock splits, dividend announcements, takeover bids, block purchases and sales, and corporate earnings reports. Most of these studies have indicated that stock prices do, in fact, respond quickly and accurately to the receipt of new information. There has been convincing, contradictory evidence reported, however. A recent study of the response of stock prices to quarterly earnings reports indicates there is a 90-day lag in the response of stock prices to earnings reports that can be considered unusually favorable or unfavorable. The magnitude of the continuing response after the report is large enough to overcome the costs of transacting to take advantage of the lag. This study is carefully done and uses a sample of observations encompassing the samples used in all previous studies that produced results consistent with the efficient market hypothesis.

In an efficient market, the expected change in security prices in any future period should be unrelated to the exhibited behavior of the security in any previous period. Again, most of the studies which have employed standard statistical procedures to search for systematic patterns in the series of stock prices have found little evidence that you can predict future price changes on the basis of past changes. However, recently published evidence indicates there is a definite seasonal pattern in stock prices. The expected rate of return to the market apparently shifts substantially to the right in the month of January. At this point, we can only conjecture as to why this happens, but the evidence that it does happen here and throughout most of the world is overwhelming.

In an efficient market, all trading rules should fail under simulation. Many trading rules have been tested and most have failed. At least one, however, has convincingly produced abnormal returns in simulations based on historical data. If the market tends to be overly optimistic and pessimistic in forecasting the earnings and dividends of firms, you can take advantage of this error by investing in stocks with low price-earnings ratios and avoiding stocks with high price-earnings ratios. Low price-earnings ratio portfolios have produced superior returns in the past, even after allowing for factors such as transactions costs, risk adjustment, statistical significance, and differential taxes. Some have argued that the price-earnings effect is really a small firm effect in disguise. However, the most recent evidence indicates that *both* effects are probably present in stock returns.

If the market is efficient, professional investors should not exhibit distinctive performance. Again, nearly all the studies of professional investment performance indicate that they don't. However, as we know, the available risk-adjustment performance measures are subject to a number of problems. One of these problems is a failure to separate returns produced by the funds when they are in aggressive and defensive positions. Failure to allow for this will tend to inflate the standard errors associated with the performance indices and reduce their apparent significance. At least one recent study which attempts to compensate for this has reported evidence consistent with the notion that fund managers can be distinguished on the basis of their skill in selecting undervalued issues. This is inconsistent with an efficient market, because in such a market there should be no undervalued issues.

Overall, the best evidence points to the following conclusion. The market isn't *strictly* efficient with respect to any of the so-called levels of efficiency. The price-earnings ratio phenomenon is inconsistent with semistrong form efficiency, and the January effect is inconsistent with even weak form efficiency. Overall, the evidence indicates that a great deal of information available at all levels is, at any given time, reflected in stock prices. The market may not be easily beaten, but it appears to be beatable, at least if you are willing to work at it.

Good luck!

QUESTION SET 1

Assume the following equation of a characteristicline for a stock A for Questions 1 through 3:

$$E(r_A|r_M) = .01 + .9r_M$$

Suppose the following represent the actual observations on r_A and r_M at several points *prior* to and including some event. The event occurred at time 0.

t	r_M	r_A
-3	.003	.0127
-2	.005	.0140
-1	.010	.0200
0	.008	.0192
$+1$	.0075	.01525
$+2$	.012	.02130
$+3$	.006	.0144

1. Compute the residuals from the characteristic line, that is, the portion of the stock's return which is not statistically associated with the market's return. Plot these residuals against values for r_M.

2. The values in the table may represent only a few of the observations used to fit the characteristic line. What must the *average* residual be for *all* of the residuals obtained in fitting the line?

3. Suppose the event was a change in the dividend. How would you use data like those given to proceed with an event study along the lines of Fama, Fisher, Jensen, and Roll?

4. From an examination of the evidence provided by Fama, Fisher, Jensen, and Roll (FFJR), could you infer that a trading rule based on split announcements would allow you to make abnormal profits? Explain.

5. FFJR interpret their results as evidence in support of efficient markets. Do the results appear to provide support for one particular form of the efficient markets hypothesis?

6. The FFJR study focuses on stock market reaction to stock splits. Since a stock split does not increase the fraction of a company held by an investor, one could argue that investors should be unconcerned with stock splits. Why, then, might a stock split be considered to be an important event for investors?

7. Rendleman, Jones, and Latané (RJL) focus on stock market reaction to earnings data. What is the specific "event" around which RJL take their measurements? What evidence is provided on the different forms of the efficient markets hypothesis?

8. What is the January effect in stock prices? Would this result be consistent with any of the forms of the efficient markets hypothesis?

9. One explanation of the January effect has to do with sales and purchases related to the tax year.
   a. Present the tax effect hypothesis.
   b. Studies have shown the January effect to occur internationally, even in countries where the tax year does not start in January. Try to speculate on a plausible reason for this.

10. In trying to test for the relationship between low price-earnings ratios and stock performance,
    a. What is the problem with simply observing the performance of a group of low price-earnings stocks that had existed from beginning to end over a period of time?
    b. How did Basu's 1977 study overcome the problem in part a, and what did he find?

11. What is the phenomenon of the size effect in stock performance, and why did some researchers claim that this effect was the real factor in Basu's "low P/E ratio effect?" Further, how does the size effect show up in the studies of seasonality?

12. What did Jensen find pertaining to the performance of mutual fund managers
    a. When expenses of the fund were deducted from returns?
    b. When expenses of the fund were not deducted from returns?

QUESTION SET 2

1. What is the January effect? Given that you are managing two funds, a U.S. treasury fund and a small-company growth stock fund, and can transfer funds with little or no cost between the two, can you devise a simple strategy to take advantage of the January effect?

2. Fama, Fisher, Jensen, and Roll studied the reaction of a stock price to the announcement of a stock split and found that the stock prices went up in response to the stock split announcement. Although the net asset value of the firm remained the same, what other factor did they consistently find that could justify the increase in price? Was their study consistent with a weak, semistrong, or strong form efficient market?

3. What are the four behavioral traits an efficient securities market will exhibit?

4. Rendleman, Jones, and Latané studied the reaction of stock prices to quarterly earnings reports. Did their study indicate a weak, semistrong, or strong form of market efficiency? Given that their study remains valid, would you, as a portfolio manager, be able to garner extra returns by investing in a stock that had much greater earnings than expected *after* the public announcement of the earnings?

5. In studies which have looked at the question of whether or not changes in stock prices are random, as the trading interval has become smaller, the correlation coefficients become significantly different from zero, usually for successive percentage changes. Can you, as an individual or portfolio manager, make use of this information to gain an incremental increase in portfolio income?

6. What is a trading rule? What time-tested rule appears to be useful to traders or portfolio managers?

7. Does Basu's study of the performance of portfolios formed on the basis of price-earnings ratios support the weak, semistrong, or strong form of market efficiency model? What weakness in other studies did Basu's study rectify?

8. If you were a mutual fund manager, would you be pleased or displeased with the results of Jensen's mutual fund performance studies? What counterarguments would you make to the study?

ANSWERS TO QUESTION SET 2

1. The January effect is the term given to the phenomenon that the average rate of return to stocks in the month of January is higher than in any other month. To take advantage of the effect under the circumstances given, you would transfer all U.S. Treasuries into the growth stock fund at the end of December and then transfer it back out at the end of January.

2. In 80 percent of the cases, the stock split was accompanied by a dividend increase, which could justify a price increase in the stock because management usually doesn't raise dividends unless they feel there has been a permanent increase in the earning power of the firm. The study was consistent with that of a semistrong form efficient market.

3. The four behavioral characteristics of an efficient securities market are
   a. Security prices respond rapidly and accurately to new information.
   b. Changes in the security prices are random.
   c. Trading rules will fail to produce superior returns.
   d. Professional investors will fail to produce superior returns either as individuals or as a group.

4. The RJL study is inconsistent with the semistrong form of market efficiency, because the stock price did not respond until a full 90 days after the quarterly earnings report was publicly released. In the case of an extremely good earnings report, you, as a portfolio manager, could reap extra returns by investing in that stock within the 90-day reaction period.

5. Even though a statistically significant relationship has been detected, it is rarely significant in an economic sense, because brokerage commissions would make the expected profits negative.

6. A trading rule is a standard guideline which a person follows in making the decision to buy or sell stock. The one rule quoted by the text as having met the test of time is the rule to buy stocks that have inordinately low price-earnings ratios and avoid stocks with inordinately high price-earnings ratios.

7. Basu's study, showing that ranking stocks on the basis of their price-earnings ratios can accrue superior returns to portfolios consisting of low price-earnings rated stocks, refutes the semistrong form of the market efficiency hypothesis. Basu's study overcame the deficiency found in earlier studies by including in his sample firms which may have gone out of business in the period studied.

8. The Jensen study showed that the performance of mutual funds, relative to his market index, was neutral; for example, you gained no extra rewards from professional management beyond what you can get by simply borrowing or lending and investing in the S&P 500 index stocks. Obviously, as a mutual fund manager, you would be displeased with this study. To counter it, you might argue that
   a. Because of time delays in large financial institutions, a discovery of a good stock purchase by a superior analyst may not work its way to the purchase decision while the investment is still available at the good price. This fact does not negate the superior

performance of the analyst, but merely indicates that the recommendation was not acted on within the correct time frame.

b. There are weaknesses in the risk-adjusted performance measures. A fund generally tries to predict the future direction of the market, and in doing so the fund's characteristic line is shifting over time. When studying the composite of the fund's returns, your single estimation of the characteristic line may thus serve to overestimate the fund's residual variance and thus the standard error in the Jensen Index. Thus the indices may appear to be statistically insignificant.

c. The Jensen result of neutral fund performance can also be questioned on the grounds that measured performance can be sensitive to the choice of market proxy.

REFERENCES

ALEXANDER, S. S., "Price Movement in Speculative Markets: Trends or Random Walk," *Industrial Management Review* (May 1965).

ALLVINE, F. C., and O'NEILL, D. E., "Stock Market Returns and the Presidential Election Cycle: Implications for Market Efficiency," *Financial Analysts Journal* (September–October 1980).

BAESEL, J., SHOWS, G., and THORP, E., "Can Joe Granville Time the Market," *Journal of Portfolio Management* (Spring 1982).

BANZ, R. W., "The Relationship Between Return and Market Value of Common Stocks," *Journal of Financial Economics* (March 1981).

BAR-YOSEF, S., and BROWN, L. D., "A Reexamination of Stock Splits Using Moving Betas," *Journal of Finance* (September 1977).

BASEL, J., and STEIN, G. R., "The Value of Information: Inferences from the Profitability of Insider Tradings," *Journal of Financial and Quantitative Analysis* (September 1979).

BASU, S., "The Investment Performance of Common Stocks in Relation to Their Price-Earnings Ratios," *Journal of Finance* (June 1977).

BASU, S., "The Relationship Between Earnings Yield, Market Value and Return for NYSE Common Stocks," *Journal of Financial Economics* (June 1983).

BEAVER, W. H., "Market Efficiency," *Accounting Review* (January 1981).

BERNSTEIN, P. L., "Efficiency and Opportunity," *Journal of Portfolio Management* (Fall 1977).

BRENNER, M., "The Effect of Model Misspecification on Tests of the Efficient Market Hypothesis," *Journal of Finance* (March 1977).

BROWN, P., KLEIDON, A. W., and MARSH, T. A., "New Evidence on the Nature of Size Related Anomalies in Stock Prices," *Journal of Financial Economics* (June 1983).

BROWN, L. D., and ROZEFF, M. S., "The Superiority of Analysts' Forecasts as Measures of Expectations: Evidence from Earnings," *Journal of Finance* (March 1978).

COOTNER, P. H., *The Random Character of Stock Market Prices*. Cambridge, Mass.: MIT Press, 1964.

CRAGG, J. G., and MALKIEL, B. G., "The Concensus and Accuracy of Some Predictions of the Growth of Corporate Earnings," *Journal of Finance* (March 1968).

DANN, L. Y., MAYERS, D., and RAAB, R. J., "Trading Rules, Large Blocks, and the Speed of Price Adjustment," *Journal of Financial Economics* (January 1977).

DeBONDT, W., and R. THALER, "Does the Stock Market Overreact?" *Journal of Finance,* July 1985.

DREMAN, D., *The New Contrarian Investment Strategy*. New York: Random House. 1982.

EMMANUEL, D. M., "Note on Filter Rules and Stock Market Trading," *Economic Record* (December 1980).

FAMA, E. F., "The Behavior of Stock Market Prices," *Journal of Business* (January 1965).

FAMA, E. F., FISHER, L., JENSEN, M. C., and ROLL, R., "The Adjustment of Stock Prices to New Information," *International Economic Review* (February 1969).

FAMA, E. F., and FRENCH, K. R., "Permanent and Temporary Components of Stock Prices," *Journal of Political Economy* (April 1988).

FINNERTY, J. E., "Insiders' Activity and Inside Information," *Journal of Financial and Quantitative Analysis* (June 1976).

FINNERTY, J. E., "Insiders and Market Efficiency," *Journal of Finance* (September 1976).

FOSTER, G., "Quarterly Accounting Data: Time Series Properties and Predictive Ability Results," *The Accounting Review* (Spring 1977).

FRENCH, K. R., "Stock Returns and the Weekend Effect," *Journal of Financial Economics,* (March 1980).

GIBBONS, M. R., and HESS, P., "Day of the Week Effects and Asset Returns," *Journal of Business* (October 1981).

GULTEKIN, M. N., and GULTEKIN, B. N., "Stock Market Seasonality: International Evidence," *Journal of Financial Economics* (December 1983).

HAUGEN, R. A., and LAKONISHOK, J., *The Incredible January Effect*. Homewood, Ill.: Dow Jones-Irwin, 1988.

JENSEN, M. C., "The Performance of Mutual Funds in the Period 1945–64," *Journal of Finance* (May 1968).

JENSEN, M. C., "Risk, The Pricing of Capital Assets, and the Evaluation of Investment Performance," *Journal of Business* (April 1969).

JENSEN, M. C., and BENNINGTON, G. A., "Random Walks and Technical Theories: Some Additional Evidence," *Journal of Finance* (May 1970).

JONES, C. D., PEARCE, O. K., and WILSON, J. W., "Can Tax-Loss Selling Explain the January Effect? A Note," *Journal of Finance,* June 1987.

KATO, K., and J. SCHALLHEIM. "Seasonal and Size Anomalies in the Japanese Stock Market." *Journal of Financial and Quantitative Analysis,* June 1985.

KATZ, S., "The Price Adjustment Process of Bonds to Rating Reclassifications: A Test of Bond Market Efficiency," *Journal of Finance* (May 1970).

KEIM, D. "Dividend Yields and Stock Returns: Implications of Abnormal January Returns." *Journal of Financial Economics,* September 1985.

KEIM, D., and R. STAMBAUGH. "A Further Investigation of the Weekend Effect in Stock Returns." *Journal of Finance,* May 1984.

KEIM, D. B., "Size-Related Anomalies and Stock Return Seasonality: Further Empirical Evidence," *Journal of Financial Economics* (June 1983).

KERR, H. S., "The Battle of Insider Trading vs. Market Efficiency," *Journal of Portfolio Management* (Summer 1980).

KON, S. J., and JEN, F. C., "Investment Performance of Mutual Funds: An Empirical Investigation of Timing, Selectivity and Market Efficiency," *Journal of Business* (April 1979).

LORIE, J., and NEIDERHOFFER, V., "Predictive and Statistical Properties of Insider Trading," *Journal of Law and Economics* (April 1978).

REINGANUM, M. R., "Misspecification of Capital Asset Pricing: Empirical Anomalies Based on Earnings Yields and Market Values," *Journal of Financial Economics* (March 1981).

REINGANUM, M. R., "Anatomy of a Stock Market Winner," *Financial Analysts Journal*, March/April 1988.

RENDLEMAN, R. J., and CARABINI, C. E., "Efficiency of the Treasury Bill Futures Market," *Journal of Finance* (September 1979).

RENDLEMAN, R. J., JONES, C. P., and LATANÉ, H. A., "Empirical Anamolies Based on Unexpected Earnings and the Importance of Risk Adjustments," *Journal of Financial Economics* (November 1982).

ROBERTS, H. V., "Stock Market Patterns and Financial Analysis: Methodological Suggestions," *Journal of Finance* (March 1959).

ROZEFF, M. S., and KINNEY, W. R., "Capital Market Seasonality: The Case of Stock Returns," *Journal of Financial Economics* (November 1976).

SCHULTZ, P., "Transactions Costs and the Small Firm Effect: A Comment," *Journal of Financial Economics* (June 1983).

SCHWERT, G. W., "Adjustment of Stock Prices to Information About Inflation," *Journal of Finance* (March 1981).

SCHWERT, G. W., "Size and Stock Returns, and Other Empirical Regularities," *Journal of Financial Economics* (June 1983).

STEVENSON, R. A., and ROSEFF, M., "Are the Backwaters of the Market Efficient?" *Journal of Portfolio Management* (Spring 1979).

STOLL, H. R., and WHALEY, R. E., "Transactions Costs and the Small Firm Effect," *Journal of Financial Economics* (June 1983).

APPENDIX 8

ADDITIONAL PROPERTIES OF THE MINIMUM VARIANCE SET

Property AI: The minimum variance set is hyperbolic in expected return-standard variance space and parabolic in expected return-variance space.

When the minimum variance set is drawn on a graph, where we are plotting standard deviation against expected return, the set takes the shape of a *hyperbola,* such as that drawn in Figure A.8.1. In this figure, the two broken lines intersect at a point called the center of the hyperbola. As we move to positions of higher standard deviation on the minimum variance set, we approach the broken lines from below and above, never quite reaching them. The slopes of the two broken lines increase, in absolute value, as we increase the cross-sectional differences in the expected rates of return between the individual stocks in the population. At one extreme, if each stock had precisely the same expected return as every other stock, the minimum variance set would be a point at the standard deviation of the global minimum variance portfolio. In Figure A.8.1 the horizontal dotted line

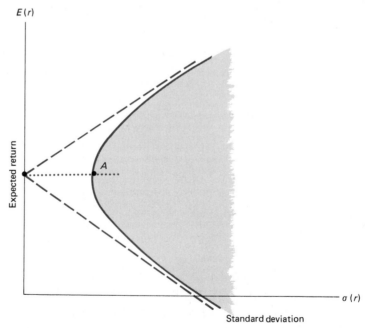

FIGURE A.8.1 Minimum variance set drawn in terms of standard deviation.

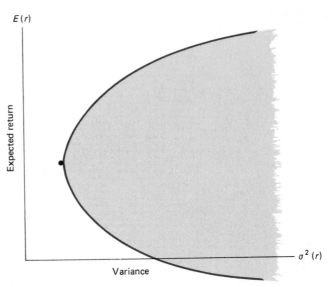

FIGURE A.8.2 Minimum variance set drawn in terms of variance.

bisects (splits in half) the angle of the two broken lines. Such a line will always go through the position of the minimum variance portfolio, in this case at point A.

Now suppose that the minimum variance set is drawn on a graph where we are plotting variance instead of standard deviation on the horizontal axis. Because we square the standard deviation to obtain the variance, the upper and lower sections of the bullet are stretched back into the shape depicted in Figure A.8.2. When drawn in this space, the shape of the minimum variance set is that of a *parabola*. A parabola is truly "bullet" shaped. Think of the path taken by a baseball when hit into the air by a batter. The ball moves upward at a decreasing rate of ascent, finally it reaches its peak, and then begins to fall. If it weren't for the friction caused by air resistance, the path of the ball going down would be the exact mirror image of the path of the ball going up, and the entire path taken would be that of a parabola. Thus, the path of the golf ball hit on the moon by astronaut Allen Shepard was that of the shape of a minimum variance set.

Another way to describe a parabola is to think of a circular cone such as "dunce cap." If you sliced the cap with a plane at an angle to its base, the slice, when superimposed on the plane, would be parabolic in shape.

Property AII: All stocks have nonzero portfolio weights in nearly all portfolios in the minimum variance set.

When short selling is allowed, we make use of each member of the population of securities available to us. This means that we are either taking positive or negative

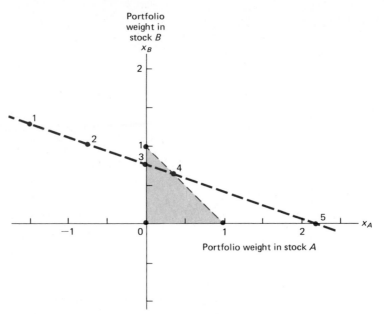

FIGURE A.8.3 Portfolio weights in ACME and Brown.

positions in every stock available. We can see this for our example involving Acme, Brown, and Consolidated in Chapter 5. The critical line for the three stocks is drawn in Figure A.8.3. With the exception of the points labeled 3, 4, and 5, for any portfolio on the critical line, the portfolio weights in all three stocks are nonzero. At points 3, 4, and 5, the portfolio weights in Acme, Consolidated, and Brown are zero, respectively, but these are the only portfolios in the minimum variance set in which any of the stocks has a zero weight. In general, the number of exceptions to property AII will be equal to, at most, the number of stocks from which we have to choose.

Property AIII: If a riskless asset exists and we can buy or sell it without restriction, we can separate the decision of how much risk to assume from what securities to buy.

The minimum variance set for the three example stocks in Chapter 5, Acme, Brown, and Consolidated, is plotted in Figure A.8.3. Suppose that a risk-free bond is available at the point labeled r_F and that we are able to buy or sell as much as we want of it. Given our discussion of the properties of combination lines in Chapter 4, we know that by borrowing or lending we can attain any position on a straight line extending from the position of the risk-free asset and passing through any available position in $E(r)$, $\sigma(r)$ space.

Given the bullet of Figure A.8.4, we can find the set of best borrowing and lending opportunities by extending a straight line up from r_F and swinging it down

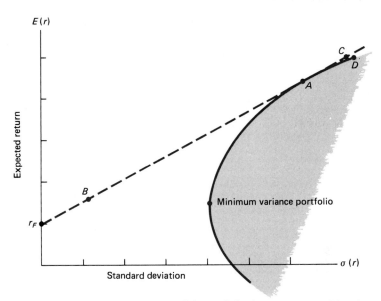

FIGURE A.8.4 Adjusting portfolio risk by borrowing and lending.

until it touches the bullet at point A. Portfolio A is the one portfolio on the bullet that has the maximum value for the following ratio:

$$\frac{E(r_P) - r_F}{\sigma(r_P)}$$

We can say that portfolio A is the best portfolio of risky stocks for us to hold, irrespective of our attitude toward taking risk. If we have a high degree of risk aversion, we should buy both the risk-free bond and portfolio A in some combination. In doing so, we might attain a position like that of point B, which dominates the low-risk portfolios on the bullet. Note that portfolio B dominates the minimum variance portfolio in the sense that it has a lower standard deviation but the same expected rate of return.

If we have a low degree of risk aversion, we might want to sell the risk-free bond and use the proceeds, in addition to our own equity, to invest in portfolio A. These levered portfolios dominate the portfolios on the high-risk segment of the bullet. Note that portfolio C, for example, dominates portfolio D, because it has lower risk and the same expected rate of return.

Thus, we can separate the decision of how much risk to take from what risky assets to hold and in what proportions. If you and I both see the same bullet, the ratio of our holdings of Acme to Consolidated will be the same in both of our portfolios, irrespective of our relative propensity to take on risk. If you are more risk averse than I, you may be buying the risk-free bond, and I may be selling it. In any case, we will adjust the risk of our portfolios through the relative amount of borrowing and lending we do and not through the composition of the portfolio of risky stocks we invest in.

Property AIV: If betas are computed with reference to an index portfolio *inside* the minimum variance set the relationship between betas and expected returns would no longer be linear.

Suppose the index portfolio selected is not on the bullet but rather slightly inside it as with portoflio M' on the left side of Figure 5.11 in chapter 5. Note that portfolio M' has the same average return as efficient portfolio M. This being the case, we may find that the relationship between betas and average returns is still positive (as long as the average return on the index is greater than the average return on the minimum variance portfolio) but that the position of each stock will not fall on a straight line.

Richard Green* has shown that the vertical distance between the position of each stock J and the line drawn based on portfolio M and property V is given by the following expression:

$$\frac{\{\bar{r}_J - z\}\sigma^2_{\varepsilon M'} - \{\bar{r}_{M'} - z\} \operatorname{Cov}(\varepsilon_{M'}, \varepsilon_J)}{\sigma^2_{rM'}}$$

where

$\sigma^2_{\varepsilon M'}$ = residual variance of the inefficient portfolio M' obtained by relating the returns on M' to the returns on the minimum variance portfolio with the same expected rate of return (in this case portfolio M)

$\operatorname{Cov}(\varepsilon_J, \varepsilon_{M'})$ = covariance between the residuals on stock J with the residuals on the inefficient portfolio

z = point of intersection with the expected return axis of a line drawn tangent to the bullet at the position of portfolio M

*See Green (1984). In the equation for the deviation from the line, the term Z is found in the same way that it was found in the case of property II, (Chapter 5), that is, with reference to a line drawn tangent to the bullet at the same average rate of return as the proxy portfolio. It should also be noted that the residuals in the equation aren't quite the same as the residuals taken from a regression of security returns on the returns to a market proxy. Rather these are the residuals taken from a regression of security returns on any two different proxy portfolios taken from the bullet. Measured in this way, the residual variance of any portfolio or security positioned on the bullet is always zero. This is true because, on the basis of property I, (Chapter 5), any portfolio on the bullet can be considered as a linear combination of any two other portfolios (say, A and B) on the bullet. As such its returns in any period can be written as follows:

$$r_P = x_A r_A + (1 - x_A)r_B$$

The returns on portfolio P are, thus, fully explained by the returns on minimum variance portfolios A and B. As such the coefficient of multiple correlation is 1.00, and the residual variance is zero. As you move to a security or portfolio positioned inside the bullet, when portfolio returns are related to the returns on any two bullet portfolios, residual variance becomes positive, increasing with the distance inside the bullet.

We know from property II that if the inefficient portfolio is positioned near the global minimum variance portfolio, the difference between $\bar{r}$ and $\bar{Z}$ will be very large. In this case even if the inefficient portfolio is positioned only slightly inside the bullet (and thus its residual variance is small), there can be a substantial scattering of the individual stocks in average return, beta space.

This property will be useful to us in assessing the performance of portfolio managers. In measuring performance, analysts frequently compare portfolios by positioning them in average return, beta space. Property AIV gives you some guidelines which show you how your relative position on such a graphing is dependent on the characteristics of the market index that was used to compute your portfolio's beta factor. Suppose, for example, that your position turns out to be unfavorable, and you are in danger of losing an account, or even your job. You can use your knowledge of property AIV to defend yourself. It is obvious from the preceding expression that, to a great extent, your positioning is dependent on the characteristics of the proxy portfolio used to estimate your portfolio beta. A case may even be made for the argument that your measured performance may be more a product of the nature of the proxy portfolio than of the quality of your management. Many different proxies for the market are widely employed, and all may fall far short of capturing the properties of the true market portfolio.

Property AV: For any index portfolio on the minimum variance set, other portfolios exist that are perfectly uncorrelated with the index portfolio. In expected return, *standard deviation* space, the expected (or average) return to all the uncorrelated portfolios is given by the point where a line drawn tangent to the bullet at the position of the index portfolio intersects the expected (or average) return axis. In expected return, *variance* space, it is given by the point where a line connecting the positions of the index portfolio and the global minimum variance portfolio intersects the expected (or average) return axis.

Consider the bullet of Figure A.8.5. Assume that we have chosen portfolio M as our index portfolio. To find the positions of all the stocks and portfolios that are uncorrelated with this index, we draw a line tangent to the bullet at point M. This line of tangency intersects the expected return axis at point Z. I now draw on the graph a line with zero slope going through points Z and Z'. The solid portion of this line runs through investment opportunities available to us that are inside the minimum variance set. We will find that each of these opportunities is perfectly uncorrelated with index portfolio M. It is easy to see why this is true, since, based on Property 2, all these portfolios must have beta factors equal to zero.

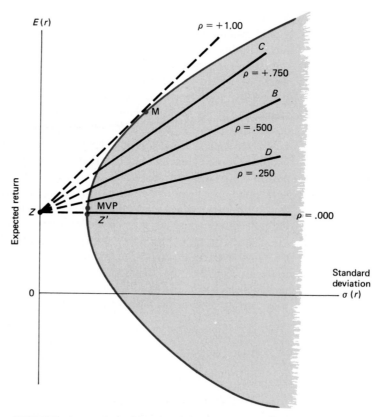

FIGURE A.8.5 Correlations of investments with a minimum variance market index.

One of the uncorrelated portfolios will have a lower variance than any of the others. This is the portfolio positioned at point Z'. This portfolio has a zero covariance with index portfolio M and a zero beta as well. It is usually referred to as the minimum variance, zero beta portfolio.

We should note that if we were to draw a line ZB, bisecting the angle made by lines ZM and ZZ', it would denote the positions of all stocks and portfolios on or inside the bullet that have correlation coefficients with portfolio M equal to .50. Likewise, line ZC, which bisects the angle made by lines ZM and ZB, denotes investments with correlation coefficients equal to .75. In the same sense line ZD denotes investments with correlations equal to .25.

The bullet is drawn in terms of *variance* in Figure A.8.6. In this space the expected return of zero beta portfolios can be found by the vertical intecept of a line connecting the positions of the index portfolio and the global minimum variance portfolio.

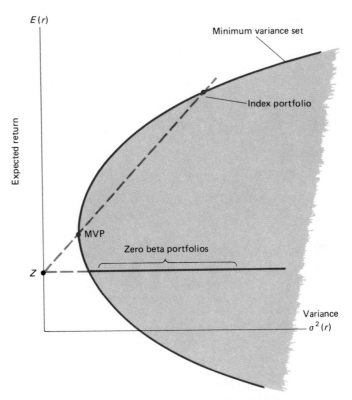

FIGURE A.8.6 Finding zero beta portfolios in expected return, variance space.

Property AVI: There will be a linear, deterministic relationship between betas, computed with reference to an *inefficient* index portfolio, and average returns for all portfolios that are, themselves, minimum variance.

Roll (1978) has shown that even if the index portfolio is inefficient, it will still be the case that, for portfolios that are minimum variance, these portfolios will all line up on a straight line in beta, average return space. Thus, in Figure A.8.7, if portfolio M is used as the index portfolio, the Xs may be considered as efficient portfolios and the points as portfolios that are inside the minimum variance set.

This property is a direct result of the fact that combinations of minimum variance portfolios are, themselves, minimum variance. Suppose we split our money equally between any two minimum variance portfolios. We would obtain another *minimum variance portfolio* with a beta and average return equal to the means of the betas and average returns of the two portfolios which were com-

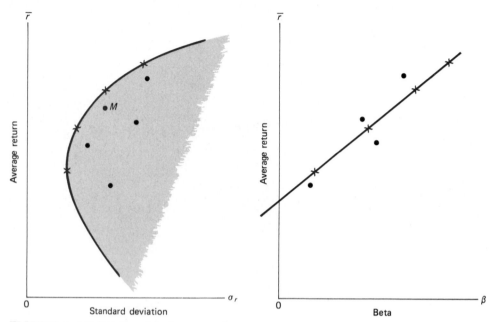

FIGURE A.8.7 Relationship between beta and average return for minimum variance portfolios.

bined. The only way that this will always happen for all combinations of *minimum variance portfolios* is if they all line up on a straight line in average return, beta space.

This property will later become significant in interpreting the results of early tests of the capital asset pricing model. These early tests grouped together large numbers of stocks into widely diversified portfolios. They then looked for a linear relationship between the betas of these portfolios and their average rates of return. As you can see from property AV, they may find such a relationship, irrespective of the position of their market index relative to the bullet, as long as the portfolios they are examining come close to being minimum variance portfolios.

GLOSSARY

American call option A contract giving the holder the right to buy a specified number of shares of stock at a given price on or before a given date.

American put option A contract giving the holder the right to sell a specified number of shares of stock at a given price on or before a given date.

Arbitrage pricing theory A theory purporting to describe the structure of security prices. The theory assumes that stock returns are produced as they would under an index model. The theory describes the relationship between expected returns on securities, given that there are no opportunities to create wealth through riskless arbitrage investments.

Arithmetic mean yield The simple average of periodic rates of return. The arithmetic mean yield relates the ending to beginning wealth associated with an investment if it is assumed that the dollar amount invested is kept constant at the beginning of each period.

At-the-money option A put or call option where the current price of the underlying asset is approximately equal to the present value of the exercise price.

Beta factor The slope of a security's characteristic line. The expected change in the security's rate of return divided by the accompanying change in the rate of return to the market portfolio.

Binomial option pricing American or European option pricing model which finds the value of the option required to deliver a risk-free return to a hedged position assuming there are two possible returns to the stock each period

Black-Scholes option pricing model A model to value European put or call options which assumes that the distribution for the instantaneous rate of return on the underlying asset is normal and constant over time. The model provides an option price that produces the risk-free rate of return to those investors who use the option to create a risk-free hedged position.

Broker An individual who acts as an agent to execute a trade for an investor and receives compensation in the form of a competitively set commission.

Butterfly spread A spread position using call options where you buy options with relatively large and small exercise prices and sell options with intermediate exercise prices. The spread position pays off when the value of the underlying asset falls within a certain range.

Callable bond A bond that can be redeemed by the issuer at a stated price (or prices which change over time) usually beginning after a period of call protection.

Capital asset pricing model   A theory which purports to describe the structure of security prices where all investors in the economic system are presumed to hold efficient portfolios in expected return, variance space.

Capital market line   A line showing the portfolio positions of individual investors in expected return, standard deviation space in the capital asset pricing model.

Cash matching   A form of interest immunization where the timing of the cash flows associated with bond investments is matched up with the timing of the required payments associated with the liability being funded.

Characteristic line   A line showing the relationship between the rates of return to a security or portfolio and the corresponding rates of return to the market portfolio.

Clearing house   An organization associated with an organized exchange for trading options or futures contracts. The clearing house stands, as a guarantor, between you and the other party to the option or futures contract.

Closed-end investment company   Similar to a mutual fund except that shares in the fund are traded by investors in the secondary market. In the case of a mutual fund, you buy and sell shares directly from and to the fund. In the case of a closed-end investment company, you buy them from other investors who happen to own them and want to sell.

Coefficient of determination   The fraction of the variability in one variable that can be associated with the variability in another.

Combination line   A line showing what happens to the expected rate of return and standard deviation to a portfolio of two securities as the portfolio weights in the securities are changed from one value to another.

Commercial paper   Short-term unsecured promissory note issued by a corporation.

Consol   A perpetual bond with a constant periodic interest payment and no maturity date.

Constant growth model   Dividend discount model in which growth in dividends is expected to be constant in perpetuity.

Convertible bond   A bond giving its holder the option of exchanging the bond for a stated number of common shares of the issuing firm.

Correlation coefficient   Statistic describing the goodness of fit about a linear relationship between two variables. The correlation coefficient is equal to the covariance between the variables divided by the product of their standard deviations.

Coupon   The interest payment on a bond.

Covariance   Statistic roughly describing the relationship between two variables. If the covariance is positive, when one of the variables takes on a value above its expected value, the other has a propensity to do the same. If the covariance is negative, the deviations tend to be of opposite sign.

Cox constant elasticity of variance option pricing model   A model to price European put and call options that makes nearly the same assumptions as the Black-Scholes model. This model, however, allows for the magnitude of the variance in the returns for the underlying asset to be a function of the level of the value of the asset. The Black-Scholes model is a special case of this model.

Cox-Ingersoll-Ross duration   A measure of the responsiveness of present market value to change in interest rates that assumes interest rates exhibit a propensity to revert to some mean level over time.

Critical line   A line tracing out, in portfolio weight space, the portfolio weights in the minimum variance set.

Cumulative average excess return   A measure of the cumulative response of security prices to some economic event. The cumulative average rate of return between two points in time is the sum of the average residuals experienced by a sample of securities in each of the subperiods between the two points.

Cumulative preferred stock   A security with a fixed periodic claim that must be paid before dividends can be paid on the common stock. If the payment is skipped, it must be later paid up in full before common dividend payments can be made.

Dealer   An individual who assumes title to and maintains inventories of particular securities and trades from them, profiting from the difference in the prices at which he or she is willing to buy or sell from the inventory.

Debenture bond   A bond that is unsecured by real property.

Delivery premium   Premium in the futures price that relates to the value of the options on the part of the seller of the futures contract to deliver various types or grades of commodities under the contract.

Delta   The expected change in the market value of your option position accompanying a small change in the market value of the common stock underlying the position.

Dividend clientele   The shareholders of a given company who are presumed by some to group themselves according to marginal tax rate, where the high-bracket investors buy stocks with low dividend yields and the low-bracket investors buy stocks with high dividend yields.

Dividend discount model   Stock valuation model which solves for the value of a common stock as the present value of future dividends expected to be received.

Dividend/price ratio   Ratio of the dividend per share of a stock to its market price per share.

Dividend yield   See dividend/price ratio.

Efficient set   The set of portfolios of a given population of securities which offer the maximum possible expected return for a given level of risk.

Elasticity of yield to maturity   Percentage change in the value of a security accompanying the percentage change in one plus its yield to maturity. The point yield elasticity is equal to the negative of some duration measures.

Equipment trust certificate   Fixed income security that is secured by a particular, designated piece of property that is both mobile and salable, such as a railroad car.

European call (put) option   Contract giving the holder the right to buy (sell) a specified number of shares of a given stock on, but not before, a given date.

Exercise price   The price at which you have the right to buy (sell) a security under a call (put) option contract.

Expected rate of return   Sum of the product of the possible rates of return on an investment and their associated probabilities.

Fisher-Weil duration   Measure of the responsiveness of present market value that assumes parallel shifts occur in term structures of any shape.

Fixed income security   A security with a defined, limited dollar claim.

Floor broker   Individuals buying and selling on the floor of an organized exchange.

Forward contract   A contract that obligates you to buy (if you buy the contract) or sell (if you sell the contract) a given commodity at a given price (the forward price) at a given point in time. There are no interim cash flows associated with a forward contract.

Fundamental beta   An estimate of the beta factor for an individual security that employs information about the nature of the company issuing the security (earnings stability, financial leverage, etc.)

in addition to the past relationship between the security's returns and the market portfolio.

Futures contract   Similar to a forward contract except that futures contracts are traded on organized exchanges and the futures price is amended from period to period so as to keep the current market value of the contract at zero. The process of debiting or crediting your account to compensate for the amendments is called *marking to market*.

Futures overlay   Position in a portfolio futures contracts that complements the risk characteristics of your cash position so as to achieve a desired risk characteristic for the net position

Gamma   The expected change in the delta factor associated with your option position accompanying a small change in the market value of the common stock underlying the position

General obligation municipal bond   A bond backed by the full faith and credit of the issuing state or municipality.

Geometric mean yield   The nth root less one of the product of one plus n periodic rates of return. The geometric mean relates the beginning to the ending wealth over the periods if it is assumed that income from the security is reinvested back into the security.

Global minimum variance portfolio   The lowest-variance portfolio achievable, given a population of securities.

Growth horizon   Length of time that the growth rate in earnings or dividends for a particular stock can be forecast with a degree of accuracy sufficient to be considered in the valuation process.

Hard floor   Floor underlying the market value of an option which is equal to the greater of zero or the difference between the underlying asset value and the option's exercise price.

Immunization Curve   Curve showing the duration of a stream of liabilities for different values of the discount rate.

In-the-money option   A call (put) option where the underlying asset value is greater (less) than the present value of its exercise price.

Income effect of a change in the money supply   Change in real rate of interest moving in the same direction as the change in money supply resulting from the change in transactions demand associated with the monetary-induced change in national income.

Index arbitrage   Taking a simultaneous hedged position in stock index futures and a cash position in the index itself to take advantage of mispricing of the futures contract.

Indifference curve   Curve tracing portfolios defined in expected return, standard deviation space that a given investor faces with indifference.

Inflation premium   The difference between the nominal and real rates of interest. The inflation premium compensates investors for the loss of purchasing power due to inflation. It is equal to the expected average rate of inflation over the term of the investment for which the interest rate is computed.

Interest immunization   An investment strategy that ensures that a portfolio will generate sufficient cash flows to meet a series of cash payments having the same present value as the portfolio.

Internal yield   The rate that will discount the cash flows associated with an investment to a present value that is equal to the present market value of the investment. The internal rate of return relates beginning to ending wealth levels if you assume that cash flows can be reinvested at the internal yield when received.

Iso-expected return line   Line, drawn on a mapping of portfolio weights, which shows the combinations of weights all of which provide for a particular portfolio rate of return.

Isovariance ellipse   Ellipse, drawn on a mapping of portfolio weights, which shows the combinations of weights all of which provide for a particular portfolio variance.

January effect   Market anomaly whereby stock prices throughout most of the world have a propensity to rise sharply during the initial part of the month of January.

Jensen Index   Risk-adjusted measure of portfolio performance equal to the difference between a portfolio's realized or expected rate of return and the return that it should have, given its risk and its designated position on the security market line.

Joint Probability distribution   Distribution showing the probabilities of simultaneously getting various pairs of returns on two investments.

Liquidity effect of a change in the money supply   The initial effect of a change in the money supply on the real rate of interest, moving rates in the opposite direction from the change in money and caused by the adjustment of portfolio positions of investors in response to the change in the supply of money.

Liquidity preference theory of the term structure   Theory which purports to explain the shape of the term structure on the basis of market expectations of future interest rates and on the basis of risk, or liquidity, premiums which may be present in the expected rates of return to bonds of various maturities.

Locked-in effect   Propensity for investors to hold on to securities on which they have accrued capital gains in order to avoid realizing them for tax purposes.

Macaulay duration   Weighted average maturity of a stream of payments where the maturity of each payment is weighted by the fraction of the total value of the stream that is accounted for by the payment. Macaulay duration is also a measure of the responsiveness of market value to a change in interest rates which assumes that parallel shifts occur in a flat term structure.

Marginal probability distribution   Distribution which shows the probabilities of getting various rates of return on a particular investment.

Marginal rate of substitution   An implicit "discount rate" for payoffs received in a particular future state of the world equal to the marginal utility associated with consumption in that state divided by the marginal utility associated with current consumption.

Market efficiency   The extent to which the market prices securities so as to reflect available information pertaining to their valuation.

Market expectations theory of the term structure   Theory which purports to explain the shape of the term structure on the basis of market expectations of future interest rates alone. Risk or liquidity premiums in expected returns on investments of different maturities are assumed away.

Market portfolio   The ultimate market index, containing a common fraction of the total market value of every capital investment in the economic system.

Market segmentation theory of the term structure   Theory which purports to explain the shape of the term structure on the basis of flows of funds between the long-, intermediate-, and short-term maturity segments of the market. Each segment is viewed as compartmentalized, and the yield in each segment is determined by the supply and demand for loanable funds in the segment.

Minimum variance set   Set of portfolios which has the lowest possible variance achievable for the population of stocks, given their expected rates of return.

Minimum variance zero beta portfolio   The one portfolio in the minimum variance set that is completely uncorrelated with the market index.

Mortgage bond   A bond secured by the pledge of a specific property.

Multi-index model   Model purporting to explain the covariances that exist between securities on the basis of unexpected changes over time in two or more indices, such as the market, the money supply, or the growth rate in industrial production.

Multistage growth model   Dividend discount model in which growth in dividends is expected to change in one or more stages.

Municipal Bond   A bond issued by a state or municipality, the interest income of which is usually exempt from taxation at the federal level.

Mutual fund   A portfolio of securities owned collectively by a group of investors. Shares in the fund are bought and sold directly from the fund.

Nominal interest rate   Interest rate relating the market value of an investment to its expected (or realized) future cash flows, unadjusted for the expected (or realized) rate of inflation. The nominal rate is comprised of the real rate and the inflation premium or the expected rate of inflation over the life of the investment.

Normal probability distribution   Symmetric, bell-shaped distribution which can be completely described on the basis of its expected value and its variance.

Out-of-the-money option   A call (put) option where the market value of its underlying asset is below (above) the present value of its exercise price.

Over-the-counter market   A trading network of thousands of dealers in particular securities.

Population value   Parameter describing the shape of a marginal or joint probability distribution computed on the basis of the values for the probabilities in the distribution.

Portfolio insurance   Using option pricing models to dynamically allocate funds between a risky portfolio and a riskless investment to provide a lower limit to the market value of your overall position.

Portfolio weight   The fraction of your money that you invest in a particular security in the portfolio.

Preferred stock   A security with a defined, fixed, periodic claim on the income from a firm. The claim isn't mandatory, but it must be paid before dividends are paid on the firm's common stock.

Price effect of a change in the money supply   The effect of a change in the supply of money on the inflation premium in the nominal rate of interest.

Price-earnings ratio   Ratio of the market price per share of a stock to its earnings per share.

Primary security   Security issued to finance a real economic investment.

Private placement   A security that is issued to a small number of investors. The terms of the offering are typically tailored to the needs of the investors.

Program trading   The simultaneous purchase or sale of a portfolio of stocks using the Dot computerized trading system.

Put-call parity   Relationship between the market values of puts and calls written on the same stock, with the same exercise price and time to maturity, that prevents the opportunity for making pure arbitrage profits by taking simultaneous positions in the put, the call, and the underlying stock.

Random walk   Property of a time series where the probability distribution for the future changes in the series is constant and unrelated to changes in the series that have occurred in the past.

Real rate of interest   The rate of return on an investment adjusted for changes in purchasing power. The real rate compensates investors for delaying consumption.

Residual   The vertical distance between the actual rate of return produced by a security and the return consistent with the return to the market index and the security's characteristic line.

Residual variance   Statistic describing the propensity for a security to deviate from its characteristic line. The probability weighted sum of the squared residuals.

Revenue bond   A bond, usually issued by a state or municipality, which isn't backed by the full faith and credit of the issuer. Rather the interest and principal are to be paid from funds derived from a particular designated source, such as the revenue from a toll bridge.

Risk adjusted performance measure   Measure of performance which purports to be unaffected by the risk of the portfolio or the performance of the market.

Sample estimate   An estimate of a population value for the underlying probability distribution obtained from observing or sampling a series of rates of return to an investment or investments.

Secondary security   A security, such as a futures contract, issued by one financial investor and sold to another. The net supply of secondary securities is zero.

Security market line   Line showing the relationship between the expected returns and betas for all portfolios and securities under the capital asset pricing model.

Semistrong efficient market hypothesis   Security prices fully reflect all information that has been made publicly available.

Sharpe Index   Risk-adjusted performance measure reflecting both breadth and depth of performance and equal to the risk premium earned on the portfolio divided by its standard deviation.

Short sale   Act of selling securities you don't own. You borrow shares from someone, sell them, repurchase them at a later date, and return them to the lender of the shares.

Single-index model   Model which purports to explain the covariance which exists between the returns on different securities on the basis of the relationship between the returns and a single index, usually the market.

Sinking fund   A provision in a bond indenture which called for the periodic retirement of the outstanding issue. The retirement can be made by purchase of the bond itself, or other similar bonds, in the open market or by redeeming the bonds at a specified call price, at the issuer's option.

Small firm effect   Market anomaly whereby small companies exhibit a propensity to produce rates of return that are larger than those predicted on the basis of the capital asset pricing model.

Soft floor   Floor underlying the value of a call option equal to the greater of zero or the difference between the market value of the underlying asset and the present value of the option's exercise price.

Specialist   Individual on the floor of an organized exchange who keeps an inventory of one or more stocks and trades with floor brokers out of that inventory.

Speculative demand for money   The demand for money as an alternative investment, usually reflected in the amounts of money kept in savings accounts.

Standard deviation   The square root of the variance. A statistic describing the propensity to deviate from the expected value.

Straddle   Simultaneous long positions in put and call options written on the same stock with the same exercise price and time to expiration.

Striking price   *See* exercise price.

Strong efficient market hypothesis   Security prices fully reflect all information that is knowable, including inside information.

Systematic risk   That part of a security's variance that can't be diversified away. In the context of the capital asset pricing model, systematic risk is equal to the square of the product of the beta and the market's standard deviation.

Tax-anticipation note   A note secured by taxes already due but not yet paid.

Term structure of interest rates   The relationship between yield to maturity and term to maturity for securities of a given risk and tax status.

Time-weighted return   Concept of rate of return on an investment in which the portfolio is divided into units, as with a mutual fund, and the return calculated for each unit.

Theta   The expected change in the market value of your options position with the passing of a day, assuming the market price of the underlying stock, the risk-free rate of interest, and the volatility of the underlying stock remain constant.

Transactions demand for money   The demand for money as a medium of exchange, usually kept in checking account balances.

Treasury bill   Security issued by the U.S. Treasury with a maximum maturity of 1 year and promising a single payment of interest and principal at maturity.

Treasury bond   Security issued by the U.S. Treasury with no maximum maturity and promising semiannual interest payments and return of principal at maturity.

Treasury note   Security issued by the U.S. Treasury having a maximum maturity of 7 years and promising semiannual interest payments and return of principal at maturity.

Treynor Index   Risk-adjusted performance measure reflecting depth but not breadth of performance and equal to the risk premium earned by the portfolio divided by its beta factor.

Two-state option pricing model   Model valuing put and call options that assumes, in any given period of time, two rates of return are possible for the underlying asset. The model values the option so as to give anyone hedging with it the risk-free rate of return.

Uniform probability distribution   Rectangular distribution relating to the ending value for an asset whereby all values between an extreme high and low value are equally probable.

Unit normal distribution   Normal probability distribution having an expected value of zero and a standard deviation equal to 1.

Utility of wealth function   The relationship between your well-being and the amount of wealth you have at any given point in time.

Value-weighted return   Return calculated as an internal rate of return, including consideration for deposits and withdrawals to and from the portfolio.

Variance   Propensity to deviate from the expected value. The probability weighted squared deviations from the expected value.

Velocity of money   Number of dollars of national income supported by each dollar in the money supply. A measure of the speed with which money turns over in the economy.

Warrant   A contract giving the holder the right to buy a specified number of shares of a given asset at a given price. The major difference between a warrant and a call option is that the former is a primary security, while the latter is a secondary security.

Weak form efficient market hypothesis   Security prices fully reflect any information concerning the future of the price series that can be obtained by analyzing the past behavior of the series.

INDEX

A

After-tax rates of return, investments, computation of, 542–44
After-tax yield to maturity, bonds, 545
American option pricing, 420, 464–75
  binomial model as American option pricing model, 472–73
  early exercise:
    call options, 470–71
    put options, 471–72
    value of, 469–72
    with no value, 469–70
  floors supporting call options, 465
  floors supporting put options, 468–69
  hard floor:
    definition of, 465
    market forces supporting, 466–67
  lower limits to value of options, 465–72
  soft floor:
    definition of, 465
    market forces supporting, 468
American Stock Exchange (AMEX), 28
Annual rates of return, common stock, 20
Arbitrage pricing theory (APT), 3, 256–69
  compared to CAPM, 256, 269
  consistency of, 268–69
  deriving of, 257–65
  empirical tests of, 265–68
    with finite number of securities, 263–64
    with infinite number of securities, 258–63
  measuring portfolio performance using, 297–300
  testability of, 266–68
Arithmetic mean:
  computation of, 343, 364–65
  deriving market's forecast of future interest rates from, 355–57
At-the-money option, 428

B

Babcock, G., 384
Banz, R. W., 654

Basu, S., 652–55
Baumol, W., 589
Beta:
  fundamental betas, sale of, 178–79
  for index models, estimation of, 180–85
Beta factor, 57–58, 117–20
  definition of, 117
Binomial option pricing, 431–41
  bias problems, 481-87
  binomial model as American option pricing model, 472–73
  over multiple periods, 436–41
  over single period, 432–36
    call options, 432–35
    put options, 435–36
BJS study of properties of stock returns, 166
Black, Fisher, 3, 166–67, 235–36, 247, 251, 265, 266, 291, 343, 432, 483, 486
Black, Jensen, and Scholes test of CAPM, 235–36
Black-Scholes option pricing model, 3, 263
  bias problems, 481–87
  estimating variance of stock's return, 448–49
  relationship between put/call values and underlying stock prices, 432, 449
  value for call options, 445–48
  value for put options, 449
  valuing options for, 441–45
  valuing options on stocks that pay dividends, 449–51
Bond futures contracts, hedging with, 530–31
Bond portfolio management, 376–85
  dividing portfolio between bonds and stock, 385
  duration of bond, formula for, 382
  expected return for portfolio analysis, estimation of, 377–82
  forecasting expected returns, 377–82
    on corporate bonds, 380–82
    on Treasury bonds, 377–80
    see also U.S. Treasury bonds
  risk of investments, estimation of, 382-83
Bonds:
  after-tax yield to maturity, 545
  interest income, taxation on, 541